Photoshop Artistry

Barry Haynes   **Wendy Crumpler**   **Seán Duggan**

New Riders

1249 Eighth Street, Berkeley, CA 94710

Photoshop Artistry

Barry Haynes, Wendy Crumpler, and Seán Duggan

Copyright © 2007 Barry Haynes and Wendy Crumpler

New Riders

1249 Eighth Street
Berkeley, CA 94710
510/524-2178   800/283-9444   510/524-2221 (fax)

Find us on the Web at www.newriders.com

To report errors, please send a note to errata@peachpit.com

New Riders is an imprint of Peachpit, a division of Pearson Education

Project Editor: *Becky Morgan*
Editor: *Anne Marie Walker*
Production Editor: *Andrei Pasternak*
Copyeditor: *Sally Zahner*
Indexer: *Patti Scheindelman*
Technical Editor: *Wayne Palmer*
Proofreader: *Liz Welch*
Media Developer: *Eric Geoffroy*
Cover Design: *Barry Haynes*
Interior Design: *Monica Whipple, Wendy Crumpler, Charlene Will, and Barry Haynes*

ISBN 0-321-34699-8

9 8 7 6 5 4 3 2 1

Printed and bound in the United States of America

About the Authors

Barry Haynes has been involved with photography since he was 14. He later became a US Navy photographer and attended most of the Navy's advanced photography courses. After getting his BA in computer science from University of California San Diego, Barry spent 10 years, from 1980 to 1990, doing software development and digital imaging research at Apple. It was a great time to be at Apple, and Barry was able to be a part of Apple's growth from 500 employees to over 10,000. He took a leave of absence from Apple in 1990 to set up a darkroom and get back to photography. He soon found himself teaching Photoshop workshops and the notes for those evolved into Barry's advanced *Photoshop Artistry* book series, the latest of these being this *Photoshop Artistry* from New Riders. His books are very popular with photographers and artists who are using Photoshop to create their final artwork.

He also teaches in-depth photography and digital printmaking workshops in Gibsons, B.C. Canada, where he has his home, gallery, and studio. Barry enjoys using his Photoshop darkroom techniques to print, show, and sell his own photography using Epson inkjet digital printers. Barry has given talks and workshops for Palm Beach Photographic Center, Santa Fe Workshops, Anderson Ranch, International Center of Photography, the Photoshop Conference, Seybold Seminars, MacWorld, the Center for Creative Imaging, advertising agencies, design firms, photography stores, and other organizations. His articles appear in *Communication Arts*, *Camera Arts*, *Photo Techniques* and other photography magazines.

Wendy Crumpler has been in advertising and design since 1980. She has worked in print, television, CD-Interactive, interactive television, and computer-based training. Prior to her discovery of the computer in 1981 and the Macintosh in 1986, she was an actress and teacher. She is the author of two versions of her popular *Photoshop, Painter and Illustrator Side-by-Side* book, from Sybex, and also *Gateway: The Andean Path to Inner Wisdom*. She has done production, illustration, design, and training for a variety of clients using many applications. She has worked for Angotti Thomas Hedge, Boardroom Reports, Deutsch Advertising, J. Walter Thompson, TBWA Advertising, Wechsler Design, Wells Rich Greene, Canon, Parke Davis, and AT&T.

Seán Duggan is a photographer and digital artist who combines a traditional fine art photographic background with extensive experience in digital graphics. He has worked as a custom black & white darkroom technician, studio and location photographer, digital restoration artist, graphic designer, Web developer, and educator. His visual tool kit runs the gamut from primitive pinhole cameras and wet darkroom alternative processes, to advanced digital techniques. In addition to providing Photoshop training seminars and digital imaging and color management consultation services, he creates illustrations and image design solutions for the Web and print-based media. He is an instructor for the photography department of the University of California, Santa Cruz Extension and the Academy of Art College in San Francisco where he teaches regular classes on Photoshop and digital imaging for photographers. His Web site can be seen at www.seanduggan.com.

Let us know what you think

There's been a lot of student and reader involvement in the shaping of this book. Listening to people who use these techniques helps us to refine and dig deeper to find solutions to our clients' and students' problems. And, we get smarter in the process. We love what we do and invite you to become part of the digital revolution with us. Let us know what you think of the book, what was helpful, what confused you. We are committed to empowering people to use their minds and spirits, computers, and software to advance their own artistic abilities and to make a difference on this planet.

Take one of our in-depth workshops

We live in Gibsons, British Columbia on Canada's Sunshine Coast. In this charming seaside village, we teach hands-on workshops for no more than six students at a time. These classes are tailored to meet the individual needs of those students. Check for the latest information about the details, times and locations for our digital imaging courses, as well as book updates, scanning and printing tips, and other useful information on our Web site, www.barryhaynes.com.

Barry Haynes Photography
P.O. Box 1748, 547 Sargent Rd.
Gibsons, B.C. V09 1V0
CANADA   direct phone: 604-886-2214 U.S. messages: 541-754-2219 email: barry@maxart.com or wendy@maxart.com

ACKNOWLEDGMENTS

We've worked with a lot of really great people over the years we've been writing *Photoshop Artistry*. But this is the best team we've ever worked with. That's saying a lot 'cause we've worked with the best. At least, now we have.

So thank-yous to:

Seán Duggan, for doing such a great job on all your chapters. We learned a lot from reading your work and discussing issues with you. Over the years you've been a great help to us and a good friend. You've influenced the way we work many times and we don't influence easily.

Becky Morgan, for giving us the time we needed to produce a really great book. Becky, we know how busy you are and we know the pressures inherent in publishing, but whenever we had personal traumas you blessed us with a sense that life was more important than the book. That is a rare gift and we appreciate it so much. You've been hands-on with this book; you helped with design, you put together a great team, you even pitched in with proofreading at the 11th hour. Pretty damn amazing. We hope you get some time off now.

Anne Marie Walker, our editor. We've said it before, "You're a great shepherd." Although at times, it must have felt like herding cats. You navigated the I/we issues with great good humor, kept track of everything, and pulled us closer together as a team. You were just wonderful to work with, patient, kind, and respectful of the authors' words, voices, and intentions. Thank you.

Wayne Palmer, out technical editor. Wayne, we waited to begin tech edits so we could work with you. It was worth the wait. Your queries, comments, and suggestions made this a much better book. It was fun talking shop with you over the Internet too!

Sally Zahner, our copy editor. Oh, Sally, wasn't this fun pushing the envelope of technology? No? Well, you did it anyway and even managed to laugh. We heard you were the best in the business and we can't argue. We loved working with you.

Andrei Pasternak, our production manager. Andrei, it's great to be able to turn over a project to someone with your abilities and sensibilities. Your down-to-earth approach to everything inspires confidence and peace. Happy music making.

Lupe Edgar, we appreciate your watching over this project and making sure the printing goes well the first time this time. Thanks for all your help over the past two and a half years. You're the greatest!

Liz Welch, our proofreader. Liz, you are the most efficient proofreader we've ever seen. Are you like a speed reader or something? Thank you for your efficiency; you really made the end of the project flow.

Eric Geoffroy, media (DVD) coordinator. Eric, thanks for all the last minute back and forth. We appreciate your commitment to excellence.

Patti Scheindelman, our indexer. Patti, we know that an index can either be a powerful tool for the reader or a real frustration. We got the power. Thanks.

Ed Hill for arranging the amazing Pulling Together Canoe Journey for Barry and the rest of humanity.

Thomas Bach for help with high-quality Epson printing questions.

Bruce Fraser, Dan Margulis, Martin Evening, and Vince Versace, whose work we always respect and check for another competent opinions.

Dan Burkholder for his advice on art papers, his amazing images, his great jokes, and for being fun to hang out with at Fotofusion.

Ben Wilmore for his great books and teaching style and for fun times together at Fotofusion.

Art and Fatima Nejame for putting on the Fotofusion conference each January at the Palm Beach Photographic Center in Florida. What a great conference and place for photographers to connect! See www.fotofusion.org.

Our friends Wolf, Zach, and Justin Wagman, and Denise Saunders. It was wonderful to have you visit and we think you make a great example.

All the photographers who let us use their beautiful images for our portfolio pages.

The people of Gibson, B.C. and the Sunshine Coast community for making us feel so welcome. We live in Paradise!

Denise Haynes. Grandma, thank you so much. We couldn't be here without your support and you give it even though we know it's difficult for you that we're so far away. We miss you and look forward to the day you are up here with us.

Our son, Max, who continues to astound, confound, delight, and make us proud. Max, you are so smart and funny and talented. Every year with you is a great adventure!

Our readers and students, who challenge us, support us, befriend us, and give meaning to our work.

From Barry to Wendy

I look forward to spending some vacation time with you, now that this book is done! I said that on the last book but this time we really need it. Kayaking together is a good start. Thanks for doing more work on this edition than everyone else put together! You are a great writer and partner too. Love you!!!

From Wendy to Barry

Not many people could do what we do. Not many relationships could handle the kind of stress we put on ours. What we have is stronger than work. We were meant to be together. I still look at you and marvel at your beauty. I love your nose. I love you.

Finally, and most importantly, our thanks to the Divine Creator for the bounty of this life and for giving us a chance to contribute in what we hope is a positive way.

In Memoriam: Adelaide S. Crumpler, March 9, 1923–March 7, 2006

This book is dedicated to

The town of Gibsons, B.C. and the Sunshine Coast of Canada

You've made us feel at home and shared your beauty with us. Thank you.

Table of Contents

17 ◆ Image Resolution and Scanning 238

18 ◆ The Master Image Workflow 254

19 ◆ Making Selections 268

20 ◆ Levels, Curves, and Hue/Saturation 278

21 ◆ Overall Color Correction 302

22 ◆ Correcting Problem Images 324

Portfolios

Foreword

This is our eighth edition of *Photoshop Artistry*. We've now been writing and improving this book for over ten years. What an amazing journey we've traveled with digital photography. Barry was there at its inception—while working at Apple, he bummed his first copy of Photoshop from Russell Brown. The application was on a single diskette in Russell's pocket. Wendy began working with the first shipped version in New York City in 1990. That was a lifetime ago.

Our first version of *Artistry* in 1995 took us just under a year to write. This edition has taken about the same length of time and that's longer than usual for a rewrite. Redesigning the book and writing new material based on our working experience with the software were important to us. We are grateful to Peachpit, who gave us the time needed to make such large-scale changes.

We three authors also had a lot of life happen to us in the last year and a half. Barry and Wendy moved to Canada, bought one house and sold another. The three of us dealt with aging parents, distance from loved ones, and death. All of us have children, spouses, and lives outside the creation of this book.

But perhaps, as is often the case in real life, the delay has been beneficial. We've taken more time with this edition than any since the first. We had more time to discuss important issues and decide what we really wanted to say. We've completely refocused the book to make it more meaningful to photographers, who are our primary audience, and to make it useful to past and future users of Photoshop, not just those using CS2. We hope you feel the time was well spent.

We want to alert you that there will be no *Photoshop Artistry* for the next version of the software. This edition will serve for the new software along with specific information available on our Web site when the time comes.

There's a lot of new material in this book. We explain image processing with Bridge and the wonders of Camera Raw. We show you how to automate our color and black-and-white workflows for digital cameras with actions, Bridge, and Camera Raw. There are also many new step-by-step examples.

However, as Photoshop continues to grow and change, our core workflow methods (adjustment layers, Levels, Curves, Hue/Saturation, and masks) get refined but can still be applied to many versions of Photoshop. If you can use the core concepts of our workflow correctly, you can create great images. The heart of Photoshop and how we direct photographers to use it has remained fairly consistent. We don't expect that to change significantly with the next version. Think in terms of SLR cameras. New models come out with new features, but if you understand aperture, shutter speed, and depth of field, any camera will serve you well. We've written this edition with the expectation of it having a long shelf life. If you know the interface of your version of Photoshop, you should be able to do the exercises contained in this book with only minor adjustments. If you have CS2 and beyond, it should be an easy fit.

We have written eight editions of *Artistry* over the past 11 years and now we need time to focus on our own artwork. Art takes time. More than just the time in front of the computer, time to explore artistic drive and impulses. Time to experiment, time to make mistakes, time to live into the art that resides within us already. Merely getting better at Photoshop does not make you an artist.

So, if being great at Photoshop doesn't make one an artist, what does? What is art?

We think art does two things. Art creates an energy bond between the creator and the viewer. What is art to one person may be merely noise to another. But there is an unspoken communication between the artist and audience that elevates both. To achieve that sort of bond, artists must put their energy, their essence into the work. That is not an offhand thing. It requires dedication and soul-searching. It requires the ability to let go of what other people think, the courage to put one's art out into the world. It requires that the creator release the creation, stop tinkering, say, "It is finished!"

Another requirement of art, we believe, is that it forces us to take another look at life, to reexamine what we think we know. We've included the work of former students in this book that we feel does just that, whether it be the abstract beauty of Mark Reid's vision or the ethereal loveliness within the challenge of Kenda North's work. Perhaps it's the spirituality implicit in a landscape, or the wonder of a moment in life captured forever by the photographer.

This book is a course in today's photography, and we believe you'll find more than just the mechanics of Photoshop here. Perhaps a bit of inspiration, or the feeling that you have partners on the path as you work to become better at the craft and art of photography. We hope this book helps you find your own way of working by presenting techniques that are grounded in solid results. You won't find a lot of gimmicks here. That's why many colleges and universities choose *Photoshop Artistry* as the text for their digital imaging courses. Photoshop is huge and there are so many ways to accomplish most any task, it's easy to get lost. We've tried to focus on what photographers need to know, and give you a place from which to soar into your own creativity. It's a bit like learning the rules of painting, so you can break them. If you know the rules, you have a sense of where you are coming from and possibly, where you are headed. We don't always show you the fastest or easiest method; we try to show you methods that will serve you on a regular basis and become the bedrock of your own workflow.

As always, we invite you to come and take a workshop with us. It's a great way to share and explore your work in a supportive environment. Our classes are small and informal and generally a great deal of fun. While we teach Photoshop and photography, we learn a lot from our students, not just about art, but about life. The Andean spiritual tradition, which Wendy has been studying for the past few years, has a term called *ayni,* which means reciprocity. As we give, we receive. We feel that about our classes. It's a two-way street, and we always come away from a workshop feeling enriched by the experience. Many of our good friends came to us as students. It's a great way to live.

So, thank you for choosing *Photoshop Artistry*. If you are new to the book, welcome. If you are returning, welcome back. Let us hear from you.

Barry and Wendy

Photoshop Artistry

1 ◆ How to Use *Photoshop Artistry*

Welcome to *Photoshop Artistry*. This eighth edition of the book represents ten years of experience in presenting a comprehensive overview of how to work effectively in Photoshop.

Those of you familiar with past editions of the book will notice the new look. We've completely redesigned the book to make accessing the information easier. We've narrowed our focus to make the information as photography-specific as possible. We don't try to show you every technique; rather, we teach a Photoshop workflow that applies to all types of photography. In some instances what we show you can be achieved by other methods, but we try to show you either the methods we use most often or the ones that illuminate underlying principles that will help you understand Photoshop at a deep level.

After ten years, we've realized that all sorts of people use this book. Although we don't consider this a beginner book, we know that some beginners choose to use this book and that some teachers of beginners require this book for courses. We have tried to include enough information to make Photoshop understandable for the novice without boring intermediate to advanced users. It's a complex balancing act.

How the Book Is Organized

This book is divided into seven sections. The first two sections contain overview chapters that present in-depth information to support you in your work with the hands-on chapters. The last five sections contain hands-on exercises designed to give you practice using the tools and techniques we've found through many years of teaching to be solid, useful, and dependable.

We do not follow this book from front to back when we teach our classes, nor do we expect that most of you will work through each chapter consecutively. The chapters are grouped more according to issues they address than level of difficulty. For instance, you might read Chapter 7, "Layers, Layer Masks, and Layer Comps," before you read and do Chapter 21, "Overall Color Correction." When you read Chapter 7, you may not understand all the points we make if you haven't actually done hands-on work with layers. On the other hand, if you read and do Chapter 21 first, you may still have questions regarding how the layers and layer masks work that can only be answered by reading the overview, Chapter 7. Whichever order you

choose, you'll find yourself coming back to the overview chapters as your understanding of techniques and processes deepens. In fact, we often have students who redo exercises as they become more advanced in their own Photoshop work. In this respect, you'll find this book to be multilayered; even the most basic chapters may throw concepts at you that you don't yet understand. Just be patient and keep working through them. You'll make the connections eventually, and when you do you'll understand this amazing application on more than a superficial level. At the end of this chapter we give you three detailed course outlines that we suggest you work from, or teach with, depending on your skill level or your students' skills and understanding.

Reading vs. Doing

Through the years we've had more and more people ask us to be very clear and specific about the actions they need to take as they read each chapter. In this edition we use a diamond bullet (◆), to let you know you need to take action. You'll find these bullets in both overview chapters and hands-on chapters. Even though it's an overview chapter, when you see the symbol, we really mean for you to stop reading and do the steps. Especially when you're working through Chapter 2, "Preferences and Color Settings," and Chapter 3, "Navigating in Photoshop," you need to make sure you've done each bulleted step. The rest of the book depends on your having done certain tasks to set up Photoshop preferences before you start the hands-on exercises.

◆ So when you see this symbol, follow the instructions.

Many of the preferences we have you set up automate your Photoshop application in one way or another. We offer a custom set of menus and shortcut keys for photographers, as well as our ArtistKeys actions. The exercises show you how to use these free Photoshop enhancements.

The Step Numbering System

The only time you will see numbers associated with the diamond bulleted steps is when you are expected to create a finished piece of artwork. In some chapters, such as Chapter 29, "Portrait Compositing," and Chapter 30, "Product Compositing," we step away from the creation of the main artwork to do a small tutorial within a tutorial. In those instances, you may already know how to use the tool we are explaining, so feel free to move on to the rest of the exercise. If you don't know how to use the tool or use it well, the tutorial gives you an opportunity to learn and practice before you have to use the tool to create artwork. The tutorials do not have step numbers, because they are not part of the actual process of creating the main image. We've maintained the step numbers in response to many requests from students who go back over the exercises for additional practice. We were asked to point out only the actions they need to take to create the image. If you are doing an exercise for additional practice and want to bypass the explanations, follow the step numbers and the bullets in those steps.

Screenshots and Commands

Almost all of the screenshots in this book are taken from the Mac. Where there are important differences between the Mac and the PC, we've tried to include screenshots of the PC for clarity. All of the keyboard commands are given first in the Mac format, then in the PC format in parentheses. Photoshop works almost identically on both platforms, aside from the keyboard differences between the Mac and PC. Whenever you see square brackets around a keyboard shortcut, such as [F9], those shortcuts refer to the ArtistKeys action set and will work only if you've loaded that action set from the *Photoshop Artistry* DVD.

A Little About the Authors

Three of us have authored this book. Each of us is highly skilled, has a well-developed artistic sensibility, and works with Photoshop in our own way. You may occasionally notice differences in style and opinion throughout this book. However, we agree on the fundamentals of what is important for you to know to work effectively. Most of the time we speak in one voice, but one of us will offer an aside from time to time. This is especially true where we talk about artwork we've created or specific types of work that one of us does exclusively or far more often than the others. All three of us have taught Photoshop for more than a decade, and that also colors how we've written the book. You may notice that we repeat important ideas several times. We do that on purpose, as we know that certain concepts are easily forgotten or difficult to grasp. In teaching the material over the course of the years, we've learned to reinforce those concepts through repetition. If you grasp it the first time, congratulations.

Using *Photoshop Artistry* to Teach Classes

For those of you who use our book to teach classes, note that each student needs to have a copy of the book and DVD to avoid copyright infringement. You may, however, load the images on each machine if each student is required to have a copy of the book as well. This cuts down on problems when students forget to bring the DVD to class.

Here is our suggested setup for your classroom computers when you teach using *Photoshop Artistry*.

Set Up Lighting in the Room

Lighting should be standardized and easily replicated from class meeting to class meeting. If you have lots of windows in the lab, you'll need to make sure you have the blinds down at all times to lessen the influence of sunlight throughout the day. We find that keeping the overhead lights off and using a desk lamp beside each computer is a good way to work. The desk lamp needs to be focused down so the student can read and see their keyboard; but the light should not hit the monitors, which would lower effective display of color and contrast. The main goal is to make sure that light doesn't fluctuate during the course of the classes, changing the way images look onscreen. USB LED lights plugged into the USB keyboard port work well.

Calibrate the Monitors

If you have a calibration device, use it. If not, you can use the built-in Adobe calibrator. On each machine, bring up the calibration image from the folder for Chapter 16, "Color Preferences, Calibration, and Printing," on the DVD. Press F to put each monitor in full-screen mode, and press Tab and then Command (Ctrl)-0 to fit the image on each screen. Look around the room. Do all the computers' images look basically the same? If you have different machines from station to station or older machines at some stations, you may notice differences in the brightness throughout the room. Correct any significant issues if possible.

Put Two Folders on the Desktop

Each machine should have a folder called Photoshop Artistry containing all the files from the DVD you're using for this class. We keep all the files online for all classes, but if you're short of space, you can load only the files for the class you are currently teaching.

The second folder we call Digital Printmaking Files Here. Each student can use this folder to hold his or her classwork. This makes it easier for them to access files for printing or for backup. Make sure students understand how to save files to this folder so their files won't end up in random places.

An Optional Folder

For our advanced classes we use a third folder that contains compensation curves for printers, print drivers, and additional profiles that might be needed for printing to special printers or papers.

Set the Preferences and Color Settings

We've included preferences files for you on the DVD in the Ch01. How To Use This Book folder. Inside that folder is one file, Adobe Photoshop CS2 Paths, and one folder, Adobe Photoshop CS2 Settings. You need to copy both of these on each machine. Copy them over the ones that already exist when Photoshop is not running.

On a Mac running OS 10.2.4 or higher, put both the Photoshop CS2 Preferences file and folder on the boot hard drive in a folder with the following pathname: Users/*YourUserName*/Library/Preferences/Adobe Photoshop CS2 Settings. On Windows XP, put these items in the following folder: C:\Documents and Settings\ *Your User Name*\Application Data\Adobe\Photoshop\9.0\Adobe Photoshop CS2 Settings.

Keep these files handy—people often make changes to preference settings and then can't figure out why their images don't look right or their readouts differ from those in the book. Also, when you run through the preferences in a classroom situation, people often miss making some of the settings. So even if you intend to walk your students through the creation of preferences, it's still a good idea to load ours again and restart Photoshop before the students work on images.

Suggested Course Outlines

On the last page of this chapter we list our suggested course outlines. Please feel free to modify them to suit your class. They are only suggestions. We advise you to demonstrate the examples for the students. Ask them to watch first. Break the examples in manageable sections. Demonstrate a section, have the students work through that section, then move on to the next section until you've completed the entire exercise. If your class size is small enough, you can have students try some of the techniques from the exercises on their own images; or, for any class size, have them practice on their own images as homework.

Working from the Menus

Although all three authors are strong keyboard shortcut users, we often teach our students (especially beginners) by pulling down the menus and showing where the commands reside. We find giving students this visual orientation helps them locate the commands and functions they need. We recommend encouraging students to learn shortcut keys, especially for tools and navigation, but we also recognize that people learn and work in different fashions, so we try to teach in a way that gives all learners the information they need.

Working on Your Own

If you are working through the book on your own, you can still follow the basic outlines included here. Unfortunately, you won't have anyone to deliver the lectures, so read those chapters instead. And consider taking a workshop. We find the interaction between students and instructors invaluable. We've made many lifelong friends through our workshops and have learned a lot ourselves.

Photoshop is a very comprehensive application. You can work at many levels, and you don't need to know everything. It's important to determine how much of the program you really need or you'll drive yourself crazy wading through all the bells and whistles. What we present here is most of what you'll need to know if you're a photographer. And trust us, if you know all there is in this book, you'll be perfectly capable of finding or figuring out anything else you need.

Remember, if you are new to Photoshop, it's a foreign language. It will take you six months to a year to learn enough to be truly comfortable. If you are new to photography, it's also a foreign language. And if you are new to computers, well...

Other Resources

Throughout *Photoshop Artistry,* we try to point you to other books, Web sites, and materials you may find helpful. Our bibliography lists some of the materials we consult and use. We also have downloadable QuickTime training videos that you may find helpful if you learn better from a demonstration than from written material. See our Web site at www.barryhaynes.com for more on these videos.

Portfolios

We've included some of our own work, as well as that of some of our students, for you to enjoy. These portfolio pages give you an idea of what you can do with Photoshop. Now, start creating your own art!

Suggested Course Outlines

R = Read   D = Do   L = Lecture

	Beginners			Intermediate			Advanced
D	CH3	Navigation	R	CH2	Preferences	R	CH2	Preferences
L	CH18	Master Image Workflow	D	CH3	Navigation	D	CH3	Navigation
D	CH19	Making Selections	R	CH18	Master Image Workflow	D	CH22	Correcting Problem Images (File 2 and 3) Steps 12–13
L	CH20	Levels, Curves, Hue/Saturation, and the Histogram	L	CH21	Overall Color Correction	L	CH9	Camera Raw
D	CH21	Overall Color Correction	D	CH22	Correcting Problem Images (File 1) Steps 1–11	D	CH11	Image Processing with Bridge (Actions and Batches)
R	CH6	Selections, Channels, Masks, and Paths	L	CH9	Camera Raw	R	CH16	Color Preferences, Calibration, and Printing
R	CH7	Layer, Layer Masks, and Layer Comps	D	CH11	Image Processing with Bridge (Image Sorting, Color Correction, and Preferences)	D	CH27	Compositing Bracketed Photos
L	CH22	Correcting Problem Images Steps 1–11	D	CH26	Restoring Old Photos	D	CH28	Compositing Multiple Images
D	CH23	Replace Color, Color Range, and Selective Color	D	CH24	Color Matching Images	D	CH29	Portrait Compositing
L	CH9	Camera Raw	L	CH16	Color Preferences, Calibration, and Printing	D	CH25	B&W and Duotones
L	CH2	Preferences	D	CH12	Essential Photoshop Techniques for Photographers	D	CH12	Essential Photoshop Techniques for Photographers
D	CH26	Restoring Old Photos	D	CH25	B&W and Duotones	D	CH10	Automating Photoshop
			D	CH30	Product Compositing			
			R	CH14	Digital Imaging and the Zone System			

2 ◆ Preferences and Color Settings

In this chapter, we'll use a step-by-step approach to guide you through Photoshop's Preferences and Color Settings. We'll also cover how to install the custom ArtistKeys actions that are on the DVD, as well as discuss how to configure other user-defined keyboard shortcuts and menus, and how to work with the Preset Manager. We'll conclude the chapter with a brief look at some important preference settings for Adobe Bridge.

Even if you're already somewhat familiar with Photoshop, this chapter is essential reading, since following the recommended settings not only ensures that you have the most effective settings for photographic work, but also configures Photoshop as it's referenced throughout this book. Before doing the color correction exercises in the hands-on chapters, you should also read **Chapter 15**, "Color Spaces, Device Characterization, and Color Management," and **Chapter 16**, "Color Preferences, Calibration, and Printing," and create the preference settings described in those chapters as well. Other chapters that are essential for understanding digital imaging fundamentals and our concept of the digital workflow are **Chapter 17**, "Image Resolution and Scanning," and **Chapter 18**, "The Master Image Workflow."

◆ Launch Photoshop CS2 if it's not already running.

◆ On a Mac, the Preferences reside under the Photoshop menu at the far left of the Menu bar. On a PC, choose Preferences/General from the Edit menu. You can also use the keyboard shortcut Command (Ctrl)-K.

The Preferences divide into nine sections, and we will go through them in the order that they appear. We will not cover every preference in detail, and some we won't cover at all. If we don't mention one, either it's self-explanatory or we are not changing it from the default setting. Our focus will be on the settings that are most important for working efficiently with photographs. In addition to reading about each preference, you can also refer to the screen shots and set the Preferences as shown in the illustrations. At the end of this process (or in the middle, if you decide to complete this section in more than one session), you will need to quit Photoshop in order to save all of the new preferences and color settings.

General Preferences

The first panel of options are the General Preferences. As the name suggests, these are not specific to any one part of the program. Many of the settings here are not vitally important, but a few warrant a closer look.

Color Picker

The Adobe Color Picker is the default setting; it gives you many more options than either the Apple Color Picker or the Windows System Color Picker. In addition, it's a great place to learn about color!

◆ Choose the Adobe Color Picker.

Image Interpolation

The Image Interpolation setting determines the default algorithm that is used for resizing images. This process is also known as resampling, and it involves either creating new pixels to make an image larger or taking some away to make it smaller. For a general setting, we recommend using the default, Bicubic, which is very good for resampling photographs. For specific cases, Bicubic Smoother is

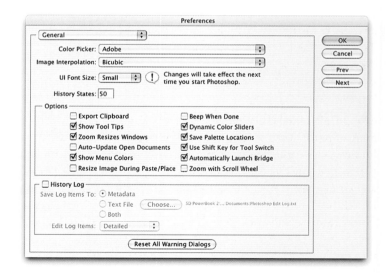

The General Preferences.

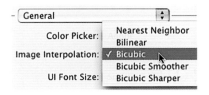

The interpolation options in the General Preferences.

best for upsampling (making an image larger), and Bicubic Sharper is better for downsampling (making an image smaller). All of the interpolation choices are also available in the Image Size dialog, which is where you would usually initiate a resampling command, and you can make different choices there if necessary. If you resample an image by using the Crop tool or the Transformation commands (which we don't recommend), then the default of Bicubic will be used. It would be nice if Adobe added the interpolation choices to the Options bar for both the Crop tool and the Transformation controls. Nearest Neighbor is the fastest interpolation method, but it's not suitable for photographs, since it offers the poorest quality. It can be useful for resizing black-and-white line art and screen captures, however, because it doesn't soften an image's sharp edges by adding transitional pixels (anti-aliasing) when you increase the size.

◆ Choose Bicubic for the interpolation method.

History States

The History States setting determines the number of versions from a single work session that Photoshop remembers. Every time you do something to an image, whether it is applying a color correction adjustment or painting an area with a brush tool, the program creates a record of the state of the image at that point in the editing history. This setting also determines the number of Undo levels you have available; they appear in the History palette as a list of previous commands called history states (the oldest state is at the top of the list and the most recent is at the bottom).

The default setting is 20 and the maximum number is 1000. Keeping track of history states does require RAM and scratch disk resources, however, so whether you can actually take advantage of a large number will depend on your system, as well as the size of the file you are working on (we will discuss scratch disks in more detail later in this chapter). When Barry is working on a very large file, he sometimes sets the number to 1 to make Photoshop perform faster, since it doesn't have to keep track of a large list of history states. As a compromise between the default of 20 and the maximum of 1000, we find that 50 works well most of the time. If you are doing spotting

or retouching where more history states may be useful, then you can always set it to a higher number for those editing situations.

◆ Set the History States number to 50.

Additional General Preferences

In the center section of the General Preferences are check boxes for 12 options. Most of them are self-explanatory (or, if you mouse over each choice, a tool tip will give you additional information about that choice). Refer to the screen shot illustration at the bottom of the previous page to see how these options should be configured. We will give background information for only the most important of these.

Export Clipboard

You need this feature only if you want to copy data in Photoshop and paste it into another program. Turning this off will make switching between Photoshop and other applications faster. You can still cut and paste inside Photoshop, just not between Photoshop and other applications.

◆ Set Export Clipboard to Off (unchecked).

Zoom Resizes Windows

If this is on, then Command (Ctrl) + (plus) or Command (Ctrl) – (minus) in Standard Screen mode will resize your window to fit the new zoom factor as you zoom in or out. Resizing windows for the Zoom tool, including for Command (Ctrl)-Spacebar-click and Option (Alt)-Spacebar-click, is controlled using the Resize Windows to Fit option in the Options bar for the Zoom tool.

◆ Set Zoom Resizes Windows to On.

Dynamic Color Sliders

Dynamic Color Sliders allows the Color palette and other areas to show you all the possible color combinations as you move each color slider. In addition to being a good way to preview color changes, this feature is also very useful to have on when you're color correcting.

◆ Set Dynamic Color Sliders to On.

Save Palette Locations

Save Palette Locations remembers where you had all the palettes the last time you quit Photoshop, and restores them the next time you open the program. We recommend taking advantage of this useful option. If you turn this off, then your palettes will appear in the default state the next time you start Photoshop.

◆ Set Save Palette Locations to On.

Use Shift Key for Tool Switch

Holding the Shift key down and then typing a tool's single-letter shortcut key will cycle through all the tools in that group. For example, holding the Shift key down and repeatedly typing L will switch among the standard, Polygonal, and Magnetic Lasso tools. Turning this feature off means that simply typing the shortcut key several times without the Shift key down will cycle through the available tools for that shortcut. It's perfectly fine to have it set up this way, but it can often be confusing for people who are unaware of the behavior. We recommend turning this option on.

◆ Set Use Shift Key for Tool Switch to On.

Automatically Launch Bridge

This is a convenience setting that will launch Adobe Bridge whenever you start Photoshop. If you use Bridge for sorting through your images and finding images to work on, then this is very useful. If you do not want to have it start up right after Photoshop, you can also leave this preference unchecked and launch Bridge from the Folder icon on the Options bar.

◆ Set Automatically Launch Bridge to On.

History Log

This option provides the ability to save a log of what you did to an image in Photoshop. The Save Log Items To section controls where the History log is saved. You can save it in the metadata of the file, to a separate text file, or to both locations. Metadata is additional information about the image that is saved with the file.

To access the metadata information, you use File/File Info, then click on the History choice to the left. Saving the History log to a file's metadata will result in larger file sizes, but since the saved log is text data, the increase may not be that significant. Saving the log to a text file saves the information about all the files you work on and everything you do in Photoshop in a text file with a name and location that you choose. The Both setting saves the info for a particular file in that file's metadata and also logs everything to the specified text file.

The Edit Log Items section determines how much information is saved. The choices are Sessions Only, Concise, and Detailed. Sessions Only just keeps track of when you open and close each file. This could be useful if you need to track the time spent on a job for billing purposes. Concise keeps the session info, as well as the history of what you did while in Photoshop.

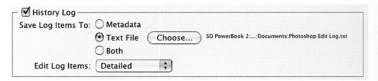

The History Log options.

A History Log can be recorded using three different methods, each more detailed than the previous one.

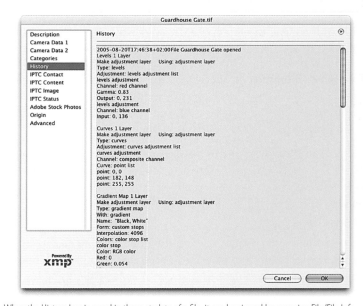

When the History Log is saved in the metadata of a file, it can be viewed by accessing File/File Info.

The Concise log lists History similar to the way the History palette lists history states. Detailed keeps track of all the Concise info, as well as all of the settings for every command you apply (for example, the exact numeric settings of a specific color correction). A Detailed log looks very similar to what an action (a recorded series of Photoshop steps) looks like if you open up all of the steps in the Actions palette to see the details of each command. The Detailed option gives you a lot of information about what you did to an image. Figuring out exactly what this information means is another matter (which could be the subject of yet another Photoshop book). Although there may be some situations where having a History log is useful, for the purposes of this book you do not need to have it turned on; we suggest turning this on only if you really need it or are curious to see what the information in a History log looks like.

◆ Set History Log to Off (unchecked).

Reset All Warning Dialogs

Various dialogs in Photoshop give you the option of turning them off so that they no longer issue a warning about their particular issue again in the future. Reset All Warning Dialogs will bring all those dialogs up again until you turn them off.

◆ Click the Next button to proceed to the next set of Preferences.

File Handling Preferences

The second panel of the Preferences is divided into three sections: File Saving Options, File Compatibility, and Version Cue.

Image Previews

The Icon option refers to the tiny picture of your image you see when you're looking at your file in the Mac Finder or in Windows Explorer. The Thumbnail option refers to the preview you see in the Open dialog on a Mac or PC. The Full Size option saves a 72-dots-per-inch full-size preview for applications that can use this feature—there aren't many. It's mostly a waste of space that makes the file size unnecessarily large, so we recommend that you leave this check box unchecked.

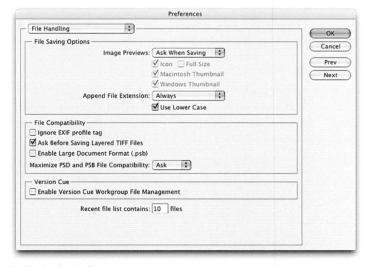

The File Handling Preferences.

When you choose the Ask When Saving pop-up choice, you have the option of including the icons or thumbnails as you save a file. You also can choose to Always Save an Icon and/or Thumbnail or Never Save one. If you are working on files specifically for the Web, it's best to set the Image Preview options to Never Save, because any type of preview will increase your file size and they are never seen by the viewer. You also might want to choose Never Save if you are working on very large files and don't want to wait for the thumbnails to be generated. The Ask When Saving option gives you the most flexibility, letting you decide on a case-by-case basis whether previews or thumbnails make sense for the image you're working on.

◆ Set Image Previews to Ask When Saving.

Append File Extension

If you turn this on (by choosing either Always or Ask When Saving), Photoshop appends the correct three-character file extensions to files so they can be understood and opened on any platform. This is very important, especially when you save more obscure file formats, like the settings from within some of the color correction dialogs. Plus, it is also quite useful, when you're looking at a list of your own files, to be able to distinguish between the different file formats you may have used.

◆ Set Append File Extension to Always/Use Lower Case.

Ignore EXIF Profile Tag

Some digital cameras tag their files with an sRGB color profile in the file's EXIF data. For certain cameras this may represent an accurate interpretation of the image's colors, while for others it is no more than an industry-standard default, which may not be the best interpretation. If this option is enabled, then digital camera files with a camera-generated EXIF tag will be treated in the same way that files with no embedded profile are treated. Generally we recommend that you leave this option off. If your color settings are configured as we recommend later in this chapter, then you will have the option to decide how to handle these files when you open them. A case where you might want to turn this option on is if your camera tags the files with sRGB but you discover that they look more accurate when viewed as Adobe RGB. With the Ignore EXIF Profile Tag option on, you could choose how to interpret the file when using color settings described later in this chapter. See also Chapters 15, 16, and 18 for more information on these subjects.

◆ Set Ignore EXIF Profile Tag to Off.

Ask Before Saving Layered TIFF Files

Let's say you open a TIFF file created by your scanning software. If you add any layers to that file and then save it, Photoshop will just save it in TIFF format, along with all the layers, because that was the original format for that file (Photoshop introduced support for layered TIFFs in version 6.0). In some workflow situations that are geared toward design and page layout, the TIFF version of the file often represents a flattened version of the main image that has been prepped for a page layout program. Turning this option on will serve as a reminder that a layered file is being saved in TIFF format so that you have the chance either to use File/Save As to save it in the PSD format or to flatten the layers before saving as a TIFF.

◆ Set Ask Before Saving Layered TIFF Files to On.

Enable Large Document Format (.psb)

When you turn this feature on, Photoshop allows you to save files in the PSB format, a special file format designed for very large files whose dimensions or file sizes exceed the limitations of more standard formats such as PSD and TIFF. The maximum pixel dimension supported by PSB is 300,000x300,000 pixels (with an RGB file, such an image would be over 251 GB!). These large files, with full layer support, can only be saved in PSB format and TIFF format (up to 4 GB). The only reason you would ever need to save in the PSB format is if you are working with massive files that exceed a dimension of 30,000x30,000 pixels, or if you are working with a large dimension, 16-bit file with many layers whose file size is larger than 4 GB for TIFF or 2 GB for PSD. Most users will want to leave this option off unless they need to work with really huge files. Files saved in the PSB format are readable only by Photoshop CS2 or CS.

◆ Set Enable Large Document Format (.psb) to Off.

Maximize PSD and PSB File Compatibility

When you save a layered file with this option enabled, Photoshop creates an additional full-resolution version that represents what the image would look like if the layers were flattened (the program refers to this as a full-resolution composite). The idea behind this functionality is to allow other programs, such as Adobe InDesign, Illustrator, or even older versions of Photoshop, to import or open the image and ensure that the appearance of the layered file is accurate. These other programs are actually using the flattened, full-res composite version. Depending on your layout workflow, another potential benefit is that you could also update the layered file, and the flattened

If the Maximize Compatibility preference is enabled or set to ask when saving, this message appears when saving a layered file in the PSD or PSB format. Unchecking the check box will save the file without the full resolution composite.

Name	Size
Max-Compatibility-OFF.psd	136.6 MB
Max-Compatibility-ON.psd	248.2 MB

With Maximize Compatibility turned off, a 200 MB file with three adjustment layers takes up just 136 MB of disk space when saved in PSD format. When Maximize Compatibility is turned on, the addition of the full-resolution composite creates a file size that is over 100 MB larger.

composite that is placed in InDesign (but linked to the layered file) would automatically be updated when the changes were saved.

But using this option exacts a significant cost—in the form of increased file sizes. This may not be a big issue for people working on modest-sized layout images or graphics for a Web design, but for some photographers, especially those working on large images, it can be critical. With Maximize File Compatibility enabled, every time a file with layers is saved, Photoshop must also save a flattened version of the file. This flattened composite version is then saved with the main layered file. Turning the Maximize File Compatibility option off saves disk space and time (the larger the file, the longer it takes to save it) when you're working on layered files. For example, let's say you're a landscape photographer accustomed to working with large scans from medium- or large-format film, and you open a 200 MB scan of a medium-format transparency. With Maximize Compatibility on, if you then add a couple of adjustment layers and save this file, it will be over 100 MB larger on disk than if you had saved the file with that feature turned off.

Another possible (but, in our opinion, unconvincing) justification for maximizing compatibility is that a visual reference for how the image should look is included with the layered file. This would be an issue only if any Blend modes were used in the layers, and if future versions of Photoshop changed the algorithm for how the blending was calculated. When using the workflow that we suggest, however, you will already have a reference in the form of a flattened file that has been optimized for making a fine print. See Chapter 18 for more on workflow issues, and Chapter 31, "Blend Modes, Calculations, and Apply Image," to learn about Blend modes.

In the past, it was much easier for us simply to recommend that most people set this to Never, because leaving it on makes your saved Photoshop files much larger than they need to be. Photographers who are working with their images only in Photoshop (and aren't switching back and forth between the current and older versions of the program) and are not using their layered files in other programs, such as InDesign, do not need this functionality and they certainly can do without the bloated file sizes.

Photographers do use other programs, however, that make use of the flattened, full-resolution composite image that is generated when Maximize Compatibility is turned on. Adobe Bridge, for example, will use the flattened composite image of a layered file if one is available. This will speed up the time it takes to create thumbnails and previews of layered images for you to browse in Bridge. (Of course, once created, the thumbnails and previews are always quickly accessible in the central cache file or in the distributed cache files used by Bridge; see the section on Bridge preferences at the end of this chapter for more on the Bridge cache files.) Other programs that use the full-res composite version are digital asset management software such as iView MediaPro and Extensis Portfolio. Both use the composite generated by the Maximize Compatibility option for creating accurate thumbnail and preview images of layered files.

If you use only Photoshop for your imaging work and do not rely on other programs that may need the full-res composite, then our recommendation is to set this option to Never. If you want the flexibility to decide whether you want to maximize the compatibility on a case-by-case basis, then set this to Ask. If you are working with 16-bit images, then the flattened composite image is saved even if you have specified Never for this functionality (see Chapter 18 for more on workflow issues with 16-bit files).

◆ Set Maximize Compatibility to Ask or Never.

Version Cue

Version Cue is a separate program that is part of the Adobe Creative Suite, but is not included with stand-alone versions of Photoshop. It allows you to manage files that multiple people may be working on, such as in a networked workgroup environment in a design studio. If you are using Version Cue in your workflow, then you should turn this on. If not, it's OK to leave it unchecked.

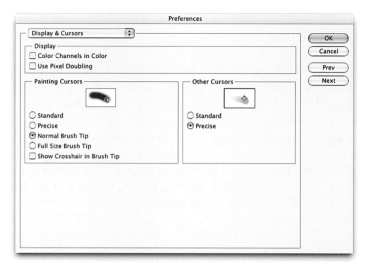

The Display & Cursors Preferences.

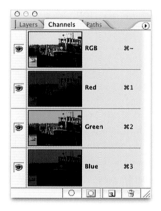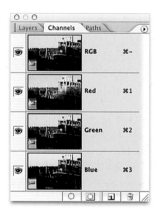

Viewing the color channels in color makes it hard to see subtle tonal details in the channels (left). Using the default grayscale display of the color channels (right) is a much better way to work.

Display & Cursors

Color Channels in Color

This option displays the Red, Green, and Blue, or CMYK channels with a bright-colored transparent overlay that makes it very hard to see image detail. Viewing individual channels in grayscale (the default setting) provides a more accurate view of the details. See Chapter 6, "Selections, Channels, Masks, and Paths," for more information about channels.

◆ Set Color Channels in Color to Off.

Use Pixel Doubling

This option speeds up screen redrawing by using a reduced resolution for the screen display when moving data such as layers or selected areas. If you have a very slow system, it might be helpful, but we have never found it to be necessary.

◆ Set Use Pixel Doubling to Off.

Painting Cursors

When Painting Cursors is set to Normal Brush Tip (the default), the cursor will appear as a circular outline that is the size of your brush. This is far more useful than the Standard cursor, which shows the Paintbrush icon, or the Precise cursor, which shows crosshairs at the center "hot spot" of the brush tip. This setting even takes into account the current zoom factor, which is very useful.

The Normal Brush Tip shows the size of the brush up to the point where the edge feathering that creates a soft edge is at 50%. There is tone being applied beyond the edges of the Normal Brush Tip, but it is so slight as to be hardly noticeable (though you can detect it by sampling with the Eyedropper tool and checking the Info palette). Photoshop CS2 has a new painting cursor called Full Size Brush Tip, which shows you the entire area of brush tip coverage out to the point where no tone is being applied. For most purposes, however, this is not very useful and may even cause confusion as to the true area that the brush will affect.

Another new option in Photoshop CS2 is the ability to display crosshairs in the center of the brush tip. We usually leave this off, because having it on with smaller brushes gets in the way of seeing what you are painting.

◆ Set Painting Cursors to Normal Brush Tip.

Other Cursors

For the Other Cursors option, we recommend the Precise setting, which gives you a very accurate crosshairs for all the nonpainting tools. If you like the visual feedback that a tool icon gives you about

which tool is active, however, then you may choose to leave this set to Standard (you can always display a precise cursor by pressing the Caps Lock key).

◆ Set Other Cursors to Precise.

◆ Click the Next button to proceed to the next set of Preferences.

Transparency & Gamut

Transparency Settings

These allow you to change the appearance of the checkerboard pattern, which represents the transparent areas of a layer. The default settings work fine for us, but for some projects, such as working with line art elements where the line art has colors similar to the transparency grid, you might need to change the settings. Clicking each color swatch will bring up the Color Picker, letting you choose new colors for the checkerboard. Careful though: You can end up with some combinations that are pretty hard on the eyes!

◆ Leave Transparency at the default settings.

Gamut Warning

When you're preparing images for CMYK, the Gamut Warning overlays the designated color (in the case of the default, a middle gray) on top of any colors in the image that are out of gamut, or that can't be reproduced in CMYK or in the color space that is being proofed. This is a useful feature because once the out-of-gamut colors have

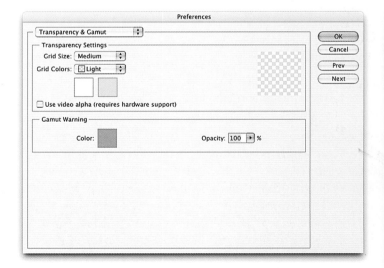

The Transparency & Gamut Preferences.

A Normal Brush Tip cursor (left) compared to a Full Size Brush Tip cursor (right). The Normal Brush Tip gives a much more accurate view of the area that will be affected by the brush stroke.

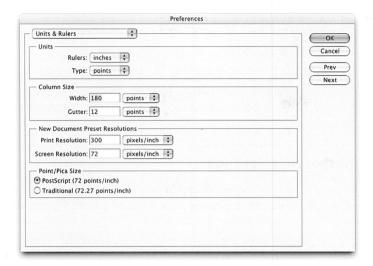

The Units & Rulers Preferences.

In addition to setting the Units in the Preferences, you can also change the Units in the Info palette by clicking the small crosshairs in the cursor coordinates section, or by right-clicking (Control-clicking with a one-button Mac mouse) in the rulers themselves.

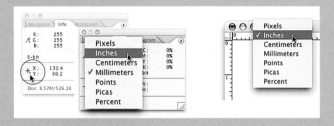

been identified, you can make further adjustments to bring them into gamut. The default gray color works very well for this purpose.

◆ Leave Gamut Warning at the default setting.

◆ Click the Next button to proceed to the next set of Preferences.

Units & Rulers

For most of these settings we don't have a definite recommendation, since they are subject to personal preference and the demands of a particular project. We do have some background information, though, on how these settings can affect different areas of Photoshop.

Units

This setting controls the scale on Photoshop's rulers, which are shown via the View/Show Rulers menu option. It also controls the dimension display settings in the Info palette and the initial dimension display when you enter the Image Size and Canvas Size dialogs.

We usually leave it set at inches, but for very detailed measurements as well as for Web and multimedia projects, we change it to pixels. Of course, if you are more comfortable with centimeters, then that may be the best setting for your work. There is also a Percent setting here, which will display your scale and, more important, record your actions using a percentage of the total image size. You should choose Percent for the Units when making actions where proportional locations and sizes are more important than actual inches, pixels, or centimeters. See Chapter 10, "Automating Photoshop," for more on working with actions.

Column Size

If you are accustomed to creating documents and pages that are based on a column layout, this is the place where you specify the exact size of the columns. The ability to specify document size in columns can be found in the New Document, Image Size, and Canvas Size dialogs.

New Document Preset Resolutions

In the New Document dialog, you can choose from many presets that represent common page and screen sizes. This setting determines the resolution for those presets. The defaults are fine.

Point/Pica Size

Software is standardized on the PostScript interpretation of the point/pica system. In the many years we have been doing digital imaging and layout work, we've never had a reason to use the Traditional scale.

◆ Set Point/Pica Size to PostScript.

◆ Click the Next button to proceed to the next set of Preferences.

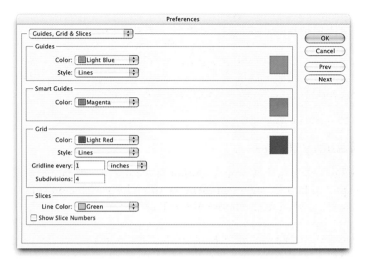

The Guides, Grid & Slices Preferences.

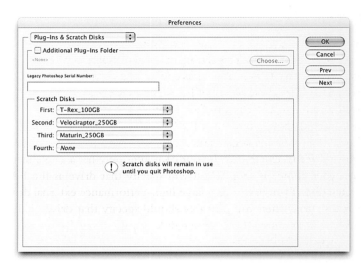

The Plug-Ins & Scratch Disks Preferences. Open the drop-down menu for the First, Second, Third, and Fourth Scratch Disks to choose from the available hard disks on your system.

Guides, Grid & Slices

As with the previous section, there are no required settings here; for our purposes, the default settings are fine. The colors you use for guides, grids, and slices are typically determined by the colors in the image you are working on (in other words, you need contrasting colors in order to see them), and the size of the grid is also usually a project-specific setting. When working on projects that use a layout grid, we use the grid and guides to help place objects precisely. When the Move tool is active, you can double-click a guide to bring up the Guides and Grid preferences to quickly change the colors and styles, and view these changes as you make them.

Slices are used for dividing an image or layout into sections that can be saved and compressed with different settings for use on Web pages. One thing you should do here is uncheck the Show Slice Numbers check box. In some instances, slice lines may also be visible over your image, and many people who don't need this functionality find this a bit irritating. To turn off the visibility of the slice lines, go to the main menu and choose View/Show/Show Extras Options. In the Show Extras Options dialog, uncheck Slices to hide them. We will not be covering slices in this book, but if you do need to divide an image into slices for a Web project, you'll want to turn Show Slices back on.

◆ Use the Default settings for Guides, Grid, and Slices, or change to specific colors and styles as needed.

◆ Click the Next button to proceed to the next set of Preferences.

Plug-Ins & Scratch Disks

Additional Plug-Ins Folder

This tells Photoshop where to find additional plug-in filters that are stored in a location other than the default plug-ins folder (the default plug-ins that ship with Photoshop are already set up when you install the program). In Mac OS X, they are in a folder called Plug-Ins, directly inside the Adobe Photoshop CS2 folder that is normally installed in the Applications folder on your boot drive. In Windows XP, the plugs-ins folder is found at: C:\Program Files\Adobe\Photoshop\Plug-Ins. You can always add more plug-ins to that folder and then restart Photoshop.

Third-party plug-ins will usually appear in their own menu section (such as Nik Color Efex Pro) under the main Filter menu. The different filters belonging to a plug-in will be listed under that submenu. If you want to get additional plug-ins from another folder that resides outside the Plug-Ins folder mentioned above, then check the Additional Plug-Ins Folder check box. Navigate to find the folder that contains the additional plug-ins, and then, on a Mac, click the Choose button at the bottom right of the dialog (don't click the Open button at that point, as you would for most other cases with an Open dialog, or you'll just open the folder to continue the search). On a PC, you click OK after clicking the folder that actually contains the additional plug-ins.

Scratch Disks

A scratch disk is temporary space on your hard disk that Photoshop uses for its calculations. This setting tells Photoshop what hard drives you want to specify as scratch disks and in what order they should be used. Even if you have plenty of RAM, in most cases Photoshop will need to use a scratch disk. In fact, Photoshop requires more scratch disk space than the amount of RAM it uses. As a general rule, you should always use the largest, fastest disk drive you can afford for your primary (First) scratch disk. If your computer only has a single drive, then your choice is simple: You will specify that drive as the First scratch disk. If you have a very large high-performance external drive or a disk array, then you probably should specify that drive or disk array as your primary (First) scratch disk, because it will be faster than your original, built-in drive.

If you have several hard drives on your system, you can also specify Second, Third, and Fourth disks on which Photoshop can store temp files when it runs out of space on the First drive. Try to leave at least five to ten times the scratch space for the size of the file you're working on, and certainly leave much more space on the disk than the amount of RAM that is assigned to Photoshop. To see how much RAM Photoshop is using for an image, open the pop-up menu at the bottom left of the document window when in Standard Screen mode (you can also see this in the Info palette by choosing it in the palette options). The Scratch Sizes option shows you on the left the amount of RAM that is being used by all open documents and on the right the amount of RAM that is allocated to Photoshop. If the number on the left is larger than the number on the right, then Photoshop is using the hard disk for scratch space. See the ReadMe file that comes with Photoshop for more information about improving Photoshop performance.

◆ Click the Next button to proceed to the next set of Preferences.

Memory & Image Cache

Image Cache

In order to increase the display efficiency when working with larger files, Photoshop makes several internal copies of the file at different zoom sizes and uses the smaller versions to update the screen quickly when the display view is zoomed out. Leaving the Cache set to 6, the new default (the previous default was 4), seems to work quite well for both small and large files. With small files Photoshop will probably be so fast that you won't notice a difference between the number of cache levels, and the extra memory overhead for the Cache is mini-

mal. The larger the Image Cache setting, the more RAM and scratch disk space Photoshop uses when you open a file. If you don't have much memory and are working with very large files, you may want to reduce the size of the Image Cache. The largest Image Cache setting is 8, and 1 turns off the Image Cache, forcing screen refreshes to wait for calculations to be finished on the entire file.

◆ Set the Cache levels to 6.

Memory Usage

Before setting the maximum amount of memory Photoshop uses, it is helpful to know how much memory you have available on your system. On a Macintosh, choose About This Mac from the Apple menu. An information window opens, showing you the total amount of memory available on your Macintosh. On a Windows system, right-click the My Computer icon on the desktop and choose Properties from the pop-up menu. The total amount of memory that is installed is listed at the bottom of the General tab in the System Properties dialog.

In Photoshop's Memory & Image Cache Preferences section, the default Memory Usage setting is 50%. For our Mac systems, which have between 1 and 2.25 GB of RAM installed, we generally allocate 75% to 85% of the available memory to Photoshop. We would use the same amounts on a Windows computer.

The more memory you have installed on your computer, the higher the percentage you can allocate to Photoshop, because there will still be enough left for the operating system and other, less memory-

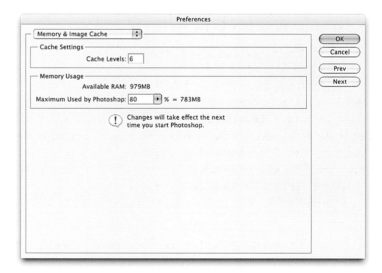

The Memory & Image Cache Preferences.

Monitoring Memory Efficiency

Photoshop has a scratch disk efficiency indicator. To access it, select Efficiency in the pop-up menu at the bottom left of the document window when in Standard Screen mode. You can also see how much RAM is being used for the file you're working on, as well as the total RAM allocated to Photoshop by choosing Scratch Sizes from the same menu. These options can also be viewed at the bottom of the Info palette by choosing them from that palette's options.

The efficiency rating changes depending on the amount of time Photoshop spends swapping image data in and out of RAM from the disk. If your efficiency rating is less than 100% for most operations, you are using the scratch disk instead of RAM. If such is the case, then you might want to add more RAM to your system to get better performance.

On the Mac, if the ✳ character follows the percentage number, your primary (First) scratch disk is operating with asynchronous I/O working. That is good for better performance because async I/O allows the disk to read or write while Photoshop does something else. If you don't see the ✳, check the folder called Enable Async I/O within the Applications/Adobe Photoshop CS2/Plug-Ins/Adobe Photoshop Only/Extensions folder. If this folder has the character ~ in front of it, remove that character and restart Photoshop. This turns on asynchronous I/O for Photoshop's primary scratch disk. If you still don't see the ✳ character, read the About Enable Async I/O document in the Enable Async I/O folder to learn how to set up the correct disk drivers for async I/O.

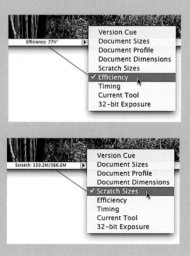

intensive applications to run efficiently. If you don't have much memory—less than 512 MB, for example—or if you want to run more than one memory-intensive application at the same time, then use the 50% default setting; if you have lots of memory, give Photoshop a higher percentage. After setting the memory usage, you will need to quit Photoshop and then restart the program for these changes to take effect (but you don't need to reboot your operating system). You can do this after you've finished setting all the Preferences (there's only one more panel to go). When Photoshop starts up, it calculates the available RAM in your system by measuring the amount of installed RAM and subtracting all that is used by software that permanently reserves RAM (including the Mac or Windows OS). Check the Scratch Size and Efficiency box at the bottom left of your open document window to see how much RAM is available and how Photoshop is using it. See the previous section on "Plug-Ins & Scratch Disks" for more information on scratch disk size and efficiency.

◆ Click the Next button to proceed to the next set of Preferences.

Type Preferences

These settings are new to this version of Photoshop and are obviously not that crucial for working with photographs. Refer to the illustration on this page to see how ours are configured. If you are working with Asian text, you will, of course, want to enable that check box.

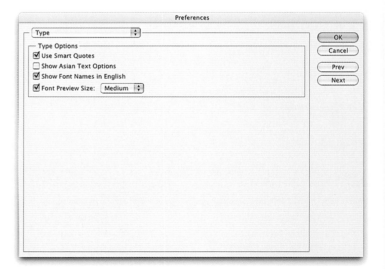

The Type Preferences.

◆ Click the OK button to close the Preferences dialog and accept the changed settings.

◆ If you want to complete the rest of this chapter at another time, you should quit Photoshop now. Performing a controlled shutdown of the program will save the new Preferences settings. If you will be continuing directly to the next section on the Color Settings, you can quit the program after completing that section.

Configuring the Color Settings

The Color Settings are "mission control" for how Photoshop handles color in the images you work with. These settings not only affect the display of images, but also control how color separations and conversions from one color space to another are made. The settings shown here are what we use for most situations, and we recommend them for general photographic use. It should be noted, however, that some of the settings, such as the CMYK and Spot workspaces, are output-specific, and the setting that you use will be determined by how the image will be reproduced on a printing press. (If you're only printing to your desktop inkjet printer, you don't even need to worry about these settings.) Our recommendations for the CMYK and Spot settings are intended only as a starting point.

In this section we will show you the settings we recommend for working with photographs. At this point in the book, however, we are not going to explain all of them in exhaustive detail, because a thorough explanation involves a lot of background material that is presented in Chapter 16, "Color Preferences, Calibration, and Printing." Instead, we will show you a quick way to set most of the settings as we recommend, and show you how to save those settings so that they appear as a menu choice at the top of the Color Settings dialog. We'll give some brief background information for some items, and you can find more detailed coverage of them in Chapter 16.

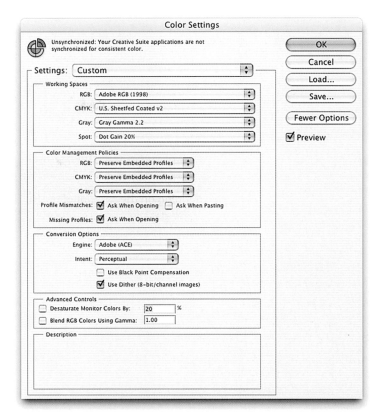

The Color Settings configured for photography work in Photoshop.

◆ Choose Edit/Color Settings, or use Command (Ctrl)-Shift-K, to open the dialog. If you have not changed any of these since installing the program, they will still be set to the defaults.

◆ In the Settings menu at the top of the dialog, choose North America Prepress 2.

This will configure most of the settings the way we want them for working with this book. One of the most important settings specifies that Adobe RGB (1998) will be the RGB working space. This has a larger color gamut than sRGB, which is the default RGB working space. Also key is that the Color Management Policies are set to preserve any embedded profiles they encounter.

◆ Set the CMYK working space to U.S. Sheetfed Coated v2. As mentioned previously, this should only be used as a starting point. Talk to your printer if you are preparing files for a real project using CMYK.

◆ Set Gray working space to Gray Gamma 2.2

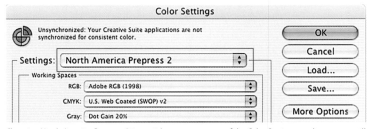

Choosing North America Prepress 2 is a quick way to set most of the Color Settings up the way we will need them for the exercises in this book.

What About Mac Gamma 1.8?

The default "standard" gamma on Macs is 1.8, but if you are using a gamma setting for the Gray workspace, we still recommend that you set the Gray Gamma to 2.2. The reason? The Mac gamma of 1.8 is a leftover from the early days of the Mac when a 1.8 gamma yielded a better match between Mac grayscale monitors (no color displays back then) and the grayscale output from Apple LaserWriters. Over the years it has become the standard gamma setting for the Mac OS.

A gamma of 2.2 (which is the native gamma on Windows computers) can also be used when calibrating the monitor on your Macintosh system. A gamma of 2.2 is much closer to the tonal response curve of displays and produces fewer aliasing artifacts and smoother tonal transitions in gradients.

The only thing to be aware of is that images you prepare in Photoshop or other color-managed applications will appear a bit darker on a Mac when viewed in a program that does not use color management.

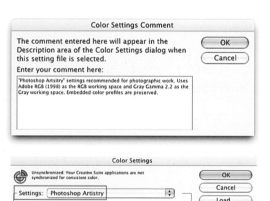

After saving the Color Settings and adding a descriptive comment (above), they will be available as a menu choice at the top of the dialog (below).

Technically, gamma settings are used for images that will be displayed on screens or published in a multimedia project, and dot gain settings are used for images that are reproduced on a printing press. For desktop inkjet printers and continuous-tone photographic printers such as the LightJet 5000, however, Gray Gamma 2.2 works fine (Mac users, see the sidebar "What About Mac Gamma 1.8?" above). If you will be preparing grayscale images specifically for press reproduction, then you will want to use a dot gain percentage that matches the conditions of the press that will print the project.

◆ In the section for Color Management Policies, deselect the check box for Ask When Pasting.

We have found that for nearly all cases, the default behavior of converting the colors of the pasted item to the color space of the destination image is the right choice, and we would rather not be bothered with this particular message box.

After you have set the Color Settings dialog to match the one in the screen shot on the previous page, click the Save button to save this configuration as a menu item that will appear in the Settings menu at the top of the dialog. Name it "Photoshop Artistry." If you want, you can add a comment describing the settings that will appear in the Description section when that menu item is chosen. Ater saving the settings, click OK to close the dialog and finish the rest of the recommended under-the-hood settings in this chapter. For more detailed coverage of the color settings recommendations made in this chapter, you should read Chapters 15 and 16. In those chapters we also explain how to create your own custom color settings.

Synchronizing Color Settings for the Adobe Creative Suite

If you have installed the entire Adobe Creative Suite 2, you can synchronize your Color Settings so they will be the same for all applications

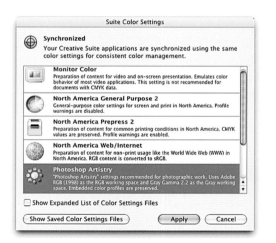

Synchronizing the Color Settings for the Adobe Creative Suite 2 from within Adobe Bridge. This option will be available to you only if you have installed the entire Creative Suite 2.

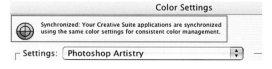

Once the Color Settings have been synchronized for the Creative Suite, you will see a status message about this at the top of the Photoshop Color Settings dialog.

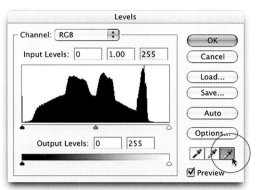

Choosing 3 by 3 Average for the Eyedropper sample size.

in the suite (you will not have this option if you use only the stand-alone version of Photoshop). To synchronize, go to Adobe Bridge and choose Edit/Creative Suite Color Settings. In the Suite Color Settings dialog, choose the saved color settings that you want to use for the entire suite. Once you do this, a Synchronized icon will appear at the top of the Photoshop Color Settings dialog.

In the Levels dialog, double-click the highlight, or white-point, eyedropper to set a target value for the highlights.

Additional Settings for Color Correction

Eyedropper Tool Setup

The default setting for this tool is Point Sample, which measures a single pixel. With this setting, especially if the display of the image is zoomed out, you might accidentally measure a pixel that is slightly different in color from those around it. The 3 by 3 Average setting measures a grid of 9 pixels surrounding the pixel you click on. When working with photographic images, this gives you a more accurate and representative measurement, because most colors are actually made up of groups of different-colored pixels.

◆ In the Tool palette select the Eyedropper tool, and on the Options bar set Sample Size to 3 by 3 Average.

> **NOTE**
>
> Setting the Eyedropper tool to 3 by 3 Average also affects how the Color Sampler tool measures color, as well as how the Magic Wand and the Color Range tools create their selections.

Setting Highlight and Shadow Target Values

The last items that you need to set up for color correction work are the highlight and shadow target values. We will show you how to set them using the Levels dialog, but they can also be set the same way using the Curves dialog.

◆ Open any image into Photoshop.

◆ From the main menu, choose Image/Adjustments/Levels, and in the lower-right corner of the Levels dialog, double-click the highlight, or white-point, eyedropper (the rightmost one).

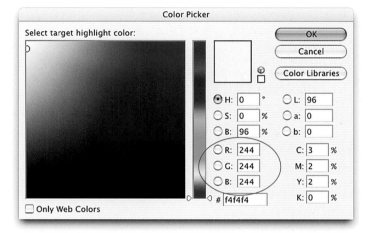

Setting the target values for the highlight eyedropper.

◆ In the Photoshop Color Picker that appears, you should set your RGB highlight target settings to 244, 244, 244 (the CMYK values that correspond to these RGB numbers will depend on your RGB and CMYK workspace settings in the Color Settings dialog we covered earlier in this chapter).

The objective with this setting is to create a target highlight tone that represents a bright, neutral white that still has tonal detail (as opposed to a blown-out white with no detail). A value of 244 for the R, G, and B colors will achieve this. The key to these values is that they are all equal. Using RGB numbers that are equal for the highlight target value will create a neutral highlight color when setting the white point with the highlight eyedropper.

◆ Click OK in the Color Picker to return to the Levels dialog.

◆ Double-click the shadow, or black-point, eyedropper (the leftmost one). In the Color Picker, set the RGB shadow values to 8, 8, 8, then click OK to return to the Levels dialog.

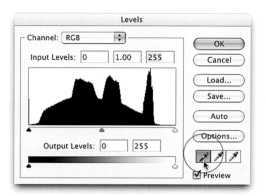

In the Levels dialog, double-click the shadow, or black-point eyedropper, to set a target value for the shadows.

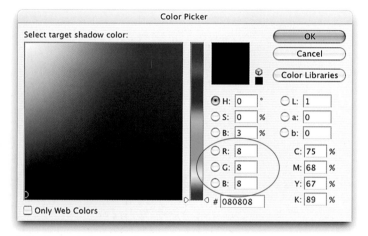

Setting the target values for the shadow eyedropper.

When you click OK in Levels after setting the eyedropper target values, you will see this message. Click Yes to save the new target values as defaults.

◆ Click OK to exit Levels. If you get the message "Save the new target colors as defaults?" click the Yes option (this is not the default active button, so don't press the Return (Enter) key or these new settings will not be saved).

To learn more about these highlight and shadow settings and how to use them to color correct a photograph, refer to the step-by-step exercise in Chapter 21, "Overall Color Correction," which takes you through the basics of color correction.

◆ Quit Photoshop to ensure that all the settings you have configured are saved in the program's Preferences and settings files. Relaunch Photoshop to continue with the rest of the setup.

In the next section we'll cover additional settings that affect some of Photoshop's palettes, as well as the loading of the ArtistKeys actions.

Using the ArtistKeys Actions Set

In the Preferences folder of the *Photoshop Artistry* DVD, we have provided a set of custom actions, called ArtistKeys.atn. We strongly recommend that you load this set of actions into your copy of Photoshop, since we will be referring to these shortcuts throughout the book. In the next section, we'll take you through this process.

Saving Any Previously Created Actions

If you have already created new actions of your own, either in a new set or as additions to the Default Actions set, you should save these actions before loading the ArtistKeys.

◆ To save previous actions, choose Window/Actions to bring up the Actions palette. If the palette is in Button mode (so that it looks like a collection of colored buttons), click the small button at the top-right corner of the palette to open the palette menu, and highlight Button Mode to show the actions as a list.

◆ In List mode, highlight the set of actions you wish to save by clicking it, then choose Save Actions from the Actions palette pop-up menu.

◆ If Default Actions is the only actions set visible, you don't need to be concerned about saving these unless you have added new actions to that set.

The Default Actions set is always available from the Actions palette by choosing Replace Actions or Load Actions from the Actions palette menu.

Loading the ArtistKeys in the Actions Palette

The next step will load the ArtistKeys into the Actions palette and leave any existing actions in place.

The Actions palette seen here in Button mode. To turn off Button mode, open the palette menu and highlight that option at the top of the menu.

◆ Choose Load Actions from the Actions palette menu, and pick the ArtistKeys.atn file from the Ch02.Preferences folder on the *Photoshop Artistry* DVD.

If you would rather replace all actions with ArtistKeys, choose Replace Actions instead of Load Actions. If you choose the Replace Actions option, be sure that you've saved any other actions you've created (this process is described earlier). Choosing Replace Actions will replace *all* actions in the palette, not just the currently highlighted set.

About the ArtistKeys

The ArtistKeys use function keys for the menu items in Photoshop CS2 you'll use most often. For example, F9 through F12 will show and hide the most commonly used palettes. We tried to assign these keys logically, so F9 is the Info palette and Shift-F9 is the Histogram palette, because both of these palettes are critical when doing overall color correction. F10 is the Layers palette and Shift-F10 is the Channels palette, since these palettes are often used together. We use

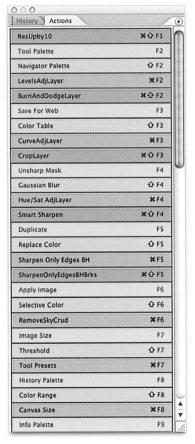

The ArtistKeys loaded into the Actions palette. This view shows only a portion of all the actions as seen in Button mode (Button mode is accessed from the Actions palette pop-up menu).

F2 through F12 to implement single menu items. We mention these keys quite often throughout the book as alternative ways of accessing menu items (the ArtistKeys are always shown in brackets—for example, [F9]—when referenced in a step-by-step chapter).

We think you'll find the ArtistKeys function key set a valuable asset when working in Photoshop. If you ever want to use one of these function keys for something else, make sure you're not in Button mode, then double-click the area to the right of the action name (double-clicking directly on the name allows you to rename the action). By setting the function key for that action to None, you can reassign that function key to another action. For more information about actions, see Chapter 10.

If ArtistKeys Don't Work

Both the Mac and the Windows operating systems reserve some of the function keys for system-specific commands. Before using the ArtistKeys, you will need to find the keyboard preferences for your operating system and turn off the default function key associations.

With Apple PowerBooks and some other laptops, the leftmost function keys (F1 through F5) control screen brightness, sound volume, and other OS settings. This behavior will normally override Photoshop-specific function keys used within Photoshop even if the ArtistKeys are loaded in the Actions palette. At the bottom left of the PowerBook keyboard is a "fn" key; holding this down while pressing a function key will override the system-level commands that are associated with the function keys and perform the Photoshop-specific shortcut that is assigned to it.

In the Apple System Preferences under Keyboard & Mouse, you can also set up the keyboard so that your custom program-specific function keys (such as the ArtistKeys) work normally and the OS-specific functions are accessed when the "fn" key is held down. Some PC laptops, depending on the manufacturer, may also have a similar feature.

This illustration shows how to configure the F1 through F12 keys for custom actions on an Apple PowerBook running OS 10.3.9.

User-Defined Keyboard Shortcuts and Menus

In addition to the ArtistKeys actions set available on the *Photoshop Artistry* DVD, you can also create your own keyboard shortcuts in Photoshop.

◆ From the main menu, choose Edit/Keyboard Shortcuts to access the dialog that controls customization of not only the keyboard shortcuts, but also the menu items.

Custom Keyboard Shortcuts

To create your own set of keyboard shortcuts without altering the default shortcuts that Photoshop ships with, you should create a copy of the default set first.

◆ To do this, click the New Set button (the obscure, inadequately labeled icon showing a floppy disk and a downward arrow), and give the new set a name.

◆ Then use the next drop-down menu to choose between shortcuts for application menus, palette menus, and tools. To change the shortcut for a given item, click in its Shortcut column and then use the keyboard to enter the new shortcut. Use the Save button (the floppy disk icon) at the top of the dialog to save the new shortcuts when you are done.

Before you begin customizing keyboard shortcuts, create a duplicate set by clicking the New Set icon.

After clicking the New Set icon, you will be prompted to choose a name for the new set of keyboard shortcuts.

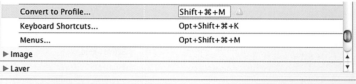

Choosing a shortcut that is already in use will prompt a warning. In this case, the existing menu item for the shortcut was one that was never used, so it made sense to replace it with a command that was used more frequently.

Just remember that creating a new keyboard shortcut for one command may invalidate another shortcut if you try to use the same keys the existing shortcut uses (a warning will appear). But if the key combination you opt for is assigned to a command you rarely use, then such a reassignment should not be a big problem.

We have created a set of keyboard shortcuts that can be used along with the ArtistKeys actions, and if you'll be using the ArtistKeys actions (as we recommend you do for this book), then you should also take advantage of these custom keyboard shortcuts. The file is called ArtistShortcuts.kys and can be found in the Chapter 2 folder on the DVD. To make these shortcuts visible in the Keyboard Shortcuts Set menu, move them into the Presets/Keyboard Shortcuts folder inside the Photoshop application folder.

Using Custom Menu Sets

You can customize menu items either by hiding certain commands or by assigning a color label to them. Barry has created a set of customized menus called ArtistryMenus.mnu that contain only the commands that he feels are most useful for photographers. You can find this in the file Chapter 2 folder on the DVD. To load these menus, do the following.

◆ Quit Photoshop. Locate the Photoshop application folder on your computer. In that folder go to Presets/Menu Customization. Open the Menu Customization folder.

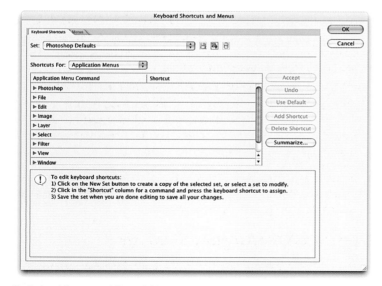

The Keyboard Shortcuts and Menus dialog.

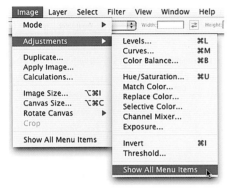

Selecting ArtistryPhotography-Menus in the Keyboard Shortcuts and Menus dialog.

If you are using a custom menu set (such as the Artistry Photography Menus) and you want to see all of the menu commands that are available for a menu, choose Show All Menu Items from the bottom of the active menu.

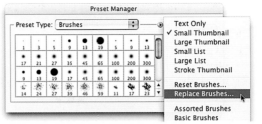

With the Brushes presets active, choose Replace Brushes and load BarrysPhotoBrushes.abr from the *Photoshop Artistry* DVD.

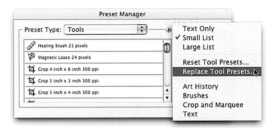

With the Tools presets active, choose Replace Tool Presets and load the ArtistryPresets.tpl from the *Photoshop Artistry* DVD.

◆ On the DVD, open the folder for the Chapter 2 and find the file called ArtistryMenus.mnu. Drag that file from the DVD into the Menu Customization folder.

◆ Relaunch Photoshop and go to Edit/Menus to bring up the Keyboard Shortcuts and Menus dialog. Open the Set menu at the top of the dialog, choose ArtistryPhotographyMenus, and click OK.

Once these menus are loaded, certain commands will not be visible. If you want to see all of the menu items that ship with the program, simply choose Show All Menu Items from the bottom of the active menu, and you'll see every menu item. The next time you use the menu it will revert back to the configuration specified by the custom menu set. Refer to Chapter 10 for more on menu customization.

The Preset Manager

The Preset Manager allows you to configure the appearance and content of several palettes such as the Brushes palette, the Styles palette, the Gradients palette, and others. To access the Preset Manager, choose Edit/Preset Manager.

For many of the palettes that you control with the Preset Manager, you have the choice of replacing the current content with the new content (such as adding new styles to the Styles palette), or appending the new content to the existing list.

Loading Photo Brushes and Tool Presets from the DVD

We have created two files you can load into the Preset Manager that contain special Brushes and Tool presets that Barry has created for his photo work. These Brushes and Tool presets are used throughout the book, so it's important that you load them before continuing with any of the tutorial chapters.

◆ In the Preset Manager, with Preset Type: Brushes selected, use Replace Brushes from the pop-up menu in the Presets dialog, and navigate to the Chapter 2 folder on the *Photoshop Artistry* DVD and select BarrysPhotoBrushes.abr to load them into the Brushes palette. You can also simply drag the file from the DVD into the Presets/Brushes folder in the Photoshop application folder (if you use this latter method, you will need to restart the program in order for the new brushes to show up in the Brushes palette menu).

◆ Next, select Preset Type: Tools, and click Replace Tool Presets to load ArtistryPresets.tpl (this file is also in the Chapter 2 folder on the DVD).

Presets That Are Accessed Indirectly

Some of the items within the Preset Manager don't have regular palettes you can access from the Window menu. Others, like the Brushes

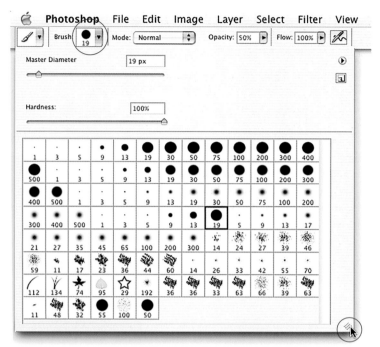

palette, can be accessed from the Window menu, as well as from inside the Options bar, depending on the currently selected tool.

The items that are not available via the Window menu are Gradients, Patterns, Contours, and Custom Shapes. You can find the Gradient Picker on the Gradient tool's Options bar, as well as in certain dialogs where gradients can be applied (such as the Gradient Map adjustment layer dialog, or the Gradient Overlay section of the Layer Styles dialog). You can access the Patterns Picker from the Fill dialog, the Options bar when using the Pattern Stamp or Healing/Patch tools, the Pattern Overlay section of the Layer Styles dialog, and the Texture section of the Bevel and Emboss style. Contours are an option for many of the Layer Styles, and Custom Shapes are accessed from the Options bar when the Custom Shape tool is selected, or in the new Shape Blur filter dialog.

After loading the BarrysPhotoBrushes set, you can drag outward on the lower-right corner of the pop-up Brush Picker to expand it to show all of the available brushes. This will ensure that the next time you click the Brush icon on the Options bar (circled in red above), the picker will open at the same size. To quickly select a brush tip and close the picker at the same time, click and hold on the Brush icon on the Options bar. Then drag down to choose the brush you want and release the mouse button. This will select the chosen brush and close the Brush picker at the same time. This is a very efficient way to select a brush with a single mouse click.

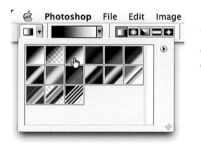

You access the Gradient presets through the Gradient Picker on the Options bar, as well as in any dialogs where gradients are used.

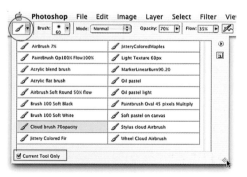

Use the same procedure described above for the Brush Picker to show a larger view of the Tool presets. To select a specific preset, click down on the tool icon on the Options bar and drag to select the tool preset. When you release the mouse button, the picker will close. Make sure the Current Tool Only check box in the lower-left corner is checked.

This Custom Shapes presets can be found in the Options bar for the Custom Shape tool, as well as in the new Shape Blur filter dialog.

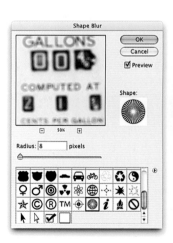

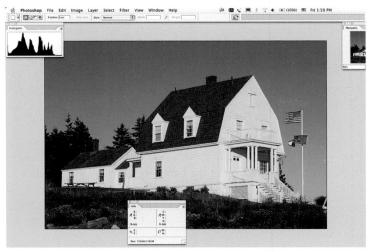

With the screen view set to Full Screen Mode, this is how we generally have our palettes set up for color correction. Once you've created an arrangement of palettes that you think you'll want to use again, choose Window/Workspace/Save Workspace and save it as a custom workspace.

Arranging Your Photoshop Workspace

When you have configured all of the preferences and color settings described so far, you should then arrange your palettes the way you think you'll like them. If you're new to the Photoshop interface and are not yet sure how to arrange the palettes, read Chapter 3, "Navigating in Photoshop." We also recommend several palette arrangements for working with this book—those are covered in Chapter 3 as well.

You can also save different palette layouts that are specific to certain types of work (say, retouching or color correction) by arranging them the way you like them, then choosing Window/Workspace/Save Workspace. The illustration at the top of this page shows the palette arrangement that we use for color correction work. Photoshop CS2 has several predefined workspaces listed at the bottom of this menu (some of which alter the keyboard shortcuts and menu items). When the Save Palette Locations option is checked in the first section of the Preferences, your palette locations will appear as you left them the last time you quit the program.

When working in Photoshop, you should close any palettes you don't need; just click the small "x" at the top of the palette in Windows, or the red button on a Mac. You can always recall palettes by choosing them from the Window menu.

Saving and Standardizing Your Preferences

For Photoshop to save changes you have made to the Preferences, Color Settings, preset configurations, and palette arrangements, you need to quit the program. If you have already done this once in a previous section of this chapter, you still need to do it again to save the most recent changes. When you quit Photoshop on a Mac running OS 10.2.4 or higher, the Photoshop CS2 Preferences files are updated, then stored on your boot hard drive in a folder with the path name Users/*YourUserName*/Library/Preferences/Adobe Photoshop CS2 Settings. In Windows XP, these files are at C:\Documents and Settings*Your User Name*\Application Data\Adobe\Photoshop\9.0\ Adobe Photoshop CS2 Settings. Quitting the program at this point ensures that Photoshop will save your preferences and other settings to these files. If your computer or Photoshop were to crash before a controlled shutdown of the program, you would lose these latest changes to the preferences, and Photoshop would revert to the settings you had in place when you last successfully quit from the program.

If you are part of a creative workgroup or a company where several people are using Photoshop, it is a good idea for everyone to be using the same Color Settings and Preferences. For any printing or publication work, it is vitally important to standardize the color separation, workspace, and profile-handling preferences if you are doing color corrections and separations. Once you set up the Preferences and Color Settings as desired on one machine, you can copy these files to the Photoshop CS2 Settings folders on all the computers running Photoshop to ensure that everyone is using the same settings.

It is a good idea to make a backup copy of your Photoshop CS2 Settings folder once you have set it up as described here. That way if Photoshop is ever acting strangely, you can replace your current settings with that backup copy. We have also placed a Photoshop CS2 Settings folder in the Chapter 2 folder on the *Photoshop Artistry* DVD. You can use the settings files contained in this folder to automatically set up your Photoshop settings by copying them to the correct location.

Bridge Preferences

With Photoshop CS2 the File Browser from the previous two versions of the program evolved into a separate application called Adobe Bridge. For those who are used to the File Browser, Bridge functionality is very similar, but it offers additional features and is a more powerful tool for sorting and organizing not just photos, but also any type of file you might use with the other Creative Suite applications.

We'll cover some strategies for working with images using Bridge in more detail in Chapter 11, "Image Processing with Bridge," but in this section we want to point out a few useful Bridge preferences. We won't mention every preference in detail, as some are self-explanatory, and others are not very relevant to working with photographs in Photoshop.

◆ Switch to Bridge if it's already open, or open it by clicking the Bridge icon on the Photoshop CS2 Options bar (the small folder with the spiral shell icon and the magnifying glass).

◆ In Bridge, go to the Bridge menu (Mac) or the Edit menu (PC) and choose Preferences. On the left side of the Preferences dialog are six sections. We'll begin with the first one, General.

Thumbnails: Background

The Background slider changes the background tone for the thumbnails from black to white. This will change dynamically as you move it so you can see the change in the open Bridge window behind the Preferences dialog.

Additional Lines of Thumbnail Metadata

Metadata is information about your image. This can include things such as exposure information, copyright notices, and keywords. These menus allow you to add to the default information about the photo that is displayed along with the thumbnail. What you display here is largely a matter of personal preference. We like to see Date Created and Exposure information, and sometimes Date File Modified.

◆ In the left column of the dialog, click Metadata.

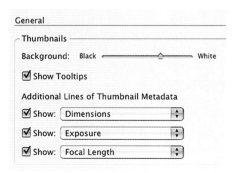

These preferences in Bridge control the appearance of the thumbnails and how much information is displayed with them.

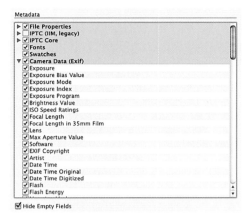

The Metadata display preferences in Bridge.

Metadata

These check boxes determine which lines of metadata appear in the Metadata tab of the Bridge browser. What you choose here will largely be determined by how you use metadata and whether you work for a company that uses some of these protocols (the IPTC CORE metadata, for example, is used by newspapers and other publications, but seeing those information fields in the Metadata tab is probably not necessary for a fine-art photographer). We generally like to see the File Properties, the Camera Data (EXIF), and Camera Raw information. Fonts and Swatches are applicable only if you also are using Bridge with Adobe InDesign or Illustrator.

◆ In the left column of the dialog, click Advanced.

Advanced

This section contains what we feel are the most important Bridge preferences for photographers. If you use Bridge to browse for large files, you should increase the Do Not Process Files Larger Than setting so that it's greater than the file sizes you want to browse. Bridge will still show a filename for files that are larger than is specified here, but it will not show a thumbnail or a preview.

Double-click Edits Camera Raw Settings in Bridge

If this check box is selected, double-clicking on a thumbnail will open Camera Raw, and you will be able to make adjustments to the file; but note that the default highlighted, or active, button is Done, not Open. This means that if you press the Return (Enter) key after changing the settings in Camera Raw, the changes will be recorded for the file and will be applied to the thumbnails and preview images in Bridge, but the file will not open directly into Photoshop. To open it into Photoshop, you would need to click the Open button.

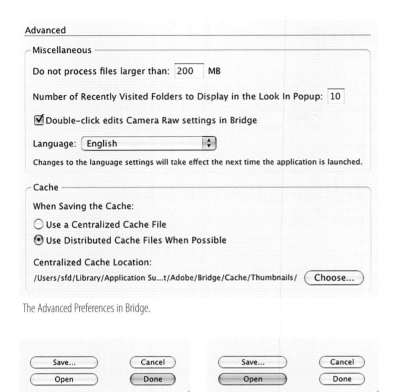

The Advanced Preferences in Bridge.

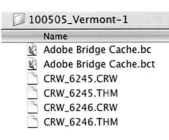

100505_Vermont-1
Name
Adobe Bridge Cache.bc
Adobe Bridge Cache.bct
CRW_6245.CRW
CRW_6245.THM
CRW_6246.CRW
CRW_6246.THM

When Use Distributed Cache Files When Possible is chosen, the the Bridge cache files are saved in the actual folder that contains the images.

When Double-click Edits Camera Raw Settings in Bridge is checked, the Done button in the Camera Raw dialog is the default active button (above left), meaning that when you press the Return (Enter) key, the changes will be applied, Camera Raw will close, and you will be returned to Bridge. When that option is not checked, the Open button is active (above right) and pressing Return (Enter) will apply the changes and open the image into Photoshop.

If the check box is not selected, then the Open button is the default active button and the file will open into Photoshop when you press the Return (Enter) key.

We recommend checking this option so that you can move quickly between Bridge and Camera Raw to make initial adjustments to your Raw files. If you decide that you are ready to open the file into Photoshop for further editing, simply click the Open button in the Camera Raw dialog.

◆ Check Double-click Edits Camera Raw Settings in Bridge.

Cache

Bridge uses a cache file to store all of the information about the images that it has browsed. The default behavior is for the program to use a centralized location for this cache file. The one potential problem with this is that the thumbnail, preview, and metadata information about any group of images is linked to their location in a specific folder. If the folder is moved or renamed outside of Bridge, then the link to that information is broken and Bridge will have to re-create all the cached information for those images (thumbnails, preview, metadata, and so on). If you have a folder containing a lot of large files, this can take a while.

To prevent this from happening, click the Use Distributed Cache Files When Possible option. This will save the necessary cache files in the same folder that contains the images. With this approach, folders can be renamed and their location changed without Bridge having to rebuild the cache. This approach is also useful for folders of images that will be burned onto CDs or DVDs, since the Bridge cache files reside in the image folders and are burned to the disc along with the images. Distributed cache files are not possible if you are browsing images on a CD, DVD, or any disc that is write-protected.

◆ Set the When Saving the Cache preference to Use Distributed Cache Files When Possible.

As with Photoshop, you should quit Bridge after changing any preferences to save those changes to the program's preferences file.

What's Next?

After following the steps in this chapter, your preferences are now set up as we recommend for working with the step-by-step tutorials in this book. In the next chapter, "Navigating in Photoshop," we cover some of the essential information you need to know for efficiently working with the Photoshop interface.

3 ◆ Navigating in Photoshop

Efficiently using Photoshop's tools, palettes, and windows makes work go faster. Here, we show you how to set up your windows, palettes, and screen to create a flexible and productive environment.

When you first open Photoshop, the palettes are in their default location and grouping. In our classes, the first thing we show people how to do is set up the screen and Photoshop so the palettes that are essential to the way we work are always available. We take some time to explain keyboard shortcuts that you must know to work efficiently, and show you how to load presets that make life in Photoshop easier. In this chapter, I'll walk you through that entire process, for our first lesson: navigation.

Arranging the Workspace

When you open Photoshop for the first time, many of the palettes you'll need to use are arranged at the right side of your screen. There are 4 palette bays containing 11 palettes. Unfortunately, some of the palettes that you need to view simultaneously are docked together— as soon as you click the tab of, say, the Info palette, you lose the Navigator palette, which moves behind it. Our first job is to separate the palettes, close the ones we don't need, and put the others into positions that make them accessible for our work. This arrangement of palettes is called a *workspace,* and you can create numerous workspaces to accommodate the different types of tasks you do.

To move a palette out of its bay, you click and drag its name tab into a new position. If it doesn't separate, you didn't drag far enough before releasing the mouse. Try again if that's the case. This will be easier for you to understand visually if you go ahead and open a file.

◆ Go to File/Open, find the *Photoshop Artistry* DVD, and navigate to the Ch03.Navigating folder. Open the produce.psd image. Type F to put the image in Full Screen mode. (Of course,

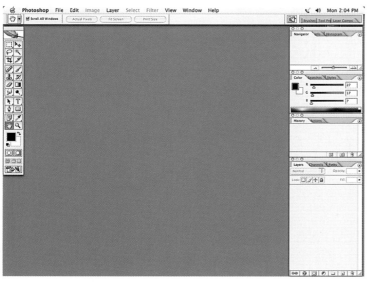

When you first open Photoshop CS2, your palettes will be arranged like this.

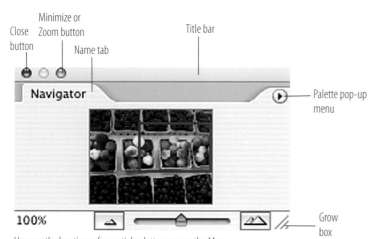

Here are the locations of essential palette areas on the Mac.

Here are the locations of essential palette areas on the PC.

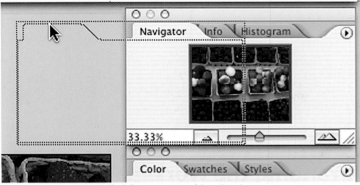

Move the Navigator palette to the left to move it out of the palette bay.

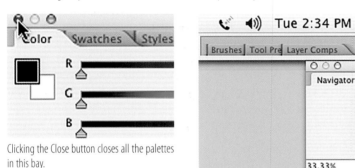

Clicking the Close button closes all the palettes in this bay.

Only about this much of the Navigator palette should show on your screen.

you don't know what that is yet, but for now just do it. We'll explain this later.)

◆ Click the Navigator tab and drag it out to the left, away from the Info and Histogram palettes. If you were successful, grab the Info palette tab and move the Info palette to the lower middle area of your screen. This is where it will stay during most of the lessons in this book.

◆ Now move the Histogram palette to the upper-left corner of the screen. It will cover part of the Toolbox. Click the Toolbox to bring it back to the front, then use Window/Tools [F2] to close the Toolbox.

◆ We don't need any of the color palettes (Color, Swatches, or Styles) in the next bay, so you can click the Close button on the Color palette to close this palette bay. On the Mac click the red button at the top left; on the PC click the red X on the top right. All the palettes in the bay close at once.

◆ After the Histogram and Color palettes are out of the way, move the Navigator palette back over to the right side of the screen.

Keep moving it until you see only the area of this palette that has the magnification setting of the currently open file.

In the next palette bay are the History and Actions palettes. We will use both of these at different points in the book, but they do not always need to be available. In Chapter 2, "Preferences and Color Settings," you loaded a set of actions, called ArtistKeys, that we created. Throughout the exercises you'll see references to these shortcut keys, such as [F10]. In Chapter 10, "Automating Photoshop," you'll learn how to set up your own actions.

◆ For now, separate these two palettes by dragging the name tab for the History palette, then close both palettes.

Finally, we come to the palette bay containing Layers, Channels, and Paths. Layers is a palette we want to have visible much of the time that we'll be working on images, and Channels is a palette that we will often reference as we are looking at the Layers palette. Because we do not need Channels all the time, we want that palette out of the way; but when we do need it, we want it to open on the left side of the screen so we can see our channels and layers at the same time. Photoshop remembers the last location of a palette and brings the palette back up in that same location. Paths, a powerful way to do some tasks, is not a palette we'll use often in this book, so we'll just close that one.

◆ Click the name tab for the Channels palette, and drag it over to the left side of your screen; then close the Channels palette.

◆ Drag the Paths palette out of the palette bay and close it.

◆ Make sure the Layers palette is on the far right side of your screen, under the Navigator palette, then close the Layers palette.

The Navigator palette is now open on the right side of your screen, the Histogram palette is at the upper left, and the Info palette is at the bottom of the screen.

Saving Your Workspace

We will use this palette configuration often as we work through examples in this book, so we are ready to save the workspace.

◆ Go to Window/Workspace/Save Workspace, and name this workspace Color Correction. For now, the only thing we want to save is Palette Locations. We will discuss the other options in Chapter 10.

Once you learn the keyboard shortcuts for the tools in the Toolbox, you'll be able to close the Toolbox. If you need to use it while you are

Your screen should look something like this before you save this workspace.

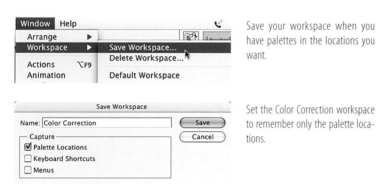

Save your workspace when you have palettes in the locations you want.

Set the Color Correction workspace to remember only the palette locations.

still learning the shortcuts, you can open it from the Window menu or use the ArtistKey [F2]. If you'd like to try using the workspace, do this:

◆ Close the Navigator palette and move the Info palette to the bottom-middle of your screen, then choose Window/Workspace/Color Correction. All your palettes should now be in the saved position.

Keys for Zooming and Scrolling

We make everyone learn certain keyboard shortcuts when we teach Photoshop. It is important that you learn them. Even if you hate keyboard shortcuts and don't want to be a power user, you need to learn these few, or you will make your work in Photoshop much harder than it should be. There are many modes in Photoshop where you can't access the tools you normally use. This can be confusing, espe-

cially for the beginner. Many processes in Photoshop come up in a modal dialog: for example, Levels, Curves, Hue/Saturation, and most of the color correction tools and filters. When you use these tools, you are in a mode because you can't go to the Toolbox and switch to, for instance, the Zoom tool. Learning the shortcut keys will help you function even when you're in the middle of an adjustment or filter. Make sure you learn the shortcuts listed in the following subheads here, and read the sections for other valuable tips.

Use the Spacebar for the Hand Tool

We can't stress enough how important it is to stay in the Hand tool most of the time. This is a nondestructive tool that does not change any pixels or settings when you use it. Therefore, if you accidentally click somewhere on your image with this tool, nothing happens—that is, nothing that has to be corrected later. Here's how to use it:

◆ Type H for the Hand tool. Click and drag the image to scroll. Now type B to access the Brush tool. Hold down the Spacebar and the icon for the Hand tool reappears. Scroll the image. Type H again.

As soon as you open an image, type H to put yourself in the Hand tool. And, as soon as you finish using any other tool, type H to put yourself back in the Hand tool. Otherwise you will inadvertently paint, crop, marquee or worse to your file. Shift-Spacebar gives you the Hand tool and scrolls all open images that are in Standard Screen mode at the same time (wonderful when comparing images).

Command (Ctrl)-Spacebar to Zoom In, Option (Alt)-Spacebar to Zoom Out

We use the Navigator palette primarily to show the zoom percentage of the file. We've found that using keyboard shortcuts to navigate is much faster. One exception to this: If you have a second monitor that you use to hold palettes, then you might want to use the Navigator palette to move to different parts of the screen. When you zoom in and out using the Zoom tool or shortcut keys, Photoshop zooms by a known amount. If you are at 100%, where you see the pixels of your image displayed at a 1:1 ratio to your monitor's pixels, then you will zoom in to 200% and then 300% and then 400%. You will find that the image is sharper at a factor of 2 from 100% than some odd percentage like 136.13%. That means 25% , 50%, 100%, or 200% is sharper than 33.3%, 66.6%, and so on.

◆ Hold down the Command (Ctrl) key and the Spacebar to get the Zoom tool, then click to zoom in on your image. Where you click will become the center of the new screen. Press Option (Alt)-Spacebar-click to zoom out.

Type Command-0 (zero) to fit your file in the window. Now hold down Command-Spacebar and drag diagonally to draw a box around an area you want to zoom in on. That portion now fills the entire window. This technique is called marqueeing, and you'll use it a lot.

By default, the Spacebar zooming options do not change the window size, unless you type Z for the Zoom tool and then turn on Resize Windows To Fit in the Options bar. With the Zoom tool active, Control-Spacebar-click (right-click on the PC) gives you a pop-up menu with various zooming options.

Command (Ctrl)-+ and Command (Ctrl)- –

You can also use Command (Ctrl)-+ and Command (Ctrl)- – (minus sign) to zoom in and out. In Standard Screen mode these keys change your window size while zooming, unless you go to Photoshop/Preferences/General and turn off the default Zoom Resizes Windows setting. You can use Command-Option (Ctrl-Alt)-+ or –, which does the opposite of the Zoom Resizes Windows preferences setting.

Command (Ctrl)-0 and Command-Option (Ctrl-Alt)-0

You can zoom so the entire image fits in the screen by pressing Command (Ctrl)-0 (zero). If you press Command-Option (Ctrl-Alt)-0, the image zooms to 100%. Both of these shortcut combinations are useful in color correction. You may be zoomed way in on an image to adjust the color of a particular area, then quickly press Command (Ctrl)-0 to see how that adjustment affects the overall appearance of the image. You can also double-click the Hand tool in the Toolbox to fit the image in the window or double-click the Zoom tool to zoom to 100%. However, we suggest learning the keyboard shortcuts because you can use them to manipulate the image even when you are in the middle of an adjustment or filter.

Other Useful Keys

You can use the Page Up and Page Down keys on many keyboards to scroll the current image a page's worth of pixels up or down. Command (Ctrl)-Page Up scrolls to the left and Command (Ctrl)-Page Down to the right. Add the Shift key to any of these to scroll 10 pixels at a time. The Home key scrolls to the top left and the End key to the bottom right.

The Menu Bar

At the top of your screen is the Menu bar. When we mention File, Edit, Image, Layer, and so on, we're referring to the items in the Menu bar. By default, just below the Menu bar is the Options bar.

The Options Bar

Most of the tools have changeable options you view in the Options bar. The beauty of the Options bar is that it's context specific. It's a very smart palette. If you are performing an action that doesn't affect an option on the current bar, that option will be grayed out and unavailable. We'll discuss the specifics of the options for important tools in Chapter 4, "The Toolbox."

If you choose a tool by either clicking its icon or using its shortcut character, the options automatically appear in the Options bar if it is present. If the Options bar is not visible, pressing Return (or Enter in Windows—you can use either throughout) brings up the Options bar. If you're using ArtistKeys, [F12] toggles the Options bar.

For tools that have brushes, gradients, or patterns associated with them, you'll see an icon on the Options bar with the current swatch. Click the swatch or the associated pop-up arrow to access further options for that brush, pattern, or gradient. When the Options bar is onscreen, pressing Return will take you to the first changeable option, generally an input area, where you can type a value. Press Tab to move to the next input area, or press Return to accept the values that you just input.

Set Tool Options

Before you use any tool, you'll want to check the Options bar and set options for this specific use of the tool. Here, we'll set options for the Brush:

Type B for the Brush tool. Click the icon to the right of the word *Brushes* to bring up the Brush Presets palette. Set the size of the brush at 20 pixels and set the Hardness to 0. Press Enter or Return to accept this size for the brush. Now press Return again to highlight the Opacity setting and type 45. Press Tab to move to the next input area and type 7 for the Flow value. Finally click the Airbrush icon beside the Flow setting to turn the Airbrush on. Press Return once more to accept all the settings for this

Here, the Menu bar and the Options bar abut each other. You can grab the Options bar at the far left side to move it away from the Menu bar if you like. The Marquee tool is active.

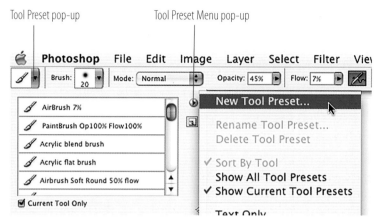

Tool Preset pop-up   Tool Preset Menu pop-up

Click the Tool Preset pop-up, then the Tool Preset pop-up menu to create a new tool preset. When you do this, a dialog will appear for you to create a name for your preset, and then your new tool will appear in the preset menu in alphabetical order.

brush. Check the Options bar. If any input area is highlighted, press Return again.

Tool Presets

At the far left of the Options bar is the icon for tool presets. Tool presets are where your saved preferences for that specific tool are kept. It gets tedious to reset all the options for a tool you use often. Creating a preset is easy, and you can have multiple presets for a tool.

◆ Click the Tool Preset icon to bring up the current tool presets.

◆ Click the Tool Preset pop-up menu and choose New Tool Preset. Name your new preset Light Small Airbrush and uncheck the Include Color box if it's checked. Click OK or press Return or Enter to create the preset.

When you've made the presets you need, be sure you save your set with a meaningful name. Using the Presets Manager, you can move tools into and out of sets, and then save very specialized and personalized tools for the way you work. This is particularly handy for use with Photoshop's brushes, where you might create a lot of brushes but want only a subset available for each type of work you do. You don't have to scroll through millions of brushes to find the one you want.

We will be using tool presets in many of our examples, and the Preferences chapter showed you how to load those presets. We prefer to use the Tool Presets palette with the Current Tool Only check box checked. This removes the clutter of having all presets for all tools displayed; we see only the ones for the tool we're currently working with. If you wanted to use the Tool Presets palette to switch to

another tool, as well as to pick its options, then you'd need to work with the Current Tool Only check box unchecked. Our predefined set of presets, called ArtistryPresets.tpl, is in the Preferences folder on the *Photoshop Artistry* DVD. If you didn't already loaded those presets after reading Chapter 2, "Preferences and Color Settings," please refer back to that chapter and load them now.

The Palette Well

If your monitor is set to at least 1024 pixels wide, then the Options bar will have a gray area at its right side called the Palette Well. You can drag palettes and drop them into this docking area. At that point the palette's title tab appears in the docking area, and you can access the palette from there by clicking on it. If you have many palettes docked, moving the mouse over the area highlights the names of the palettes without opening one. Click the mouse on the title of the palette you want to open. The Palette Well keeps occasionally used palettes handy. The good point is that you don't have to go to the Window menu to open or close a palette. The bad point (or sometimes good point) is that the palette closes once you return to your file to work. Any palette that you need to refer on a regular basis, such as the Info palette, should be pulled out of the dock and left open on your desktop. To remove a palette from the docking area, just click and drag the palette's title tab where you want it. Truthfully, we never use the Palette Well, as we prefer to use the ArtistKeys to open and close palettes. Whether you use the Palette Well will depend on how useful (or annoying) you find it.

Context-Sensitive Menus

Control (right)-clicking opens up a context-sensitive menu of commands you can execute with the current tool, and/or the options you can set. This is a very powerful feature, because the items in this context-sensitive menu may actually come from several different regular menus in Photoshop and are chosen based on Photoshop's state when you Control (right)-click. We point out some of these context-sensitive menus as we go through the exercises. Each tool has at least one context-sensitive menu. This can be a great time-saver. Mac users with a 2-button mouse can right-click as well.

The Photoshop Screen Modes

In the beginning of this chapter, we asked you to type F for Full Screen mode. You can view any open file in one of three screen modes, which the icons toward the bottom of the Toolbox denote. The leftmost icon denotes the Standard Screen mode, the middle icon shows the Full Screen mode with the Menu bar, and the rightmost icon shows Full Screen mode without the Menu bar. We often refer to this last one as Presentation mode. Typing F cycles through the three different screen modes. If you find that the screen looks different than what you expected, try typing F again until it looks the way it should. If other images cover the one you want to see, you can find it using the list of open files at the bottom of the Window menu in any of the three screen modes.

Standard Screen Mode

All Photoshop files initially open in Standard Screen mode. When you first open a file, the window will be a Macintosh or PC window with scroll bars and a grow box in the lower-right corner, and all the rest of the standard fare. At the top of the window, in the title bar, is the name of the file as it was last saved, as well as the current color mode (RGB, CMYK, Lab, etc.), the bit depth (8 or 16), the current layer (in a layered file), and whether you are working on the layer mask. If you see an asterick after the number 8 or 16, this tells you that the file has an embedded profile other than the working RBG profile. This is a lot of information to take in, but after reading the rest of this book, you won't find it overwhelming, merely helpful.

In Standard Screen mode on a typical Mac or PC window, the cursor often fluctuates between displaying as the tool you are using or as the arrow cursor for the scroll bar when you move the mouse ever so slightly while at the edge of the window. If you are making an edit along the edge of the image, you may want to make the window a little bigger than the image. Doing so adds Photoshop gray space between the edge of the file and the window's scroll bars so you can more easily make these edge edits.

Although we recommend doing most of your work in Full Screen mode, Standard Screen mode is the one to use when you want to copy pixels or layers between images.

Full Screen Mode

Full Screen mode places the active, top document in the center of the screen, surrounded by a field of gray, which hides the other documents from view. Working in Full Screen mode with the Menu bar offers many advantages. If you are working on a small monitor, Full Screen mode doesn't waste the space that scroll bars normally take up. Full Screen mode allows you to see the corners of your image and to move the image with the Hand tool (hold down the Spacebar when in a different tool) to different areas of the screen. On the Mac, accidentally clicking in the gray area while in Full Screen mode doesn't switch you to the Finder or some other application.

The gray area is especially useful when you're making selections that need to include the pixels at the very edge of the document. Using any of the selection tools or the Cropping tool, you can actually start or end the selection in the gray area, which ensures that you have selected all the pixels along that edge. Full Screen mode removes all other distractions from your screen and allows you to focus on your beautiful image surrounded by nondistracting neutral gray. On the PC, Photoshop offers this advantage in any screen mode. That is,

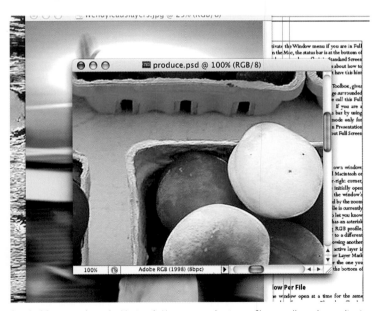

Standard Screen mode on the Macintosh. You can see other image files as well as other application files and the desktop.

In Full Screen mode, all other images and applications are hidden behind the active image.

Full Screen Presentation mode turns the background black and removes the Menu bar.

When you press Tab and hide the palettes, Full Screen Presentation mode looks like this.

when the Photoshop screen area is maximized in the Windows user interface, it covers all other programs.

Full Screen Presentation Mode

The rightmost screen mode icon, at the bottom of the Toolbox, gives you a mode similar to Full Screen mode, but with the image surrounded by black instead of gray, and the menu bar removed. We call this Full Screen Presentation mode, or just Presentation mode. If you are a Photoshop power user, you can work without the Menu bar by using command and function keys—but we generally use this mode only for presentations. In this book, we won't be using Full Screen Presentation mode, so when we refer to Full Screen mode, we're talking about Full Screen mode with the Menu bar.

The Status Bar

On the PC you can use the Window menu to show or hide the Status bar, which offers additional information about the current file and Photoshop, while in any of the screen modes, although you need to use Alt-W to activate the Window menu if you are in Full Screen Presentation mode. When you maximize the window, the Status bar drops to the bottom of the screen. On the Mac, the Status bar is at the bottom of the current window and only shows up when a file is in Standard Screen mode. Photoshop CS2 allows you to put additional infomation on the Info palette regarding status issues. On the PC, the Status bar gives you additional hints about how to use the current Photoshop tool—useful for the beginner. The Mac Status bar lacks this hint information.

Comparing Images

There are times you need to compare one area of in image to the overall image, or one image to another image. Photoshop makes this simple to do.

More Than One Window Per File

You can have more than one window open at a time for the same Photoshop document. To do this, go to Window/Arrange/New Window to open a second window of the same file. Utilizing this capability, you can, for example, have one window showing a section of the file up close and the other window showing the entire file. You can also use this technique to have one window display a particular channel or mask of the file, while another window shows the RGB or CMYK composite version. There are many uses of this feature, and one of the best is to have one window showing how the image will look when printed on one printer, say the LightJet 5000, and a second window showing how it will look when printed on the Epson 2200, 4000, or 7600. To find out exactly how to do this, see Chapter 16, "Color Preferences, Calibration, and Printing."

Quick Reorganization of Open Windows

You can use Window/Arrange/Cascade to stack all the open windows on top of and slightly overlapping each other. You can use Control (Ctrl)-Tab or Control (Ctrl)-Shift-Tab to scroll through your open windows and bring each one to the front (use these keys to scroll through open files regardless of their organization or screen mode).

Also under Window/Arrange are the Tile commands. You can tile your windows either horizontally or vertically. This is really useful when you have several versions of the same image open and you

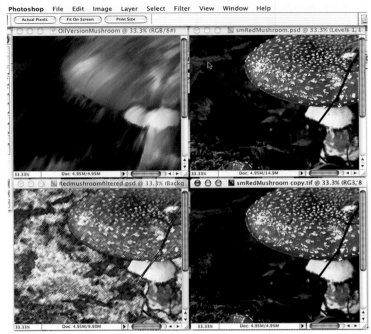

These four versions of an image have been tiled horizontally and matched in both zoom factor and location.

want to check how adjustments have affected a particular area. The windows tile in the middle of the screen, keeping clear of whatever palettes you have open on the sides; so if seeing as much of your images as possible is important, make sure you press the Tab key first to hide all the palettes before you tile. Once you've tiled your images, you can match the location or zoom factor for all the open windows. Or you can choose to match both the zoom and the location. Again, this is very useful for comparing versions of an image. If you Shift-Spacebar-drag with the Hand tool (or if you've turned on Scroll All Windows in the Hand tool options), all the images inside the windows will scroll at once. However, if one of your images is in Full Screen mode, tiling it will put it back in Standard Screen mode.

If you're on the Mac, you can click the yellow Minimize button or double-click the title bar to put your file on the system dock, keeping it handy but out of the way. In Windows, clicking the Minimize button causes the window to be minimized to the bottom of the Photoshop workspace as a small title bar.

Palette Management

Photoshop contains a lot of different palettes, which control different sets of functions. The Toolbox is the main palette. Its functions are discussed in Chapter 4. The color-picking palettes are discussed

in Chapter 5, "Picking and Using Color." The Channels, Layers, Layer Comps, and Paths palettes are discussed in both Chapter 6, "Selections, Channels, Masks, and Paths," and Chapter 7, "Layers, Layer Masks, and Layer Comps." What we discuss in this chapter is how to most efficiently use all the palettes on the Photoshop screen.

Accessing Palettes

All palettes can be accessed from the Window menu. Any currently open palette will be marked in this menu with a check mark. An open palette that is obscured by another is marked by a dash before its name. You can use the Window menu to open or close a particular palette even when you're in a filter or adjustment. You may notice when you click the Window menu that modifiable keyboard shortcuts are already set up for many of the palettes. We recommend using the Actions palette to define function keys that will bring up and close the palettes you use most often. Barry has created a set of function keys for you, called ArtistKeys, which we explained how to install in Chapter 2. We talk more about actions in Chapter 10. The function keys that you use in the Actions palette will override any keyboard shortcuts that you have set. However, if you are in a mode such as Curves or Levels, the ArtistKeys shortcuts will not work and the ones listed on the Window menu will. For this reason, it's a good idea to modify your keyboard shortcuts for accessing palettes to match any actions you've set up.

Tab to Hide Palettes

Pressing the Tab key makes the Toolbox—and all other visible palettes—disappear. Pressing Tab again brings all these palettes up in their previous locations. Pressing Shift-Tab opens or closes the other palettes without changing the status of the Toolbox and Options bar. You can close any of the palettes, except the Toolbox, by clicking the Close button in the top-left corner of the palette on the Mac or the top-right corner in Windows. If the Tab key does not make the palettes go away and come back, the cursor is probably within a text field on the current tool's Options bar. Just press Return (Enter for Windows) to deactivate that field, and the Tab key should hide the palettes again.

Palette Locations

You can move palette groups or single palettes around the screen by clicking the title bar at the top and dragging the palette to a new location. Photoshop opens the palettes in the same location that they were last used unless you turn off the Save Palette Locations option in Photoshop's General Preferences. If you find your work goes faster having palettes in particular locations, you can save the locations (and settings) of open palettes using the Window/Workspace/Save Workspace command.

Grouping and Separating Palettes

Early in this chapter, we separated palettes that were in a palette bay by clicking the name tab of a palette and pulling it out of the bay. To move palettes *into* a group, click the name tab of the palette you want to add and then drag it over the group window. New palettes in a group are added to the right. If you have a small monitor, you may want to group more of your palettes together to save screen space. Switch between palettes in the bay by clicking the name tab of the palette you want or by choosing the palette from the Window menu. If you hide any of the palettes within the group, the whole group gets hidden. You can also compact and collapse palettes by clicking in the green Zoom box at the top left of the Mac window. On the PC this button is on the right and has a minus icon.

Collapsing Palettes

On the Mac, clicking the first time on the Zoom button (the green one) at the top resizes the palette so that it just holds the things within it: If the palette was open larger than the information inside it, the palette closes down to fit. If the palette was not open enough to show you all its contents, it opens up to do that. In Windows clicking the rightmost box closes the palette, and the box just to the left of it duplicates the behavior we describe here.

Clicking the button a second time, or double-clicking the title tab or title bar, resizes the palette to show just the name tab.

Clicking again in this palette's grow box or Zoom button expands it to the compact size that just shows all the contents. The compact

The Layers palette options are the ones you'll probably use most often.

paletter can be left at the bottom or top of your monitor until you need it without taking up much screen real estate. If you hold the Shift key down and drag a palette toward the top or bottom of the screen, it will snap to the edge of the screen, then neatly open or close at the top or bottom of the screen when you double-click the tab or click the Zoom button. If you are in a modal dialog and you need to minimize a palette or bring one back open that is currently minimized, double-clicking the title bar will do it; using the Zoom button will not.

Palette Options

Most palettes have a menu that you can access by clicking the Menu icon at the top right of the palette. The palette options show you different ways to display the palette, as well as commands that are often represented by buttons on the bottom of the palette. You should check out the palette options on all the palettes that have them, but pay particular attention to the Layers palette options. They are important and we use them often in this book.

Special or Important Palettes

Using the Info Palette

The Info palette [F9]) is one of the most useful tools in Photoshop. Not only does it measure colors like a densitometer (something we will do extensively in the color correction exercises in later chapters in this book), but it also gives you important measurements any time you are scaling, rotating, making, or adjusting a selection. The location of the cursor, the size of the box you are drawing, the degree of rotation, and many other useful measurements are always present in

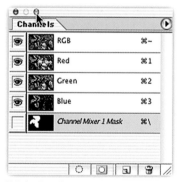

Click the Zoom button to get a compact palette like the one in the figure at the upper right.

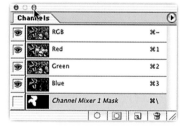

Clicking the Zoom button on a compact palette gives you a collapsed palette like the one below.

Click the Zoom button on this palette and it expands to the compact version seen above.

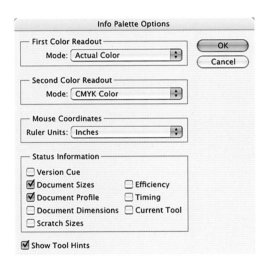

In this illustration, our top-left values are set to 8-bit RGB values and the top right are set to 8-bit CMYK values. Barry likes to keep his second readout in RGB but showing the 16-bit values. To change either readout, click the tiny triangle beside the eyedropper for that readout. Also, we've set two color sampler points: #1 for our white or highlight point and #2 for the shadows.

You can now choose to show more information in the Info palette about the file itself. This makes the Info palette on the Mac now function more like the Status bar on the PC.

the Info palette. This is a good one to keep up on the screen most of the time. See Chapter 13, "Color Correction Tools," and Chapter 18, "The Master Image Workflow," for a discussion of the important Color Sampler part of the Info palette. If you are using the ArtistKeys actions from the book's DVD, then use [F9] to access this palette. The built-in default Photoshop function keys use F8 for Info and you can access the Info palette by pressing F8 from within a modal dialog if you have not loaded our keyboard shortcuts. If you click the palette pop-up menu and select Palette Options, you can choose additional information for the Info palette to display. This is especially helpful when you are working in Full Screen mode and no longer have a Status bar onscreen showing you information.

The Navigator Palette

Photoshop's Navigator palette [Shift-F2] allows you to zoom in and out to quickly see where you are in an image and efficiently move to a particular spot in that image. This palette contains a small thumbnail of your entire image with a red box, called the View box, on top of the thumbnail that shows you the part of the image you can currently see in your window. As you zoom in, you will notice this box getting smaller because you are seeing less and less of the image area. You can click and drag this box or just click where you want to be in the Navigator palette, and your window will display what's inside the box. Though the Navigator is quite useful, we actually use only a few of its capabilities, preferring to use keyboard shortcuts (remember those?) to navigate our images.

In the bottom left of the Navigator palette is the numeric text box that shows you the current magnification of your image. We always keep this portion of the Navigator palette onscreen. You can type in the exact zoom factor that you need in this area if you are at some funky magnification value. Again, we have found that images are a little sharper on the screen when zoomed to a divisor or multiple of 100% (25%, 50%, 100%, 200%, 400%, and so on).

The Actions Palette

Check out Chapter 2 to learn how to set up the Actions palette with the ArtistKeys command set so that you can quickly configure function keys to show and hide any palette. You will notice, throughout the book, references like [F11]. These show you places where we have created shortcuts for you using the Actions feature. Actions can be used to automate either a single menu choice, such as bringing up a palette, or a whole sequence of events, such as complex functions for sharpening and removing noise from an image. Please read Chapter 10 to learn about the wonderful ways you can automate repetitive tasks using actions! Most of the color separations in this book were produced automatically with actions included in the ArtistKeys set.

The Brushes Palette

Most of the retouching and painting tools allow you to access the Brushes palette from the Options bar. A few, like the Healing brush, only allow you to make minor changes to their brushes, and some, the Gradient tool for example, do not use the brushes at all. You'll know whether the tool has access to the complete Brushes palette when you see the small Brushes palette icon on the right of the Options bar just to the left of the Bridge icon (a folder with a seashell).

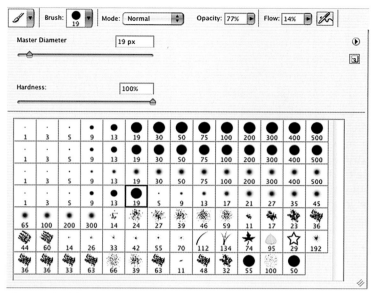

When you've loaded BarrysPhotosBrushes.abr and opened the Brush Picker palette, it should look like this. This arrangement allows you to pick most brushes with a single movement.

The default way the Brush Picker displays the brushes shows a single application of the brush tip along with the diameter of the tip in pixels, and then a preview of what a brush stroke will look like with that brush tip. Although the stroke thumbnails can be useful, we prefer to use the small thumbnail view since it displays more brushes at once. You should have BarrysPhotoBrushes.abr already loaded, but if not, go back to the Preferences chapter and do that now.

The quick way to select a brush is to choose from a thumbnail in the Brush Picker. But first, the Picker palette must be in Small Thumbnail view, and large enough to show you all the thumbnails:

◆ Type B for the Brush tool. Now, click the Brush Tip icon in the Options bar and click on the small button at the top-right corner of the Brushes drop-down picker to choose Small Thumbnail from the pop out menu.

◆ Move your cursor to the grow box in the bottom-right corner of the Brush Picker palette, and click and drag to increase the size

of the picker. It will be a very wide window with the first row of brushes going from a 1-pixel brush to a 500-pixel brush. Make the palette deep enough to display all the brushes. Press Return or Enter to close the Brush Picker palette. Photoshop will save this as a preference when you next open the palette.

To select a particular brush via the Options bar, click and drag on top of the Brush icon (not the Brush Presets icon) at the left of the Options bar until the cursor is over the brush that you want. When you find the brush you need, release the mouse button and the Brushes palette will disappear and leave you with the new brush selected. This allows you to get a new brush with only one mouse click and also without having the Brushes palette on the screen all the time. If you simply click the Brush Size icon to open the Picker palette and click on a Brush icon, you'll need to press Return or Enter to exit the palette. The palette also disappears when you begin to paint, but sometimes it's confusing whether or not you've laid down the first stroke if you let the palette close automatically. Another quick way to choose a brush is to Control-click on a one-button Mac mouse (right-click) in the image with a painting tool; the Brush Picker will open at the location of your cursor.

Use [Shift-F12] to open the Brushes palette, or F5 if you use the default keyboard shortcut. The Brushes palette that is accessed from the Window menu has many more options for configuring the behavior of the brushes; you can find out how to use them in Chapter 4, "The Toolbox," and Chapter 32, "Digital Paint."

History Palette

Every time you use a Photoshop command that changes your image, that command gets saved in the History palette as a History state. It may be creating a new layer, painting a brush stroke in your image, or even using the Levels command. In the History palette, you see a list of all the commands you have invoked in order from the oldest on top to the newest on the bottom. As it has always been done, Command (Ctrl)-Z toggles between Undo and Redo of the last command you did. Command-Option (Ctrl-Alt)-Z moves back up the history chain, undoing command after command. Command (Ctrl)-Shift-Z goes back and redoes those same commands in the same order they were originally done.

When you click the name of any History state, Photoshop takes you back to the image as it existed when the state was created. By default, all subsequent changes to the image are lost if you begin working on the document from that state. Non-linear history, which we discuss later in this section, retains all the history up to the limit set in Preferences.

Non-Linear History

Here's a history lesson for you. After we opened the Produce file, we duplicated the Background layer because we wanted to run a filter while keeping our original intact. We then used the Colored Pencil filter on this copy of the Background. Next we changed the Blend mode of the duplicated layer to Soft Light. Then we clicked the Colored Pencil state in the History palette to take the image back to that stage, and we ran the Dry Brush filter on the Colored Pencil version. You can see in the third illustration that the Blending Change state in the History palette did not disappear as it would have if we had used the History palette without Non-Linear History. Finally, we went all the way back to the Duplicate Layer state and ran the Dry Brush filter on the copy of the Background layer itself. You see the results of that filter in the fourth image. You can click on any of the History states and continue manipulating the image. Any new step you take will be recorded in the History palette up to the limit set in your preferences. However, you can also see that it might get confusing to remember steps you took to achieve any specific effect, because the History is not, well, linear.

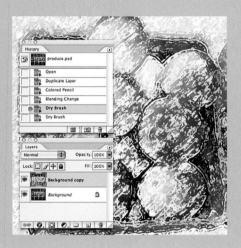

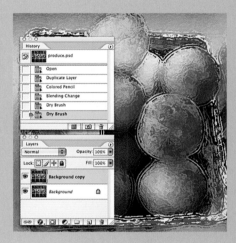

At any time, you can create a snapshot that will remember the state of your image at that particular point. You can have multiple snapshots—they are all saved at the top of the History palette. Photoshop by default automatically takes a snapshot of your image when you first open it. This snapshot is used to implement the Revert to Saved type commands. In the history options that are accessed from the History palette, you can also choose to have a new snapshot created whenever you save your image. In addition to being able to undo to previous snapshots and History states, you can use snapshots and History states as the source information for the Fill command, the Eraser, the History Brush, and the Art History Brush. That means if you use one of those tools or commands, you can choose a state in the History palette and paint or fill information from that state onto your image. To use the History palette in this manner, simply click in the left column beside the snapshot or History state that you

want to use when painting, filling, or erasing. However, as with the rest of History, snapshots disappear when you close your file. If you think you might want to retrieve information from a History state or snapshot for future editing, you can save a duplicate of the image directly from the History palette. Just click the name of the state or snapshot that you want to duplicate, and then click the first icon on the bottom of the palette. This creates a completely new file that you can save for future use.

The History Brush is a special painting tool that paints from your image as it existed at a particular state within the History palette. Clicking in the leftmost column of the History palette next to any snapshot or History state sets the History Brush to paint on your current image with the data from the image as it looked at that previous point in history. In general, the brush paints from the state of a single layer into that same layer unless you are using a merged snapshot as your source.

For most photographers, the History palette is a convenient way to move back several steps to the image as it was before you made a series of missteps. If, for instance, you were cloning part of another photo into a window and realized that after 15 passes with the Clone tool you had cloned into the wrong section of the window, you could click the History state from just before you started using the Clone tool, and begin again—much faster than doing Command-Option (Ctrl-Alt)-Z 15 times.

For some photographers, however, the History palette is a way to try several different possibilities before deciding on the direction that best serves the image, especially if you have Allow Non-Linear History turned on in the History palette options. For instance, let's say that you have created a composite image and you want to try some artistic filters. You might merge the visible layers, then try the Angled Strokes filter. After seeing that version, you could go back in the History palette to the Merge Visible Layers History state and run a different filter, maybe Rough Pastels. At the bottom of the History palette you would see a state for the Angled Strokes filter, then a state for the Rough Pastels filter. If you go back to the Angled Strokes state and add a colored overlay in Multiply mode, a New Color Fill Layer state will appear at the bottom of your History palette. But unlike in Linear History, this state will not reflect the state immediately above it. Rather, it will have skipped over the Rough Pastels state. In Linear History, when you click a previous History state and do something to the image to change it, all the subsequent History states are cleared from the palette. In Non-Linear History, only the preference setting for the number of states affects how many states are saved.

Save, Save As, and Save As a Copy

When you are working in Photoshop (or any application for that matter), you'll want to save your work—not just when it's completely finished, but in intermediate steps along the way. The first time you save your work, you are doing a Save. When you go to File/Save or type Command (Ctrl)-S, Photoshop gives you a dialog to name your image and choose where to file it. How this dialog looks depends on your system and which options you want Photoshop to show you. Besides an input area for name and destination for your file, you also choose the format (most often you'll be using the Photoshop format) and whether you want to save your layers, alpha channels, and profile for the document. Once you've done the initial Save, you can use Command (Ctrl)-S to save the document in stages without being presented with the dialog. You may not even be aware that Photoshop

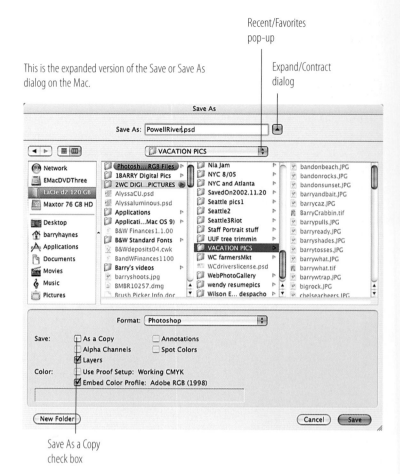

Recent/Favorites pop-up

This is the expanded version of the Save or Save As dialog on the Mac.

Expand/Contract dialog

Save As a Copy check box

is executing the Save command if your file is small. If it's large, you may have a moment's lag and see the spinning wheel or hourglass as the Save happens.

As you work, you might want to save a version of your file. Here, you have two choices: Save As, which appears on the File menu, and Save As a Copy, which is an option at the bottom of the Save As dialog. When you execute a Save As, you choose the name for the file and its destination just as you did in the original Save, but you choose a different name, possibly giving some information about what state the file was in at the point of the Save. For instance, if your orignal was called BlueTiger.psd, your Save As version might be BlueTigerLayers.psd or BlueTiger8x10.psd. The main thing to remember is that when you choose to Save As, you do not overwrite the original file, and the open document will be named with the new name. In other words, you have kept the original intact.

Save As a Copy also does not overwrite the original but rather saves the current state of the document as a new, unopened file.

Save a Version is available only if you are using Version Cue to keep track of projects. Unless you are in a workgroup environment, you will probably not use Version Cue.

Bridge

Photoshop 7 introduced the File Browser, and Photoshop CS gave us some nice upgrades. Photoshop CS2 presents a more robust version of the file browser called Bridge, a stand-alone application. Bridge is how most photographers navigate through their folders of images. Bridge has also evolved enough to do many of the organizational tasks that photographers need, as well as handle more advanced automation to make your work smoother and faster. We'll talk more about how we use Bridge in the next chapter.

Bridge is now a separate application that can run outside of Photoshop, unlike the old File Browser. Depending on how you've set your Bridge preferences, you can view other types of files and open those files and applications with a double-click. If you want Bridge to open automatically when you open Photoshop, you can click Automatically Open Bridge in Photoshop's General preferences. Whether or not you choose to have Bridge open automatically, you can always acess it from the Bridge icon on the Options bar in Photoshop. Clicking the icon will open Bridge if it is not already open; it brings Bridge forward if it is already open.

Basic Organization

By default, Bridge is divided into several areas—the Menu bar at the top; the Look In (navigation) menu at the top left; the shortcut icons at the top right; panels for Favorites, Folders, Preview, Metadata and Keywords in the left section; Content (thumbnails and other information) in the right center section; and status information at the lower edge of the window. You can resize the panels by dragging the dividing lines between the sections, similar to changing the window size in Microsoft Excel or other applications. When you find an arrangement that works well for you, save it as a Bridge workspace using Window/Workspace/Save Workspace.

Reorganizing the Bridge Window

The panels in the left section can be moved to different locations (though remaining on the left side) by dragging the title tab to a new location. We have found that moving all the tabs in this section up to the top is a better organization scheme for viewing both information and previews. It allows you to see most of the information you need from any panel instead of having to scroll that panel. Then, opening

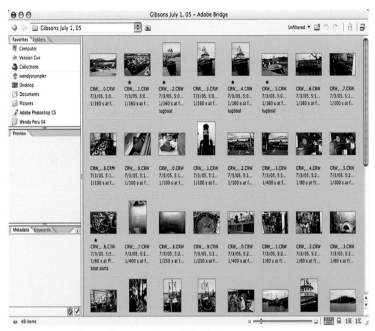

When you open Bridge initially, your workspace looks like this.

As soon as you get the blue box around the upper panels, you can release the mouse.

Move the boundary between the sections to the right.

up the Preview panel so that you have a large preview is the next step towards using Bridge more efficiently. Let's set this up now:

◆ Click the Preview panel's name tab and drag it up toward the Favorites and Folders tabs. As soon as you see the blue box around the upper panel, you can release the mouse and the Preview panel will dock in the top section. Do the same for the Metadata and Keyword panels. Now grab the vertical bar that separates the panels on the left from the thumbnails on the right and move it to the right until only one column of thumbnails shows on the right side. Use the slider bar at the bottom of the window to increase the size of the thumbnails. You can now use the arrow keys to scroll through your images. Use Window/Workspace/Save Workspace to name this workspace PreviewBig.

Save a Bridge workspace that looks like this. This gives you a large preview of the selected image and a fair-sized thumbnail on the right as well.

Alternative Views

Wendy uses the view to the right to compare photos before deciding which one to open or use. This is particularly useful when working with portraits. You build this view by moving the divider between the Thumbnails and the Preview to about the middle of the window, then use the Thumbnail slider at the bottom of the Thumbnails section to create a large thumbnail. When you use this view, don't scroll through your images with the arrow keys. Instead, use the scroll bar so that the image on the left stays put as the images on the right change. If you find this layout helpful, don't forget to save it as a workspace.

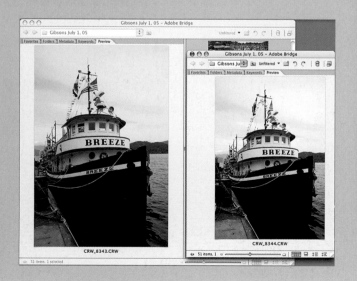

You can also compare photos by opening a second window in Bridge using File/New Window. Make a large preview in both, but only scroll through the thumbnails on one. You need to move the vertical bar separating the panels in both windows until you can see the preview of both. We've made the second window here smaller so you can see how large the underlying Thumbnails panel is. Even though you don't see the thumbnails on the top window, you can still scroll through them using the arrow keys. This use of Bridge allows you to compare images in different folders.

Portfolio

Kenda North

Kenda is Professor of Photography at the University of Texas at Arlington. This is an image she worked on in one of Barry's advanced printmaking classes. Her whole series of underwater shots is spectacular. See them at www.kendanorth.com. The photographs speak of the conflict between nature and culture.

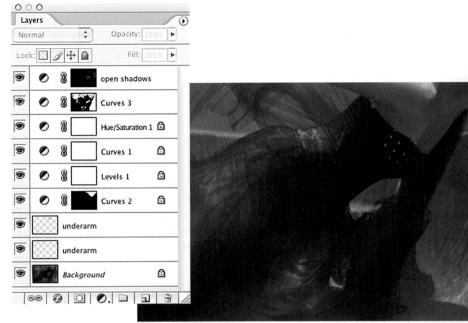

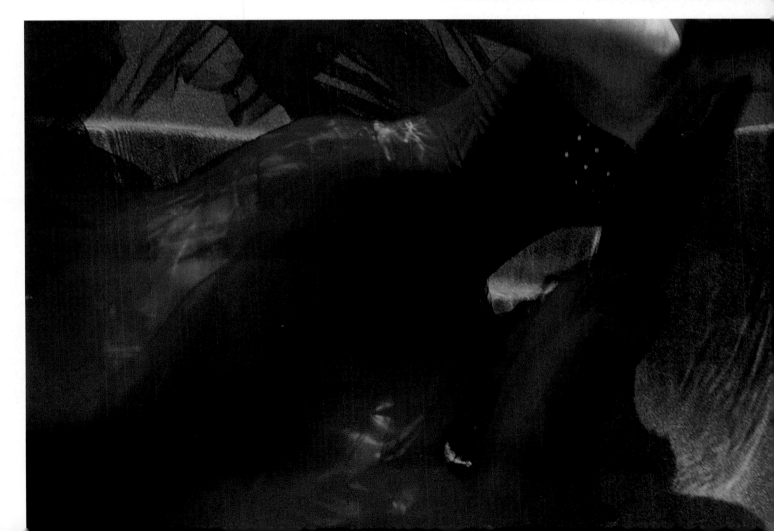

4 ◆ The Toolbox

The Toolbox is the vertical palette on the left of your screen where Photoshop stores its tools. Rather than offering an exhaustive tour of every tool with all its possibilities and applications, we'll focus on just the information you need for working with photographs. For the most part, we say very little about the tools we don't use. In some cases, though, such as with the Type tool, we will show you as much as we can, even though we don't actually use the tool in any of our examples, because we realize that you may need to work with type at some point.

We'll point out important options you should know about, tell you about Tool presets we have created for specific tools, and show you context-sensitive menus that are particularly helpful.

Rather than reading this chapter front to back, you may want to use it as a reference for more information on the specifics of certain tools than the other chapters provide.

The Tool Groupings

The tools in the Tools palette are divided into groups that suggest their use. The top section of the palette contains the tools that are used to make selections and slices; move selections, slices, or layers; or crop files. You might think of this grouping as having to do with boundaries or borders. The slice tools are applicable only for Web work such as creating image maps and rollovers, and we do not cover them in this book.

The second section contains image editing tools used for painting, erasing, sharpening, retouching, and adding effects. If you want to manipulate the actual pixel information of a file or layer, you will probably use one of these tools.

The third section contains drawing tools for dealing with vector shapes, whether Bezier curves, custom shapes, or type.

The fourth section holds tools used for viewing the file (Hand and Zoom), making annotations (Notes), and sampling color (Eyedropper).

Some of the tools in the Tools palette have a little arrow in their bottom-right corner indicating that hidden tools are nested in this same tool bay. Clicking the arrow and holding down the mouse button reveals the other tools that you can access from the same icon area. As a default preference, typing Shift plus the keyboard shortcut for that tool will cycle you through the available tools in most cases. I'll note exceptions in the information for specific tools.

Tool	Shortcut		Shortcut	Tool
Marquee	M		V	Move
Lasso	L		W	Magic Wand
Crop	C		K	Slice/Slice Selection
Spot Healing/Healing/ Patch/Red Eye	J		B	Brush/Pencil/ Color Replacement
Clone/Pattern Stamp	S		Y	History/Art History
Eraser/Background/ Magic Eraser	E		G	Gradient/Paint Bucket
Blur/Sharpen/ Smudge	R		O	Dodge/Burn/Sponge
Path Selection/ Direct Select ion	A		T	Type
Pen	P		U	Shape/Line
Notes	N		I	Eyedropper/ Color Sampler/Measure
Hand	H		Z	Zoom
Foreground Color	—		X	Exchange Colors
Default Colors	D			Background Color
Selection Mode	Q		Q	Quick Mask
Screen Modes	F			
Jump to ImageReady	—			

The Selection Tools

In the first section of the Tools palette are the three primary tools for making selections, as well as tools for moving, cropping, and making slices for Web work. In conjunction with items from the Selection menu and the Pen tool (which we discuss later), you can isolate portions of your image for editing by making a selection. Which tool you use depends on the type of image you are using and the type of selection you need. Sometimes, it is not readily apparent which tool will do the best job. We will give you the basics of how they work here, but know that you will need to practice with all of them to understand how to use them and to be able to choose the right tool for the job. Chapter 19, "Making Selections," gives you more information and practice with the selection tools, and Chapter 6, "Selections, Channels, Masks, and Paths," gives you more information on how selections are used.

Important Selection Tool Options

You will find the following options on some or all of the selection tools.

Selection Interaction When you use the Marquee, Lasso, or Wand tool, the four icons to the right of the Tool Presets icon on the Options bar control how a selection should interact with any current selection. The default is New Selection; that is, any selection you make will replace the current selection. Next is Add to Selection, a function you also can accomplish by using the Shift key as you make your new selection. (It helps if you begin the new selection outside the old one.) Then comes Subtract from Selection, which you can do by using this icon or by holding down Option (Alt) and dragging from within the current selection. Finally, there is Intersect with Current Selection, which takes only the overlapping area of both selections and makes a new selection from it. You also can use Shift-Option (Alt)-drag to intersect selections. If you use the keyboard shortcuts, you'll see the icons on the Options bar activate as you hold down Shift, Option (Alt), or both keys.

Feather The Feather option found on the Options bar for the Marquee and Lasso tools allows you to set the amount of blend on the

A filled selection made with Anti-aliased on.   A filled selection made with Anti-aliased off.

Layer Properties...
Blending Options...

Duplicate Layer...
Delete Layer

Group into New Smart Object

Rasterize Layer

Free Transform

Color Range...
Load Selection...
Reselect

Most selection tools show you these options when you Conrol-click on the Mac or right-click on the PC.

edges of your selection. A softly blended selection is often preferable both for color correcting and compositing. A larger feather radius gives you more of a vignette effect. The amount of feather is calculated in both directions from your selection border. For example, a 15-pixel feather measures both 15 pixels to the outside of your selection area and 15 pixels to the inside, giving you a total feather effect of 30 pixels. We rarely set a feather radius on our selection tools; we prefer either to make a selection and then use Select/Feather from the Menu bar to set the feather, or to create a mask from the initial selection and then blur the mask. This way, we can change our radius if we are unhappy with the effect. Also, if you make a selection with the Rectangular Marquee and the feather is zero, you can later choose Image/Crop to crop to that selection. If you set the feather to a nonzero value, on the other hand, Image/Crop is disabled.

Anti-aliased Anti-aliased subtly blends the edge of your selection with the surrounding area, so you usually want to leave it on. It is not an option on the Rectangular Marquee because straight edges need no

Along with using keyboard shortcuts to control selection interaction, you can choose these icons from the Options bar. From left to right they are New Selection, Add to Selection, Subtract from Selection, and Intersect with Current Selection.

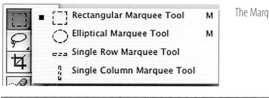

The Marquee tools.

Fixed Aspect Ratio allows you to click and drag until you have a crop that you like, while being assured that the width-to-height ratio will be what you need.

When you use Fixed Size for the Marquee tool, you can input mixed units of measure for Width and Height, such as 3 inches by 400 pixels.

anti-aliasing. Making selections with Anti-aliased off gives you hard edges that are jagged on diagonal lines and curves.

Marquee Tool (M)

You use the Marquee tool to make rectangular or oval selections, something you do quite often in digital imaging. The other tool choices in this tool bay, Single Row and Single Column, you'll probably use less often, but these tools are useful for selecting 1-pixel-wide rows or columns of artifacts introduced by scanners or bad media and then deleting or cloning into the selected area. If you need these two tools, you have to choose them from the Toolbox, as there are no shortcut keys for them.

When you look at the Options bar for the Marquee tool, you see basic selection tool options as well as the following areas:

Style The Style pop-up menu allows you to choose a fixed aspect ratio or a fixed size for either the Rectangular or the Elliptical Marquee. You would use a fixed aspect ratio if you were making a selection that you knew needed to have a 4:5 ratio, for example, or a 1:1 ratio for a perfect square or circle. When you choose this option, you can't input a unit of measure in the Width or Height entry field.

A fixed size is useful when you know the exact size of the print you want to make and you want to crop to that size. Here, if you click with the Marquee tool, you get a rectangular selection of the size that you specified. By keeping the mouse button down while moving the mouse, you can move the selection around the image to find exactly the crop you desire. Of course, you also can use this option simply to select and edit an area of a specific size.

Modifier Keys Holding down the Shift key while using the Marquee tools constrains your selection to 1:1; that is, you get a perfect square

or a perfect circle. Be sure you release the mouse button before you release the Shift key. However, if you already have a selection, the action is different. The Shift key causes Photoshop to add a new, unconstrained selection to your original selection.

Holding down the Option (Alt) key while drawing forces the selection to draw from the center where you first click down. This can be extremely useful, as you will see in Chapter 19.

Holding down the Shift and Option (Alt) keys while dragging gives you a perfect circle or perfect square drawn from the center.

Be careful how you click in a file with an active selection. If you click inside the selection, you may inadvertently move the selection slightly. If you click outside the selection, you lose it.

If you press and hold down the Spacebar after starting a selection, you can move the selection while making it. Release the Spacebar to continue changing the selection.

Move Tool (V)

You use the Move tool to move the contents of a selection or a layer. Click and drag the contents to move them to a new location within your document. You can also use the Move tool to drag and drop a

Use the Move tool with the Control key on the Mac to find out what layers exist at a particular location in your file. Right-click on the PC.

Show Transform Controls reveals where the pixel information is on that layer. If you move one of the handles of the bounding box, you will be in Free Transform mode and the Options bar will reflect that.

layer from one document to another. If you are using any other tool, you can hold down the Command (Ctrl) key to temporarily access the Move tool without deselecting the currently active tool.

Auto Select Layer This allows the Move tool to activate the layer of the object that you click. This can facilitate moving objects around if the boundaries of the object you're selecting are clear. If you're having trouble selecting the appropriate layer, hold down the Control key on the Mac, or right-click on the PC, and choose the layer from the pop-up menu. Only layers that have pixel information under the location of the cursor will show on the list.

Auto Select Group This feature is available only when Auto Select Layer is turned on. It selects not only the topmost layer that contains pixel information at the spot you clicked, but all the layers of the group to which the selected layer belongs.

Show Transform Controls This gives you a rectangle with handles that encompasses the area of that layer that contains pixels. If you move one of the handles, you are immediately in Free Transform mode and the Tool Options bar will reflect that.

Alignment Alignment options are available when working with linked layers, with a selection and one or more layers, or with multiple components of a single path (including multiple shapes on a single-shape layer). If you have only two elements selected, you will activate only the first set of alignment icons, which allow you to align edges or entire elements with each other. If you select three or more elements,

the second group of alignment icons will also activate, allowing you to distribute the space among the edges or the entire elements as well.

Lasso, Polygonal Lasso, and Magnetic Lasso Tools (L)

We use the Lasso and Polygonal Lasso all the time to make selections. Sometimes either Lasso is the only selection tool we need to make adjustments. More often, it is just the beginning of the mask making process. We get close with our selection tool, then use the Brush on the mask.

Lasso

You use the Lasso tool to make freehand selections. Although drawing with a mouse is a little clunky, you'll find yourself using this tool a lot. You can always get a graphics tablet if you want to draw with a pen. Clicking and dragging gives you a line that follows the track of your mouse. Draw as close to the object you are trying to select as you can to select it. If you take too much or too little, you can use modifier keys to add to or delete from your selection. For a smoother transition between the selected and nonselected areas, you can use a feather value, although if you needed to be exact with your mask, you would not use a feather on the Lasso but, rather, a blur on the mask once you created it.

After starting the selection, if you hold down the Option (Alt) key and click, let go of the mouse button, and then click in a new spot, you can draw with straight lines between mouse clicks. You can continue clicking this way to make geometric shapes, or you can hold down the mouse button and draw freehand again. When you let go of the mouse and the Option (Alt) key, a straight line connects the beginning and ending points of your selection, so be careful not to let go of the Option (Alt) key until you finish your selection. Because the Option

To change the color of this barn, we made a loose selection with the Lasso using a 2-pixel feather. We added a Hue/Saturation adjustment layer that used the selection for its mask. We could adjust the Reds in Hue/Saturation without making any further selections, because there is very little red in either the sky or the foliage.

If you have linked layers and you are in the Move tool, you'll see icons for alignment.

(Alt) key in Photoshop is used for subtracting from a selection, you have to press Option (Alt) after starting the selection to get the straight-line behavior.

Polygonal Lasso

The Polygonal Lasso comes in handy when you need to make a selection that has at least some straight edges to it. Most often we switch to the Polygonal Lasso by adding the Option (Alt) key as we draw the selection. If you prefer to use the Polygonal Lasso tool, you can draw straight lines at every click, without using the modifier key. In the Polygonal Lasso tool, using the Option (Alt) key after starting the selection enables you to draw in freehand. The Polygonal Lasso tool requires you to click on the selection starting point again to complete a selection.

Magnetic Lasso

We rarely use the Magnetic Lasso because we are more adept with the Pen tool, if we need a hard edge selection, or the Brush, if we need a soft edge for a mask. However, when you have good contrast between the object you are selecting and its background, the Magnetic Lasso can be a great first selection tool. With the Magnetic Lasso tool, you can set a contrast value for the edge that you're trying to capture, then draw freehand around that edge and let the Lasso decide how to draw the selection. Position your cursor over the edge of the object you want to select, and click to set the first fastening point. As you move the mouse, the Lasso lays down more fastening points to define the edge. You can click down at any time to manually place a fastener or hold down the

We used the Magnetic Lasso with an Edge Contrast setting of 40% to make this loose selection of the red rock. Depending on what sort of adjustment we do, this selection may work as an adjustment layer mask if we only add a little blur to the mask.

Option (Alt) key and either drag to access the regular Lasso or click to access the Polygonal Lasso. Draw until you reach the starting point and you get an icon that looks like the one in the Tools palette. If you let go of the mouse, the selection is made. If you double-click or press Enter before you get to your starting point, a line is drawn from the current mouse position to the starting point to complete the selection. Hold down the Option (Alt) key and double-click to draw a straight-line segment between the mouse position and the starting point. With experimentation, you can get a pretty decent first selection using this tool, and then finesse the selection with some of the more sophisticated selection methods we'll discuss in later chapters.

Width Set your Magnetic Lasso width wide enough to cover the object edge you plan to trace, but not so wide that you take in many additional areas around the edge. You can use the bracket keys to change the width as you drag if necessary, if Pen Pressure is not active.

Edge Contrast Edge Contrast is the minimum contrast that you want Photoshop to consider when trying to discern the edge. The lower the contrast between the edge you're outlining and the background, the lower you need to set the Edge Contrast.

Frequency Frequency governs the number of "points" that the Lasso automatically puts down to define the selection.

Pen Pressure Click this icon if you want the Lasso width to respond to the pressure you exert on your stylus when using a pressure-sensitive tablet. The harder you press, the smaller your Lasso width. Make sure this is not turned on when you are using a mouse.

Magic Wand Tool (W)

Whereas the Marquee and Lasso tools make selections based on physical proximity of pixels, the Magic Wand makes selections based on the color values of adjacent pixels. This is a very valuable tool; it's the simplest way to select a colored area. All of the options are significant, but the Tolerance setting is especially important to understand.

Tolerance The tolerance that you set determines how close in value pixels must be before they can be selected. The lower the tolerance, the more similar the colors must be; the higher the tolerance, the greater the range of colors.

Contiguous You can choose whether you want Photoshop to select only those pixels within the tolerance value that are beside each other, or to search the entire image and select all pixels that fall within the tolerance. Where you click makes a difference.

Here's the selection that I got using the default tolerance of 32 and clicking in the upper-right area of sky with the Contiguous button checked.

Clicking in the same spot with Contiguous unchecked gives me a selection that would make a pretty good mask.

The Grow and Similar Commands

The tolerance value that you set on the Magic Wand also affects which pixels you select when you use the Grow and Similar commands from the Select menu. The Grow command selects adjacent pixels that fall within this tolerance, whereas the Similar command selects pixels throughout the entire image that fall within the tolerance range. You can also change the tolerance setting on the Magic Wand between uses of these two commands, to select a larger or smaller range of colors.

Use All Layers The Use All Layers option makes its selection based on a merged version of all the currently visible layers. Whether you want this option on or off depends on the type of image you are working with and the kind of selection you wish to make. If another layer affects the colors of the object you want to select, you probably want this option on. If all the colors you want to select are on only one layer, leave it off. But remember: Regardless of whether your selection is based on one layer or on merged layers, the edits that you make affect only the currently active layer.

The Crop Tool (C)

How you crop a photo can make an enormous difference in its impact. Although we sometimes use the Rectangular Marquee tool and the Image/Crop command to crop an image, the Crop tool is more powerful because it gives you the ability to change the boundaries and even the perspective of your crop. To use the Crop tool, click and drag a box around the area you want to crop. The area that will be cropped from the image darkens. Click and drag one of the handles (the little boxes in the selection corners and edges) to change the

size of the crop area. To cancel the crop, press the Escape key or the Cancel button on the right end of the Options bar. To accept the crop, press Return (Enter), or click the Commit button (the checkmark) on the right end of the Options bar.

Width, Height, and Resolution You can enter proportions for the crop manually. Whatever crop you make will be constrained to these proportions, and it will be resampled to exactly these specifications when you accept the crop by pressing Return (Enter). Leave the Resolution blank to maintain the specified aspect ratio and let Photoshop resample the file if necessary. For example, if you ask for your crop in inches, and the dimensions are larger than the area you selected, Photoshop lowers the resolution of the file after the crop but does not resample the crop area. However, if you ask for your crop in pixels and the crop is larger than the current file, it maintains the resolution of the image but adds pixels; in effect, it upsamples the image. Click Clear to clear all input areas.

Front Image When you click the Front Image button in the Tool Options bar, the exact dimensions and resolution of the currently active image appear in the input areas.

Delete or Hide In general, when you use the Crop tool, you delete the area that you want removed from your image, so Delete is the default here. However, you can choose to simply Hide the other areas of the file, then use the Move tool to relocate the image and decide on the final crop. If you are in a file that has only a *Background* layer, you'll need to turn the background into a regular layer by double-clicking and naming the layer.

Before you make a selection with the Crop tool, the Tool Options bar looks like this. Here, we've decided to make a 5x4 crop. We left the Resolution blank because we prefer to use Image Size to change the resolution of the file.

After you make a selection with the Crop tool, the Tool Options bar looks like this.

Shield Cropped Area After you make a selection with the Crop tool, the Options bar changes and allows you to cover the area that you want to crop out with a colored overlay. You can choose the color and opacity. This flexibility helps you check the placement of your crop for more pleasing results. Barry usually keeps the opacity at 75%

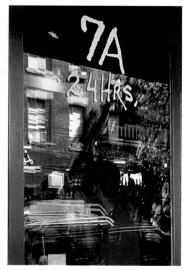
This is the result of the previous crop using Perspective.

Click the Perspective button to allow irregularly shaped crops. Using the Shield option colors the area to be deleted with an overlay. Changing the shield color to red gave us a better idea of the area of the crop.

The result of the rotated crop.

Because we wanted to rotate our crop from the lower-right corner, we moved the center point there before beginning the rotation.

until he decides how he's going to crop, then changes it to 100% to check the look before making the actual crop.

Perspective Click this button if you want to change the dimensions of your crop disproportionately. This will stretch the image after the crop to fit a rectangle based on the area and shape you chose. You use this option primarily to correct the perspective distortion that occurs when you take a photo at an angle.

Moving and rotating Click in the middle of the selected area to move the crop boundary without changing its size. Click outside the crop box corners when you see the curved double-arrow Rotate icon, and drag to rotate the crop boundary. You can move the "center point," or point of transformation around which you will rotate the selected area, by dragging it.

The Image Editing Tools

Open the files BarryCrabbing.psd and MarinaHouse.psd in the folder for this chapter on the *Photoshop Artistry* DVD to try the tools in the next part of this chapter.

The Tool Cursor options you set in your File/Preferences/Display and Cursors preferences control how your tool cursor appears. In general, we use Brush Size for the Painting Cursors and Precise for the Other Cursors. Before we explore each tool, we need to discuss the Brushes palette and some options that are standard to all the tools.

The Brushes Palette

Most of the image editing tools get their brush tip information from the Brushes palette. To see this window, choose Window/Brushes, or click the Brush palette pop-up on the far right of the Options bar when you are in a tool that uses brushes. The brushes you'll see (though not all the brush options) are the same for all the tools except the Pencil tool, which has only hard-edge brushes. The Gradient, Paint Bucket, Healing tools, Color Replacement tools, and special Erasers are image editing tools that either do not use brushes or have limited brush options available.

Each tool retains the brush-and-option set last used for that tool. You can add and save brushes or groups of brushes using the pop-up menu at the top right of the Brushes palette.

Brush Presets When you open the Brushes palette, the first area you enter is the Brush presets. Here you'll see either icons or the names of the currently loaded brushes. This is where you start to create a brush. Choose a preset by clicking it and you can see which options are turned on for that brush by looking for the checks in the boxes

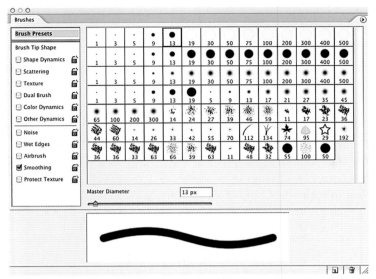

This is the full Brushes palette that you get when you choose Window/Brushes or click the Brush Palette icon on the far right of the Options bar. The abbreviated palette below allows you to choose a different brush directly from the Options bar. In both instances, we've expanded the palette to show all the brushes and used Small Thumbnail view.

Use this pop-up to show the currently loaded brushes.

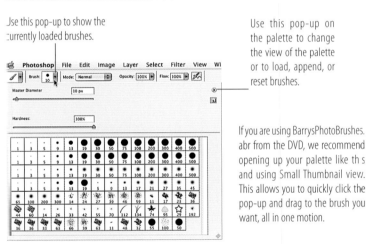

Use this pop-up on the palette to change the view of the palette or to load, append, or reset brushes.

If you are using BarrysPhotoBrushes. abr from the DVD, we recommend opening up your palette like this and using Small Thumbnail view. This allows you to quickly click the pop-up and drag to the brush you want, all in one motion.

placed together on the screen (the default value for this is 25%, which causes a 75% overlap of each dab, so that it looks like a continuous stroke). To learn about spacing, set it to 100%, and then paint using the Paintbrush tool with a big, hard-edge brush. At 100%, the dabs are tangent to each other on the canvas. Now try turning the spacing off (uncheck the Spacing box). With spacing off, the spacing is controlled by how fast you move the brush.

You can change the angle and roundness of the brush by typing values in the dialog or by using the handles and arrow on the brush definition area at the lower left of the palette. The Brush icon on the palette illustrates what that brush will look like.

For more on the specifics of the other Brush options, see Chapter 32, "Digital Paint."

Common Image Editing Tool Options

The following options work primarily the same way for all the painting tools.

Painting Modes In Photoshop, you can paint with more than just the current foreground color. By changing the Painting mode, you can get many different results from your brush. These Painting modes are essentially the Blend modes that we cover in Chapter 31, "Blend Modes, Calculations, and Apply Image." If you read that chapter (and experiment with painting), you'll get a feel for what each of the modes can do. If you are a photographer who works in a realistic style, you won't often use modes while painting, but they are good to understand for the special situations that sometimes present themselves, such as when you need to paint color on an object without disturbing its underlying grayscale values.

on the left of the palette. The only thing you can change about your brush in this area is the master diameter.

Brush Tip Options Click the words *Brush Tip Shape* to enter this area. Here you can change the diameter of the brush (up to 2500 pixels), the hardness of the brush, and the spacing. When you set the hardness to 100%, you get very little or no blending between the color or image you are painting and the background. A hardness of 0% gives maximum blending with the background. Try the same large brush with different hardness settings to see how it can affect the stroke. The spacing controls how closely dabs of the Paintbrush tool are

To Access Specific Blend/Painting Modes

Macintosh Option-Shift		Windows Alt-Shift	
plus			
Normal	N	Soft Light	F
Dissolve	I	Hard Light	H
Behind	Q	Vivid Light	V
Clear	R	Linear Light	J
Darken	K	Pin Light	Z
Multiply	M	Hard Mix	L
Color Burn	B	Difference	E
Linear Burn	A	Exclusion	X
Lighten	G	Hue	U
Screen	S	Saturation	T
Color Dodge	D	Color	C
Linear Dodge	W	Luminosity	Y
Overlay	O	Airbrush On/Off	P

You can toggle through the different Blend modes as you paint by pressing Shift-+ (plus) to move forward or Shift-− (minus) to move backward through the various modes. In addition, see the chart on this page for the specific keystrokes for each Blend mode. You can also use these keys to change the Blend modes for layers when you are not in a painting tool.

Opacity and Flow The default Opacity setting for brushes is 100%. However, any new Brush preset you choose will retain the opacity, flow, and paint mode of the last-used brush. This is not true for Tool presets; they maintain the settings that were used when you created the preset. You can change the opacity of a brush by typing in a number from 0 to 9 while using one of the brush tools (1 equals 10%, 2 equals 20%...9 equals 90%, and 0 equals 100%). If you type two numbers quickly, like 25, you can set the opacity to that double-digit percent. Opacity and Flow work hand in hand to determine the amount of paint laid down. We like to think of the opacity as controlling the transparency of the medium and flow as controlling how fully you've loaded your brush. To mimic watercolor, a very transparent medium, keep the opacity low. For a thick oil paint effect, you would set a high opacity, though you might also lower the flow to get more of a blended effect. When Flow is present on the Options bar (and Airbrush is not active), pressing Shift along with a number will set the amount of flow.

When you're painting with the Pencil or Paintbrush, the Opacity setting from the Brushes palette is not exceeded as long as you hold the mouse button down, even if you paint over the same area again and again.

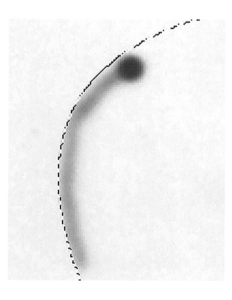

Here, we used a soft-edge brush with the Airbrush tool. As we got to the top of the stroke, we held the mouse down, and as you can see, the paint built up in the shape of the brush.

Modifier Keys If you hold down Shift when using any of the painting tools, you draw vertically or horizontally. Also, if you click once with the tool, release the mouse button, and then Shift-click somewhere else, you get a straight line between these two points with the current brush.

Airbrush Airbrush is an option on many of the painting tools rather than a tool unto itself. When you turn on the Airbrush option, paint will continue to be laid down when you hold the mouse in one spot until the maximum opacity is reached. When the Airbrush option is checked (either on the Options bar or in the Brushes palette), any settings you input control the amount of flow rather than the opacity. To set the opacity in this case, hold down the Shift key as you type the numbers. The opacity of one application of color using the Airbrush option will never exceed the current opacity setting no matter how long you hold down the mouse.

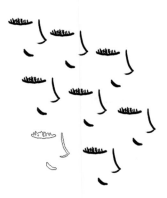

You can create a pattern, marquee it, and define a brush or pattern from it.

Here we've clicked several times with the brush we just defined.

The Healing brush and Patch tool use pixel information from a source—either a sampled area or a pattern—and then blend those pixels with existing pixels from your image. These tools are similar to the Clone Stamp, but the healing tools don't take the information verbatim; instead, they interpolate it to blend the pixels seamlessly with those from the existing image. The Spot Healing brush uses the same sort of interpolation, but it does not require that you set a source for its transformations. Instead, it looks at the pixels over which the brush passes and makes some assumptions about what should be kept and what needs to be healed.

Spot Healing Brush

The Spot Healing Brush is now the default healing tool in the palette and is probably the tool you'll use most often, especially for facial retouching, because of its ease of use. You simply click and drag over the area you want to heal, and let Photoshop do all the work for you. Be careful when you're in an area that has hard edges. Because Photoshop searches the edges of your brush for information, it may pick up unwanted colors or patterns. If this happens, undo the stroke and try a different direction for the stroke, use Replace mode rather than Normal mode, choose the Create texture option

Defining a Custom Brush In addition, you can define a custom brush by drawing a rectangle or an elliptical selection around all or part of an image and choosing Edit/Define Brush. You can use a color or grayscale selection to define your brush, though the brush appears as grayscale in your palette. Consequently, if you build your brushes in grayscale with a white or transparent background, your results will be more predictable. Painting with any brush uses the density of the gray in the brush to determine the amount of foreground color to lay down. After you have defined your custom brushes, you can use Save Brushes from the Brushes palette menu to give your new set of brushes a distinctive name. You can save the brushes wherever you like, but if you've hit on something you think you're going to use again, save your brushes in the Photoshop/Presets/Brushes folder, and they will show up in the easily accessible Brushes palette pop-up menu.

Photoshop includes several custom brush palettes inside this folder already. You can load these palettes or any palette you create by using Load Brushes from the pop-up options, or if you want to add those brushes to the current palette, choose Append Brushes. Reset Brushes restores the default Brushes palette.

Spot Healing Brush, Healing Brush, Patch Tool, and Red Eye Tool (J)

If you do much retouching in your work, Photoshop will make you very happy. You'll have opportunities to work with these tools in Chapter 26, "Restoring Old Photos," and Chapter 29, "Portrait Compositing." For now, here's a bit about how these tools work. If you'd like to erase a few wrinkles from Barry's face (he'd appreciate it, no doubt), you can open BarryCrabbing.psd from the DVD and try your hand.

This is the original, somewhat shiny nose.

Using Proximity as the sampling option with the Spot Healing brush can sometimes give you unexpected results.

If that happens, you might try Create Texture as the sampling option.

You sample an area for the Healing brush just the way you do for the Clone Stamp—by Option (Alt)-clicking.

As you stroke with the Healing brush, you see a representation of the area from which you are taking information. After a few seconds, the calculations are made and the stroke is blended with the image.

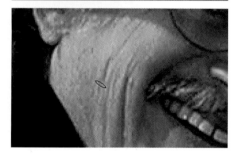

The Spot Healing brush does not require you to choose a sample location; you only need to drag the tool. This works well on the small wrinkles. Note the angled brush.

rather than the Proximity option, or make a selection first of the area to be healed that does not include the hard edges. For more control over exactly where Photoshop looks to get the healing information, switch to the Healing brush.

Healing Brush

To use the Healing brush, select the brush and options from the Brushes palette and the Options bar. If you want to use a sample from a file, Option (Alt)-click with the brush to set the sample start point. If you want to use a pattern, click the Pattern button and choose the pattern from the pop-up. When you use the brush, you lay down a stroke and then wait. Photoshop calculates how to blend the information together, then changes the pixel values. For this reason, it's best to work in short strokes and check that the effect is what you want before continuing. You can work with several different Blend modes, but there is no Opacity slider. Therefore, you might want to make a copy of your layer before you retouch it, then change the opacity of the layer if you want more control over the

When you need to cover an area with information that is completely different, you need to switch to the Clone Stamp.

blending of the effect. Photoshop can heal onto an empty (transparent) layer as well, giving you another option to maintain the integrity of your original.

Patch Tool

The Patch tool works from the same premise, matching the lighting, texture, and shading from the sample with the source image. Rather than making brush strokes, though, you select an area to work with. The radio buttons on the Options bar now ask you to state whether the selection you make is to be the Source or the Destination for the transformation. If you choose Source, drag the selection you've made to the area that has the information you want to incorporate, or click the Use Pattern button to use the current pattern. If you choose Destination, drag the selection to the area that you want to heal. The selection marquee now moves to that location. You can drag this same selection to new locations to heal other areas. At any point during this process, you may click the Use Pattern button to use the current pattern instead of the pixels from the original selection. Clicking the Transparent button for either Source or Destination will give you texture but maintain more of the underlying color and contrast. Wendy loves the Patch tool for correcting larger areas that might need several strokes with the Healing brush. Plus, using Source, you get to move around the image until you find an area that you feel is a good match.

Still, there are times when you'll find you need the Clone Stamp to create information, and there's no clear-cut formula to say when you'll need which tool. Spot Healing, Healing, and the Patch tool work best when you are correcting small areas that are not significantly different from what you want the final product to look like. They are not as good for detail work due to the unpredictability of the averaging they perform. If you have to completely cover an area that includes a lot of detail, the Clone Stamp may still work best. We use all the tools for retouching in Chapter 26.

Red Eye Tool

Using the Red Eye tool, you can quickly get rid of "red eye" by choosing the pupil size and darkening amount you want for the eyes, then clicking on the red color. The process sometimes takes a few seconds, and you may need to change the options to get a realistic result, but it's worth the effort. It works so well, it virtually ends the need to even consider using a red-eye reduction method on a camera. We use the tool in Chapter 29.

Brush, Pencil, and Color Replacement Tools (B)

The Brush tool is one of the most important tools in the Toolbox. Because we do so much of our work with masks, we use this tool constantly, switching back and forth between the default colors by typing X. Yes, it's a good tool for painting as well, but most of what we do we accomplish by using adjustment layers and masks, rather than by creating with paint. The Brush tool has anti-aliased edges that make the edge of where you paint blend more evenly with what you are painting over. When you use the Pencil tool, the edges of your drawing are jagged because there is no anti-aliasing. Use the Pencil tool when you want to be sure to get a solid color even on the edge of the painted area. When you switch from an anti-aliased painting tool, such as the Paintbrush, to the Pencil tool, the brushes in the Brushes palette switch to hard-edge brushes.

If your work is primarily realistic, you won't need a lot of the available brush options. You need to understand the Hardness setting and how that affects the blending together of edges, and you need to learn the keyboard shortcuts for making your brush larger and smaller.

See Chapter 32 to learn more about how to use the Brush and the Brushes palette.

The Color Replacement tool replaces areas of a targeted color in your image with the foreground color in the Toolbox. We never use the Color Replacement tool, preferring to change the color of objects with a Hue/Saturation adjustment layer and a layer mask.

Clone Stamp and Pattern Stamp Tool (S)

With the Clone Stamp, you can copy information from an image onto itself, from one layer of an image to another layer, or from one photo to another. Though much of the work of the Clone Stamp was usurped by the introduction of the Healing brush, it is still an indispensable tool. Healing works well in areas of generally uniform color, where you need to cover only minor imperfections. Cloning works better when you have a lot of detail you need to match or for areas with distinctive edges.

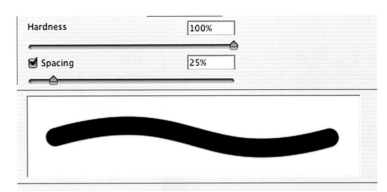

At 100% Hardness, the edges of your brush are crisp and well defined. At 0% Hardness, the brush has a soft edge, allowing your stroke to blend with the existing image pixels.

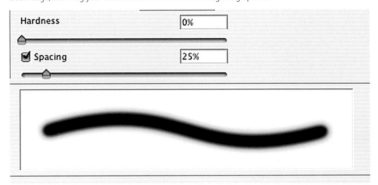

With the Pattern Stamp, you can lay down a pattern from the currently loaded patterns using a brush rather than the Fill command.

Aligned Both tools allow you to choose Aligned if you want to paint a continuous image or Pattern, even if you let go of the mouse or stylus. Aligned is the option you will use most often with the Clone Stamp. You can use it to remove spots and scratches, and also to copy part of an image from one place to another. To use it, pick a brush size from the Brushes palette, then hold down the Option (Alt) key and click at the location where you want to pick up the image (called the *pickup location*). Now, without holding down the Option (Alt) key, click the place where you want to clone the new information (called the *putdown location*). As long as you hold down the mouse, information copies from the pickup location to the putdown location. Icons for both of these locations move correspondingly when you move the mouse. When you release the mouse button and then move it and click down again, the relative distance between the pickup location and the putdown location remains the same, but both move the offset distance that you move the mouse. Therefore, you can clone part of the image, stop for lunch, and then come back and finish the job without worrying about misaligning your clone. This makes Aligned very good for removing spots. You also can clone from one image or one layer to another by Option (Alt)-clicking the pickup image or layer and then clicking to clone in the putdown image or layer.

You would uncheck Aligned to copy the same object to various places within the image. When you disable Aligned, the pickup location remains the same when you move the mouse and click down in a new putdown location, which allows you to copy the same part of the image to multiple places within the image. When you want to change the pickup location, you need to Option (Alt)-click again. Non-aligned would work better if you needed to copy, say, one star or apple over and over.

We Option (Alt)-clicked the Wheel image to set our pickup location.

In this image of the Grand Canyon, we can fix this scratch quickly because it's a straight line. First we Option (Alt)-click to set our source location.

The putdown location is in a different file on a new, blank layer.

Once you've chosen your source location, you can click one end of the scratch, then Shift-click the other end. The CloneSstamp draws a straight line to cover the scratch.

We moved the cloned layer and added a layer mask.

Use all Layers If you have a composite that uses layers, you can clone from the entire image without flattening first by turning on the Use All Layers option. This will clone from whatever is currently visible, so you can turn layers on and off for different effects, even between strokes with the tool.

Pattern Stamp

Patterned cloning uses the current Photoshop pattern and copies it wherever you paint with the mouse. If the Align box is checked, painting the pattern is consistent; the patterns line up even if you've released the mouse button and started drawing more than once.

To define a pattern, you select a rectangular area with the Rectangular Marquee, and then choose Edit/Define Pattern. Your new pattern is then added to the current Patterns palette. If you've added patterns that you really like and want to keep, be sure you save your patterns to a file via the Preset Manager.

The History and Art History Brush (Y)

As we mentioned in Chapter 3, "Navigating in Photoshop," we use the History palette mainly as a tool to move back through the steps of creating an image. Occasionally one of us may make a snapshot of work at a certain point so we can decide which direction to take, but more often we use Layer comps. So we don't generally use the History brush, which works in conjunction with the History palette to give you multiple levels of undo and multiple snapshots from which to paint. One of the primary uses for the History brush is to recapture effects or states that you used earlier in your work but lost via Undo or further manipulation. But we are more likely to use layers, because layers generally give you more flexibility. The position of the History Brush icon in the History palette determines the state of the file from which you will paint using the History/Art History brush.

If you decide to use History, remember that it is layer dependent and dependent on the pixel dimensions of the file. That is, you can paint to a layer only the information that has existed on that layer. You can't paint information from a different layer's History state. Also, if you crop the file, you can't paint from a History state that existed before the crop. And, unlike layers and layer comps, when you close the file, the History states vanish.

The Art History brush attempts to increase the capabilities of Photoshop to create artwork from photographs. Although you can achieve some interesting results with this tool, it's unpredictable, and discovering methods that are particularly useful takes a lot of practice. Our suggestion: If you want to create naturalistic artwork from your photos, invest in Corel Painter. See Chapter 32.

Both the History and Art History brushes can use any brush shape currently loaded, and both can use Blend modes, though not all are available to the Art History brush.

Eraser, Background, and Magic Eraser Tools (E)

The Eraser tool erases to the background color in the *Background* layer and to transparency in any other layer. The default background color is white but can be any color. Erasing a layer to transparency allows you to see through the erased area to the layers below it.

You can choose from three options for the type of eraser nib: Brush, Pencil, and Block. The first two give you eraser nibs that act exactly like their painting tool counterparts with respect to style, so refer to the Paintbrush and Pencil sections of this chapter. The Block option is most like the Eraser from early versions of the program. It does not have anti-aliased edges, and the size of the area you erase is determined not by brush size but rather by the magnification of the image you are working with. The higher the magnification of the image, the smaller your erased area, until the eraser is the same size as a pixel and you are erasing individual pixels.

Erase to History This option erases to the current position of the History brush source in the History palette. Click this option or hold down the Option (Alt) key as you use the Eraser to use Erase to History. You usually use the Eraser when you want to completely remove something in a small area. With Erase to History, you are replacing rather than removing pixels.

We don't use the Eraser all that much because we generally work with layer masks. On a mask you use the Brush tool to paint with white or black to indicate which portions of the layer should be visible.

Background Eraser

The Background Eraser is a tool that some people use when compositing to remove the background from images they wish to composite. The main deficiency of this tool, however, is that (like the Magic Eraser) it deletes image information and replaces it with transparency. So always copy the layer, so that the Background Eraser performs its deletion on the copy and not the original image (be sure to turn the Eye icon off for the original, so that you can see the tool's effect). This working method preserves a backup copy of all your image data in case you need to fill in any areas where the eraser's choices were less than satisfactory.

The Options palette for the Background Eraser has three main settings that affect how it performs pixel deletion.

Limits Discontiguous will erase the sampled color wherever it occurs in the layer; Contiguous will erase areas that contain the sampled color and are connected to one another; and Find Edges will erase the sampled color in contiguous areas, but do a better job of preserving the sharpness of object edges.

Sampling From the Sampling options, you can choose Continuous to sample colors continuously as you drag through the image. This option is best for erasing adjoining areas that are different in color. The Once option will erase only areas containing the color you first click. This is best for deleting a solid-colored area. The Background Swatch option will erase only areas containing the current background color.

Tolerance You set a Tolerance value similar to that of the Magic Wand tool. A low tolerance erases areas that are very similar to the sampled color, and a high tolerance erases a broader range of colors.

Once again, we rarely use this tool, and if we do, we use it only to create our initial selection for a layer mask.

Magic Eraser

We do not use this tool. It's rare in our type of work to find large areas of flat color that we need to erase, which is what this tool does; and even if we did, we'd probably use a layer mask to remove unwanted areas from our image.

Gradient Tool and Paint Bucket (G)

The Gradient tool is a very important aid in masking. Any time you want to fade two images together, or fade an adjustment in or out, you'll need to build a gradient on layer masks. The other use for this tool is to unify or intensify color in your image. In both instances, the Gradient tool imitates adjustments made with graduated filters during shooting. If you'd like to experiment with the tool, open the MarinaHouse.psd file from the DVD.

The basic function of the Gradient tool is to make a gradual blend in the selected area from one color to another color. You blend by clicking and dragging a line the length and angle you want the blend to appear. The line drawn indicates the area in which the transition takes place. The Gradient tool is often used in a mask channel to blend two images together seamlessly by making a blend from black to white. Black represents one image and white the other. Although it is rare for us to need complicated gradients, it does happen from time to time. For example, one of our students, a studio photographer, had a shot with a painted backdrop of a twilight sky. The backdrop was good but not the exact colors that she had envisioned. We showed her how to

Here's the original MarinaHouse image. Marina house is a lovely old bed and breakfast right on the water here in Gibsons.

We created a Channel Mixer adjustment layer to create a black-and-white image; then, using the default colors and a linear blend, we made a gradient blend on the adjustment layer. The red oval shows the length of the drag we used to create the gradient.

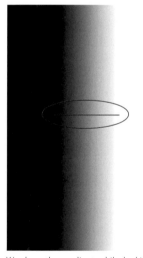

We drew the gradient while looking at the image itself so we could decide about where we wanted the effect to begin and end. Here's what the mask for the Channel Mixer layer looks like, and an approximation of the line we drew for the gradient. The fall-off of color on either end of the line we drew is very subtle. Beyond either end, the color is either pure black or pure white.

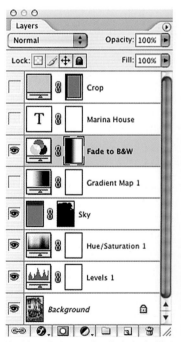

Here's how the Layers palette looks for the MarinaHouse image when the onscreen image looks like the illustration on the next page.

The gradient mask allows the color to fade out of the image.

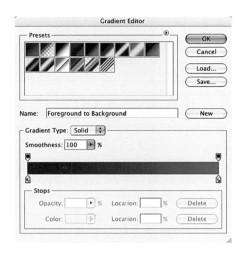

The Gradient Editor showing a Foreground to Background gradient using two shades of blue. You access the Editor by typing G to get to the Gradient tool, then clicking once on the color swatch on the Options bar. We used a gradient similar to this on the Sky layer in the MarinaHouse image.

build a custom gradient with the colors that proved more pleasing in the final print.

You choose the gradient you want to use via the Gradient palette. The palette appears when you click the pop-up on the Gradient Color swatch on the Options bar. The default setting, Foreground to Background, will compute a gradient for you based on the currently selected foreground and background colors. Using the default palette, the second icon is for Foreground to Transparent. The final icon in this palette is Transparent Stripes, which also uses the current foreground color as the stripe color. Double-click a swatch to view its name or to rename it. Clicking the color swatch once brings up the Gradient Editor, which is discussed later in this section.

The Default Settings When you set the Blend mode to Normal, the Type to Linear, and the Gradient to Foreground to Background, everything from the edge of the selection to the first click on the line is solid foreground color. Everything from the mouse release to the other end of the selection is solid background color. Along the line, there is a blend from foreground to background color, and at a place 50% along the length of the line, the two colors are blended each at 50%. In the MarinaHouse image, we used this type of blend on the layer mask for the Channel Mixer adjustment layer to fade the image from black and white to color. We also used this type of gradient to darken the sky in the Sky layer.

Gradient Types Photoshop has five types of Gradient blends: Linear, Radial, Angle, Reflected, and Diamond. These are represented by the group of five icons on the Tool Options bar. We use Linear about 95% of the time, most often in masks to fade an effect in or out of an area. The other types that we use are Radial and Reflected. Linear is the default and makes a blend based on a straight line that you draw at any angle. Radial creates a radial blend done as a circle. If Gradient is set to Foreground to Background, the first click of the mouse is the circle's center using the foreground color, the line length that you drag is the circle's radius, and the mouse release location is at the outside edge of a blended circle using the background color. The Angle blend gives the effect of sweeping a radius around a circle. The line you draw is the "angle" of the radius in the foreground color (or first color of the blend) that then sweeps around the circle, changing gradually to the background color (or that moves through the colors of your selected blend). The Reflected gradient reflects two symmetrical linear gradients outward from your starting point, and the Diamond gradient uses the line you draw as one of the corners of the diamond shape that is created.

Blend Modes and Opacity You can set the Blend mode and opacity of the gradient you are about to create using these settings in the Gradient Options palette. We discuss the various Blend modes in Chapter 31. However, you might want to try some of the modes, such as Color, Multiply, Difference, and Hard Light, as you explore the Gradient tool.

The Dither Option Leaving the Dither option on results in smoother blends with less banding. We recommend that you leave it on unless you want a banded gradient.

The Gradient Editor

Click the Gradient Preview swatch on the Options bar to access the Gradient Editor. The currently active Gradient palette appears, along with the controls to create or edit any gradient. If you want to base your new gradient on an existing one, click the swatch of the existing gradient or use the Load button to load any other palette shipped with Photoshop or created by you. To modify an existing gradient, just select it and start making changes. When you have something you like, type in a name and click the New button. Your gradient will be added to the palette. If you want to save the gradient permanently, click the Save button and give your palette a distinctive name. Otherwise, when you reset the palette, reset your preferences, or re-install Photoshop, you will lose your gradient. To remove a gradient, hold the Option (Alt) key and click the swatch.

Each square above or below the color bar represents a stop for either color or transparency in the gradient. When you click a stop, you can change the color or transparency of the gradient. To remove a stop from the gradient, simply pull it away from the color bar.

Stops below the color bar represent different colors. You can add a new stop by clicking anywhere below the bar, and you can move this point by dragging left and right. The Location box tells you the location of this color as a percentage of the length of the line you draw to create the gradient. You can set a point to a particular color by first clicking that stop and then either clicking the color box below and to the left to display the Color Picker and pick a new color, or using the automatic Eyedropper to sample a color from any currently open file. The color point you are currently working on will have its triangle top highlighted in black. The little diamond points under the colored bar represent the halfway point between the color to the left and the color to the right of that diamond point. Click and drag it to have the

Location window show you the location relative to the percentage of distance between these two points. The default location of the diamonds is always 50% of this distance, but you can move them left and right.

Click above the color bar to change the transparency of the gradient at points along its length. You can turn off the transparency of any gradient by deselecting the Transparency check box on the Tool Options bar when you are using the Gradient tool. Try turning off Transparency and then using the Foreground to Transparent option: You get just the solid foreground color. The length of the bar again represents the length of the line you draw when making the gradient. You can place Opacity stops anywhere along the bar by clicking above the bar. When you click a stop, the bottom of it turns black, indicating that it is the stop you are currently editing. The Location window shows you the location of this point relative to the total length of the line, and the Opacity entry field shows you its opacity. The diamonds between stops show you the midpoint between the Opacity stops. Bring the Gradient Editor up and play with it a bit, and it will become obvious how it works.

Noise Photoshop has the capability to build a gradient based on a range of colors. The application computes a gradient composed of colored bands spaced irregularly. The Roughness setting controls how radical the transitions are from color to color, with a lower setting giving you more of a standard gradient and a higher setting giving you something out of a technicolor nightmare. Use Restrict Colors to keep the colors from oversaturating. Transparency removes or partially removes colors from the gradient. Try using a Noise gradient

The bottom row of stops are the Color stops. Click one to activate the controls for that stop. In this illustration, the bottom stops use the foreground color on the left and the background color on the right. These stops look a bit different than ones you add yourself.

The top row of stops are the Opacity stops. Click one to activate the controls for that stop.

This is a noise gradient applied as a Gradient Map layer to the MarinaHouse image. You can turn this layer on in the file included on the DVD and turn the Fade to B&W layer off. If you double-click the adjustment layer icon for this layer, you can take a look at the gradient that produced this.

as a Gradient Map adjustment layer. Turn on the Preview button and experiment with the sliders, buttons, and Roughness setting. As a gradient map, these gradients offer a quick way to explore color choices that would take much longer to generate as a gradient that you build yourself.

Paint Bucket Tool

The Paint Bucket tool, which is in the same tool bay as the Gradient tool, is similar to the Magic Wand in that it fills an area based on the tolerance value set in the Options bar, and the pixel on which you click. We seldom use the Paint Bucket. The Paint Bucket is, however, very useful for colorizing black-and-white line drawings such as cartoon drawings, animations, or solid-color areas.

Blur, Sharpen, and Smudge Tools (R)

The Blur, Sharpen, and Smudge tools are a rarely used set of tools. The Blur tool softens the variations between pixels so that edges blend better. However, we perform most blurs with the Gaussian Blur filter. Using the filter gives you the opportunity to preview how the blur will affect your image. There are a few instances where we may use the Blur tool on a mask to correct some small flaw, or on a copy of portions of the image for retouching, but hardly ever do we apply it directly to the pixels of an image. The Sharpen tool, which makes the variations between pixels greater to produce more of an edge, we use even less than Blur. For sharpening we use Unsharp Mask or Smart Sharpen. We might use the Smudge tool, which pulls color from one area into another, for an effect, but we're not big on effects. Wendy has used it for painterly effects, but is more likely to use Painter.

Dodge, Burn, and Sponge Tools (O)

We also seldom use the Dodge, Burn, and Sponge tools. In Chapter 12, "Essential Photoshop Techniques for Photographers," we demonstrate nondestructive methods of dodging (lightening areas) and burning (darkening areas) using layers and masks. Seán occasionally uses the Dodge and Burn tools for correcting masks because you can limit the tools' influence somewhat by choosing highlights, midtones, or shadows to work with. Our major complaint with the tools is that there are no parameters for exactly what Photoshop considers a highlight, midtone, or shadow to be, and if you use the tools on image pixels, you can't easily undo their effect. Using a Curves adjustment layer or a Dodge/Burn layer set to Softlight, we can be more exacting and have more flexibility.

Here is a grayscale mask of a portion of the house before dodging with the Dodge tool.

With the tool set to dodge Highlights at 20% Exposure, we can selectively dodge only the lighter areas of the mask without having to be overly cautious about our brush strokes.

The Sponge tool can saturate or desaturate areas, but you get more control and flexibility using a Hue/Saturation adjustment layer along with a mask.

Vector Tools

The third area of the Toolbox contains tools that work with vector shapes rather than pixels. If you use the Pen tool to create a path, draw a shape with a Shape tool, or set type, you have created a mathematical equation within your document. This equation can be interpreted to be the same shape by any printer capable of working with vectors, and can be printed at any resolution or size. Pixel-based images begin to break up if they are printed larger than the size for which they were originally intended. The primary reason to use a vector path, mask, or shape is the sharp edge that can be delineated with vectors.

Some photographers who work only with soft-edged selections may never use the Pen tool to build a vector mask or path, but if you do compositing, it's worth some time and effort to learn these tools.

The Path Selection/Direct Selection Tool (A)

If you are used to working in Illustrator, you'll feel right at home in Photoshop. If you're not used to the vector world, you may find these tools difficult to work with at first. To experiment with them, try the hands-on tutorial on the Pen tool in Chapter 28, "Compositing Multiple Images."

Once you have an existing path, you can use the Path Selection tool to select the entire path. You can move the path by dragging it or copy the path by Option (Alt)-dragging it.

If you use the Direct Selection tool, you can choose a particular point to work with. If you use this tool to click a point connected to a curved segment, you get "handles" that allow you to change the shape and length of the curve. If you are in the midst of using the Pen tool and hold down the Command (Ctrl) key, you can also access the Direct Selection tool.

Subpaths

If you draw more than one vector shape while in a single path in the Paths palette, those shapes are considered to be subpaths of the main path—that is, the one you name in the Paths palette. Each successive shape is "stacked" on top of the preceding shapes whether they overlap or not.

You can have multiple subpaths included as part of a path and these subpaths can be combined in different ways depending on their stacking order to create intricate masks or selections. The interaction icons on the Options bar are similar to the selection interaction icons with one additional icon, Exclude, which excludes the overlapping section of paths in determining masks or areas to be filled or stroked with color. Combining subpaths may be helpful if you are trying to make some complex selection with very sharp edges, but such a selection would more likely be used by a graphic designer than a photographer.

If you have more than one active subpath, you can use the same type of alignment options that are available when you select multiple layers of a document. You can also copy and paste subpaths to other paths.

The Temple door.jpg file included in the Chapter 4 folder on the DVD contains several paths to work with if you would like to see some of the available options.

The Type Tool (T)

Most photographers have little need to set type on an image, and none of our examples in this book use type. However, we include some information here for those of you who may need type from time to time.

When you use the Type tool, you enter text by clicking the image in the location where you want to insert the text, or clicking and dragging to create a bounding box for paragraph type. If you choose either the Horizontal or the Vertical Type icon, type is added to your image as a new layer with the type surrounded by transparency. The layer is named using the characters that you just typed in, which makes identifying the layer easy. The two Type Mask tools add a selection of your type boundaries to the currently active layer. This is done by adding a Quick Mask overlay that remains active until you hit the numeric keypad's Enter key or click the Accept icon (it looks like a checkmark) on the Options bar. The regular Enter (Return) key just adds a new line for text. You can add layer masks and vector masks to type layers as you would to any other layer.

You can change the color of type, kern it, track it, baseline-shift it, and change the attributes character by character. If that's not enough, you can transform the layer or add layer effects and still have vector text. Vector text is primarily important if you are printing to a press rather than a desktop printer. Using vector text ensures that the letterforms will be sharp and crisp rather than jagged, as often occurs with bitmap text.

You access type layers through the Layers palette, where you can modify the opacity and the Paint mode of the layer. You can't do this on a character-by-character basis.

The Character and Paragraph palettes give you more extensive information than what is available on the Options bar.

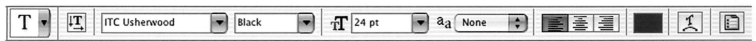

Here's the Options bar for the Type tool. The first two icons are for Type tool presets and Change Type Orientation. The first pop-up is for the typeface or font family, then weight, size, and amount of anti-aliasing. Then come three icons for alignment, the Color square, the Warp Text button, and the Palettes button for accessing the Character and Paragraph palettes.

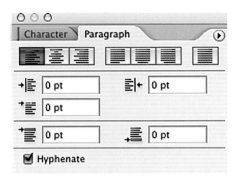

The options on the Paragraph palette work only if you have set paragraph type.

The Character and Paragraph Palettes

The Character and Paragraph palettes appear when you click the Palettes button on the Type tool Options bar. Here's a quick rundown of what you'll find on these palettes.

Font The first entry field of the Character palette is for the font or typeface name. Generally, you look for the name of the typeface, such as Times or Garamond (we used Trajan Pro in the previous illustration), and then select the weight of the face that you wish to use, such as light, book, bold, or italic. Photoshop gives you a preview beside the name showing what each face looks like so you can choose even if you don't know the faces by name.

Weight The second entry field is for the weight of the face, which may be book, bold, light, and so on, or may be prefaced by a number that describes the weight.

Size The size at which text appears depends not only on the size you choose in the Type tool Options bar, but also on the resolution and dimensions of the image you set using the Image/Image Size command. Luckily, if you resize your image, Photoshop sizes the type accordingly. To resize the type with a keyboard shortcut, use Command (Ctrl)-Shift-> to increase type by 2 points or pixels, and Command (Ctrl)-Shift-< to decrease size by 2 points or pixels.

Kerning Photoshop allows you to kern letter pairs—that is, change the amount of space between any two characters. A positive number gives you more space between the letters; a negative number tightens the space. Click between a pair of letters you want to kern, then either type a number in the input field or use the pop-up. Use Option (Alt)-right arrow or Option (Alt)-left arrow to kern via the keyboard. If you do set your own type, kerning is one area that shows the difference between people who know type (designers and production artists) and those who don't. Wendy likes to think of the space between letters as a rhythm. Unless you are going for some weird effect, the rhythm should be steady and flowing. It should seem that the letters have the same amount of space between them. Certain pairs of letters

tend to look more open or tight than others, and the space between them often needs to be adjusted. In body copy, it generally doesn't matter. But if you are typesetting display type (say for a poster or rack card advertising your work) it is worthwhile to look closely at the type for gaps or letters that collide. Good kerning will give your work the professional appearance that it so rightly deserves.

Leading Leading (rhymes with bedding) is the amount of vertical spacing between the baselines of the lines of text. A positive number gives you more space between the lines, and a negative number, less space. If you set type in all capitals, a negative number usually gives better spacing between the lines. If you want to change all the text on a layer, click the layer in the Layers palette but do not click in the text itself with the Type tool. Use the Character palette to change the spacing. To change the leading of existing type you need to select the line or lines you want to change. You can then either set a value in the Character palette or use Option (Alt)-up arrow to tighten the leading and Option (Alt)-down arrow to give the leading more air.

Tracking Tracking refers to the horizontal letter spacing of the text. Whereas kerning is the space between any two characters, tracking is the space between more than two characters. As in kerning, a positive number gives you more space between the letters, spreading them out, and a negative number draws the letters tighter together. Use the same keyboard shortcuts as with kerning when you have whole words or paragraphs highlighted.

Scaling You can scale some or all of the letters vertically, horizontally, or both by highlighting them and inputting values in the two fields at the top of the third section of the Character palette. Values are written as a percentage of the normal scale of the letters.

Baseline Shift Some or all of the letters may be shifted up or down from the normal baseline by inputting a value in this field. A positive number shifts the letter up; negative numbers shift the letter down. Use Shift-Option (Alt) plus the up or down arrows to shift letters via the keyboard.

The letter spacing on the top word is just as it appeared when typed in Photoshop. Kerning some of the letter pairs closer together in the lower version helps the word hang together better.

Color The text color comes in as the current Color square on the Options bar. You can highlight portions of the text later and choose a different color in the Options bar, the Swatches palette, or the foreground Color square. You can click the Color square to change the color of the type at any time. You change the color of all the text when you click the Color square with a type layer active but no text selected. Use the Type tool and select letters to change attributes individually. If letters on a type layer are colored differently, the color square in the Options bar will display a question mark when differently colored text is highlighted or when the entire layer is activated in the Layers palette.

Character Styling You can find styles for faux bold, faux italics, all caps, small caps, superscript, subscript, underline, and strikethrough at the bottom of the Character palette. In addition, if you are using OpenType fonts, you have other options available to you via the palette pop-up.

Alignment The first three icons at the top of the Paragraph palette (they appear on the Type tool Options bar also) are for alignment: flush left, centered, or flush right.

Justification The last four icons at the top of the Paragraph palette are for justifying paragraphs. All four justify the paragraph; only the last line is treated differently. You can align the last line left, centered, right, or (the icon that's set apart on the far right) force justification. The specifications for how to justify the paragraph are set using Justify from the Paragraph palette pop-up menu.

Indents The second section of the Paragraph palette controls indents. You can make left, right, and first-line indents, which means you can set hanging indents. You also can set hanging punctuation from the Paragraph palette pop-up menu.

Space Before/After The third section of the Paragraph palette allows you to control the amount of space before and after your paragraph.

Hyphenation If you want Photoshop to automatically hyphenate a paragraph for you, click the Hyphenate button. Hyphenation is set according to the settings you use in the Hyphenation dialog, which you access via the Paragraph palette pop-up menu.

Composition Photoshop is able to use both Single-line and Every-line methods of text composition. Composition controls how type is fitted into a text box. Every-line is the default and usually results in better line breaks over the paragraph. Use Single-line if you want more manual control over the breaks.

Warp Text Photoshop has a fairly robust engine for generating warped type. Click the button on the right of the Options bar to enter this area.

Text on a Path Photoshop can set type on a path. You can draw a path with the Pen tool or use a custom shape to create a path. If the path is open, you are only allowed to put type on top of the path. If, however, your path is a closed shape, you can put type either on the outside or the inside of the path. Look at the illustrations below to see the different cursors that appear in each instance.

Check Spelling/Find and Replace Text Photoshop has the additional capacities to check spelling and replace text. Both of these options are found under the Edit menu.

The Pen and Freeform Pen Tools (P)

For a hands-on tutorial on the Pen tool, see the "Paths and the Pen Tool" section of Chapter 28.

The Pen tool works by placing points and connecting those points with line segments to form paths. You connect the segments by either

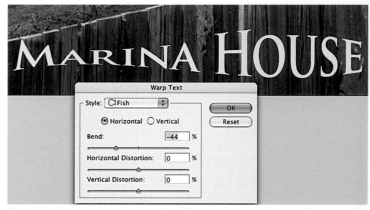

Warping text can create some interesting effects. The type is still editable and the effects are modifyable unless you rasterize the text.

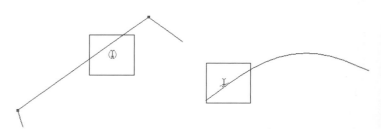

When your cursor looks like this, the text will appear within the boundaries of the closed path as you type.

When your cursor looks like this, the text will appear along the top of the path as you type.

clicking from point to point, or clicking and dragging. A segment can be either straight or curved. Each segment has two points associated with it, a beginning point and an endpoint. Points that control curved segments have handles. A corner point (that is, a point that connects two straight-line segments) has no handles. A smooth point connecting segments in a continuous curve has two handles that are dependent on each other. If you adjust the direction of one of the handles, you affect the other handle in an equal and opposite manner. Simple enough so far. However, a corner point can also join two curve segments that are noncontinuous and abut sharply, as in the two curves forming the top of this lowercase *m*. In that case, the anchor point would have two handles that work independently of each other. And finally, a straight-line segment that joins a curve segment does so via an anchor point that has only one handle, which controls the direction and height of the curve. This type of point is sometimes referred to as a *cusp*.

To draw straight-line segments with the Pen, click where you want to place anchor points. To draw a curved segment, click and drag. To make a corner point with handles that work independently, click and drag out a handle, but after you drag, hold down the Option (Alt) key to access the Convert tool. Use the tool to drag the handle in a different direction. The handle that controls the previous segment will not change, but when you place a new anchor point, you'll have a corner rather than a smooth curve.

There are actually three types of pens you can use. The Pen tool works like Illustrator's Pen tool and basically the same as it has for many years. Recent versions of Photoshop also include the Freeform Pen, which allows you to draw freehand style and place points as you go, and the Magnetic Pen (an option you access from the Freeform pen), which judges the contrast between two edges to help you draw a path for use as a selection.

You can use the Magnetic Pen tool to help you draw a path around an item. However, most of the time "automatic" tools are really only useful as a starting point for creating what you need. We think you'd do better to use your time learning how the Pen tool works (and practicing) rather than spending time correcting a path from the Freeform or Magnetic Pen.

When you begin to use the Pen tool to create a new path, be sure you show the Paths palette. This is where you will save and name the path, fill or stroke it, turn the path into a selection, or turn a selection into a path. You can also duplicate or delete a path. These options are available as icons at the bottom of the palette and from the pop-up menu. In the Layer menu you can designate a path as a vector mask.

You'll get your feet wet actually using the Pen tool in Chapters 28 and 30.

The beauty of the Pen tool is that once you make a path, it is infinitely editable. You can add or delete points, change the height or direction of curves, and even turn a curve into a straight-line segment or vice versa. You will use the Pen tool mostly for making selections where a crisp, hard edge is needed—primarily in compositing, though you may find instances where it's great for creating the initial selection you need for color work as well.

The Shape Tool (U)

You can use the Shape tools in three different ways. You can make a shape layer, a work path, or a filled region on an existing layer. These three options are the first three icons on the Options bar. The first two options create vector paths that can be edited and are device independent, that is, they can print at the resolution of any printer. The third option makes a selection and fills it; you change the pixels and you can't undo it later except via the History palette.

The next set of icons are where you choose the tool or shape you want. The first two icons are the Pen tool and Freeform Pen tool, then come rectangles, rounded-corner rectangles, ellipses, polygons, lines, and custom shapes. Click the shape you want, and then click the pop-up menu to access the settings for that particular shape. The last icon in the group is the gateway to the Custom Shapes palette. Choose from the default shapes, load a larger Custom Shapes palette from the Presets folder, or create your own shapes and save them to a new palette. If you have some cool shapes already built in Illustrator, paste them as paths into Photoshop, and then use Edit/Define Custom Shape to save them to the Shapes palette. Save the palette with a new name if you want to make sure you keep all your shapes. You might also use the Custom Shape tool to create a shape for a special mask. Most photographers do not use the Shape tool often, at least not for realistic imagery. It is more of a design tool.

As you draw shapes, you need to be aware of the shape interaction icons on the Options bar. These icons are similar to the selection interaction icons. They determine whether the next shape you draw will be a new shape (in this case a new shape layer), added to the existing shapes, subtracted from the shapes, intersected with the shapes, or excluded from the shapes. Once you have several shapes on a layer, you can select two or more with the Path Selection arrow to align or combine them.

The Shape tool can help you determine the crop for a photo. In Chapter 21, "Overall Color Correction," we show you how to use

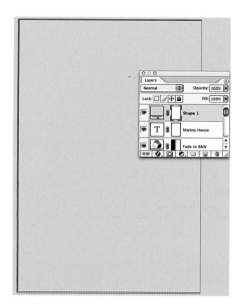

To create a Cropping layer first create a solid-color fill layer that covers the entire photo.

Before you draw the second path, set the interaction icon to Subtract.

When you draw the next shape, you create a window through which to view the image. Use the Direct Selection tool to click and drag the interior boundaries to resize the crop. Use the Shift key as you drag to maintain the rectangular aspect.

a selection with a Solid Color adjustment layer to determine your crop. An as alternative, you could use a vector mask instead of a layer mask for the adjustment layer—it lets you move the boundaries of the crop more precisely. To create a crop layer you first choose the rectangular Shape tool. On the Options bar, you then choose a color for the outside border of the crop. You might use black, white, or the midtone gray of your Photoshop work area.

Make sure the Shape Layer icon is active on the Options bar, then draw a rectangle around your image. This will give you a solid-color layer that blocks out your photo. Now use the shape interaction icons to draw a new shape that subtracts from the first; it's the middle interaction icon. Drag the Shape tool to about the size you need. Your image will reappear and you now have an interior rectangular path that you can modify with the Direct Selection tool.

Other Useful Tools

Notes and Audio Annotation Tool (N)

Although we don't use the Notes tool, it could be used to attach a note to a client about certain corrections that will be made to the image.

To attach a written note, choose the Note tool and click where you want the note to appear. You can also click and drag to create a notes box in which to input your message. Click in the input window to type your note. The color indicator on the Tool Options bar shows the color of the note and the author's name. This can be changed from note to note—a quick way to identify the author. You can resize the input window and move the Window and Note icons independently of each other.

To delete a note, click the icon once or Command (Ctrl)-click it and press the Delete key. You can click the Clear All button on the Options bar to delete all annotations at once.

Eyedropper, Color Sampler, and Measure Tools (I)

You use the Eyedropper tool to choose the foreground and background color within an image onscreen. With the Eyedropper selected, you click the color that you want to make the foreground color, or Option (Alt)-click in the image to get the background color. You access the Eyedropper tool by holding down the Option (Alt) key when using any of the painting tools and then clicking where you want to pick up a new foreground color. You can choose to have the tool sample only one pixel to choose the color, or get an average color of 3x3 or 5x5 pixels. A sample of 3x3 is better for color correction as areas of color that look homogenous are actually a collection of colors. Choosing a single pixel can give you a false reading.

The Color Sampler tool allows you to place point samples in up to four locations in your file. During manipulation of your image, you can watch how your changes are affecting the areas where you placed samplers. You can move point samples after you've placed them by Shift-dragging them, and hide them completely by using the Info palette pop-up. You can change the readout values from RGB to

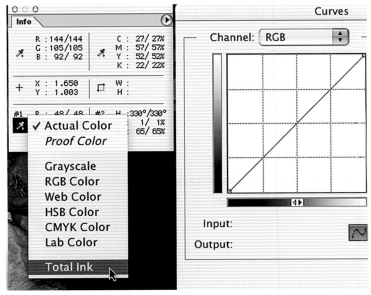

You can set up to four Color Samplers and change the readout at any time. Here, we've changed Sampler #1 to give us the Total Ink percentage while in the middle of a Curves adjustment.

> **NOTE**
>
> The Eyedropper tool automatically appears whenever you are in Levels, Curves, Color Balance, or any of the color correction tools and you move the cursor over the image. This allows you to see the color values of any location in the Info and Color palettes while you are correcting and changing those values.

CMYK, Grayscale, HSB, Lab, Actual Color, or Total Ink percentages, even in the middle of making adjustments to the file, by clicking the specific sampler pop-up triangle. You can delete a sampler from the screen by dragging it off the image, or by Shift-Option (Alt)-clicking the sampler. We use color samplers all the time in our initial color correction to keep track of whether adjustments we make are creating color casts in the highlights or shadows of an image. To see how you can use the Color Sampler tool to match color between objects, read Chapter 24, "Color Matching Images."

None of us use the Measure tool, but if you need to measure the distance between areas of your image, you can simply drag the Measure tool from point A to point B. However, Wayne Palmer, our technical editor, finds the Measure tool, when used in conjunction with Rotate Canvas/Arbitrary, to be invaluable for straightening images. The Measure tool measurements can be viewed on the Options bar as well as in the Info palette. If you create a line for measuring, it stays in place even when you switch tools and come back to it, although you don't see it when you are in another tool. The measurement does not stay once you close a file. When you draw a new measure line, the old one disappears. You can also click the Clear button to get rid of a line.

Hand Tool (H)

Use the Hand tool to scroll to a different part of your image. You can access the Hand tool more efficiently while working in another tool by using the Spacebar on the keyboard along with a mouse click, which you can do any time. If you double-click the Hand tool in the Tools palette, the image resizes to the largest size that fits completely within the current screen and palette display. This is the tool that we recommend you come back to by typing H after you have done any work with other tools. It will not harm your image if you use it inadvertently as the Crop or Brush tool might.

Zoom Tool (Z)

Use the Zoom tool to magnify the image and, with the Option (Alt) key, to shrink the image. The location where you click is centered within the bigger or smaller image. Using this tool is like moving a photograph you are holding in your hand either closer to your face or farther away. The actual size of the photograph doesn't change, only how closely you are looking at it. It is best to access the Zoom tool using Command (Ctrl)-Spacebar-click to zoom in, or Option (Alt)-Spacebar-click to zoom out. You can use these command keys any time, even when a dialog, like Levels, is up. If you double-click the Zoom tool within the Tools palette, the image zooms in or out to the 100% size. At 100%, the image may be bigger than the screen, but you see every pixel of the part of the image you are viewing. Use this for detailed work. The Resize Windows to Fit option resizes your normal window to surround your zoomed size, if possible. We leave it off because we don't like our windows automatically resizing.

5 ◆ Picking and Using Color

When you first went to elementary school, you began learning color theory. Three pencils—red, yellow, and blue—and all other colors could be created from those primary colors. If you went on to art school you probably still worked with those same basic color principles. When you start painting with light, which is where Photoshop excels, how you think about and choose color changes dramatically.

Paint, Ink, and Light

Most painting manuals talk about the color wheel with red, blue, and yellow as the primary colors. Green, orange, and violet are the respective complementary colors, created by combining two primary colors. Six tertiary or intermediate colors use one of the primary colors and one of the secondary colors. Twelve basic hue ranges include red, red-orange, yellow, yellow-green, green, and so on.

You do, from time to time, find color manuals for paints that specify the primary colors not as red, blue, and yellow, but as magenta, cyan, and yellow. If you've printed to a four-color press, you know these printing inks as CMY, with K (the black ink) used as a fourth color. In this context, magenta and yellow produce red, cyan and yellow produce green, and magenta and cyan produce blue. If you divide the wheel into the same 12 areas, you still have 3 primary colors, 3 secondary colors (or complements) produced by combining primaries, and 6 intermediate colors.

If you work with the spectrum of light, you still have three primary colors, only here they are red, green, and blue. Red and green light combine to create yellow, not brown as they would if you were working with pigments. Green and blue combine to make cyan, and blue and red combine to make magenta. In other words, the three primary light colors RGB are complements of the three primary ink colors, CMY.

Warm or Cool Colors

We usually think of red, orange, and yellow as being warm colors. These are sometimes called aggressive colors because they seem to move toward you or to be closer to you in a painting. Blues, greens, and violets are usually considered cool colors, sometimes called receding colors because they seem to move objects into the background or cause them to recede in a painting.

In reality, however, there are warm reds that contain more yellow and cool reds that contain some blue. The same is true for greens, blues, violets, and yellows. The color you actually see is relative. A certain red on a warm yellow background looks different than the same red on cool blue. Choosing colors that complement your image or achieve certain effects can become a complex process. That is why there are color wheels for every single type of artist, designer, or craftsperson, as well as libraries of books on color theory.

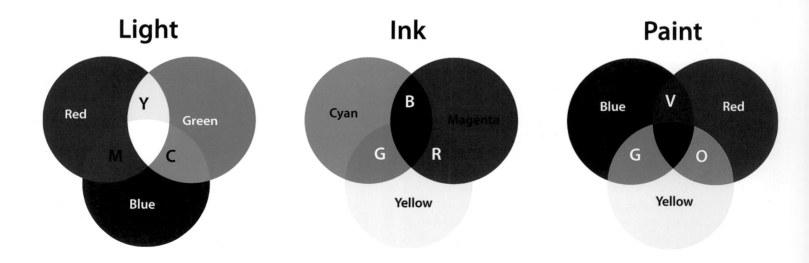

 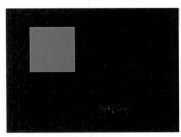

The orange and blue squares are exactly the same color in both of the illustrations above. In the purple background the orange becomes brighter, the blue duller.

Photoshop Color Modes and Models

Photoshop has different color modes that you can use for different purposes at different times. These color modes are based on different color models or methods of measuring and naming color values. The color mode you work in will determine the number of colors and channels in a document, as well as which tools and file formats you use. Instead of working in just one color mode, like RGB or CMYK, it is a good idea to learn the advantages and disadvantages of the different color modes and models. Photoshop has various tools for picking and saving colors. We summarize these color mode issues in this chapter, mostly concerning how they relate to picking and choosing color. For more information on setting up and using the RGB, CMYK, and Lab color modes in Photoshop CS2, see Chapter 15, "Color Spaces, Device Characterization, and Color Management."

The RGB Color Mode

For overall color correction and ease of work, using the red, green, blue (RGB) color mode offers many advantages. We recommend keeping your final master files in RGB format. Red, green, and blue are the additive colors of light that occur in nature. White light consists of wavelengths from the red, green, and blue spectrums. All scanners, even high-end drum scanners, actually have sensors that originally capture the data in RGB format. You can use RGB for final output to computers, multimedia and TV monitors, color transparency writers, digital video, Web sites, and most digital printers, because these all use RGB as their native color space. Plus, RGB files are smaller than CMYK files because they have only three components of color instead of four.

The CMYK Color Mode

Cyan, magenta, and yellow are the complementary colors to red, green, and blue. Red and cyan are opposites, so if you remove all the red from white light, you're left with cyan. Cyan is formed by mixing green and blue light. Similarly, green and magenta, and blue and yellow, are complementary colors. When you print on a printing press, the colors of ink used are cyan, magenta, and yellow. These are called subtractive colors because when you view something that is printed, you actually see the light that's reflected back: For example, when white light, which contains all the colors, hits a surface painted cyan, you see cyan because the cyan paint subtracts the red from the white light, and only green and blue reflect back for you to see. To print red using CMY inks, you use magenta and yellow inks. Magenta subtracts the green light and yellow subtracts the blue light, so what reflects back to your eyes is red light. The cyan, magenta, and yellow dyes that make up printing inks are not pure, so when you print all three of them at the same time, instead of reflecting no light and giving you black, you get a muddy gray color. Because of this problem, the printing trade adds black ink (the K in CMYK) to the four-color process so that the dark areas are as dark as possible.

Even though you can convert your file to CMYK and do all your color corrections in that space, we do not recommend it as the normal workflow. This is because most images today are used for multiple purposes and CMYK is a much smaller gamut of color than RGB. Keeping your image in RGB until you are ready to make separation plates for printing gives you (and your printer) more control over how much color ink and how much black ink to use in creating your image on press. Your RGB master can be used for Web display, digital printing, or broadcast without suffering the color-gamut limitations that CMYK would impose. So keep your master file in RGB format for the highest quality and versatility across all media.

The Hue, Saturation, and Brightness Color Model

Another color model Photoshop uses is Hue, Saturation, and Brightness (HSB). Although you can't convert an image to HSB mode, many color tools allow you to think about and massage color using the HSB color model. Instead of dividing a color into components of red, green, and blue, or cyan, magenta, and yellow, HSB divides a color into its hue, its saturation, and its lightness. The hue is the actual color, or the radius of the color wheel (see the illustration on the next page) and can be any of the colors of the rainbow. A particular red hue differs from a purple, yellow, orange, or even a different red hue. The saturation refers to the intensity of that particular hue. Highly saturated colors are quite intense and vivid, so much so

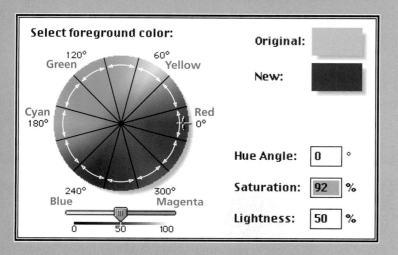

Select foreground color:

120° Green   60° Yellow
Cyan 180°   Red 0°
240° Blue   300° Magenta

Original:

New:

Hue Angle: [0] °

Saturation: [92] %

Lightness: [50] %

RGB and the Color Wheel

The old Apple Color Picker can help you understand how Photoshop delineates Hue. We've divided the color wheel into 30° segments with black lines, and typed the names (in green) of the six true color segments. Photoshop considers red hues to be the area from 345° to 15°, with 0° being pure red. Cyan hues (red's complement) range from 165° to 195°, with 180° being true cyan. The in-between ranges (red/yellow, yellow/green, green/cyan, and so forth) are considered the fall-off ranges when you adjust the hue in Photoshop.

that they almost look fluorescent. Colors of low saturation are duller and more subtle. The lightness of a part of an image determines how light or dark that part is in overall density. Lightness is the value in the image that gives it detail. Imagine taking a black-and-white image and then colorizing it. The black-and-white image originally had different tonal values of gray. The details show up based on the lightness or darkness of the black-and-white image. Removing the lightness value would be similar to removing this black-and-white detail part from a color image. If you increase the lightness, the image starts to flatten and show less depth. If you increase the lightness all the way, the image loses all its detail and becomes white. If you decrease the lightness, the image may appear to have more depth, and if you decrease it all the way, the image becomes black. To work with an image using the HSB color space, you use Image/Adjust/Hue/Saturation or Image/Adjust/Replace Color. The Color Picker and the Color palette also allow you to choose color in the HSB color model.

The Lab Color Mode

The Lab color mode is a device-independent color space that has as its color gamut the colors that the human eye can see. The Lab color model is used internally by Photoshop to convert between RGB and CMYK, and it can be used for device-independent output to Level 2 and Level 3 PostScript devices. The Lab color mode is quite useful for some production tasks. For example, sharpening only the Lightness channel sharpens the image without "popping" the colors. You can also use Curves on the Lightness channel without worrying that you are shifting colors. Although you can work in Photoshop using Lab color, it can be confusing, and some filters don't work with images in Lab. Our rule of thumb is to work in RGB, and to choose Lab if a particular task can be best accomplished there.

Using the Color Picker

Photoshop's main tool for picking colors is the Photoshop Color Picker. You access the Color Picker by clicking the foreground or background color swatch at the bottom of the Tools palette or by clicking the color swatches in the Color palette. You can use this picker in Hue, Saturation, or Brightness mode; or in Red, Green, or Blue mode. Or you can use Lab color to select a color using Lightness, the "a" channel, or the "b" channel. See the diagrams on the next page for an explanation of each mode. In addition, you can set a specific color by typing in its Lab, RGB, HSB, or CMYK values.

The Color Libraries button brings up the Color Libraries Picker for choosing PANTONE, TruMatch, Toyo, and other standard colors. You can use these as separate color channels within Photoshop's Multichannel mode, choose one or more colors for Duotone mode, or set spot color channels in CMYK or RGB mode if you need color to print with special inks. If you don't choose one of the above options, the color automatically converts to RGB or CMYK for painting, depending on the active color space.

Using the Color Palettes

Besides the Color Picker that you access from the Tools palette, you can also access the Color palette and the Swatches palette from the Window menu. Normally these are grouped together on the desktop, but you can separate them by clicking their name tabs and dragging each of them to some other location on the desktop. Because the big Color Picker is a modal dialog, it stops the normal functions of Photoshop until you close the dialog. So you can't access it on the fly to quickly change color when using the painting tools. The Color

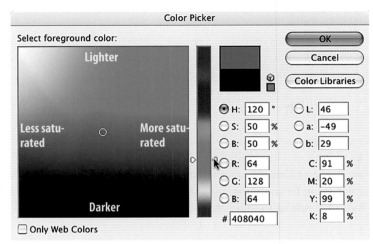

This is the Color Picker in Hue mode, the default. The slider (shown next to the black arrow cursor) changes the hue of the color as you move it up or down. The small circle in the middle of the color square changes the saturation as you move it left and right, or the brightness as you move up and down. Even though you are using HSB to choose the color, the corresponding values appear in RGB, CMYK, and Lab modes. The hue here is absolute green because the H value is 120°. If you wanted a warmer color, toward the red/yellow end of the spectrum, you would move the slider down. For a cooler hue of green you would move the slider up toward cyan.

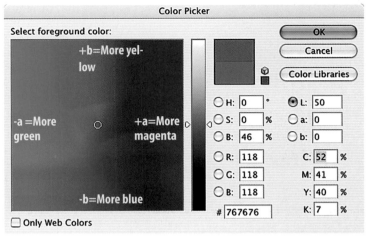

The Color Picker in Lab mode. This color space encompasses all colors and is so large that even minor changes can make a big color difference. Look at the Lab numbers for the colors in the two other Color Picker illustrations to get an idea of how the "a" and "b" channels work. Here, because the L channel is highlighted, the slider adjusts only the Lightness of the color; and because the "a" and "b" channels are both zero, the color is a neutral gray.

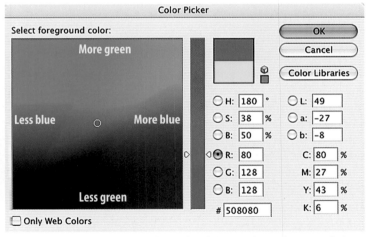

This is the Color Picker in Red mode. The slider on the color bar now changes the amount of red in a color. The small circle in the middle of the color square changes the amount of blue as you move it left and right, or the amount of green as you move it up and down. Clicking the G radio button gives you a slider with green values; the colors on the large color square will be more or less green and blue. With the the B radio button selected, the slider will change to blue values; you change red and green values by moving the circle in the color square.

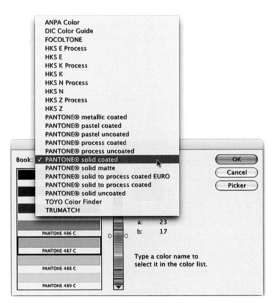

When you need to specify colors that you want to print or show exactly as expected, you need to use a color library. For the cover of our book, we usually specify a PANTONE color for the background to ensure consistency of coverage. Inside colors are generally specified in TruMatch because we know those colors are printable using CMYK inks. To access this list, click the Color Libraries button in the Color Picker.

and Swatches palettes come in very handy for getting the colors you need quickly.

The Color Palette

In the Color palette, you can move the color sliders to create a color that you like. You pick this color for the foreground or background depending on which of the swatches is active in the Color palette.

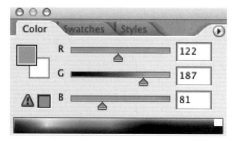

The Color palette shown as it is normally grouped with the Swatches and Styles palettes. The foreground and background colors are shown to the left. You can tell that the foreground color is currently active because of the double line around it. If you move the sliders, you adjust the foreground color. If you click the background color (in this case the white square), it becomes the active color, and moving the sliders modifies it. If you click either color square, you get the Color Picker. This palette also shows you the CMYK Gamut Warning icon, the triangle with the exclamation point. If you click the colored square beside the triangle, a new, in-gamut color will be chosen. It will be the closest printable color to the one you originally chose.

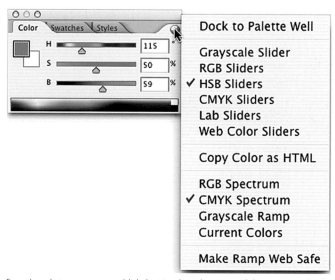

From the palette pop-up menu (click the triangle at the upper right), you can set the display of the Color palette to Grayscale, RGB, HSB, CMYK, Lab, or Web color. You can also dock the palette in the well from here. The pop-up menu also brings up options for how to display the color bar at the bottom of the Color palette. You can choose a foreground color by clicking a color in the color bar; Option (Alt)-click for the background color; or choose either black or white from the two swatches at the right side of the bar. Here, the palette is set to HSB and the color bar is set to CMYK Spectrum.

The upper swatch is the foreground color, and the lower is the background color. The active swatch has a bold, black line around it. You can change the display mode of the sliders in the Color palette by using the palette's pop-up menu. You can also pick colors from the color bar, called the ramp, along the bottom of the palette. This color bar offers different display modes to choose from using the Color palette's options.

The Color palette is useful, as it remembers the colors you last selected with the Eyedropper tool when using color correction tools like Levels and Curves, and it shows you how the color adjustments you're making change the color of that location. See Chapter 24, "Color Matching Images," for more details.

If you use Photoshop for painting, the HSB color palette is particularly useful. You can move the H slider to the basic hue that you want, then use Saturation and Brightness as if you were creating a tint or shade of the color. Lowering the Saturation is akin to mixing your color with white paint, and lowering the Brightness value is akin to adding black paint to dull the color. The nice thing is you can then use the Hue slider to move your color right or left to warm it or cool it.

The Swatches Palette

If you were a painter, you'd mix colors on a palette and then make some notes or keep a swatchbook that reminded you what to mix to get the shade you needed. The Swatches palette is where you store frequently used colors in Photoshop. The palette gives you access to a library of swatch sets, and allows you to save, and then later load, your favorite set of custom swatches. Clicking a color swatch using the palette's Eyedropper tool will give you a new foreground color. Command (Ctrl)-clicking picks a new color for the background. You automatically get the eyedropper when the cursor moves over the swatches area. If you've chosen a color from your image, or mixed a color with the Color palette, you can save the current foreground color in the Swatches palette; simply position your cursor over the empty gray area at the end of the swatches. Your cursor becomes a paint bucket, and when you click, you're prompted to name your color; the new swatch is added at the end of the existing swatches. If you want to skip naming the color, you can hold down the Option (Alt) key as you create the swatch. Pressing Option (Alt) while hovering your mouse over an existing swatch gives you scissors, which remove the swatch when you click. Once you've added or deleted all the colors you think you'll need, you can use the Swatches pop-up menu to save your palette with a name that reminds you what colors

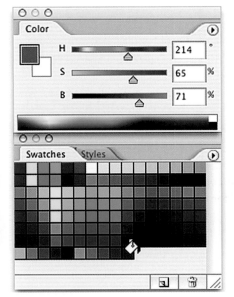

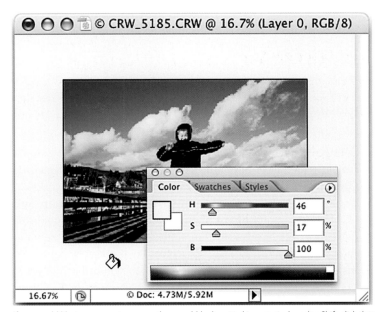

In this illustration, we've mixed a blue color to use for designating a certain type of retouching. We used the sliders on the Color palette to mix the color, and we want to save it to use on several images. When we move the cursor over an empty space on the Swatches palette, it becomes a Bucket, and clicking pours the color into a new swatch. A dialog appears, allowing us to name the color if we like. If this is a color that we'll be using often, we would delete unneeded colors from the palette by Option (Alt)-clicking them, then save this palette with a descriptive name.

If you would like to see your images as they would look matted in a particular color, Shift-click that color with the Paint Bucket in the window area.

are included. In some instances this is the name of the client or the name of a project or product.

If you are working on files with different color profiles attached (see Chapter 15), you may see differences in the same Color palette from file to file. Although the color itself doesn't change, different devices may not be able to render that color. The Swatches palette updates to give you a preview of how certain colors will change depending on how they are used. This helps ensure that the color you choose will render as intended.

Using Custom Color Libraries in Photoshop

Photoshop does allow you to choose colors from custom libraries. If you know that a product uses a particular PANTONE ink for its boxes, you can choose that PANTONE color either by clicking the foreground color and using the Color Picker's Custom Libraries button, or by loading the appropriate PANTONE swatches in the Swatches palette and choosing the color there. Remember, however, that if you paint with a custom color, it is converted to the current color mode (RGB, CMYK, and so on) and does not separate as a custom color plate. To have Photoshop designate a color as a custom separation, you must paint a channel with a gray value (100% black for full coverage, 0% black for no coverage) and designate that channel as a spot color. For more on this see "Bump Plates, Custom Separations, and Spot Colors" in the next section.

Practical Applications of Choosing Colors

You may never need to mix a color or save a swatch, but here are some ways we typically find ourselves needing particular colors.

Masking

Most every time you work on a mask for a portion of your image, you first type D for the default colors of white foreground and black background. You can then simply type X to exchange colors. When you do a lot of masking, this will become second nature. Even though it's only black and white, you don't want to have to choose these each time from the Color palette or the Color Picker. Like all keyboard shortcuts, this will speed your work and reduce inconsistencies.

Matting

If all your photos get matted with a certain color, say ivory, you might want to use the Paint Bucket tool to change the background of your Photoshop window when you're in Full Screen mode or you've zoomed out to make space around your image. When you choose a custom matte color, you always see your print as it will look when matted—and all your color corrections may change subtly when you view the image against something other than middle gray. To do this, mix the color that you want or choose it via the Color Picker or

Swatches palette. Type G (or Shift-G if the Gradient tool is selected) to get the Paint Bucket, then Shift-click the gray window area of any open image. All open images will now have the chosen color as the window color. Set the R, G, and B values all back to 192, and Shift-click the window to go back to the default middle gray.

Choosing Compatible Printing Inks

You can use Photoshop to determine what colors will work well with your image in print. Set your Eyedropper to select a Point Sample, and enlarge the image until you start to see individual pixels. Using the Eyedropper, find colors in the image you think might work. For each color, use the Color palette in CMYK slider mode to record the CMYK values. If you are doing the layout for your ad, poster, or book in a page layout or design application, input those values in your page layout program to set up colors for borders, backgrounds, or text. To make sure the colors you've chosen will print in CMYK, it's a good idea to have a TruMatch swatchbook on hand. TruMatch is a color identification system that identifies CMYK ink percentages that print with good results. Choose the TruMatch color that best approximates the ones you sampled from the image. Those colors are guaranteed to print in CMYK. If your budget allows printing with special inks, such as PANTONE colors, you could choose a matching PANTONE color this same way. Use a swatchbook from PANTONE, TruMatch, or another ink specification system to choose your colors, as the swatchbooks will give you a truer representation of the actual printed color than your monitor.

Retouching

When retouching portraits, we often sample a color from the image to correct some photographic defect in the eyes or hair. Using the Color palette with HSB sliders allows us to modify that sampled color using Hue, Saturation, or Brightness to repair the area if we need variations. We sometimes mix colors to wash over the cheeks or lips, as if applying blush or lipstick. If you are hand-coloring black-and-white images, you'll also use the Color palette to choose those colors.

Callouts, Dingbats, and Special Characters

Any time you need callout rules, arrows, asterisks, or other special characters to mark areas of your photo, it's a good idea to mix your color and pour a swatch in the Swatches palette to ensure consistency. In Chapter 26, "Restoring Old Photos," we use color to indicate which tool to use. We mixed each color and put a custom swatch in the Swatches palette. Although you can sample the color from a previously created image, that image may not be open when you

need it. Photoshop will keep the swatch until you load replacement swatches. Even if you think you'll never load other swatches, use the Swatches palette menu to save your set, so in case you have to reload Photoshop (or need to send colors to another user) you'll have a swatch set with exactly the colors you used before.

Bump Plates, Custom Separations, and Spot Colors

As you'll see later in this book's exercises, if you plan to print your work at a commercial printer, you'll most likely have to convert your images to CMYK. And the exercises will illustrate that CMYK conversion can sometimes alter bright colors, causing a drab appearance. Although highly specialized print shop masking is generally done by a production person, as an artist you might want to request that the printer use an extra color plate, called a bump plate, for certain colors that are not reproducible with CMYK inks. Bump plates are often the only way to get bright or saturated colors to reproduce accurately.

Another reason to use custom colors that need special plates is for setting type on an image. For the cover of our books, we generally choose a special PANTONE ink so we can get the rich, vivid color we want.

When you need to designate areas of your image that are to print with inks other than the standard CMYK inks, you need to create a Spot Color channel that shows the printer the area to be printed with that ink. Depending on the coverage of the specific ink (ask your printer what percentage of the ink to use), you may be able to make a selection from one of your channels, or you may need to create the Spot channel and then simply use the Brush tool to paint areas that require the additional ink. To create a Spot channel, you can use the Channels palette pop-up menu and choose New Spot Channel. You'll be prompted to choose your ink color. You can also select an area of your image first, then choose New Spot Color to create a new Spot Color channel. If you've saved a selection as a Mask channel, you can double-click that channel and designate it as a Spot channel as well. Although you won't see the spot color on any layer, Photoshop will approximate its effect when you turn on the Eye icon for that channel.

Whatever your reason for wanting a special color plate, Photoshop can accommodate you.

Portfolio

Mark Reid

Gentle, whimsical, insightful, and philosophic, Mark Reid is a one-of-a-kind photographer who sees things most of us miss. Mark is an abstract painter who just happens to paint with the camera, primarily a 4x5 film camera. He's also a very giving artist who inspires others to pursue their art. We are so excited to show his work here. See more of his abstracts and landscapes at www.markreidphotography.com.

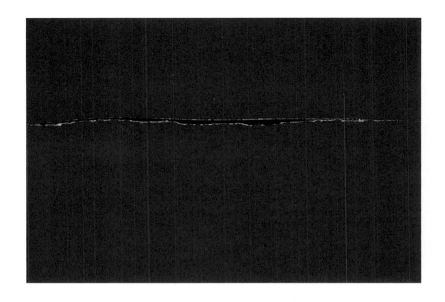

6 ◆ Selections, Channels, Masks, and Paths

No matter what type of Photoshop work you do, you will most likely have to make selections. Spot color corrections require selections. Compositing requires selections. Retouching requires selections. Even cropping requires selections. When you make a selection, you are choosing part of the image to work with, to the exclusion of the other part. The better your selection techniques, the better your work will look. While making selections is one of the most basic Photoshop tasks, mastering the creation and use of selections may take you quite some time. In our classes, we often find students happy to make selections, but the minute we mention channels, masks, and paths, eyes glaze over and palms get sweaty. In reality, those techniques are all about selections—how you make them, save them, and use them. Selections, masks, channels, and paths are all a way to isolate a portion of the image.

Making Selections

Let's start by talking about the concept of a *selection*—an isolated part of an image that needs special attention. You may want to make this part of the image lighter or darker, change its color altogether, sharpen it, or filter it. Or you might select something in an image that you want to copy and paste into a different image. Photoshop offers two basic methods of making selections. The first is based on shape and uses the Marquee and Lasso selection tools that we discussed at length in Chapter 4, "The Toolbox." The second selection method is based on color or luminosity.

To learn more about using the selection tools, go to Chapter 4 and Chapter 19, "Making Selections."

Shape-Based Selections

You can make selections using various tools. The simplest are the Rectangular and Elliptical Marquees, which allow you to draw a box or an ellipse around something by clicking to one side of the area you want to isolate and then dragging diagonally to the other side. This will create a box- or oval-shaped selection that is denoted by a dotted line, often called "marching ants," around the edge. The next level of selection complexity involves the Lasso tool, which allows you to draw a shape around objects to select them. Using Photoshop's Lasso, you can draw either freehand or straight-line segments, or combinations of both. The Magnetic Lasso is a variant of this tool that snaps

the selection marquee to an area based on its contrast with its surroundings.

Color-Based Selections

Photoshop makes color- and luminosity-based selections for you all the time when you use commands such as Hue/Saturation, Curves, Extract, or Replace Color. You won't see the marching ants, but Photoshop recognizes the invisible selections those commands create. However, some other tools and commands in this category do allow you to see what you're selecting. These commands—including the Magic Wand tool, and the Select/Color Range, Select/Grow, and Select/Similar commands—produce the marching ants. The Magic Wand allows you to click a certain color in an image and automatically select pixels based on the color you chose and a tolerance value controlling the range of deviation from that color. The tolerance value, which you set on the Options bar, is also used by the Select/Grow command, which selects adjacent pixels to any that are currently selected *and* fall within the tolerance value, and the Select/Similar command, which selects pixels throughout the image.

Moving Selections

After you create a selection (and sometimes while you're creating it), you may need to move it around on the image to select the exact area you want to work with. When using the Marquee tool, you can start your drag to make the selection, then hold down the Spacebar to interrupt the drawing of the marquee and move its selection boundary

Using the Magic Wand and a tolerance value of 65 selects most of the red rosehip.

around the image. Once you've placed the top-left corner of the selection where it needs to originate, let go of the Spacebar and continue your drag to complete the selection. Let's try it out.

◆ Navigate to the Ch06.Selections Channels Paths folder on the *Photoshop Artistry* DVD, and open TheNewParisDog.psd image.

◆ Type M for the Marquee tool. If the Rectangular Marquee is not selected in the toolbox, type Shift-M until it is the current tool.

◆ Click anywhere on the image and begin to drag diagonally. With the mouse button still pressed, hold down the Spacebar and move the marquee around the image.

◆ Release the Spacebar but keep pressing the mouse down and finish creating your selection.

If you need to move a selection after you've drawn it, you can use the Marquee tool, the Lasso tool, or the Magic Wand. With one of these tools selected, click *inside* the selection boundary and drag. (If you click outside the selection boundary, you deselect the area.) To move the boundary just a pixel or two, you can use the arrow keys, but you must be using one of those tools. If you use the Move tool, you will move the actual pixels of your image rather than just the selection boundary.

Changing a Selection

If you make an initial selection and it's not exactly what you need, you can edit the selection rather than starting from scratch. This method also lets you use multiple tools, enabling you to make more-complex selections than any one tool could give you.

Selection Interaction

When you use any of the selection tools in the Toolbox, you'll see a set of four selection interaction icons on the Options bar. The first, default, icon for each of the three selection tools is New Selection. If you have an existing selection and you click outside it, Photoshop assumes you want to deselect the current area and make a new selection. The next three icons add to the current selection, subtract from the current selection, or take the intersection of the current and new selections. You can also add to any selection using the Marquee, Lasso, or Magic Wand selection tools by simultaneously pressing the Shift

As you Option (Alt)-drag with the Lasso, you see the area you'll subtract from the selection.

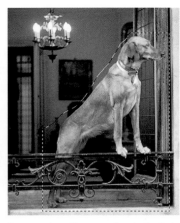
Once you release the mouse, the selection looks something like this.

key when you create the new selection. You can subtract from a selection using one of these tools by holding down Option (Alt) to define the area you want to subtract. Shift-Option-drag (Shift-Alt-drag) takes the intersection of the two selections. We recommend learning the shortcut keys for selection interaction, because it's easy to forget you've clicked on a selection interaction icon and leave your selection tools in that state. This can really confuse you. So if you use the icons on the Options bar (and they do make additions and deletions easier), make sure you click back on the default New Selection icon before moving on to the next tool.

◆ Make a rectangular selection around the dog. You may find it easier to start your drag from the upper-right side of the dog's head, then drag diagonally down to the feet.

◆ Type L for the Lasso tool and hold down the Option (Alt) key as you drag around areas that you want to subtract from the selection of the dog. Try to get as close to the dog as possible without deleting parts of the dog from the selection. If you delete portions of the dog, you can hold down the Shift key as you draw with the Lasso to add those parts back in.

Inversing Selections

Use the selection you just created; or if you like, use Select/Load Selection to load DogMask—a selection of the dog we saved with this file. When the dog is selected, anything we do (painting, changing color, and so on) can happen only within the boundaries of the selected area. If you were to compare working on an image in Photoshop to painting a wall, selecting just the dog would be equivalent to putting masking tape everywhere on the wall that you don't

You can use the selection interaction icons at the left of the Options bar to always make a new selection, or add to, subtract from, or intersect with the current selection.

When you load the DogMask, your selection looks like this. Any painting or adjustments that you do will happen only on the dog's body.

When you use Select/Inverse, everything except the dog becomes the selected area, so any painting or adjustments will not affect the dog.

want to paint, say the bricks at the top edge or the planter boxes. If we choose Select/Inverse, then everything except the dog becomes the selection. So any time you have a selection of an object, you also have, via Select/Inverse, a selection of everything except the object. Continuing with the wall analogy, using Select/Inverse would be like removing the masking tape from the bricks and planter boxes and taping over the rest of the wall.

◆ Use Select/Inverse or its keyboard shortcut, Command (Ctrl)-Shift-I, and notice that the marching ants are now around the outside edges of the image as well as around the dog.

Select/Transform Selection

OK, you've moved your selection, added to it, and inversed it. But what if you need to make it larger or smaller, or skew it in some fashion? Then you need to use Select/Transform Selection. Chapter 8, "Transformation of Images, Layers, Paths, and Selections," deals with this topic. When you invoke this command, you get the same handles and capabilities you get with Edit/Free Transform (a command we use a lot in this book), except that the transformation does not affect pixels—only your selection boundaries.

Setting the Feather Value

Using most of the selection tools in their default mode is similar to placing masking tape along the edge of the selection, in that there is a defined, sharp edge to the selection. Such a selection is said to have a feather value of 0 (zero). The selection feather determines how quickly pixels transition from being in the selection to not being in the selection. With 0 feather, the boundary is absolute—a pixel is either within the selection or outside of it. You can change the feather of a selection using the Select/Feather command. If you change the feather to 20, the transition from pixels being fully selected to being fully unselected would happen over the distance of 40 pixels (at least 20 pixels on either side of the 0-feather selection line). If you used this type of feathered masking tape to paint the selection of the dog green, the feather would cause the green paint and the yellow of the dog's fur to fade together slowly over the distance of 40 pixels. Whereas setting the feather value of a tool before you use it constricts you to that particular feather value, using Select/Feather is a bit more flexible, allowing you to try out different feather values as you copy and paste selections or make adjustments. There are reasons to use both commands.

◆ Use File/New and choose 2 x 3 from the preset menu. Make sure Mode is set to RGB at 8 bits.

◆ Type M for the Rectangular Marquee tool, and make a large rectangular selection.

◆ Type B for the Brush tool, and choose Paintbrush Op100 Flow100 from the Tool presets pop-up menu on the left of the Options bar. Choose any color and paint the left half of the rectangular selection with this brush.

The left side of the rectangle was painted with no feather on the selection. The right side had a 20-pixel feather when it was painted. In the middle, you can see a bit of overlap.

◆ Now go to Select/Feather and enter a Feather value of 20. Paint the right side of the rectangle with the same color and the same brush.

◆ Close this window without saving it.

It's easy to see what the feather value did to the application of the paint using exactly the same selection and the same tool. Often when you make an adjustment to your file using Levels or Curves or when you run a filter, you'll use a feathered selection.

Quick Mask

Sometimes, no amount of moving, transforming, or feathering gives you exactly the selection you need. In those cases, Quick Mask might be the answer. A mask, like a selection, is a way to isolate a part of your image. Quick Mask allows you to see your selection graphically, with a colored overlay masking out the nonselected portions of the image. There are sharp edges where you've made the selection with no feather, and soft edges where you used a feather value. More important, Quick Mask allows you to modify your selection with painting tools, giving you the flexibility to make better selections. Unlike most masks, however, Quick Mask does not allow you to save your selection somewhere in your document.

You invoke Quick Mask mode by clicking the Quick Mask icon in the Toolbox. In its default state, the command produces a red overlay on all the areas not currently selected, and no color at all over your selected areas. Using the Brush tool you can paint with black everywhere you want to extend the masked-out areas, and paint with white where you want to extend the selection. Because you can use brushes of different size, shape, hardness, opacity, and flow, you have unlimited ability to alter your mask. When you click back on the selection icon, you get the marching ants again.

If you have spent any amount of effort making your selection, it would benefit you to save it so you could reuse it—or modify it. Unfortunately, Quick Mask has no save function. It is only a temporary way of making a selection. Once you deselect, it's gone. This is one reason we save complex selections either as mask channels (if the selection is not currently modifying a layer) or as layer masks (if the selection needs to actively alter a layer).

Another problem with Quick Mask is that you can switch the command to apply the overlay color to the *selected* areas rather than the *masked* areas, by double-clicking the Quick Mask icon and setting the option. While this is sometimes useful for creating the selection you want, if you forget to switch back to the tool's default mode, new

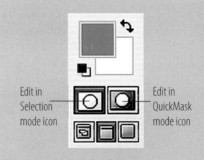

masks you create will use black for the selected portions of the image and white for the masked areas. Very confusing.

Mask Channels

You can save a selection to a mask channel (some authors call these channel masks), which allows you to use it again later or to do further selection editing on the mask with the painting tools. This is especially useful for a complicated selection that you don't want to have to remake later. To save your selection, choose Select/Save Selection, or just click the Save Selection icon at the bottom of the Channels palette. The new mask channel you create by doing the Save Selection is named by default Alpha 1 unless you name it. Adobe used the term *alpha channel* in its initial release of Photoshop, when there was only one mask channel you could use. You had to create your mask, use it, then lose it if you needed to mask a different portion of the image. Now you can have up to 56 channels in an image—and that includes color channels. The mask channels are still often referred to as alpha channels.

Sometimes people get confused about the need to have both selections and mask channels. Remember, a selection actually masks out the nonselected areas of the currently active color channel(s) and layer, so those areas can't be edited. After you create a selection or do a Load Selection, you can change which color channel(s) or layer within a document is active, and the selection will remain. It always affects what you do to the active color channel(s) or layer. A mask channel is just a selection saved for later use. Unless the mask channel is currently loaded as a selection, it doesn't affect any other channel(s) or layers or anything that you do to them with the painting tools or filters. You can load any mask channel as a selection at any time. A layer mask, on the other hand, is a mask channel associated with a particular layer. It is always removing the black areas of the mask from view in that layer. We will talk extensively about layer masks in Chapter 7, "Layers, Layer Masks, and Layer Comps."

We do many things with mask channels in this book. Sometimes we use the terms *selection* and *mask* interchangeably (although, as we explained, the terms are not exactly equivalent), because they both refer to an isolated part of an image. A mask is simply a selection that has been saved somewhere. To modify an image with a mask that is saved in a mask channel, you must first load the mask as a selection. Choose Select/Load Selection from the Menu bar, or click the mask channel you want to load and drag it to the Load Selection icon at the bottom left of the Channels palette. You also can load a selection by Command (Ctrl)-clicking on the channel you want to load. This is the method we use most often, because it works not only with mask channels but also with layer masks and transparent areas on a regular layer. When a selection is loaded, you can see the marching ants.

Whereas you invert a selection by typing Command (Ctrl)-Shift-I, you invert a mask channel either when you load it or, more permanently, by typing Command (Ctrl)-I. And just as a selection can have a feathered edge, a mask channel can be blurred. Let's see how this works.

◆ Go to File/New and once again choose 2 x 3 as the Preset size.

◆ Type M for the Rectangular Marquee, and make a rectangular selection in the middle of the image.

◆ Type B for the Brush tool, choose a bright color, and paint the left half of the inside of the rectangle.

◆ Use Select/Save Selection, and name the selection No Blur. If it's not open already, open the Channels palette using Window/Channels to see what your new channel looks like in the palette.

Look at the painted edge close up to see the difference between how the paint is laid down on a nonblurred edge versus the 20-pixel blur.

Although your colors may be different, your painting should look very similar to this.

◆ Drag the No Blur channel to the Create a New Channel icon at the bottom of the Channels palette.

◆ Type Command (Ctrl)-D to deselect your selection, then go to Filter/Blur/Gaussian Blur to put a 20-pixel blur on this channel. Double-click the name of this channel and rename it Blurred.

◆ Use Select/Load Selection, and load the Blurred channel.

◆ Paint the right side of the rectangle with the same brush you used for the left side.

◆ Now go to Select/Load Selection and choose No Blur from the pop-up menu for selection. Click the Invert check box to load the area outside the rectangle as the selection. Make sure that New Selection is on in the Operations section of the dialog.

◆ Choose a contrasting color for your brush, and brush the outside of the rectangle on the left side.

◆ Use Select/Load Selection to load the inverse of Blurred. Make sure the Invert box is checked and New Selection is on, then paint the right side of the image.

◆ Type Command (Ctrl)-D to deselect the Marquee, and look at the edges you've painted.

◆ In the Channels palette, click the thumbnail for the No Blur channel. Look at the edges. Now click the thumbnail for the Blurred channel. Look at its edges.

◆ Keep this file open; we'll use it again later in this chapter.

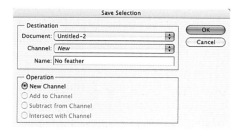

When you save a selection using Select/Save selection, you are given the opportunity to name your new channel. If you click the Save Selection as Channel icon on the bottom of the Channels palette, your new channel will automatically be named Alpha 1, and subsequent channels will be named Alpha 2, Alpha 3, and so on.

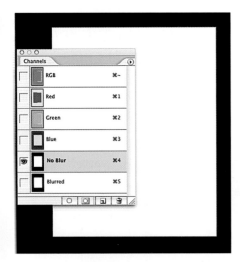

When you view only the No Blur mask channel, you can see in black and white how sharp the edges of the mask are.

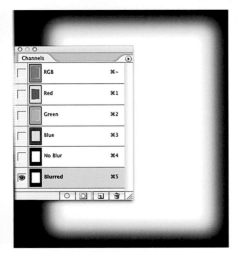

The 20-pixel blur value you entered for the Blurred mask actually creates 40 pixels of softness—20 pixels on either side of the selection boundary.

How Mask Channels Work

When you save a selection to a mask channel, the parts of the image that you selected show up as white in the mask channel, and the nonselected parts (the masked parts) show up as black. Our technical editor, Wayne Palmer, suggests a mask mantra: "White reveals, black conceals." When you have a blend between two partial selections, it shows up as gray in the mask channel. Feathered or blurred selection areas also show up as gray. A mask channel has 256 possible gray values (32,768 in 16-bit), just like any other grayscale image. A *layer mask,* which we discuss in the next chapter, is just a mask channel that is being used to mask out (remove) part of a layer. You can also save a selection to a layer mask, using Layer/Add Layer Mask; that will usually hide the nonselected parts of that layer.

Editing Mask Channels

You activate a channel for editing by clicking its name in the Channels palette or by using the shortcut key for that channel, such as Command (Ctrl)-1 for the top channel, Command (Ctrl)-2 for the next channel, and so on. The Eye icons on the Channels palette control what you see onscreen as you edit.

You can edit a mask channel just as you would edit any grayscale image—using painting tools or filters. Often, you make an initial selection using one of the selection tools, then save it to a mask channel, where you have the flexibility of working with the painting tools for complex editing. White in a mask means an area is totally selected and black means it's totally unselected. Gray areas are partially selected. You can edit a black area and make part of it white; doing that adds the white part to the selected area. Sometimes your initial selection may not need further editing; in that case, you just save it so you can use it again later.

You can rename a mask channel by double-clicking the channel, entering the name you want, and then pressing Return (Enter). You can also use the channel options on the Channels palette pop-up menu. If you Option (Alt)-click the Save Selection icon, or choose Select/Save Selection, you can type in the new name and save the name in the New Channel dialog box.

All mask channels are visible at all times within the Channels palette. By contrast, layer masks are visible in the Channels palette only when that layer is active. In the next chapter you'll see that when you're on a layer containing a layer mask, that layer mask name appears in italics in the Channels palette to denote that its presence in the palette is temporary. As soon as you activate a different layer, the previous layer's mask will no longer show up in the Channels palette.

Combining Mask Channels

When you load a selection, you can combine it with an existing selection. But when you Command (Ctrl)-click a mask channel or layer mask, it loads as a new selection and replaces any existing selection. If you want to add that new selection to an existing one, Command (Ctrl)-Shift-click the mask channel. Command-Option (Ctrl-Alt)-clicking a mask channel subtracts the new selection from from an existing one; and Command-Option (Ctrl-Alt)-Shift-clicking a mask channel intersects the new selection with the existing selection, giving you the parts that the two selections have in common. If you don't want to remember all these keyboard shortcuts, they show up in the Load Selection dialog box, which you can also access by choosing Select/Load Selection. Try this.

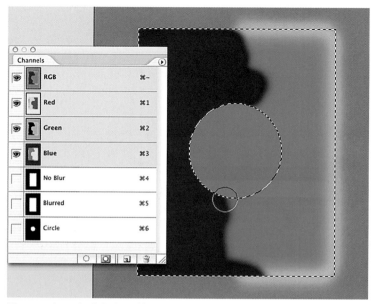

When you subtract the Circle channel from the No feather channel, you get a selection that looks like this. The magenta paint is constrained inside the rectangle but not allowed inside the circle. Using the Add, Subtract, and Intersect functions while loading selections gives you the ability to create complex selections without a lot of hard work.

◆ Use Command (Ctrl)-D to deselect any current selection. Now type M or Shift-M, and use the Elliptical Marquee to draw a circle in the middle of the image. Use Select/Save Selection, and name this channel Circle.

◆ Once again, use Command (Ctrl)-D to deselect the circle. Command (Ctrl)-click the No Blur channel thumbnail to load that channel as a selection.

◆ Use Select/Load Selection and choose the Circle channel, but instead of making a new selection, click the Subtract from Selection button.

◆ Type B for the Brush tool, choose a third color, and paint. Paint will be applied within the rectangle, but not inside the circular area because it is not part of the selection.

You effectively cut a hole in the middle of the rectangular selection when you used the Subtract command. When you start to build complex masks with hard and soft edges or gradients over only portions of the mask, you'll understand the vital importance of the channels' selection interaction capability.

Deleting, Moving, and Copying Channels

You can remove a mask channel from the Channels palette either by clicking that channel's thumbnail and choosing Delete Channel from the Channels palette pop-up menu, or by clicking the channel and dragging it to the Trash icon at the bottom right of the palette. If you delete the Red, Green, or Blue channel this way, Photoshop will assume that you want to produce spot color plates of the other two channels and will give you Cyan, Magenta, or Yellow channels, depending on which of the RGB channels you trashed. If you look at Image/Mode, you'll see that you are now in Multichannel mode. Designers sometimes use this process of deleting color channels after converting to CMYK in order to produce a duotone effect without using additional inks that add to the printing costs.

You can copy any channel, including the Red, Green, and Blue channels, by clicking the channel and dragging it to the New Channel icon at the bottom of the Channels palette. You also can make a copy of a channel by choosing Duplicate Channel from the Channels palette pop-up menu.

You can move a channel from one location to another in the Channels palette by clicking the channel and dragging it until the line between the two channels where you want to put this channel becomes highlighted. You then release the mouse button. You cannot, however, change the location of the original Red, Green, and Blue channels if you're in RGB mode, or the Cyan, Magenta, Yellow, and Black channels if you're working in CMYK.

Color Channels

A *pixel* is the basic unit of information in a digital image. In a black-and-white, 8-bit image, each pixel contains 1 byte of information, which allows it to have 256 possible gray values. A *channel* refers to a two-dimensional array of bytes. A black-and-white image has one color channel—black. An RGB color image has three color channels (for Red, Green, and Blue). A CMYK image has four color channels. You can see these channels by choosing Window/Channels and looking at the Channels palette. In an RGB file, Channel 1 is red, Channel 2 is green, and Channel 3 is blue. There is also a composite Channel-~, which allows you to see the red, green, and blue channels at the same time. (This is how you see color.) Also called the RGB channel, Channel-~ is an imaginary channel because as a composite view of the three color channels, it doesn't take up any additional space beyond that which the red, green, and blue channels take up. In RGB, Photoshop assumes Channels 1, 2, and 3 are Red, Green, and Blue, and that Channels 4 and higher are mask channels. When

Your Channels palette and Layers palette will look like this when you are viewing TheParisDog layer.

You can edit the mask while looking at the RGB image.

If you reload the mask channel as a selection, the selection shows the results of the painting you did.

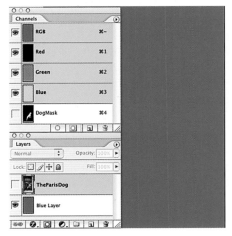

When you turn off the visibility for TheParisDog layer, the Channels palette reflects what you see onscreen. However, TheParisDog layer is still the active (highlighted) layer. If you try to paint now, Photoshop won't let you because the layer that is active is no longer visible.

you're working with a grayscale image, Photoshop assumes Channel 1 is the image and Channels 2 and higher are mask channels.

The Relationship Between Active and Visible

One of the challenging aspects of using channel masks is that you need to pay attention to several things at once. You need to know which layer is active, which channel is active, and which channels and layers you are currently viewing. Notice that the Channels palette has two columns. The left, thin column contains the Eye icons, which signify the channels you are currently seeing. The right column shows each channel's name and thumbnail. Clicking in the right column for a particular channel highlights that channel, indicating that you are working on it. That makes it the *active* channel.

Clicking in the right column for Channel ~ (the RGB composite channel) highlights the Red, Green, and Blue channels.

The Eye icons for the Red, Green, and Blue channels normally are turned on, and those channels are highlighted when you're working with an RGB image. However, what you see in those channel thumbnails will change depending on what is currently visible in the Layers palette. We'll talk more about the relationship of layers and channels in the next chapter. For now, try this:

◆ Reopen the TheNewParisDog image if it's not currently open. Go to Window/Layers [F10] to show the Layers palette if it is not already onscreen.

◆ Look at the thumbnails in the Channels palette.

◆ In the Layers palette, click the Eye icon for TheParisDog channel to turn off its visibility, and look at the thumbnails in the Channels palette again.

When TheParisDog layer is visible, it blocks out all of the underlying Blue layer, so what you see in the Channels palette looks like different black-and-white versions of the dog layer. When TheParisDog layer is not visible, all you see is the Blue layer. The channels then look like three gray panels. The amount of gray in each of the Red, Green, and Blue channels lets you know how much of each color needs to be combined to represent that particular shade of blue. In the next chapter, you'll see how the Channels palette looks when part of each layer is visible.

Here, DogMask is the active channel. If you paint now, you will be painting the mask. The foreground color will be white, black, or some shade of gray.

Although what you see onscreen looks exactly the same, the RGB channels are now active, and when you paint you'll be painting on the image itself. So look before you paint: The foreground and background colors are a clue. If they are colors other than black, white, or gray, the RGB channels are active.

Editing a Mask Channel While Viewing RGB

There are times when you need to finesse a selection after you've already created the mask channel. If you click the right column of the DogMask channel—the column with the name—that channel becomes the active one. It shows up in black-and-white, and if you do any editing with the painting tools, you do so in black-and-white in the DogMask channel. The Eye icons for the RGB channels turn off now. Occasionally, working on this black-and-white channel with the painting tools gives you all the information you need to tweak an edge or fill in some holes. Most of the time, though, you'll want to see exactly what part of the image will be affected by the mask.

If you want to edit the mask channel while also seeing the RGB image, do the following.

◆ Make DogMask the active channel by clicking its thumbnail in the Channels palette. Next, click the Eye icon column of Channel ~, which turns on the Eye icons for RGB.

◆ Type B for the Brush tool, and use the bracket keys to make your brush small enough to paint out the railing in front of the dog's body. Type D for the default colors, then X to exchange the foreground for background. Paint the railing to add it to the selection area.

Changing the Color of the Mask Overlay

In the illustrations here, we made our mask channel overlay green to make it easier to see. To change the color, double-click the mask channel thumbnail to bring up its channel options, click on the color swatch, and change its color in the Color Picker to something that is not prominent in the image. (Neon color often works well.)

To change the color of the Quick Mask overlay, double-click the Quick Mask icon in the Toolbox.

Be sure to leave its opacity at lower than 100% so you can see the picture through the overlay.

You see the RGB channels, but they're not active, so they're not highlighted. Instead, the DogMask channel is highlighted, because you are still working on it. The parts of the mask that are black will show up with an overlay color, usually the default red. If you paint in black with the Paintbrush tool, you add to this black part of the mask, which would represent the nonselected area. The paint shows up in the overlay color. If you paint with white, which normally represents the selected part of the mask or layer mask, you subtract from the overlay color. This is very much like painting in Quick Mask mode, except that when you use a mask channel you are saving your changes as you paint. You can also view the mask while working on the RGB image if you activate the RGB channels (Channel ~), so that when you paint with the Paintbrush, you modify the RGB image. If you click the Eye icon of the mask channel, you see this channel as an overlay while you're working in RGB. Once again, this can be confusing, because what you see onscreen looks exactly like painting the mask channel while seeing the RGB image. If you paint now, though, the paint is applied to the image itself. So before you paint, take a moment to look at the Channels palette and make sure which channel is active.

Paths

A totally different way to make selections is to use the Pen tool. The Pen tool creates selections, called *paths,* which are mathematical descriptions of points joined by straight and curved line segments. With the Pen tool, you can create the most exact paths along subtly curved surfaces. This is not a tool we use often, but we all know how to use it, and we *do* use it. The Pen tool is a one-of-a-kind instrument. The edges it makes are precise, its curves elegant. Often, it's the best tool for selecting hard-edged objects away from their backgrounds.

Chapter 28, "Compositing Multiple Images," contains a tutorial on the Pen tool. You'll also work with this tool in Chapter 30, "Product Compositing."

Converting Between Paths and Selections

We include the Pen tool here because paths can be converted back to normal selections when you're ready to use them to modify your image. You create a path using the Pen tool or one of the vector shape tools in the lower portion of the Toolbox. You must have the Paths palette open to use and save these paths. You use the Make Work Path and Make Selection commands in the Paths palette to convert between selections and paths, and vice versa. To use a path, you usually convert it into a selection and then maybe into a mask channel or a layer mask. You can use the Layer menu to convert a path directly into a different kind of layer mask called a vector mask, which maintains a crisp edge no matter what your print resolution.

The Interactivity of Selections, Mask Channels, Layer Masks, and Paths

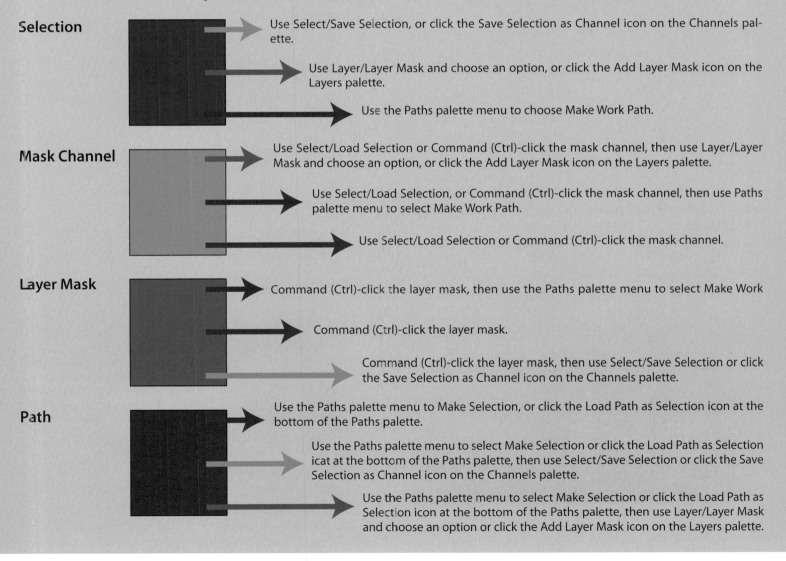

Selection

Use Select/Save Selection, or click the Save Selection as Channel icon on the Channels palette.

Use Layer/Layer Mask and choose an option, or click the Add Layer Mask icon on the Layers palette.

Use the Paths palette menu to choose Make Work Path.

Mask Channel

Use Select/Load Selection or Command (Ctrl)-click the mask channel, then use Layer/Layer Mask and choose an option, or click the Add Layer Mask icon on the Layers palette.

Use Select/Load Selection, or Command (Ctrl)-click the mask channel, then use Paths palette menu to select Make Work Path.

Use Select/Load Selection or Command (Ctrl)-click the mask channel.

Layer Mask

Command (Ctrl)-click the layer mask, then use the Paths palette menu to select Make Work

Command (Ctrl)-click the layer mask.

Command (Ctrl)-click the layer mask, then use Select/Save Selection or click the Save Selection as Channel icon on the Channels palette.

Path

Use the Paths palette menu to Make Selection, or click the Load Path as Selection icon at the bottom of the Paths palette.

Use the Paths palette menu to select Make Selection or click the Load Path as Selection icat at the bottom of the Paths palette, then use Select/Save Selection or click the Save Selection as Channel icon on the Channels palette.

Use the Paths palette menu to select Make Selection or click the Load Path as Selection icon at the bottom of the Paths palette, then use Layer/Layer Mask and choose an option or click the Add Layer Mask icon on the Layers palette.

7 ◆ Layers, Layer Masks, and Layer Comps

There are artists who create beautiful art in Photoshop without the use of layers, but they are few and far between. Everything we do, we do with layers, adjustment layers, and layer masks, because of the flexibility they offer. Layers are an integral part of Photoshop, and this chapter is one of the most important for you to understand. Here you will get an overview of layers, the different types of layers, and the overall functionality you'll need to understand when working with layers and masks. You'll actually create interesting images with layers in the step-by-step exercises in Chapters 19 through 32.

A layer of a Photoshop file is like the layer of a cake. Some cakes have only one layer, others have several of different types. Just as a completed cake could contain layers made variously of cake, fillings, and frosting, Photoshop can have layers made of images, adjustments, and fills.

Think of each image layer in an RGB Photoshop document as a separate RGB file. Each layer has its own Red, Green, and Blue channels. As you look at the layers in the Layers palette, imagine that the one at the bottom of the palette is a photographic print lying at the bottom of a pile of prints on your desk. Imagine that each layer above that in the Layers palette is another photographic print on top of the bottom one in the order you see them in the Layers palette. You have a pile of photographic prints on your desk. Some prints may be smaller or have shapes cut out of them, but the stack is always stable and never topples over. When you look at this stack from above, it looks like one image. Now imagine that each image in that stack is an inch deep and has information written on its edge to help you identify it, such as Boy, Boat, Lake, Sky, Fish. You can look from the side and see all the components of that image and tell what order they are in. Looking at that image from above is like looking at your onscreen Photoshop file. Looking at that stack of images from the side is like looking at the Layers palette.

Using Photoshop is better than having your stack, because it lets you control how much of each photo you see, as a percentage of the whole, or what parts of each photo you see. You can apply a variety of effects on each photo in the pile, so the possible combinations of ways you can view them all together number in the millions. You can change the order of the photos in the pile, move them and distort them in relation to each other, and save different versions of your stack of photos. All these things and more are what Photoshop layers allow you to do.

RainInCostaRicaFinalCC.psd— an image with many layers. Here we see the final composite. This image is included in the Chapter 7 folder on the DVD; open it and follow along while reading this section.

These four images were used, along with layers and masks, to create the composite to the left.

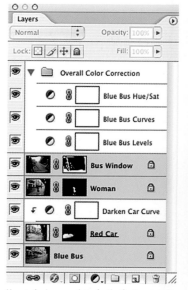

Here is the Layers palette for the final composite. We've highlighted the four image layers.

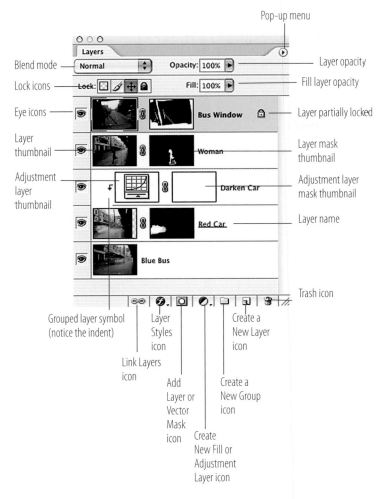

Pop-up menu

Blend mode — Normal
Lock icons — Lock:
Opacity: 100% — Layer opacity
Fill: 100% — Fill layer opacity
Eye icons
Layer thumbnail
Adjustment layer thumbnail
Bus Window — Layer partially locked
Woman — Layer mask thumbnail
Darken Car — Adjustment layer mask thumbnail
Red Car — Layer name
Blue Bus
Trash icon

Grouped layer symbol (notice the indent)
Layer Styles icon
Link Layers icon
Add Layer or Vector Mask icon
Create New Fill or Adjustment Layer icon
Create a New Group icon
Create a New Layer icon

The Layers Palette

To work with layers, you use the Layers palette, which you activate via Window/Layers [F10]. The Layers and Channels palettes work similarly: You move, copy, or delete their contents in the same ways. In Chapter 3, "Navigating in Photoshop," we asked you to separate the Layers and Channels palettes, because if you use layers and channels at the same time, which you often do, you will understand their relationship more quickly when you can see them both at the same time. Make sure you've done this before reading the rest of this chapter.

The Palette Icons

As you can see in the above illustration, the Layers palette is awash with icons. Don't panic—you'll quickly learn which ones you need. In this chapter we'll concentrate on the Create a New Layer icon and the Add Layer Mask icon, as well as the Eye icons, which control layer visibility. The other most often used icons for photographers are the

Lock icons, the Create New Fill or Adjustment Layer icon, and the Opacity and Blend mode settings.

The Palette Menu

When you click the palette pop-up at the upper-right side, you get the Layers palette menu, which has many of the same commands you see under the Layers menu. In reality, it doesn't matter whether you choose your commands from the Menu bar or the Layers palette pop-up, or for that matter whether you use actions or keyboard shortcuts to execute commands. All three of us use actions or the Layers palette menu and icons rather than the Menu bar, because it's faster for us. When you are just learning the application, though, you may want to use the Menu bar more often just to familiarize yourself with where the commands are. We'll talk about the menu items in the appropriate section for each command.

The Palette Options

At the very bottom of the Layers palette pop-up menu are palette options. You won't need these often, but you should be aware of a couple of issues. First, if you have a lot of layers, you may want to set Thumbnail Size to the smallest one (not None—it's too confusing if you can't see at least whether you are using an image layer or an adjustment layer). This will save you screen space. If you use the next size up, however, you will get different thumbnails for each type of fill or adjustment layer. This is a helpful quick reference to what's going on in your file, especially for beginners. Second, it's easier to see how each layer relates to the image as a whole if you keep Thumbnail Contents set to Entire Document. The Use Default Masks on Adjustments check box simply controls whether Photoshop will automatically create a new layer mask with each adjustment you

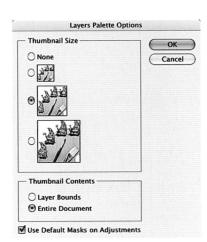

For beginners, we recommend using the Options in this state. More advanced users can use the thumbnails one size smaller.

add. Because you'll often paint on the masks for adjustment layers, to limit where that adjustment happens, we suggest you keep this on.

Layer Basics

Creating Layers

There are several ways to create layers, and the method you choose will often depend on the type of layer you need to work with. You can create a new, blank image layer by using Layer/New/Layer, by choosing New Layer from the Layers palette menu, or by clicking the Create a New Layer icon at the bottom of the Layers palette. Layers that you create this way will be completely transparent until you put image information on them.

If you copy something from your current image or any other image and then use Edit/Paste, you create a new layer with image information already on it. You'll also find a couple of very useful commands on the Layers menu: Layers/New/Layer via Copy and Layers/New/Layer via Cut. Use these when you have a selection that you want to duplicate or cut to a new layer.

Naming Layers

When you first create a layer using any of the Layer/New commands, you can name the layer. If you have already created a layer, you can name it by double-clicking the name in the Layers palette or by choosing Layer/Layer Properties from the main Menu bar or from the Layers palette.

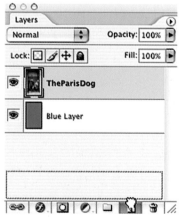

Drag TheParisDog layer to the Create a New Layer icon at the bottom of the palette to copy it.

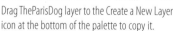

When you initially copy a layer, it has the name of the one you copied from plus the word *copy*. Double-click the name in the Layers palette to change it.

Copying Layers

You can make a copy of any layer by clicking the layer and dragging it to the Create New Layer icon to the left of the Trash (garbage can) icon at the bottom of the Layers palette. You can also make a copy of the active layer by choosing Duplicate Layer from either the Layers palette's pop-up menu or the Layer menu. The copied layer will have the same name but with "copy" appended to it.

◆ Go to File/Open and navigate to the folder Ch07.Layers Masks Comps on the *Photoshop Artistry* DVD. Open TheNewParisDog. psd image.

◆ Use Window/Layers [F10] to show the Layers palette if it is not currently on screen.

◆ Click TheNewParisDog layer and drag it to the Create New Layer icon at the bottom of the palette to make a copy of the layer.

Copying a Layer to Another Image

Using the Move tool, you can click a layer in the main document window or the Layers palette in one image, and drag and drop it on top of another image's main document window to create a new layer in the second image. You can also drag and drop a whole group of layers if they're linked together or you are moving a Layer Group. See the "Layer Groups" section later in this chapter.

Layer Visibility

The far left icon of any layer in the Layers palette is the Eye icon, which controls the layer's visibility. If you see the eyeball, the layer is considered to be visible, even if another layer covers it completely. Simply click the Eye icon to turn visibility on and off. If you need to turn visibility on or off for several layers, you can click and drag up or down this Eye icon column to quickly affect many layers. We often turn off visibility for all the layers in an image we're working on. Then we turn on the Eye icons one at a time, working from the bottom up, to see how each adjustment has changed the image. This helps isolate each adjustment from the overall effect and allows us to determine if we must do further work on any adjustment. We'll work with visibility later in this chapter, and, trust us, you'll get a lot of practice with this.

Blend Modes and Opacity

At the top of the Layers palette are two very important pop-ups, those for Blend mode (also called Blending mode) and Opacity. Blend modes are special formulas for how image pixels in layers combine.

Although you may think the Blend modes are for designers and people who work with effects, let us disabuse you of that notion. Blend modes have many practical applications for photographers, and we use them throughout the hands-on exercises in this book. In fact, we devote a whole chapter to them: Chapter 31, "Blend Modes, Calculations, and Apply Image." Opacity, the second pop-up, is a slider that lets you change the transparency of the currently active layer. This setting is important for both compositing and correcting images, as it allows you to blend effects or images together with great flexibility and accuracy. When tools other than painting tools are active, typing a number (or a two-digit number) changes the Opacity of the current layer.

Fill

The Fill pop-up is not one that photographers often use, but it could be useful for some effects. If you had a layer that uses layer styles such as Outer Glow, Drop Shadow, or Stroke, you could lower the Fill opacity, causing the image part of the layer to become more transparent without affecting the layer style. If you wanted the style and the layer to be more transparent, you would use the regular Opacity setting. To affect only the layer style, you'd use the setting for that specific style.

Layer Groups

A great feature of Photoshop is layer groups (these used to be called layer sets). These allow you to group layers into logical sets and then, if necessary, collapse a finished group into a single element within your Layers palette. This is for people who have a large number of layers and who want to be able to organize them into functional units. Once layers are combined into a layer group, you can turn the group's visibility on and off by clicking the Eye icon for the group folder. You can move the group within the Layers palette or to another image, as well as scale and transform (scale, rotate, skew, and so on) the group contents. You can add a layer mask or a layer vector mask to a layer group. This applies the mask or path to all the layers within the group as a unit. You can create a new document from the group using Duplicate Group from the Layers palette menu. A group also has an opacity and Blend mode. When you first create a layer group, the default opacity is 100% and the default Blend mode is Pass Through. Pass Through is a Blend mode created for groups; it specifies that all the Blend modes in all the layers within a group set will behave as they would if the set didn't exist and each of those layers existed independently of the set. You can now nest (put one group inside another) up to five levels of layer groups. In a very complex composite, this can help you keep track of the different elements.

The Lock icons from left to right are: Lock Transparent Pixels, Lock Image Pixels (which locks transparent pixels as well), Lock Position, and Lock All.

Locking Layers and Groups

In Photoshop you can lock layers and Groups. This can prevent you from accidentally moving a layer, which can easily happen if you press the Command (Ctrl) key, putting you into the Move tool, at the same time as moving the mouse with the button down. If you are working on a complex composite or a color correction where multiple copies of the same image have to line up exactly, we recommend that you lock any layers that you don't want accidentally moved later. Do this by clicking in one of the four lock options at the top of the Layers palette while the layer you want locked is active. You can also lock an entire group similarly. From left to right the Lock icons are Lock transparent pixels, Lock image pixels, Lock position, and Lock all. If you turn on Lock all, that must be turned off before you can set one of the other locking options. Lock transparent pixels stops you from painting in or changing the transparent parts of the layer, Lock image pixels locks both the transparent and non-transparent areas, and Lock position stops you from moving the layer with the Move tool. Lock transparent pixels does not stop you from painting on the parts of a layer that are made transparent with its layer mask if image pixels exist in those locations. To stop this as well as to stop painting onto a layer mask and to stop changing a layer clipping path, you need to choose Lock all. None of the lock options stops you from changing the stacking order of the layers in the Layers palette. Once a layer is locked, you will get the universal Not symbol if you try to paint on it, and you will get a warning message that the layer is locked if you try to move it with the Move tool. Using these features at the right times could save you a lot of grief by removing the possibility for costly accidents!

Linking and Aligning Layers

By clicking the Link icon at the far left on the bottom of the Layers palette, you can link two or more layers together so they move and transform as a group. Select the layers you want to link by Shift-clicking adjacent layers or Command (Ctrl)-clicking nonadjacent layers. When you click the Link icon, it will show up on the right side of the palette to let you know these layers are linked together. If you only need the layers to be linked temporarily, such as when you're moving several layers to a new file, you only need to Shift-click them. Linking is for layers that need to perform as a group for

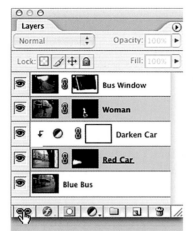

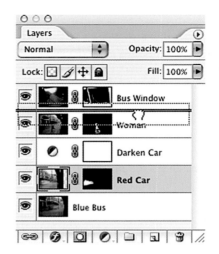

In this illustration, we clicked and dragged the Red Car layer upward in the palette. If we let go of it now, it will move above the Woman layer. Notice the heavy black line between the Bus Window layer and the Woman layer telling you where the layer will appear when you release the mouse button.

Because we want to be able to move the Red Car and the Woman layers at the same time, maintaining their relationship, we have selected them for linking. We Command (Ctrl)-clicked the two layers because they are not adjacent to each other in the palette.

Once you link the layers, by clicking the Link icon at the bottom of the palette, the link icon appears on the far right side of the palette for those layers. You can now move the layers in the image window, transform them, or copy them to another file as a unit.

a longer period of time. Linking allows you to insert layers in the stacking order before or after a linked layer, maintaining the ability to transform the linked layers without affecting those that are not linked. If you group the layers and need to insert a layer in the stacking order of the group, that new layer becomes part of the group and transforms with the group.

If you have layers selected or linked together and one of them is the active layer, you can use Layer/Align to align the rest of the linked layers with the active layer in one of six ways: Top Edges, Vertical Centers, Bottom Edges, Left Edges, Horizontal Centers, or Right Edges. Remember, the results of the Layer/Align command will depend on the layer that is currently active. There is also a Layer/ Distribute Linked choice that will space out the linked layers evenly in the same six ways. The Options bar for the Move tool also displays clickable icons for any of these 12 choices that apply to the currently active layer and any other layers that are linked to it. If you currently have a selection on the screen, you can use Layer/Align to Selection to align the currently active layer and any that are linked to the selection in the same six possible ways.

Moving Layers within the Image Window

You can move a single layer, multiple layers, or a group of linked layers, from side to side or up and down using the Move tool. Just click to activate the layer you want to move in the Layers palette, then select the Move tool from the Tools palette. Click the layer in the main

document window, and drag it to its new location. If you have all the Eye icons on, you can see its relationship to the other layers change. To select multiple layers with the Move tool, you Shift-click them or Command (Ctrl)-click if the layers are not adjacent. To nudge the layers one pixel at a time, use the arrow keys on your keyboard. If you think you're going to need to move layers together a lot, think about linking them or grouping them.

Changing the Stacking Order within the Palette

You can change the stacking order of layers in the Layers palette by clicking the layer you want to move and dragging it until the line turns into a double line between the two layers where you want to put this layer. Let go of the mouse at that point, and the layer is moved. When you move a layer, it changes the composite relationship of that layer with the layers around it.

Deleting Layers

You can remove a layer by clicking it and choosing Delete Layer from either the Layers palette's pop-up menu or the Layer menu, or by clicking the layer thumbnail and dragging it to the Trash icon at the bottom right of the Layers palette. If your layer has a layer mask, make sure that you grab the layer thumbnail and not the thumbnail for the mask, or else Photoshop will assume that you merely want to delete the layer's mask.

Merging Layers and Flattening

At any time, you can merge two or more layers into one. Choose one of the merge options from the Layer menu on the main menu or the Layers palette. Merge Down merges a layer onto the one beneath it. Merge Visible merges all layers whose Eye icons are turned on into the lowest visible layer. Flatten merges all layers, visible or not. You will be asked whether you want to discard hidden layers. If you meant to have the hidden layers be part of the image, you need to turn on their visibility before you invoke the command. One way that we use the Merge command often is to merge all the visible layers into a new layer in order to run some filter, such as Sharpen or Blur over the entire image. To do this, hold down the Option (Alt) key when you choose the command. We never use Flatten, because we always keep our layered file for future changes. If we want a flattened version of the layered file, we use Image/Duplicate and check Duplicate Merged Layers Only.

Layer Styles and Blending Options

If you double-click the area to the right of the layer name in the Layers palette, use Layer/Layer Style, or choose Blending Options from the Layers palette menu, you get the Layer Style dialog. All of the features in the Layer Style dialog could fill a book in itself, and as photographers you won't need many of them, so we'll cover the most important in much more detail in Chapter 33, "Contact Sheets, Picture Packages, Slide Shows, and Web Photo Galleries."

Types of Layers

The *Background* Layer

If you open a single-layer image in Photoshop and look at the Layers palette, you'll notice that the image's layer is called *Background*. It is called *Background* in italics because the *Background* layer differs from a normal layer. There are restrictions on what you can do with the *Background* layer that do not apply to normal image layers. The restrictions apply as long as the layer is named *Background;* these limits are in place as a safeguard. If you have an image with multiple layers and you choose Layer/Flatten Image, all your layers will be compressed into a single layer. This single layer will become a *Background* layer.

The *Background* layer, when it has that name, must be the bottom layer and cannot have any transparent areas. If you make a selection in the *Background* layer and clear or delete that selection, the selected area fills with the background color. If you delete a selection in any other layer, that area fills with transparency (the checkerboard pattern) if you view the layer by itself. If there are other layers below the active layer, you will not see the checkerboard pattern but, rather, the visible layers below it.

You can't move other layers below the *Background* layer or move the *Background* layer above other layers. To convert a layer from a *Background* layer into a normal layer, just double-click it and give it

a new name or accept the default name, Layer 0. It then becomes a normal layer and you can move it above other layers, as well as create transparent areas in it. Barry usually does this when working with images, because he prefers all the layers to have the same full Photoshop capabilities, such as stacking order and masks, which a *Background* layer does not.

The *Background* layer, or the first layer in a document, determines the initial canvas size for your layered document. You want to make sure the canvas is large enough to encompass the parts you want to see in all your layers. Therefore, you may want to put your largest picture element—often your main background—down as your first layer. If you add additional layers that are larger in horizontal or vertical pixel dimensions than this bottom layer, you can see only as much of the image as fits on top of the bottom layer onscreen. However, you can still move these other layers by typing V for the Move tool and moving the layer to expose parts left hanging outside the canvas area. In Photoshop, parts that hang off the edge are permanently cropped only when you use the Cropping tool (unless you choose Hide Cropped Areas on the Options bar) or the Image/Crop command. To expose these parts of the image, you can always increase the canvas size using Image/Canvas Size or by choosing Image/Reveal All. This will add a solid color (the background color) to the edges of the *Background* layer or the bottom layer if you have converted the Background layer to a normal layer.

Image Layers

The layer types that you will most often work with are pixel or image layers and adjustment layers. A pixel-based layer is one that has image information on it. The thumbnail will show you a tiny picture of the image information on the layer. These layers require the most memory, so if you have a complex composite like the RainInCostaRica image, your file grows large very quickly. If you create a new layer that is completely filled with pixel information, the file size will double. A layer that is not filled with pixel data will not be as large. You can paint these layers, use layer effects, and filter the layers. A pixel-based layer is the most versatile layer type. When you create a new layer by clicking the Create New Layer icon at the bottom of the Layers palette, this is the type of layer you create. It will be completely transparent when it appears.

Adjustment Layers

If pixel-based layers are the most versatile, adjustment layers are certainly the most useful. Adjustment layers hold information on proposed changes to your file. You use these layers to change the color or tonal values in an image without having to make those changes

👁 ⬜	◼	🎱	**Color Fill 1**			
👁	▨	🎱	Gradient Fill 1			
👁	▮	🎱	Pattern Fill 1	👁 ⬜	⬭ 🎱	Selective Color 1
👁	🏛	🎱	Levels 1	👁 ⬜	🌍 🎱	Channel Mixer 1
👁	📈	🎱	Curves 1	👁 ⬜	▨ 🎱	Gradient Map 1
👁	◔	🎱	Color Balance 1	👁 ⬜	📷 🎱	Photo Filter 1
👁	◪	🎱	Brightness/Contrast 1	👁 ⬜	◧ 🎱	Invert 1
👁	▨	🎱	Hue/Saturation 1	👁 ⬜	▬ 🎱	Threshold 1
				👁 ⬜	◆ 🎱	Posterize 1

Here are the icons for the 15 different types of fill and adjustment layers. The ones we use most often are Curves, Hue/Saturation, Levels, Photo Filter, Channel Mixer, and Threshold.

to the actual pixels of the image. In other words, an adjustment layer is nondestructive. You can create an adjustment, then change your mind later and use different settings without having to create a new image, layer, or adjustment layer. This capability is vitally important, as a change that you make to the file at the beginning of the color correction process may be not exactly what you want after you have made other changes.

An adjustment layer's Layer thumbnail (the leftmost one) tells you the type of adjustment layer it is. Each different adjustment layer has a different icon design, which you see if you have your palette thumbnail option set to the middle or large size. When you double-click the layer thumbnail, the dialog for that adjustment reappears and you can change your initial settings. By default, a layer mask is added to the layer when you create the adjustment. Any painting, filtering, or effects you add to the adjustment layer actually happen to the mask.

Although an adjustment layer does add size to your image, it does not make you pay the price of adding another set of RGB channels for the new layer. For a 2 MB file, adding a Curves adjustment layer would make the file only about 0.1 MB larger. Adding a layer mask that is painted will make it a bit larger still. The color correction adjustments you make in the adjustment layer apply to all the layers below that adjustment layer. You can turn this correction on and off simply by turning the Eye icon on or off for that particular adjustment layer.

As a photographer, you will use adjustment layers for basic color correction, spot color correction and enhancement, and retouching.

Fill Layers

Fill and adjustment layers share the same Create icon at the bottom of the Layers palette, though they differ from each other somewhat. When you create a fill layer, you automatically get a layer mask as an adjustment layer, but a fill layer covers all the information below it unless you lower the opacity, use a Blend mode, or mask out part of the layer. There are three types of fill layers: Solid Color, Gradient, and Pattern. Whichever type you use, you can access the preset libraries to choose the content of the fill layer. We sometimes use fill layers to correct texture in blown-out areas of an image, or to build custom gradients for skies or packaging.

Now you're going to add a Pattern fill layer to TheNewParisDog image, which will make the image look as if it's being viewed through a curtain; then you'll desaturate with a Hue/Saturation adjustment layer to make the image look old and faded.

◆ Return to TheNewParisDog image and use Layer/New Fill Layer/Pattern, and use the Pattern thumbnail to choose one of the black-and-white patterns. Click OK to accept the pattern and create the Fill layer.

◆ Use the Blend mode pop-up at the top of the Layers palette to change the Blend mode of this layer to Overlay.

◆ Now, use the Create New Fill or Adjustment Layer icon at the bottom of the Layers palette to create a new Hue/Saturation adjustment layer. You have to click the icon and drag to the type of adjustment you want.

◆ When the Hue/Saturation dialog appears, move the Saturation slider to the left to about −40 to remove most of the color from the underlying layers. Click OK to create the adjustment layer.

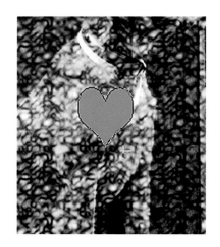

After you create a shape, the path for the shape is highlighted. Depending on how your interaction icons are set on the Options bar, you can now draw a new shape layer or add, delete, intersect, or exclude shapes from this layer. To edit the path for this shape, choose the Direct Selection tool from the Toolbox, click the path, and move its points or segments.

Shape Layers

These vector-based layers are not used as often by photographers as they are by designers, but if you need a solid-color shape with sharp edges that will print at any resolution, you create a shape layer. A photographer might use such a shape as a logo or trademark. If your studio is Swan Studios, for example, you could create a custom swan shape and draw that shape onto any image in any color. Shape layers work just like Solid Color fill layers you create with an active path. They automatically have a vector mask associated with them. You can choose a shape tool and simply drag to create that shape on the image, and a new shape layer will appear with a shape that's the same color as the foreground color. All shapes on the layer are the same color. You can later rasterize shape layers (that is, turn them into pixel-based layers), so that you can paint or filter them, by using Layer/Rasterize and then choosing Shape, Fill Contents, Vector Mask, or Layer. Just as with paths, you can use a shape layer to create a shape and later turn it into a selection. This comes in handy for making unusual masks.

- In the Toolbox, click the Shape tool and choose the Custom Shape tool. It looks like a soft star.

- On the Options bar, make sure that the first icon after the Tool presets pop-up is highlighted, so that you'll create a Shape layer when you draw rather than a path or a filled image area. Next, click the Custom Shape icon and choose the heart shape. (If the heart shape is not loaded, you can choose any shape available.) Also, on the Options bar, click the color swatch and choose a color from the Color Picker for the heart you are about to draw.

- Drag the Custom Shape tool on top of the dog's chest to create the new shape layer.

Text Layers

Once again, this is more a tool for designers, but you might want to put text in an image at some point. Just as you might use a shape layer to put a symbol on an image, you might use the text tool to place a copyright mark or include the studio name. When you choose the Type tool from the Toolbox, Photoshop knows you're going to create a text layer. The text will initially be in the foreground color and whatever typeface was last used. You can change these before you type, or you can highlight text after it has been created and change either the type specs or color. The text remains fully editable unless you rasterize the layer.

- Click the Type tool in the Toolbox. On the Options bar, choose a typeface and size (12 or 14 point is probably big enough) and type a word on top of the dog. I used "heart."

- Press the Enter key on the numeric keypad or click another layer in the Layers palette to exit the Type tool—using the Return key on the regular keypad will put a carriage return in your text rather than exit the tool.

After you create the text layer, the name of the layer will change to whatever words you used on that layer. If you don't like the placement of the word, use the Move tool to move it around the image. If you click the text layer in the Layers palette while you are in the Type tool, you can change the typeface, size, or color of all the letters at once by changing those options on the Options bar. If you highlight individual letters with the Type tool as you would in a word processor, you can change the specifications for those letters only, leaving the others in the original style you used.

Smart Objects

This is a new type of layer that allows you to place art in a Photoshop file and still have that art be editable in its native format. This means that you can place art from another program, as well as other layered Photoshop files, into a Photoshop document and they remain linked to and editable in their source program. For example, you can place artwork from Illustrator into Photoshop and still edit it in Illustrator. If you double-click the layer thumbnail for the Smart Object layer, it opens a child file with all the original art and layers intact. Recolor them, move them, or change them however you please. When you use File/Save on the child, the edits you made appear in the Photoshop parent document. Conversely, you can make transformations to your Smart Object in Photoshop without degrading the quality of the original artwork. For photographers, one great use of this feature is that you can place a Camera Raw file as the basis for an image and later change your adjustments in Camera Raw (we'll demonstrate this in Chapter 22, "Correcting Problem Images.")

You can group layers in a Photoshop file into a Smart Object if you want the ability to transform those layers as a single object. And, creating the Smart Object from the layers will make your file smaller. However, if you ask Photoshop to make your Smart Object a layer again, you do not get those separate layers back with their accompanying masks. Any layer mask associated with the Smart Objects layer gets applied and you get a single layer with transparency. Be careful how you use this.

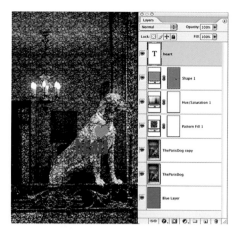

Here's what your Layers palette will look like before you collect the layers for a new Smart Object.

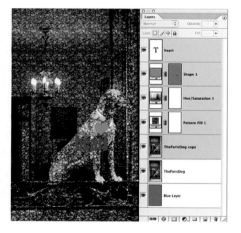

Shift-click these layers so Photoshop knows which ones you want to group.

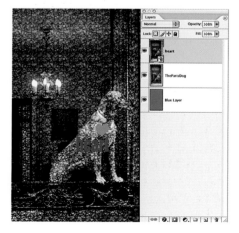

Once you create the Smart Object, your palette looks like this.

Now that we have created several layers we can try out Smart Objects.

◆ In the Layers palette, click the Text layer that you just created, then Shift-click TheNewParisDog copy layer. This will highlight all of the layers in between as well.

◆ From the Layers palette pop-up, choose Group into New Smart Object.

◆ Double-click the layer thumbnail for the Smart Object that you just created. A new window will open with the layers that you used to create the Smart Object.

◆ Double-click the layer thumbnail for the Pattern Fill layer, and change the pattern that you are using.

◆ Use File/Save, then File/Close on this image.

◆ Look at TheNewParisDog image to see how it has changed.

Besides increasing your flexibility in using Camera Raw, Smart Objects are useful if you have a composite image that needs to be part of other files but may change before final usage. Let's say you have a composited a product shot with a logo that's going to go in several images of different sizes. The client hasn't made final choices on logo design, placement, or color. You could go ahead and build the composite with the files that you currently have and place that file as a Smart Object in all the various images to be used. When the client makes the final decisions, you merely update the Smart Object, and all instances where it is used update automatically.

Layer Masks

A layer mask is a way to isolate a portion of a layer. Using layer masks on image layers, you can hide certain parts of the layer or make parts visible. By using a layer mask on an adjustment layer, you can restrict the adjustment to specific areas. There's a joke in Barry's classes that no matter what question you ask, he'll reply: "Use an adjustment layer and a layer mask." While that's not quite true, it's a fact that we use that combination a great deal. And we don't just use layer masks on adjustments. You'll see later in the hands-on chapters that we create layer masks for all of our composites and most spot-color adjustments. In fact we rarely make anything but rudimentary selections anymore, preferring to use masks to accomplish most of the work. Let us make this clear—using layer masks is the way we all work. It's the easiest, fastest, most flexible way to achieve a wide variety of effects.

You use a layer mask when you want part of a layer to be temporarily removed or made invisible. The black parts of the layer mask make

The Choices for a Layer Mask

If you've made a selection and you have an active layer, you'll see four choices if you decide to create a layer mask by using Layer/ Layer Mask. To the right, here, is the initial file with two layers, the *Background* layer which is orange, and the Maple Leaf layer, which is smaller than the background and has transparency surrounding it. Here are what the four scenarios for creating layer masks look like. Notice that each time you create a mask, the mask immediately becomes active. You can tell whether the layer or the mask is active, because it has a border around its thumbnail.

The original file with no layer mask and an active selection.

If you choose Reveal All, you get a completely white layer mask. The entire layer shows and if you have a selection, it is not deselected when you create the mask. This is the default mask that is created if you click the Add Layer Mask icon at the bottom of the palette without an active selection.

If you choose Hide All, you get a completely black layer mask. The entire layer is hidden, and if you have a selection, it is not deselected when you create the mask.

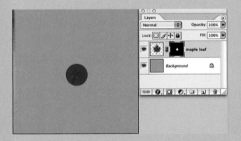

If you choose Reveal Selection, you get a mask that is white within the boundaries of the selection, but black elsewhere. This hides the layer except for the selected area. This is the default mask that is created when you click the Add Layer Mask icon at the bottom of the palette with an active selection.

If you choose Hide Selection, you get a mask that is black within the selected area and white elsewhere. This hides the selection.

the layer transparent in those areas, which allows you to instantly view that layer and its composite with the other layers without seeing masked-out areas. Layer masks are nondestructive to the file and can be altered without degrading the image.

Adding a Layer Mask

In Photoshop, you can create a layer mask on an image layer by choosing Layer/Add Layer Mask or by clicking the Add Layer Mask icon, which is third from the left at the bottom of the Layers palette. If you use the menu method, the choices that appear there depend on whether or not you have a selection active at the time you invoke the command. If no selection is active, you can choose between Reveal All or Hide All. If you choose Reveal All, you get a layer mask that is completely white. If you remember mask channels from the last chapter, you know that anywhere a mask is white it reveals the selec-

tion, or in this case, the layer. A completely white mask is what you get if you click the Add Layer Mask icon on the palette, so you might consider that the default. You also get a completely white mask on adjustment layers automatically unless you have turned this option off in your Layers palette preferences. If you choose Hide All, you get a completely black mask and none of your layer shows. If you Option (Alt)-click the Add Layer Mask icon on the Layers palette, a completely black mask will result as well.

If you have an active selection when you create a mask, the selected area will become the only thing that is white in the mask and therefore the only visible part of that layer when you click the Add Layer Mask icon or choose Layer/Layer Mask/Reveal Selection. If you choose Layer/Layer Mask/Hide Selection or you Option (Alt)-click the New Mask icon, everything except the selected area will now be visible and the selected area will be rendered black in the layer mask.

If you have a path on your screen, Command (Ctrl)-clicking the Add Layer Mask icon will create a vector mask that, like a layer mask, just shows you the area within the path. When you have a layer vector mask, you can later edit that path, now part of the layer, to change what you actually see. In general you should use a layer mask for any mask that you want to be able to soften or blur. When you want a very sharp edge that is mathematically accurate no matter what the image size, the layer vector mask is the way to go. Most photographers rarely if ever use vector masks. When you create a fill or adjustment layer, you automatically get a Reveal All layer mask. However, just as with a regular layer, if you already have a selection when you create an adjustment layer, the adjustment layer's layer mask will be a copy of that selection, and so the adjustment will affect only the selected area. If you have an active path before creating an adjustment layer, that path will be turned into a layer vector mask for that adjustment layer and will affect only the part of the image within that path. You can have both a layer mask and a layer vector mask at the same time for any layer. In that case, there will be two mask thumbnails for that layer. The vector mask will always appear on the far right of the Layers palette thumbnails.

You can also add a layer mask to a Smart Object.

♦ Click the Smart Object layer in TheNewParisDog image. Your layer will be named with whatever word you typed before making the Smart Object. This is now the active, highlighted layer.

When you create the layer mask for the Smart Objects layer (in this case the layer named "heart"), the only visible areas of the layer are where the layer mask is white. Notice the icon at the lower right of the layer thumbnail informing you that this is a Smart Object.

♦ Open the Channels palette if it is not onscreen by using Window/Channels [Shift-F10]. Command (Ctrl)-click TheDogMask channel to load it as a selection.

♦ Use Layer/Layer Mask/Reveal Selection or click the Add Layer Mask icon on the bottom of the palette to add a layer mask to this layer.

Editing a Layer Mask

You don't know exactly how a layer mask is going to work until you see it in action. You may have painstakingly created what you expect to be the perfect mask, and yet when you add it to the layer or adjustment layer, it simply doesn't look right. You need to edit the mask. Just like editing mask channels, this means using the painting tools, filters, and gradients to achieve the look you want. We rarely worry about our initial selections, preferring instead to make easy, rough selections, then finesse them with the painting tools when we see how that layer or adjustment layer affects the entire image. This is true for both compositing and color correction. So, effectively editing a layer mask is an extremely important skill.

The first thing to remember is which layer you are on and whether you are on the layer or the mask. In our beginning classes, people will sometimes paint for a long time wondering why they aren't seeing any results. Then they realize they've painted black all over portions of a different layer. Let us reiterate: Look at the Layers palette and be sure of not only which layer you are on but whether you are on the layer or the mask. Look at the Channels palette to make sure you are working with the correct channel or channels. In the "Seeing Layers in Action" section later in this chapter you'll see the Layers and Channels palettes for the RainInCostaRica image, as well as what your screen looks like when different layers or masks are active.

When you first add a layer mask, the mask's thumbnail has a double-line border around it in the Layers palette and is highlighted and active in the Channels palette. When you activate a layer that has a layer mask, that mask is added to the channels in the Channels palette temporarily. It appears in the Channels palette only while you have that layer activated. The mask first appears when you create it in the mode in which you can edit the mask and also still see the RGB image. Option (Alt)-clicking this layer mask thumbnail in the Layers palette at this point switches you to the mode in which you can edit and see only the mask. The Eye icon is now on for the mask and off for RGB in the Channels palette. Option (Alt)-clicking again returns you to the original mode where you can edit the mask and see the RGB image. If you paint with black in the main document window

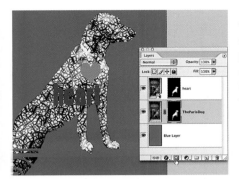

When you first create the layer mask for TheParisDog layer, your image looks like this. The masks for the two upper layers are identical, so the dog in the heart layer completely covers the dog in TheParisDog layer.

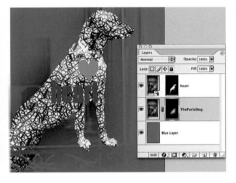

When you filter the layer mask and blur it, both the image and the layer mask look different.

while the layer is in this state, you add the black to the layer mask and remove those areas from view in the associated layer.

If you want to edit a layer mask while looking at the mask itself, Option (Alt)-click the layer mask's thumbnail in the Layers palette. The main document window now displays just the black-and-white mask, and your Layers palette has all the Eye icons dimmed out. The Channels palette now shows this layer mask channel as active, with its Eye icon on. This is the best way to check your mask for tiny problems that show up more clearly in black and white than when you are looking at the image's pixels. We often do this if we have used a brush on a mask to remove areas from a composite but want to check that we haven't missed spots. You might also switch to this mode to check the edges of your mask for trouble spots. We edit masks looking at the RGB or looking only at the mask depending on what we're looking for. When we edit a mask looking at RGB, we are most likely looking at how that mask blends the layer or the effect into the other layers.

To go back to editing the layer itself and also see it, click the layer thumbnail in the Layers palette. Now the black double line is around the Layer thumbnail. For each regular layer in the Layers palette, the layer thumbnail is the one to the left and the layer mask thumbnail is the one to the right. The item you are editing, either mask or layer, will always have a double-line border around it.

◆ In the Layers palette, click TheParisDog layer thumbnail to make this the active layer.

◆ Command (Ctrl)-click the layer mask thumbnail for the Smart Objects layer (ours is called "heart") to load that mask as a selection.

◆ Click the Create Layer Mask icon at the bottom of the Layers palette to add a layer mask to TheParisDog layer. The layer mask is now active and has a double line around it.

◆ Choose Filter/Blur/Gaussian Blur, and blur the mask by 40 to 50 pixels. You see the result in the RGB because the RGB channels are currently visible in the Channels palette.

◆ Option (Alt)-click the layer mask thumbnail for this layer, and you will see what your edit did to the mask itself.

Show/Hide Layer Mask

If you need to see the layer without its mask, turn off the layer mask by Shift-clicking the mask thumbnail. You'll get a big red X across the mask to remind you that you've turned it off.

◆ Shift-click the layer mask for TheParisDog layer.

Delete the Layer Mask

If you decide you don't need the mask for that layer at all, you can drag it to the Trash icon at the bottom of the Layers palette to throw it away. Make sure you click the layer mask thumbnail before you start your drag, or you might inadvertently throw away the layer itself. When you drag the mask thumbnail to the trash, Photoshop will ask you if you want to apply the mask before deleting it. Applying the mask will remove the portions of the layer that were previously masked out. We don't recommend this in general, as once you've deleted pixel

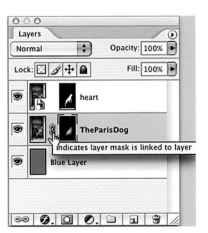

If you need to move the mask and the layer independently of one another, click the link icon to unlink them.

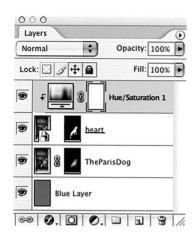

The Hue/Saturation adjustment layer is grouped with the heart layer. Only the portions of the image that are visible through the heart layer mask will be affected by the adjustment.

information, you can't get it back after you have exhausted your maximum number of undos. It's safer to just Shift-click the layer mask to turn it off, or delete the mask without applying it.

Unlink a Mask from the Layer

You may in rare cases want to unlink a layer mask from its layer so you can move the two independently of each other. This is particularly true when you are compositing images. You may have created a layer mask and situated it exactly where you need it (for instance, a mask of a television screen), but you need to move the contents of the layer itself (what is showing onscreen) over a bit. Simply click the link icon between the layer and its mask, click the layer thumbnail to make the layer itself active, then use either the Move tool or the arrow keys to move the layer. It's a good idea to relink the layer and its mask after you've done this. Usually you want the layer and its mask to move together.

Clipping Groups

A layer can be grouped with the layer or layers below it. The bottom layer in a group determines the transparency for the entire group and is called the clipping mask. The visibility of upper layers will be restricted to the shape of the bottom layer. This also means that if the bottom layer in the group has a layer mask that removes its center portion, that same center area will be removed from all the layers in the group. We often group layers when we repair or spot-color-correct areas. For instance, you may have to add a Channel Mixer layer to repair damage to one channel of an image. You create the Channel Mixer adjustment layer and edit the mask to affect only the portion of the image that needs correction. However, Channel Mixer tends to desaturate the colors when used this way, so you may need a Hue/Saturation adjustment layer to correct that. By grouping the Hue/Saturation layer when you create it, you can use the mask that

controls the Channel Mixer adjustment layer and not have to edit the Hue/Saturation mask in exactly those same areas. Again, you'll see how we used this in the RainInCostaRica image.

To group a layer with the one below it, choose Layer/Create Clipping Mask. You can ungroup a layer later by choosing Layer/Release Clipping Mask. Command-Option (Ctrl-Alt)-G is a command you can use as a toggle to create or release a clipping mask. You can also group or ungroup a layer with the one below it by Option (Alt)-clicking the line between the two layers. It is obvious when layers are in a group, because the name of the bottom layer in the group is underlined. This bottom underlined layer determines the transparency for the group. The other layers above it in the group are indented to the right with dotted lines between them.

Seeing Layers in Action

Let's take a look at the RainInCostaRica composite image with its five different layers to see how visibility and editability of layers and layer masks work.

◆ From the Chapter 7 folder on the *Photoshop Artistry* DVD, open the RainInCostaRicaFinalCC.psd file.

◆ Open the Channels palette if it is not onscreen by using Window/Channels [Shift-F10].

In the Layers palette for RainInCostaRica, you see that this image has four image layers and one Curves adjustment layer. There is also a layer group at the very top of the palette. For our work in this chapter, we are going to ignore the layer group and focus on the other five layers. Currently, we are looking at all of them because the Eye icons in the left column of the Layers palette are all on. For details about how this composite was created, check out Chapter 28, "Compositing Multiple Images."

Imagine that all the layers are in a pile, with the bottom layer, here called Blue Bus, at the bottom of the pile. As you add layers on top of this, like Red Car, Woman, and Bus Window, they are blended with the layers below them. The active layer that is highlighted, Bus Window, is the layer that is modified by changing the settings for Opacity and Blend mode at the top of the Layers palette. The active layer will also be changed by anything you do with any other Photoshop tools such as the Paintbrush, Levels, or Curves. If you do something to the active layer while all the other layers' Eye icons are on, you can see the changes to this layer as they are combined with the other layers, but the other layers themselves do not change.

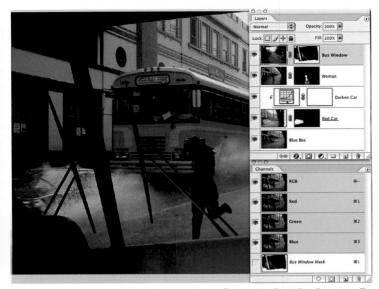

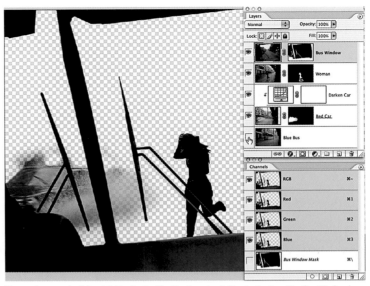

These are the states for the layers and channels when you first open the RainInCostaRica image. The Bus Window layer is active, and because it has an associated layer mask, that mask shows up in the Channels palette. All the layers are currently visible with Eye icons turned on, and the Channels palette thumbnails reflect that.

Here, we've turned off the visibility for the Blue Bus layer by clicking its Eye icon. The Bus Window layer is still active, however, and any changes that you make with painting tools or filters will happen on that layer. The Channels palette reflects the fact that much of what you now see is transparent due to the layer masks in the Bus Window, Woman, and Red Car layers.

The Channels Reflect the Layers

What you see in the Channels palette thumbnails depends on the layer you have activated and which other layers have their Eye icons on.

◆ Turn off the Eye icon for the Blue Bus layer by clicking it.

◆ Look at both the Layers palette and the Channels palette.

Notice that if you turn off the Eye icon for the Blue Bus layer, not only does the main part of the image turn into the transparency pattern, but you also see that pattern in the Channels palette's thumbnails. Layers whose contents are smaller than the *Background* layer show up with transparency (a checkerboard pattern) surrounding the image pixels. Areas of an image that are hidden by a layer mask also show with transparency. Through these transparent parts, when all the Eye icons are on, we will see the composite, the rainy Costa Rican street scene. The Bus Window layer is still the active layer, so the Channels palette also contains a temporary thumbnail, that of the Bus Window layer mask.

View a Single Layer

If you want to work on a layer and see only that layer, you can click the Eye icons of the other layers to turn them off. A quicker way to turn them all off is to Option (Alt)-click the Eye icon in the Layers palette of the layer you want to see. Doing this also changes the RGB

display of the channel thumbnails in the Channels palette so that you see just the Red, Green, and Blue channel info of the one layer. To turn all the other layers back on again, just Option (Alt)-click the same layer's Eye icon in the Layers palette. The RGB channel thumbnails in the Channels palette will once again show a composite of all the visible layers. Please be aware, however, that when you Option (Alt)-click the Eye icon of a layer to make it the only visible layer, that does not necessarily make it the active layer. To activate the layer itself, you must click its name in the Layers palette.

◆ Option (Alt)-click the Eye icon for the Blue Bus layer.

◆ Look at both the Layers palette and the Channels palette.

Even though you see only the Blue Bus layer, the Bus Window layer is still the active one. If you try to paint with the Brush at this point, you'll get a warning that the target layer is hidden. If you want to work on the Blue Bus layer, you have to click it in the Layers palette to activate it.

◆ Option (Alt)-click the Eye icon for the Blue Bus layer to turn on all the layers' visibility again.

View the Layer Mask Only

For those times when you need to check your mask in black and white, you'll want to turn off the visibility of everything except the layer mask for that layer.

When you Option (Alt)-click an Eye icon for a layer, you turn off visibility for all layers but the one you clicked. This does not necessarily make the visible layer active, though, as seen in this illustration. The Bus Window is still the active layer here. You know that because it has the blue highlight in the Layers palette, and its mask thumbnail still shows in the Channels palette. If you want to make the Blue Bus layer the active layer, you need to click the layer thumbnail in the Layers palette, not just the Eye icon.

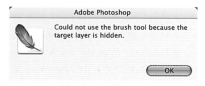

If you try to paint when there are no active pixels visible, you get this warning.

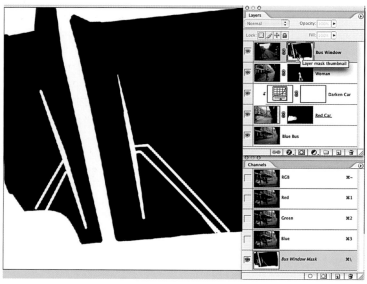

Here, we Option (Alt)-clicked the layer mask thumbnail for the Bus Window layer. This activated the layer mask for editing in the Channels palette and dimmed the visibility icons of the other layers in the Layers palette.

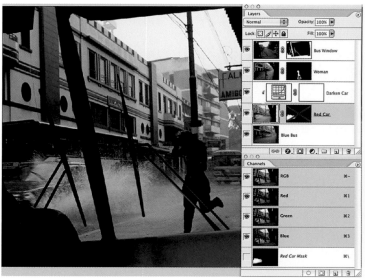

If you want to see how a layer mask affects the layer, you can turn the mask off and on by Shift-clicking it in the Layers palette.

◆ Option (Alt)-click the layer mask thumbnail for the Bus Window layer.

◆ Look at the Layers and Channels palettes.

The RGB channel thumbnails in the Channels palette still show you the information for the Layers palette visibility states, but with an important difference. The Eye icons for the RGB channels are turned off. Only the Eye icon for the mask channel, *Bus Window Mask*, is turned on. In the Layers palette, the Eye icons for all the layers are turned on but are dimmed.

◆ Option (Alt)-click the layer mask thumbnail for the Bus Window layer to turn on visibility for the layer thumbnails.

Turn Off a Layer Mask

◆ Shift-click the layer mask thumbnail for the Red Car layer.

You just turned off the mask for the this layer. The big red X is there to graphically remind you that the mask is off. In this composite, you now no longer see the most of Blue Bus layer, because the Red Car layer covers it almost completely. By turning off the mask, you've created a different view of a rainy street in Costa Rica. The RGB channels in the Channels palette update as you turn the mask on and off.

◆ Shift-click the layer mask again to turn it back on.

Here, we've turned on the Eye icon for the Red Car Mask channel in the Channels palette to be able to see the mask overlay. However, because we were on the Red Car layer itself before we turned on the overlay, we needed to click the Red Car Mask channel in the Channels palette or the Red Car layer mask thumbnail to activate the mask itself for editing.

Edit Using a Layer Mask Overlay

There are times when you want to see both the layer mask and the RGB image while editing. One way to do this is to turn on the layer mask overlay by turning on the visibility for the layer mask in the Channels palette.

◆ In the Layers palette, make sure the Red Car layer is active.

◆ In the Channels palette, turn on the Eye icon for Red Car Mask channel by clicking it.

The red overlay shows you where the masked-out areas of the image are. These areas are black on the layer mask. The transparent areas in the overlay are where the layer mask is white. Areas in the overlay that are not completely red are shades of gray on the layer mask and partially transparent. The color of the overlay is controlled by double-clicking the mask thumbnail in the Channels palette. You can edit either the layer itself or its mask in this configuration, but generally you'll be working on the mask when you set up your file this way. But before you paint or filter, make sure you look at the Layers palette to see whether you are on the layer or the layer mask.

NOTE

We've said it a couple of times already in this chapter, but it's so important, we want to say it once more: To understand the relationship of layers, masks, and channels, you need to have both the Layers palette and the Channels palette open onscreen. Before you paint on anything, take a look at the both palettes. Which layer is active? What channel are you on? Is the layer or the layer mask active?

The Layer Comps Palette

Once you've added, moved, scaled, masked, and otherwise edited your layers to create a composite for your ad, poster, newsletter, or fine art, you'll most likely want to save several different variations of the file to determine which version is perfect for the project. In the old days, you had to do just that—save lots of different files with different version names. Now, however, Adobe has come up with a way for you to do this with only one file via the Layer Comps palette. This palette is capable of saving the Eye icon state, the main window position, and the effects for each layer. Once you've created a version you like, you click the New Layer Comp icon at the bottom of the palette. You can name your composite, choose which of the three options you need to remain constant, and make notes regarding that comp. You can make adjustments to the file and then update a composite by clicking the name of the comp first, and then clicking the Update button (the one that looks like a circle). To view the composite state, you must click the icon to the left of the comp name. Use the forward and backward arrow buttons at the bottom of the palette to quickly cycle through the comps and evaluate them. The Layer Comps palette can't move layers up and down in the Layers palette hierarchy, though, so it's not a tool to use at the beginning of your artwork process; history states and snapshots would be better suited for that. We show you how to use the Layer Comps palette in Chapter 26, "Restoring Old Photos" and we also use it in Chapter 30, "Product Compositing."

8 ◆ Transformation of Images, Layers, Paths, and Selections

One of Photoshop's strengths is its ability to work the way you work—numerically, if you're a by-the-numbers person, or intuitively, if you just like to move things around until they look right. Transforming images, layers, selections, and paths is one area where you'll appreciate this capacity.

This chapter talks about how you can use the Edit/Free Transform command, as well as Edit/Transform/Scale, Rotate, Skew, Distort, and Perspective, to distort a version of a file, layer, or path. In addition, you can use Select/Transform Selection to make the same types of changes to an active selection. We will start with a simple situation and then move into more complicated transforms. First we want you to know that whenever you are doing a transform, the Info palette and the Options bar will show you your progress by displaying the current change in angle, position, or dimensions. At any time during a transform operation, you can use the Options bar to see what you have done to the item so far and to modify those changes numerically.

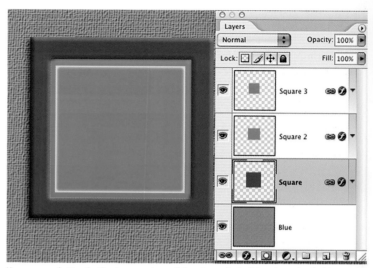

Here we see a button that has been made up of three layers. Each of these layers has had layer styles applied to give it shadows, beveled edges, and so on. Because the layers Square, Square 2, and Square 3 are all linked together, any transformation done to any one of them happens to all three of them. Because each layer is an object surrounded by transparency, we do not need to make a selection before transforming the entire object. The transparency itself is assumed to be the selection.

All the Transform commands, along with Free Transform, are interrelated, and you can switch from one to the other during a transform.

Transform Commands

Let's take a look at each of these Transform options. Then we'll discuss how they can be combined using Free Transform and the Edit/ Transform menu. Look at the Square button in the figure above. It is a simple shape, but you will soon see that we can do a lot to it. Whatever we do to the Square button, we could do to any image or any piece of an image that is pasted into Photoshop as a layer.

◆ Open the SquareButton.psd file in the Ch08.Transformation folder of the *Photoshop Artistry* DVD. Type F to put the image in Full Screen mode, then type Command-Option (Ctrl-Alt)-0 to zoom to 100%. Bring up the Info palette [F9] and the Options bar [F12] so you can see numerically what you are doing as you move the cursor during each transform.

Here we see the Transform menu with all its individual options. You can choose any item from this menu to transform the image in one way at a time. While you are in the middle of a Free Transform, you can still choose any single option from this menu, which allows you to combine single transformation elements, working on them one at a time, before you have to accept any changes. This way, instead of having to type in a Scale value and press Return (Enter), type in a Rotate value and press Return (Enter), and type in a Skew value and press Return (Enter), you are able to begin the Free Transform, choose each option separately, set its value, and press Return (Enter) only once at the end to make all the changes you entered. This gives you more control than simply dragging handles in a Free Transform.

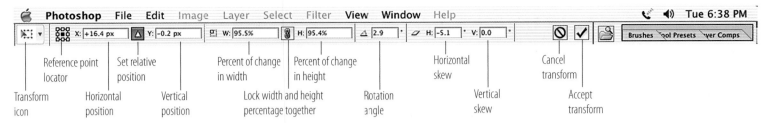

X: +16.4 px   Y: -0.2 px   W: 95.5%   H: 95.4%   2.9°   H: -5.1°   V: 0.0°

Reference point locator | Set relative position | Percent of change in width | Percent of change in height | Horizontal skew | Cancel transform

Transform icon | Horizontal position | Vertical position | Lock width and height percentage together | Rotation angle | Vertical skew | Accept transform

◆ Make sure Square is the active layer in the Layers palette, then choose Edit/Transform/Scale. Click the top-right handle and drag it up and to the right.

◆ Press and hold the Shift key while dragging the corner to force the scale to be proportional.

◆ Scale the layer to 125% with the Shift key down while looking at the Info palette. If you can't get 125% exactly, you can actually type this number into the X scale factor on the Options bar; then click the Link icon to make the Y scale factor the same.

◆ Now release the mouse, choose Edit/Transform/Rotate, and use the same top-right handle to rotate the image −14° by dragging up and to the left after clicking the handle.

◆ Now choose Edit/Transform/Skew and drag the top-middle handle to the left until the horizontal skew angle is 9.6°.

◆ Finally, choose Edit/Transform/Perspective and click the top-right handle again. Drag it down until you see the dimension of the right edge decreasing from both the top and bottom at the same time.

The Options bar shows you the cumulative results of the four transforms you've made so far. The Rotate and Skew angles have changed due to the effects of the Perspective command you invoked at the end.

Edit/Transform/Distort allows you to click a corner handle and independently drag that corner in any direction while leaving the other corners alone. You can also click one of the handles in between two corners, which allows you to distort that entire side of the image as a unit. Play around with Distort for a while, and remember that if you don't like the results, you can always exit and cancel the entire transform by pressing the Escape key or clicking the Cancel Transform (check mark) icon at the right side of the Options bar. If you cancel, though, the image returns to the original rectangular button. While you are entering the individual Transform commands, Photoshop keeps track of all of them while showing you a quick preview. When you press Escape or Cancel Transform, they all go away, and when you press Return (Enter) or click the Cancel Transform icon, the commands are all executed in the final high-resolution image. This final high-res transform may take a little while to render, especially on a large file. However, what you see in the preview is merely a proxy; the high-res version won't be pixelated, so it's worth the wait.

Let's make the button appear as though the bottom of it is closer to you and the top is farther away.

◆ Go to Edit/Transform/Distort, bring the top-right and bottom-left edges toward the center, and move the top-left edge a bit until it looks right to you.

◆ Now press Return (Enter) to finish the transformation, and you will notice that it doesn't look as pixelated as the preview did.

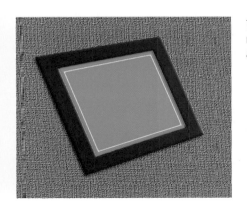

The image after scaling to 125%, rotating by −14°, skewing by 9.6°, and then applying perspective.

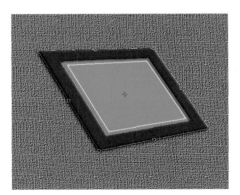

The image after using Edit/Transform/Distort to make the bottom seem closer and the top farther away.

Edit/Free Transform

If you have several transformations to make on a single object, or if you are unsure of which transformations you'll need, you'll probably want to use Edit/Free Transform. Because you can access all of the transformations through this command, it's the one we almost always use. If at any time during the Free Transform you need to perform one specific transformation such as a Scale, you can go back to the Edit menu and choose it. When you want to use Free Transform again, return to the the Edit menu once more and choose it.

◆ Choose File/Revert to revert your image to the Square button again, and do the previous transformation all in one step.

◆ Choose Edit/Free Transform. To Scale to 125%, click the top-right handle and drag up and to the right with the Shift key held down until you see 125% in the Info palette. Make sure you release the mouse button before the Shift key to keep things proportional.

◆ Now move the cursor a little above and to the right of the top-right handle, and you should see a cursor curving to the left and down. This cursor is telling you that if you click and drag at this point, you'll rotate your object. With the curved cursor visible, click and drag up and to the left until the angle in the Info palette is −14°.

◆ To do the Skew, Command (Ctrl)-click the top-middle handle and drag to the left while keeping the mouse down until the delta H angle is 9.6. Don't move the mouse up or down while dragging to the left, or you will also be changing the vertical scaling, and it may be hard to get the angle exactly at 9.6 without the scale changing, too. When you get the angle to 9.6, you can release the Command (Ctrl) key; you are then just adjusting the vertical scaling.

Because Free Transform does many things at once, keeping a particular component of your transform exact can be hard, and you may have trouble getting back exactly to 125% scaling. The way to fix this is to release the mouse, then go into the Options bar to reenter 125% and adjust any other values. Since you are still in Free Transform, let's do some more transformations before we finish.

◆ To change the Perspective, hold down Command-Option (Ctrl-Alt)-Shift and then click and drag the top-right handle down and to the right.

◆ Finally you Distort by just holding down the Command (Ctrl) key while you click and drag in any corner handle and then move

The default location for the reference point is in the center of the object's area. We have placed the cursor on top of it, and you can see the little black circle at the bottom-right of the cursor. This tells you that you can now click the reference point and drag it to its new location. Use the Reference Point Location icon at the top left of the Options palette to place this rotation point exactly in the center or on the corners or middle edges.

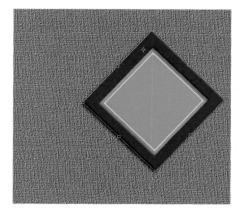

Here we are rotating the above button around a reference point that was moved to the upper-right corner of the button. Now that we have rotated the button, the reference point appears just to the left of the top of the button. You can see the curved rotation icon at the bottom below the center of the button.

it to where you want it. You can now press Return or Enter to finish the Free Transform.

Changing the Reference Point

A very useful feature is the ability to change the point of transformation during a transform.

If you open the original SquareButton file again from the DVD and type Command (Ctrl)-T or choose Edit/Free Transform, you will notice in the center of the button a small crosshairs with a circle in the middle of it. This is the reference point of any transformation you make. That is, any transformation you do will move out from this point. If you scale, the object you transform gets larger from the center out. If you rotate, you rotate around the center. When you put your cursor on top of the reference point, the cursor gets a small circle at its lower right, as in the figure at the top of this page. At this point, you can click and drag this reference point anywhere on the screen. When you release the mouse, this new location becomes the new reference point of transformation. After releasing the mouse, move the cursor to just outside one of the button's corner handles until you see the Curved Rotation icon. Click and drag at that point to rotate the button, and you will see that it is rotating around the reference point wherever you placed it. You can even place it outside of the button's area. It is very powerful to be able to transform around any point. If, for example, you need to composite a different eye in a portrait, you can line up one corner of the eye to the one you are replacing, then set the reference point of transformation at that corner of the eye. Then, when you free transform, you can more easily match the size and rotation of the original eye. You can, of course, move the reference point over and over again, and then make changes around that new reference point. If you want to get the reference point back to the center of the object, just drag it to the vicinity of the original center and it will snap and lock on to the center when it gets close enough. You can also use the Reference Point Location icon at the top left of the Options bar to exactly locate the reference point at the center, corners, or middle edges.

Transforming the Contents of a Selection vs. Transforming the Selection Itself

When you have a selection, if you choose Edit/Free Transform and then do a transformation, you transform the contents of the selection within that layer, not the selection boundary itself. To transform the selection boundary and not its contents, you need to use Select/Transform Selection.

◆ Choose File/Revert and click the Square 3 layer in the Layers palette to activate that layer.

◆ Command (Ctrl)-click the thumbnail for that layer to load the layer's transparency as a selection.

Actually, the pixels that are not transparent are loaded as the selection. This layer has the Inner Glow effect on it to create the highlight around the green area in the center of the button. Let's say we want this area to be smaller in the center of the button.

◆ Type Command (Ctrl)-T or choose Edit/Free Transform, then Option (Alt)-Shift-click the top-right handle and keep the mouse button down while you drag that handle toward the center to make this center square smaller.

Remember that the Shift key forces the Scale to be proportional. The Option key makes the transformation happen symmetrically around the center of the area to be transformed.

◆ Press Return (Enter) after you have made the square smaller, as shown in the bottom figure.

We just did a Free Transform of a selection's contents. Your selection should still be there, but if it's not, just Command (Ctrl)-click the Square 3 layer again to reload it.

◆ Choose Window/Show Info [F9] to bring up the Info palette. This time, choose Select/Transform Selection, which puts you in a Free Transform mode where you are working on the selection itself.

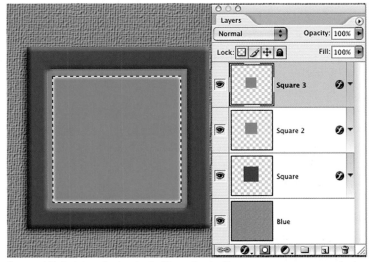

Command (Ctrl)-clicking the thumbnail of Square 3 to load its nontransparent area as a selection.

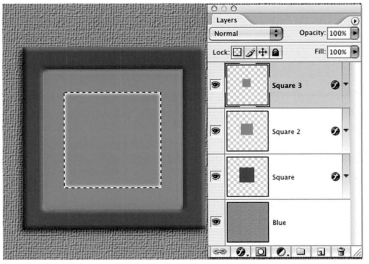

Square 3 after making it smaller with Option (Alt)-Shift-click-and-drag using Free Transform of the layer, then Return (Enter) to finish that Free Transform.

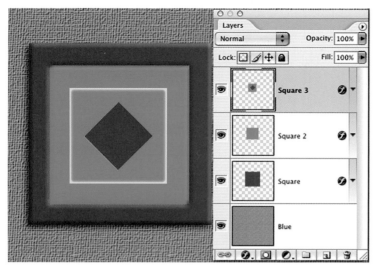

The final button after using Select/Transform Selection to create the center diamond area and then filling it with red.

Using a simple Elliptical Marquee and Select/Transform Selection can help speed some tasks. By rotating a simple elliptical selection with a feathered edge, we can apply corrections such as curves to this young woman's face.

◆ Now hold down Option (Alt)-Shift while you drag the top-right handle and scale the selection inward until it's at 50% in the Info palette. Move the cursor just outside the top-right handle to get the rotate cursor, which looks like a curved double arrow, then rotate the selection up and to the left until you get −45° in the Info palette.

Notice that the values in the Info palette and Options bar change on the fly as you move the mouse with the button held down. If you can't get the exact values you want in the Info palette, get them close using the mouse, then release the mouse button to edit the values inside the appropriate text boxes on the Options bar.

◆ Press Return (Enter) to finish your transform.

This time you have transformed the selection itself and not the contents of the selection. Again, the only difference is that to transform the selection itself, you start the process with Select/Transform Selection instead of Edit/Free Transform or Edit/Transform.

◆ Type I to get to the Eyedropper tool, and click the red color on the outside of the button to load it as the foreground color.

◆ Choose Edit/Fill or type Shift-Delete (Backspace) and use the pop-up to fill that selected area using the foreground color. Your image should now look like the image at the top of this page.

Transform Path

If you have an active path and go to the Edit menu, you'll see that the Transform options are now Free Transform Path and Transform Path. With an active path, you get these options even if you have a selection marquee active at the same time.

◆ Click Square 2 in the Layers palette to make it the active layer. Command (Ctrl)-click the Square 2 thumbnail to load a selection of the nontransparent area of this layer.

◆ Choose Window/Paths [Shift-F11] to bring up the Paths palette.

◆ Choose Make Work Path from the Paths palette menu to turn this selection into a path, and click OK when asked if you want the Tolerance set to 2.0. You now have a path of the area around the edge of this layer.

◆ Choose Edit/Free Transform Path.

◆ Command (Ctrl)-drag the top-right point of the path down and to the left until that point is at the top-right highlight on Square 3. Command (Ctrl)-drag the bottom-left point up and to the right until it is at the bottom-left highlight on Square 3.

◆ Press Return (Enter) to complete the path transform, then choose Fill Path from the Paths palette menu to fill this area with the red foreground color.

◆ Drag the Work Path to the Trash icon in the Paths palette. You should now have the Double Diamond image on the next page.

Moving the path points with the Command (Ctrl) key held down while in Free Transform Path.

The final Double Diamond button after filling the path with red.

Linked Layers Transform and Move as a Group

The three square layers in this example are all linked together, which you can see by noticing that the Link icon at the right of each layer is on for the other two layers whenever one of the square layers is active. Had we not loaded a selection to do the transformations on Square 3, all three layers would have transformed in the same way. Try this to see for yourself.

◆ Type H for Hand tool to get out of the Pen tool and be able to access Free Transform again.

◆ Use File/Revert to go back to the original file on the DVD; then click the Square 3 layer, and, without loading a selection, choose Edit/Free Transform.

◆ Start to scale the image and you'll notice that all three layers—the entire button—scale together.

If you use the Move tool to move any of these layers, they will also all move together because they are linked. This is a very useful feature when you create an object that is made up of more than one layer but you want to move it or scale it as a whole. You can also drag and drop this linked object to another document, and all the layers will be copied to the other document with the same names that they have in your current document. Combining all the layers that make up this button into a layer group makes this even more convenient.

◆ Press Escape or Command (Ctrl)-Period to cancel this transformation, then from the Layers palette menu choose Select Linked. Now you can type Command (Ctrl)-G or use Layer/Group Layers to move these linked layers into a group.

◆ Double-click the name of the group and rename it Button.

Layer groups and linked layers allow you to create component documents that contain standard objects, such as buttons. When you need one of these objects, you open the container file and drag and drop that component into your current working document. To unlink a layer so that you can move or transform it on its own, you need to click the Link icon at the bottom of the Layers palette while that layer is active. This unlinks that layer from the others. You can now

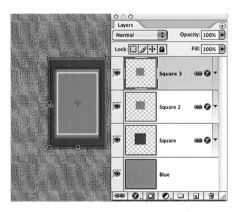

Here, even though Square 3 is the active layer, all three layers transform because they are linked.

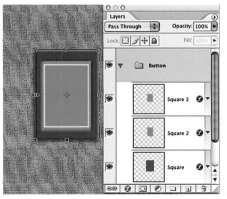

In this case, all three layers transform because you are actually transforming the group named Button.

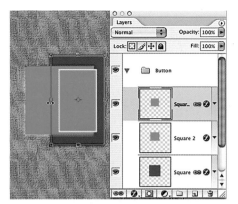

In this instance, the two linked layers transform, but Square 2 does not, even though it is part of the group called Button. This is because you are transforming the Square 3 layer and that transformation affects only the active layer and any linked layers.

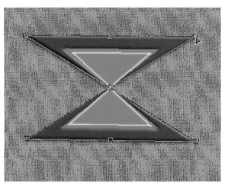

With Free Transform, you can hold down the Command (Ctrl) key and drag a point all the way across the object being transformed. Here, we transformed the group, Button, by moving the top corner points across the button to the opposite sides.

transform or move the current layer. If you want to relink the layers after the change, just reclick in the Link icon. You can also Shift-click or Command (Ctrl)-click layers to do a group link or unlink in one step.

Edit/Transform/Rotate and Flip vs. Image/Rotate and Flip Canvas

With a layer, choosing Edit/Transform/Rotate or Edit/Transform/ Flip rotates or flips, respectively, the currently active layer and any other layers that are linked to it. These commands also affect a layer group full of linked or unlinked layers if the layer group is active in the Layers palette. Image/Rotate Canvas/Rotate or Flip rotates or flips the entire document, including all layers whether they are linked or not.

Warp

The ability to warp information as you transform means that you are no longer constrained to straight lines as you composite images together. You can, if needed, achieve something like a square peg in a round hole using Photoshop.

Warp uses an "envelope" technology that may be familiar to any of you who have worked with type, where the Warp feature has been available for a while. When you select Edit/Transform/Warp, a grid appears that has four corner points with handles as well as two vertical and two horizontal grid lines that can be manipulated to create the shape of the envelope you need. In addition, you can choose preset envelope shapes from the Options bar.

Also on the Options bar is an icon that allows you to switch between Free Transform and Warp. It's just to the left of the Cancel Transform icon. However, switching between Warp and the other transformations is confusing. If you use Distort first, for instance, then switch to Warp, some of the handles you use to warp an image may be locked. If you use Warp first and then switch to a different transformation, you get a bounding box that is rectangular even though your image may be anything but rectangular at that moment. If you are going to use Warp to manipulate an image, we suggest that you start with an

The original iMac image.

The second image is composited using Edit/Transform/Warp. Lowering the opacity of the layer while within the Warp transformation allows you to see where to place the points, handles, and grid lines of the transformation.

The composited image. We kept the opacity of the layer at about 50% so the reflections of the original monitor show.

Once you define the four points of a plane in Vanishing Point, Photoshop builds a grid for you. You can extend or reposition it as necessary.

image that is about the size you need or just a bit larger. Keep the number of transforms you need to a minimum, and use Warp exclusively if possible. If you'd like to practice using Edit/Transform/Warp, you can open the iMac.tif and Wendyleads.tif files from the DVD for this chapter.

Warp does a good job of wrapping images onto curved surfaces, but if you need to work with perspective planes, the inability to set additional anchor points limits the effects you can create. If images on planes is what you need, you may do better with the Vanishing Point feature.

Vanishing Point

Photoshop has the capability of cloning or copying items in perspective using Vanishing Point. To use the feature, it's generally best to create a new, blank layer for information that is being created rather than copying or cloning onto an existing layer. That way, if you need to make changes or tweak what you've done, you have more flexibility.

When you first choose Filter/Vanishing Point, you need to define the planes that make up the image. Flat walls, sides of buildings, sidewalks, or streets can give you guides on which to build grids. If you don't have straight or flat planes in your image, it will be more difficult to discern where the vanishing points of the perspective planes lie. Once you click four points to define the plane, you can move or extend that plane to other areas of your image. You can have more than one plane in the image, and Photoshop will remember the planes you have created whenever you invoke the filter again. If you open the ColonyLobby.psd image from the folder for this chapter on the DVD, you can see the grids we used if you choose Filter/Vanishing Point.

Once we had our grid for the wall, we extended it to include the area of the curtains, then chose the Stamp tool to clone the curtains in perspective on the blank layer we created before entering Vanishing Point. The Stamp tool inside Vanishing Point works just like the

Clone Stamp in the regular Photoshop Toolbox. Option (Alt)-click to establish the pick-up location, then click and drag to clone. There's also a Brush tool here that can act as a healing brush to attain better blending with the cloned material.

If you need to clone a fairly rectangular area, you can select the area you want to change with the Vanishing Point Marquee tool. The selection is created in the perspective of the plane in which you drew it. If you Option (Alt)-drag this selection, it becomes a floating selection. If you Command (Ctrl)-drag, you actually copy information into the selection. We copied information using both the Stamp tool

Here we are cloning the curtains within Vanishing Point. Notice the outline of the perspective grid.

As you move a pasted object into a grid, it will take on the perspective of the grid.

If your grid is yellow or red, you need to move the corner points until the grid turns blue for Photoshop to properly calculate the vanishing point perspective.

and the Marquee tool for the curtains in this image. We got better results on the top edge using the Marquee tool, but better results on the bottom of the curtains using the Stamp tool. You can use the tools in combination to achieve the your desired results. And Vanishing Point offers multiple undos, so you can change your mind, go back several steps, and try a different tack if needed.

Another way to use Vanishing Point is to paste information into a grid. We created a second grid in the interior of the mirror (although we could have simply extended the original), and pasted the poster into another blank layer. When you paste, the pasted image appears at the left of the window, so you'll need to move it into the appropriate grid, where it will take on the perspective of that grid. Once in the grid, you can resize the pasted image if needed by typing T. Please don't click the Marquee tool on a grid before you resize the pasted image. Once you click on a grid, the pasted object no longer floats and can't be resized.

If your grid is not blue, that's a clue that there are some problems with the grid. Red means the aspect ratio of the plane can't be calculated, and yellow means that not all of the vanishing points of the plane can be resolved. Just use the Edit Plane tool (the black arrow) to move corner points on the plane until it turns blue.

Lens Correction

Transformations are sometimes needed because of the lens that was used to shoot the original picture. Photoshop can handle many of these problems in one place, the Lens Correction filter. You'll find Lens Correction in the Distort filters, and it's a real powerhouse. Here you are able to correct problems with barrel and pincushion distortion, chromatic aberration, vignetting, and perspective.

In our example, there's a bit of distortion toward the edges of this family photo Barry shot with a 90mm lens on his 4x5 camera. It's most noticeable with the two faces to the far right. The faces seem to be pulled into the center of the image—called pincushion distortion. There's a small amount of darkening around the edges as well—what's called vignetting. To correct these problems, we went to Filter/Distort/Lens Correction and entered the values you see on the next page. We used the Remove Distortion slider to set the basic value we wanted to use, then used the up and down arrows to move the slider in small increments. You could also use the first tool in the Toolbox at the left of the Lens Correction window, which is the Remove Distortion tool. To use it, you drag either from the center out to correct for pincushion distortion, or from the edges into the center to correct for barrel distortion. If you use the tool rather than the slider, remember that a little movement goes a long way. We found the slider to be more exacting and easier to use.

The second tool is the Straighten tool. This one can be very useful if a line or edge in your image should be vertical or horizontal. If so, simply drag the tool across that edge, and the image will straighten around the line of your drag. If the problem is with the vertical or

Here are the settings we used on the McNamaras image to correct the slight pincushion distortion and lighten the edges.

horizontal perspective of the image, there are sliders for each issue on the right side of the window. In that same area is an angle of rotation setting that lets you rotate the entire image.

When you first enter the Lens Correction filter, a grid is drawn over your image to help you discern what type of corrections you want to make. You can turn the grid on and off from the check box at the bottom of the window, resize or recolor the grid, or use the third tool in the Toolbox to reposition the grid.

At the very bottom of the Lens Correction window are settings for specifying how you want to handle any blank areas that are created by adjustments you've made in the filter. You can choose to scale the image so those edges are cropped out of the photo, or use the Edge pop-up to choose to fill those areas with the background color, transparency, or repetitions of the edge pixels. If the blank space is minimal, Edge Extension might be acceptable, but for large areas you would probably want to finish your adjustments in Lens Correction, then either crop your photo or use the Clone Stamp to fill in those areas with appropriate content.

Chromatic aberration in a lens shows up in your image as a colored line on one side of objects in the image. The Chromatic Aberration feature of the Lens Correction filter works similarly to Camera Raw's Chromatic Aberration feature. See Chapter 9, "Camera Raw," to learn about this important feature.

In the original McNamaras photo, the two people on the far right are a bit distorted due to the wide-angle lens. We've hidden the grid so you can see the faces better.

Here are those same faces after the Reduce Distortion settings, shown at top left, have been applied.

9 ◆ Camera Raw

In the early days of digital cameras (which was really not that long ago), the Raw file format was offered on only a few high-end cameras and was used mainly by professsionals and techie types. But in recent years a steady change has been afoot, and now anyone with a decent digital camera that supports the Raw format can access those files. Whereas understanding the nitty-gritty of how to process Raw files was once considered the province of advanced photographers only, knowledge of this technique is now regarded as important, yet basic, information that any halfway serious digital photographer needs to understand. In this chapter, we'll explain just what a Raw file is, discuss its advantages and disadvantages as compared with JPEG, offer some recommendations for the best way to expose your images, and cover how to process your files using Adobe Camera Raw.

What Exactly Is a Raw File?

The word *Raw* conjures up associations of uncooked foods or something that is rough, unrefined, and unpolished. When applied to a Raw file from a digital camera, those connotations are not far off the mark.

When a digital camera is set to save images as JPEGs or TIFFs, the initial Raw data from the image sensor is processed by the camera's onboard computer. Color, tonal, and contrast adjustments may be applied according to specific formulas the manufacturer has developed for making the images "look good." In addition, if left to its own devices, the camera may be applying other adjustments as well, such as saturation and sharpening. Finally, if you are using the JPEG format, the file is compressed, which means that some information is discarded, and the file is then written to your memory card as an 8-bit file.

With a digital Raw file, none of that extra processing takes place. It consists simply of the Raw data that the camera's image sensor has recorded. Along with this basic exposure data—which basically is a record of what was photographed—Raw files also contain metadata about the exposure. This metadata will differ from camera to camera, but it includes such things as white-balance and exposure information, the focal length of the lens, the metering pattern that was used, whether the flash fired, and so on.

Not All Raw Files Are the Same

The term "Raw file" is a generic umbrella term that describes several different proprietary file formats that have been created by different camera makers (such as .NEF for Nikon and .CRW and .CR2 for Canon). There is no such thing as a single Raw file format that is the same for every camera. Each camera, and even different camera models by the same manfacturer, has its own Raw format that has been designed to produce the best image possible from that camera's image sensor. As sensors evolve, so does the Raw format they use. At the time of this writing, Adobe Camera Raw 3.4 reads more than 100 different Raw formats from a variety of professional and midrange cameras. The software is periodically updated when new cameras are released, and you can download these updates for free from the Adobe Web site; but if you buy a new camera, it may be a few months before an update for Camera Raw that supports your camera's Raw format becomes available.

How Digital Camera Sensors Work

Before we get into what a Raw file converter like Adobe Camera Raw is doing to your file, it helps to understand what image information a Raw file actually contains, so let's review the basic functionality of a digital camera's image sensor.

The sensor in a digital camera contains a mosaic array of smaller sensors called photosites that represent each pixel in the image. The photosites create a voltage charge in response to the amount of light that strikes them during the exposure. The mosaic grid of photosites is covered with colored filters in an alternating pattern. A common

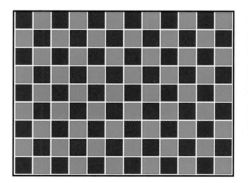

The Bayer Pattern uses alternating pixels of red, green, and blue to record a digital image. The camera's onboard computer, or a Raw convertor such as Camera Raw, fills in the missing colors using a process of color interpolation called de-mosaicing.

arrangement used by many cameras is the Bayer Pattern that alternates between green and blue pixels in one row and red and green pixels in the next row. The green-blue and red-green rows themselves alternate, with the result that twice as many green pixels are recorded as red or blue. The reason for this is that human vision is more sensitive to the green range.

It's important to note that the sensor is not actually capturing a color image as we normally think of a color photo. The photosites on the sensor are recording only brightness or luminance values. The images that virtually all digital cameras produce are actually grayscale files. The tiny color filters over the sensors serve as a reference to what color a pixel should be. If you are shooting JPEG, it is the job of the camera's onboard computer to interpret this information and interpolate the missing color data into a full-fledged color image. If you are shooting Raw, that task, called *de-mosaicing,* falls to the Raw conversion software you are using. In addition, Raw format lets you control any other interpretive adjustments to be applied to the file. Instead of letting the camera make all the creative decisions about how the image should look, you get to make them.

Pros and Cons of Raw Files

Whether you feel that the ability to process the Raw files yourself is a wonderful thing, or too much hassle to bother with, really boils down to how comfortable you are with digital editing software. One of the primary aims of this chapter is to demystify the Raw conversion process and show that it's really not such a big deal. Having said that, we do acknowledge that, depending on your situation and what you are photographing, the Raw format does have both advantages and disadvantages. As nature and fine art photographers, we feel that the pros far outweigh the cons, but here's a rundown of both.

Advantages of Raw

In our view, the main advantage of Raw is that it allows us to interpret the file ourselves and not leave such important creative decisions to the camera. When working with Raw files, you have tremendous latitude for correcting exposure and white balance errors that you don't have with JPEG files. With JPEG, exposures must be more accurate, because they're 8-bit files and the corrections required for poorly exposed shots (especially underexposed ones) can result in banding or posterization, especially in the shadow tones. And since it's a high-bit-depth file, a Raw file has much more tonal overhead for when you need to make major corrections. With Raw we can also choose to interpret the same file in many ways without ever altering the original file produced by the camera. Finally, only by shooting in

Depending on the size of your camera's memory buffer, how fast it can write files, and the speed of your memory card, shooting in Raw may not be ideal if you are photographing fast-action sequences with a motor drive.

Raw do we have access to the high-bit-depth information captured by the image sensor. On most current cameras, that translates into a 12-bit image, or 4096 tonal values per color channel. With JPEG you are limited to 8-bit files (256 tonal values per channel).

Disadvantages of Raw

The primary disadvantage of Raw is that it creates an extra step in your workflow. Raw files cannot be used immediately in other programs because they have to be processed first some (some cameras do allow you to shoot Raw + JPEG). If you are unfamiliar with how to process Raw files, the array of settings and controls in a Raw converter can seem confusing. If you're used to the more compact file sizes of JPEGs, then Raw files may seem too large, especially since you can fit fewer images on a memory card. For some photographic situations, especially those where you are shooting fast action with a motor drive, the Raw format may actually slow you down, because it takes longer for the camera to write Raw files than it does JPEGs. This speed hit is also influenced in part by the write speed of your memory card, but typically it takes longer for the camera to deal with Raw files. For situations where you are shooting lots of images under controlled, unchanging light and you have your exposure dialed in to produce good images, Raw capture may be overkill, especially if the images don't require significant corrections and have a short "shelf life" (say, senior prom portraits taken in a portable studio set up at the dance).

Proper Exposure for Raw Files

At the time of this writing, digital SLRs have image sensors that can capture approximately six stops of dynamic range. *Dynamic range,* also known as *exposure latitude* or *contrast range,* is the range of tonal values from the darkest to the brightest that can be recorded in a single exposure. As stated earlier, in a camera that can record 12 bits of information, this translates to 4096 possible tonal values.

Since digital sensors record data in a linear fashion, the brightest stop of exposure contains fully half of the available tonal levels. In a typical camera with a six-stop dynamic range, this translates to 2048 values. Since each stop of exposure below the brightest represents half as much light, the next stop would contain 1024 values and the next stop down from there is halved to 512. The stop after that contains 256 values, then 128, and finally 64 levels in the darkest shadows.

You may have heard that it is a good idea to underexpose your digital camera captures so that you don't risk the highlights being blown out to white. While this will, indeed, control the highlights, it also means that you are not utilizing all of the available tonal levels that your sensor is capable of recording. Looked at another way, if the tonal data does not extend into the right-hand side of the camera's histogram, it means you are using far fewer tonal levels than the camera is capable

NOTE

For more detailed information on linear gamma and exposure considerations for Raw images, you can download two PDF articles by Bruce Fraser, "Understanding Digital Raw Capture" and "Linear Gamma," on the Adobe Web site: http://www.adobe.com/products/photoshop/cameraraw.html

of capturing. While you can certainly lighten an underexposed image in Camera Raw, this would mean redistributing the 64 levels in the dark shadows into the brighter areas of the tonal range, and on some exposures this could introduce noise into the midtones or shadows.

The linear nature of how the information is recorded by the sensor means that ideally you want to have the data in the histogram as far to the right side (the highlight side) as possible without any clipping taking place. Highlight clipping in a histogram can be seen when the data appears to be clipped off, or tall spikes are visible on the far right side. Put another way, it means that you want the highlights in the image to be as bright as possible without having them become a total white with no detail. With such an exposure, the image may appear to be too bright and washed out when you preview it on your camera's LCD screen, but you can easily adjust that in Camera Raw without any of the negative side effects that come from trying to open up the dark shadows on an underexposed shot. In addition, Camera Raw does possess some amount of highlight recovery ability so even an image that appears to show slight highlight clipping on your camera's LCD display may be salvageable with the proper adjustments in Camera Raw.

Camera Raw Philosophy

Camera Raw is for making global adjustments to your image, and the more you can do to get the image looking good in Camera Raw, the better. Corrections to specific areas (such as darkening a sky or lightening the shadows on someone's face) need to be applied in Photoshop where selections, adjustment layers and layer masks can be used. Your primary goal when adjusting a Raw file in Camera Raw is to adjust the overall tonal range until the image looks the way you want it to. Depending on the photo, this could include making sure that you have bright highlights and rich shadow tones, but that you also preserve important detail in those key areas. If there are color casts caused by lighting or white balance errors, you can address these using the white-balance controls. As you will see later in this chapter, this is especially effective if there are tonal areas in the image that should be neutral.

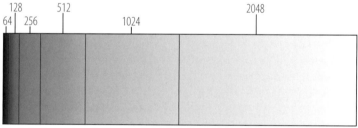

128 512   2048
64 256   1024

Due to the linear nature of a Raw capture, fully half of all the tonal levels that your sensor is capable of capturing are recorded in the brightest stop of exposure. The illustration above shows the linear gamma for a six-stop exposure range.

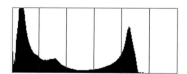 

To ensure that you are taking advantage of all the tonal levels your camera sensor can capture, the ideal histogram for a Raw exposure should have the data as far to the right as possible, but without any highlight clipping. The histogram on the left is not making full use of the right side, where the majority of tonal values are recorded. After you've made an exposure adjustment in the camera, the histogram on the right shows the data spread across the full width of the tonal range, with data being recorded in the vital right-hand side that represents the brightest stop of exposure.

Apart from tonal and color adjustments, you can also address noise issues in Camera Raw, though the controls it offers are no magic bullet that will totally remove noise from an image. You can also choose to apply input sharpening. It is important to differentiate the sharpening that you apply here from the final sharpening that is applied to prepare the file for output. If you apply any sharpening in Camera Raw, it should be subtle and designed to restore some of the original sharpness that is lost when a continuous-tone real-world scene is digitized into a mosaic of square pixels.

The Camera Raw Interface

In this section we'll explore the Camera Raw interface and all of its controls and functionality. We'll walk you through the different options using a selection of different Raw files that are included in the folder for this chapter on the *Photoshop Artistry* DVD. For most of this chapter you do not even have to have Photoshop running. We can access the files and open them into Camera Raw using Adobe Bridge.

◆ In Adobe Bridge, navigate to the Ch09.CameraRaw folder on the DVD and open the file called Queen Mary Table.CRW.

The Camera Raw dialog will open and display a preview of the image. In the upper-right corner of the preview, you may see an exclamation mark in a yellow triangle for a few seconds. This means that Camera Raw is still building the preview from the information in the Raw file. The image may appear to be a bit fuzzy while the preview is generating, but it will get sharper, and the warning icon will disappear, when the preview is complete.

We'll start off with a general view of all of the controls that the dialog offers, then we'll get more specific in our explorations by using actual image examples to explain how the settings work.

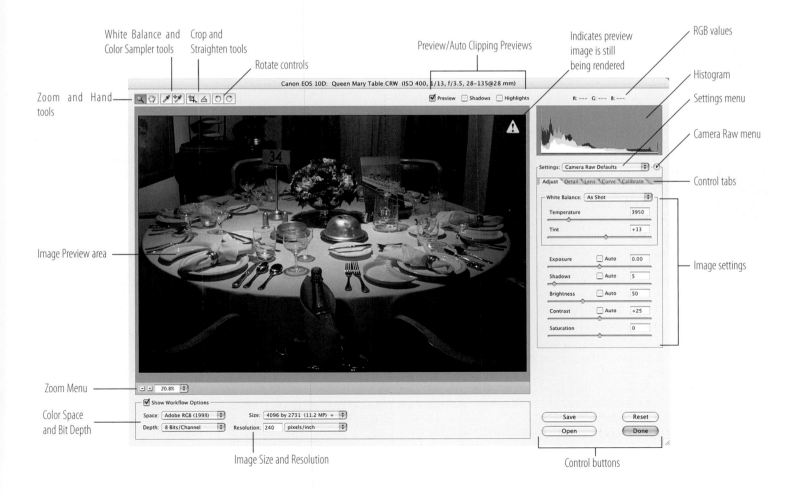

The Camera Raw toolbar.

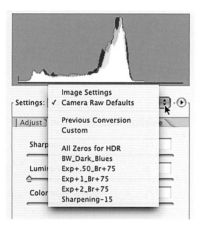

The Settings menu. The six choices at the bottom of the menu are custom settings that were created for specific editing situations.

Tools, Previews, and the Histogram

At the top left are a series of six tool icons (in previous versions of Camera Raw, these used to run vertically along the left side). The tools are grouped in pairs. The first two control basic navigational functionality such as zooming and scrolling; the next pair are Eyedropper tools for setting white balance and placing Color Sampler points. These are followed by the Crop and Straighten tools, and finally the Rotate tools for rotating the preview image.

Moving to the right along the top you will see check boxes for turning the preview on and off and also for displaying color overlays that alert you to highlight clipping (red) and shadow clipping (blue). A full color histogram is on the far right and above that is an info display that shows the RGB values for the cursor location as you move it over the preview image.

Settings Menus

Just under the histogram is the Settings menu. This contains options to use previously applied settings or to revert to the Camera Raw defaults for the camera that created the image. You can also choose to apply the Previous Conversion if the current image can use the same

NOTE

The minimum monitor resolution required to show all of the Camera Raw dialog (as well as some other dialogs in Photoshop) is 1024x768.

adjustments as the previous one. At the bottom of this menu you will also find any custom settings that you've saved.

If you click the small triangle button to the right of the Settings menu, a fly-out menu will appear that offers the ability to save and load settings, to turn the Auto adjustment off or on, to save new Camera Raw defaults (or reset to the standard defaults), and to access the Camera Raw preferences.

The Save Buttons

At the lower right of the Camera Raw dialog are four buttons, for Save, Open, Cancel, and Done. Save opens another dialog and allows you to save the adjusted Raw file as a TIFF, PSD, JPEG, or DNG file. We'll cover that dialog later. The Open button processes the Raw file with the selected adjustments and opens it into Photoshop. The Done button applies the adjustments and closees Camera Raw, returning you to Bridge. Cancel is self-explanatory—it cancels the entire process without applying any of the adjustments.

If you press the Option (Alt) key, the functionality of some of the buttons will change. The Save button will skip the Save dialog and apply the settings that were used the last time the Save dialog was accessed. The Cancel button will change to a Reset function, allowing you to clear out any settings you have made and start over.

If you have chosen to open the image into Photoshop CS2 by using the contextual menus in Bridge (right-click a thumbnail or Control-click with a Mac one-button mouse), then Option (Alt)-clicking the Open button will change it to an Open a Copy button. This allows you to open a copy of the image using the current changes, but it does not record those changes into the file's metadata. This is useful

When a Camera Raw session is initiated from Bridge, the active button is the Done button; clicking it will apply the changes and return you to Bridge. When Camera Raw is hosted by Photoshop, the Open button is active; clicking it will convert the Raw file and open it into Photoshop.

When a Camera Raw session is initiated from Photoshop, Option (Alt)-clicking the Open button will open a copy of the file and not apply the latest image adjustments to the XMP sidecar file that keeps a record of the changes. This is a good way to explore different interpretations of an image but not overwrite the basic Raw corrections for the file.

The Original Raw File Is Never Changed

When you make changes to an image using Camera Raw, the original Raw file created by your camera is never altered. The adjustments that you make are stored as a set of instructions in a sidecar XMP file that references the Raw image file. This is how you can quickly restore the image to the default Camera Raw settings for that particular camera model. If you use Bridge to move files around on your system, then the XMP files will always travel along with their associated Raw file. But if you move the files yourself using the Mac Finder or Windows Explorer, then you need to make sure that you are also moving the XMP files that go with the Raw image files.

CRW_8636.CRW	Raw files with their corresponding
CRW_8636.xmp	XMP files that contain the Camera
CRW_8637.CRW	Raw adjustments.
CRW_8637.xmp	

for when you want to process the Raw file twice to address specific areas in the image, or if you simply want to create a different interpretation, such as a black-and-white version of the image. In such a case, you would not necessarily want the black-and-white adjustments to be recorded to the XMP file that contains the Camera Raw instructions for that image.

Workflow Options

Finally, along the bottom of the dialog under the preview image are the Workflow Options. These allow you to choose the Color Space that the image is processed into, as well as the file's bit depth, pixel dimensions, and resolution. We will discuss these in more detail later in the chapter.

Auto Adjustments

Now that we have had a good overview of all the features available in Camera Raw, let's get to work and explore them in more depth. We'll start with the Queen Mary image we already have open in Camera Raw and begin our explorations with the Adjust tab.

If you are used to the previous version of Camera Raw that shipped with Photoshop CS, one of the first new things you may notice is the presence of four Auto check boxes above the Exposure, Shadows, Brightness, and Contrast sliders. These do a very good job of making many images look better by ensuring that there are bright highlights,

dark shadows, good midtones, and a dash of contrast, all depending on the actual content of the image.

But they still represent a canned, formulaic adjustment that is not ideal for all images. Photographs made at night or twilight are never interpreted very well by the Auto adjustments, since they are trying to redistribute the tones to create a brighter highlight. And if you have bracketed your shots by using different exposures, those subtle differences between files will be lost when you view the images in Bridge, as the Auto adjustments are trying to make the images look similar.

Turning Auto Adjustments Off

You can turn the Auto adjustments off for a given setting by moving the slider for that setting. You can also simply click the check boxes to turn them off individually. If you want to toggle them all off and on at the same time, you can use Command (Ctrl)-U. You can also reach that command from the Settings fly-out menu.

◆ Press Command (Ctrl)-U a few times to turn the Auto adjustments off and on. With the Queen Mary Table photo, you'll notice

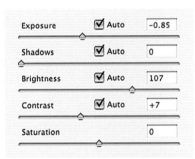

The Auto adjustment check boxes.

The Auto adjustments are not ideal for certain types of images, or for instances where you have bracketed your exposures. The top row of Bridge thumbnails shows three frames where the exposure was bracketed one stop apart. The bottom row shows how the same images look if the default Auto adjustments are left on in Camera Raw.

The Queen Mary Table image with no Auto adjustments applied.

The Queen Mary Table image with Auto adjustments applied. Since the Auto adjustments address only brightness and contrast, the image becomes only slightly brighter and the yellow color cast is not fixed.

that the image is significantly brighter with the Auto Adjustments applied, but they do nothing to fix the color cast caused by the interior display lighting on this exhibit. The Auto adjustments affect only brightness and contrast. Take a moment to also see how the histogram changes with the adjustments on or off.

Saving No Auto Adjustments as a New Default

Turning the Auto adjustments off using these methods will affect only the active image. If you want to configure Camera Raw so that they are never applied (unless you choose to do so), follow these steps:

◆ Open any Raw file into Camera Raw. Open the Settings menu just below the histogram, and make sure that it is set to Camera Raw Defaults.

◆ From the Settings fly-out menu on the right side of the Settings menu, choose Use Auto Adjustments to turn them off (you can also use the Command (Ctrl)-U shortcut).

◆ From the same Settings fly-out menu, choose Save New Camera Raw Defaults. Click Done to exit Camera Raw and apply the new preference.

These default settings are camera-specific, so you will need to repeat these steps with Raw files from your other cameras if you want to turn off the Auto adjustments for all your camera files.

Image Adjustments

Camera Raw keeps the majority of its controls grouped in five control tabs on the right side of the dialog. This is where you will be applying most of the changes to your images. The control tabs each address specific areas of the Raw conversion:

Adjust

This area controls color balance and basic tonal adjustments.

Detail

This tab contains controls for sharpening and noise reduction.

Lens

The Lens tab addresses chromatic aberration and vignetting, specific issues that are caused by optical imperfections in lenses.

Curve

This functions much like the Curves dialog in Photoshop and allows for precise contrast and brightness adjustments.

Calibrate

The Calibrate tab lets you affect the hue and saturation characteristics for the red, green, and blue color ranges in an image. It is also useful for fine-tuning the default camera profiles that ship with Camera Raw.

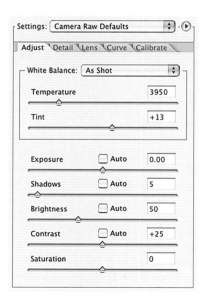

The Settings menu and the five image adjustment tabs, with the Adjust tab active.

The Adjust Tab

Let's take a more detailed look at the controls offered in the Adjust tab. We'll continue using the image of the Queen Mary dinner table, because it has some qualities that we can definitely improve with the Camera Raw controls.

◆ First, make sure the Settings menu under the histogram is set to Camera Raw Defaults. If the Auto adjustments are on, turn them off by using the Command (Ctrl)-U shortcut.

Though the White Balance controls appear first in the Adjust tab, we will actually start our tour by discussing the Exposure, Shadows, and Brightness controls. For most images, we like to adjust the overall tonal balance before addressing white-balance issues. Plus, in images where the color casts are very subtle, it is much easier to see changes in white balance after the overall brightness of the image has been adjusted.

Exposure, Shadows, and Brightness

For many images, the Exposure, Shadows, and Brightness sliders will let you accomplish a good deal of the work you need to do. If you are familiar with the Levels command, you'll notice similarities between these settings and the Input Highlight, Shadow, and Midtone sliders in Levels.

Exposure

The Exposure slider controls the highlights in Camera Raw, letting you determine the brightest tone in the image while proportionately remapping the rest of the tonal scale. Though the effect may seem to be the same as with the Input Highlight slider in Levels, the Exposure slider is affecting the high-bit linear data of a Raw file, so it is able to apply changes that are not possible when you're working in Levels. One of the most significant of these changes is the ability to recover highlight detail that seems to be blown out.

◆ To Explore these controls, go to the Settings menu and choose Camera Raw Defaults to return the image to its original state.

◆ At the top of the dialog, click the Highlights and Shadows check boxes to turn on the automatic clipping display. In this image you can see that there is some minor shadow clipping in the dark areas of the image and highlight clipping on some of the items on the table.

◆ Move the Exposure slider to the right to lighten the brightest highlights, as well as the entire image. Watch how the histogram changes shape as you move the slider.

The automatic highlight and shadow clipping display will add a red overlay to areas where the highlights are clipped, and a blue overlay to areas where the shadows are clipped. These overlays will show when there is clipping in at least one of the color channels. With this display there is no way to see which channel has the problem, or if all channels are affected.

◆ Move the Exposure slider to the left to darken the image. When you get far enough to the left, the red clipping display will no longer be on the plates, but it will still show on the bright reflection on the serving dish.

The red overlay shows you where in the image tonal values are being brightened to a total white with no detail. There are some types of highlights where clipping is acceptable, such as bright reflections on water, glass, or metal, as we see in this image; but in general you don't want to adjust normal highlight detail to where it is a total white. The plates and the tablecloth in this image are a good example of that. While they are certainly bright, those areas still contain plenty of detail, and we don't want them to be a total white.

◆ Set the Exposure value to 0.00 to clear any changes you have made.

Shadows

The Shadows setting in Camera Raw functions similarly to the Input Shadow slider in Levels. Both let you set the darkest point in the image, and the middle tonal values will darken in proportion to that adjustment.

◆ Move the Shadows slider to the right to darken the shadows. The more you move the slider to the right, the more areas will be covered by the blue clipping display. If you move the slider all the way to the left, the clipping overlay should disappear entirely.

The blue overlay shows where tonal values have been forced to a total black with no detail. Shadow clipping is generally not as critical as highlight clipping, simply because it occurs in darker areas and is harder to see. Some minimal shadow clipping is OK, especially if it occurs in areas where you would not expect to see any detail anyway. The main point is to make sure there is no clipping in areas that contain shadow details you care about preserving. If you have doubts about this, it is best to adjust the shadows so that there is no clipping and then make final shadow adjustments in Photoshop.

◆ After you are finished exploring the Shadows slider, set the slider value to 5.

Alternate Clipping Display

You can also display clipping by holding down the Option (Alt) key as you click and hold on the Exposure or the Shadows slider. This feature has been a part of Camera Raw since the first version and it corresponds to how the clipping display is shown in the Levels dialog. For the highlights, the image will turn black, and as you hold the Option (Alt) key down and move the Exposure slider to the right, parts of the image will turn different colors if clipping is occurring only in one or two channels, or they will turn white if detail is being clipped in all three channels. For the shadows, the image will turn white as you hold the Option (Alt) key down and move the Shadows slider to the right. The image will turn different colors if clipping is occurring only in one or two channels, or black if detail is being clipped in all three channels.

We usually prefer this method of seeing clipping, because it shows us whether clipping is happening in all three channels, or only in one or two. With highlight clipping, if the latter is the case, then there is a chance that Camera Raw may be able to use the existing information in the channels that do contain detail in order to "recover" the lost detail in the one or two channels where it is clipped.

◆ If they are currently checked, click the Highlight and Shadow clipping display check boxes at the top of the dialog to turn them off.

◆ Hold down the Option (Alt) key and move the Exposure slider, and then the Shadows slider, to the right to see how this version of the clipping display works.

A good way to approach Camera Raw adjustments is to use this clipping display until you can just start to see clipping in the highlights, and then back it off a bit. Do the same with the shadows: Move the slider until you can just begin to see shadow areas that are clipped, and then move the slider back to the left a bit. Keep in mind that not

The highlight clipping display created by Option (Alt)-clicking the Exposure slider.

The shadow clipping display created by Option (Alt)-clicking the Shadows slider.

After setting the highlight and shadow endpoints, the image looks very dark. This will be fixed once the Brightness is increased.

every image should have a bright highlight, so for some images the actual adjustment you make may result in slightly darker highlights.

◆ Hold down the Option (Alt) key and move the Exposure slider left to –1.00 until the plates are no longer being clipped. You will still see clipping on the brightest metallic reflections, but that's OK for this image.

◆ Hold down the Option (Alt) key and move the Shadows slider right until the value reads 10. Though this does cause some clipping in the deepest shadows, those areas are not important to the image and don't contain detail that we care about.

Now the image is much too dark overall. We'll fix that in the next section, when we discuss the Brightness adjustment.

How to Interpret the Clipping Colors

When you use the Option (Alt) key in conjunction with the Exposure and the Shadows sliders to see the clipping display for the highlights and shadows, you will see a range of colors depending on which channels are being clipped. Here's how to interpret what those colors are telling you:

Highlight Clipping: White shows that there is clipping in all three channels. Red, green, or blue indicate that clipping is occurring only in those channels. Yellow indicates there is clipping in the Red and Green channels. Magenta reveals clipping in the Red and Blue channels. Cyan shows clipping in the Green and the Blue channels.

Shadow Clipping: Black shows clipping in all three channels. The concept of opposite colors is at work when clipping occurs in one or two channels. Cyan shows clipping in the Red channel. Magenta indicates clipping in the Green channel. Yellow reveals clipping in the Blue channel. Blue shows that there is clipping in the Red and Green channels. Red reveals clipping in the Green and Blue channels. Green indicates that shadow values are clipped in the Blue and Red channels.

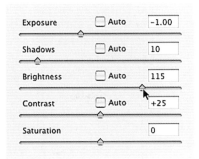

These are the settings we used to adjust the Exposure, Shadows, and Brightness for the Queen Mary Table photo.

Brightness

The Brightness slider adjusts where the midtone of the image is mapped along the tonal scale without affecting either the white or the black point. This is similar to how the Input Midtone slider functions in Levels.

- Move the Brightness slider to the left and right to see how it affects the image. Notice how the histogram changes in response to these moves. Adjust the Brightness slider to the right until you feel the overall brightness for the image looks good (we used a value of 115).

- If you Option (Alt)-click the Exposure slider, you will see that, even though the plates have been significantly brightened, no highlight clipping is occurring there.

Now that we have adjusted the highlights, shadows, and overall brightness, we can move on and use the White Balance controls to address the color cast issues in this image.

White Balance

The human visual system is always compensating for different colored light as we view the world. This is why we don't see fluorescent lighting as an unpleasant green color, or tungsten light as being overly reddish yellow. A digital camera relies on white-balance settings or an auto feature that evaluates the brightest tones in a scene that it thinks should be white and adjusts them so that they are white. The camera's auto white balance for the Queen Mary dinner table image failed because several reflective highlights in the image are already pure white.

Even though you can choose a specific white-balance setting on your camera, or use auto white balance, the nature of a Raw file means that the setting is never permanently applied to the image. It is only noted in a metadata tag that is saved with the file. Camera Raw displays the image using this white-balance setting when you first open it, but you can change the setting if you want to.

White Balance Presets

At the top of the White Balance section of the Adjust tab, you will see that the menu is set to As Shot, which means it is being displayed with the white balance that was used by the camera, either as a chosen setting or from the auto-white-balance feature (in this case, the latter). If you open this menu, you will see a total of nine choices that represent most of the white-balance settings that are commonly found on digital cameras. These settings tell Camera Raw that the image was photographed under those conditions, and the color balance is adjusted accordingly. The Cloudy and Shade settings will both make the image noticeably warmer, because those types of lighting are generally cooler (bluer) in appearence than regular daylight. The Tungsten setting will add blue to the image to compensate for the warm yellow color cast created by tungsten lightbulbs. The Auto setting tells Camera Raw to evaluate the image and apply what it thinks is a good white-balance correction. Essentially, this is the same thing

After adjusting the Exposure, Shadows, and Brightness, this is what the image looks like with White Balance set to As Shot.

The Tungsten White Balance is a big improvement, but it's still not perfect.

Using the Tungsten setting as a starting point, we adjusted the Temperature and Tint sliders to create this result. The tablecloth looks much better here than in the version with the Tungsten setting.

Color Temperature and the Kelvin Scale

The Kelvin scale for measuring color temperture of light may seem counterintuitive if you are not familiar with it. We are used to thinking of "warmer" as being a higher temperature and "cooler" as being a lower temperature. But that refers to the thermal properties of heat.

With the color temperture of light it is the opposite. Lower color temperatures result in a "warmer" color of light that is more red/yellow (typical household lightbulbs are about 2500K). Higher color temperatures cause light to be "cooler" and biased more toward the blue part of the spectrum (open shade on a clear day is closer to 9000K). Light that is neutral, meaning that it imparts no color cast to a scene, is generally identified as Daylight and ranges between 5000 and 5500K.

that happens with a camera's auto-white-balance setting, only it happens after the image has been photographed.

◆ Try out both the Auto and the Tungsten settings to see how they work with this image. Both represent a significant improvement over the original capture, though neither is what we would call perfect. The Auto setting seems to be a bit better than Tungsten, but both are very similar in how they affect the image.

Temperature and Tint Sliders

Below the White Balance Settings menu are the Temperature and Tint sliders, which allow you to brew your own, custom white-balance setting.

The Temperature slider controls the blue-yellow color balance of the image. Moving the slider to the left adds blue and moving it to the right adds yellow. You can also enter a color temperature value in degrees kelvin, and Camera Raw will then apply an appropriate

compensation for it. So if you have a scene that is illuminated by the reddish-yellow light of candles or firelight, for example, you would move the slider to the left, resulting in a lower color temperature reading and the addition of blue to compensate for the reddish-yellow color balance. Of course, it's important to realize that reality is not always neutral and not all color casts are bad. For some images, such as those shot in candlelight, you might want to keep the reddish-yellow color cast.

The Tint slider allows for fine-tuning of the adjustments you make using the Temperature slider. Moving it to the left adds green, and moving it to the right adds magenta. You should always start your custom white-balance adjustments with the Temperature slider or the White Balance tool (more on that shortly) and then use the Tint control for final tweaks.

◆ If you have experimented with these sliders, choose Auto from the White Balance menu.

◆ The image still seems a bit yellow. Change the Temperature value to 2650. This will add a bit of blue to the image, which helps to clean up the whites of the tablecloth.

◆ Change the Tint value to +10 to add a touch of magenta to compensate for the slight greenish cast.

The White Balance Tool

Among the tool icons at the top left of the dialog is a white-balance tool (the eyedropper on the left) that is very useful if your image contains an area that should be neutral. Unlike the eyedropper tools in

Using the White Balance tool to click the shadowed tablecloth to the right of the champagne bottle.

The result produced by the white-balance eyedropper tool.

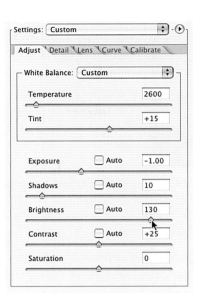

These are the final values that we used for all of the Adjust tab settings.

Levels or Curves, this tool does not change the brightness of the tone you click on, nor can you select a target color; but it does do a very good job of neutralizing the tone you click on, and in the process it adjusts the color balance for the entire image.

The key concept with this tool is that you need to use it on an area that should be neutral. This can include any range of tones from dark shadows up through brighter highlights, but it works best on middle or lighter gray tones.

- Return the White Balance menu to As Shot. Select the white-balance eyedropper tool from the upper-left part of the dialog.

- Click the shadowed part of the tablecloth just to the right of the champagne bottle and under the two forks.

With one click of the white-balance eyedropper, the color cast has been greatly improved. If you look at the Temperture value, it should be close to 2600 (we chose 2650 when we made the manual adjustments to the sliders).

- Try clicking other areas of the tablecloth, napkins, and place settings. You will find that some corrections will be cooler than others.

The white-balance eyedropper is very effective for clearing up color casts when an image has areas that should be neutral. Sometimes, however, a numerically neutral tone may be too cool for your taste. If when using this tool you find the adjustment a bit too blue, simply adjust the Temperature slider to the right to add more yellow, and fine-tune with the Tint slider if needed.

Although the white balance eyedropper did a great job of cleaning up the yellowish color cast, the image still seems a bit too dark. The solution for that is to make another correction to the Brightness slider.

- Adjust the Brightness slider to the right to 130.

Contrast and Saturation

The default Contrast setting is 25. This is a fairly moderate increase in contrast that can help a lot of images, but we usually prefer to apply contrast adjustments using the Curves tab simply because it gives us more control over where on the tonal range the contrast is adjusted and by how much.

- Change the Contrast to 0 to see how it affects the image. It opens the shadows by making them a bit lighter. This softens the overall effect of the image and works well for this scene.

Compared to the subtleties of using a curve, a simple slider leaves much to be desired, but it's fine for quick adjustments. We'll explore contrast tweaks using the Curves tab in the next section.

The Saturation slider increases or decreases color saturation. In many cases, we prefer to apply saturation changes using an adjustment layer in Photoshop, since it provides a bit more flexibility as well as control over specific colors, but if the saturation changes are minor, there is nothing wrong with making them here in Camera Raw.

- Move the Saturation slider to the right and left to experiment with how the saturation changes affect the image. Moving the slider all the way to the left will totally desaturate the colors and

Moving the Saturation slider all the way to the left removes all color from the image and creates a gray-scale version.

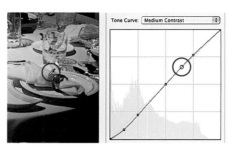

Holding the Command (Ctrl) key down as you move the mouse over the image will show a circle on the curve to indicate where that image tone can be found on the curve.

give you a grayscale interpretation of the file. This can be a good way to get a quick preview of how the image might look in black and white (though, depending on the image, it may not be the best way to create a grayscale version).

◆ Move the Saturation slider to +15 to slightly boost the color saturation in the photo. This will be most noticeable in the flowers, the picture of the ship, and some of the wood tones.

Curves

After we have made overall adjustments to the color and tonal balance of a file using the controls in the Adjust tab, our next stop is usually the Curves tab to apply additional fine-tuning to the tonal map for the image.

◆ Click the Curves tab.

The default setting will apply a Medium Contrast curve to the file. From the drop-down Tone Curve menu, you can also choose Strong Contrast, Linear, or Custom. Any time you manually adjust the curve, the menu will show Custom. If you are interested in creating custom curves, it is often helpful to start out with a Linear curve that has no points on it.

◆ In the Tone Curve menu, choose Linear. This sets the curve to a diagonal line and represents no adjustment at all.

◆ Hold down the Command (Ctrl) key and move your cursor over the image. This will display a small circle on the curve that shows where the image tone you are sampling can be found on the curve. Command (Ctrl)-clicking the image will set a control point on the curve at that location.

The preceding steps are similar to how you locate image tones in Photoshop's Curves dialog. The only difference is that in Photoshop you only have to hold down the mouse button to show the tone indicator circle on the curve. There are other similarities to the Photoshop Curves dialog as well. You can remove a point from the curve in several

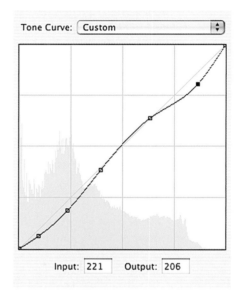

This curve slightly darkens the highlights on the front part of the table so there is a more even transition to the tones at the back of the table.

The table image before the custom curve shown above. The front part of the table is much brighter than the back part.

The table image after the custom curve designed to even out the highlight tones between the front and back parts of the table.

ways: click it and drag it out of the curve grid, Command (Ctrl)-click it, or click to select it and then press the Delete key. Control-tab will select the next point on the curve and Control-Shift-tab will select the previous point. You can also select multiple points by Shift-clicking them. If dragging the control points seems too cumbersome, you can use the arrow keys to move them by one level, or add Shift to the arrow keys to move them in increments of 10 levels.

◆ When you have finished experimenting with the Curves tab, click the Done button in the lower-right corner of the dialog. This will close the file and apply the settings that you have made. In Bridge the thumbnail and the preview will update to reflect the changes.

The Detail Tab

The Detail tab contains only three settings, and as the name of the tab suggests, these affect an image's details. You can apply overall sharpening, as well as noise reduction. To properly evaluate these features, we need to open different images.

Sharpening

We'll start by taking a look at the Sharpening control. We'll stay on the good ship Queen Mary to do this, but we'll step outside the dining cabin and take a look at the top deck of the ship.

◆ In Bridge, navigate to the Ch09 folder on the DVD, and double-click the file Queen Mary.CRW. Click the Detail tab.

◆ To really see how the sharpening is affecting the image, zoom in to 100%. You can do this by double-clicking the Zoom tool in Camera Raw, using the Zoom Level menu in the lower-left corner, or pressing Command-Option (Ctrl-Alt)-0.

In the default setup for Camera Raw, the Sharpness is set to 25. Sharpening at this point in the image editing workflow should be used to restore some of the sharpness that was lost when the scene was converted into an image made of pixels. Output sharpening is applied in Photoshop toward the end of the process and is meant to sharpen the image for the intended type of output.

On the left, a 100% view showing the effects of no sharpening (0). On the right, a 100% view showing the effects of a sharpening setting of 25 (the default).

◆ Press the Spacebar to get the Hand tool, and click and drag to show an area of the image that has good detail in order to evaluate the sharpening effect. The lifeboat davits and guy-wires near the closest funnel is a good area.

◆ Lower the Sharpening to 0 to start off with no sharpening. Raise it back up to 25 and see how the sharpening affects the contrast edges in the image.

Although the default setting of 25 is a fairly low level of sharpening, we like to have more control over the sharpening process, and that means handling it later in Photoshop. In the Camera Raw preferences you can specify that the sharpening be applied only to the preview image that appears in Bridge. That way the previews will look good, but you can still have control over the sharpening process.

◆ From the fly-out menu to the right of the Settings, choose Preferences. You can also access this by pressing Command (Ctrl)-K. In the Camera Raw Preferences, open the menu for Apply Sharpening To, and set it to Preview images only. In the Detail tab it will be noted that the sharpening will be applied only to the preview image.

Keep in mind that Camera Raw never changes the original Raw file, so the sharpening is applied only to the processed copy of the file that is opened into Photoshop, or saved as another file format. If you ever need to quickly prepare images for client approval, you can always use a sharpening setting that works well for the size of images you need to present. An even more flexible way to handle this (though it requires an extra step) is to create an action that applies sharpening to the converted presentation images. Actions and other aspects of automation are covered in Chapter 10, "Automating Photoshop."

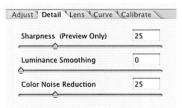

The Detail tab. In the Camera Raw preferences, we have set the sharpening to apply only to the preview images, not to the actual file that is converted and opened into Photoshop.

In the Camera Raw preferences, there is a setting for applying sharpening only to the preview images.

◆ Click the Cancel button to close this file without applying any changes.

Noise Reduction

There are two controls for reducing noise in Raw files, Luminance Smoothing and Color Noise Reduction. Each one addresses a different aspect of digital noise. Luminance noise is the grayscale speckled pattern that looks similar to film grain (though if you appreciate grain, noise is unfortunately not nearly as attractive as film grain). Color noise shows up as colored speckles. To properly evaluate how these controls work, we need to open a file with significant levels of noise.

◆ In Bridge, find the Chapter 9 folder on the DVD and double-click the file HatStand_ISO1600.CRW.

Before we can evaluate the noise levels or how successful the noise reduction controls are, we need to clean up the strong yellow color cast and lighten the image a bit.

◆ Brighten the image by moving the Exposure slider to the right until the value for that setting is at +0.75. Move the Brightness slider to the right until its value is set at 95.

◆ To correct the yellow color cast, open the White Balance menu and select Tungsten.

◆ Click the Detail tab and then double-click the Zoom tool to display the image at 100%. Press the Spacebar to get the Hand tool, and drag the image until you can see a section of the straw hat and the wooden hatstand and wall to the right of it.

Luminance Smoothing

Of the two types of noise that Camera Raw addresses, luminance noise is the hardest one to deal with. This is because the speckled pattern of the noise is more a part of the visible pixel structure of the image, and therefore it is harder to smooth this noise pattern without also softening fine image details that you want to remain sharp.

◆ Click the numeric value field for Luminance Smoothing. Press Shift and the up arrow key on the keyboard. This raises the value in increments of 10 (Shift-down arrow lowers the setting in increments of 10). Press Shift-up arrow again to raise it to 20. Continue this until you reach 40.

◆ Turn the Preview check box off and on to compare it with the unsmoothed version (the preview will only show you the before and after of the changes you have made in the currently active tab).

Although the hard edges of the speckled noise pattern are being smoothed by this adjustment, there is also an overall slight softening of all image details (notice the weave on the straw hat). The other thing to be cautious about is that when Luminance Smoothing is applied at really high settings, image detail suffers.

◆ Set the Luminance Smoothing to 100 to see how image detail is affected by such a high setting. Return the setting to 40 when you are done.

Color Noise Reduction

The Color Noise Reduction feature is much more successful than Luminanace Smoothing simply because it is only dealing with the colored mottling and not trying to smooth the underlying structure of the noise pattern. The default setting is 25, which works quite well on many images—So well, in fact, that you will need to lower it to 0 to actually see the color noise in this image.

A 1600 ISO image with the Luminance Smoothing value set to 0.

With the Luminance Smoothing value set to 40, there is a noticeable softening of the noise pattern.

When the Luminance Smoothing value set to 100, fine details in the image, such as the weave on the straw hat, become overly soft and lose edge definition.

Color Noise Reduction set to 0: A mottled pattern of colored noise is visible in the image.

◆ Set Color Noise Reduction to 0 so that the color mottling becomes visible, then raise it to 25 again. As you can see, this feature does an excellent job of removing the noisy colored speckles from the image.

Generally, for images shot with plenty of light at low ISOs, we leave the Color Noise Reduction set to 0 or to a very low amount, such as 2. We typically do not use higher amounts unless we have an image with obvious noise problems, such as the example photograph of the hatstand. You'll notice that when Color Noise Reduction is used, even at 25, it reduces the saturation of colors in the image and can also affect subtle colors in the three-quarter tone and dark shadow areas. For example, if you have an image of leaves that contains highly saturated areas that do not reflect actual detail in the original image, that would be an example where Color Noise Reduction would be effective. You can also process one version of the image with Color Noise Reduction and another version without, put the two as layers on top of each other, then just paint in the Color Noise Reduction in the areas where you really need it. See Chapter 27, "Compositing Bracketed Photos," for the details of how to composite two versions of an image together and then get the best of each image.

◆ Click Cancel to close the hatstand file without making any changes.

The Lens Tab

The controls in the Lens tab address two problems that originate in the lens of a digital camera: chromatic aberration and vignetting.

◆ From Bridge, open the file Nevada Time.CRW from the DVD. Click the Lens tab. This image of Hoover Dam was photographed at 28mm with a 28 to 135mm zoom lens.

Color Noise Reduction set to the default value of 25: The colored noise is removed.

Chromatic Aberration

Some wide-angle lenses, especially wide-angle zooms, do not evenly focus the red, green, and blue wavelengths of light. This can result in color fringes—typically red and cyan, but also blue and yellow—that are visible along high-contrast edges. The problem usually becomes more pronounced toward the edges of the image.

The Chromatic Aberration R/C slider adjusts the size of the Red channel relative to the Green channel. The Chromatic Aberration B/Y slider adjusts the size of the Blue channel relative to the Green channel. If you hold the Option (Alt) key down while moving the slider, the other Chromatic Aberration problem channel will be turned off so you can view and solve one problem at a time. For example, if you are working with the R/C slider, holding the Option (Alt) key down will turn off the visibility of the B/Y problem, making it easier to see when you've fixed the R/C one. These Chromatic Aberration corrections happen to a greater extent as you move away from the center of the image, where no correction is needed.

Chromatic Aberration is typically not visible in an image until you zoom in to at least 100%. The areas we will be looking at in this photo are highlighted in red.

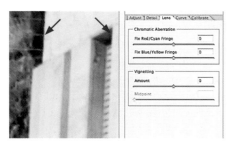

Chromatic Aberration is visible as a slight red fringe on the left side of the image.

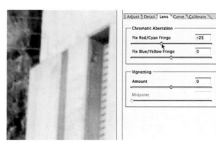

The red fringe is removed by adjusting the Red/Cyan Fringe slider.

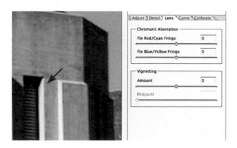

The top-right edge of the intake tower in the background shows both red and cyan fringes.

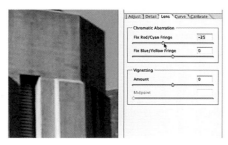

The adjustment to the Red/Cyan Fringe slider corrects the chromatic aberration.

◆ Click the Zoom tool, and click and drag a zoom marquee around the top-right corner of the intake tower in the background. In the Zoom menu in the lower-left part of the dialog, make sure the zoom is set to 200%. You will see some red fringing on high-contrast edges there and also a cyan fringe on the the edge of the tower.

◆ Double-click the Hand tool to fit the image onscreen, then hold down the Command (Ctrl) key and click and drag a zoom marquee around the top-left corner of the foreground tower on the left. Use the Zoom menu to set the view to 200%. You will see a very noticeable red fringe there.

◆ Move the R/C slider all the way to either side; it will give you an idea of how it shifts the size of the channels to try and remove the fringing. Reset the value to 0 before continuing.

◆ Place your cursor in the numeric field for the R/C controls. Hold the Shift key and press the down arrow key. This changes the value in increments of 10 points in the negative direction. Press Shift-down arrow again, and you will see the red fringe start to shrink. Press Shift-down arrow one more time to bring the setting to −25. This removes the red fringing very effectively.

◆ Double-click the Hand tool to show the entire image in the preview window, and Command (Ctrl)-click and drag a zoom marquee around the top-right corner of the background tower to check how this setting affects that side. Once you are zoomed in, you can turn the Preview check box off and on to compare the correction with the original file.

Vignetting

Vignetting refers to the slightly darkened corners in an image that result from a lens that does not evenly distribute light across the entire image sensor. It is usually more apparent on wide-angle lenses, with cheaper lenses more likely to show this effect.

Positive vignetting values will correct for this by lightening the corners, while negative values will darken the corners. Once you change the vignetting amount, the Midpoint control becomes active and lets you control how far out from the center of the image the correction starts to take effect. The higher the number, the closer it is to the corners before the adjustment starts to happen. Lower numbers will begin to apply the effect closer to the center of the image.

The Calibrate Tab

The Calibrate tab is designed to let you customize the built-in camera profiles that ship with Camera Raw. There are a few reasons you might want to do this. One would be to compensate for any variations between your individual camera and the one that was used to create the built-in profiles that represent that model of camera (for instance, even though Camera Raw has a profile for a Canon 5D, the 5D that you own wasn't used to make that profile). Another reason to tweak the built-in profile would be if you were always making the same adjustments for shots taken under a specific type of lighting—say, open shade. By fine-tuning with the Calibrate controls, you could save a setting that was customizeded for exposures made by your specific camera under open-shade lighting conditions.

Calibration Overview

To calibrate your camera to a certain shooting situation, photograph a GretagMacbeth ColorChecker chart, or similar calibrated target, using your camera's Raw format. The chart should be evenly illuminated and lit by the light source that you'd like to calibrate to (such as open shade, studio lighting conditions, and so on). You can purchase a ColorChecker chart at most professional camera stores for about $75.

Open the Raw photograph of the ColorChecker chart into Camera Raw, and choose Camera Raw Defaults from the Settings menu. That will display the ColorChecker image on your calibrated monitor using the standard profile that Camera Raw uses for your camera model. Place the actual ColorChecker chart in a 5000K viewing box or under 5000K lights. If the image on the screen does not match the ColorChecker chart, first make changes to the overall brightness and contrast using the controls in the Adjust tab and then fine-tune the colors in the Calibrate tab to try and create a better match.

When you are done, open the fly-out menu to the right of the Settings menu and choose Save Settings Subset. In the Save Settings Subset dialog, open the menu and select Calibration so that it is the only check box selected, and click Save. In order to have it available as a menu choice in Camera Raw (and also in Bridge's Apply Camera Raw Settings menu), you need to save it to the Camera Raw Settings

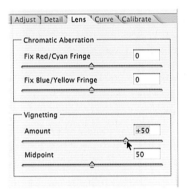

Positive amount values will lighten the corners of an image, correcting for darkened corners due to uneven lens illumination.

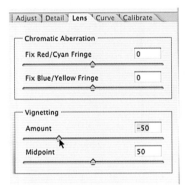

Negative amount values will darken the corners of an image.

Positive midpoint values will apply the effect closer to the corner, while negative midpoint values will apply it closer to the center of the image.

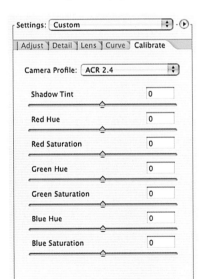

The Calibrate tab.

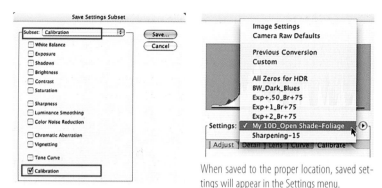

The Save Settings Subset dialog showing that only the Calibrate settings will be saved.

When saved to the proper location, saved settings will appear in the Settings menu.

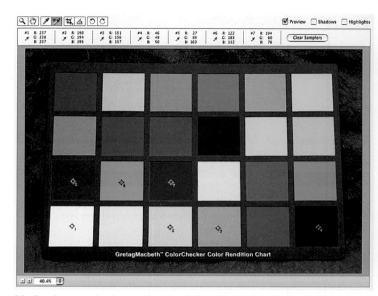

Color Sampler points placed on specific paths of a GretagMacbeth ColorChecker chart. The info readouts for the point samples appear above the preview image.

folder. On a Mac you can find that at User/Library/Application Support/Adobe/Camera Raw/Settings. On Windows you'll find it at: Documents and Settings\User\Application Data\Adobe\Camera Raw\Settings. For a detailed description of creating a custom calibration setting for a camera, see Bruce Fraser's *Real World Camera Raw with Adobe Photoshop CS2* (Peachpit Press, 2005).

Placing Color Sampler Points

To get a sense of how the Calibrate controls work, the best way is to open up a file and see how actual colors in an image are affected. To make it easier to see the differences, and also to demonstrate some Camera Raw functionality that we have not covered yet, we'll use a file of a GretagMacbeth ColorChecker chart.

◆ From Bridge, navigate to the Chapter 9 folder on the DVD and open the file ColorChecker.CRW.

◆ Make sure the Settings menu is set to Camera Raw Defaults and the Auto adjustments are not checked, and click the Calibrate tab.

Although you can see differences in the color patches just from visual observation alone, sometimes it's useful to see the changes in the actual numeric values that represent a given color. To do this, we can place up to nine Color Sampler points in our image so that we can easily track the changes to the color swatches as we adjust the Calibrate controls.

◆ In the row of tools in the top left of the dialog, click the Color Sampler tool (the eyedropper on the right).

◆ Click the white patch in the lower left of the ColorChecker to place a point sample. Skip the second patch in the bottom row and repeat the process to place a point sample on the two middle neutral swatches. Skip the fifth patch from the left and place a

point sample on the black patch. Finally, place a point sample on the red, green, and blue patches. This will let us see how the changes we make are affecting the main colors as well as the neutrals.

The info readouts for the Color Sampler points are arranged above the preview image. If you need to move a point sample, simply click and drag it to a different position. If you want to delete a point sample, hold down Option (Alt) and click it. To remove all of the point samples, click the Clear button next to the Sampler info readouts.

The Calibrate Controls

The easiest way to see what the sliders do is to make large movements in either direction. There is no real step-by-step in this section, just an invitation to explore the controls and pay attention to the image and the numbers in the info readouts. We'll explain how each control affects the image. Before you move on to the next slider, be sure to reset the previous slider to the midpoint (0).

Shadow Tint

The Shadow Tint slider affects the green-magenta balance in the shadow tones. Moving the slider to the left (negative values) adds green, and moving it right (positive values) adds magenta. If you wanted to make sure that the dark shadows in an image were neutral, you could place a point sample there. For this test image, you can refer to the values for the darkest neutral patch on the right.

Red Hue and Red Saturation

Red Hue changes the character of the reds by adding green and subtracting blue (positive values), which makes the reds more orange; or by adding blue and subtracting green (negative values), which makes them more magenta. Red Saturation decreases (negative values) or increases (positive values) the saturation of red.

Green Hue and Green Saturation

Green Hue changes the character of the greens by adding blue and subtracting red (positive values), which makes the greens more cyan; or by adding red and subtracting blue (negative values), which makes them closer to a yellow-green. Green Saturation decreases (negative values) or increases (positive values) the saturation of the greens.

Blue Hue and Blue Saturation

Blue Hue changes the character of the blues by adding red and subtracting green (positive values), which makes the blues more purple; or by adding green and subtracting red (negative values), which shifts the blues closer to cyan. Blue Saturation decreases (negative values) or increases (positive values) the saturation of the blues.

Parallels to the Hue/Saturation Dialog

One thing to notice is that the behavior of the Hue sliders in the Calibrate tab is essentially the same as the Hue slider for the same colors in Photoshop's Hue/Saturation dialog. The primary difference is that with the Hue/Saturation command you can shift the colors much farther in either direction. The Saturation slider functions quite similarly, but it does not allow for the total desaturation or saturation of colors that is possible in the Hue/Saturation dialog.

You should also take a look at the info readout for the red, green, and blue patches as you move their Hue sliders in the Calibrate tab. The value for the color you are adjusting actually remains more or less constant; it's the other two colors that are changing and thus influencing the hue of the color you're modifying. This is also how hue modifications work in the Hue/Saturation dialog. If you open the ColorChecker image into Photoshop; place Color Sampler points on the red, green, and blue patches; and then go to the Hue/Saturation dialog (Command (Ctrl)-U) and choose Reds, Greens, and Blues from the Edit menu at the top of the dialog, you will see the same behavior in regard to the info values for the color being adjusted.

The Calibrate Controls for Color Correction

After you learn how the Calibrate controls really work, it might seem logical that you can use them for actual color correction work on your Raw images. While this is certainly possible for minor tweaks, it is not ideal when you need to make more significant changes. Keep in mind that corrections you apply in Camera Raw are global, meaning they affect the entire image. The goal when working is to get the overall image looking as good as possible. If you have specific regions or colors that need more targeted corrections, you should bring the image into Photoshop where you can use adjustment layers with layer masks to apply the corrections only to the areas of the image that really need them.

Crop and Straighten

You can apply flexible crops in Camera Raw and straighten images where the horizontal or vertical lines are a bit off. Since the original Raw file is never altered (all modifications are written into the XMP metadata for the file), any cropping or straightening that you do here can always be changed or undone, even after the file has been processed. In this section we'll cover how to use these tools. Although this is not a step-by-step section, the images featured here are included in the Chapter 9 folder on the DVD.

The Crop Tool

By clicking the Crop tool in the Camera Raw toolbar, you can access a menu that offers several standard aspect ratios. Choosing one of these will restrict the cropping box to those proportions. For example if you want a square crop, choose 1x1, and if you want a crop that will yield an 8x10 proportion, choose 4x5. If you choose the Custom option, you can enter in a custom aspect ratio, or even a specific size in pixels, inches, or centimeters. Of course, you can also just select Normal and draw your cropping box exactly how you want it.

Click and drag across the image to define the cropping box. Drag the square handles to resize it or change its proportions (if you have chosen an aspect ratio from the Crop menu, you have to select Normal from the menu before you can change the proportions). The areas that will be cropped off are covered with a semi-opaque gray overlay. To cancel the crop, even after the file has been processed, simply choose Clear Crop from the Crop menu. When you click Open, the crop is applied to the version of the image that opens in Photoshop. The thumbnail and preview that are displayed in Bridge also show the cropped version of the file.

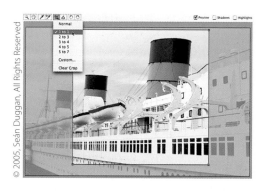

The Crop menu offers a selection of common aspect ratios, as well as a feature where you can specify a custom aspect ratio. To get rid of a crop, use the Clear Crop option at the bottom of the menu. This illustration shows a cropping box that uses a square, 1 to 1 aspect ratio.

Use the Straighten tool to trace along a line that should be horizontal (in this case, the horizon) or vertical, but that isn't.

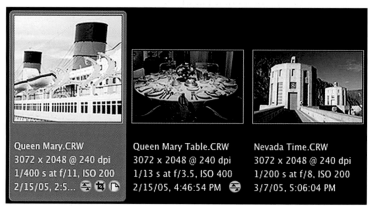

Queen Mary.CRW
3072 x 2048 @ 240 dpi
1/400 s at f/11, ISO 200
2/15/05, 2:5...

Queen Mary Table.CRW
3072 x 2048 @ 240 dpi
1/13 s at f/3.5, ISO 400
2/15/05, 4:46:54 PM

Nevada Time.CRW
3072 x 2048 @ 240 dpi
1/200 s at f/8, ISO 200
3/7/05, 5:06:04 PM

When a crop has been applied to a Raw file, the thumbnail and preview in Bridge are updated to reflect the crop. A crop symbol in the lower-right corner of the thumbnail indicates that a crop has been applied to the image. The icon showing the sliders means that the image has been adjusted in Camera Raw, and the document page icon means that the image is currently open in Photoshop.

After using the Straighten tool, an angled crop box will appear over the image. The actual straightening effect is not applied until you open the image into Photoshop or click the Done button. The thumbnail and preview image in Bridge will be updated to reflect the correction.

The straightened image.

The Straighten Tool

To straighten an image that is slightly askew, select the Straighten tool. Find a line that should be horizontal or vertical. Click on one side of this line and drag across the image, following the line with the dotted line created by the tool. When you let go of the mouse button, a cropping box will appear at an angle over the image. The straightening correction will be applied when you click either the Open or the Done button, and the processed image will then reflect the correction.

Workflow Options

At the bottom of the dialog are the Workflow Options for setting the working space, color depth, size, and resolution. We mentioned these briefly in the first part of the chapter, but now we'll go into them in more detail.

Working Space Considerations

A Raw file created by your camera is unprocessed and is really just a recipe for making an image. As such, it does not have any working space characteristics associated with it until you make that choice during the Raw conversion process. Some digital SLRs do allow you to choose Adobe RGB (1998) as a color space, but that applies only to JPEG files and not to Raw captures.

There are four color space choices in this menu: Adobe RGB (1998), ColorMatch RGB, ProPhoto RGB, and sRGB IEC61966-1. The workflow we describe in this book involves creating a master image file where the majortiy of the editing and enhancements take place. Any derviative files that will be used for specific purposes (such as fine art prints, publications, Web site use) are generated from this master file. In terms of the working space we use for our master file, our aim is to preserve as much of the file's color information as possible. This means choosing a working space with a large color gamut.

The Workflow Options.

In light of this approach, only two working spaces in this menu make any sense: Adobe RGB (1998) and ProPhoto RGB.

Adobe RGB (1998)

Adobe RGB (1998) has long been our standard working space. It has a larger color gamut than either sRGB or ColorMatch RGB, making it a good choice to use as a working space for your master files. If you are relatively new to Photoshop, or if you are primarily processing your Raw images into 8-bit files (more on bit depth in the next section), then we recommend this working space.

In the past, it was always a clear choice to use Adobe RGB. Recent technical developments in the landscape of both high-end digital SLRs and inkjet printers, however, have made an alternate choice very viable as a working space.

ProPhoto RGB

ProPhoto RGB is a very wide gamut working space, much larger than Adobe RGB. It was originally specified by Eastman Kodak as a way to describe all of the rich, saturated colors that certain Ektachrome transparency films were capable of producing. In the past it was not recommended as a working space for most uses (other than high-end scans of Ektachrome transparencies) because it was deemed far larger than the majority of capture or output devices could match. But as we mentioned earlier, the digital imaging landscape is evolving, and there are now reasons that make ProPhoto RGB worthy of consideration as a working space for some photographers.

The primary issue at play here concerns color gamuts and clipping. Certain digital SLRs and the newer Epson Ultrachrome K3 inks have color gamuts that are larger in some areas than what can be contained by Adobe RGB (see the gamut mapping illustrations below). This means that if you process a Raw file from one of these cameras and you convert it using the Adobe RGB working space, you are irretrievably clipping some of the colors in your master working file. Of course, you can always go back to the original Raw file and process it again using ProPhoto RGB, but if you have done significant work to the master file in terms of adjustment layers, layer masking, or compositing, then you will have to redo much of that work.

If you have an Epson printer that uses the K3 inks (and, presumably, newer ink sets that have not been released yet), those printers are capable of producing colors that fall outside of the Adobe RGB gamut. By converting your Raw file using Adobe RGB, you are closing the door on the ability to take advantage of your printer's larger color gamut.

The four color-space options in Camera Raw.

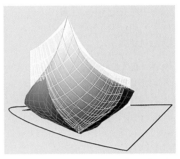

The color gamut of a Canon 5D (ghosted wireframe) compared to Adobe RGB (colored wireframe). The camera has a much larger gamut.

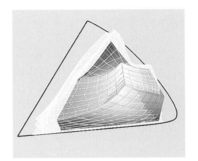

The color gamut of Adobe RGB (ghosted wireframe) compared to an Epson R2400 using premium luster paper (colored wireframe). Some of the colors this printer can print will be clipped by Adobe RGB.

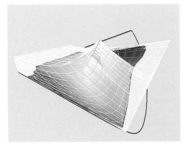

The color gamut of ProPhoto RGB (ghosted wireframe) compared to a Canon 5D (colored wireframe). The ProPhoto color space contains nearly all of the colors that a 5D can capture.

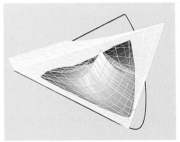

The color gamut of ProPhoto RGB (ghosted wireframe) compared to an Epson R2400 using premium luster paper (colored wireframe). The ProPhoto color space contains all of the colors that this printer can reproduce.

When to Use ProPhoto RGB

Due to the expansive size of its color gamut, ProPhoto RGB is well suited for digital camera Raw files, where you want to preserve as much of the color information from the original capture as possible. In this regard it is ideal as an "archival" working space so that your images can take advantage of the much larger printer gamuts that will very likely be possible in the not-too-distant future. But it is not for every situation, and there are some things to be aware of when using it.

First, as already stated, it's best suited for Raw files or for scans that have been captured at a high bit depth. Due to the very large gamut, there is not much point in using it with 8-bit files; you should think of it as a working space to use with 16-bit files. Second, since the color gamut is so much larger than anything that can be displayed on a monitor, you should familiarize yourself with using Photoshop's soft-proofing capabilities and different rendering intents to preview how the image will look when printed.

Depth

Apart from the tremendous flexibility you have in how the image can be interpreted, or in salvaging exposure errors, one of the primary reasons to shoot in Raw is to have access to the high-bit data that your camera's image sensor can generate. With this in mind, it probably comes as no surpirse that we recommend processing Raw captures as 16-bit files. An 8-bit file has only 256 tonal levels per color channel, but a Raw file converted as 16-bit into Photoshop has thousands of levels. All of those extra levels give you much more tonal flexibility when making edits to the file, especially if significant tonal editing is required. While it is true that 16-bit files are twice as large as 8-bit files, the advantages that a 16-bit file provides are well worth the extra storage space they require.

Size

The Size menu allows you to process the file at the size of the camera's image sensor (the dimension without a plus or minus symbol) or at several smaller or larger sizes. If you know that you will be using the file for making larger prints, you'll get better results resizing it with Camera Raw than using Image Size in Photoshop to do a one-shot resizing. Barry has compared the two methods and found that the version resized in Camera Raw had fewer sharpening artifacts later in the process. Another approach would be to bump up the resolution in 10% increments using Photoshop's Image Size dialog. The 10% increment approach does appear to work a bit better on some digital images. If you do an Image Size of 110% seven times,

The Size menu in Camera Raw.

that results in a file that is very close to double the original size. In the ArtistKeys action set there is an action called ResUpby10—[Command (Ctrl)-Shift-F1]—which does exactly that and gives you a file that is 5987 pixels wide instead of 6144 when starting with a 3072-pixel-wide image. Barry has tried this and believes it produces a resizing that is a bit cleaner than doing it in Camera Raw.

The "acid test" for your own standards, of course, would be to resize the same image using each method (Camera Raw, one-step Image Size using Bicubic Smoother, and the ResUpby10 action), sharpen, and make test strips of each file on the paper you like to print on. Make a note of each method on the back of the test strips, then turn them over, mix them up, and see which one looks best to you.

Resolution

The Resolution setting does nothing to the file size or the number of pixels in the file. All it does is set the number of pixels per inch that will be used when the file is printed. In this sense it is no more than a convenience setting. You can always change this later using Image/Image Size in Photoshop, but if you always print at the same resolution, then you might as well set it here.

Adjusting Multiple Files

In Bridge you can select several Raw files at once by clicking one and then Shift-clicking another at the end of a series (or Command (Ctrl)-click files that are not contiguous to each other). From the Bridge File menu, choose Open With if you want to process the files into Photoshop, or Open in Camera Raw if you just want to apply edits to the Raw files without opening them into Photoshop. You can also right-click (Control-click on a Mac one-button mouse) to access these same choices.

In Camera Raw

In Camera Raw, the multiple files will show up as thumbnails along the left side. You can click back and forth between them to compare the images, apply adjustments individually, or even batch process them. This technique makes sense if you have several files that all share the same exposure and look like they might benefit from the same adjustments in Camera Raw.

To apply the same corrections to several files, make your adjustments to one file, then click the Select All button above the thumbnails (if you don't need to select all the files, instead of using the Select All button, simply Command (Ctrl)-click the ones you do want to select). When the thumbnails are highlighted, click the Synchronize button, and the settings from the first file you adjusted will be applied to all of the files.

In Bridge

You can also apply Camera Raw settings to many files at once in Bridge. To do this, chose a file that is representative of the group you want to adjust. Open this file in Camera Raw, make your adjustments, and click the Done button. In Bridge, select the other files that can use the same adjustment, right-click them, and from the contextual menu choose Previous Conversion.

Another way to do this, especially if you need to apply settings that are not from the previous conversion, is to right-click the thumbnail of the file that has the settings you want, and from the menu choose

Copy Camera Raw Settings. Then select the other thumbnails, right-click them, and choose Paste Camera Raw Settings. In addition to right-clicking or Control-clicking with a one-button mouse, all of these choices for applying settings are also available in Bridge's Edit/Apply Camera Raw Settings menu. You can find more information on the integration between Bridge and Camera Raw in Chapter 11, "Image Processing with Bridge."

The Camera Raw Save Options

When you have several images open in Camera Raw, you can click the Save button and perform the Raw conversion in a way that will bypass Photoshop completely and save the files in one of four file formats. This can be quite useful, for example, when preparing quick proofs for a client—you can spin off a copy directly from Camera Raw.

The Save Options dialog lets you specify a destination folder for the saved files, choose a naming scheme, and select from the following file formats: Digital Negative (DNG), JPEG, TIFF, and Photoshop (PSD).

Select several thumbnails in Bridge, Control-click on a one-button mouse (right-click) and choose Open in Camera Raw to open all the files.

Four files open at the same time into Camera Raw. The first file has been adjusted and the Select All button has been clicked. By clicking the Synchronize button, the adjustments that were applied to the first image (highlighted above in blue) will be applied to all of the selected files.

Applying the Previous Conversion to two selected files in Bridge.

Copying the Camera Raw settings from a selected file in Bridge.

Pasting the copied Camera Raw settings onto two other files.

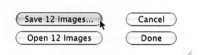

When you have multiple files open in Camera Raw, the Save and Open buttons indicate how many files will be processed.

When you return to Camera Raw after clicking the Save button in the Save Options dialog, a save status indicator appears just above the Save and Open buttons.

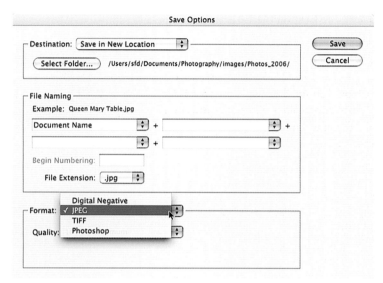

This Camera Raw Save Options dialog.

Saving Files and Processing New Images

The save feature in Camera Raw is very versatile, allowing you to process and save multiple files and work on other Raw images at the same time.

When Camera Raw Is Hosted by Bridge

There are some differences in the functionality of Camera Raw depending on how you have initiated the Camera Raw session. You will have the most flexibility if you have accessed Camera Raw through Bridge, either by double-clicking a Raw file (if the Bridge preferences are set to have Bridge "host" Camera Raw), or by using File/ Open in the Camera Raw menu in Bridge. When you click Save in the Save Options dialog, Camera Raw will begin to process and save the files in the background. You will see a progress message just above the save buttons in the lower-right corner of the dialog. If you still have images in the filmstrip queue in the Camera Raw dialog, you can do more work on them if you like. Or you can close the Camera Raw dialog and return to Bridge for sorting, ranking, adding keywords, or even starting a new Camera Raw session. In any new Camera Raw sessions you start, you will see the save status progress displayed above the save buttons. You can even choose to open a new

Raw file into Photoshop, or work on other images in Photoshop while the save continues in the background.

When Camera Raw Is Hosted by Photoshop

If you have opened Camera Raw through a Photoshop command (such as by choosing Open in Photoshop CS2 from the Bridge File menu), clicking Save in the Save Options dialog will return you to the main Camera Raw dialog. You can choose to do additional work here, just as you could when the session was launched from Bridge, but if you close the Camera Raw dialog, you won't be able to do anything in Photoshop until the saving process has finished. You can return to Bridge, as well as work on Raw files that are hosted from Bridge, but Photoshop will be unavailable while the save is still in progress. You will see a Save Status dialog that lists how many files remain to be saved.

DNG: Digital Negative

One of the format choices in the Save Options dialog is Digital Negative, or DNG. This warrants some further discussion simply because it is a Raw format that has some special properties that will interest digital photographers.

Future Accessibility to Raw Files

One concern about the proprietary Raw formats created by camera vendors is that they are not openly documented. In order for Camera Raw to decode your Raw files, Adobe has to get ahold of a camera, create some test images, and reverse engineer the files. The concern among some photographers is that the undocumented nature of Raw files does not bode well for being able to access those files 10, 15, or 25 years in the future. If the camera vendor is still around, there is a good chance they will still support their files from a decade or more in the past, but is there any guarantee that they will do so,

If Camera Raw is hosted by Photoshop, closing out of Camera Raw will show you a status message showing how many files still need to be processed. At this point you cannot do anything else in Photoshop until the file saving is done.

or even that they will still be in business? If that seems far-fetched, just consider that shortly before this chapter was written, two long-established camera vendors, Konica-Minolta and Mamiya, decided to throw in the towel, quitting the camera business entirely. How much longer will the Raw files from cameras made by those two companies be supported?

DNG: A "Future-Proof" Raw Format

Adobe created the DNG format specifically to deal with these concerns about the future accessibility of Raw files. It is openly documented, and the file documentation required to program a DNG converter can be obtained by anyone for free. Apart from its other benefits, DNG is worth considering for this reason alone. Although no one can tell for certain what the future will hold, the fact that the format is openly documented means that it's arguably more future-proof than the undocumented formats created by camera vendors.

Advantages of DNG

The fact that a DNG Raw file is more likely to be accessible for many years into the future is its primary advantage, but there are others.

No XMP File Required for Metadata

Unlike regular Raw files, DNG files do not require a separate XMP file to hold the metadata and Camera Raw adjustment instructions. All of that can be contained within the DNG file, without ever permanently altering the actual Raw data. In addition, keywords and other metadata can be written back into a DNG file after it has been created, even from other applications, such as asset management programs like iView Media Pro.

Ability to Embed the Original Raw File and Previews

The DNG format is a Raw file. The Raw data from the camera's image sensor is saved when you convert to DNG. But if you are leery of totally getting rid of your original camera-vendor Raw format (such as, the NEF format for Nikon or the CR2 format for Canon), you can choose to embed a copy of the original camera-vendor Raw file in the converted DNG, which can be extracted later. The only reason to do this would be if at some point in the future you wanted access to vendor-specific metadata tags or functionality that the vendor's Raw conversion software offered. This does increase the file size, of course, but the option is there.

You can also choose to embed a full-sized JPEG preview that you can use to quickly generate proofs, to create Web site images, or to display your adjusted Raw file accurately in a photo-cataloging program. Those programs do not understand the XMP files generated by Camera Raw, so any adjustments you make in Camera Raw are not reflected when the programs create thumbnails and preview images.

The DNG Converter

Although you can use the Save dialog in Camera Raw to convert files to the DNG format, for batch processing it is much more convenient to use the free DNG Converter that can be downloaded from the Adobe Web site. This will convert a folder of files and place them into a destination folder without overwriting the original Raw files. Plus, as a separate application, it works in the background, leaving you free to do other work in Photoshop, Bridge, or Camera Raw.

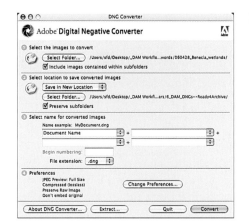

The DNG Converter.

10 ◆ Automating Photoshop

Automating your work will save you time and money, two valuable benefits of the features Photoshop offers. If you feel that getting your work done faster and more efficiently could be useful, there is something in this chapter for you. You may have noticed the proliferation of function keys—such as [F10] or [Shift-F4]—throughout this book. These are the ArtistKeys actions that we set up for ourselves. We use them all the time and we give them to you in the hope that they will start you off in automating your own work. We showed you how to load the ArtistKeys in Chapter 2, "Preferences and Color Settings."

Photoshop offers several levels of automation, from the very simple to the complex and incredibly powerful. In this chapter we'll walk you through how to accomplish simple to moderately complex actions, explain some of the actions you'll find in the ArtistKeys set, and point out some advantages of scripting. No matter what type of work you do, automation can remove some of the drudgery, giving you more time for the fun stuff.

First Steps

You don't have to do a thing to Photoshop to start being more productive—you only have to learn a few shortcuts. Do you use the Magic Wand a lot to make selections? Learn to type W to access the tool. Or type B for Brush, or C for Crop—most of the frequently used tools have easy-to-learn shortcuts. Photoshop comes with a large number of keyboard shortcuts, but if a command you use a lot lacks a shortcut, you can set one up. If you are more of a menu-driven user, you can create your own set of custom menus to speed up searching through the menus.

Customized Menus

Barry and Wendy use a set of customized menus when they teach their classes, as some students prefer to work from the menus rather than palettes or the keyboard. However, some menus list a lot of items we don't use, which can make scrolling through all the choices laborious. To be more efficient, we hid all the commands that we rarely or never use. You may have loaded the customized menu, ArtistryMenus, when you read Chapter 2. We suggest that as you work through the book you use either our custom menu or the Photoshop default menu. But maybe you'd like to know how to set up your own special menu. Let's do it.

◆ Go to Edit/Menus.

◆ For the Set, choose Photoshop Defaults if that's not the currently chosen option. In the Menu For pop-up choose Application Menus.

◆ Click the triangle beside the File menu to open it.

◆ Click the Visibility icon for Edit in ImageReady, a command we rarely need. This will remove the command from the File menu.

◆ Turn off any other commands in the File menu that you don't need on a regular basis, then do the same thing for each of the other menu items.

◆ Click the Menu For pop-up again and choose Palette Menus. Open any palette that you use on a regular basis, and turn off items you rarely need.

◆ Once you have made all the adjustments you want, click the Create a New Set icon at the top of the dialog to name your menus, and save them in your Presets/Menu Customization folder.

Here we've opened the File menu to change its appearance.

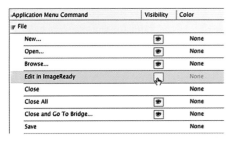

Turn off the Eye icon for each menu item you don't want to see.

Click the Create a New Set icon to save your menus.

You can save different sets of menus for the different types of tasks you do—say, one for color correction, one for compositing, one for retouching. In fact, if you look at the Set pop-up, you'll see that Adobe has created several already. In these special menus, colors are assigned to the most often used items. You can start with a menu Adobe (or we) provide, then turn items on or off depending on how you use Photoshop. We do not use the color option, preferring to just turn off the menu functions we don't use, but if it helps you organize your workflow, by all means use color as well. If you want to keep your version of the menu—that is, overwrite the one that loaded with the application, use the Save Changes icon (the one on the left) at the top of the dialog. To get rid of special menus that you don't use, click the Trash icon. To access commands hidden by a special menu, you can choose Show All Menu Items from the bottom of a menu to temporarily return it to its default state.

Customizing Keyboard Shortcuts

All of Photoshop's tools, as well as the most often used commands and menu items, have keyboard shortcuts. There are special shortcuts for tools in modal dialogs like Liquify and Extract. Yet the beauty of Photoshop (as well as most other Adobe applications) is that you can make the application work the way you do, instead of the other way around. So if a certain key makes more sense to you than the one that ships with Photoshop, you can change the shortcut to the key you like.

Unlike actions and scripts, which can handle many commands with a single stroke, each keyboard shortcut you set will pertain to one and only one menu item. A keyboard shortcut doesn't remember any settings either. But if you find yourself constantly going up to the Menu bar or to a palette pop-up for the same item over and over, a

keyboard shortcut is just what you need. It doesn't have to be a task that you'll be doing in the future either; keyboard shortcuts can be set for a short period when you're doing something repetitive, then deleted when the project is completed. As soon as you realize you're going to use a command a lot, set up a keyboard shortcut for it. It's quick and easy to do.

◆ Go to Edit/Keyboard Shortcuts and use the pop-up in the middle section to choose the menu or tool for which you want a new or different shortcut.

◆ Click the Shortcut column for that item, then type the key combination you want to use.

If that combination is already in use for some other command, an alert will appear telling you which command currently uses that shortcut. You are then given a chance to disable the current shortcut so you can use the keys you input, or you can simply type a different combination. You must include either the Command (Ctrl) key or a function key in the keyboard combination, except for the Tool shortcuts, where a single alpha character is acceptable. All 26 characters are currently assigned, however, so if you want to set a new key for a tool, you will have to change the key for some other tool. Let's see how that works.

We rarely use the Dodge, Burn, Sponge tool. The keyboard shortcut for that tool is O. Let's say that we use the Elliptical Marquee a lot and find switching between the Rectangular Marquee and the Elliptical Marquee a hassle. Because there's a shortcut we seldom use, we can use it for the Elliptical Marquee.

◆ Use Edit/Keyboard Shortcuts. If you've loaded the customized ArtistryMenus, you'll need to first go to Edit/Show All Menu Items, then choose Keyboard Shortcuts. Or you can use the keyboard shortcut to start out with, which is Command-Option-Shift (Ctrl-Alt-Shift)-K.

◆ From the Shortcuts For pop-up, choose Tools.

◆ Click the Shortcut column for the Elliptical Marquee and type O.

◆ An alert like the one on the next page will appear.

The first keyboard shortcut we'll change is a tool key.

Tool Palette Command	Shortcut
⬚ Rectangular Marquee Tool	M
○ Elliptical Marquee Tool	O⚠
⋯ Single Row Marquee Tool	
⋮ Single Column Marquee Tool	

Type the letter that you want to use as a keyboard shortcut.

⚠ **The shortcut O is already in use and will be removed from Dodge Tool, Burn Tool and Sponge Tool if accepted.**

If you type a letter that is already in use, both the shortcut area and the bottom of the dialog will display the alert icon. The alert at the bottom of the window will also tell you what the conflict is.

At this point, you have several options. You can click Accept, which deletes the shortcut completely from the original tool; you can click Accept and Go to Conflict, which sets your new shortcut but takes you to the tool from which you took the shortcut so that you can create a new one for it; or you can Undo the change. If you get confused about the keys you've set, you can click the Use Default button to go back to the original shortcut key for that tool. You need to click one of the Accept buttons for each shortcut you set. If you're using the Photoshop Defaults shortcuts, the set will be renamed Photoshop Defaults (modified). Clicking the Create a New Set icon at the top of the palette at this point will give you an opportunity to save your modified set with a new, more meaningful name. This is great when multiple people use the same system. Save the set in the Presets/ Keyboard Shortcuts folder, and it will be included in the Set pop-up the next time you access the dialog. You can also duplicate a set before you start to make changes. If you switch sets, an alert will ask if you want to save changes to the current set before you make the change.

The Summarize button creates an HTML document that opens in your default browser and allows you to print out all your new keyboard shortcuts.

We've included a set of keyboard shortcuts on the DVD in the Ch02.Preferences folder called ArtistShortcuts.kys. If after reading this chapter you plan to use ArtistKeys actions, we suggest you load the keyboard shortcuts as well. They work in conjunction with each other. To access the shortcuts, copy them from the DVD into the Presets/Keyboard Shortcuts folder in your Photoshop folder. When you restart Photoshop they will appear in the Keyboard Shortcuts Set pop-up menu.

Actions

Actions allow you to record and edit a single menu item or a very complicated sequence of events. You can then run that menu item or series of events on an entire folder full of files. You can execute these

events with the press of a function key or a click of a button onscreen. You choose Window/Actions [F11] to bring up the Actions palette. To create new actions or edit existing ones, you need to turn off Button mode in the Actions Palette menu. After you define all your actions, you can turn on Button mode, which shows you the function key associated with an action and also turns the Actions palette into a series of buttons you can click to play an action.

ArtistKeys to Set Up Your Actions

In the Ch10.Automating Photoshop folder on the *Photoshop Artistry* DVD, we have given you our predefined set of actions called ArtistKeys. We use these keys a lot in the book and you'll learn them faster if you work through the exercises with them. If you haven't already loaded the set into your copy of Photoshop, refer back to Chapter 2 and do it now. If you feel you've loaded the actions correctly but they're not functioning, refer to the chapter's sidebar on what to do if your ArtistKeys actions don't work.

We've used these actions for years. Barry developed most of them before there were shortcut keys to show and hide many of the palettes. So you may notice that our action keys for showing and hiding palettes differ from the Adobe default keyboard shortcut keys. If you load our keyboard shortuts, ArtistShortcuts, you'll see that they work in conjunction with the ArtistKeys actions. Later in this chapter, we'll show you how to change the function key assigned to any action.

Record a Single Item Action

You work the way you work. Photoshop gives you multiple ways to achieve a desired result, and your way may differ from that of other photographers. Because of this, you may need to use a menu item that others don't often need. If you want to set up an action with a function key to perform any menu item, even from the palette menus, here are the steps to take. You're going to create a new set to contain your actions and then add to it as we go through this chapter.

Let's say you often need to retouch the *Background* layer. You can go to the Layers palette and drag the *Background* layer to the Create a New Layer icon, you can go to the Layers menu and choose Duplicate Layer, or you can set up an action with a function key so you only have to press a key to complete the process.

◆ Open the file SunsetfromDakotaFlat.psd from the folder for this chapter on the DVD.

◆ Turn off Button mode by using the Actions palette menu if you are currently using buttons.

- Click the Create a New Set icon at the bottom of the Actions palette (it looks like a file folder). Name your new set My Actions.

- Create a new action by clicking the New Action icon at the bottom of the Actions palette, or by choosing New Action from the Actions palette menu. Name the action Duplicate Background.

- Click the Record button.

- Choose Layer/Duplicate, then click the Stop Recording button at the bottom of the Actions palette.

Click the Create a New Action icon.

Now, even though we named this action Duplicate Background, and it did indeed duplicate the *Background* layer of this file, in reality this action will duplicate whatever layer is currently active in the Layers palette when you run the action. So any time you use this action, you need to be on the *Background* layer first. More on this later in the chapter.

Choose a Function Key

You can choose a function key when you create an action, or you can assign a key at a later time.

- Double-click the white area to the right of the action's name, Duplicate Background, to bring up the Action Options dialog. Double-clicking the name merely lets you rename the action.

- Click the Function Key pop-up and choose an available key for your new action.

- Click OK to close this dialog and assign the function key.

Click the Stop Recording icon when you think you're finished with the action.

The keys that are available to you in this dialog will depend on what other sets of actions are loaded in the Actions palette at the time you assign the function. Photoshop allows you to use the Shift and Command (Ctrl) modifier keys as well if those are not in use. If you assign a key and later load an additional set of actions that contains some of the same function keys, the keys in the most recently loaded set will not appear and will not function. So try to organize your sets in ways that do not cause conflicts.

Insert a Menu Item

When you click the Record button, you can record a single menu item simply by choosing Insert Menu Item from the Actions palette menu. Doing so opens the Insert Menu Item dialog. You choose the menu item that you want to automate from either the main Menu bar or a palette menu, and its name then fills the text box. Often, this technique is used to insert commands that are not recordable when you're recording multiple command actions. If you want the user to

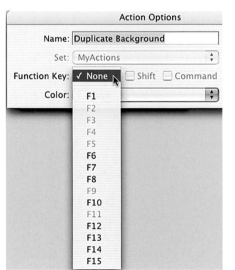

Only the function keys that are still available for use will show up in the Function Key pop-up.

always enter the values for a particular command (such as a filter) when using the action, you need to use the Insert Menu Item option from the Actions palette menu when recording that command, and then choose that command as the menu item to insert. Recording a command this way doesn't actually execute the command until the user plays the action, so the user must enter the values at that time instead of having you set the default values at the time you record the action.

In our hypothetical situation of retouching the *Background* layer, let's say that you always start your retouching while viewing the image at 100% magnification (not a bad idea for retouching). So you'd not only like your action to duplicate the *Background* layer, but also immediately change the magnification to 100%. Many of the commands in the View and Window menus do not record if you merely execute them during the recording of an action. Here's what you do.

◆ Click the Duplicate Layer command in the Duplicate Background action.

◆ Choose Insert Menu Item from the Actions palette menu.

◆ Choose View/Actual Pixels.

You can see that there is now a command in your action called Select Actual Pixels menu item. This command will run as part of the action. To try it out, type Command (Ctrl)-0 to fit the image onscreen, then click the action name and run the entire action.

Record Multiple Commands

To record an action with a sequence of events, you run through a series of steps rather than stopping the recording after a single menu item. Each recorded menu item in the sequence is called a command. Because you want to run this sequence on many other files, you need

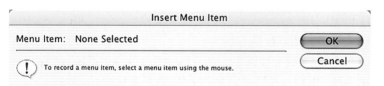

When you first choose Insert Menu Item you get this dialog. Once you choose the menu item (and, remember, you can choose from palette menus as well), you get a dialog like the one below.

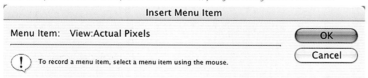

to be aware of the state of the file when you start recording. All subsequent files will have to be in the same beginning state for the action to work properly. Actions are like computer programs; they have no intelligence to pick the right layer within the file or to make sure the file was saved before you start—you'd need a script for that. (See "The Big Guns: Scripts" later in this chapter.)

In Chapter 11, "Image Processing with Bridge," Barry explains how to use an action to create adjustment layers for a set of files all shot at the same time and location. Let's say you just did 300 product shots in your studio and you need to quickly color correct them all to hand them over to a client. The following action will do the lion's share of the work for you. We're using six images of the tugboats in the following sections to walk you through the process of using actions, but after you set up your action, feel free to try it on another set of images. Make copies of all your images before you run any test actions!

Build a Sample File

We're going to color correct the first image with adjustment layers, then save the settings for each of those layers. Next we'll throw away the adjustment layers and go through the entire process again, but the second time we'll be recording an action. You could actually record the action now, as you build the file, but we find that doing this one extra step of first running through all the things you are going to do lessens the fumbling when you record your action. If you have not already worked through Chapter 21, "Overall Color Correction," you might want to save the rest of this chapter until you've done that exercise. That way, you'll know how to color correct the image.

◆ Create a folder on your desktop called ActionTest.

◆ Open the file Tug12.psd from the Original Tugboats folder in the Chapter 10 folder on the *Photoshop Artistry* DVD.

◆ Use Layer/New Adjustment Layer/Levels [Command (Ctrl)-F2] to create a Levels adjustment layer. Set your highlight, shadow, and midtone brightness, and correct for major color casts with this adjustment layer.

◆ Use Layer/New Adjustment Layer/Curves [Command (Ctrl)-F3] and set your contrast curve for this image.

◆ Use Layer/New Adjustment Layer/Hue/Saturation [Command (Ctrl)-F4] and saturate the image.

◆ Create another Curves adjustment layer [Command (Ctrl)-F2] and open the shadow areas of this image. Type Command (Ctrl)-I to invert the mask for this adjustment layer. You do not need to do any painting on the mask at this time.

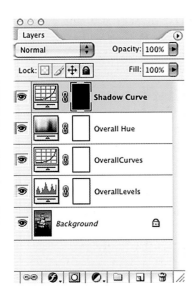

Once you've created all the layers that you are going to use for this action, your Layers palette looks like this.

Save the Necessary Settings

You now have all the layers that you need to do the initial color correction on all the images. We created an additional Curves adjustment layer, because the images we'll be working with all have shadow areas that need to be lightened. We're going to save the settings for the layer (indeed, all of these layers); but if we work on a different set of images, the action we're about to create will still be useful because we can edit it to load different settings when needed.

◆ Double-click the Levels adjustment layer icon. In the dialog box, click Save to save your levels setting here. Call it TugOverallLevel. Photoshop will append a .alv extension. Save it in your ActionTest folder.

◆ Double-click the Overall Curves adjustment layer icon. In the dialog, click Save to save your Curves setting. Call it TugOverall-Curve. Photoshop appends a .acv extension for Curves. Save it in your ActionTest folder as well.

◆ Double-click the Hue/Saturation adjustment layer icon. Click Save and name your adjustments TugOverallHue, and save this setting in the ActionTest folder. Photoshop appends a .ahu extension.

◆ Finally, double-click the Shadows adjustment layer and save its setting. Because this is another curve, Photoshop will again append the .acv extension, so make sure you name this differently than the first curve setting. You'll be choosing them later by name as you build your action. A name like ShadowCurve should be sufficiently descriptive.

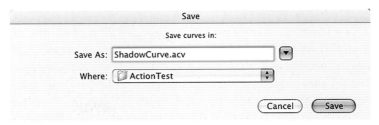

Save each curve with a distinctive name.

Create the Action

Now we need to get our test file back to the state it was in when we opened it. Then we'll we record the action. If you have been using the ArtistKeys actions to create your adjustment layers, *do not* use them for this step. Use either the Layer menu or the Create a New Fill or Adjustment Layer" icon at the bottom of the Layers palette.

◆ Drag each of the four adjustment layers you just created to the Trash icon at the bottom of the Layers palette.

◆ Click the Create a New Action icon on the bottom of the Actions palette. Name the action CCTugboats and click the Record button.

◆ Create a Levels adjustment layer and load the TugOverallLevels. alv file from within the ActionTest folder.

◆ Create a Curves adjustment layer and load TugOverallCurve.acv.

◆ Create a Hue/Saturation adjustment layer and load TugOverall-Hue.ahu.

◆ Create a second Curves adjustment layer and load ShadowCurve. acv. Now type Command (Ctrl)-I to invert the mask for that layer.

◆ Do a Save As, saving your file with the same name, and make sure As a Copy is unchecked. Save it in the ActionTest folder.

◆ Click the Stop Recording button at the bottom of the Actions palette.

You did the Save As step to give yourself more flexibility in how you use this action. You'll learn more about this in the next step.

The Actions palette icons are, from left to right: Stop Playing/Recording, Begin Recording, Play, Create New Set, Create New Action, and Delete.

Editing Actions After Recording

If you followed all the preceding steps to the letter, your action should work perfectly. Look in the ActionTest folder to see if a file named Tug12 exists. If not, repeat the steps in the "Create the Action" section. If you do have a file in the folder, congratulations. You've created an action that will serve you well through all your color corrections.

Adding a Command

You may have noticed that the file is still open in Photoshop. This is great if you want to edit the file further. However, if you need to process several files, you might not want them all to be open at once. You need to tell the file to close after it saves. For this, you need to record an additional command.

◆ Click the name of the action, CCTugboats, then click the Record button at the bottom of the Actions palette or choose Start Recording from the palette menu.

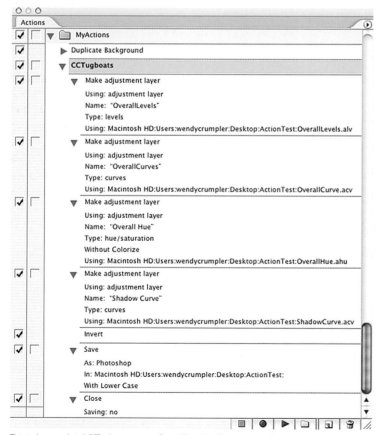

This is the completed CCTugboats action after adding the Close command.

◆ Close the file and stop recording, either by clicking the square Stop Recording button on the palette or via the palette menu.

When you record any new command while the name of the action is active, the command appears at the bottom of the list of commands—which in this case is exactly where we want it. If you want a command to show up in a specific place in the sequence of commands, activate the command that occurs before the one you are about to record. The new command will appear after the highlighted command.

Because we just saved this file, you should not receive a dialog asking if you want to save the changes. We did a Save As and navigated to a different folder so that we wouldn't overwrite our original files. We did not give our file a new name, because Photoshop would record that new name and give every succeeding file the same name. By not doing anything to the name input area, Photoshop assumes that all files should maintain their original names. Because of our workflow, we'd actually like to have those files named Tug12Layers, Tug13Layers, and so on, but a single action can't know how to do that. A batch action can, however, and we'll be using this same action to process a batch of files in a moment.

Stop Message

If you are the only person who is going to run your action, you're finished at this point. If, however, you are going to have studio assistants run the action and you want them to understand just how things are to be done, you can include Stop Messages to inform others of special issues. Just like when you insert menu items, the Stop Message will appear after the highlighted command. And just like with any inserted command, if it shows up in the wrong place you can simply drag it up or down the palette to move it.

If you need a Stop Message, use the palette menu to select Insert a Stop Message. Whatever you type in the entry area appears as an alert to the user of your action. You have a choice when creating the message of completely stopping the sequence of commands or giving the user a choice to continue the action. You might choose to stop the action completely if you want the user to airbrush areas of shadow detail before continuing. You might choose to allow the user to continue

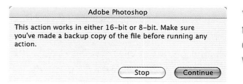

Your stop message will appear like this to the user of the action if you click the Allow Continue check box when you enter the message.

(as we have in this Stop Message) as long as they have satisfied certain criteria (in this case, having already made a backup of the file).

Modal Break Points

There are two narrow columns on the left side of the Actions palette. The first has check marks; the second column has what look like tiny black or red boxes with a few dots inside. Both are very important toggle switches that give you more control over the action, making it even more versatile.

Let's talk about the little boxes first. Adobe calls these modal controls. If you've ever done any programming, you may know these as break points. Any time you record a command that requires interaction with the user through a dialog (such as the Levels dialog), the action will insert one of these boxes in the column to the left of that command. If you look at a large set of actions, such as our ArtistKeys set, you'll see that this box can be empty, gray, black, or in some cases red. If the box is empty, the command's modal dialog is turned off. The command runs transparently to the user, and whatever settings are included in the action are the ones that will be used. If the box is gray, the modal dialog is unavailable and cannot be turned off. If the box is black, the command is on and the modal dialog will appear to the user, requiring the user to click, type, or input settings. The red boxes appear only at the action level, that is, for the name of the action. These boxes indicate that there are modal dialogs in different states within the action—some on, some off. If all dialogs are on, this box would be black. If all were turned off, this box would be empty.

Now why would you want to turn these dialogs on or off? Our CCTugboats action offers a good illustration. If you have 300 images to process, you will want to batch process them. If you turn all the modes off, your action will run without any input from you—you can walk away from the computer and go have a cup of coffee while the action does all the work. If, on the other hand, you need this same set of layers for a fine-art print that you are doing, you might want to turn all the dialogs on so you can create customized settings for each adjustment layer as you go. With the dialogs on, you can set the parameters for the adjustments you use. When you accept any of the dialogs, the action will move you to the next command automatically.

Command Toggles

The check boxes in the first column of the Actions palette are switches that turn the entire command or action on or off. You might turn off the Stop Message once everyone in a workgroup environment has used the action and knows what the Stop Message has to say. Or you might have a set of images where the overall contrast is

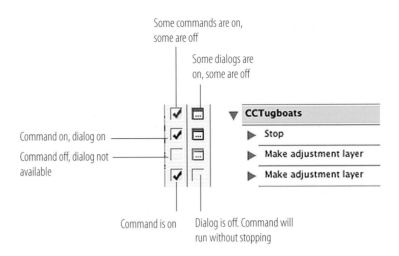

Some commands are on, some are off

Some dialogs are on, some are off

Command on, dialog on

Command off, dialog not available

Command is on

Dialog is off. Command will run without stopping

fine and you feel you won't need that Curve for this set of prints. If you turn off the modal dialog, the Curve will still run, just without your intervention. If you turn off the command toggle, the Curve command will be skipped completely. Because this is an action you use all the time, you don't want to delete the command by dragging it to the Trash icon; you just want to temporarily turn it off.

Record Again

We've been hinting that you can use this same action for other groups of images where you might need different settings. One way to accomplish this is through the use of modal break points. Another way is to record the necessary commands again. One of the reasons we set up this action by loading the settings for each adjustment layer is so you can save settings for a different group of images and load those settings when you process that group. Think of it—if you have three or four basic setups that you use in the studio, you could save a group of settings for each, then simply record those settings again when you want to process files.

When you want to rerecord a command, activate that command and choose Record Again from the palette menu, or simply double-click that command in the Actions palette.

Photoshop will take you back through whatever steps the command requires. When you finish those steps, the command will be modified.

Further Refinements

Duplicating and Moving Actions and Commands

To make a copy of a command, you can click an existing command and drag it to the New Action/Command icon, at the bottom of the

The ABCs of Actions

Always make a backup copy of your images before you run any action, even an action you've tested.

Be careful how you choose your commands. Choosing from the main or highest-level menu minimizes the possibilities for actions that don't run as expected.

Continue to save your set of actions as you make modifications. Do this in the Actions palette by clicking the name of the set you want to save, then choosing Save Actions from the Actions palette menu. Photoshop only saves what you've explicitly told it to save. If Photoshop crashes before all your commands are saved, you'll have to rebuild your actions.

Duplicate your set somewhere outside the Photoshop Presets folder. Then if you have to reinstall Photoshop at some point, you can copy your actions instead of having them overwritten by the installation process.

Actions palette. You can then drag that copy, or any command, to another location in the current action or in another action. This means if you already have a command that creates a Curves adjustment layer in one action, you can make a copy of it and drag that into another action without having to record the process.

Playing Part of an Action or a Single Command

If you want to start playing an action in the middle, just click the command at the point at which you want to begin and choose Play from the Actions palette menu or click the Play icon at the bottom of the Actions palette. The action will play through the sequence of commands from that point onward. If you want to play only that one action and not the rest of the sequence, you can Command (Ctrl)-click the command.

Functions That Actions Don't Support

Some menu items in Photoshop don't do anything during the recording of an action. If, while recording, you choose a menu item, click a tool, or do some operation, and a new command doesn't show up in the Actions palette, then that function is not recordable. For instance, most of the commands under the View menu do not record. If you want to include that function as part of an action, and the function can be chosen from a menu, you can choose Insert Menu Item, which will play that menu item when the action plays. You can't insert default values into these commands, but at least you can get the user to respond to them.

Other Actions Features

Actions can be organized into different sets. To create a new set, choose New Set from the Actions palette menu or click the third icon from the right (it looks like an empty folder with a tab) at the bottom of the Actions palette. You can then drag actions into the set. Use sets to organize your actions into different functional groups. You could have a Color Correction set and a Compositing set. A set for Weddings and a set for Portraits. You get the idea. The function keys operate globally across all the sets, so you can't use the same function key for two different actions, even if they are grouped in different sets.

Button Mode

Button mode shows you each action as a single button with its associated function key if there is one, and in the color you chose for the action when you recorded it. When they teach, Barry and Wendy print out a TIFF file of the ArtistKeys actions and tape it to the side of each student's monitor as a quick reference guide. It helps students learn the shortcuts more quickly. We've included ArtistKeys.tif on the DVD for this chapter so that you can make a printout as well. Button mode also lets you run an action by simply clicking a button (then you don't have to remember any key at all). You can't record or edit your actions in Button mode, however.

Useful Actions in ArtistKeys

The Sharpen Only Edges BH, RemoveSkyCrud, and Process Color actions included with ArtistKeys are useful, but they need some explanation. In the sidebar on the next page are screen shots

Toolbox	F2	Navigator Palette	⇧F2	LevelsAdjLayer	⌘F2	BurnAndDod...	⌘⇧F2
Save For Web	F3	Color Table	⇧F3	CurveAdjLayer	⌘F3	CropLayer	⌘⇧F3
Unsharp Mask	F4	Gaussian Blur	⇧F4	Hue/Sat AdjLayer	⌘F4	Smart Sharpen	⌘⇧F4
Duplicate	F5	Replace Color	⇧F5	Sharpen Only Ed...	⌘F5	SharpenOnly...	⌘⇧F5
Apply Image	F6	Selective Color	⇧F6	RemoveSkyCrud	⌘F6	Image Size	F7
Threshold	⇧F7	Tool Presets	⌘F7	History Palette	F8	Color Range	⇧F8
Canvas Size	⌘F8	Info Palette	F9	Histogram Palette	⇧F9	Flatten Image	⌘F9
Color Palette	⌘⇧F9	Layers Palette	F10	Channels Palette	⇧F10	Save & Close	⌘F10
Actions Palette	F11	Paths Palette	⇧F11	Horizontal Web	⌘F11	Button Mode	⌘⇧F11
Options Palette	F12	Brushes	⇧F12	Bridge	⌘F12	ResUpby10	⌘⇧F1
Sharpen Only Edge...		Sharpen Only Edge...		Vertical Web		Sharpen Only Edges	
To Gray		To CMYK		Process Gray		Process Color	
Process Color USM 100		Tile Horizontal		Duplicate Background		CCTugboats	

The ArtistKeys in Button mode.

Two Actions from ArtistKeys Explained

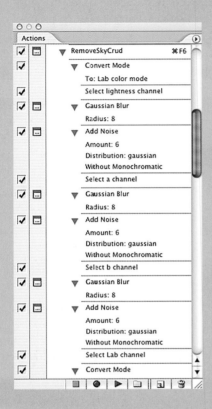

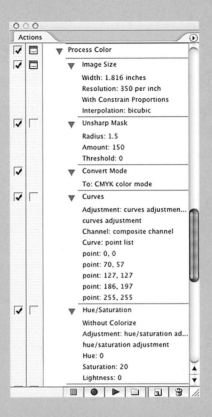

The RemoveSkyCrud action is sometimes useful on images that have a large, clumpy grain pattern in the sky area or other locations that don't have details in them, such as shadow areas. To use this action, first use Image/Duplicate to make a flattened copy of your Master Image, then run RemoveSkyCrud on it. This turns the copy into Lab color mode, then blurs each channel separately; it also uses Add Noise after the blur to return a more even grain pattern to the channel. When finished, this action converts this copy of your image back to RGB color using your RGB working space. Then use the Move tool with the Shift key held down to drag and drop this copy of your image back on top of your master image layers. Finally, add an all-black layer mask to this Crud Removed layer and use a soft Airbrush with a low Opacity, like 7%, to paint white in the mask only in the areas where you need to remove the clumpy grain in the sky area. Depending on the amount of grain in your master image sky, you may want to change the Radius values, within this action, for Gaussian Blur and Add Noise.

Here we see the Process Color action, which is in the ArtistKeys set but doesn't have a function key assigned to it. This is a generic version of the basic action we used to process all the screen shots within *Photoshop Artistry*. The Image Size command within this action has a break point attached to it, which allows us to set the width we want for this particular screen shot. The other commands here will always just run and do the same thing. After resampling the screen shot to 350 dots per inch (the width of its box in InDesign, our current page layout program), the file is then sharpened, it's converted to CMYK, it has a Curve run on it to compensate for contrast loss due to CMYK conversion, and it has Hue/Saturation run on it to saturate the colors again after the CMYK conversion. Notice that there is a similar action called Process Color Breaks that has break points on the Unsharp Mask step and the Hue/Saturation step. We use this action when we want to double-check the amount of sharpening or the amount of color saturation.

of RemoveSkyCrud and Process Color, along with detailed captions that explain how to use them. The third, and very important script, Sharpen Only Edges BH, is explained and used in Chapter 12, "Essential Photoshop Techniques for Photographers." Please let Barry know, at barry@maxart.com, how useful you find these actions, and if you discover any new and better variations of them.

Batch Files and Droplets

File/Automate/Batch is an incredibly useful command that can be run from within Photoshop or Bridge. If you have to process more than just a few images the same way, a batch process is what you want to use.

Batch Files

With batch processing you can run an action on all the open files, or specify an action along with a source and destination folder for that action; or if you are in Bridge, choose the folder or images that are selected in Bridge and run an action from Photoshop. You can also import images from a digital source such as a camera, but we're not recommending that because it is too easy to modify your images incorrectly without having first saved backup files. If you specify a source folder and a destination folder, Photoshop opens each file in the source folder and runs the action on the file and then saves that modified file in the destination folder. If the source folder has subfolders, you can choose to have Photoshop also process the files in the subfolders. You do not have to put Open or Close commands in your action; the Batch command automatically adds these at the beginning and the end. If your action contains an Open command to open a specific file, the Override Action "Open" Commands check box in the Batch dialog lets you tell it to ignore that command. Another check box lets you tell the Batch command to ignore any Save commands. You select the action you want to perform by using the Action pop-up menu in the Batch dialog and choosing the Source and Destination folders by clicking their respective Choose buttons. If you choose None for the Destination setting, Photoshop leaves the modified files open. If you choose Save and Close, the files are saved back in the folder in which they started, under the same name. If you want to run several actions on the same set of files, create an action that plays each individual action on a file, and then save it. Use it for the Batch action.

Photoshop also has the capability to log batch-processing errors to a file, whose name and location you choose. After the error is logged, the action continues. When you're running actions on a large group of files within a folder, this allows the action to process the other files

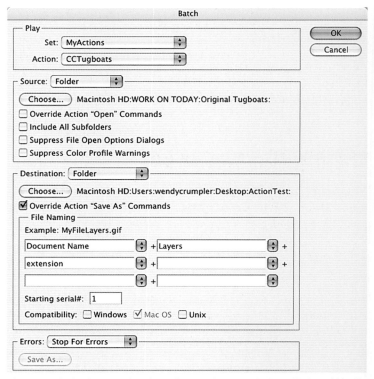

When we run this batch process, Photoshop will open each image in the Original Tugboats folder (the source), run the action CCTugboats on it, then do a Save As to the ActionTest folder (the destination) and close the file. We do not have to override the Open command, because there is no such command in our action. Our files are already in our color working space, so there's no need to suppress color profile warnings either. We did choose to override the Save As command that is in our action because we want Photoshop to rename our images as it processes them. Note the addition of the word Layers between the document name and the extension.

even if there is an error with several of them. When an error comes up, you can also choose to have Photoshop stop the action and display an error message on the screen.

Droplets

Droplets take the process one step further by allowing you to create a small applet that can reside on your desktop or in a folder on your hard drive. All you need to do to run a batch process is to drag a folder of images on top of the droplet. You don't even need to have Photoshop up and running. Photoshop will open and run the appropriate action on all the files and subfolders depending on how you have saved the settings in the File/Automate/Create Droplet command.

This is how the droplet looks on the Mac desktop. You simply drag a folder onto the pointing arrow. The highlighted folder is the destination. It's a generic folder that we created before we created the droplet. Once we run a folder of images, we'll file them appropriately, leaving this folder open for the next batch.

The Big Guns: Scripts

When you need more capabilities than actions can provide, you'll want to learn some basic scripting (and, for you true production geeks, some not-so-basic scripting). Photoshop actions can't speak to other applications, nor can they be set to run differently depending on file variables. Scripts can do all of this and more.

Photoshop can be scripted using a variety of languages. The scripting language you use depends on the platform you'll be using to do your production, and to some extent on your previous scripting experience. The most often used languages are Microsoft Visual Basic and JavaScript on the PC side, and AppleScript and JavaScript on the Mac side. If you've already had to learn some JavaScript to accomplish your Web work, you'll be able to extend that knowledge now to help you with simple production tasks directly in Photoshop. If, on the other hand, you've worked in AppleScript with QuarkXPress or FileMaker, or VisualBasic in Windows, you might want to stick with one of those languages.

Another important consideration is whether you need only Photoshop to do the work, or whether another application or part of your operating system will need to interact with Photoshop. If Photoshop will stand alone, JavaScript gives you the flexibility of being completely cross platform. If you need application interaction, other languages may be more appropriate.

Automation Included in Photoshop and Bridge

Contact Sheet II, Picture Package, and Web Photo Gallery are all explained in Chapter 33 "Contact Sheets, Picture Packages, Slide Shows, and Web Photo Galleries," and we show you some of the highlights of the Merge to HDR script in Chapter 27, "Compositing Bracketed Photos."

Photoshop automatically installs several JavaScripts that you can find under the File/Scripts menu. These scripts can export layers of a multilayered Photoshop document to separate files for building effects and animations, or they can create separate documents and Web photo galleries out of the comps you've created in the Layer

Comps palette. The Image Processor can save different versions of a file for you and/or run an action on every image in a folder, and the Script Events Manager can attach and run JavaScripts or actions to Photoshop events. Although we haven't used the Script Events Manager yet, we like the idea of being able to run an action to save a copy of an image to a daily backup folder each time we close a file. Little mind-numbing tasks that are easy to forget can happen automatically.

These are the scripts that show up in the menu, but there are many more sample scripts for you to view and begin to work with.

Where to Learn More About Scripts

The first place to go when you want to start learning about scripting is the Photoshop Scripting Guide in the Scripting Guide folder. Start with this guide rather than the one to the specific language because it covers very important concepts specific to how Photoshop is set up for scripting. Understanding these concepts will make it easier to comprehend what's being described by a particular script.

Also in the Scripting Guide folder are PDF guides to the three major scripting languages, as well as sample scripts for each one. Most of these scripts are mere snippets, but they employ some core functions and can serve as the basis for more complicated scripts.

The Adobe Web site has more information, and you can download (or upload) scripts from http://share.studio.adobe.com.

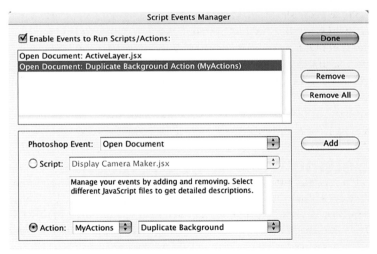

You can run multiple scripts or actions on the same event. Here, we've set up the Script Events Manager to run the JavaScript—ActiveLayer.jsx—then the action—Duplicate Background—every time we open a document. Unfortunately, only JavaScripts run from the Manager, though any action can. You can add and remove commands as you need them. All of the currently active commands are listed at the top of the dialog.

11 ◆ Image Processing with Bridge

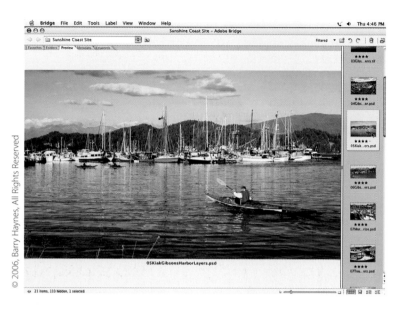

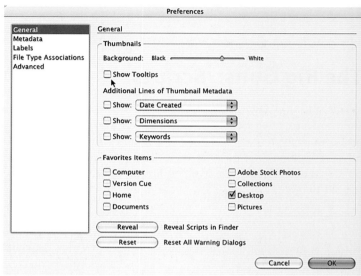

The General Preferences for Bridge. Make sure you set yours up similarly.

Bridge, which comes with Photoshop CS2, is Photoshop's image editing application. You'll find it to be a very helpful application. But while this chapter covers Bridge, it also discusses ways of improving your workflow and quickly processing those hundreds and thousands of images you'll now be capturing. Many of these techniques will work for film images, too, but the chapter's main focus is on digital files. It wasn't until I, Barry, spent a lot of time last year using Bridge to sort and process my Camera Raw files that I began taking full advantage of the benefits of converting to a digital camera. I want to pass on to you what I've learned about image processing with Bridge.

Setting Up Bridge Preferences

Before we get into the details of using Bridge, you need to make sure that you have your Bridge Preferences set up properly to work with this chapter. Please go through the Preferences dialogs in these first pages and make sure that you set up the options in your version of Bridge to match the settings shown here. You get to the Bridge Preferences by choosing Bridge/Preferences. Click the General tab at the top left to see the items discussed in the first dialog on this page.

General Preferences

In General Preferences, I usually turn off Tooltips because they get in the way when using Bridge. When you first start with Bridge, you may want them on for a couple of days to help explain what things do. I also turn off the Additional Lines of Thumbnail Metadata; when editing images I don't want to see the date, dimensions, or keywords of each image. The Favorites Items is also something I don't use, so I turn all of them off except for Desktop. Seán and Wendy like the Favorites feature and find it useful for creating a list of frequently used folders. Some items here are obviously of personal preference.

The Labels Preferences

In the Labels Preferences area, the only change I make is to turn off the Require the Command (Ctrl) Key to Apply Labels and Ratings check box. This allows you to change an image's rating by just typing a number from 1 to 5 instead of having to type Command (Ctrl)-1 to Command (Ctrl)-5, which is the default method. In this chapter, we'll show you how to use Ratings to sort your images.

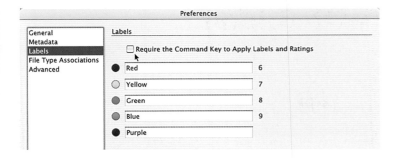

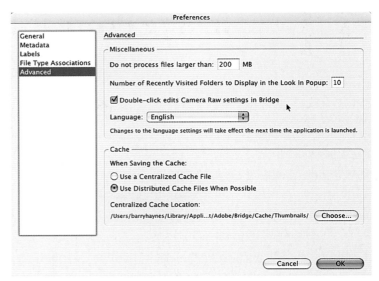

Advanced Preferences

In the Advanced Preferences dialog, I recommend that you check the box for Double-click Edits Camera Raw Settings in Bridge. Now when you double-click a Raw file, Camera Raw mode will run within Bridge instead of within Photoshop. This way you can more quickly go back and forth between Bridge and Camera Raw to do initial Camera Raw edits. While you are doing this, Photoshop can be occupied doing something else or can even not be open. When you click the Done button in Camera Raw, the default for the Return (Enter) key with this option checked, you'll automatically go back to Bridge. If you want to open the Raw file into Photoshop after editing in Camera Raw, then you click the Open button.

If you uncheck Double-click Edits Camera Raw Settings in Bridge, then double-clicking a Raw file will open Camera Raw within Photoshop, and the Open button will be the default for the Return (Enter) key, which Opens the raw file into Photoshop. Now when you click the Done button, Camera Raw will close but you won't return to Bridge automatically—you'll just sit there in Photoshop with no files open. You'll have to click back on Bridge to return to it and process another file. We find this unchecked setting less productive.

The Do Not Process Files Larger Than 200 MB option allows you stop Bridge from taking up too much processor time calculating previews for really large files. Depending on the speed of your computer and the number of really large files you have, you can set this according to your needs. With a fast Mac G5, for example, 200 MB works fine, but on a slower G3 it's better to set this to 50 MB.

Use Distributed Cache Files When Possible is the option to choose in the Cache area. This places Bridge files in the same folder as the images represented. This way when you copy a folder full of images to another drive, or make a backup copy to DVD, you also copy the Bridge preview pictures and other info for those images. This saves

Bridge from having to generate those previews again when working on another drive or computer.

Organizing Bridge for Photography

When you initially install and open Bridge, it opens in the default layout, as shown the illustration. You can change this layout; if you've worked through Chapter 3, "Navigating in Photoshop," you may have already created a Bridge workspace called PreviewsBig. Once the Preview, Metadata, and Keywords tabs have been dragged up to the top pane of the Bridge window, you get a much larger area for looking at Folders, Preview images, Metadata, or Keywords. Click the top left of the tab you want to view, and most of your page will fill with that information. We have three Bridge workspaces that we use all the time. When we created them we set up shortcut keys for each one. They are FoldersBig [Command (Ctrl)-F9], PreviewsBig [Command (Ctrl)-F10], and PreviewsBigLightBox [Command (Ctrl)-F11]. These are all illustrated on the next page. You should set up these three workspaces now as part of your Bridge working environment and Preferences. Use the Window/Workspace/Save Workspace menu to set up each of them, following the illustrations here.

◆ Move the middle vertical divider by clicking in the center of it and dragging to the right. This makes the frames to the left of the divider larger and the thumbnail area to the right smaller. Leave enough space on the right pane for one row of thumbnails.

◆ Click the Preview tab in the middle section, then drag it up to the top and release when it's next to the Folders tab.

◆ Drag the Metadata and Keywords tabs to the top of the window as well.

◆ Use Window/Workspace/Save Workspace, as shown here, to save this layout as PreviewsBig. Specify the function key Command (Ctrl)-F10 for this workspace.

You now have a small vertical row of thumbnails on the right side of the window; when you click one of them, a big preview of that image fills most of the window to the left.

◆ Click the double-arrow toggle in the lower-left corner of the Bridge window to fill the screen with just the thumbnails.

◆ Save this workspace as PreviewsBigLightBox and set Command (Ctrl)-F11 as the function key.

To fill the screen with just one preview—the PreviewsBig work-space—you can actually click the double-arrow toggle in the lower left corner of the Bridge window. I find toggling with the two function keys, F10 and F11, quicker. Plus, the toggle switch toggles you between the last workspace you used and a full page of thumbnails. So if you used a different view than PreviewsBig—say, the built-in Adobe Filmstrip view—you would toggle between the Filmstrip and Thumbnails views.

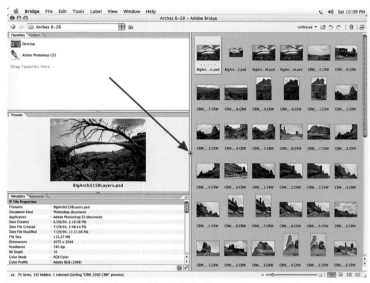

Here we are moving the middle vertical divider. In the illustration below, we've dragged this vertical divider most of the way to the right so we can only see one column of thumbnail images.

This is the default Bridge layout, which you can always return to by choosing Window/Workspace/Reset to Default Workspace as shown in the menu choice here.

Here we are dragging the Preview tab up. When we also drag the Metadata and Keywords tabs up to the top, then we'll have a much larger Preview area, as shown in the layout on the next page.

- Go to PreviewsBig view and click the Folder tab at the top of the left pane. Now move the central divider until you see lots of thumbnails in the Thumbnails pane and the long list of folders on the left.

- Use Workspace/Save Workspace to name this view FoldersBig, and set Command (Ctrl)-F9 as the shortcut key.

Any time you see a group of thumbnails in the File Browser, if you type Command (Ctrl)-T, you'll see those thumbnails without the filename, date, and so on underneath each image. This allows you to see more images without being distracted by all that text.

Shooting, Archiving, Updating

Those of you who have been shooting with digital cameras for a while will know some or most of this information. For those who have just switched from film to digital, though, there may be some important things you haven't figured out yet. I've seen the full range of knowledge in my workshop students and even some longtime professional photographers we've come across are new to computers and need some of these tips.

See how the Preview area looks after also dragging the Metadata and Keywords tabs to the top. Assign the keyboard shortcuts as you save the workspace.

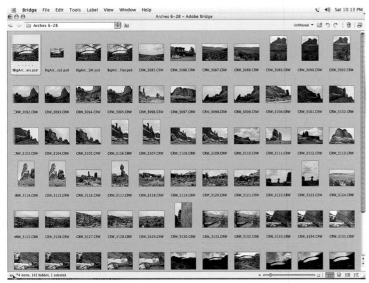

Our PreviewsBigLightBox workspace is a window that is entirely filled with thumbnails from the currently selected folder.

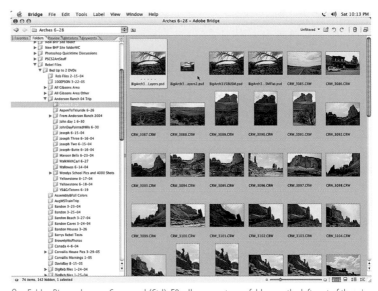

Our FoldersBig workspace, Command (Ctrl)-F9, allows you to see folders on the left part of the window; then when you click a folder, you see thumbnails of images in that folder in the rightmost window. You should also create a workspace like this one, with this same name and shortcut key.

Here we see a portable computer hooked to a LaCie card reader, front right, a LaCie portable FireWire drive, back right, and an Apple iPod to the left. The card reader allows you to quickly transfer digital images from the camera's memory card to the computer. Using the card reader is often faster than attaching the camera directly to the computer. The FireWire drive and/or iPod are for making extra copies of your camera's files.

Equipment to Take on a Digital Shoot

When you're out shooting in the field with your digital camera, you want to make sure you bring enough CompactFlash cards, or whatever memory-card format your camera uses, for a day's shooting. And, of course, you need to bring enough film if you're using a film camera for your entire trip. Actually, it's best to have enough memory cards for two days' shooting, just in case you don't have time in the evening to offload your files. But what you want to do when you do have some extra time is to take your camera memory cards and put them into a little card reader as you see pictured above. This one is made by LaCie, costs about $30, and is a great little reader. You can plug the reader into a setup like the one shown here. This setup includes a portable computer and card reader, but also a little LaCie pocket drive, which is a 20 GB FireWire drive that requires no external power source. On the left side, you can see an Apple iPod, which is another choice you could use for backing up files. You can plug these into your portable computer without an external power supply, and they will show up on your desktop as a hard disk. You can plug in the card from your camera, open the card as a folder on your desktop, then drag the files to your hard disk, portable drive, or iPod. What we suggest doing with these portable devices is to make a second copy of

all your images and then keep these little devices in your camera bag. That way, if your portable is stashed in the trunk while you're eating dinner and somebody breaks into the car and steals it, you've always got your camera bag and all your files with you. When you're on a long trip, you don't want to lose all your images. That's the nice thing about digital cameras—you can always make extra backups.

You can also buy portable, battery-operated hard disks that have a little screen on them (in fact, the more expensive iPods do this) where you can see the photographs too. Personally, I don't think that feature is all that valuable, because it's still a dinky little screen like the one on your camera, and what you really want to do is see the images on your portable or, better yet, on your calibrated monitor back in your studio. I prefer to be able to see a bigger version of each photograph to judge how well I've done. Out in the field, just looking at the histogram on the camera will tell you what you need to know. You can also get little portable, battery-operated devices, or use built-in drives on your portable, to burn your images onto CDs or DVDs as backups in the field. This would allow you to mail backup CDs or DVDs to your studio while on a long trip.

Copying the Digital Files onto Your Computer

When you plug a card reader into your computer, you want the files show up on your desktop as if they were an extra hard disk. Then you can use the Finder on the Mac or Explorer on the PC to copy the files from your card directly to your hard disk. From there you can access those files from Bridge or Photoshop.

You want to control what software, if any, runs when you plug a memory card or camera into your computer. I gave a talk to a group of professional photographers in New York, and one of their most common questions concerned how to cancel those "irritating applications" that automatically appear when you plug in your camera.

On the Mac

You want to make sure that in Mac OS X your CD and DVD System Preferences, in the Hardware section, are set up so that when you plug in camera cards or a camera, the Mac's default iPhoto or Image Capture software doesn't automatically launch.

◆ To do this choose Apple/System Preferences from the top-left corner of your screen, then click on CDs & DVDs in the Hardware section of the System Preferences window. This brings up a dialog with a set of options. By default, when you plug in a CD or camera, Max OS X opens iPhoto. Instead, you want the files to show up on your desktop, where you can copy them without any processing. You want to switch the When You Insert a Picture

Change this setting to Ignore in Mac OS X so iPhoto does not open when you insert a camera card or an image CD, or plug in a camera.

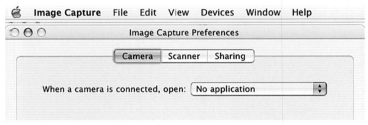

In the Applications folder in OS X is an application named Image Capture that can activate when you plug a camera or card into your Mac. Open Image Capture and choose Image Capture/Preferences, then set When a Camera Is Connected Open: to No application. This will stop Image Capture from running when you plug in a card or camera.

CD option to Ignore. In fact, I set all the different choices here to Ignore; that way, if I'm inserting a CD or a DVD for some other purpose, it doesn't start up some application that I don't want.

◆ If the Image Capture app shows up when you plug in cameras or memory cards, see the illustration directly above for how to cancel this.

On Windows

If you are using Windows XP and you plug in a card, it will show up as another drive in Explorer. Some PCs have programs installed that try to be helpful by launching an auto-download package to download your files. There are so many different types of PCs and PC programs that can do this, we can't cover all the ways to cancel or control them here. You'll have to access the documentation that came with your particular brand of PC if this is a problem for you.

Hard Drive Organization and Making Backups

It's a good idea to have several hard drives so that if one fails you have backups on other drives. Keep track of the files you are currently working on so you can back them up to a different drive at the end

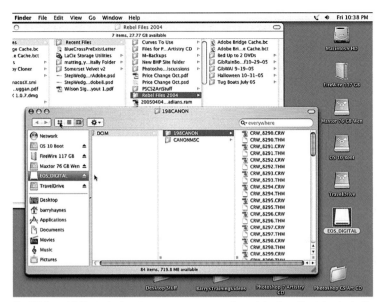

The EOS Digital folder in the front is a camera memory card containing Raw files. It just looks like a hard disk on the Mac desktop. To copy the Raw files to a hard drive, you just do a Select All on the files in the 198Canon folder, then drag and drop them on a folder on the hard disk wherever you want them.

of each day. After you get a certain amount of backup information on your backup drive, copy that to a backup DVD.

Organize your files so you can easily find things, especially images, again at a later date. For each photo shoot, for example, you could put all the files for that shoot in a folder having the name and date of the shoot. That folder could be easily backed up to another hard drive and/or a DVD. When you back up to DVD, make two copies and store one of them at an off-site location. Having two copies is good insurance, because sometimes CDs and DVDs fail. Having one at an off-site location gives you extra protection from losing your images to theft, fire, earthquake, and so on.

Burning CDs and DVDs

When you make backup CDs or DVDs, set the format to one that is readable by both Macs and PCs. This will be the format of the directory or table of contents on the DVD itself, not the format of the actual files on the CD. If this directory format is not readable by both Macs and PCs, then you may not be able to access your DVDs on the other platform. Imagine if you switched platforms, then went back and tried to read some old CDs, and found that you couldn't read the directory format.

I know lots of PC users who have switched to the Mac and a few who have switched the other way. Now Macs have started using Intel chips, so who knows what will happen next! Many people, like the three of us authors, have to be able to work with both platforms. Some CD and DVD writers, especially on the PC, don't use a format that will work for both platforms. You also have to be careful that the filename formats don't use special characters that the PC or Unix won't recognize. This can be a problem when you create files for Web use. If the server where the files are stored is a Unix server, for example, some special characters that Macs and PCs may use in filenames won't work on Unix systems. Avoid punctuation characters in general. If you want to put dividers between words in a filename, use underlines or hypens. Any other punctuation character may indicate something else depending on the platform. Extra-long filenames seem to often cause problems with CD and DVD writing software on either platform, and especially when switching from one platform to another.

Updating Software and Hardware

In the digital world there are always new versions of everything, and you are always encouraged to update, especially when you are hooked up to the Internet. This automatic updating may seem easy, and it can be sometimes. But! When you update something, the new version may then be incompatible with something else you have on your system, so then you'll have to upgrade that, too. A single upgrade that you initially "automatically" updated over the Internet can cause a chain reaction headache and it can take $ out of your wallet to purchase yet other upgrades for things that are no longer compatible with the first upgrade. This process can eat up a lot of your time and money, and cause great frustration. So we don't upgrade things unless we need a particular feature in a new version, and when we do upgrade, we try to update a group of things at the same time and then work with those for a couple of years until we have to do the next round of upgrades.

Bridge's Automatic Raw Settings

When you enter Bridge and are looking at newly copied Raw files, Bridge will create new previews for those images. If you open a new Raw file into Camera Raw, you'll notice that it has automating settings that you can turn on for Exposure, Shadows, Brightness, and Contrast in the Adjust section. You can also automatically run a curve on the image from the CS2 Curve section. The default Medium Contrast curve works well for previews, but you might want to turn it off if you are trying to bring out shadow detail in a more final ad-

The Camera Raw default settings that help us sort images in Bridge are to have the four Auto check boxes selected in the Exposure section to the right, setting Sharpness to Preview Only and Color Noise Reduction to 12 in the Detail section, and leaving the Curve section set to Medium Contrast. Choose Save New Camera Raw Defaults from the pop-down menu to the right of Settings menu in the Camera Raw dialog.

justment. These automatic settings will make the previews of unedited Raw images look better while you sort and evaluate them in Bridge. We like to change the automatic settings a bit from the defaults. We recommend setting sharpening so that it only happens to the preview pictures, since we want to do final sharpening after all color correction has been applied to the image. Also in the Detail section, we set Color Noise Reduction to 12 instead of 25, since 25 is usually more than you need for ISO 100 images shot in bright light. We don't usually use these automatic settings for final color correction—just to get better previews while editing in Bridge. At the bottom left of the main Camera Raw dialog, we also set Space to Adobe RGB, Depth to 16 Bits/Channel, and the Resolution to 270, which usually fits our print sizes well. If you want to change these automatic settings to be the defaults for all your unedited Raw files, then choose Save New Camera Raw Defaults from the pop-up menu to the right of the Settings menu inside the Camera Raw dialog. After changing the Camera Raw Defaults, you'll notice that Bridge will update all the previews for images that have not been previously adjusted by you in Camera Raw. These issues will be covered in more detail in Chapter 9, "Camera Raw."

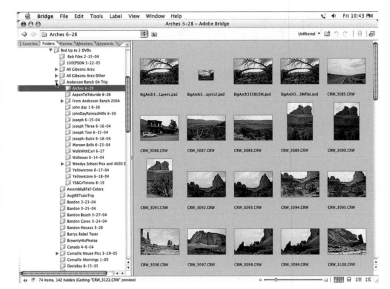

Keeping all your digital images online makes them much easier to access. For example, I taught a workshop at Anderson Ranch in 2004 and actually drove out there from Oregon, so it was more than a two-week trip taking hundreds of images each day. If I use the FoldersBig workspace to open up that Anderson Ranch folder in Bridge, I have a subfolder for each of the different places I went along the way. This makes it quick and easy for me to use Bridge to find any image I took on that trip. With the auto settings we'll show you, Bridge does a nice job of displaying these images even though many of them have never been named or color corrected and are still stored in their original Raw format.

Sorting Images with Bridge

We three authors have found that Bridge has greatly improved our ability to sort our digital images. Here are some tips we've discovered.

Sorting a Single Folder Shoot

You can try this out by locating a folder full of digital camera images on your hard disk.

◆ Finding the folder to sort is usually easier when using the FoldersBig workspace, Command (Ctrl)-F9. To sort a group of new images, first click the folder for that group of images. Now use Command (Ctrl)-F10 to put Bridge into the PreviewsBig workspace you set up earlier in this chapter. Click the first image at the top right of your screen. The right arrow key will take you to the next image and the left arrow key to the previous one. You can also type a number rating for each image as you go along. By default, the rating is Command (Ctrl)-1 to Command (Ctrl)-5, but the preferences we set at the beginning of this chapter allow us to change this rating by typing a simple 1 to 5.

Here you see my Tugboat shoot after I narrowed the pictures down to ones that have a 2-star rating using the steps outlined below on this page. Notice the Filtered pop-up in the top-right corner that you use to choose which set of star ratings you'll display. Also notice the Image Size slider at the bottom right of the window. You can use this to make the thumbnail images in your Bridge window bigger or smaller depending on your needs. Finally don't forget to use Command (Ctrl)-T if you want to get rid of the text below the thumbnails and have more screen real estate to see just the images as you edit them.

◆ First type a 1 on the images that you like; after going through all the images, use the Filtered pop-up at the top right of your Bridge window to show only images with a rating of 1 or more stars.

◆ Now you can go back through these images, now just the 1-star rated ones, and type a 2 for the images you think are the best of the 1-star set. After this second pass, you can use the Filtered menu again to show just the images that have a 2-star or better rating.

◆ Now you can switch to Command (Ctrl)-F11, your PreviewsBigLightbox workspace, to see all of those 2-star images. Use Command (Ctrl)-T to remove the text below these images, then use the slider at the bottom right of your Bridge window to make the images bigger until they just fill the window but you can still see all of them. These are all the images with a rating of 2 stars or more.

You can continue this process of paring down your images until you get just the ones that have 5 stars. Usually after paring down to 3 or 4 stars, you've got the few best images from a shoot. These are the ones you'll want to do custom work on with Camera Raw and then Photoshop adjustment layers, and finally maybe even print.

Re-Sorting a Large Group of Many Shoots Each in Its Own Folder of Images

The following example illustrates how I, Barry, have used Bridge to greatly improve the access to and usage of my images. You can do a similar thing with yours.

I had lots of folders of images shot in the area of our new home in Gibsons, British Columbia, on the "Sunshine Coast" with my Digital Rebel. Since we first came here, I've shot thousands of photos, but I hadn't sorted the images into the particular local areas because I wasn't sure how to categorize them. After being here a while and learning the Sunshine Coast better, I wanted to re-sort those photos into specific categories in different folders than where they were originally organized.

To do this I made a new folder inside Bridge called All Gibsons Area; within that folder I made the subfolders that I then wanted to sort my images into. You can create new folders in Bridge using File/New Folder, or you can create them in the Finder or Explorer. In a Bridge

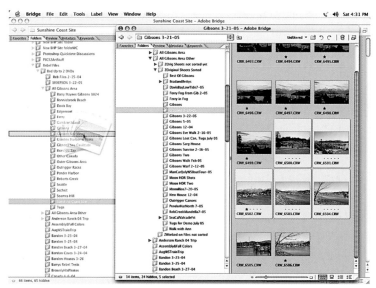

The Bridge window to the left has my All Gibsons Area folder opened, so I can see the different category folders inside it. The Bridge window to the right is opened to the Gibsons shoot I did on 3-21-05 before I knew how I wanted to organize my images. I've selected five images in this folder to the right by clicking the first image, then Shift-clicking the last image. If the images were not all in a row, I could instead Command (Ctrl)-click each image that I wanted. To move the images, just click the white border around one of the selected images and drag it on top of the folder you want to move or them to. At that point you release the mouse button and the images are moved. To copy the images, do the same thing, but hold the Option (Alt) key down as you do it. This is very easy to do with Bridge!

window with the FoldersBig workspace, I set up my All Gibsons Area folder so I could see all the subfolders that I wanted to sort images into.

Then I used File/New Window to open a new Window in Bridge and navigated to one of the original shoot folders that I wanted to copy images out of. I then used Bridge to select the images that I wanted to move or copy, and transferred them to the new folders.

To move images with Bridge, you just click them to select them, then drag and drop them onto the new folder you choose. If you want to make a copy of those images in that new folder, then you need to hold the Option (Alt) key down while dragging and dropping the images onto that new folder. This will copy each image; and if it's a Raw file, it will also copy its XMP file. See an illustration to the left of this Bridge file-copy process in action.

XMP files contain additional information about a file, like its changed Raw settings, added after the original camera shoot. The Finder or Explorer won't automatically copy XMP files for you!

To finish sorting your images, you can just use Bridge to drag and drop images from the original shoot folders into the new category folders you made. Doing this in Bridge works great because you can see previews of the images even if they are Raw files that haven't been opened into Photoshop before.

When you are doing this sorting process, remember that you can first rate the files in the original shoot folders using the 1-star to 5-star system we showed you in the previous section. After rating them, you only have to view the better images in a particular shoot folder and consider them for copying. You can select the images that you want by clicking the first one and then Command (Ctrl)-clicking others you'd like. If you want to select a group of images that are all together,

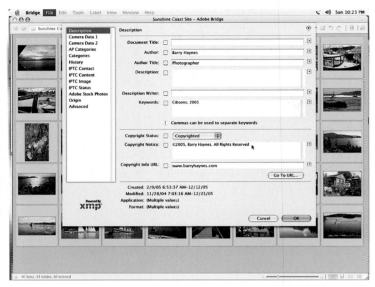

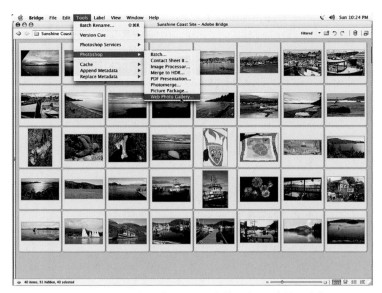

After selecting all the images that you want to put on your Web site, use File/File Info to bring up this dialog and enter your name, keywords, copyright info, and so on into the metadata for each image. This way if someone grabs a file off your Web site, that information will be in the file, so the person can use it honestly if they want to. At the top-right corner of the File Info dialog is a pop-down menu allowing you to save any set of information you've entered here as a template. You can also load templates that you've previously saved so that you don't have to enter your name and copyright info each time.

Here I've selected 40 images in Bridge and are using Tools/Photoshop/Web Photo Gallery to create a Web site for these 40 images. The features and options for Web Photo Gallery are covered in Chapter 33, "Contact Sheets, Picture Packages, Slide Shows, and Web Photo Galleries."

click the first one, then Shift-click the last one, and all the images between will be selected too.

Creating a Web Site from a Group of Images

A great way to automate with Bridge is to select a group of files using Bridge, then use Bridge's Tools/Photoshop menu to run a Photoshop Batch, Contact Sheet, Photo Merge, Web Photo Gallery, or other automation feature. Bridge will then send Photoshop a list of the filters to use in that automation feature. That is how we are going to create a Web site. If you browse to www.barryhaynes.com and then click the link *Our new workshop location: Gibsons B.C. "the Sunshine Coast,"* you can see the Web site that I made by starting in Bridge via this technique.

◆ Sort all the images that you want for a Web site, and put them into a named folder. For this example you want to have 40 images, so star rate them, as we showed you earlier in this chapter, then just continue to show only the images with higher star numbers until you get about 40 images.

◆ Before outputting these to the Web site, you want to put your copyright info, your name, and your Web site address into each image. To do this you select all the images in Bridge; choose File/File Info, and enter your name, location, copyright notice, and Web site location; then click OK to add that information to each image file.

It's a good habit to add your name and copyright info to all files right after you shoot them and before archiving them to CD or DVD. That way the info will always be there, and you won't have to remember to add it later when you've edited the file and sent it off to some magazine, Web site, or the like.

◆ Choose Tools/Photoshop/Web Photo Gallery to create your gallery. To learn about the options of Web Photo Gallery, see Chapter 33.

After your gallery is created, you can use Adobe GoLive, or another Web site editing package, to edit the text description of each image and make other changes and improvements. The rest of the work of creating the Web gallery is done by Bridge and Photoshop.

When Photoshop creates an image gallery, it automatically scales each thumbnail and larger image to the sizes you specify. One problem is that Photoshop doesn't sharpen the images after scaling them. You can make your Web images look better by later sharpening them in Photoshop. This process can be automated using Bridge and a Photoshop Batch and Action. To do this, you want to initially set the JPEG quality to Maximum (10) in the Web Photo Gallery dialog. This allows you to reopen the images, after the gallery is generated by Photoshop, and sharpen them a bit without the quality degrading too much. Normally you don't want to reopen a JPEG image and do any further processing on it. In this case, though, you just sharpen them slightly, then resave the sharpened images with a JPEG quality setting of 8. We show you how to do this in Chapter 10, "Automating Photoshop."

Automating Camera Raw Production

In this section we'll cover several topics. We'll show you how to set up the FinalCorrectionDefaults and explain what they do. If you have groups of pictures from a photo shoot that are similar, we'll show you how to apply the same Camera Raw settings to all of them and then tweak those settings for each image. We'll show you how to create a set of adjustment layers for one image and copy those to other similar images. In addition, we'll show you how to select a group of images in Bridge and then run a Photoshop batch on them to open them into Photoshop and add the same set of adjustment layers to each.

Use the Same Camera Raw Settings

Let's say you're in Bridge and you've identifed a group of pictures that you want to color correct.

◆ You can find the three tugboat images we use here in the folder Ch11.Image Processing W Bridge on the *Photoshop Artistry* DVD. You can also find a similar group of your own images to work with. You want to find a group of images that you would like to color correct in a similar way. Use Bridge to pick the one that is an average of the others to start out with. If you're using the tugboat images, start with the one shown in the illustration above

NOTE

You should read and study Chapter 9, "Camera Raw," and Chapter 10, "Automating Photoshop," before proceeding further in this chapter. Here we'll summarize features from both those chapters, as well as other parts of Photoshop, as we show you how Bridge helps you get those areas to work together in automating your workflow.

These are the three tugboat images that you can open from the *Photoshop Artistry* DVD: this one, in the middle; the one right above it, showing foreground detail; and the one below, showing sky detail. You want to adjust them all similarly. Start out with the middle one, since it has the most in common with the others. Double-clicking this image brings it up in Camera Raw.

on this page. Double-click that image to bring it up in Camera Raw.

Default Raw Settings for Final Correction

We mentioned earlier how you want to have the automatic settings in Camera Raw turned on so Bridge will do automatic and basic corrections when you first look at new digital files. Sorting color-corrected pictures, even if they are not perfectly color corrected, is easier than sorting flat and desaturated Raw files. When you're actually doing your final color correcting on an image, you'll usually get better results without the automatic settings, because this will give you more detailed control of each image.

When doing final correction on an image, for best results start over on the image and correct it manually. Before I start manually adjusting a Raw file, I choose a set of Raw settings I call FinalCorrectionDefaults. What those settings do in Camera Raw is turn off the automatic adjustments in the Adjust area. In the Detail area they set Sharpness to 0 and Color Noise Reduction to 12, our recommended default settings. The other setting change for final correction is to have the Curve set to Linear instead of to the automatic Medium Contrast curve.

◆ To initially set up the FinalCorrectionDefaults, you go into Camera Raw, with any Raw image, and set all the settings the way we just described here; then you use Save Settings from the pop-up menu to the right of the Settings menu. You name these settings FinalCorrectionDefaults. You should create this FinalCorrectionDefaults setting now. You only have to do it once, and it will remain part of your Camera Raw preferences.

◆ To start adjusting an image with the FinalCorrectionDefaults settings, you open that image into the Camera Raw filter, then choose FinalCorrectionDefaults from the Settings menu. Do this to the image you now have open in Camera Raw. From Bridge you can also choose Edit/Apply Camera Raw Settings/FinalCorrectionDefaults without even opening the image into the Camera Raw filter.

We don't usually choose these settings until we're ready to do final color correction, because they may initially make your Raw preview and thumbnail look worse.

The Adjust Section of Camera Raw

There are seven sliders you could possibly set in this section. We usually leave the White Balance sliders alone, as our camera does a reasonable job with these, and we can make further refinements in Photoshop with adjustment layers.

◆ While holding the Option (Alt) key down, move the Exposure slider over to the left until you get any lost highlight details back, or to the right until you just start losing highlight detail, then

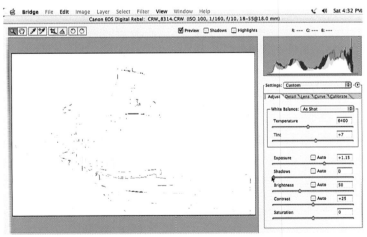

Adjusting the Shadow setting with the Option key held down so no important shadow details are lost. We've already set the Exposure in the same way. Notice that the histogram is not losing any details from either end. If it were losing details, a vertical bar would appear on one end or the other. Later in Photoshop adjustment layers, we can decide if we want to throw a little more highlight or shadow detail away. Doing this with adjustment layers allows us to change things more easily than if we had to go back to Camera Raw.

back off a bit. Lost highlights show up as nonblack when the Option (Alt) key is held down. As soon as you start seeing anything that's not black, you're losing some highlights. It's the same with the Shadows slider when you see nonwhite areas with the Option (Alt) key held down, so adjust that, too.

◆ We usually just leave the Brightness and Contrast adjustments and do them in Photoshop, unless we've got a really big problem; we do the same with the Saturation adjustment. They can be done with more control as adjustment layers in Photoshop.

The Detail Section of Camera Raw

◆ In the Detail area, set the Sharpness to 0 and Color Noise Reduction to 12. We find that the Adobe default of 25 usually removes too much shadow color detail with our cameras. Increase the Luminance Smoothing setting from 0 only if you have a really noisy image, which usually happens with low-light shooting or high ISO camera settings. Keeping the ISO under 400 when shooting with most digital cameras reduces the likelihood of this type of noise problem.

The Lens Section

Adjustments in this section are more likely to be required when you're using less expensive wide-angle zoom lenses at their wider settings. Chromatic aberration is caused by an imperfection in how camera lenses (usually wide-angle zoom) bend different colors of light. This causes the Red channel details to register in a slightly different location than the same details in the Green channel.

◆ With the Option (Alt) key held down, look around the edges of your image to see if there's any chromatic aberration. See that little red or green line in the illustration on the next page? That shows chromatic aberration. You want to zoom in to 400% and look at objects with distinct edges around the sides of the image—that's where you'll see the aberration. You can see that the red lines are on the right side of an edge and the green lines on the left, but if you move the slider the wrong way, the colors will switch sides. Now the green lines are on the right and the red lines are on the left. When the red/cyan fringe is removed, look for the blue/yellow fringe, also with the Option (Alt) key held down. The blue/yellow fringe can be harder to see and is sometimes just not there, although it's easier to see once the red/green one is fixed.

◆ After fixing the fringe in one location, do Command (Ctrl)-0 to zoom back out, then go and check the fringe in some other parts of the image. You want to look around the edges of your image.

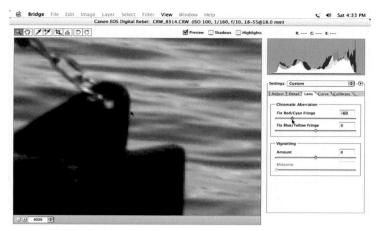

In this Tugboat image we are adjusting the red/cyan fringe to remove it. The fringe you see here, that red line to the right of the object and the cyan line to its left, is exaggerated so that you can see it in this book image. When you actually move these sliders back and forth, you want the Option (Alt) key down, which isolates the fringe to either the red/cyan or blue/yellow colors that you are trying to remove. Move each slider until the fringe is completely gone or is as small as possible.

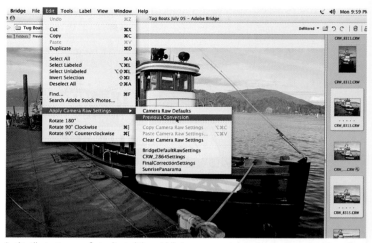

In this illustration, we first adjusted the middle image separately in Camera Raw, then chose Done from Camera Raw. That returned us to Bridge, where we selected the other two images and gave them the same settings by choosing Edit/Apply Camera Raw Settings/Previous Conversion.

Sometimes you have to balance the fringe adjustment between one location and another. When you turn the Preview check box off and then turn it back on, you should see a lessening of the fringe with the Preview on.

◆ To zoom in on an image, press Command (Ctrl)-Spacebar, which puts you into the Zoom tool. Now simply clicking and dragging with the mouse button allows you to drag a box around the area you need to see up close. You want to zoom in to 400% and then turn the Preview button on and off to make sure the aberrations are gone.

The Curves Section

Just leave this Curve set at Linear, which FinalCorrectionDefaults set for you, because you want to see all the shadow details from inside Photoshop.

◆ If the image looks really flat, try the Medium Contrast curve instead. You first want to see what Linear looks like; otherwise there may be shadow details in this image that you didn't know were there. At this point click Done, and these settings will be applied to the image, and you'll return to Bridge, where you can apply the settings to the other images.

Applying Camera Raw Settings to Other Images with Bridge

Now that we've applied the initial Camera Raw settings to the first image in the group, we want to apply those same settings to the other images in this group.

◆ Click the first of the next images, then Command (Ctrl)-click the second one to select them both. If you have more than two other images, either Command (Ctrl)-click or Shift-click to select the group. Now choose Edit/Apply Camera Raw Settings/Previous Conversion and those same Camera Raw settings will be applied to the other selected images. You'll notice that the Bridge thumbnails for those other images will update to show the differences these changes have made to them.

Opening These Images into Photoshop

Now you want to open these images into Photoshop so you can add adjustment layers and make more detailed color corrections.

◆ Click and Command (Ctrl)-click to select all images.

◆ If you then choose File/Open With/Adobe Photoshop CS2, the images will open into the Camera Raw filter, but that filter will reside within the Photoshop application.

In this illustration we first chose all three images, then opened them into Camera Raw. We clicked the center one and made the adjustments to it. Finally we clicked the Select All button at the top left, then clicked Synchronize to set all three images to the settings we chose for the center one. Now we can further customize the other two in turn by clicking one of them and adjusting its settings.

◆ If you instead choose File/Open in Camera Raw, or Command (Ctrl)-R, then all the files will show up in Camera Raw, but the filter will still be in the Bridge application.

◆ In either case, when you open more than one image at a time into Camera Raw, all the images will show up in a thumbnail list on the left side of the Camera Raw filter. You can click any of these thumbnails, now inside the Camera Raw filter, to work on that particular image.

◆ If you are using the tugboat images, click to select the middle image that we started out with before. Otherwise, click the image of yours that you adjusted in Camera Raw a minute ago. Another way to apply the Raw adjustments from this image to the other images would be to click the Select All button at the top left of the Camera Raw filter, then click the Synchronize button that became enabled after you clicked Select All. Synchronize causes the adjustments from the selected image, with the blue outline around it, to be applied to the other ones. First a Synchronize dialog will appear allowing you to choose the particular adjustments you want applied to all images. Usually the choice you want is all of the adjustments except White Balance and Crop.

The advantage to applying the settings to all images this way is that you can then click one of the other images, while still in Camera Raw, and tweak any of these settings that appear to be a bit off for

that image. Most of the settings will be the same, but you might want to change the Exposure and/or Shadows setting a bit, for example.

◆ Now, if you want to open all three of these into Photoshop from Camera Raw, you can click Select/All again and then click Open 3 Images, and all three of those will open into Photoshop. Those Raw adjustments you made for each of these images will also be saved in each image's XMP file.

◆ If you want to continue to sort and correct images in Bridge, you can click the Done button. If you entered Camera Raw using File/Open in Camera Raw, then you will have accomplished all this without even entering Photoshop! If you entered Camera Raw using File/Open With/Adobe Photoshop, when you click Done you'll be sitting there in Photoshop and will have to navigate your way back to Bridge to get more work done.

Creating Photoshop Adjustment Layers and Applying Them to Several Images

You should read Chapter 21, "Overall Color Correction," and maybe Chapter 22, "Correcting Problem Images," so you'll have a deeper understanding of the possibilities touched on in this section. In this section we briefly mention a color adjustment workflow, but cover it more completely in those chapters. We're going through this workflow here because I find that my workshop students, even though they understand Photoshop quite well, often have trouble integrating Photoshop steps and actions with Bridge and Batches. Here we'll put it all together.

Getting Raw Corrected Images into Photoshop

◆ Make a fresh copy of the Chapter 11 folder from your *Photoshop Artistry* DVD to your desktop. This will give you a copy of the three tugboat files, along with their XMP files, with my adjustments from the Camera Raw filter. Navigate Bridge to that fresh copy of this folder on the desktop, and select all three of these GibsonsTugBoats files from inside that newly copied folder. Use File/Open in Camera Raw to open all three at once into the Camera Raw filter within Bridge as you learned in the previous section.

◆ Click the Middle image, number 8314, which already has the initial corrections I have done to it with Camera Raw. These same corrections have already been applied to the other two images, but those two need to be tweaked.

- Click the top 8313 image and you'll notice that the right side of the histogram is losing highlight details. With the Option (Alt) key down, move the Exposure slider to the left until the highlight details are restored.

Again, this process is explained in great detail in Chapters 9, 21, and 22. Here we are integrating them into a total workflow.

- The rest of the adjustments for image 8313 are fine left the same as those for 8314. Now click the bottom, 8315 image. Here the Exposure setting can be moved a little bit to the right, again with the Option (Alt) key held down to see what highlights are clipped.

- Now Click Select All in the top-left corner and click Open 3 Images at the bottom right, and these three images should open into Photoshop. Now in Photoshop, choose GibsonsTug-Boats8314 from the Window menu, and the middle image should come to the front. Type F to put that image in Full Screen mode. Use Command (Ctrl)-0 to zoom in, and use [F9] to bring up the Info palette.

Use Threshold

Now you'll do the overall color correction steps in Photoshop. The first of these steps is to set the highlight and shadow points using Threshold. Refer to step 3 of Chapter 22, or all of Chapter 21, if you need more help understanding this step.

- Go to Layer/New Adjustment Layer/Threshold to find your highlight and shadow. With Preview on, move the slider to the right till the brightest highlights show in white. Zoom in to the highlight area, then Shift-click to set a Color Sampler there. Zoom out and then move the slider to the left until you see the darkest area. Zoom in to that area, and Shift-click to add a second Color Sampler there. The highlight will be out on the cloud on the right edge of the image, and the darkest point will be on the bow of the boat. Shift-click each of these to set Color Samplers, then cancel out of Threshold.

Use Levels

The second step in overall color correction is to do the main color adjustment using a Levels adjustment layer. Refer to step 4 of Chapter 22 if you need further help with these Levels adjustments.

- Type [Command (Ctrl)-F2] to bring up a Levels adjustment layer. Now hold Command (Ctrl)-Spacebar down, then click and drag a box around your highlight spot, and set the highlight on that cloud where you put the Highlight Color Sampler. Use Com-

mand (Ctrl)-0 to zoom back out and then zoom back into the bow area of the boat and set your shadow at the Color Sampler you put there.

- Use the RGB midtone slider to lighten the image a little, then look at the color balance. The image is a bit blue, so go to the Blue channel and add some yellow to make it warmer. Setting the middle slider to about 94 or 95 should do it.

- We're also going to add a tad of magenta, so go to the Green channel and do this by eye. We used a setting of 98 for the middle slider here. Remember, once you have clicked on a slider, you can use your arrow keys to move that slider value in increments of 1.

Use Curves

The third step in overall color correction is to do the overall contrast adjustment using a Curves adjustment layer. Refer to step 5 of Chapter 22 if you need further help with these Curves adjustments.

- Use [Command (Ctrl)-F3] to create a Curves adjustment layer, and do a little S-curve to increase the contrast. Just Option (Alt)-click in the curve diagram till you get the diagram that has only four dividers. Click a point in each of the intersection points down the middle diagonal line. Drag the topmost point up and to the left. Drag the bottommost point down and to the right. This makes an S-curve and increases the contrast. Click OK to exit Curves.

Use Hue/Saturation

Hue/Saturation is covered in step 6 of Chapter 22, so look there if you need help with this correction tool.

- Use [Command (Ctrl) F4] to do a Hue/Saturation adjustment layer, and saturate all the colors by about +12 with Edit set to Master. We usually use somewhere between 10 and 20.

- Set Edit to Blues to tweak the blue colors a bit. Saturate the blues by about +15, and if you want to make sure that you're picking the blues in the water and the sky, use the +Eyedropper tool and drag across the blue areas in the image that you want to make sure are included in the adjustment.

- Move the Hue slider for the blues. To the left, the blues become more cyan; to the right, they become more magenta.

- Now go to Red and saturate the reds a bit, maybe about +8. Make sure you click the Preview button off and on again to see the before and after effect.

Open the Shadows

There were your three basic overall adjustment layers. Now for specific adjustments. Let's say you want to open up the shadow detail a bit. You'll add a curve to accomplish this. This type of adjustment is covered in step 7 of Chapter 22.

◆ Use [Command (Ctrl)-F3] to create another Curves adjustment layer. Name this adjustment layer OpenShadows. While looking at the shadow part of the image, hold the mouse button down and measure the shadow areas you want to adjust. Notice where the circle moves on the curve graph. Click where the these values are on the curve graph, and drag the curve up and to the left. Don't look at the overall image—look only at the darkest areas and lighten those as much as you think you want. Click OK.

◆ Choose Image/Adjustments/Invert, or Command (Ctrl)-I, to invert the layer mask on that adjustment layer. Type B for the Brush tool, then choose the Airbrush 7% setting from the Tool presets pop-up. Now type D for Default colors so that you're painting with white. You now want to paint with white on the mask for the adjustment layer.

◆ Zoom in on the dark areas, use the right bracket key to get a bit bigger brush, and paint with the white brush to lighten some of those shadows. You are painting white in the mask, which slowly adds the curve adjustment you made above to the areas where you paint. Hold your Spacebar down to scroll around. Any other places that you see where you want to open up detail can be airbrushed at this same time using this same curve.

◆ To see what you've just done, type H to put yourself back in the Hand tool, zoom back out and type [F10] to bring up your Layers palette, then turn this adjustment layer off and on to check the adjustment. If you want to open the shadows more here or in a different area, type B to go back to the Brush tool. When you're finished with your painting, type H to put yourself back in the Hand tool.

These would be the basic Photoshop adjustment layers for this image, and we've quickly shown you the steps to create them.

Automatically Apply Those Adjustments to Other Images

Now that we have these adjustment layers, one way to apply them to the other images is to create a new Layer group.

◆ To do this, hold the Shift key down and select all four adjustment layers in the Layers palette. Then go to Layer/New/Group from Layers. Name this group "For All Images." What we want to do now is drag this group of layers over to the other images.

◆ Put this first image into Normal Screen mode by typing F twice, and make sure the other images are showing onscreen behind this image. Click the For All Images layer group folder and hold the mouse down as you drag this folder on top of one of the other images. Hold down the Shift key as you drag to center the layer

Here in the Layers palette you see the four adjustment layers we created to color correct the initial image. We're choosing to put those four layers into a group so they can be more easily moved to other images using drag and drop.

Here we see the group that we created in the image to the left. We have put the three images into Normal Screen mode so we can see them all. With the image containing the Ggroup on top, we click the group in the Layers palette, then drag it and drop it on one of the other two images. Once you see the gray boxlike icon on the second image, you can release the mouse button to add the group of layers to that image.

After dragging the group of layers to the lower image, we've filled the shadow detail mask with black and are now painting white in that mask with the Airbrush 7% Brush in the areas where we want to bring out more shadow detail. We'll go through all these color adjustment and masking techniques in detail in Chapter 21 and 22. What we want you to learn from this chapter is how you can use Bridge, Camera Raw and Photoshop together to automate the process of working with many images.

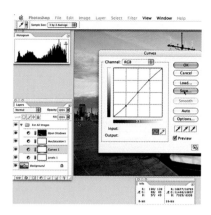

Saving the Curves setting so we can use it to create an action. Just double-click the Curves thumbnail to bring up this dialog, then click the Save button and put the setting file in the BridgeAutomationDemo folder.

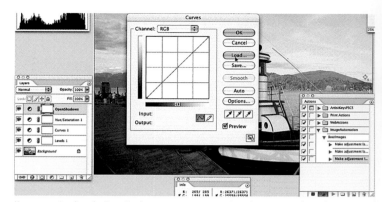

Here we are Loading the OpenShadows curve as we are making the action to adjust a large group of images. You can see the layers we are creating to the left, and the action in the Actions palette to the right.

group over the other image. Release the mouse button before releasing the Shift key, and this will make a centered copy of all these layers on the other image. Repeat this process to drag a copy of the layer group to the other image.

Now you have applied that same set of adjustments to the other two images by dragging a copy of all the adjustment layers to those images.

◆ To tweak one of these other images, click that image and type F for Full Screen mode, then zoom in. Click the gray triangle to the left of the For All Images group folder to open the folder and show all the layers. The mask on the top adjustment layer will need to be different for each of these two new images. Click the rightmost mask thumbnail of the OpenShadows layer to make it active. Now choose Edit/Fill or type Shift-Delete (Backspace) and choose Black as the color to fill it with. Refill this layer mask with 100% black.

◆ Type B for the Brush tool and D for default colors, and paint the mask for the OpenShadows adjustment of this image in the places where you want to open up, or lighten, the shadows. Now fix the mask on the third image, and you've color corrected all three images.

Using a Batch to Adjust a Larger Set of Images

Another way you can apply a set of layers from one image to another is to go back to the original image where you created the layers and make an action script to create those layers. Because we've already

made the set of layers for one image, we can just remember the settings for each of those layers.

Save Layer Settings

◆ To do that, double-click each one of the adjustment layer thumbnails, which will bring up the Adjustment dialog. Click the Save button, then create a new folder on your desktop with a name that indicates what these layers are for. Call it BridgeAutomationDemo. Inside that folder, save your Levels settings, again using a name that makes sense to you. After you save the settings, you can cancel out of the dialog without making any changes to the current image. Save your Curves settings, Hue/Sat settings, and Open Shadow curve settings in the same fashion and in the same folder.

Create an Action to Make these Adjustments

Once you've saved the settings, you want to create an action that will create adjustment layers with those same settings in the other images that we want to apply them to. The easiest way to do this is to throw away the group from this first image and then re-create the adjustment layers here.

◆ Bring up the Actions palette [F11]. If Button mode is on, use the Actions menu to turn off Button mode. Click the Actions palette pop-up menu and choose New Set for a new set of actions. Name this set Image Automation. We created a new set so it would not be part of any other set of actions, like ArtistKeys. Again go to the Actions palette pop-up and choose New Action. Name this action with a name that indicates what shoot you are going to process; in this case we used BoatImages.

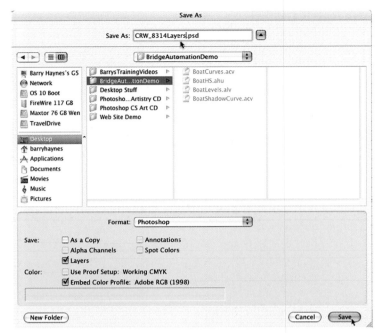

Here we see the Save As dialog. The important points are that we've added the word *Layers* and we are saving into the BridgeAutomationDemo folder.

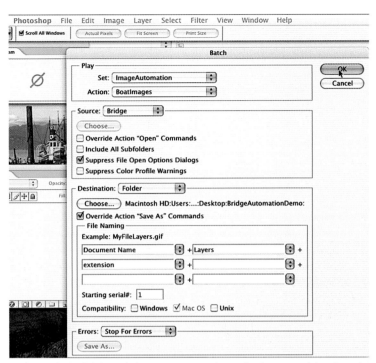

Here we see the Batch dialog with the correct settings as discussed in the main text below. Note what you do in this dialog to add the word *Layers* to the filenames.

If you were in the studio and you had shot a couple hundred images, it would be much quicker to set up an action like this rather than manually drag the group of layers to every image.

◆ Click Record in the New Action dialog to begin recording the action. Now you'll go through the steps that you used to create the adjustment layers, but you can go really quickly since you already have your settings for each layer saved.

◆ Type [Command (Ctrl)-F2] to make a new Levels adjustment layer, click OK to the New Layer dialog, then click Load to load the saved Levels setting from the BridgeAutomationDemo folder. The three-letter extension for Levels is .alv. Click OK to close Levels.

◆ Type [Command (Ctrl)-F3] to make a new Curves adjustment layer, click OK, then load the Curves setting for the overall curves. The 3-letter extension for curves is .acv. Make sure you load the Overall curve and not the one for the shadows. Click OK to close Curves.

◆ Type [Command(Control)-F4] to make a new Hue/Saturation adjustment layer, click OK, and load the overall Hue/Sat settings that you created. The three-letter extension for Hue/Sat is .ahu. Click OK to close Hue/Saturation.

◆ Finally, type [Command (Ctrl)-F3] again to make another Curves adjustment layer that will be the Shadow adjustment for each image. Name this layer OpenShadows, click OK, load the Shadow curve, and then click OK to close Curves. For this particular adjustment, you want to invert the mask; so use Image/Adjust/Invert, but don't bother painting on this layer because the placement of the shadows will be different in each image. So you will have to paint in the areas where you want to open the shadows separately for each image.

◆ After you have created all the adjustment layers, you need to do a File/Save As to direct the action to the folder where you want all your images saved. Add the word *Layers* to the end of the filename (but before the extension), then save the image in Photoshop format. Once the image is saved, make sure you click the Stop Recording button on the bottom of the Actions palette or use Stop Recording from the Actions palette pop-up menu.

Applying the Action to Other Images

Now we'll use Bridge to apply the action to whatever images we want. It's faster and easier to select the images from Bridge than it is to open them from Photoshop. This is especially true of large groups of Raw images that haven't been named or color corrected, since Bridge still shows us good-quality previews of those images.

◆ When you want to apply that action to some other images, click the action in Photoshop, then go back to Bridge. Click and select all the other images that you want to apply the action to, then choose Tools/Photoshop/Batch to run the Photoshop Batch on all your selected images.

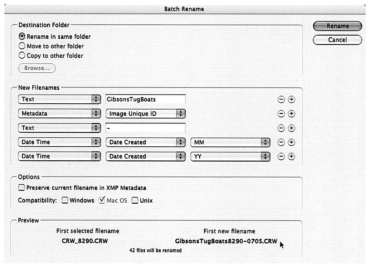

Here in the Tools/Batch Rename dialog we are renaming all the files in the Tugboat shoot, which, as you can see at the bottom in the Preview area, started out as Raw files in the format CRW_8290.CRW. We want the new format to have the name GibsonsTugBoats, which we put in the first Text field. You can add a new field by clicking the + radio button to the right of the current field. We next added a field from the camera's metadata, which is the Image Unique ID. This is the number the camera gave this image, and we wanted to keep it. Next we added a text field so we could put a dash in the filename. We wanted the month and year, but the Date Time menu didn't have that as an option. It did have just the month, so we chose that. To get the year we used the +, then added another Date Time part and set that to just the year. As you can see in the Preview area at the bottom, the final filenames have this format: GibsonsTugboats8290-0705.CRW.

The Batch Dialog

Look at the illustration of the Batch dialog on this page as we go through the different settings with you.

◆ In this Batch dialog, make sure you have the right set of actions, and the correct action within that set, selected. The Source files are going to be coming from Bridge, and the Suppress File Open Options Dialogs check box should be on. Set the Destination menu to Folder, then click the Choose button and navigate to the BridgeAutomationDemo folder you created earlier.

◆ Make sure the Override Action "Save As" Commands box is also checked. When you first turn that check box on, you'll get a rather obscure warning. What it actually means is that you have to have a Save As step in the action, otherwise the files won't actually get saved. We have a Save As step in there, but now we're going to override that step with these instructions. The instructions are to add the word *Layers*. So it's going to be the old filename, plus the word *Layers*, plus the file format extension. Now the files should actually be saved in that correct folder when we run the action.

When running a Batch, it's best to place the destination files into a different folder than where they were stored originally. That way if a Batch error overwrites your original files, you won't lose your originals. Our technical editor, Wayne Palmer, added this comment here: "I would really emphasize this if you were to create an action that ever changes the size of the file. I can tell you horror stories!"

Click OK and See What Happens

When you click OK to run your Batch, you should see the Actions palette running through each step of the action for each image you've chosen. The actions run so quickly that you might not see the actual layers being created, but you should see the progress bar come up for each image as it's being saved.

◆ You can close the Actions palette in Photoshop now. If you go to the Finder or File Manager and look in that destination folder, you should see that those files have been added and are now all set up for you to dodge that final layer. You can simply open each one, type B for the Brush tool, D for the Default colors, and then paint white to open up the shadows where you need to. Use Command (Ctrl)-S to save the file again when you've done this step.

A Batch That Leaves Files Open in Photoshop

When you run a Batch and you want your files just to be left open in Photoshop, you can choose None in the Destination pop-up and the files will be left open onscreen. However, if you are running the batch on a hundred or so files, you probably want the Batch to automatically save and close them.

Renaming Files

A great feature of Bridge is the ability to easily rename a large group of files that usually have meaningless names assigned by a digital camera.

◆ To rename all the files in a particular shoot, you first select all those files using Bridge. Then choose Tools/Batch Rename to specify the details of the new names. It will be easier for you to understand if you read how to specify the details of the names while looking at the Batch Rename dialog at the top of this page. Also see the name-specification info in the caption for that dialog.

The Edit/Find Command

If you use keywords a lot or descriptive filenames, then the Find command can be useful for finding images of a certain category. Look at the Find dialog, and its features, to the left. I personally don't look for images this way, as my brain remembers based on where I put the images. I usually leave images from a particular project in one folder with that project's name and date. Once I get to that folder, I can find the image I'm looking for visually with Bridge. For someone doing stock photography, though, keyword searches could be very useful, provided you take the time up front to enter descriptive keywords for each image. You'd enter those in the Metadata area of Bridge, which we'll talk about next.

Bridge Keywords and Metadata

Bridge has an extensive set of things that you can do with Keywords and Metadata. These features are best explained while looking at the appropriate part of Bridge.

◆ Use Command (Ctrl)-F9 to bring up the FoldersBig workspace. Click the Keywords tab to see keywords instead of folders. At the top left of this page you see Bridge's Keywords tab, along with details of how to add new keywords and use them with your images.

◆ Keywords you use a lot, like *Gibsons* or *Corvallis* for me, can be added to your Bridge keyword set via the New Keyword menu, which pops up from the little pop-up menu at the top right of

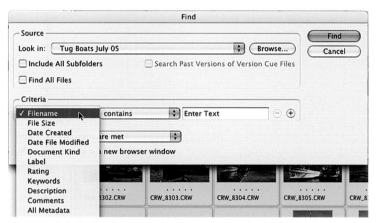

Here we see the Bridge Find dialog. Notice from the pop-up menu that, besides text searches, you can also search by File Size, Date Created, Document Kind, and other categories.

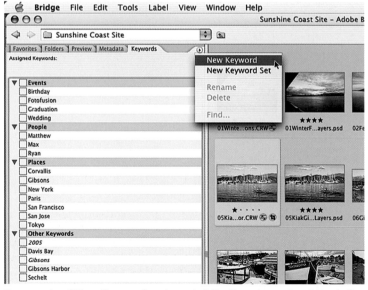

Here we see how Bridge will appear after going to the FoldersBig workspace, then clicking the Keywords tab. Notice in the pop-down menu in this dialog that you can also create new keyword sets. These are the different categories of keywords that show up here to the left in bold type. You create keyword sets to store keywords in particular categories that you use a lot.

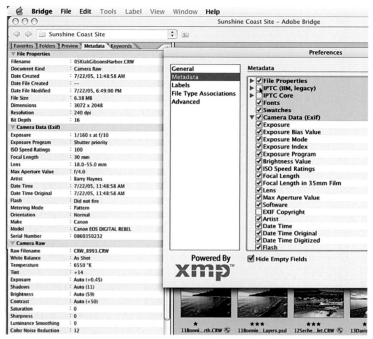

To the left in this illustration you see the metadata display that you get when clicking the Metadata tab after choosing the FoldersBig workspace—Command (Ctrl)-F9. You call up the Metadata Preferences, to the right, by clicking the pop-up menu at the top right of this Metadata area. You can also access these Preferences using Bridge/Preferences, then clicking the Metadata option.

Here we see the list of File Info categories. Description is the default category, and of course we know what Camera Data is. AP Categories and IPTC Contact, Content, Image, and Status are both standard photograph categories used by national and international photography organizations. If you were shooting for AP—the Associated Press—for example, you could enter all that standard information about your images here.

the keywords area. If you want to add a particular keyword to the currently selected file(s), just click the check box next to that keyword. These keywords will then later show up in the File Info for those files even if you save them in Photoshop, TIFF, or JPEG format. You can then use Bridge to search for these keywords and find all files that contain them.

♦ Below you see how to access and use the files' metadata information by clicking the Metadata tab. Choose Command (Ctrl)-F9 to pick the FoldersBig workspace, select an image in one of your folders, then click on the Metadata tab. The Metadata preferences, shown to the right below, choose which metadata categories, like File Properties and Camera Raw, and which items within each category show up in the Metadata display.

A lot of useful information from your digital camera (shutter speed, aperature, date, and so on) gets saved along with the Raw or JPEG files from your camera. By using File/File Info, you can also add many different categories of file info, which will also show up in the Metadata display if you have that category turned on. I myself don't modify the keywords and metadata fields of my images very often, although I do use a few keywords from time to time, and I also always put my name, copyright, and Web site information in images that get sent out into the world. We show you how to do that for a group of files earler in this chapter in the "Creating a Web Site from a Group of Images" section. Once you've added this info to your files, the info will show up in the Metadata area.

For someone who is a new photographer or a commercial shooter, and/or someone who distributes their images over the Web or via stock agencies, these features are very useful, so check them out! There is a great book called *The DAM Book: Digital Asset Management for Photographers* (O'Reilly 2005), by Peter Krogh. This volume has lots of helpful and detailed information about how to manage your files, keywords, and metadata.

Conclusion

This chapter has focused on showing you the parts of the Bridge application that we feel are most important for photographers. We spent a lot time showing you how to set up Bridge for efficient use. We also showed you how to use Bridge in combination with Camera Raw, Photoshop Actions, Batch, and other automation features. Automating your image processing in these ways is really the most important thing you can do with Bridge. We did not go through every last feature of Bridge. You can find that menu-by-menu type of information in other books, as well as in the Adobe Help files and manuals that come with Bridge. Have fun processing your images!

Portfolio

Kirsten Shaw

Kirsten took this shot on a recent trip to Iceland. Because she was there in the fall, the colors were wonderful, but it was almost always raining. She brought this image to Wendy's intro class hoping to find a way to show its true beauty. "When you are there," she said, "you see past the rain, and this is what you see."

12 ◆ Essential Photoshop Techniques for Photographers

We wanted to have a chapter where photographers could go and quickly access essential techniques that they will use every day. Sometimes those techniques will be explained in this chapter, and in other instances we'll refer you to other chapters, sections, and pages in this book. Enjoy while learning to master these important techniques! The big purple starfish above reminds us of SpongeBob's best friend Patrick. Our 10-year-old son, Max, watches *SpongeBob SquarePants,* and we can just imagine Patrick and his friend taking in the rays at the Davis Bay beach on the "Sunshine Coast" in B.C.

A selection by itself isn't actually doing anything to this image. It's a mask with no action associated with it until you do Levels or Curves or Paint or something. It's still a mask, though, in my mind.

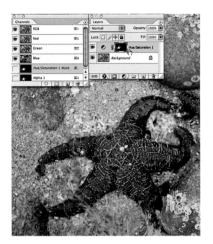

Now we've saved this selection when creating a Hue/Saturation adjustment layer and the selection has become an adjustment layer mask. The white parts of that mask are controlling where that adjustment will happen to the cumulative parts of all the layers that are below this adjustment layer. Just one at this point. This mask is actually affecting the image. Channel 4 is still sitting there doing nothing.

Thinking About Masks

You'll find it helpful if you simplify your thought process by realizing that selections, channels, adjustment layer masks, and regular layer masks are all really something of the same concept. They are all ways to isolate or separate one part of an image from the other parts. They are just different applications or uses of the same concept. I, Barry, strongly believe in the KISS principle: KEEP IT SIMPLE, STUPID! Not that anyone is stupid at all—it's just an engineering expression that applies here because people tend to make selections, masks, channels, and layer masks too complicated. Don't be afraid of them! When you learn to think about all these concepts as the same thing, really, you're just applying the KISS principle.

Selections

When you use the Lasso tool or the Marquee or Magic Wand, you are making a selection (creating a mask) that has no permanent loca-

Now we've saved this selection in the Channels palette, and it shows up with the default name Alpha 1. We could deselect the selection, close the file, and come back another day, then Command (Ctrl)-click this to load it as a selection again. This Alpha 1 channel is still a mask—just a mask that isn't doing anything to the image.

tion. The selection just floats on your screen, and you can apply it to, or have it affect, whatever layer is active. Just click a different layer, and that selection will now be applied to that layer. Adjustment layer masks or regular layer masks are selections (masks) whose nonblack areas are already applied to a particular layer, and, unless they are totally black, they are actively doing something to the cumulative composite that creates your final image. When you have a selection on your screen, you then have to do something else, like run a Levels or Curves adjustment, to have that selection actually affect the image. The process here is to first make the selection, then do something the selection will affect. If what you do is create an adjustment layer, then that selection gets permanently saved as the adjustment layer's mask. This is the best way to work.

Channels

A channel just gives you a place to save a selection that you might want to use later. If a layer has a layer mask, that mask shows up in the Channels palette as channel \ only when that layer is active. If the channel is #4 or greater in an RGB image, it isn't doing anything to the image; it's just sitting there as a selection that has been saved.

Adjustment Layer Masks

When you have a selection that has been converted into, or was created as, an adjustment layer mask, it is actively doing something to the image. If that layer is active, then that layer's mask shows up in the Channels palette; otherwise it just shows up in the Layers palette.

Regular Layer Masks

A regular layer mask is also actively doing something to the image. The nonblack parts of the layer mask are controlling the parts of the

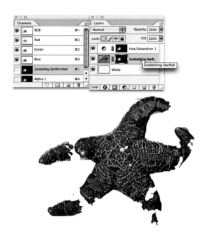

This regular layer mask is now removing the parts of this image where this mask is non-black. We call it nonblack because even gray areas of a mask will reveal part of the image in those areas. It's not just the white parts that affect the image. Another way to think about it is "white reveals, black conceals, and gray partially reveals."

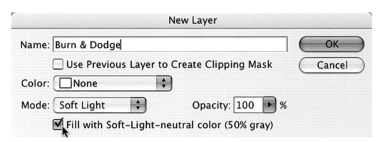

Here is the New Layer dialog as it needs to be set up for a Soft Light Burn & Dodge layer. [Command (Ctrl)-Shift-F2] will make one of these for you using ArtistKeys.

layer that are visible. A regular layer mask shows up in the Channels palette only when that layer is active.

Again, these are all examples of the same concept of isolating a part of the image—the concept is just applied in different ways. If you Command (Ctrl)-click any channel, adjustment layer mask, or regular layer mask, this turns the nonblack areas of that mask into a selection that you can then use to affect another layer by just clicking that other layer and doing something with the selection.

Look in Chapters 6, 7, 19, 21, 22, 23, and beyond for many different applications of masks, and you'll learn more about them. Just don't get carried away trying to make something complicated out of something that's actually very simple. So many people have made comments to me like, "I'm starting to understand layers a bit, but I don't understand channels at all." Now you know that saving a selection in a channel just parks it there, period. It's that simple. When a selection (mask) is a layer mask of some kind, then it's actually doing something to the image.

Burning and Dodging

I never use the Burn and Dodge tools! The reason I don't use them is because when you, for example, burn (darken) some pixels, you are changing the actual pixel values in your *Background* or other real layer to make them darker. If you later decide that you burned them too much and go back to dodge (lighten) them, you'll find that the quality of those lighter pixels isn't as good as that of the original pixels, especially if they were burned heavily. Shadow details will have been lost in the burning, and you won't be able to get them back. To do your burning and dodging, it's much better to use the Soft Light Burn & Dodge layer or a Curves adjustment layer, as we'll show you here. Also, when you use the Burn or Dodge tool, your choices are

limited to working with Shadows, Midtones, or Highlights. You can make that choice much more accurately when you burn or dodge with a Curves adjustment layer.

Soft Light Burn & Dodge Layer

As a final step in making a master image, I always put a Burn & Dodge layer at the top and make any adjustments that are needed to the lighting of the entire image. This is always a great last step and can make the difference between an OK image and a great image. Here are the steps to make a Softlight Burn & Dodge layer that will allow you to burn or dodge anything in your image, as all other layers will be below the layer we are about to make.

◆ You can try this with any of your images, or you can open the Starfish9217Layers.psd file from the Ch12.Essential PS Techniques folder on the DVD. Just bring up an image and follow these steps. Before I start this final Burn and Dodge, I usually press Tab to remove all the palettes and then type Command (Ctrl)-0 to zoom the image to Fit on Screen. This way the image fills the screen without any palettes getting in the way of artistic perception. Now press [F12] to bring up just the Options bar.

◆ Make sure the top layer in your Layers palette is active. Choose Layer/New Layer, naming this layer Burn & Dodge, then set the Mode to Soft Light and check the Fill With Soft-Light-Neutral Color (50% Gray) option. When you click OK, you'll get a solid-gray layer, yet the image won't look any different because 50% gray doesn't show up in Soft Light mode.

◆ Type a B for Brush and choose the Airbrush 7% option from the Tool Presets pop-down to the left side of the Options bar. (These presets and the Artistry brushes need to be set up as we explain in Chapter 2, "Preferences and Color Settings.") Now type D for default colors, and you will be painting with black.

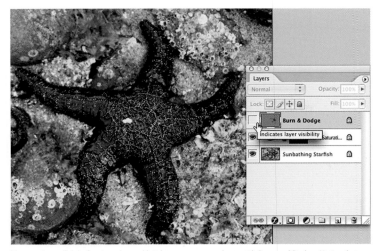

The purple starfish before its color and brightness are evened out with Burn and Dodge. Notice that we just turned the Eye icon off on the Burn & Dodge layer to see this.

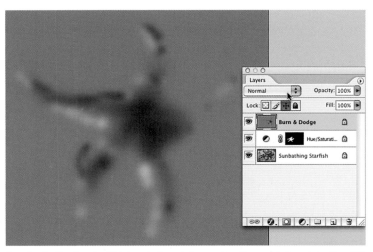

Changing the Blend mode of this layer to Normal shows us how the areas that are darker than 50% gray are making the starfish darker, and the lighter areas are brightening things up.

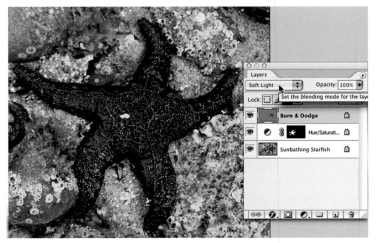

The starfish after its color and brightness are evened out with Burn and Dodge. Notice that we just turned the Eye icon back on in the Burn & Dodge layer to see this version. Open the Starfish-9217Layers.psd file from the Ch12.Essential PS Techniques folder on the DVD if you would like to experiment with these layers and masks.

When you type D on a regular layer, you get black as the foreground color and white as the background color. Remember that this is the opposite when you are working on a mask.

◆ Now paint with the black soft brush wherever you want to darken, or burn, the image. The darker you make it, the darker the underlying image will get. If you want to lighten, or dodge, the image, type an X to exchange the colors and paint with white. This also works for painting over areas that you've burned too much.

The original image with the final Burn & Dodge layer off.

Now with the Burn & Dodge layer on showing more details in the rocks around the starfish, too.

Remember that the left bracket key will make your brush bigger, and the right bracket key will make it smaller. I sometimes change the

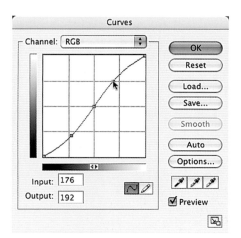

This is a midtone curve that I applied to increase the contrast of areas around the edges of the starfish. I looked at those areas while creating this curve, clicked OK, inverted the mask, then painted in the areas where I wanted to apply this curve using a soft white brush.

Starfish contrast mask with increased contrast areas being the nonblack areas.

Starfish contrast before applying this curve.

Starfish contrast after applying this curve.

Brush Flow from 7% to 4% when doing this. That allows me to make more subtle changes and ensures that I don't overdo it.

Burn or Dodge with Curves

When you have to do more serious burning and dodging, using a curve gives you a lot more control. This is usually done after the overall color correction steps of a Levels, Curves, then Hue/Saturation adjustment layer. At this point there is sometimes a shadow area that is too dark but also too flat. It might also be a highlight area that is too washed out and/or too flat. You can also use this technique for midtones or any tonal range area of the image that needs to be lightened or darkened but also needs to have its contrast or even its color balance changed.

Focus on the Area in Question

◆ In this curve process you want to zoom your image so that you're looking at the area you want to fix but you can also see the relationship between that area and the surrounding parts of the image. You then choose Layer/New Adjustment Layer/Curves [Command (Ctrl)-F3] and make a curve that will adjust the important area the way you want; you can even overdo the curve a bit because you will be applying it using a soft Airbrush, and you can also later decrease the opacity of this layer to reduce the effect.

It is quicker to reduce the effect with the Opacity setting than to have to go back into the curve and further tweak it. Also, during this step you don't have to worry if this curve totally destroys other parts of the

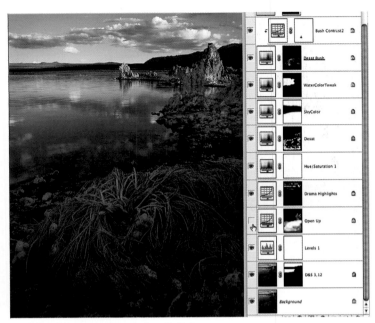

Barry's Mono Lake image without the Open Up Dodge curve.

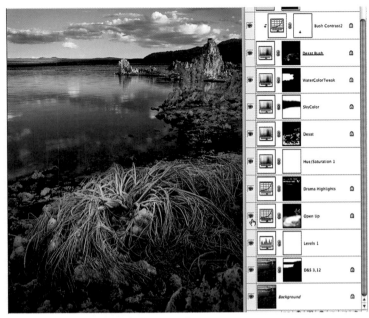

The same Mono lake image with the Open Up Dodge curve on.

image, since the mask you will make will stop that from happening. When you are finished with your curve, click OK in the Curves dialog.

Invert the Mask and Paint in Your Effect

Invert is the best way to make this mask black, because it always works, it's very fast, and it doesn't depend on the state of the foreground or background colors, which some Fill options do.

◆ Use Image/Adjustments/Invert (Command (Ctrl)-I) to invert the mask of the Curves adjustment layer and make it black.

◆ Now type B for the Paintbrush, choose Airbrush 7% from the Tool Presets pop-up at the left of the Options bar, and type D for default colors. This gives you a 100-pixel soft brush and sets you up for painting with white. You should now be looking at your image the way it appeared before you made this curve.

◆ Painting on top of the areas you wanted to modify will slowly bring up the changes you created with the curve. It is better to do it slowly. And remember that in Airbrush mode, which you are now in, the longer you hold the mouse button down, the whiter the mask gets in that area and the more your effect gets applied. This is so cool! If you overdo it and apply too much of the effect, just type X to switch the foreground color to black, and paint over your area with some black to lessen the effect.

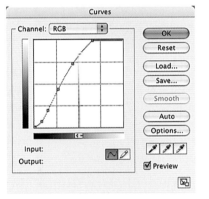

The Open Up curve that allows the above improvement to the Mono Lake image. Of course this curve is applied only in the areas where the mask for this adjustment layer is white. To see that mask, open the Mono-LakeDriedBushLayersSm.psd file from the Ch22.Correcting Problem Images folder on the DVD. Then Option (Alt)-click the layer mask thumbnail for this Open Up layer.

It Gets Even Better—You Can Tweak the Curve

Now that you have a mask created in the areas you want to fix, there are several ways to further tweak your fixes. In the first technique, you have to switch to the Hand tool because typing a number while in the Paintbrush will change the Flow rate of the brush instead of the Layer Opacity.

◆ If the fixes are all overdone, then just type an H to move into the Hand tool, then type a number between 1 and 9 to change the Opacity setting of the layer. The Layer starts out at 100% Opacity, so if things are really too hot, type a 5 for 50%. I'll often just type a 1 for 10%, then move on up the keyboard—2 for 20%, 3 for 30%, and so on—until I get where I want to be. If you type two numbers together quickly, like 35, you'll get 35% instead of the 30% and then 50% you would get if you typed slowly. Remember that 0 puts you back at 100%.

◆ If the curve just wasn't strong enough to produce the effect you wanted, or if it needs some other change, just double-click the leftmost Layer thumbnail to bring the Curves dialog back up again. You already have a mask that is nonblack in the areas that you want to change, so when you change the curve now, only those nonblack areas will be modified by this curve change.

Again, I'm using the expression nonblack here to emphasize that even areas where the curve is a dark gray will be affected just a little by this curve. The subtleties you can get with this method are awesome.

Mouse to Locate Image Areas on the Curve

These techniques can often help you to decide what areas of the curve to initially modify, and now it can help you decide how to change the curve to make it even better.

◆ Another thing to remember here is that if you hold the mouse button down over the areas in the image you want to modify, a small circle will appear on the curve graph showing you where those areas actually are in the curve. As you are changing the curve, turning the Preview button off shows you the way the image was in the previous version of the curve, and turning the Preview button on shows you the image with this curve. When you think you are finished with your changes, it is always best to do the Preview button test; if you like the image better with the Preview button on, then click OK to accept the changes. If it looks better with the Preview button off, then you can Cancel this round of Curves changes.

Actions Give More Control Than Shadow/Highlight

Adjusting shadows, highlights, and midtones with curves and masks gives you way more control than you'd have with the built-in Shadow/Highlight tool, and you can create the effect just as quickly as with Shadow/Highlight by using an action. If you'd like, open the file GibsonsTownMorningLayers.psd from the Ch22.Correcting Problem Images folder on the DVD. Notice the layers named OpenShadows, AddHighlightDetail, and AddMidtoneContrast. They were all added using the BarrysColorCorrectionTemplate action, which sets up the normal Burn and Dodge Curve layers you might use while doing color correction using the workflow described in this book. Turn the Eye icons off for these three layers, then turn them on again and notice how much more control they gave me than Shadow/Highlight would have. Look at the GibsonsTownMorningTemplate file from the

same folder. This shows the image right after running the template action. With what you learn in Chapter 10, "Automating Photoshop," you can create your own color correction template action. The BarrysColorCorrectionTemplate action is also available in the Actions section of www.barryhaynes.com.

Other Artistry Examples of Burn & Dodge Curves

For other examples of how to use this type of curve effect in a variety of situations, see Chapters 21, 22, 25, and 28.

Spotting

Spots on film can come from schmutz inside the camera when the film is shot, from dirt in the film processing, from dirt where you store your film, and finally from the scanning process. To thoroughly spot (that is, remove spots from) your image, it is a good idea to look at every inch of your image at 100%. This is essential when working with a scan from film, since a dust spot could be anywhere on the film, and if you're not careful, there can be a lot of dust everywhere. When you're working with a digital camera, dirt can get on your digital sensor when you're changing lenses or through some other form of contamination. When this happens, you'll see a spot or spots in the same locations on each image since the sensor has contamination at that spot until you remove it. Digital cameras can also come with or develop faulty sensors, which would also cause a dirty or defective spot in a fixed place. When you first get a digital camera, it's probably a good idea to shoot a very clean, solid, neutral item so that item fills your screen. You can then run the spotting procedure I'll show you here to see if your camera has any initial defects.

When and Where to Spot

For the when, some people like to spot their images as soon as they scan or capture them. I believe this is premature for several reasons. The simplest one is that after you start to color correct this image, you might decide you don't really like it that much and that you'd rather work on another image. What a waste of time if you already spotted it!

I'd advise that you wait until you have finished the color correction of your master image, then spot that master image as one of the last steps before you archive all of your master layers. In the color correction process, you generally increase the contrast and saturation of your images. This higher contrast and saturation will make the spots show up more clearly. When the color correction is finished, you can then go back to the bottom, or Background, layer, or to a copy of that bottom layer or Smart Object, and do your spotting. So the "When to Spot" is after your master color correction layers have been added, and the "Where to Spot" is at the bottom of the master layers stack. We'll give you more good reasons for these rules of thumb below. You don't want to have to spot your image twice!

Smart Objects

You can't spot a Smart Object directly, so you have to spot a copy of the Smart Object that was turned into a normal layer.

◆ To do this, click the Smart Object, then choose Layer/New Layer via Copy (Command (Ctrl)-J). Now choose Layer/Smart Objects/Convert to Layer, and you'll have a normal layer that looks just like that Smart Object. You will spot that layer, realizing that if you later wanted to change the Smart Object's Raw interpretation, you'd have to re-spot that layer.

Another way to do spotting would be to use Layer/New Layer to add a layer at the top of your master layer stack. This layer would be transparent. You could turn on Sample All Layers in the Clone Stamp tool or in the Healing brush tools, and clone your changes up into this layer. This would now be a layer of just the changes; but the catch is that if after making test prints or at some point later you decided to change the color adjustments on some of underlying adjustment layers, the cloning you did on this layer with Sample All Layers on would

This is how your screen should look when you are ready to start spotting. You've used the Home key to scroll to the top-left corner, you are in the Clone Stamp or Healing brush tool, and all palettes but the Options bar are put away. In this case, I've held the Spacebar down for the Hand tool, and moved the window down and to the right just a tad so I can see the gray area to the top and left of the image. This just reassures me that I'm in the right spot, and also makes it a bit easier to get spots along those edges without autoscrolling happening.

no longer be totally correct, and you could possibly have to redo it. Had you done your changes to the copy of the Background or Smart Object layer at the bottom, this would not be a problem, because the changes to adjustment layers above would propagate upward.

Strategy and Tools for Individual Spotting

When spotting, do the following to set up your image on the screen.

◆ You want your active layer to be that *Background* or other layer we mentioned in the last section. Type F to put your image into Full Screen mode. Press the Tab key to remove all palettes from the screen, then [F12] to bring just the Options bar back to your screen. With your preferences set up as explained in Chapter 2, you can also choose Window/Workspace/Options Bar to set up just this palette and remove the others. Now choose View/Actual Pixels—Command-Option (Ctrl-Alt)-0—to zoom your image to 100%.

Home, Page Up, and Page Down

◆ Now you want to press the Home key on your keyboard to scroll your image to the top-left corner. This key, on my Mac keyboard, is above the arrow keys and right below the F15 key in the group of keys between the rightmost keypad group and the main group of keys on the left. It may be in a different location on your keyboard if you have a PC or Mac portable. After pressing Home, you are looking at the top-left area of your image at 100% and no palettes are in your way. Scan this area for spots, and if you find one, fix it. To fix it you'll use either the Clone Stamp tool (S) or the Spot Healing brush and its variants (J). We'll discuss these spotting tools in a minute; here we're covering a workflow to make sure you get all the spots.

◆ Scrolling to the Right: Once you've fixed all the spots on this screen, use Command (Ctrl)-Page Down to move one full screen to the right. The Page Down key is just to the right and below the Home key. After spotting this screen, continue to use Command (Ctrl)-Page Down to move one screen to the right until you've reached the top-right corner of your image, and spot it, too.

◆ Scrolling to the Left: Now press the Page Down key without the Command (Ctrl) key, and you will scroll your image one page down. Fix any spots on that screen. Now use Command (Ctrl)-Page Up to scroll one page to the left and fix spots on that page. Continue to do this until you reach the left edge again.

Here we see a spot in the clouds on the edge of a section of blue sky. The Spot Healing brush doesn't handle this too well because of the two different colors along which the spot exists. With the Clone Stamp tool here, we are Option (Alt)-clicking right on that line in a clean area just next to the spot. This is where we'll copy from.

When we hold the mouse button down on top of the spot, the + shows us where we are copying from and the circle shows us where we are copying to. Since we are able to copy from exactly on that line, the Clone Stamp tool makes an easy job of this issue.

The Spot Healing brush leaves this blue blob along the line where the spot was previously.

The regular Healing brush does better than Spot Healing because, like with the Clone-Stamp tool, we can first Option (Alt)-click on the line to pick the place we are sampling from.

◆ Now use Page Down again to scroll one page down, and repeat the Scrolling to the Right and Scrolling to the Left instructions above until you spot your entire image.

It is best to do this from left to right and from right to left, instead of top to bottom and then bottom to top; by going left to right and vice versa, the subject matter and tonalities will usually be similar all across the screen. This is less likely to be the case when you are working up and down. Doing all of a similar area at the same time will help you make consistent choices, which will make most images look better and more natural.

Over the years, one of the most common mistakes of students in my workshops is to spot their images while some palette is on the screen, like the Tools palette, and then miss some spots because they were under that palette. Not spotting at 100% is also a common mistake. When working with large files, people also make the mistake of looking at an 8x10 test print and assuming all is well because they see no spots. When they later make a 24x30 print, they can be frustrated to see spots that didn't show in the smaller print. If the spots are only a couple of pixels wide in a large file, they commonly won't show in the 8x10 print. If you spot your entire image at 100%, like we showed

you here, you shouldn't get surprise spots that show up only in large prints.

Clone Stamp or Healing Brushes?

Photoshop has always had the Clone Stamp tool for removing spots and scratches. It's the original tool for this purpose, and I've gotten very good with it over the years.

◆ To use it you type S, for Stamp, then pick a brush that is just a little wider than the spot, scratch, or piece of dust that you want to remove. You Option (Alt)-click next to the spot in a nearby area whose color and texture will best cover the spot by replacing it with a brushful from that area. Next, you move the cursor over the spot and click without the Option (Alt) key held down. If you hold the mouse button down for a minute, you'll see a + where you are copying from, and in the place you are copying to you'll see a circle indicating the brush's size. The nice thing about the Clone Stamp tool is that you can choose the exact pixels that will replace the spot every time.

As a general rule with the Clone Stamp tool, always dab—don't make strokes with the brush. Strokes can produce a slight blur, which will show your work. If the spot is on the edge of something, then you can Option (Alt)-click on that same edge but further along, where there is no spot. The Spot Healing brush doesn't work as well in difficult areas like this, but it is great for spots in the middle of solid blue sky, for example. With the Spot Healing brush, you just click down on top of a spot without having to Option (Alt)-click anywhere. The regular Healing brush also has a feature similar to the Clone Stamp, in which you Option (Alt)-click where you want to copy from. With the Healing brush you are copying texture from that area more than copying all the pixels, as you are in the Clone Stamp tool. Learn more about all these tools, as well as the Patch tool, in Chapter 26, "Restoring Old Photos." That chapter has many examples of how to use these tools under a variety of circumstances.

Try Out the Clone Stamp Tool and Healing Brushes

Now we'll try this out on Barry's MonoLakeDriedBush image. We will be talking about the color correction of this image in Chapter 22, "Correcting Problem Images." This is a low-resolution version of a much larger image Barry shot with his Pentax 6x7 camera on 120 film. Since it was shot with film, it's more likely to have dust spots than an image from a digital camera.

◆ Open the image MonoLakeDriedBushLayersSm.psd from folder Ch22.Correcting Problem Images on the *Photoshop Artistry* DVD. Type F for Full Screen mode. Press [F10] to bring up the Layers palette, then click the Background layer to activate it, and turn off the Eye icon for the D&S 3,12 layer right above the Background layer. We'll talk about this layer in just a bit. So that we can remove these spots in several ways, click the word *Background* and make a copy of the *Background* layer by dragging it to the Copy icon, next to the Trash icon at the bottom of the Layers palette.

◆ Bring up the Navigator palette, [Shift-F2], so you can see your zoom factor. Use Command (Ctrl)-Spacebar-click a few times to zoom into 300%. Normally you'd remove spots at 100%, but we are zooming in further here since this is a low-res image. Press the Tab key to remove all your palettes, then use [F12] to bring up just the Options bar. Press the Home key to bring yourself up to the top-left corner as we discussed in the previous section. Now type S to choose the Clone Stamp tool, and pick a 5-pixel hard-edge brush from the top-left area of the Brushes pop-up on the Options bar. The Mode should be set to Normal, with Opacity and Flow both set to 100%. Aligned should be on and Sample All Layers should be off.

◆ Move next to a spot and Option (Alt)-click on a nearby area that appears to be the right color and texture to cover the spot. Now move the brush circle over the spot. The circle should be slightly larger than the spot. You can use the left and right bracket keys (to the right of the P key) to make the brush smaller or larger. Click the spot, and remove it by copying from where you Option (Alt)-clicked and using those pixels to cover the spot. Move around on the screen and try other spots.

With Aligned on, the relationship between where you Option (Alt)-clicked and where the cursor currently is will remain the same, so you should be able to just click on other spots and have them go away. You'll notice that some of the spots in the clouds will require Option (Alt)-clicking in a different location to get the right color and texture match to properly remove the spot.

◆ When you've removed all the spots on the first screen area, use Command (Ctrl)-Page Down to move one screenful to the right. There is a really big spot that will require several clicks or switching to a bigger brush. Several clicks is usually faster and more transparent.

◆ Type a J to switch to the Healing brush. Shift-J will toggle between its variations. The Spot Healing brush has a small circle to the left of its thumbnail. Try this on some of the spots to see how it works. You don't need to Option (Alt)-click first with this tool—just click on top of a spot. If you need more spots, drag this layer to the Trash icon at the bottom of your Layers palette, then

When the Threshold is set to 0, that means that any difference in pixels can potentially be considered dust or scratches, and so everything is blurred and you even lose your grain pattern. This is too much blurring.

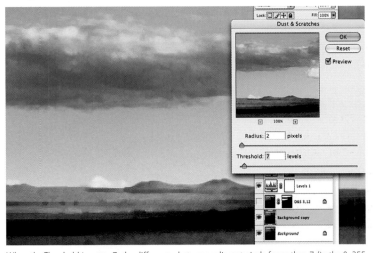

When the Threshold is set to 7, the differences between adjacent pixels fewer than 7 (in the 0..255 range) will not be blurred, as they are not considered dust and/or scratches. In this image, the grain pattern consists of values less different from each other than 7. This value will be different for various images and different types of film and digital camera files.

make another copy of the Background layer with a new set of spots. You may notice that this tool does not always work perfectly with spots in the clouds or spots on the lake.

◆ Use Shift-J to switch to the regular Healing brush and try it out. To start it going, you'll need to Option (Alt)-click on a clear sky area next to one of your spots, then just click on the spot like you did with the Clone Stamp tool. With this image, the regular Healing brush appears to do a slightly better job than the Spot Healing brush, especially if you click just to the right of the spots on the

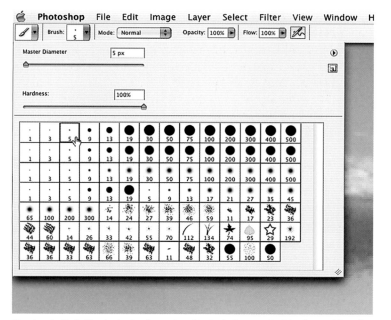

Choosing the 5-pixel hard-edge brush to paint white in the layer mask of the Dust and Scratches layer. This Brush pop-up menu sometimes reverts to Stroke Thumbnail mode and also changes size at random. This is a Photoshop bug, and when it happens, you just need to use the pop-up menu to the top right to return to Small Thumbnail mode, and use the grow box at the bottom right to change the size of the box so the top three rows end in a 500-pixel brush. I hope this bug is removed for CS3 and beyond. It's an intermittent bug, which is why the Adobe folks have probably had trouble reproducing it.

lake so that the correct water pattern texture can be applied to the spot.

Dust and Scratches Filter to Remove Spots

When there are a lot of dust spots in a nondetailed area, like a sky or lake, the Dust and Scratches filter can sometimes save you time. You don't want to use it on image detail, as this filter does blur details. The D&S 3,12 layer you initially turned off in the MonoLake image actually removed most of the spots in this image.

◆ Throw out your extra copies of the Background layer by dragging them to the Trash icon at the bottom right of the Layers palette. Now make yourself a new copy of the *Background* layer by clicking the word *Background* and dragging it to the Copy icon to the left of the Trash icon at the bottom of the Layers palette. You still need to be zoomed into 300%, since this is a low-res image. Turn on the Eye icon again for the D&S 3,12 layer, and you'll notice that all the spots go away. Notice that the layer mask for this layer is white only in the areas of the sky, so the detail parts of the image didn't get blurred by the filter. Turn the Eye icon off again

for this layer, and make sure your copy of the *Background* layer is active.

◆ Choose Filter/Noise/Dust and Scratches. Set the Radius to 2 and the Threshold to 0.

The radius is the number of pixels around a scratch that the filter will modify to get rid of the scratch. You generally increase the Radius setting until all your most common-sized spots and scratches are removed. Notice now that the entire image is blurry and you've also lost your grain pattern.

◆ Increase the Threshold to about 50, and you'll notice that your spots and the grain pattern come back. Now lower the Threshold until the spots are gone but the grain pattern is still there. At a Threshold of about 7, you are where you want to be. Turn the Preview check box off to see the original Background image, then on again to see what the filter has done to it. Click OK to complete the filter, then double-click on the name Background copy and change it to D&S 2,7.

Even though the grain pattern is not modified in the sky, some details in the clouds and certainly on land have changed and blurred out. This setting of 2,7 will work, but we want a mask that is white only where the spots are. In my original, much larger, version of this image, I had set the Radius to 3 and the Threshold to 12. That is why I named the image D&S 3,12, so I would know what settings I had used in case I wanted to change them later.

◆ Now choose Layer/Layer Mask/Hide All to add a layer mask that is all black. Type B for PaintBrush and choose PaintBr Op100% Flow100% from the Tool Presets pop-up at the top left of the Options bar. Type D for default colors so that you are painting with white. Now just click down wherever a spot is, and you'll be painting white in the layer mask. This replaces that spot with the version of it that Dust and Scratches has removed. On really big spots, like the one in the middle of the sky on this image, Dust and Scratches won't have totally removed them, and you'll have to remove them in the *Background* layer with the Clone Stamp tool. If you've already revealed the blurred-out big spot from the Dust and Scratches layer, make sure you first paint that layer's mask black in the big spot area before trying to fix the spot in the *Background* layer. Otherwise, the spot in the Dust and Scratches layer will continue to override whatever you do to the Background layer. That complication is a disadvantage to this technique.

File Size Issues with This Technique

Since we used a copy of the *Background* layer to run the Dust and Scratches filter on, the size of our layered file increased significantly by having two copies of the *Background* layer. This can be an issue when you are dealing with large files from film, like this MonoLake image, which started out at 500 MB before the addition of any layers. If size is an issue for you, you can always drag the Layer Mask thumbnail (the rightmost thumbnail) of your Dust and Scratches layer to the Trash icon at the bottom of the Layers palette. When you're asked "Apply Mask to Layer before Removing?" you click Apply. This deletes all of this layer except for the parts of it being used to remove spots. When you save your file, it will then take up less space. The only problem with this method is that if you discover more spots after making a test print, you won't be able to remove them as easily as just clicking another white spot in your Dust and Scratches mask, because the rest of this layer will now be gone. Hard disks, extra RAM, and DVDs are relatively cheap these days, so I'd just keep the layer and the mask!

Removing Noise

The best thing to do about noise is to avoid having it in your file in the first place. This means using a fine-grain film and exposing and processing it properly. Processing it properly is getting difficult these days, though. Maybe we'll all have to send our film to Duggal, a big lab in New York. Actually, I just looked at Google, and plenty of places are doing Dip and Dunk processing in Vancouver, B.C. If you use film, Dip and Dunk is the way to go because the film doesn't get put through a machine with rollers that can put scratches on it. Bad processing can mean dirt on the film and too much noise in the emulsion!

For those of you using digital cameras, try to test the camera before you buy it. I have a 2 1/2-year-old Canon Digital Rebel; I compared it to other cameras when I bought it and found the noise levels to be very low, even better than some more expensive cameras on the market at the time. Currently, I'm testing an 8-megapixel point-and-shoot that shoots Raw, but the files on this camera have more noise in them than the ones from my Rebel. Even though this camera is 8 megapixels, I bet I could make just as big or maybe a bigger print with a Rebel image because it has less noise. Maybe this camera has a smaller sensor, which generally means more noise. Test a camera. Just borrow one from a camera store for a few minutes, or rent one for a day, and shoot some sample shots of the type of material you're interested in. Then compare the noise to other cameras you already own or other cameras you're testing. Not all megapixels are the same!

If you shoot in Raw mode, you are more likely to be able to remove the noise before you get into Photoshop by using the Luminance Smoothing and Color Noise Reduction options in the Detail section of the Camera Raw filter. I won't buy a digital camera unless it has the option of shooting in Raw mode. If you are shooting in JPEG mode, see if your camera's options allow you to turn off the automatic sharpening that most cameras do to JPEG files. See what options are there for controlling noise before the JPEG is created, and test them.

Shooting in low-light situations with either film or digital cameras causes the most noise in the film or in the digital file. Try to make sure there's enough light for a correct exposure! For more info on using digital cameras correctly, see Chapter 9, "Camera Raw," and Chapter 11, "Image Processing with Bridge." Now we'll discuss Photoshop techniques you can use to reduce noise once it's in your files.

Channel Mixer Techniques

Seeing the noise and recognizing it is the first step toward removing it. Digital camera noise often shows up better if you look at each of the Red, Green, and Blue channels separately. You can do this with the Channels palette, as you will see below. We are going to look at a file that I shot in JPEG mode without a flash. This is not optimal lighting for a camera, so this image has a fair amount of noise.

◆ Open the file named KitchenLayers from the Chapter 12 folder on the *Photoshop Artistry* DVD. Using the Layers palette [F10], turn off the Eye icons for the Channel Mixer and Hue/Saturation layers. Now use [Shift-F10] to bring up the Channels palette, and click the word Blue in the Blue channel to activate just that channel. You will need to turn the Eye icons off for the Red and Green channels if they are still on. Notice how noisy this Blue channel is in the area of the background wall and the white wall where the plug is. Now turn the Eye icons on for the Channel Mixer and Hue/Saturation layers, and notice how the Channel

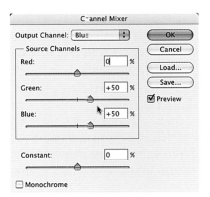

The Channel Mixer settings for the Blue channel. We are making a new Blue channel by using 50% of the original Blue channel and 50% of the original Green channel, which is much less noisy. If you double-click on the Channel Mixer adjustment layer thumbnail, you'll see that we did a similar adjustment to the Red channel. The Green channel was left alone because it was quite clean to start with.

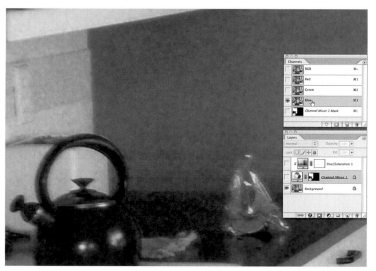

The original Blue channel before the Channel Mixer is applied to remove the noise. Notice the noise on the brown wall to the back, middle, and right, and also on the white tile where the wall plug is. This noise caused faint colored spots when the image was viewed in RGB mode.

The Blue channel after the Channel Mixer has been applied to remove some of the noise in the wall in the background and also on the white kitchen tile.

Mixer cleans up this noise by creating a new, less noisy Blue channel. Try the same procedure with the Red channel.

◆ Double-click on the leftmost layer thumbnail for the Channel Mixer layer to bring up the Channel Mixer dialog.

The Channel Mixer allows you to create a new set of Red, Green, and Blue channels for an image using a mix of opacities from the existing Red, Green, and Blue channels. When you choose Blue for the Output Channel, you can then pick the mixture of the existing

channels to be used to make the new Blue channel. Many digital cameras actually capture better information in one of the colors, usually Green, then use that information to enhance what is captured for the other colors. The Blue channel is often more grainy than the other two. With this image both the Red and Blue channels are grainy. Since we are using more of the cleaner Green channel to improve both the Red and Blue channels, the colors in the image become flatter. That is why I added a Hue/Saturation layer to help resaturate those colors. The adjustment layer mask on the Channel Mixer is white only in the areas where the original image has a lot of noise. Those are often lower-light areas and also areas of flat color. Only areas where the mask is white are affected by the Channel Mixer and also by the Hue/Saturation adjustment layer, since it's in a Clipping Group with the Channel Mixer layer below it. Clipping Groups allow both layers to share the mask belonging to the Channel Mixer layer. They will be explained more later in this book.

Channel Mixers are a good way to reduce noise in digital files. You'd only want to use them after already trying to remove the noise using Color Noise Reduction in Camera Raw. Since this image was shot as a JPEG, there was no chance to use the Camera Raw Color Noise Reduction. That is one reason I don't recommend shooting in JPEG unless you really have to.

New Reduce Noise Filter

Photoshop CS2 has a great new Reduce Noise filter that does far more to reduce existing noise than any previous Photoshop filter. Remember that it is better not to get noise in your image to start with but if you do have to work with a noisy image, this filter can be a big help.

Setting Up to Filter

◆ To try this out on the kitchen image we were using above, turn off the Eye icons for the Channel Mixer and Hue/Saturation layers, then click the word *Background* and drag it to the Copy icon at the bottom right of the Layers palette just to the left of the Trash icon. This will make a copy of the *Background* layer, which you can use to run Reduce Noise on. Running any filter on a copy layer allows you to use a layer mask to selectively apply or remove that filter. With that Background copy layer active, choose Filter/Noise/Reduce Noise. Click the Advanced button to get more options. Make sure the Preview check box is checked. With the Overall tab chosen, you'll have the options shown in the illustration on the next page. Play with each of these settings as we discuss them until you understand their differences.

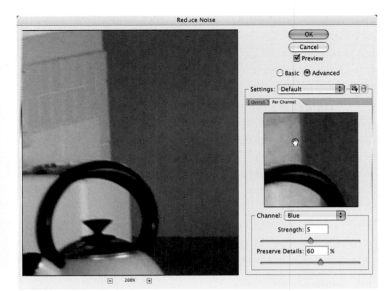

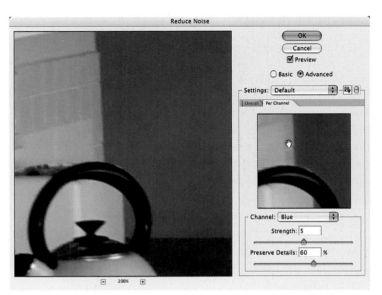

Reduce Noise Per Channel, looking at the Blue channel with the mouse button held down where you can see the Hand cursor in the black-and-white window to the right. When you hold the mouse button down, you see color on the left and black-and-white per channel on the right before the noise is removed. When you lift up on the mouse button, you then see both after the noise removal. This is a good way to preview your settings while in the tool.

Here we see the same image that is shown to the left, but now the mouse button is released so we can see it after the noise is removed. Notice how much sharper both images are. By turning the Preview button off and then on again, you actually see a before and after version of the sharpening filter on your entire screen. Since this filter is quite complex, though, you have to wait until the flashing dash below the Preview button stops to know that all the calculations are done and that this before/after preview will work properly.

Trying the Main Reduce Noise Controls

◆ The Strength setting is just a general gas pedal for the filter, so the higher you set it the more Luminance noise will be removed. In Camera Raw, removing too much Luminance noise can blur the file, so be careful with this one. If you set it too high, then real details will also be removed by accident. The higher you set Preserve Details, the more effort the filter will take to try not to blur real details while removing noise. Play with Preserve Details and Strength to see how they interact with each other on each particular image. Reduce Color Noise will remove the subtly colored spots you initially see in neutral-colored flat areas, like the background walls. Move the setting to 0%, then back to 50%, then up to 100% to see the differences. Sharpen Details will actually sharpen edges and details a bit so they don't get destroyed when noise is removed. Noise removal traditionally can blur the image somewhat, so Sharpen Details acts against that problem. Try it.

Here you see the Overall settings I used in the Reduce Noise filter for this image. Clicking the Per Channel tab brings up the Red, Green, and Blue channel settings as shown to the left.

Remove JPEG Artifact

◆ The Remove JPEG Artifact setting tries to remove a special kind of noise caused when images are JPEG compressed files. I had this turned off with this image because sometimes trying to remove this artifact actually creates more noise. Try it with your JPEG images and see if it helps. You can just turn that feature off and then on again to see if it helps in your particular situation.

The Per Channel Tab

Notice that the Arrow cursor is over the Per Channel tab in the screen shot on the previous page. Clicking that Per Channel tab gives you the options shown in the three illustrations on the previous page. The Per Channel options give you separate Strength and Preserve Details controls for each channel. This is a very useful feature, since the noise is often more centralized in the Blue channel and sometimes in the Red channel. The Green channel seems to be the cleanest with most digital files. Again, this has to do with how the digital camera captures and stores the images in its own internal, compact format.

◆ Click on Per Channel and try these options.

The Remove Sky Crud Action

There is a certain kind of image noise that doesn't get removed that well with the Reduce Noise filter. I call this large, clumpy noise. Sometimes you get these large blobs of noise in skies or other relatively low-detail parts of your image. These are really large chunks of grain that I'd have to just call clumps. They usually have an irregular pattern to them, so they stick out in a sky or other flat-colored part of the image. The Remove Sky Crud action script was developed to deal with this type of problem. If you go to a few pages from before the end of Chapter 10, you'll see a sidebar entitled "Two Actions from ArtistKeys Explained." There you'll see a screen shot of the RemoveSkyCrud action, and an explanation of how to use it. Try this action if the Reduce Noise filter is not doing the trick. I used it the other day and was pleasantly surprised. If you do decide to try it, though, you need to read the directions for it in that chapter, because you run this action on a copy of your image and there are several other steps required to use it properly.

Sharpening

The ability to easily sharpen images was one of the things that initially gave digital prints a big advantage over traditional, darkroom prints. Properly sharpening your images without oversharpening is one of the most important skills to learn.

Origin of the Term Unsharp Mask

There are ways to sharpen optically in the darkroom, and one that I learned in a Cibachrome masking workshop I took from Charles Cramer back in the late '80s is called making an Unsharp Mask. In the darkroom this involves sandwiching an unexposed sheet of high-contrast copy film next to your original film, with a piece of partially translucent material between them. You then expose and process the copy film. Since it was not in direct contact with your original film and this translucent material was between them, that copy film is an unsharp, contrasty copy of your original. To make your prints, you then sandwich this copy so that it's lined up exactly with the original film, and project your darkroom print through both of them. Projecting through this sandwich optically produces a sharper-looking print by increasing the contrast along edges. Edges are abrupt changes in contrast or color. This process is where the term Unsharp Mask came from; but Photoshop's version is so much easier to use.

The Amount, Radius and Threshold Settings

With both the Smart Sharpen and the Unsharp Mask sharpening filters, the Amount setting is the overall gas pedal for sharpening, and the Radius controls the number of pixels that can get changed around an edge. When you are sharpening, an edge is a change in color or contrast, and sharpening is achieved by increasing the contrast along edges. The Unsharp Mask filter also has a Threshold setting, which controls what Photoshop considers to be an edge. With the Threshold set at 0, everything is a potential edge, so everything gets sharpened. With the Threshold set at 10, for example, only pixel changes greater than 10, in the digital 0–255 range, get sharpened. This Threshold setting in the original Unsharp Mask filter is a very powerful option that is unfortunately missing from the newer Smart Sharpen filter. Notice that we don't even use the Sharpen, Sharpen Edges, or Sharpen More filters because they have no options. Now we'll go through several sharpening options in Photoshop so you can see how to combine them with layers and masks to get the best from each in your images.

Image/Duplicate to Sharpen a Flattened Copy

You don't want to sharpen your master layers file! That gets archived and saved in case you want to make further color changes, which you often will. You'll use Image/Duplicate to make a flattened copy of your master layers file. If you need to upsample that copy, you want to do that in 10% increments after the Image/Duplicate but before the sharpening. We'll go through the steps here so you know all the details of this process to prepare your image for sharpening.

◆ Open the file GibsonsTownMorningLayers.psd from the Ch22. Correcting Problem Images folder on the *Photoshop Artistry* DVD. This is the final layers file for a color correction example we go through in Chapter 22. Choose Image/Duplicate and check the Duplicate Merged Layers Only check box, which will flatten the image as it is copied. Now click OK in this dialog, and you will be working on a flattened copy of your master layers file. Once you have the flattened copy, you can switch to your master layers file, which has previously been saved, and use File/Close.

◆ Now you should be working on the flattened copy, so use [F10] to bring up the Layers palette. Type F to put this copy into Full Screen mode. Double-click the one layer in the Layers palette and name it Not Sharpened. Use [Shift-F10] to bring up the Channels palette, then Command (Ctrl)-click on the "CropLayer Mask copy" channel to load the crop from the CropLayer. Now use Image/Crop to crop the image. Click the Lock Position icon, second from the right, in the Lock areas of the Layers palette to lock this layer from accidental movement. Click on Name Not Sharpened and drag it to the Layer Copy icon, just to the left of the Trash icon at the bottom of the Layers palette. This will make a copy of this layer just above it named Not Sharpened copy. That copy should now be the active layer.

Smart Sharpen

We generally find that Smart Sharpen does a better job of bringing out shadow and highlight details in digital files. As discussed further in the captions on this page, both the Shadow and Highlight areas of the Smart Sharpen dialog have their own Radius setting, and they also have a Fade Amount setting, which can reduce the intensity of what is being done to the Highlights or Shadows. If the sharpening is blowing out highlight detail, then you want to use the Fade Amount slider to reduce this effect, as we have done here.

◆ Use View/Actual Pixels to zoom into 100%, then choose Filter/Sharpen/Smart Sharpen, [Command (Ctrl)-Shift-F4] to bring up the Smart Sharpen dialog. Refer to the two screen shots and captions to the right on this page as we go through the Smart Sharpen settings.

◆ Once you click OK in the Smart Sharpen dialog, you're going to learn how to combine the effects of Smart Sharpen with Unsharp Mask. Double-click the name Not Sharpened Copy and rename it to "SS," for Smart Sharpen, adding numbers for your Overall Sharpen Amount and Radius settings and then numbers for your Shadow and Highlight settings.

I named my layer "SS 200,1.5,1.5,1-20". The 1-20 means we set the Highlight Radius to 1 and used 20 for the Fade Amount. The Tonal Width controls the range of Highlight or Shadow, and I usually leave it at 50%. With some digital images I can make a fine print after this Smart Sharpen step; with others I need to go further, so we'll go through all the options here.

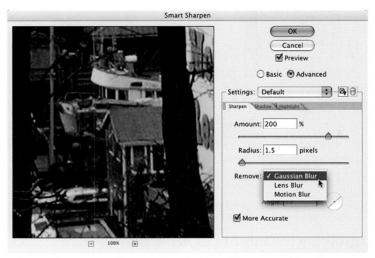

With Smart Sharpen you usually want to have the Advanced button set and have Remove set to Gaussian Blur, which will be the most common type of blur you are sharpening. I think of this as a random blur. If the Preview check box is selected, then you'll see a preview of the sharpening setting within your currently active Photoshop window. I recommend the More Accurate setting—why be less accurate? For this particular image, I set the overall Sharpen settings to Amount of 200 and Radius of 1.5. This was a handheld shot where I was standing on top of a fence, so it required more sharpening than the usual settings of 100% and .7 to 1 for the Radius. If the image starts out a bit soft, increasing the Radius will have a big effect on removing that initial softness.

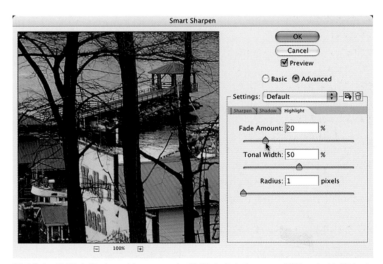

We left the Highlight Radius at 1 but we set the Highlight Fade Amount to 20% so the highlights in the trees wouldn't get too blown out. The Fade Amount reduces the effect of either the Highlight or the Shadow part of this Smart Sharpen filter. The usual Radius setting we'd use for Shadow would be 1, but we used 1.5 for this image because this image started out a bit soft. We left the Shadow Fade Amount set at 0 because we wanted more shadow detail.

The setup situation for using the Sharpen Only Edges action. When you run this action, the first step it takes is to convert your image into Lab color. If you've already made a Smart Sharpen layer, you'll be asked here if you want to merge the layers. You need to choose the Don't Merge option, which is not the default here so be alert when you are doing this or you will lose your Smart Sharpen layer, which you need to keep.

The Sharpen Only Edges BH Action

Using Layers we're going to set up a system where you can choose to combine several sharpening options to create your final image. Sharpen Only Edges BH is an ArtistKeys action that uses Unsharp Mask for its sharpening within a layer the action creates, but first this action creates a mask so that only the parts of the image that really need to be sharpened are used from this layer.

◆ Now drag your Smart Sharpen layer to the bottom of the Layers palette, and click back on the Not Sharpened layer, which is now on top, to activate it. Use [F11] to bring up the Actions palette, then use the Actions palette menu to turn off Button mode. Find the Action named SharpenOnlyEdgesBHBrks and click the gray arrow to its left to open it, as shown in the illustration above. Click on SharpenOnlyEdgesBHBrks, then use Play from the Actions palette menu to play this action. Make sure you click the Don't Merge option when the dialog comes up, as discussed above. For each of the Median, Maximum, and Gaussian Blur steps, where the action will stop, go through the details in the captions to the right on this page as you decide which setting to use in each step.

◆ When the action is almost finished, you'll get the Stop Message: "The next step is Unsharp Mask. Start with a setting of 350,1,0. Smaller images may work better with smaller Amount and Radius settings. Bigger images may look better with bigger settings. Now Continue." A Stop Message is just a way for an action script to give you some information. Click the Continue button, and you will go into the Unsharp Mask filter.

You are now running Unsharp Mask on the Lightness channel of this image. The action converts the image to Lab color so only the Lightness values in the image need to be sharpened. This allows you

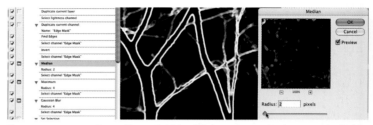

The action we are using here is SharpenOnlyEdgesBHBrks, so there are break points at the Median, Maximum, and Gaussian Blur steps to allow you to modify their settings based on the image you are working with. What you see if you turn off the Preview button at the Median step are the results of the Find Edges filter, and the edges will be many and fine. When you turn the Preview button on here, the Median filter will have spread and blended those edges a bit. You want bright, distinct edges in the mask for the main edges of things, but you don't want those edges to be too wide. The default setting of 2 here works fine for this image.

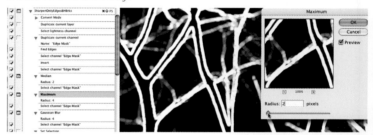

The next break point in this action is the Maximum filter, whose default of 4 spreads the edges of the branches too much. If there is too much white around edges in the mask, then the oversharpening that the mask allows you to get away with will be revealed in white halos around sharp edges in the image. Here we changed the radius to 2, which will lesson that effect around the many tree branches in this image.

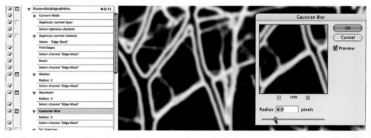

The final break point of significance allows you to change the Radius setting on the Gaussian blur step. With most masks you want the edges to be soft so that there is a smooth transition between where the sharpening is showing and not showing. Sharp edges on masks tend to show jaggy details in your images; on the other hand, if you blur the edges too much, you sometimes create halos around transition edge details.

to sharpen without changing the colors of the image as much as sharpening in RGB would do. The Unsharp Mask dialog is automatically set to 350, 1, and 0 by the action.

◆ The Amount is the overall gas pedal for sharpening, and 350 is more than I would normally do, especially for a film image. Because the mask is stopping the grain from being enhanced in nondetailed areas like sky, we can use larger amounts. Play with the Amount setting here as you read the information in the caption at the bottom of this column. I actually bumped the Amount setting to 450 because this image is a bit soft.

♦ Try setting the Radius to 1.5 and notice that halos start to show around the edges of the trees. A Radius of 1.5 might sharpen other parts of this image better, but then we'd have to darken the mask around the edges of all the trees, which would be too much work, I believe.

When using SharpenOnlyEdgesBH, we can usually leave the Threshold set to 0, since the mask stops too much grain from showing in skies and other nondetailed areas. This will be more of an issue when working with images from film cameras since they have more grain that can look ugly if oversharpened. This entire SharpenOnlyEdgesBH or BHBrks action does an even better job with images from film and is the main way I sharpen images from film. Try it alone, without the Smart Sharpen step, on some of your film images, and I believe you'll be impressed.

Tweaking the Masks of Your Sharpening Layers

Now you have three layers to create your final sharpened image: The Sharpen Only Edges Layer is on top, the original unsharpened image is in the middle, and the Smart Sharpen layer is on the bottom. We'll show you how to tweak the masks to get the best from each!

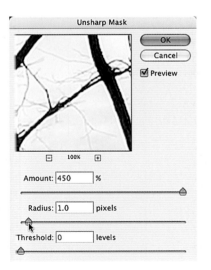

At the end of Sharpen Only Edges BH, or Sharpen Only Edges BHBrks, you are brought into the Unsharp Mask filter, and you need to pick your settings for the image you're working with. The default settings are 350,1,0, which is a more radical sharpening that one would normally use. The mask that Sharpen Only Edges creates allows you to do more sharpening because that mask reveals the sharpening only on main edges where it needs to be applied. At the end of the action, you are applying this Unsharp Mask filter through that mask, and you are only sharpening the Lightness channel of the Lab format image. Due to the softness of this image, I bumped the Amount to 450, but I left the Radius at 1 here because a setting of 1.5 produced halos around the edges of the tree branches. Without the Sharpen Only Edges mask, a Threshold setting of 0 would show too much grain in the flat sky areas. The mask blocks that grain from view!

♦ Once you click OK in the Unsharp Mask filter, double-click its Not Sharpened Copy name and rename it to "SOE *Amount Value, Radius Value, Threshold Value*" from your Unsharp Mask settings. My name was "SOE 450,1,0."

✳ Now you can type B for Brush, choose the Airbrush 7% Tool preset, and type D for white. Click back on the Not Sharpened layer to activate it, then choose Layer/Layer Mask/Hide All to create an all black layer mask for this layer. Use the Home key to scroll to the top-left corner of your image and the Tab key to remove your palettes, then [F12] to bring back just the Options bar.

You are now seeing the revealed parts of the Sharpen Only Edges layer on top and the Smart Sharpened layer at the bottom, with none of the Not Sharpened layer revealed. If you see too much grain in the sky, like at the top right of this image, paint white into the Not Sharpened layer's mask until that grain is removed. Make sure you don't paint white where the tree branches are, though, or they will be reduced in sharpness.

♦ To see the image without the Smart Sharpen effect, Shift-click the Not Sharpened layer's mask to turn it off so you are seeing the Not Sharpened layer at 100%. Shift-click again on this mask to turn it back on. If you want to turn off some of the Smart Sharpen layer's effects, just paint white in the layer mask for the Not Sharpened layer, and that area will override the image from the Smart Sharpened layer at the bottom.

♦ If you want to see all of the Sharpen Only Edges layer, without its mask, Shift-click that mask. If you see more sharpening that you want from that layer, Shift-click on it again, then paint white there until the amount of sharpness you need from it is revealed.

Here we see the final USM Layers palette. The bottom layer was sharpened with Smart Sharpen, and we named that layer so that we can remember the Smart Sharpen settings. The middle layer is the nonsharpened, flattened copy of your master layers file. The top layer was sharpened with Sharpen Only Edges BHBrks with the Unsharp Mask settings of 450, 1, and 0. Each of these layers has their position locked, so one can't be accidentally moved relative to the others. Clicking on the highlighted Lock icon in the Layers palette allows you to Lock a layer's relative position, as we have done here.

This is the final mask for the Not Sharpened layer. Because this image had a lot of detailed areas that needed maximum sharpening, most of this mask is black so the midtone and shadow detail from the Smart Sharpen layer at the bottom is revealed. The white areas to the top right of this mask show areas where there is plain sky and we didn't want the extra sky noise produced by Smart Sharpen.

You can now get whatever you want from each of these layers by manipulating the two layer masks. Notice my final Layers palette and also my final Not Sharpened and SOE masks in the illustrations on this and the previous page.

Unsharp Mask by Itself

Your can also run just the Unsharp Mask filter on an image, which I find sometimes works fine on the very unnoisy bright daylight images from my Canon Digital Rebel. For extra control, run this filter on a copy of the Background layer; that way, you can mask out any areas that are too sharp or have too much grain. I like the control that Threshold, in the Unsharp Mask filter, gives you over Noise. It seems unfortunate that Smart Sharpen doesn't also have a Threshold option. Maybe it will in the next version of Photoshop?

Here is the final mask for the Sharpen Only Edges layer originally created by the action. Notice the soft-white areas toward the bottom, where more of this sharpened layer was brought in by painting white with the Airbrush 7% brush. This brought out a little more highlight details in the boat and pier areas of the town.

Conclusion

We hope you've found this "Essential Photoshop Techniques for Photographers" chapter helpful. Look in the step-by-step chapters, starting with Chapter 19, "Making Selections," for more examples of many of these techniques. For more and future information, check the Workshops, Videos Links, and Actions sections of www.barryhaynes.com.

Portfolio

Maria Ferrari

Maria Ferrari (www.mariaferrari.com) considers herself a still life photographer, but really, we haven't seen anything that she can't do. Here are a couple of our favorites, a Diné father and daughter, and the annual Coney Island Polar Bear Swim.

13 ◆ Color Correction Tools

Photoshop offers many tools for adjusting color and modifying image gamma or contrast. This chapter gives you a quick overview of what the different tools do and when to use each one. Both in this chapter and in this book, we talk about the tools we use that are important for photographers. We don't waste time and space on tools we don't find that useful or productive. The color correction tools are in the Image/Adjustments menu, and most are also available as adjustment layers. Levels, Curves, Hue/Saturation, Replace Color, Selective Color, Color Balance, Channel Mixer, Invert, Threshold, and Exposure are the color correction tools we use most. Auto Levels, Auto Contrast, Auto Color, Brightness/Contrast, Desaturate, Gradient Map, Match Color, Photo Filter, Shadow/Highlight, Equalize, Posterize, and Variations are the ones we don't use as much. The tools we don't use much have actually been removed from our working ArtistryMenus. mnu, but if you are using this custom menu set, you can always access these tools by choosing Show All Menu Items from the bottom of any menu. You will notice that throughout *Photoshop CS2 Artistry* we color correct mostly with adjustment layers because those corrections can be changed as many times as you like without destroying the integrity of the file. Starting with hands-on Chapter 19, "Making

The Color palette remembers the values at the last location you clicked with the Eyedropper. If you made that click after entering a color adjustment tool, this palette will then show you how the values at the point you clicked change as you make adjustments using that same color adjustment tool.

The Info palette with the "before" values to the left of the slash and the "after" values to the right. In this Info palette we have created two Color Samplers: #1 for the highlight position and #2 for the shadow position.

Selections," and beyond, we actually go through the details of each tool's features and how they're used by giving real-world examples.

Using the Info/Color Sampler and Color Palettes

When you use any of the color correction tools, it is very helpful to have the Info palette, and sometimes the Color palette, visible onscreen. Use Window/Show Info [F9] and Window/Show Color [Shift-F9] to bring up these palettes. While you're working in any color correction tool, Photoshop automatically gives you the Eyedropper tool for measuring colors in the image. The Info palette shows you the digital RGB, Lab, and/or CMYK values of the pixel or group of pixels you currently have the Eyedropper tool above. It shows you these values both before (left of slash) and after (right of slash) any changes you have made during the current iteration of the color correction tool you are now using. The Color palette has a subtle but important difference from the Info palette in that it displays the values of the last place you clicked with the Eyedropper versus wherever the Eyedropper might currently be located. This allows you to click on a picture tone or color area and see how the pixel values of that particular area change as you make adjustments with the color tool you are currently working with. The Color palette also has colored sliders that give you hints as to how a certain color change, like adding red, will affect the color of the location where you last clicked.

The color correction tools are in the Image/Adjustments menu. When you use them from here, they permanently modify the pixels they are adjusting in the currently active layer. Changing the pixels over and over again can damage the integrity of the image.

Doing an adjustment using an adjustment layer creates a special layer above the currently active layer, which allows you to change this adjustment as many times as you like without modifying or damaging the original pixels or the integrity of the image. It also keeps a record for you of the changes you have made.

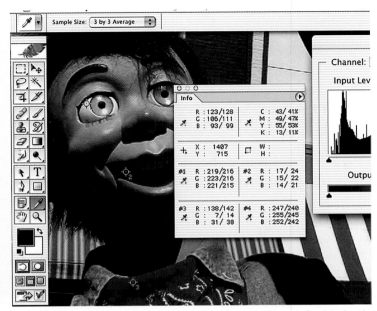

By Shift-clicking on the screen while in a color correction tool, you can place up to four Color Sampler points whose values will show up at the bottom of the Info window and will continue to update as you make color changes. These locations continue to update throughout your editing session, even as you switch tools and measure other locations with the regular Eyedropper.

The Color Sampler tool, an option of the Eyedropper in the Tools palette, allows you to click (Shift-click while in a color tool or the regular Eyedropper) up to four locations where you want to monitor the color of your image while working. These four color values show up at the bottom of the Info palette. This is a great feature because you can see how the color values at these four locations change throughout your color correction process. You don't have to measure them again; their values will constantly update as you work. Each open image can have up to four Color Samplers attached to it.

When adjusting a digital image, you usually want to make as few separate file modifications as necessary to achieve the desired result. A file modification is when you click the OK button for any of the color correction tools and you are not in an adjustment layer. Each file modification changes the original data, and too many changes can eventually degrade the quality of the data. Therefore, you don't want to constantly go from one color correction tool to the other frantically trying to get the effect you need. You want to use these tools intelligently, knowing what each one is good for and keeping the total number of uses to the minimum required to do the final adjustments on a particular image. If you do your changes using adjustment layers, the actual image pixels do not change until the image is flattened. Adjustment layers allow you to go back and change the color over and over again without suffering from this cumulative degrading effect on the digital values.

Common Color Correction Techniques

All the color correction tools share a few things in common. When using any of them, you need to turn the Preview check box on to see the changes happen to the image. With the Preview check box off, you are seeing the image as it appeared prior to the changes made by the current invocation of the tool you are using. You can see before and after by quickly turning the Preview check box off and on.

When working with a selected subarea, comparing one window to another, or adjusting an area in one layer to blend with nonadjusted items in other layers within Levels, Curves, Color Balance, or Brightness/Contrast, you usually work with the Preview button on so you can compare the changes you make to the selected area to the rest of the image.

In any of the color correction tools, you can Option (Alt)-Cancel to stay in the tool but cancel any changes you have made in that tool so far. When you do this the word Cancel changes to Reset. Many of these tools also let you load and save a collection of settings. This is useful when you have many very similar images in a production situation. You could carefully make your Levels settings for the first image and then use the Save button to save those settings in a file. If you have subsequent images in the group, you can use the Load button to automatically run the same settings or load them into an adjustment layer. You can also drag and drop adjustment layers between images.

Levels and Curves

The Levels and Curves tools have the broadest range of capabilities of any of the color correction tools. When you color correct an image from its original capture, you want to do so in a particular order. (We discuss that order in great detail in Chapter 18, "Master Image Workflow," and you should read that chapter as a first step in understanding that order.) The first step after image capture is to do overall color correction; that is, correct the complete image without any selections. Levels is the best tool to use because it gives you a histogram of the data in the image, as well as a quick way to pinpoint the lightest and darkest spots of your image. You can use the histogram to judge the quality of a capture and to fix many scanning problems. You can also use Levels to precisely adjust the highlight and shadow values, the overall brightness and contrast, and the color balance, while viewing the results onscreen and in the histogram. You make all these changes in one step and must choose OK only once after making all these improvements. When using an adjustment layer, you can go

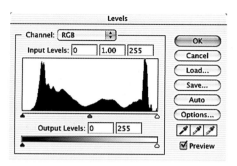

The Levels tool with its histogram is best for doing the overall color correction right after bringing in a scan or a digital camera image.

can have histogram data available to you while you are in Curves or a Curves adjustment layer.

Levels and Curves are the most powerful color correction tools. See Chapter 21, "Overall Color Correction," for a detailed introduction to Levels and Curves; Chapter 22, "Correcting Problem Images," for good discussions about using Levels and Curves in the ways for which they are best suited; and Chapter 14, "Digital Imaging and the Zone System," to understand how Levels histograms and Curves relate to the original photograph.

The Hue/Saturation Command

back in and tweak your Levels settings as many times as you like. Levels is the color correction tool we most often use first.

You can also use the Curves command to do your initial overall color adjustments of the entire image. Curves enables you to do all the same adjustments that Levels does plus more specific adjustments in particular image data ranges. The Curves command has a different user interface than Levels, however. Instead of furnishing a histogram, it provides the curve diagram shown here. The horizontal axis of the diagram represents the original image values with black and shadows on the left and white and highlights on the right. The vertical axis represents the modified image values with the shadows at the bottom and the highlights at the top. When the curve is a straight diagonal, as shown here, the image has not been changed. Moving the curve down in the middle darkens the image, and moving it upward lightens the image. The endpoints of the curve are used to change the highlight and shadow values. Using Curves, along with your mouse, on the image, you can measure individual colors, see the range of values they represent on the curve, and then change only that color range. Curves' advantage is that it allows you to independently modify specific portions of the image's tonal range in different ways and with more flexibility than Levels. With the Histogram palette, you

We often use Hue/Saturation to increase the saturation of all the colors by 10% to 20% after doing the overall color correction using Levels and Curves. This change is done with the Edit menu set to Master. With Edit set to Reds, Yellows, Greens, Cyans, Blues, or Magentas, you can change the hue, saturation, or lightness of objects in the image that have one of these standard colors as their primary color without actually making a detailed selection. You can then fine-tune these color selections further using the Hue/Saturation Eyedroppers. You should use Hue/Saturation when you want to change the color, saturation, or lightness of a particular object or color range without changing its gamma or other characteristics. The

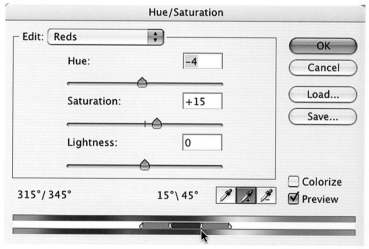

The Hue/Saturation tool. Usually you want the Preview button on when using Hue/Saturation. Notice the color bars and sliders at the bottom of the dialog. These, along with the Eyedroppers, allow Photoshop to do a much better job of picking a color range to modify with Hue/Saturation. The color bars are always visible. When you make an adjustment, the bottom color bar will change to show you how the colors are being shifted. If you are adjusting one of the component colors from the Edit pop-up, you also get the sliders between the two color bars. This shows you the range of colors that Photoshop is considering when making an adjustment. Using the Eyedroppers can expand or contract that range to make your change more exact. You can move the sliders manually as well.

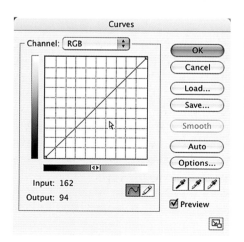

The Curves tool with a curve showing no adjustments to the image. The horizontal axis shows the original image values and the vertical axis shows these values as modified by the curve. Option (Alt)-clicking on the graph toggles it between the 4x4 default divisions and the 10x10 divisions you see here.

first part of the process is to select the object(s) you want to change and use the Hue/Saturation Eyedropper-plus and Eyedropper-minus tools to get a model of the representative color. This model shows up in the Color Strip at the bottom of the Hue/Saturation window. This Color Strip shows changes to your representative color as you make them.

The Hue slider looks at hues in a circular fashion, sort of like the Apple Color Picker or a rotary color wheel–type color picker. The initial Hue value, 0, is the degree value where you find your initial color. To change just the color, slide the Hue slider to the right (like rotating counterclockwise on the circular Apple Color Picker). If your initial color was red, then red would be your 0. A Hue change of 90 degrees would make the color green. A Hue change of −90 degrees would make your color purple. A Hue change of 180 or −180 would yield the opposite of red, which is cyan. Sliding the Saturation slider to the right makes the selected items more saturated, and sliding to the left makes them less saturated. This is like moving further from the center or closer to the center on the Apple Color Picker.

Moving the Lightness slider to the right takes away gray values, and moving it to the left adds gray values (similar to the sliding bar on the right side of the Apple Color Picker). See Chapter 21 and Chapter 24, "Color Matching Images," for more information on the Hue/Saturation tool.

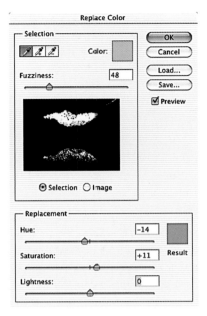

The Replace Color Command

The Replace Color command allows you to make a selection based on color and then actually change the color of the selected objects using sliders built into the command's dialog. The selections are similar to selections made with the Magic Wand, but this tool gives you more control over them. The Magic Wand requires you to make a selection by using a certain tolerance setting and clicking a color, and then selects adjacent areas based on whether their colors fall within the tolerance value you set. If the selection with the Magic Wand is incorrect, you need to change the tolerance and then select again. This process can take a lot of time and iteration. The Replace Color command allows you to change the tolerance on the fly while viewing the actual objects or colors you are selecting.

The tolerance here is called Fuzziness. Increasing the Fuzziness, by moving the slider in the dialog to the right, enlarges your selection, and decreasing it shrinks the selection. You see a preview of what is happening with the selection in a little mask window in the dialog.

After you perfect the color selection, you then use the Hue, Saturation, and Lightness sliders in the Replace Color dialog to change the color

of the selected objects. You can see this color change in the image by clicking the Preview box; the Preview box also allows you to make further tweaks to the selection while actually seeing how they're affecting the color change. Replace Color changes the color of the objects it picks from the parts of the entire image selected with the selection tools before you entered Replace Color. To learn more about using Replace Color, see Chapter 23, "Replace Color, Color Range, and Selective Color." Even though Replace Color isn't available as an adjustment layer, Chapter 23 will show you how to transfer a color selection from Replace Color over to Color Range and then get the same result as with an adjustment layer.

The Selective Color Tool and CMYK

The Selective Color tool works great when you're working with CMYK images. It's a good tool for making final tweaks to CMYK colors after converting from RGB to CMYK. With this tool, you adjust the amount of cyan, magenta, yellow, or black ink within the red, green, blue, cyan, magenta, yellow, black, neutral, or white colors in the selected area. It's also a great tool for exercising fine control when fixing color areas that fade a bit when converted to CMYK. For more information about using this tool, see Chapter 23 and Chapter 24. You can also use Selective Color on RGB images.

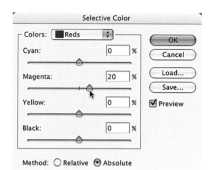

The Selective Color command is used for adding or subtracting the percentage of cyan, magenta, yellow, or black inks within the red, green, blue, cyan, magenta, yellow, black, neutral, or white colors in the selected area of a CMYK image. These percentages of change can be relative to the amount of an ink color that is already there or they can be absolute percentages.

Using the Channel Mixer and taking some of all three channels gives you better contrast in the buildings and more detail in the trees in Central Park.

The Channel Mixer

The Channel Mixer allows you to take a percentage of the color from one channel and use it to create part of another channel. You can use this technique to improve CMYK separations and also when creating a black-and-white image from a color image. In addition, it's very useful in repairing images where one of the emulsion layers of the film may have been exposed improperly or may have been damaged over time. I've found this happens often with digital cameras, where the Blue channel is sometimes poorly exposed. Because you can use the Channel Mixer as an adjustment layer, you have the advantage of being able to create several versions and select areas that work via layer masks. If you work a lot with grayscale images, go to the Videos section of www.barryhaynes.com to try Barry's downloadable Convert to Grayscale action and QuickTime training video, which gives you even more options and control.

If you simply go to Mode/Grayscale with the Manhattan Sunrise picture, this is the result.

Color Balance, Brightness/Contrast, and Variations

You will notice that we don't use the Color Balance, Brightness/Contrast, and Variations tools much in this book. We consider them less precise than the other, previously mentioned color correction tools. We explain the advantages and disadvantages of using these

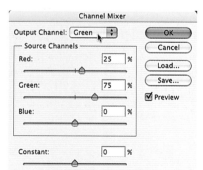

The Channel Mixer allows you to take a percentage of the color from one channel and use it to create part of another channel. Here, we are taking 25% of the Red channel and 75% of the Green channel and using it to create a new Green channel.

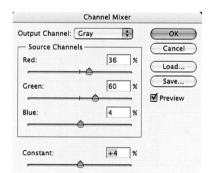

Here are the settings we used to convert the Manhattan skyline photo from RGB to Grayscale. We used the Channel Mixer as an adjustment layer in case we wanted to make changes later. For even more control over the tones in the image, we would use Curves adjustment layers with layer masks.

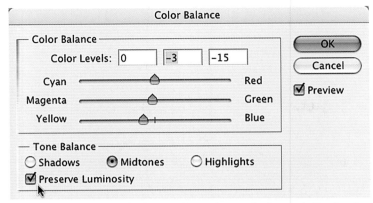

The Color Balance tool. Color levels of 0 means that no adjustment has been made. Negative values mean adjustments in the CMY direction, and positive values mean adjustments in the RGB direction. Preserve Luminosity is the main feature this tool has that allows it to do something that you can't do using Levels or Curves—namely, to change color without changing brightness or contrast.

three tools in this section. In general, they are geared more for color beginners and don't offer as much control as the Levels, Curves, Hue/Saturation, Replace Color, Selective Color, and Channel Mixer commands.

The Color Balance Tool

The Color Balance tool shows the relationship between the additive colors (red, green, and blue) on the right and the subtractive colors (cyan, magenta, and yellow) on the left. You move three sliders, the Cyan/Red slider, the Magenta/Green slider, and the Yellow/Blue slider, either to the left to get the CMY colors or to the right to get their complementary RGB colors. If you don't understand the relationship between RGB and CMY, this tool makes it a little easier to see. When you use Color Balance, you need to adjust your shadows, midtones, and highlights separately, which can take longer than using Levels or Curves. The best feature of Color Balance is that you can make adjustments with the Preserve Luminosity check box on, which allows you to radically alter the color balance of a selected object toward red, for example, without the object becoming superbright, like it would if you made such a radical adjustment in Levels or Curves. The Preserve Luminosity option can be useful when you need to remove a color cast from the image without changing its brightness and contrast.

In general, the Color Balance tool is much less powerful than Levels or Curves because you can't set exact highlight or shadow values, and you don't have much control over brightness and contrast. Moreover, if you have a setting that you use all the time in Levels, Hue/Saturation, or Curves, you can save it in a file and load it later to use on a similar image. This can be very useful when you want to save

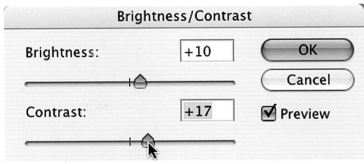

The Brightness/Contrast tool. Moving the sliders to the right increases the brightness or contrast, generating positive numbers in the respective boxes. Moving the sliders to the left decreases brightness or contrast and results in negative numbers.

time and make similar color adjustments to a group of images—once again, the Color Balance tool doesn't have this option. However, as we've said, there are times when this tool will be useful, especially as an adjustment layer that can be tweaked at will. Generally, we would say that the Color Balance tool is more of a beginning color correcting tool and not the main tool we would recommend for imaging professionals.

The Brightness/Contrast Tool

The Brightness/Contrast tool allows you to adjust the brightness and/or contrast of your image using Brightness and Contrast sliders. Usually we adjust the brightness and contrast using Levels or Curves because those tools allow you to adjust the color balance and highlight/shadow values at the same time, as well as to Save and Load adjustment values. Like the Color Balance tool, we would classify Brightness/Contrast as more of an entry-level tool. Most professionals use Levels and Curves. The only time you might use Brightness/Contrast is when you don't need to make any color adjustment and you need only a subtle brightness or contrast adjustment.

The Variations Tool

You might think the Variations tool is a neat idea, but it has several serious flaws. Variations is useful for the person who is new to color correction and may not know the difference between adding a little cyan and adding a little green to an image. When you use the tool, you see the current image surrounded by different color correction choices. The main problem with Variations is that you can't zoom in on the current image or any of its new choices to see the details of what will happen when you make possible changes. We don't use Variations in this book.

Mary's photo has been color corrected.

LuAnn was shot after the Oregon clouds rolled in, and no correction has been done.

This is the result of the correction. No other adjustments have been made to the image.

Match Color

Adobe lists two uses for Match Color. The first is correcting the color in a single image where the image is both the source and the target. The second is matching color between images, layers, or selections.

The first instance is one of those adjustments we feel is for people who have neither the time nor the inclination to actually learn the

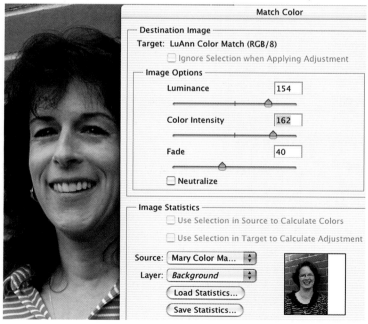

Fading the effect by 40% and bumping up the luminance and saturation gave a pretty good and very quick match.

application. It's fast, and it does an OK job on some images, but it's extremely limited. There's a button to neutralize color casts, but how in the world does it judge what the color is supposed to be? And, yes, you can brighten the picture and increase or decrease its saturation, but there are better tools.

However, there are times when you need to match the color of the light between two photos. This might happen when you have portraits of several people, taken by different photographers or at different times, that need to have a unified look—say, for a spread about a Board of Directors. If time is short, this might be the tool for you.

We don't want you to think that this tool is a magic bullet, though. We had to search to find photos that worked well with it, and as we're sure you'll notice in the case of these portraits, the background is the same in each one—only the time of day is different. One reason we don't foresee anyone using this tool a lot is that you can do virtually the same thing with adjustment layers and have a lot more flexibility. In the portraits here we could have made a layer set of the adjustment layers used to color correct one photo and then simply dragged the entire set over to the other image for the initial adjustment.

If you do decide to use the tool, make sure that the layer you plan to change is active when you enter the dialog. If you intend to modify a layer that has important information, make a copy of the layer first. Also, make sure that the layer you use as the source has all the color information you intend to use. If it is being affected by adjustment layers, you'll need to flatten the image first, or select the Merged option in the Layers pop-up in the dialog's Source section.

In some instances you will want to use only selected colors to modify your target image. In this case, make a selection in the source image first, then switch to the target image, selection, or layer and invoke the Match Color command. You can also make a selection in the target image if you want to modify only that area (such as a face), but unlike with an adjustment layer, where you can modify the layer mask if your selection is not perfect, you need to have a really good selection. If you're going to go to all that trouble, it's just as easy to use adjustment layers and masks. Easier, really.

The default values in the Shadow/Highlight adjustment are for a backlit subject like this man's face.

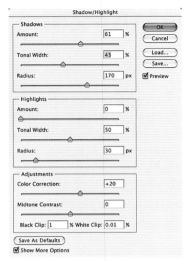

Here are the settings used to lighten the man's face below leftt.

This is the result using only the Shadow/Highligh adjustment settings shown above.

With a few adjustment layers to open and color correct the face a bit more, you have this.

Shadow/Highlight

Adobe continues to add "automatic" adjustments to Photoshop, some of which are more successful than others. With the Shadow/Highlight adjustment, we have a semiautomatic adjustment that's very good at what it does within certain limits. We've found that we can get much better results using one Curves adjustment layer for highlights and another for shadows. This allows us to adjust the masks ourselves. If Shadow/Highlight actually output the masks and curves it creates and let you fine-tune them as masks and curves in adjustment layers, then we'd find this tool more useful. You'll see how to do Shadow and Highlight adjustments with curves and masks in Chapters 21 and 22 and in other step-by-step examples in this book.

Photo Filters

If you've sometimes wished that you had shot a certain scene with a color filter, here's your chance to apply the filter after the fact.

Photoshop has a list of standard filters that can be accessed as either an adjustment or an adjustment layer. Using one of these filters is similar to setting a solid color layer above your image in Color Blend mode at a low opacity, but look closer and you'll see that it's not the same.

What Adobe has attempted to do here is correct for exposure issues, just as you might judge a situation when you're shooting by metering the highlights and shadows of the scene and choosing a filter to compensate for problems that you expect. We recommend that you turn off the Preserve Luminosity check box to more closely mimic exposure compensation. Photo Filters give you some filters that you'll immediately recognize, and the option to set your own colors. Also, because you can use the Photo Filters as adjustment layers, you can mask out all or some of the effect wherever you need to.

The Auto Levels, Auto Contrast, Auto Color, Desaturate, and Gradient Map Commands

The Auto Levels command does an automatic Levels color correction of your image; Auto Contrast does an automatic contrast adjustment. Auto Color does an automatic color correction of your image. We would not recommend using these for quality color control, but it's OK for a quick fix to an FPO (a production term meaning For Position Only) proof or for low-end reproduction. If you are in a production environment where speed is of the essence and you decide to use these tools, make sure you set up options that will work for the majority of photos that come in. To do that go to Levels or Curves (you can do this in an adjustment layer as well) and click the Options button. This allows you to set target values for the highlights, shadows, and midtones, as well as clipping percentages for black and white pixels. Save the values you set as defaults.

Where to Learn More

To learn more about the color correction tools mentioned in this overview, read Chapter 14, "Digital Imaging and the Zone System," and Chapter 18, "The Master Image Workflow," and do the step-by-step examples in Chapter 21, "Overall Color Correction," Chapter 22, "Correcting Problem Images," Chapter 23, "Replace Color, Color Range, and Selective Color," Chapter 24, "Color Matching Images." Chapter 27, "Compositing Bracketed Photos," and Chapter 29, "Portrait Compositing," also have valuable color correction techniques.

14 ◆ Digital Imaging and the Zone System

Images in the real world that you see with your eyes have the greatest beauty, because they usually are illuminated by wonderful light and have a depth and subtlety that is possible only from a firsthand experience of the scene. The range of light and tonality that is reflected from reality to our eyes, from the darkest black shadow to the brightest sparkling highlight and all the subtle transitions in between, is far greater than we can reproduce in any printed or screen image. Our eyes can quickly adjust as we gaze into a deep shadow or squint to see a bright detail. Our eyes, along with our brain, instantly perform an automatic white balance when we encounter light of varying color temperatures. When you look at a scene in nature, it has the best quality and the finest detail because you are using the most advanced and sophisticated imaging system ever invented.

Transitions to the Digital World

In this chapter we will discuss the Zone System, a method for controlling exposure first developed by Ansel Adams in 1940, and we'll show how it relates not only to good exposure practices, but also to working with photographs in the digital world. Many people who take our workshops and classes are photographers who already have an understanding of the Zone System, and they find that discussing it and how it can be applied to working on digital images is often the key that opens the doorway between the world of film and darkroom and the realm of digital imaging with Photoshop. For those of you who are new to the Zone System, think of this chapter as a combination of photographic history and a new way to think about the tonal relationships in the original scene, and how to control and improve your interpretation of it in the digital world.

Achieving Your Visualization

The Zone System gives photographers a way to measure an image in nature and then capture it on film so it can be reproduced with the photographer's intentions in mind. Adams used the term "visualization" to explain a technique where photographers imagine what they want the scene to look like as a photographic print before they actually expose the film. Once this image, the visualization, is in mind, the photographer uses the Zone System to get the correct data on the film so that the visualization can be achieved in the darkroom, where the final print is made.

Although Adams was writing about perfecting images in a traditional chemical darkroom, the concept of getting the right data on the film is also applicable to the act of translating a film image into a scanned digital image. When working with film, you want the film to have as much information about the scene as possible in order for the scanner to translate that analog tonal information into digital data.

If you are not using film anymore or (as is the experience of many younger photographers) have never used it and are photographing with a digital camera, capturing good information in terms of exposure and tonal range is vitally important to the success of your work with the image once you bring it into Photoshop.

In this chapter, we use the Zone System as a framework to explain what the right data is, how to get that data onto film, and what to look for to ensure that the film image is scanned correctly, so that all of that important tonal information is captured in the digital version of the image.

Capturing the Dynamic Range

When you look at a scene that you want to photograph, you can use a photographic light meter with a special spot attachment to measure the range of brightness in the scene. To a certain extent, you can also do this with the built-in light meter in an SLR camera, especially if it has a spot metering mode. On a bright, sunny day you will have a very large range of brightness values between the brightest and darkest parts of your image area. This range, from the darkest to the brightest tones, is called the dynamic range, or contrast range. Every photographic film emulsion and every digital camera sensor has its own specific range of tonal values, from brightest to darkest, that can be recorded in a single exposure. With film, this range is typically called the exposure latitude, while with digital cameras (and also scanners) it is referred to as dynamic range. The important thing to note here is that for the purposes of our discussion, dynamic range, contrast range, and exposure latitude are all essentially the same thing.

Most films and digital cameras can't capture the full dynamic range of brightness that is present in an original scene and that can be perceived by the human eye, especially on a bright, contrasty day. Most of us have taken photographs where the prints don't show any details ir the dark shadows or where a bright spot on a person's forehead o- in the sky is totally washed out. These are instances where either the full dynamic range of the scene was not captured in the original image, whether film or digital, or where the dynamic range of the photo paper was not large enough.

The objective with the Zone System is to use a light meter to measure the brightness range in the original scene and then adjust your camera so the parts of that brightness range that you want to capture are exposed properly onto the film or digital sensor.

Dividing a Scene into Zones

The Zone System divides a scene into 11 zones, from the brightest to the darkest. Ansel Adams used Roman numerals to denote the zones, from 0 to X. These zones in the final printed image reference how light or dark each area will be. In a photograph, a Zone 0 area would be solid black, with no detail showing whatsoever; in a halftone (the translation of a continuous-tone photographic image into dots for reproduction on a printing press) you would see no white dots in the solid black ink. Zone I is still a very dark black, and it has no real measurable detail, but it is not pure black. If you look at a Zone I halftone with the naked eye, it still looks black without detail, but if

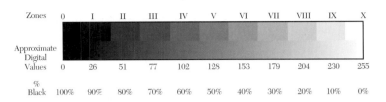

A stepwedge file of the 11 zones in the Zone System, along with the approximate corresponding digital values and percentages of black ink. The digital values shown here fall somewhere in the center of each zone. Where the actual zone values and digital values appear for each image depends on the type of output you choose. You have more latitude as to where the Zone I detail begins and Zone IX detail ends when you print at a higher resolution and line screen. If you are printing to newsprint, all of Zone I may print as 100% black and all of Zone IX as 100% white.

you were to use a loupe or other magnifier, you would see very small white dots in a sea of black ink.

On the other end of the scale, Zone X is solid white. In a print this would be the color of the paper; in a halftone there would be no dots in a Zone X area. You would use Zone X to represent a specular highlight like the reflection of the sun on chrome, water, or glass. Zone IX is a very bright white without detail, but, again, using a loupe you can see some very small halftone dots, or ink dots from an inkjet printer. The range of image brightness areas that have obvious

Ansel Adams, the Zone System, and Digital Imaging

We give thanks to Ansel Adams, perhaps the most well-known nature photographer, and his great series of books, *The Camera*, *The Negative*, and *The Print* (Bullfinch, 1995), for our introduction to an understanding of artistic photography and the Zone System. *Ansel Adams: An Autobiography* (Bullfinch, 1985) is also a wonderful book.

If you want to know more about the Zone System and how to take the best photographs using black-and-white film, you should read *The Negative*. It also shows you some very good techniques for extending or shortening the exposure latitude of your film by under- or overdeveloping. Another great book on the Zone System is *The New Zone System Manual*, by White, Zakia, and Lorenz, from (Morgan & Morgan, Inc., 1990).

Many of Adams's discussions in his books are about black-and-white photography, but the concepts still apply to color photography and even digital imaging. The depth and joy of his philosophies and his passion for the art and science of the photographic process are something that all people who deal with images should have a feeling for.

Although he died in 1984, several years before digital imaging became easily available and popular, Ansel Adams was ahead of his time and could see the changes that the coming years would bring to the photographic landscape. In his book *The Negative*, he wrote:

"I eagerly await new concepts and processes. I believe that the electronic image will be the next major advance. Such systems will have their own inherent and inescapable structural characteristics, and the artist and functional practitioner will again strive to comprehend and control them."

Middle Gray Brightness and Your Camera's Light Meter

The importance of a middle gray brightness value comes into play with light meters, both the handheld kind and the one in your SLR camera. Light meters are programmed to measure the brightness values in a scene and then average them together to create an exposure that yields an overall brightness result of middle gray. This has nothing to do with color. Light meters are color blind and see only varying levels of brightness.

If it seems odd to you that all your fancy camera's light meter is doing is returning a result to create a middle gray tone, this classic "Intro to Photography 101" experiment shows this concept in action: With your camera set on autoexposure mode (make sure the flash is turned off), take a close-up photo of something black, something white, and something middle gray. When you download the images and look at them in Photoshop with no adjustments made, you should have three exposures that are all a similar tone of gray.

The components of the exposure experiment.

The black scarf.

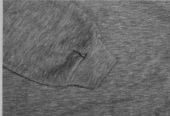

The gray sweatshirt.

The white paper.

All three close-ups were photographed outside on an overcast day with a digital SLR set to Program (all-automatic) exposure mode, with no exposure compensation corrections. No adjustments have been made to the images.

---

detail in the printed image include Zone II through Zone VIII. Zone VIII is very bright detail and Zone II is very dark detail.

In the middle of this tonal area of print detail is Zone V. In a black-and-white image Zone V would print as middle gray, halfway between pure black and pure white. In a color image, a Zone V area would also represent a middle tone brightness value no matter what the specific color of that value was. Keep in mind that there is a difference between brightness or luminosity values and color values. The Zone System is used to measure and identify the brightness values in an image, not the color values or the color saturation.

Getting a Good Exposure

Let's walk through the process of how you take a photograph with a camera and get a good exposure. We will use black-and-white negative and color positive transparency film as examples in this discussion. Normally, when you take a transparency picture with a camera, you measure the range of brightness in the original scene and set the exposure on your camera so as to reproduce that range of brightness on the film. Today's automatic cameras have computerized light meters that do all this for you, although you sometimes still need to make manual adjustments to get exactly what you want, especially if you

are photographing a subject that is either very bright or very dark (see the sidebar "Middle Gray Brightness and Your Camera's Light Meter" above). When you use a manual camera with a handheld light meter, all the exposure calculations are done manually. Even though most of you probably have automatic cameras, as we do, let's describe the manual camera process so we all understand what needs to happen to take a good picture. This discussion also applies to getting a good exposure with a digital camera.

Measuring the Brightness

To get a good exposure, you need to measure the brightness range of different areas within the scene. Let's say you are taking a photograph of a Spanish home in Costa Rica (see the images on the next page). You want to set the exposure somewhere in the middle of the brightness range that occurs naturally in the setting. That middle position, wherever you set it, then becomes Zone V. A handheld spot light meter allows you to point at any very small area in a scene and measure the amount of light reflected from that area. The light meter measures the brightness of the light—the luminance—that is reflected from the metered part of the image. Unless you plan to use filters or different film to modify the light's color, this is all you really need to measure, whether you're taking a black-and-white or color photo.

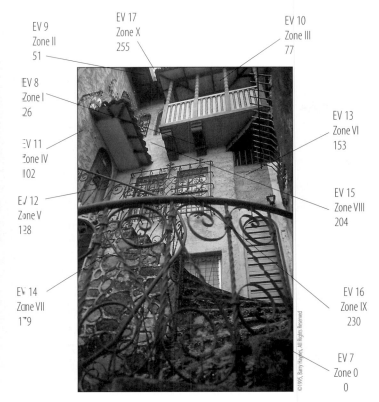

EV 9
Zone II
51

EV 17
Zone X
255

EV 10
Zone III
77

EV 8
Zone I
26

EV 13
Zone VI
153

EV 11
Zone IV
102

EV 12
Zone V
128

EV 15
Zone VIII
204

EV 14
Zone VII
179

EV 16
Zone IX
230

EV 7
Zone 0
0

The Spanish home in black and white showing the exposure value (EV) for different tonal areas (read by an exposure meter), the corresponding zones, and lastly the digital value, from 0 to 255, based on placing Zone V at exposure value 12 on the door.

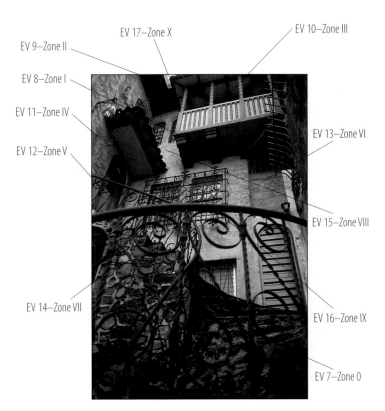

EV 9–Zone II

EV 17–Zone X

EV 10–Zone III

EV 8–Zone I

EV 11–Zone IV

EV 13–Zone VI

EV 12–Zone V

EV 15–Zone VIII

EV 14–Zone VII

EV 16–Zone IX

EV 7–Zone 0

The Spanish home in color showing the exposure value for different areas read by an exposure meter and the corresponding zone based on placing Zone V at exposure value 12 on the door. For the color image, the RGB digital values vary for each color channel depending on the color of the area.

In the Spanish home picture, the brightest areas are the little bit of sky at the top and the reflection of the sun on the right side of the window frame at the bottom. The darkest areas are the shadows in the bottom-right corner. Measuring these with a light meter that allows spot readings might produce readings like exposure value (EV) 17 for the bright section of sky at the top and EV 7 for the dark shadow at the bottom. Each jump in the exposure value represents twice as much light.

In the photograph of the Spanish home, if we have exposure value readings from 7 in the darkest area to 17 in the brightest area, there is a difference of 1024 times the brightness from the darkest amount of light to the brightest amount of light. Here's how we get arrive at that figure: EV 7 = 1 (the lowest amount of light), EV 8 = 2 (twice as much light), EV 9 = 4, EV 10 = 8, EV 11 = 16, EV 12 = 32, EV 13 = 64, EV 14 = 128, EV 15 = 256, EV 16 = 512, EV 17 (the brightest reading) = 1024. This is 1024 times as much light from the darkest area to the brightest.

Placing the Zone V Exposure

After measuring the range of exposure values within a scene that you want to photograph, you usually set the camera's exposure to a value in the middle of that range. The value that you set your exposure to causes the areas within the scene that have that exposure value to be recorded as a middle gray brightness value on the film. Where you set your exposure on the camera is called "placing your Zone V exposure." In the sample image of the Spanish home, we have placed our Zone V exposure at exposure value 12, the reading we got from the door. Usually you set your exposure to the area within the image that you want to be a middle brightness value. If a person were standing on the steps in this photo, you might set the exposure by taking a meter reading from the person's face.

When you decide where to set the exposure, you affect what happens to each of the zones within the image area, not just Zone V. If the Spanish home image were a transparency, it would reflect an exposure where you set Zone V based on the reading taken from the middle of the door. If the film were then processed correctly, the middle of the door in the transparency would look correct, as though you were looking straight at it with your eyes adjusted to it. When you set the exposure to the middle of the door, the areas around it that are lighter or darker, the zones above and below Zone V, would become correspondingly lighter or darker on the film. The bright window, at exposure value 16, would then be placed at Zone IX and would show up as very bright and with almost no detail on the film. This is because it is 4 zones above, or 16 times brighter than, where we set our exposure (at exposure value 12).

If you were to set the exposure on the camera to exposure value 16, the exposure value for the bright window, you would do to the camera and film what happens to your eye when you move up very close to the bright part of a contrasty scene. The iris of your eye closes and you start to see a lot of detail in that bright area. It is no longer a white area with no detail, because the focus of your field of vision moves up and your eyes adjust to encompass just that area. If you set the exposure on your camera to exposure value 16, that bright window area in the picture would show up as a middle gray for black-and-white or a normal color in a transparency. By changing this exposure, you would then be placing Zone V at exposure value 16. Now the door would be at Zone I, 16 times darker, and everything darker than the door would be in Zone 0, totally black. This would give you details in the highlights, but you would lose the details in the darker parts of the scene. By measuring the scene and noticing that the bottom of the stairs has exposure value 7 and the sky has exposure value 17, then setting the exposure on your camera in the middle at exposure value 12, you place Zone V at exposure value 12, thereby obtaining the full range of these values on the film.

Utilizing Exposure Latitude

Different films and different digital cameras have different exposure latitudes. The exposure latitude of a film is the number of different exposure values it can record at once. The Zone System covers a span of 11 exposure values, a range of brightness from 1 to 1024 times as bright. Most films can't capture detail in so broad a range of lighting situations. This range of light would be found in a contrasty scene on a sunny day with the sun shining directly on it. Some films can capture detail over a range of seven exposure values and some over a larger range.

In Adams's description of his zones, detail is captured only from Zone II through Zone VIII, or over a seven-zone range. Image areas in Zones 0, I, IX, and X are pretty much void of detail and are either black or white. Some high-end studio digital camera backs have a larger dynamic range than most film. If you know the exposure latitude of your film or digital camera when taking a picture, you can determine which parts of the picture will have detail and which will be black or white by measuring the range of your image area and setting your exposure, your Zone V area, so that the other zones or brightness ranges you need will be placed where the camera will capture them.

We could have gotten more details in the highlights in the Spanish home by placing Zone V, our exposure setting, at exposure value 13 or 14 instead of 12, but then the shadow areas at exposure values 8 or 9, the areas underneath the roof and balcony overhangs, would have shown up as totally black. Some pictures will not be very contrasty, and you will know by taking light measurements that the exposure latitude of your film or digital camera can handle the total number of zones in the image. All you need to make sure of, then, is that you set the exposure in the middle of that range so all the areas of different exposure values fall within the latitude of the film or digital camera, enabling you to record detail in those tonal areas.

With a digital camera, you can immediately look at the histogram of the image you shot and see if you have lost highlight or shadow details on either end. Depending on the shape of the histogram, you can also get some idea of how the different parts of the image are represented in the shot. If you don't like what you see, you can take another shot using a different exposure. Barry sometimes uses his digital camera to preview a scene before shooting it on film with his Pentax 6x7 film camera.

If your digital camera allows to you shoot Raw files this will give you much more control over the image data, especially if you use Adobe Camera Raw to "process" the Raw file. Additionally, shooting in Raw will allow you to bring your images into Photoshop as 16-bit files, which gives you more "tonal overhead" for making adjustments.

The Advantages of a Digital Image

When you look at the histogram of an image using the Levels dialog or the Histogram palette in Photoshop, you see all the tonal values in the image represented as a bar graph. Using tonal or color correction commands such as Levels or Curves, you can redistribute the tonal values and adjust them to be either lighter or darker with much more precision than you could ever have done in the darkroom. In addition, most decent digital cameras let you see the histogram on the camera back, and with many models this can be programmed to display right after you have taken the shot. One quick look tells you if you've captured the tonal information you need for a great print.

Looking at the histogram of the Spanish home image, we can actually see approximately how many values in the image fall within each zone (the height of the histogram bars correlates to the number of pixels in the zone: higher bars equal more pixels). Notice that in this image many values fall in Zones I, II, and III. That's because this photograph has a lot of dark areas. There are not many values in Zones IX and X because the scene does not have many very bright areas.

Although the Zone System was originally developed for film photography with large-format view cameras, and having in-depth knowledge of it is not crucial for working in Photoshop, it can be a very useful way to think about the tonal structure of a photograph. And anything that deepens your understanding of the balance of tones that create an image will almost certainly help you as you work to become better at Photoshop. In later chapters, we'll delve deeper and show you how to use Levels, Curves, and other tools to precisely modify the tonal and color qualities of an image.

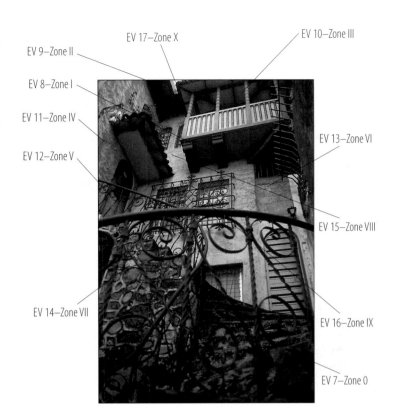

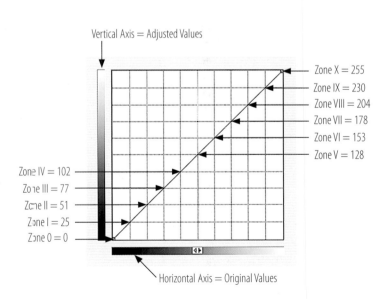

The Curves tool is one of the most precise tonal correction features in Photoshop. This illustration shows the graph section of the Curves dialog showing a 10x10 grid with the grid intersections identified with their digital values and the corresponding zones.

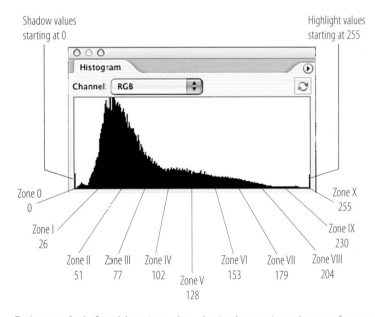

The histogram for the Spanish home image above, showing the approximate placement of zones on the bar graph of the tonal scale. The approximate digital value, from 0 to 255, is also shown for each zone.

15 ◆ Color Spaces, Device Characterization, and Color Management

In this chapter we will discuss how color is perceived by the human eye and how different light sources have a variety of qualities. We'll explain what a color gamut is, and how various color devices have different color gamuts. We'll talk about measuring or characterizing a color device and also about understanding RGB and other color workspaces in Photoshop. All of these topics are background information you'll need in working through other parts of *Photoshop Artistry*.

Color and How the Eye Sees It

It's night and you can barely see; then the sun slowly comes up, and you begin to recognize things. The light from the sun is allowing you to see more and more. In that early morning light, things seem very warm and yellow. Then, as the sun gets higher in the sky, that warm yellow fades away and you get a whiter light. That white, midday light is made up of many wavelengths of light. Light is actually waves of excited electronic particles, and those waves come in different lengths. When light waves hit a surface, each different type of surface absorbs some of the wavelengths of light, and other wavelengths are reflected back toward you if you are looking at that surface. Now, instead of the white light that comes from the sun, you see only part of that light reflected back from a surface. The part, or wavelengths, reflected back to you determines the color of that surface.

The human eye has sensors called rods and cones. The rods sense brightness or light intensity, but it is the cones that actually detect

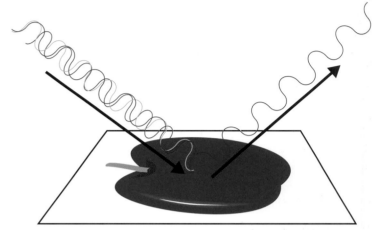

Color we see from a non-light-source surface is the color of light reflecting back off the surface while the other colors are absorbed by the surface.

color. There are three different types of cones, each sensitive to a different wavelength of light. One type of cone is more sensitive to red light, one is more sensitive to green, and the third is more sensitive to blue.

An Image on Paper

When you look at an image printed on paper, the color you see depends on the color of the incoming light that is illuminating the paper; that incoming light supplies all or most of the wavelengths of light that you could possibly see, although there might be several different types of light illuminating the paper—increasing the possibilities. The color and surface texture of the paper itself will subtract some of the wavelengths from the incoming light source and give the paper a certain color. The inks or other types of color that are painted on the paper will subtract further wavelengths from that original light and will reflect back different colors that are the remaining non-subtracted wavelengths. The angle from which you view the paper might also influence how much light is reflected back. When you are considering how a particular image might look on a certain printer, a number of factors—the digital values in the original image, the type of inks you use, the type of paper you print on, and the way the printer puts the ink on the paper—work together to create a specific range of colors you can see in that one situation.

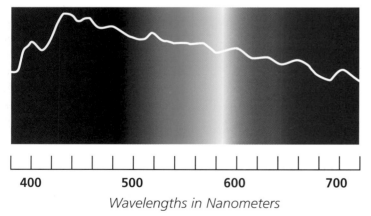

400   500   600   700
Wavelengths in Nanometers

The wavelengths of light and how you see them. The white line is an approximation of daylight wavelengths.

An Image on a Computer Monitor

Color on a CRT computer monitor comes from particle energizers, a type of light source behind the monitor's glass that hits the coating on the inside of the monitor glass and produces different colors and light intensities depending on the numerical values that are driving the different colored particle energizers. Similarly, an LCD's light source comes from behind the liquid crystals and shines out to your eyes, sort of like a backlit transparency. This is different from reflected light that allows you to see a print. With both types of monitors, light also hits the monitor from the outside due to other light sources within the room, and this "ambient" light, too, will affect the color and brightness that you see from the internal monitor light source. The way you see color on a computer monitor is quite different from the way you see it on a printed piece of paper. It is difficult to exactly match the brightness, color, and contrast characteristics of these two media. We will show you how to get as close as possible to a match using calibration.

A Slide on a Light Table

When you look at a slide on a light table, the color you see depends on the color of the light source behind the slide, the colors in the emulsion of the slide material, and the amount and intensity of the other light sources in the room.

Color Gamuts

There is a very large range of colors—wavelengths of light—that the human eye can see. There are also wavelengths of light that the eye can't see. A particular range of colors is called a color *gamut*. The

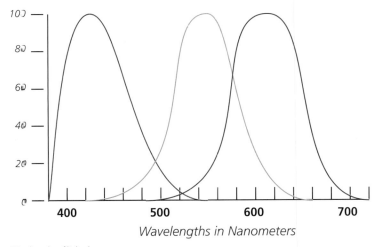

Wavelengths of light the eye can see.

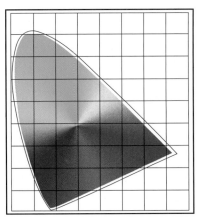

A CIE xy chromaticity diagram showing the Lab color space.

color gamut of the human eye is described in a color space called Lab color. A *color space* is a description of a range of colors to be used for a particular purpose. In the 1930s, an organization called the CIE (Commission Internationale de l'Eclairage) did a bunch of scientific measurements with human observers to develop a description of the colors the human eye could see. Without filling in all the details here, this description has evolved into two very useful tools we will use in this book for measuring and quantifying color. One of these tools that Photoshop supports is the Lab color space, which consists of a color gamut of the range of colors that the human eye can see. The second tool is the CIE xy chromaticity diagram, which shows these colors on an xy graph, again representing the colors the human eye can see. This CIE xy chromaticity diagram is useful for plotting other color gamuts and comparing one against another. When you are working on a project using the Lab color space, you won't be throwing out colors that the eye can see and you won't be working with any colors that the eye cannot see. Using the Lab color space, you would potentially be working with all the colors the eye can see; however, the eye can actually see more colors than most of the cameras, monitors, and printers you work with can reproduce. To learn more about Lab color see *Photoshop LAB Color: The Canyon Conundrum and Other Adventures in the Most Powerful Colorspace,* by Dan Margulis (Peachpit, 2005). To learn a lot more about the CIE and color history and theory, we recommend *The Reproduction of Colour,* by Dr. R.W.G. Hunt, Fifth Edition (Fountain Press, 1995). Another great and more up-to-date book is *Real World Color Management,* by Bruce Fraser, Chris Murphy, and Fred Bunting (Peachpit Press, 2005).

Measuring Color

To measure color, you need to be able to measure wavelengths of light. A device called a spectrophotometer does this best. We will be explaining how a spectrophotometer, used along with color calibration

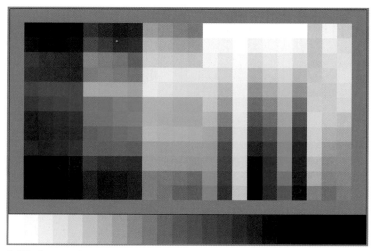

An IT8 color-measuring target.

software, improves how effectively and accurately you use digital color. You want to be able to measure the colors that a particular film or digital camera can record, a particular scanner can scan, a particular monitor can display, and a particular printer can print. To do this, people have developed test target systems, such as the IT8 color target from the CIE, to measure color. In its purest form, this IT8 target consists of a group of many color swatches—light wavelength descriptions—covering a large range of colors that the human eye can see, and that various films could capture, scanners could scan, monitors could display, and printers could print. We use the word *could* here because you need to know that each color device—each film, digital camera, scanner, monitor, or printer—has its own color gamut. The color gamut of a device is the range of colors that particular device can detect, reproduce, or display. With a spectrophotometer, you can use the IT8 target or one of many other similar targets to measure the color gamut of any particular device.

Measuring the Gamut of a Film

To measure the gamut of a film, you photograph a scientifically printed version of the IT8 target when that target is illuminated by a known type and color temperature light source. (Note: You can buy light sources in known color temperatures, and you can also measure the color temperature of a light source.) You then process that film exactly and use the spectrophotometer to measure each swatch in the target as it is reproduced on that film. Different film manufacturers will sell you film swatches with IT8 targets already correctly exposed on them for you to scan and measure. The film needs to be illuminated by a known light source while you're taking the measurements. Those measurements are then entered into a profile-making soft-

ware program, which generates a color profile of that film based on a standard created by the International Color Consortium, or ICC. An ICC profile is a description of color in a standard format that can be recognized by many different color software applications, including Adobe Photoshop and Elements, Apple ColorSync, QuarkXPress, Adobe Illustrator, and Adobe InDesign. The profile-making program knows the empirical values each swatch is supposed to have—and did have—on the scientifically produced original that was photographed. Based on the differences between the original values of each swatch and the values actually recorded on the film, an ICC profile is generated that characterizes that particular film. A *characterization* is a description of the differences from the original empirical values; it ends up also telling you the color gamut or range of colors that film can represent.

Characterizing a Scanner

To measure the color gamut of, or to characterize, a scanner, you need a scientifically produced IT8 target on film, which you can get from the film manufacturer or on a printed medium that can be scanned with the scanner. The resulting digital values the scanner gets are entered into the profile-making software to produce an ICC profile that describes that particular scanner. In Chapter 16, "Photoshop Color Preferences, Calibration, and Printing," we'll talk about several packages you can use to make custom scanner profiles.

Characterizing or Calibrating a Digital Camera

To measure the color gamut of, or to characterize, a digital camera, you could photograph an IT8 target or a GretagMacbeth ColorChecker and then compare the colors in the digital file on your screen to the actual colors on the target. To make a profile for the camera you'd have to feed the file the camera captured, without any post-processing, into a profile-making package. To calibrate the camera, though, you could adjust the Calibrate section of the Camera Raw dialog to tweak the target colors until they were correct. You can usually find GretagMacbeth ColorChecker charts for around $75 US in professional camera stores.

Characterizing a Monitor

To characterize a monitor, a scientifically created digital file of the IT8 target or some other target is measured with a colorimeter or spectrophotometer while being displayed on the screen in a room lit with controlled lighting conditions. Then those measurements are entered into the profile-making software to generate the ICC profile of that monitor. In Chapter 16, we'll show you several hardware/software packages you can use to calibrate your monitor.

Characterizing a Digital Printer

To characterize a particular digital printer or printing press, the scientifically produced digital version of the IT8 target, or some other target, is printed on that printer or press using the standard process for outputting to that device. Then the results are measured with the spectrophotometer, and the profile-generating software creates an ICC profile from those results.

Now you know what ICC profiles are and how they are made. By the way, there are various targets that the industry uses to create ICC profiles—the Kodak IT8 is just an example—and there are various companies that produce ICC profile-making software. These companies and their products include MonacoEZcolor, Proof and Profiler; ColorVision OptiCal with SpyderPro; GretagMacbeth Eye-One Photo and ProfileMaker; and many others. When you are using this calibration process to characterize, or describe, the color gamut a particular device can record, scan, display, or print, the accuracy of this characterization depends on how accurately the test was performed and measured. When you make a profile or have a profile made, make sure it is done properly, or the profile you get might actually do you a disservice. In the next chapter, we will talk about the process of making profiles using some of the more popular products now on the market.

Choosing Your Color Working Space

When you are working in Photoshop, you have the option of choosing different color spaces as your working color space. Color spaces available with Photoshop use either the RGB, Lab, or CMYK color model. Each color space also encompasses a particular color gamut. So when working in Photoshop, you need to decide which color model—RGB, CMYK, or Lab—makes the most sense for your type of work, and then, within that model, what color gamut you need for the work you are doing.

Let's first discuss the color gamut issue. For any particular body of work that involves human viewing, you will probably not need to work with colors outside the gamut of Lab because this is the set of colors the human eye can see. If you are outputting your work on color film, digital printers, computer monitors, or printing presses, you also need to consider the color gamut of those devices. It turns out that the color gamut of a CMYK printing press is much smaller

than that of the human eye, the Lab color space. If you are only outputting to CMYK presses but you are working within the Lab color space, you may be constantly disappointed because many of the colors you see on the screen may not actually be reproducible on a printing press. The color gamut of computer monitors, color film recorders, and some of the new digital color printers is much larger than that of a CMYK press. So if you are also outputting to devices other than a press, you would not want to limit your gamut to colors available only on a press, especially if your goal is to produce art prints for gallery use or exciting, colorful images for the Web and multimedia. The ideal circumstance would be to work in a color space that encompasses the entire color gamut of all the input scanners or digital cameras, display monitors, output color film recorders, photographic and ink-based printers, digital printers, and CMYK or 6-color presses that you would be outputting to now and in the reasonable future.

We got the term "reasonable future" from our friend Bill Atkinson, and it seems like a good term because "foreseeable future" could include a time when we all wear special glasses, like Geordi La Forge on *Star Trek*, that increase the gamut of what the human eye can see. That would complicate things too much. We could measure the gamut of each of those devices and plot those gamuts on a CIE chromaticity diagram. If we then created a color space that encompassed the gamut of all those devices, we would be set!

Now let's discuss the color model issue. What you have available in Photoshop is Lab, RGB, and CMYK. The Image/Mode menu also includes Index color, Duotone, and Grayscale, but we would put those in the category of special-case models that we work with only under certain circumstances.

The Lab Working Space

The Lab model has the advantage that its color gamut encompasses all the colors that the human eye can see. This is a very wide gamut and

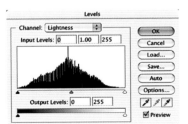

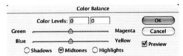

The Color Balance tool gives you different controls when you're working in Lab color, and you may find that you use it more in this color mode.

The Lightness channel in a Lab color image looks similar to an RGB histogram, but on the next page check out the "a" and "b" channels, where very small adjustments can make major changes.

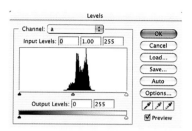

The "a" channel of a Lab image. There is a lot of unused space on either end of the histogram that could be used for a more detailed spec of this color if this were a reduced-gamut Lab space like Lab LH.

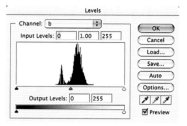

The "b" channel of this same Lab image.

would certainly encompass the devices we would be working with in the reasonable future. There are certain features of Photoshop that are not available when you're working in Lab color. To see what these are, use Image/Mode/Lab Color to convert one of your RGB images into Lab, then browse through the Photoshop menus and notice the ones that are now disabled—shown in light gray.

Barry has used the Lab color space for his art prints, but the potential problem with the Lab space is that it encompasses a larger gamut than most of the output devices we have used or will be using. The printers Barry uses now are the Epson 2200, 2400, 4000, and 7600. Another potential problem with Lab is that the tools for working in Lab within Photoshop are sometimes not as easy to work with as the tools for working in RGB. In the Lab space, there are three channels: Lightness, "a," and "b." The Lightness channel allows you to adjust the brightness and contrast of the image, as well as sharpen the image without modifying its color. Being able to separate the colors in an image from the brightness values is a big advantage of Lab. Using Levels to look at a histogram of a Lab image's Lightness channel is similar to looking at a histogram of RGB—all three channels at the same time. The color values in Lab are stored in the "a" and "b" channels. The "a" channel controls the red/green range of color, and the "b" channel controls the yellow/blue range. Most people are used to working with color using red, green, and blue along with their complements of cyan, magenta, and yellow. Using "a" and "b" takes a little getting used to. It works pretty well in Photoshop if you start out with a scan that is very close to what you want. Making major color shifts with the "a" and "b" channels in Photoshop can be more difficult.

The other thing about the "a" and "b" channels in Lab images is that if you look at their histograms, you will see that the values are usually all within the center part of the histogram. The blank parts on the left and right sides of the "a" and "b" histograms represent colors that are in the very wide-gamut Lab space but were not captured by the film or scanner, and therefore don't get represented in most Lab images. A better way to deal with the large Lab color space, which Photoshop CS and CS2 now allow even when you're using adjustment layers, would be to work with Lab images that have 16 bits per channel of color information. You'll notice, though, that some Photoshop functions—some filters mostly—still don't work with 16-bit Lab color. When you are working within an RGB space, both lightness and color values are represented in each of the Red, Green, and Blue channels, so it is harder to adjust one without the other changing as well. As we mentioned earlier in the chapter, to learn more about Lab color read Dan Margulis's excellent book.

The RGB Working Space

Working in RGB is probably the most common way people work with digital images. Scanner sensors scan in RGB format, digital cameras capture images in RGB, and most digital imaging software uses RGB as the default space. RGB is the format for images on the Web, it's used for printing on the LightJet 5000 and Fujix digital printers, it's the preferred format for Epson and Hewlett-Packard printers, and the format is used to print to color film recorders. There are lots of reasons to work in RGB, and it is the color model that Photoshop most fully supports. Working in RGB is a way to look at and interpret color data, but within the RGB world there are also different interpretations of RGB data.

If you scanned the same transparency with several different scanners, you would get different numerical results, and the colors and contrast would also probably look somewhat different. Before Photoshop 5, there was really no way to quantify those differences; all those files were just RGB files and you brought them into Photoshop and adjusted them to get what you wanted. ColorSync is Apple's system-level color management model that allows different applications to work intelligently with color. Starting with version 5, Photoshop began supporting ColorSync and color management. Now you can actually make profiles for each of those scanners, and then when you bring those files into Photoshop, you can convert them from their respective scanner profiles to a standard RGB color space that you want to work with in Photoshop. If done properly this should make these different scans look more similar and also look more like the original transparency as you view them on the screen within your standard Photoshop working space. Photoshop allows you to view each of these files on the screen in either a standard RGB working space or the working space of the scanner itself by working on them in the color space of the scanner's profile.

When using the RGB color model in Photoshop, you usually want to pick an RGB working space for each file you work with. Older versions of Photoshop, before Photoshop 5, assumed that the gamut of your RGB space was the gamut of your monitor as described by the old Monitor Setup dialog. This caused colors outside of that space to be clipped (thrown out) even though those colors might have been printable on wider-gamut output devices like color film recorders or the Epson 2400 digital printer. With Photoshop you use the Photoshop/Color Settings dialog in the Working Spaces RGB area to specify the gamut and other characteristics of your RGB space. You can choose an RGB color space that has a wider gamut than your monitor, and Photoshop will adjust the display of your space to pre-

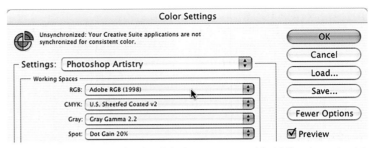

You can use the RGB pop-up in Photoshop/Color Settings to set your default RGB workspace; here it is set to Adobe RGB, which is what we recommend for most photographers.

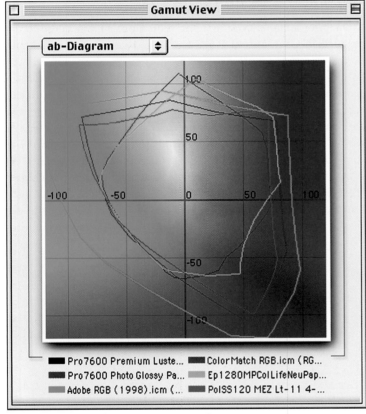

In the ab-diagram above, the Lab color space includes all the colors in the diagram. The Adobe RGB space is all the colors inside the green line, ColorMatch RGB includes the colors inside the blue line, the black line and the red line right on top of it are the profiles for the Epson 7600 Premium Luster and Premium Photo Glossy papers, the cyan line is a Monaco Proof profile Barry made for his Epson 1280 printer, and the purple line is the Polaroid SprintScan 120 film scanner. Notice that the Adobe RGB color space encompasses all or most of the colors defined by any of the spaces shown here. In Photoshop you can preview an image within a CMYK or RGB printing space using the View/Proof Setup dialog. It is a good idea to do this before printing to be sure those nonprintable colors don't spoil the effect of your image. This process is explained in detail in Chapter 16.

view as accurately as it can on your monitor, but it will not clip the colors that are outside of the monitor's gamut from your RGB file. That way you will still see those colors when you print the image.

In Photoshop, you can work on many files at the same time—each with a different RGB workspace—and yet each file will be displayed correctly on the screen. Photoshop will simultaneously display files in Lab color and various CMYK color spaces correctly on the screen as well. The RGB Working Space that you set in Photoshop/Color Settings is the RGB space that will be assigned to and used to view new RGB files and is also the space in which untagged files—those with no assigned profile—will be viewed on the screen.

Using the RGB pop-up menu, you can choose from the default RGB spaces Adobe has provided. Of the spaces provided by Adobe, only three of them have much interest to people dealing with professional images. We will describe those here; you can look in the Photoshop Help or printed documentation for information about the other spaces if you like. The four most commonly used spaces are ProPhoto RGB, Adobe RGB, ColorMatch RGB, and sRGB.

ProPhoto RGB

The widest gamut of these spaces, ProPhoto has been around for a while but was a larger space than was needed for most digital cameras and printers. This meant you were capable of creating colors in your file that were outside the gamut of your printer and therefore not printable. However, with the advent of more powerful camera sensors and wider latitude inks, many of those colors can now be captured and printed, making it worthwhile for some photographers to switch to this larger space. For more about the trade-offs between ProPhoto RGB and Adobe RGB, see Chapter 9, "Camera Raw," and Chapter 16.

Adobe RGB (1998)

Adobe RGB was originally a proposed standard for HDTV production. Some people call this Adobe RGB (1998), but we just call it Adobe RGB. The gamut of Adobe RGB essentially includes the entire CMYK gamut and more, because it also better encompasses the gamut of things like color RGB film recorders, the LightJet 5000 digital printer, various Epson and HP printers, and other color output devices. If you set your RGB working space to Adobe RGB, you will be least likely to throw out values that you'll be able to see in most of today's digital output devices, and yet the gamut is not so large that you'll be wasting a lot of your color space and risking posterization problems. With Adobe RGB you will be able to see more colors on a good monitor than you'll be able to print in CMYK on a press. Barry usually uses Adobe RGB when working with art prints in the RGB color space. However, he's been testing ProPhoto RGB with the Epson 2400 and will probably move to it full time when he gets the Canon 5D.

ColorMatch RGB

The ColorMatch RGB space's gamut is smaller than Adobe RGB but bigger than sRGB. This space is based on the Radius PressView monitor, which was an earlier industry standard for quality color work. The advantage of the ColorMatch RGB space, especially for people who are doing print work, is that it has a fairly large gamut, at least for CMYK print work, and it is a well-known space within the color industry.

sRGB

The sRGB color space is the current default for Photoshop CS and CS2. This space is good for people who work primarily on Web images and want to see what the images are going to look like on a typical PC monitor. The problem with sRGB is that it is the smallest gamut space of the three RGB spaces, and working in it will mean that you are potentially throwing out certain colors, even for CMYK print work, and you are certainly throwing out colors if you are planning to output to an Epson or HP digital printer. Photographers working on art prints should certainly change their RGB working space to something other than sRGB. If you are working in a larger gamut space, like ProPhoto RGB, Adobe RGB, or Lab, and you want to create an image for the Web, you could use Edit/Convert to Profile (Image/Mode/Convert to Profile in Photoshop CS or version 7) to convert a copy of your file from the larger space into sRGB for Web use. This would allow you to do your main work in a larger space to keep more colors, and then use sRGB to preview the work as it will

look on the average PC Web user's monitor. You can resave the file under a different name, or in JPEG format for your Web consumers, in the sRGB space that is optimized for that market. Many digital cameras also default to sRGB without the possibility of changing that. If you are opening an sRGB file from a digital camera and you are planning to color correct the file, you should use Convert to Profile to convert it to Adobe RGB. This can also be done automatically in the Open dialog. If you are not going to color correct the digital camera file, and thus increase the color saturation, you can just leave it in sRGB and it will be displayed or printed correctly. You'd use sRGB as your RGB working space if you only created images for the Web.

Other RGB Working Spaces

Some photographers and imaging professionals may choose to develop their own custom RGB working space. You can do this by creating an ICC profile of a certain film or digital camera that you like to work with. You can also do it by modifying an existing RGB working space to add a wider range of color in a particular area, like reds or greens, for example. If you go to the top of the pop-up menu for your RGB Working Spaces, you can choose Custom and then edit the Gamma, White Point, and XY Primaries to create your own custom color space. To be sure he can work with all the colors his film captures, Joe Holmes, a well-known photographer, created his own Ektachrome RGB space, which is bigger than Adobe RGB. Unless you have the tools available to measure the gamut of your input and output devices and to create your own RGB workspace, you should

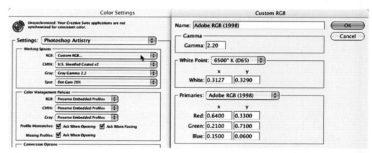

When you pick an RGB working space, that also sets up the default Gamma, White Point, and CIE xy Primaries values that describe that workspace. With More Options chosen, you can go in and modify any of these by hand by choosing Custom RGB from the top of the RGB pop-up menu. Modifying any of the values of the standard RGB spaces will change them from that space to another of your own making, so be sure to change the name of the space too so you don't overwrite the standard. An example where you might want to define your own space this way would be if you measured a particular new film or digital camera that you are using and determined from its ICC profile that the Adobe RGB Primaries did not contain a small portion of the film's color range. You could then change the Red, Green, or Blue xy values of Adobe RGB to extend the range of the Adobe RGB space. You'd want to call it something like Adobe RGB Plus!

probably pick one of the spaces provided by Adobe, or one that seems to be moving toward becoming some sort of an industry standard.

CMYK Master Workspace

The CMYK print gamut is smaller overall than the gamut of any of the RGB color spaces we just discussed, but there are a few colors CMYK can print that sRGB doesn't include. These days, it is not that common for people to have images that are only used in CMYK print. Even if you are using an image for just CMYK print, it is likely that you may have to print that image several times, at several sizes, and on different types of paper. For these situations, it is better if you have your master image in RGB or Lab; then when you resize the file, you can get more exact sharpening and you can also more accurately generate new CMYK separations for different papers and presses. Most people will be using the same image in print, on the Web, and for output to several digital printers. Because the RGB and Lab spaces are each bigger in color gamut than CMYK, it makes more sense these days to leave the master image in RGB or Lab format.

Some of the Photoshop filters don't work in CMYK, either. While viewing your CMYK images on the screen, even if the separations were done elsewhere, Photoshop compensates for the appearance of the image on the screen based on the CMYK profile the image is tagged with. If the image isn't tagged with a profile, Photoshop will display it using the CMYK settings you set for your CMYK working space using Edit/Color Settings in CS2 or Photoshop/Color Settings in CS. If you open an image that was separated to be used in a 20% dot gain situation and then display it in Photoshop with a CMYK working space set up for a 30% gain, the image will appear too dark on the screen. When you reset the Photoshop settings to 20%, the same image will appear correctly again. For those of you not involved in printing on a press, dot gain is just the spreading of printer dots due to paper absorption and the pressure of the printing plate. Dot gain makes images darker and must be compensated for. You need to be careful when opening untagged CMYK images that your preferences are set up correctly for their display. You'd only work in a CMYK space if your work was directed toward a printing press.

Working with 16-Bit-Per-Channel Scans and Files

A very useful technique, especially when working on the highest-quality art prints and on grayscale images, is to do 16-bit scans, or digital capture, then work in 16-bit-per-color-channel mode instead

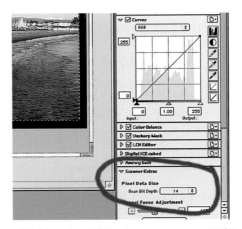

Here are the controls for the Nikon 8000 scanner set up to do 16-bit-per-channel scans. This scanner actually scans 14 bits of information per channel, but in Photoshop the two choices are either 8 bits per channel or 16 bits per channel, so when you actually do 12 or 14 bits in your scanner and save this as a TIFF file, it will show up as 16 bits within the Photoshop user interface.

of 8-bit color. This gives you up to 16 bits per Gray, RGB, Lab, or CMYK channel of information instead of the usual 8 bits. Photoshop CS and CS2 now have full layer and adjustment layer support for 16-bit files, as well as support for many other features in full 16-bit mode. The filters that photographers use for regular photography are supported in 16-bit mode, but many of the effects filters work only in 8-bit mode. To convert an image to 16-bit color, just choose Image/Mode/16 Bits/Channel; but to actually get the extra info that 16 bit is great for, you need to scan or digitally capture in 16-bit mode to start with.

Most of today's scanners get more than 8 bits per channel of RGB information when they scan. They may get 12, 14, or even 16 bits per channel. When you adjust the Curves and other controls in the scanner software, what you are really doing is deciding how to convert from the more than 8 bits of information that the scanner gets to the 8 bits of information per channel that is in a standard RGB file. When you do that conversion to 8 bit, you are throwing away information that you got from the scanner, and often you end up throwing away the wrong information or you want some of it back later. At this point, you may need to rescan your original to get that information. Most scanners these days allow you to save all 16 bits per channel of information exactly as it comes from the sensors on the scanner—a raw scan. Because Photoshop works in either 8-bit or 16-bit mode, make sure you work in 16-bit mode if your scanner or camera captures more than 8 bits per channel. This way, assuming you have a great scan from a great scanner, you might never need to scan the original again. Now, with Photoshop CS and CS2, you can permanently leave your file and layers in 16-bit-per-channel color!

Check out Chapter 17, "Image Resolution and Scanning," to get a lot of good ideas of options to consider when making 8-bit or 16-bit per channel scans.

16 ◆ Color Preferences, Calibration, and Printing

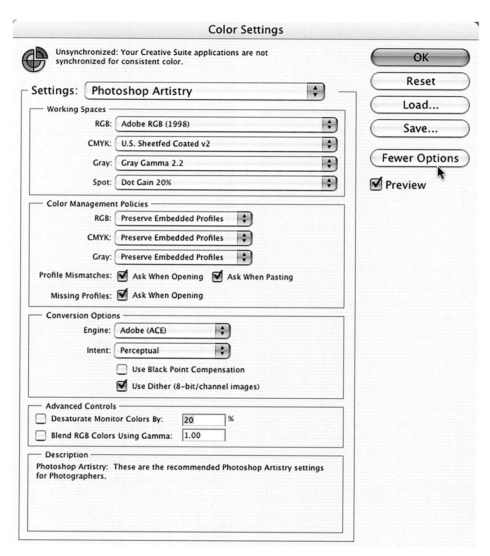

In the first part of this chapter, we will go through the Photoshop Color Settings dialog, above, and describe each setting and our recommended choice for it and what that choice means. Later in the chapter we will discuss a strategy for calibrating your monitor and printer—two tasks that can dramatically affect the quality and predictability of your results. We'll also discuss monitor soft proofing and other calibration issues.

To fully understand this chapter, you should also read Chapter 2, "Preferences and Color Settings," Chapter 15, "Color Spaces, Device Characterization, and Color Management," and Chapter 18, "The Master Image Workflow."

Setting Your Photoshop Color Preferences

You should bring up Photoshop's Color Settings dialog and possibly adjust your changes as we discuss them in these first sections.

◆ With Photoshop CS2, go to Edit/Color Settings, Command (Ctrl)-Shift-K, (Photoshop/Color Settings in CS on the Mac) to bring up the Color Settings dialog. Make sure to select the More Options button, on the right side, so you see the entire dialog. Once you have all your color settings the way you want them for a particular type of project, click the Save button to save them in a file that you can later reload in one step using the Load button.

In the dialog you see here, we've saved the color settings as the Photoshop Artistry settings. If you've gone through Chapter 2 and set your preferences, then you will have set these up already. We will be working with this dialog for some time as we describe each of the settings, why you make a particular choice, and the effect that choice will have on your images. If you don't have time right now to go through this whole discussion, just choose the settings on the left and then come back and read the chapter later. The color settings and calibration are one of the most important things in Photoshop and will dramatically affect the quality and accuracy of your results. If you are not happy with the results you are getting, make sure you understand the issues in this chapter before you continue.

Working Spaces

The top section of the Color Settings dialog is called Working Spaces. Now we'll take a tour through the different subsections of Working Spaces.

RGB Working Space

Choose Adobe RGB (1998) in the first RGB pop-up menu. After making this choice, notice that if you put the cursor on top of that same menu, the Description area at the bottom of the dialog will tell you something about the setting you have chosen. We recommend that you take advantage of these descriptions as you explore each of the settings.

We have now set the RGB working space to Adobe RGB. The RGB working space is the space that will be assigned to new files that you create using File/New, and it is the space that you will view untagged files in on the screen, even if you don't tag them with Adobe RGB when you open them. Files that are already tagged with some other color space, like some of the files on the *Photoshop Artistry* DVD

that are tagged with ColorMatch RGB, will usually be opened and viewed within that other color space, unless you choose to do otherwise in the next section, "Color Management Policies." To learn more about the Adobe RGB color space and the other default RGB spaces, see Chapter 15.

If you are a photographer and don't have another default custom RGB space you want to work in, such as the color space of your film, then Adobe RGB is a good space to choose. It's the space that most photographers use and that most books recommend. ProPhoto RGB is another RGB color space you might consider. It gives you a wider gamut than Adobe RGB and may be better for newer digital cameras shooting in Camera Raw and for the newest Epson printers. Look in Chapter 9, "Camera Raw," for more information about this color space. If you are doing Web work exclusively, then you might want to choose the sRGB space. If you are doing only work for CMYK print, then you might want to choose ColorMatch RGB. Setting your RGB working space causes certain things to happen in Photoshop in conjunction with how you set the Color Management Policies for RGB in the next section of this dialog. We'll talk about those issues there.

If you are a photographer printing RGB files to a color inkjet printer, you usually don't need to worry about the CYMK, Grayscale, or Spot color settings and you should just set them as we did in the dialog at the start of this chapter. If the CMYK, Grayscale, or Spot color sections prompt additional questions, we suggest that you review Chapter 15.

CMYK Working Space

You generally use the CMYK color space when preparing content for a printing press. Converting from RGB to CMYK is traditionally called making color separations. For the CMYK working space pop-up menu, we recommend that you choose the U.S. Sheetfed Coated v2 setting, which has worked very well for us when doing CMYK work for books and magazine articles. Most of our day-to-day printing is of our landscape art prints on the Epson 2200, 2400, 4000, and 7600. All of these printers require RGB files, and in most cases we're converting RGB or Lab master files to a custom profile for those prints. Our printing press CMYK experience involves doing all the color separations for 11 years' worth of books, including *Photoshop 3 Artistry* through this new *Photoshop Artistry,* and also Wendy's book *Photoshop, Painter, and Illustrator Side-by-Side.* We also do magazine articles and brochures, as well as effects for magazine covers or advertisements—we usually separate these, too.

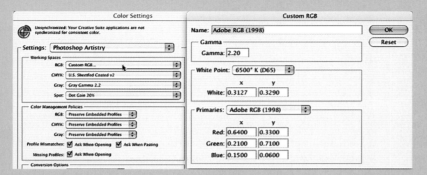

Editing Color Spaces

When you pick an RGB working space, that also sets up the default Gamma, White Point, and CIE xy Primaries describing that working space. You can then go in and modify any of these settings by choosing Custom RGB from the top of the RGB pop-up menu. Modifying any of the values of the standard RGB spaces will change them from that space to another of your own making, so be sure to change the name of the space too, so you don't overwrite the standard. An example where you might want to define your own space this way would be if you measured a particular new film or digital camera that you are using and determined from its ICC profile that the Adobe RGB primaries did not contain a portion of the film's color range. You could then change the Red, Green, or Blue xy values of Adobe RGB to extend the range of the space adding those colors. You'd want to call it Adobe RGB Plus or something like that!

The earlier *Artistry* books were printed on sheetfed presses; since *Photoshop 7 Artistry,* however, they've been printed on web presses. Traditional web presses used more black ink and less colored ink than sheetfed presses would to print the same images, so we had to do the color separations differently for web presses. When *Artistry* converted to web presses, Barry did some tests with the printer's Kodak Approval proofs comparing these same settings of ours with the settings normally recommended by the printer. Our settings actually produced more shadow detail and brighter colors on the Approval proofs (*approvals* are digital proofs that actually show the dot patterns that will appear on the direct-to-plate printing plates). When you're printing on a press, proofs are usually used because it is too expensive to just try some images on the press. The Sheetfed CMYK settings use more color ink and less black ink. Traditional web presses couldn't handle that much colored ink, but today's web presses have quality more like that of the sheetfed presses of ten years ago.

You may think you'll never need this information, but many of our workshop students have published books of their images. We provide images all the time for CMYK print projects including local brochures, tourist magazine photographs, and magazine articles we write. If you're going to publish your images, especially for your own marketing print matter, you'll want to be able to control the quality and colors of the CMYK images yourself. You'll be much happier that way!

Gray Working Space

For the Gray pop-up menu, we're using the Gray Gamma 2.2 option, which matches the gamma that we've set our Mac monitors to—a

setting we've used with grayscale images in the past. Photoshop tags grayscale images with a profile showing the gamma that they have been created or adjusted with. The most important thing with grayscale images is that you stay consistent with the gamma that you use, either 1.8 or 2.2, because the appearance of the image will change dramatically if you view a gamma 1.8 image within a gamma 2.2 environment, or vice-versa. There are other choices available for your Gray working space, including pre-set dot gains from 10% up to 30%. You can also choose Custom Gamma to set the grayscale gamma to any custom value, and Custom Dot Gain to set your own dot gain curve. You would use these options when printing grayscale images on presses and on papers with different dot gain values, or when you needed a gamma value other than 1.8 or 2.2.

Photoshop provides these CMYK default settings. We used the U.S. Sheetfed Coated v2 settings for the more color-critical pages in this book. If the settings I recommend on this page are not working for you, you may want to try the appropriate setting for your type of press and paper shown in this screenshot. It's also a good idea to talk to the print shop in advance, if possible, and see what they recommend.

Spot Working Space

For your Spot working space, which controls the dot gain on Spot Color channels, you should choose a dot gain comparable to the dot gain you are using with your CMYK working space. If you are adding a spot color plate to a certain print job, the dot gain for that plate should be similar to the dot gain you're getting at that printer in CMYK. I've set mine to the Dot Gain 20% setting, corresponding to my CMYK settings, but you might want to check with the print shop that is running a spot color job for you and see what they suggest. You can also choose Custom Dot Gain from the top of the Spot Working Space pop-up menu. This allows you to enter a custom dot gain curve, something you should do only if you know what you are doing and have specific dot gain measurements from the print shop.

Color Management Policies

The "Color Management Policies" section helps you deal with files that are different from what you normally expect. Photoshop assumes that you will normally be working with files that are tagged with profiles from your RGB, CMYK, or Grayscale working spaces. When you open or paste from a file that is tagged with a profile that is different from your working spaces or that isn't tagged with any profile, Photoshop lets you choose what to do. The settings we recommend will always warn you when you open or paste from an untagged file or a file that is tagged with a profile other than your working spaces. When I'm working on photographic images, I usually have my RGB working space set to Adobe RGB. Setting the Color Management Policies as shown here will always give you a heads-up when you are opening a file that is different from your current settings. If you always leave your working spaces set to the same values and you are

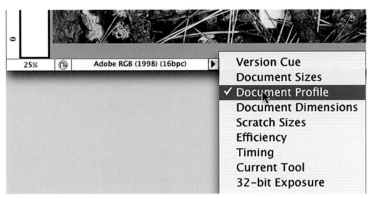

If you often work with files from different color spaces, it might be a good idea to set the info area at the bottom of your window to show Document Profile. You will then see the profile that Photoshop has assigned to that particular document. In the case of an untagged document, that document will normally be displayed using the default RGB or CMYK working space.

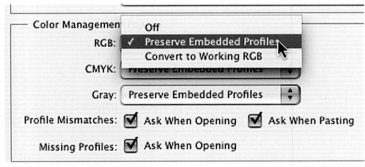

In the Color Management Policies section, you have the same three choices in each of the RGB, CMYK, and Gray pop-ups. For each one, we recommend that you choose the middle choice, Preserve Embedded Profiles. We also recommend that you turn on Ask When Opening for Profile Mismatches and Missing Profiles that happen when you open a file, and turn on Ask When Pasting for Profile Mismatches that happen during a paste.

always working with files in those same spaces, you should never encounter the warning dialogs these settings can cause.

If you often work with files from other color spaces, the default settings we recommend will cause Profile Mismatch dialogs to appear when you open a file or paste from a file in a different color space. The dialogs also alert you when a certain file is from a different color space or doesn't have a profile at all. Because Photoshop allows you to work with several files from different color spaces on the screen at the same time, there is no need to convert a file into your working space or to change your working space in order to correctly display a file from a different space.

Embedded Profile Mismatch

When you open a file from a different color space and get the Embedded Profile Mismatch dialog, you will usually want to use the embedded profile. An exception to that would be if you are going to color correct a digital file that was initially set to the sRGB space or the color space of your digital camera or scanner. You'd want to first convert that file into the larger-gamut Adobe RGB space before starting the color corrections.

Paste Profile Mismatch

If you will be combining or pasting from a file with a different space into a master file that is in your working space, it might be faster to convert the file into the working space now. Otherwise, every time you copy or drag and drop from that file into your master file within the working space, or within any different space for that matter, you will get the Paste Profile Mismatch dialog and will have to consider doing the conversion then.

Color Management Policy Dialogs

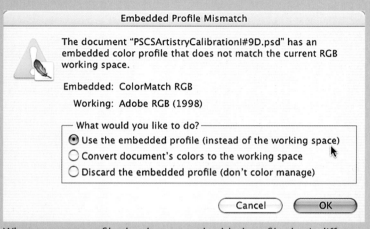

When you open a file that has an embedded profile that's different from your working space, you will get a dialog like the one above. If you choose "Use the embedded profile", the image will be correctly displayed on the screen, taking that profile into consideration, and it will continue to use that profile. If you choose "Convert document's colors to the working space," the colors in the document will be converted so the document looks correct when displayed in the working space, and the document will be tagged and displayed with the working space. If you choose "Discard the embedded profile," the profile will be tossed but the document will be displayed using the working space. To no longer get this dialog, turn off the Ask When Opening check box for Profile Mismatches; you will then automatically get the behavior chosen in the Color Management Policy pop-up for that RGB, CMYK, or Gray file type. This saves time if you are always opening files from another space and always want to make the same choice.

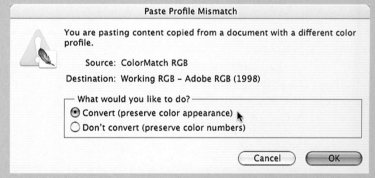

When you open a document that doesn't have a profile, you will get the Missing Profile dialog. We believe that the standard default here is to assign the working space, but this dialog is sticky. That means that if you make a particular choice, Photoshop will remember that choice and offer it next time. When working with this book, we usually assign the Adobe RGB profile to our screenshots, so Photoshop has remembered that and now offers it to us as the default. Notice that you can also assign a profile and then convert the file to your working RGB space. This option is useful, for example, when opening files from a scanner that doesn't save a profile with its files but that you have made a profile for and want to always convert from the scanner profile to your working space. To no longer get this dialog, turn off Ask When Opening for Missing Profiles.

Actually, even when Ask When Opening is turned off, Photoshop will present this dialog to let you know that the embedded profile will be used instead of the working space. Notice, however, that if you click the Don't Show Again check box here, this warning message will not show again unless you click the Reset All Warning Dialogs button in Photoshop/Preferences/General.

When you paste from a document having profile A onto a document having profile B, you get this dialog, and usually you will want to choose Convert to have the colors of the pasted image look correct within the document you pasted it into. If you don't convert the colors, the pasted image may look wrong!

Missing Profile

Opening an image that has no profile attached will bring up the Missing Profile dialog. This dialog allows you to leave the file as is (without a profile) or to assign the working space profile, or to assign some other profile you can choose from a pop-up menu. If you make this last choice, you can also turn on a checkbox to convert the file from that profile you assign into the working space.

To Stop These Dialogs

If you turn off the Ask When Opening options for Embedded Profile Mismatch and Missing Profile, or the Ask When Pasting option for Paste Profile Mismatch, you won't get the dialogs, but you will still get the behavior from the appropriate pop-up menu in this Color Management Policies section. We recommend not turning off these warning dialogs unless you are sure you understand what you are doing, and you are really bothered by the them. If you choose Preserve Embedded Profiles for RGB and you've turned off the warning dialogs, when you open a file that has a different profile from the RGB working space, that file will automatically open and be displayed correctly using the RGB profile that was attached to that file. If Convert to Working RGB is your menu choice, the file will automatically be converted to the RGB working space, but you will receive no notice of this conversion. If your RGB Color Management Policy is set to Off, then that file will be opened without any profile attached. If you look at the Document Profile name in the lower-left corner of that image's window, it will be named Untagged RGB. The pixels in the file will still be displayed on the screen using the RGB working space.

Summary of Color Management Policies

In this section we summarize the three Color Management Policy settings, and what they do in different situations. Unless you are always working with the same type of files, it is important that you understand these policies and their subtleties. The three policies are:

1. Off
2. Preserve Embedded Profile
3. Convert to Working RGB, CMYK, or Gray

When Creating New Documents

New documents are tagged with the current working space profile unless Color Management is set to Off, in which case they are left untagged.

Opening an Untagged Document

When opening an existing untagged document, all three policies will use the existing working space for viewing and editing the document but they will leave it untagged.

For Documents Tagged with the Current Working Space

When you open an existing document tagged with the current working space, that document will remain tagged with the current working space. All three policies view and edit this in the current working space and also leave it tagged with that space.

For Documents Tagged with Other Than the Current Working Space

When opening an existing document tagged with a profile other than the current working space, the Off policy untags the document and displays it in the current working space. The Preserve Embedded Profile policy preserves the embedded profile and displays it correctly in that profile's space. The Convert to Working policy converts the document from the other profile's space into the current working space and then retags the document with the current working space.

When Pasting or Importing

When pasting or importing data into an existing document, the Off policy just pastes the color numbers without doing any conversions. The Preserve Embedded Profile policy converts if the data has a source profile, but if not, or in the case of CMYK data, the numbers are pasted without any conversions. The Convert to Working option converts the data to RGB or CMYK unless it comes from a source without a profile.

Conversion Options

Now we'll discuss the Conversion Options section of the Photoshop Color Settings dialog. These influence what happens when an image is converted from one color space to another using Image/Mode/RGB, Lab, Grayscale, or Edit/Convert to Profile (Image/Mode/Convert to Profile in CS or before).

Use Dither

The Use Dither option should usually be on. This option makes it less likely that you will get undesirable banding when converting from one color space to another.

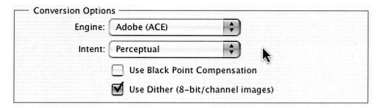

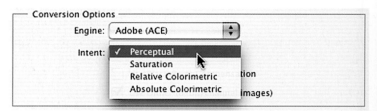

This Conversion Options section controls some of what happens when an image is converted from one color space to another using Image/Mode/RGB, Lab, or Grayscale or Edit/Convert to Profile. The Use Dither option should usually be on, because it will reduce the chance that you will get banding when converting from one color space to another. Banding appears as a choppy gradation of subtle color changes and is not usually desirable. We usually leave the Use Black Point Compensation option off when converting from one RGB space to another, like from Adobe RGB, or even from Lab, to an ICC profile for my Epson 2400 printer or the LightJet 5000. If you turn this off and then you don't like the way your blacks and dark shadows look, try the conversion again with Use Black Point Compensation on.

The Perceptual Intent setting is usually what photographers want for photographs because it preserves the overall look and feel of the image. For my RGB and Lab conversions for Epson 2200 and 2400 output, I use Perceptual with Black Point Compensation off. Relative Colorimetric with Black Point Compensation on is the Photoshop default. You may want to try that combination if the Perceptual choice is desaturating your images too much. The Saturation option is useful when you want intense colors, like for business graphics. Absolute Colorimetric is not the choice most photographers will want because the white points of the source and destination are not compensated for. You may find it useful if you're trying to match the look of one type of media, like a Press Proof for example, on another type, like an Epson printer proof.

Use Black Point Compensation

We usually leave the Use Black Point Compensation option off when converting from one RGB space to another. If you have this option off and don't like the way the blacks and dark shadows look in your prints, redo the conversion with Use Black Point Compensation on. Having it on has not helped Barry's images when he's worked with color prints on the Epson 2200, 2400, 4000, or 7600 using Epson or Bill Atkinson profiles. For him, turning this on seems to make the blacks more muddy and gives him less snappy shadows. It may give you more "Shadow Detail," but muddy shadow detail doesn't look good in most prints, and that is what we've found leaving it on gives us. What you get will depend on the images you are working with, as well as what software and settings were used to generate their source and destination profiles. If your printed blacks are coming out too dark or plugged up, try reprinting with Use Black Point Compensation on.

Engine

In general, you will want to set the Engine to Adobe (ACE), the built-in Photoshop conversion software. An example where you might want to use Apple ColorSync or Apple CMM instead would

be if a new version of one of those packages contained a feature that ACE didn't support or if that feature was more accurate using ColorSync or some other engine.

Intent

Setting Intent to Perceptual, with Black Point Compensation off and Use Dither on, is a common setting for photographers when converting an RGB or Lab master image, with a large gamut, to a CMYK or RGB print image within a smaller gamut printer space. If you find that the Perceptual setting is desaturating your colors too much, you might want to try the Relative Colorimetric setting with Black Point Compensation on or off. A good way to compare these settings is to use the wonderful Photoshop onscreen soft proofing feature while comparing several versions of the same image on the screen. For more info about this, see "Getting Accurate Soft Proofs of Your Output to RGB Printers" later in this chapter. For the ultimate test, you can also print several versions of the same image, converted with different Conversion Options, and compare the printed results.

Advanced Controls

Most people will want to leave the Advanced Controls off unless they are using a very wide gamut RGB space, one that is much wider than Adobe RGB. If you are using such a space, see the illustration and caption about the Advanced Controls dialog.

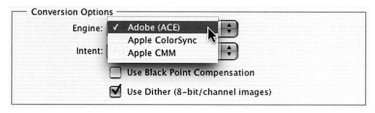

The Engine pop-up controls which software actually does the conversion. Adobe (ACE) is the built-in Photoshop software that you should normally use.

Playing with Conversion Settings

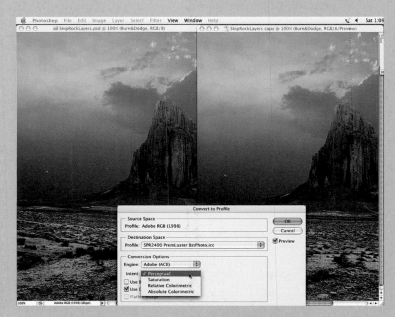

To set up the two-image comparison shown to the left, I started with my Adobe RGB master version of this image on the left of the screen. I then used Image/Duplicate to create the copy to the right and arranged the two windows so I could see both at once. While working on the version to the right, I chose Edit/Convert to Profile and picked the profile for Epson Premium Luster paper with my Epson 2400 printer. With the Preview button on, I can then choose either the Perceptual or Relative Colorimetric Intent options, and turn Use Black Point Compensation on and off while looking at a preview of the printed results in the image to the right. For this particular image, the Perceptual choice with Black Point Compensation off seemed to match my original Adobe RGB version the best.

Another thing you could do is use Image/Duplicate to make several copies of the image and convert each one in a different way with different settings. You could also compare these onscreen. The final step in the test would be to make and compare test prints after converting the image with one setting versus the other. The onscreen preview should simulate the results you get in your test prints if your monitor is correctly calibrated and you are viewing your test prints with the correct viewing light. Remember that there are many variables involved in getting this process right. I sometimes have to add a curve or Hue/Saturation adjustment layer to get the printed images to more closely match my monitor. We show you how to do that later in this chapter. Another way to use screen previews to compare printer profiles is to use View/Proof Setup/Custom. We describe this later in this chapter—check it out!

Other Preferences Relating to Color

Eyedropper Tool Setup

Usually when you measure digital image values in Photoshop, you want the Eyedropper set to measure a 3x3 square of pixels. That gives you a more accurate measurement in a continuous-tone image, because most colors are made up of groups of different pixels. If you were to measure a point sample, the default, you might accidentally measure the single pixel that was markedly different in color than those around it. We show how to set this preference correctly in Chapter 2.

Highlight and Shadow Preferences

The last preferences items that you need to set up for proper color corrections are the Highlight and Shadow settings, which you can reach by choosing either Image/Adjust/Levels or Image/Adjust/Curves. Please also refer back to Chapter 2 to see how to correctly set these.

The Advanced Controls should be left off unless you are using a very wide-gamut color space. If one were using such a wide-gamut space, it would only be really useful in 16-bit color mode, but it is unlikely the colors in that space could be accurately represented on a normal computer monitor. If you were using a large-gamut space, you could turn on Desaturate Monitor Colors By to try to somehow estimate your colors on the screen. If you did this, the screen display would probably not be able to match your printed output.

Blend RGB Colors Using Gamma controls the blending of RGB colors, probably from one layer into the next. When it is turned on, RGB colors are blended using the chosen gamma. A gamma of 1 is considered colorimetrically correct and is supposed to create the fewest edge artifacts. When this option is disabled, RGB colors are blended within the document's RGB color space, which matches what most other applications do.

Calibration of Monitors, Printers, Cameras, and Scanners

One of the most common questions we get from the readers of our *Photoshop Artistry* books and students in our digital printmaking workshops has to do with how they can better calibrate their monitors, printers, and scanners. Calibration can allow you to get from your printer the same color and contrast that you see on your monitor, to get very similar color and contrast when printing the same image on a number of different papers and/or printers, and also to improve the results you get from a scan or digital capture. Apple ColorSync and Photoshop CS provide an effective framework for people to accurately calibrate the production of digital images using Photoshop on the Macintosh and to also get accurate soft proofs of printed images on the screen. Calibration can also work well in a Windows XP environment.

Performing calibration accurately, however, requires color measurement instruments and calibration software. In previous versions of our books, we went into a lot of detail about making scanner profiles, printer profiles, and camera profiles, and a variety of software required to accomplish those tasks. Over the last two years, however, much of this time, effort, and expense has been rendered unnecessary, thanks to the high-quality printer profiles provided with photographic-quality Epson and HP printers, for use with the Epson and HP papers that get used with those printers. If you are using third-party papers, you shouldn't consider using them unless the third-party paper company also provides similar high-quality profiles—and the best paper companies now do. The industry has simplified this problem by combining consistent ink and paper quality with good printer profiles. We've also found that making scanner or digital camera profiles is not really necessary either. Today's film scanners and digital cameras do a good enough initial job that you can usually color correct their output files easily in Photoshop to get the result you want. The main thing we profile these days are our monitors, and for that we've been using the Spyder ColorVision products with OptiCAL now for the last three years. The latest of these products is Spyder2Pro which allows calibration to variable gamma and color temperature values. The Monaco Optix and Gretag Eye-One Display monitor calibrators also work quite well.

What Are Calibration, ColorSync, and ICC Profiles?

Calibration is the process where you measure the color gamut of a particular monitor, printer, or scanner and produce a detailed description of this color gamut in the format of an ICC profile. A device's color gamut is the range of colors that it can reproduce. The ICC, an international standards organization, has developed the ICC Profile format, which has become an industry standard for describing and dealing with the color gamuts of different color devices. ColorSync is a system software component built into the Macintosh that provides a framework for other applications, like Photoshop, Illustrator, Quark, and others, to use ICC profiles to accurately deal with the differences in color input and output on different devices. ColorSync allows the user to get matching, or close to matching, color on each device. For calibration to work correctly, someone needs to accurately make an ICC profile of each device and then correctly use these ICC profiles within ColorSync-savvy applications. The PC has a similar system for color management.

Do You Need to Calibrate?

If the color on your monitor matches the color on your digital prints, and if you and your clients are pleased with the results of your digital image creations, you may not need to calibrate any further. Seriously! This happy scenario is more likely to be the case if your Epson, HP, or other printer is the only output you're interested in and you are lucky enough to have a monitor that matches your particular printer's output.

If images on your monitor don't match your printer, though, then you should certainly pay close attention to the rest of this chapter. I'm interested in matching, as exactly as possible, my Epson 2200, 2400, 4000, and 7600 prints to my monitor, and also in matching Epson 2200, 2400, 4000, and 7600 prints to each other on several different papers. To do this I, Barry, used to create my own ICC profiles for each printer and ink combination. The canned profiles that come with the Epson 2200, 2400, 4000, and 7600 for Epson papers, as well as Bill Atkinson's profiles, are very good, and much better than the canned profiles that came with older Epson printer models, like the 1270 and 2000P. Epson profiles come with the printer software that ships with the printer. To get updates for profiles or printer software, go to the Epson Web site; Bill Atkinson's profiles are now available on his Web site. See the Links section of www.barryhaynes.com to access these and other site addresses.

When my prints from one Epson printer don't match those from another, I've often found them close enough that I can get them to match by creating subtle Photoshop adjustment layers that get added for prints on a particular printer/paper combination. Once I've made them, I can use these adjustment layers over and over. We'll show you how to make them later in this chapter.

If I were using a third-party paper or ink, then I'd be more likely to need to make my own printer profiles. These days, though, many third-party paper companies, like Red River Paper and Hahnemuhle also provide good canned profiles on their Web sites.

Most people should buy their own monitor calibrator and calibrate their own monitors. These systems work quite well for CRT or LCD monitors if you have a decent monitor. If you are using an Epson 2200, 2400, 4000, 4800, 7600, 7800, 9600, or 9800 and Epson papers, you probably won't need to make printer profiles, because the profiles that come with these printers are quite good. If the canned profiles are not working for you, you should make sure your Print dialogs are set up correctly before you decide to make your own profiles. See "Making Epson Prints with Canned or Custom Profiles" later in this chapter to learn how to set up Epson printer dialogs correctly. Using the wrong Print dialog settings is the most common cause of poor print color among the people who take my workshops.

Monitor Calibration for Free?

Photoshop 6 and older versions came with a tool called Adobe Gamma, which allowed you to visually calibrate your monitor. Photoshop Elements and Photoshop CS2 for Windows still come with Adobe Gamma. On the Mac in System Preferences/Displays/Color/Calibrate, there is a built-in visual calibrator. This system works similarly to the old Adobe Gamma.

We calibrate our monitors to a color temperature of 6500 Kelvin and a gamma of 2.2, which works well for printed photographs. We've found it hard to correctly and consistently calibrate many monitors to these settings using visual calibration techniques like Adobe Gamma. Even if you calibrate one monitor correctly, it is harder to match the results on other monitors each time. Most modern monitors also have buttons on the front of the monitor that allow you to set the color temperature and gamma; these are sometimes quite accurate, but often not. If you have a good eye for monitor color and some patience, you may be able to get reasonable calibration on some monitors using one of these visual techniques. If this doesn't work, or your prints are not matching your monitor, then you should try one of the third-party hardware monitor calibration techniques discussed later in this chapter. In general, the hardware calibrators from ColorVision, Monaco, and GretagMacbeth work very well these days and will usually calibrate your monitor more accurately and consistently than you can do visually.

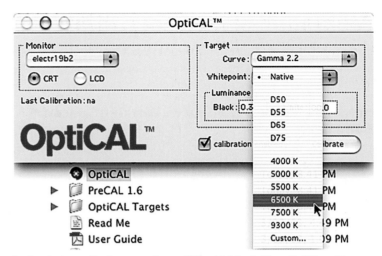

Lately we've been calibrating our monitors to 6500 and 2.2. Spyder2Pro or OptiCAL provides many choices for gamma and color temperature. The custom choice allows you to type in any white point or gamma. This can be a useful option if the standard choices (6500 and 2.2, 5000 and 1.8, and so on) don't precisely match your monitor to your prints.

Inexpensive Monitor Calibration Systems

The products described in this section all include software and a USB hardware device to measure and calibrate your monitor's contrast, white point, and color. These products also work fine with both CRT and LCD monitors. We believe all three products are priced at under $250 for the software and hardware. Prices change from month to month so we're not going to quote exact figures for each system.

The ColorVision Spyder2Pro with OptiCAL (or previous and future versions) is a good product that Barry has been using for several years on a variety of monitors. The nice thing about OptiCAL is that it allows you to choose any color temperature or gamma, instead of just the standard 5000, 6500, 1.8, and 2.2. That gives you more monitor tweaking options when your monitor image doesn't exactly match your prints.

The Monaco Optix product is also great for just calibrating your monitor. Optix allowed me to correctly calibrate external monitors attached to several iMacs with old built-in monitors that were no longer capable of being calibrated. CRT monitors wear out over time, and after three to five years get to the point where you can't correctly calibrate them. In that situation OptiCAL recognized that OptiCAL was attached to an iMac so OptiCAL didn't allow me to use the more advanced features I wanted for the external monitor. In all other cases, both OptiCAL and Optix worked fine and similarly. These products have new versions all the time so what we say about a particular version may not apply to the next version.

The GretagMacbeth Eye-One Display monitor calibration system is also a great entry-level product. It uses a measuring device that calibrates only monitors. The more expensive Eye-One Photo or Match products have the Eye-One Pro measuring device, which can calibrate monitors, printers, scanners, and other devices.

Hardware Monitor Gamma vs. Working Space Gamma

Another thing you need to consider when working in Photoshop is the hardware gamma your monitor is calibrated to and whether you work in an RGB working space that is 1.8 or 2.2 gamma. If you are using your monitor to work with images that are for CMYK print output, you may be better off if your monitor hardware gamma is set to 1.8, which is the standard gamma of Mac systems. If you are primarily doing output to the Web, you may want to set your monitor hardware gamma to 2.2, which is the typical gamma of PC systems. The gamma of your RGB working space, however, is a different story. Regardless of what you have your monitor gamma calibrated to, as long as your monitor is calibrated accurately, Photoshop should compensate for a different gamma in your RGB working space if necessary to give you a correct display of your images on the monitor.

An RGB working space that has a gamma of 2.2 more evenly displays the values in a histogram and allows you to see more separation in the shadows. Your shadow detail will likely be less posterized. Many people in the print world are used to working with the ColorMatch RGB working space with their gamma set at 1.8. In general, people who work in print have been working with a working space that has a gamma of 1.8, and people who use the Web or work on the Web are more likely to use a working space with a gamma of 2.2. If you open a file that has been color adjusted in a gamma 1.8 space into a gamma 2.2 space without converting, the file will seem darker and more contrasty. Similarly, if you initially corrected the file in gamma 2.2 and then opened it into a 1.8 space without converting, the file will seem too flat and light. Whatever space you adjust your files in, you'll get used to it and make appropriate color adjustment choices. When you open or print that file into a different gamma environment without compensation, you'll notice a problem.

From the Chapter 16 folder on the *Photoshop Artistry* DVD, open the ArtistryCalibColMatch.psd image, which was corrected and tagged with the gamma 1.8 working space ColorMatch RGB, and then choose Edit/Assign Profile (Image/Mode/Assign Profile in CS or 7) and assign Adobe RGB to this file without conversion. See how this changes the appearance of the file? Although we are Mac users and the default Mac monitor gamma is 1.8, these days we calibrate

our monitors to 6500 and 2.2, and we color correct in Adobe RGB, which is a gamma 2.2 color space. These settings seem to do the best overall job in Photoshop of matching our various monitors to the canned Epson paper profiles and Bill Atkinson profiles that we use on our Epson 2200, 2400, 4000, and 7600 printers. Because of the larger color gamut the camera can capture, will be looking more closely at using the ProPhoto RGB color space as our default for working with the Canon 5D or newer digital cameras; and you should consider that space if you have a newer larger-gamut camera.

Calibrating Scanners, Cameras, and Printers

You only need to calibrate your printer if the canned profiles are not working for you and/or you need to make profiles for third-party papers. If the canned profiles make good prints, then all you may need is one of the monitor calibrators described earlier. You only need to make a scanner profile if it is important to you to have your original scan match the original film as closely as possible. Because my prints always are corrected to look better than the original film and because I also like to work with raw scans, I, Barry, don't worry too much about having a scanner profile. If you do need to make camera, scanner, or printer profiles, buy the book *Real World Color Management* by Bruce Fraser, Chris Murphy, and Fred Bunting (Peachpit, 2005). Since I no longer find the need to make these types of profiles, I can use the time and money I would have spent on that endeavor to take more pictures and make more prints!

Making Epson Prints with Canned or Custom Profiles

We cover Epson printers here because we've found that the majority of accomplished photographers use Epson printers, and because over the years Epson has made a commitment to the art and photography community where other printer companies have been focused more on home and business solutions. Having very consistent color output with color inks that are long lasting and also having the ability to print on a variety of art papers is essential for the gallery community. When working with a calibrated color printer, you need to know that the inks and papers won't change from month to month when you buy more supplies. Epson has learned to honor those needs, where many other companies cater mainly to home or business users, where cheaper is always better and consistency doesn't matter as much.

When you print an image using an Epson canned or custom profile, the easiest way to print is to convert to the printer profile

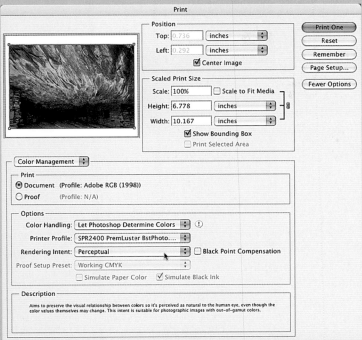

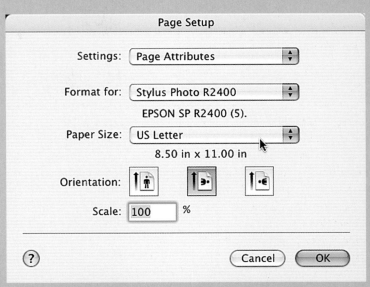

The correct Photoshop CS2 Print with Preview dialog when printing a file that you want Photoshop to convert on the fly while printing from your default color space to a canned or custom printer profile. In this case, the Print/Document space will be the name of your default color space (like Adobe RGB, Lab, or ProPhoto RGB) and the Options/Color Handling will be set to Let Photoshop Determine Colors. The Printer Profile is set to the name of the profile for your printer/paper combination. In this dialog I have this set for Epson Premium Luster Photo Paper on the Epson 2400 printer. The profiles for this printer come in PhotoRPM, BestPhoto, and Photo configurations. PhotoRPM is for 5760x1440, BestPhoto is for 1440x1440, and Photo is for 1440x720. I find that BestPhoto is the one I usually use. This would be just 1440 dpi on the 2200, 4000, or 7600. I usually set the Rendering Intent to Perceptual with Black Point Compensation off. If you don't like the results with that setting, try Relative Colorimetric with Black Point Compensation on or off. Black Point Compensation appears to have a larger effect with Relative Colorimetric Rendering Intent.

When you click Page Setup from the Photoshop Print with Preview dialog, you get this. Choose the printer you want to use from Format For and the paper size from Paper Size. If you need to define a new paper size, choose Custom Paper Size from the Settings menu.

within the Print with Preview dialog—Command-Option (Ctrl-Alt)-P—as shown in the "Photoshop Print with Preview and Page Setup Dialogs (Mac)" sidebar. By "an Epson canned profile" we just mean the profiles that get installed on your system when you install the software that comes with your printer. The Bill Atkinson profiles for Epson printers or a profile you made yourself are examples of a custom profile. Check the text in the sidebar for details of the

settings you should use. That Print with Preview dialog is causing Photoshop to convert the image from your default Adobe RGB color space into the color space defined for your printer by the profile you choose in the Options/Color Handling section.

The Page Setup dialog within the same sidebar is the second step in the Mac print dialog options setting process. Press the Page Setup button in the Print with Preview dialog once your Print with Preview

The Print Dialog and Save As

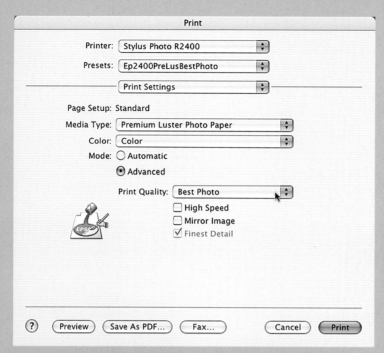

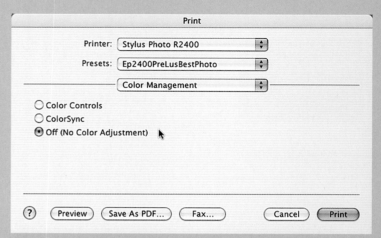

After choosing Print Settings, shown above, choose Color Management and set it to No Color Adjustment. The profile you chose in the Print with Preview dialog is doing your color management for you, and you don't want to color manage twice!

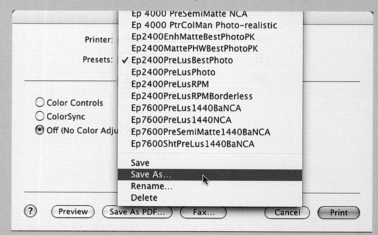

After setting your profile and Rendering Intent and then doing the Page Setup, clicking the Print button in the Print with Preveiw dialog brings up this dialog. First choose your printer from the Printer section. After choosing the printer, go into Print Settings shown here. Now you want to choose your Media Type. This is our recommended setting for Epson Premium Luster Photo Paper on the 2400 when using the Best Photo profile. Click Advanced Settings, then set Print Quality to Best Photo and turn off High Speed if you want the best print quality. If you are using a 2200, 4000, 4800, 7600, 7800, 9600, or 9800, then you'll choose the printer dpi setting of 720, 1440, or 2880 depending on the paper and printer you have. This setting just needs to match the profile you chose in the Print with Preview dialog. On the PC these settings will look slightly different, but they should all be there.

Once you've set your Print Settings and Color Management choices, you can choose Save As from the Presets menu to create a new preset with these settings. The next time you make a print, all you have to do is choose the Printer, then choose this Preset instead of going into the Print Settings and Color Management areas again.

settings are correct. Check the details of the Page Setup text as shown in the sidebar, then choose OK in that dialog to return to the Print with Preview dialog.

After returning to the Print with Preview dialog, press the Print button at the top right of the Print with Preview dialog to bring up the

dialog shown in the "The Print Dialog and Save As" sidebar. Read the sidebar for details of what you have to do there. In this dialog you have to choose your printer again. We've found that when printing over a network on the Mac to a different printer, it is best to always rechoose the printer and presets in this Print dialog each time, even if the correct printer appears to be shown. Sometimes the operating

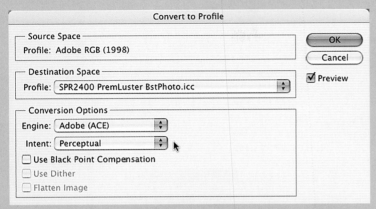

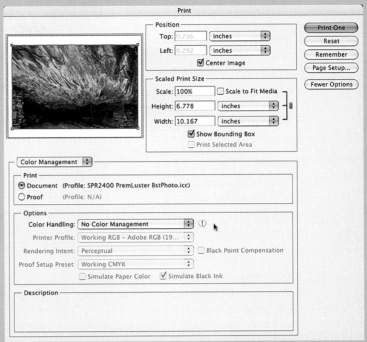

When printing an image using a canned or custom profile, I sometimes first use Edit/Convert to Profile from Photoshop to convert my flattened, sharpened master image from its default color space—Adobe RGB in this case—into the space defined by the custom profile. I then print the image using the Print with Preview settings to the right. Depending on the image I'm working with, I may set the Intent to either Perceptual or Relative Colorimetric, and I may occasionally turn on Black Point Compensation. With the Preview check box selected as shown here, you should get an accurate onscreen preview to help you in making those Conversion Option decisions. My most common choice for Epson printers is Perceptual with Black Point Compensation off.

The correct Photoshop CS2 Print with Preview dialog when printing a file that you have converted using Edit/Convert to Profile from your default color space (like Adobe RGB or Lab) to a canned or custom profile for your printer. In this case the Print-Document space will be the name of that custom profile and Options-Color Handling will be No Color Management. The Page Setup and Print Print Settings and Color Management dialog settings would be the same as before on the previous page.

system appears to get confused when a network is involved, so we always recheck each setting. When the printer is hooked up to your dedicated machine, this recheck isn't usually needed. In the Print dialog you have to specify the Print Settings and Color Management options as discussed in the sidebar. In this same sidebar, we explain how to use Save As to remember the Print Settings and Color Management options and save time with future prints.

In Photoshop CS2, sometimes you may have previously used Edit/Convert to Profile (Image/Mode/Convert to Profile with CS and previous Photoshop versions) to convert your image to the color space of a custom printer profile for a specific printer, paper, and/or ink combination. In this case in the Print with Preview dialog, Print-Document space should be the name of your custom printer

profile and Options-Color Handling should be set to No Color Management. See the Print with Preview dialog in the "Printing Something Already Converted to the Printer Profile" sidebar to see how this looks in CS2 and beyond. Using Edit/Convert to Profile allows you to see a few more conversion options, like changing the Conversion Engine and turning Dither on or off; it also allows you to see onscreen previews of these different options while in the Convert to Profile dialog. That is one advantage to that approach.

You should develop a workflow and try to make your prints the same way each time. That way, you are less likely to make mistakes due to inconsistencies in the way you make prints. You only use the Edit/Convert to profile approach if you want to add an adjustment layer after doing the conversion but before outputting to the printer. This

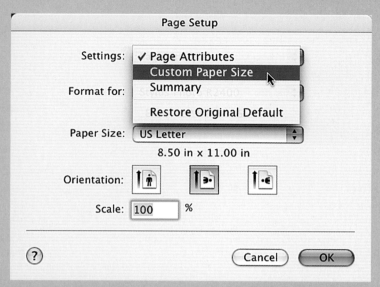

If you have an Epson 4000, 4800, 7600, 7800, 9600, 9800 or other Epson printer that uses roll paper, you will often need to define a custom paper size. In Mac OS X you do this by choosing Custom Paper Size from the Settings menu in the Page Setup menu. This gets you into the Custom Paper Size dialog on the next page.

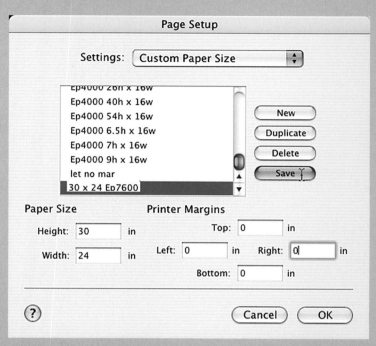

The Custom Paper Size dialog where you need to first choose the New button and then name your new paper size. After that, set the Width, Height, and Margin sizes using the text boxes toward the bottom of this dialog. The width here is 24 inches, which is the physical width of my paper on the 7600. Finally, click the Save button to save your new paper size. When you leave this dialog, by choosing Page Attributes from the Settings menu, then you have to choose this new paper size from the Paper Size menu before leaving the Page Setup dialog.

adjustment layer would be a tweak for this paper and printer only. This gives you a way to edit a profile without having to use expensive profile-editing software. For more info on this process, see "Editing Profiles Using Photoshop Adjustment Layers" later in this chapter.

The printer screenshots you see on these pages are from Mac OS 10.3.5 using Photoshop CS2 and the Epson 2400 printer. With Windows systems or different printers, the dialogs will look somewhat different, but you'll find the same functionality and workflow options. If you are using an Epson 2200, 2400, 4000, 4800, 7600, 7800, 9600, or 9800 or some other Epson pinter, you'll be able to use a similar workflow and you'll also find similar dialogs, but you'll notice that an option here or there will be different.

Notice, as shown in the "The Print Dialog and Save As" sidebar, that you can save Print dialog settings, which will make it unnecessary to reset the Print Settings options and Color Management options each time you make a print. The "Custom Paper Size" sidebar shows you how to define custom paper sizes for Epson printers that handle roll paper. Roll paper is much easier to use on the bigger 7600, 7800, 9600, and 9800 printers because you don't have to manually feed each sheet of paper. On the other hand, sheet paper is easier to mount and stack because it doesn't curl due to rolling. The 2200, 2400, 4000, and 4800 have a tray where you can load a stack of sheet paper. These printers also use roll paper but only up to 13 inches wide. If you are using roll paper, it helps to have set of art storage drawers where you can let prints flatten out for a few days before mounting. It is good to let prints dry for a week before putting them into a frame with glass

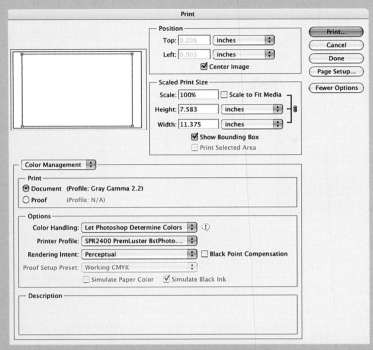

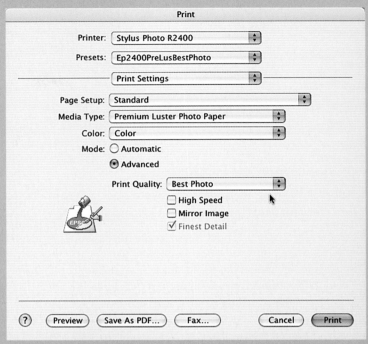

Here is how I've been setting the Print with Preview dialog to print grayscale on the Epson 2400. The settings are the same as I would use with Color except the Print-Document area is showing the grayscale color space on my grayscale image.

In the Print dialog for black-and-white images, I initially liked the shadows on black-and-white prints better when using this setting versus the new Advanced black-and-white Photo settings. I'll be doing more tests with these new settings on other papers in the future, as I haven't tried all the variations.

or plexi covering. This assures that there is no out-gassing of the print chemicals onto the back side of the glass or plexi.

Further Comments About Epson Printers

We've found that the Epson and Bill Atkinson profiles available for free with the Ultrachrome K3 printers are the best so far. These printers have the deepest blacks and also work very well for black-and-white prints. The bronzing issues on the earlier printers are pretty much gone. For printing black-and-white images, Barry has been using the same print dialog settings that he uses with color images and has had great results, even better than he initially got with the new black-and-white settings described in the Epson manual. Other photographers we know who have the 4800 and 9800 are very impressed and happy with these new printers and also what they do with black-and-white.

Barry also likes using ColorByte Imageprint for printing black-and-white prints with his Epson 4000. On that printer, and the origi-

nal Ultrachrome printers in general (2200, 4000, 7600, and 9600), Imageprint does a better job of printing black-and-white than the Epson drivers. If you have one of those printers and are not happy with black-and-white, try Imageprint or one of the other third-party rips you can download over the Internet. The term rip here is actually a bit misleading. Originally a *RIP* (Raster Image Processor) was a special computer for converting and creating image halftone patterns for an imagesetter to go to a CMYK press. These current products, like Imageprint, are actually just separate software applications that run on your Mac or PC and provide an alternative set of printer drivers for your Epson printer. Imageprint also comes with a variety of profiles for the more popular papers.

For color prints, we're actually still very happy with the quality of prints we are getting with our Epson 2200, 4000, and 7600, especially with Bill Atkinson profiles on the 7600. Since we have Imageprint for the 4000, this also makes it a great black-and-white printer. The 4000 is the only Epson printer in this series that has all the possible inks

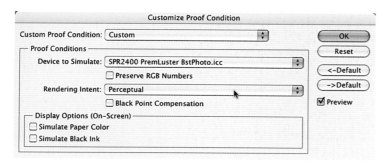

Here you see the View/Proof Setup/Custom dialog. You use the Profile pop-up menu to select the printer profile for your printer, and the Intent menu to select your rendering intent, which is usually Perceptual when working with photographs (though not always).

When you turn Proof Color on for a particular set of Info palette display values, you'll see the numbers that you'd get at that location if you did Image/Mode/Convert to Profile using the Profile currently set up in View/Proof Setup. You're seeing Proof Color values when the *R:*, *G:*, and *B:* letters are displayed in italics.

installed all the time, including both Photo black and Matte black. These three printers all use the original Ultrachrome inks.

The new Ultrachrome K3 inks have deeper blacks and more neutral black-and-white prints, and offer less possibility of any metamerism so they are certainly the best so far. Metamerism is the problem of colors looking different under various light sources. See the "Printing Black and White" sidebar for the print dialogs we have been using with those printers. The new K3 printers did return to the issue, though, of which black ink to install, the Matte black or the Photo black. The Photo black is the best ink for Premium Glossy and Premium Luster papers, and the Matte black is better for most of the matte papers. Some papers, like Epson Enhanced Matte, will work with either black ink, but the Matte black gives you deeper blacks. When you switch black inks, this wastes ink because the old ink has to be flushed out of the printer. On the Ultrachrome models, like the 7600, this was about $80 worth of ink that got flushed because it flushed all the inks. On the new Ultrachrome K3 printers, only that one black ink line gets flushed, and we believe that costs less than $15.

A 2200, 4000, 7600 or 9600 is still a great printer for color. If you can only afford a used one of those, or you can't afford a new K3 printer, don't feel that you are missing out continuing to use the original Ultrachrome printers...they are still great! If your main focus is black-and-white and you don't already have Imageprint or a RIP that works for you, then I'd definately get the new Ultrachrome K3 printers and that will probably be the end of darkroom chemicals for you, even with black-and-white prints!

Papers to Try

The papers we use most are Epson Premium Luster Photo Paper and Epson Premium Semimatte. Try Epson Premium Glossy if you like glossy prints. These three papers require the Photo black ink. The Epson Enhanced Matte paper works with either Photo black

or Matte black ink and has nice bright whites. Crane Mills' new Museo Silver Rag has good blacks when used with Photo black or Matte black ink using the Ultrachrome K3 printers. This paper works well for both color and black-and-white prints. Another one to try is Museo Max, a textured paper for Matte black inks. Hahnemuhle Photo Rag and its other matte papers are also very popular and work well with ImagePrint on Barry's 4000.

Getting Accurate Soft Proofs of Your Output to RGB Printers

One of the best features Photoshop gives you is the capability to accurately preview your printed images using the monitor. To do this for an RGB device, like a LightJet 5000 or Epson 2200, 2400, 7600, 7800, and so on, you will need an accurate ICC profile of your RGB printer when printing using a particular ink and paper combination. This could be a canned profile that comes with your Epson printer, or a profile that you or someone else made for that printer. You can compare the way the image will look when printed using this profile to the way it looks within your Lab or RGB working space. Start by choosing Window/Arrange/New Window to get an alternate window on your image. This is not another copy of the image, like you would get with Image/Duplicate; it is just another way to look at the same file you have open. Now arrange the original window of the image and the new window so you can see them side by side. Then choose View/Proof Setup/Custom to bring up the Proof Setup dialog, where you choose the Profile you will use when printing to your printer and also the Rendering Intent you want for this image.

Here is my Crater Lake image as shown on my screen in Lab color. This image has very deep, saturated blue colors, as does Crater Lake, one of the clearest lakes in the world.

Even using the Premium Luster with Gamut Warning on, there are a few colors out of gamut in the water highlights around the boat. I often print images with small gamut warnings anyhow, and they usually look fine. Using Command (Ctrl)-Y to get the onscreen preview often tells you the most about whether you will like the image using a particular printer, ink, and paper.

Here is the same Crater Lake image after using Command (Ctrl)-Y to get a CMYK preview.

Using Command (Ctrl)-Shift-Y to get a gamut warning for a CMYK version of Crater Lake, you see that the entire blue image is out of gamut.

Here it is previewed using the profile for the Epson 2400 printer on Enhanced Matte paper with the Best Photo Profiles This deep blue is way out of the CMYK gamut and is also partially outside of the gamut for my Epson 2400 on this paper.

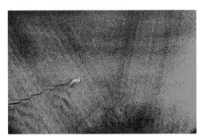

A gamut warning with the ICC profile for the Epson 2400 printer on Enhanced Matte paper with the Best Photo Profiles shows that many blues are out of gamut, but not as many as with CMYK. This is one of only a few of my images that have a gamut problem with this printer and paper combination.

With the Preview box checked, you can actually try out several profiles and rendering intents to see which settings come closest to matching the original image, in the other window, in your Lab or RGB working space. You can then use Window/Arrange/New Window again to create a third view and set that one up to do a soft proof to a different printer. This allows you to compare how the image will look on a LightJet 5000 versus your Epson 2400 versus the original in Adobe RGB or Lab. Or you could compare printing it with Relative Colorimetric and Black Point Compensation turned on in one window, and with Perceptual and Black Point Compensation turned off in another window. With a well-calibrated system, as Barry's is, the images on the screen are a very accurate simulation of what the print will look like. This is a great way to compare one profile to another, one rendering intent to another, or even one paper or printer to another. To use this method accurately with RGB printers, you will need an ICC profile for your printer, an accurate calibration of your monitor, and the correct viewing lights for comparing your prints to your monitor.

Using Proof Colors and Gamut Warning

To get soft proofs for your RGB files or to see how they will look on CMYK printers or CMYK presses, you can just choose View/Proof Colors (Command (Ctrl)-Y), and Photoshop will show you how the file will look when printed on your RGB printer or in CMYK, depending on your View/Proof Setup/Custom choices. If you have already converted the file to CMYK, then you are already seeing it as it should print on your CMYK device, provided your system is calibrated correctly. It is very important that your CMYK settings in the CMYK working space area of Photoshop/Color Settings be set correctly when you're using Command (Ctrl)-Y to preview RGB files as they will look within CMYK. If you open an existing CMYK file, it should display correctly on the screen, provided that the file has an embedded ICC profile and that your screen and output devices are correctly calibrated.

Changing the View/Proof Setup Defaults

When you initially choose View/Proof Setup, it is set up so that using Command-Y to see Proof Colors will show you how your RGB file looks when separated into CMYK using the current settings specified for the CMYK working space in the Color Settings dialog. If you choose View/Proof Setup/Custom, as we mentioned, you can change that default for the current file to show the preview using an ICC profile for your printer or other output device. When you choose View/Proof Setup/Custom while working on an open file, this sets the preview on a file-by-file basis, or actually on a window-by-window basis. If you open Photoshop and then immediately go into View/Poof Setup/Custom while no files are open, this sets the default proofing environment for Photoshop, which is normally set to Working CMYK when you install Photoshop. You can change this setting to that of an ICC profile for your RGB printer, or some other profile, by setting it when no files are open and then immediately quitting the program. When you later restart Photoshop, you will notice that Command-Y now shows you how your RGB file will look when printed on your printer using that profile.

Notice that if you choose View/Gamut Warning, Command (Ctrl)-Shift-Y, Photoshop will show you the colors in your RGB file that are outside the gamut of the proofing profile that is currently set in View/Proof Setup. If you want that to show the out-of-gamut colors for your current CMYK settings, then View/Proof Setup should be set to Working CMYK. If you want it to show you the out-of-gamut colors based on the ICC profile for your RGB printer, then you need to use View/Proof Setup/Custom to set Device to Simulate to the ICC profile for your printer.

Editing Profiles Using Photoshop Adjustment Layers

Once you make a profile or have one made for you, or even if you use a canned profile, you can edit the profile to change it and fix small areas you are not happy with. According to my friend Bruce Bayne, a color management expert, it is very common to have to make small edits to many of the profiles that are created. You will want to have this capability even if someone else makes a profile for you. Many of the profiles we have made were essentially good except for some minor flaw, like having a magenta cast in the 20% and 10% highlight areas.

We use a GretagMacbeth ColorChecker chart, available at good camera stores, to compare the neutrals in a test print with standard neutrals in the ColorChecker. If the *Photoshop Artistry* calibration image

prints correctly using a particular profile, with totally neutral gray values as well as good contrast and saturation, you may not want to tweak that profile but instead change the calibration of your monitor so the onscreen version of the image matches the print. It is usually easier to change the monitor calibration than to get a really great profile. You change the monitor calibration using one of the tools we discussed earlier in this chapter. On many monitors, you can also use the buttons on the front of the monitor to set a certain color temperature or change the color balance, brightness, or contrast. If the print itself is not neutral or if it has inadequate contrast or saturation, then you might do better editing the profile. If the profile is really far off, you should either get or make a new profile.

Many profile-making packages now contain profile editors. These allow you to edit and improve a profile after making it. The canned profiles that come with the Ultrachrome K3 printers are so good, though, that most people, including me, no longer make profiles. Another technique that I, Barry, have found to be very useful, and fairly easy to use, is to create a Photoshop Curves or Hue/Saturation adjustment layer to edit a profile, or to edit what that profile does anyway. Let's say you try a profile, and then test it with your images, or with the calibration image in the Chapter 16 folder on the *Photoshop Artistry* DVD. Say you find that the entire image has a green or magenta cast, or it's a bit too flat or contrasty, or when looking at the gray swatches you see a magenta cast in just the 10% and 20% swatches. For all such problems, you can often create an adjustment layer to fix this problem. The steps to take are as follows.

1. Make sure your monitor is correctly calibrated. Bring up the ArtistryCalibColMatch.psd file from the Chapter 16 folder on the *Photoshop Artistry* DVD, and leave it in the ColorMatch RGB color space.

2. Choose Edit/Convert to Profile (Image/Mode/Convert to Profile in older Photoshop versions) to convert this test image from ColorMatch RGB into the color profile you are using for your printer.

3. Print this image using the Print with Preview dialog shown at the top-right of page 227 of this chapter. Follow the directions in that section to set up the rest of your Page Setup and Print dialogs correctly for your printer and paper combination.

4. Make a print and let it dry for an hour for Ultrachrome or Ultrachrome K3 prints (Epson 2200, 2400, 4000, 4800, 7600, 7800, 9600, and 9800), and for at least 48 hours for dye-based inks like the Epson 1270 and 1280. This will allow the colors to stabilize.

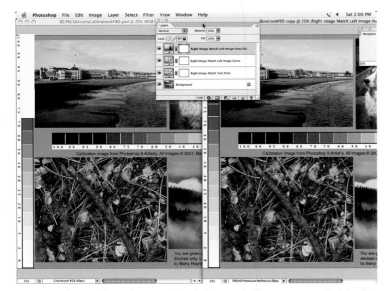

Here you see the setup for tweaking a profile, with the original calibration image on the left, still in the ColorMatch RGB space, and the copy of it on the right, which has been converted to the profile we are trying to tweak. The bottom adjustment layer in the Layers palette was used to get the rightmost image to match the test print. That was created in step 6. Then in step 7 we created the topmost two adjustment layers, which make the rightmost image match the original on the left. These topmost two are the ones whose settings you save and then later load when making future prints to that printer with that profile.

5. Bring up the original ArtistryCalibColMatch.psd on the screen, then use Image/Duplicate to make a copy of it. Choose Edit/Convert to Profile to convert this copy from ColorMatch RGB into the color profile you printed your test print with. Arrange your windows so that the original calibration image is on the left and the copy is on the right, and you can see the same parts of each. If your monitor is correctly calibrated, the image on the right should give you an accurate onscreen proof of your print.

6. The problem is that sometimes your print does not match this screen correctly. If that is the case, then create Levels, Curves, Hue/Saturation, or other adjustment layers to modify the rightmost image on screen until it looks like your print. These layers should all have names starting with "MatchPrint." Make sure you are viewing your print with a standard lighting setup that you will use all the time.

7. Once the rightmost image onscreen looks like your print, you can then create yet another adjustment layer, or two, to modify that image onscreen to make it look the way you really wanted your print to look, namely, like the original image on the left. Each adjustment layer needs to start with the name "MatchLeft." Once

you get the rightmost image to match the leftmost one, use the Save button in each adjustment layer's color correction tool to save only the adjustment layer settings you added in step 7. Just save the "MatchLeft" layers.

8. Now make another test print by first turning off the Eye icons for all the layers whose names start with "MatchPrint." Print this using the same print settings as described in step 3. After your test print dries for the correct amount of time, see if your adjustments improve the results. When you get the printed calibration image to look like the original, leftmost calibration image onscreen, then you can use those same saved "MatchLeft" adjustment layer settings to adjust all your images for this printer, ink, and paper combination. You usually have to go through steps 7 and 8 several times until you get adjustment layers that do exactly what you want with the profile. Remember to turn the Eye icons back on for the "MatchPrint" layers before you try to tweak the "MatchLeft" layers a second time.

9. When using this technique after getting your "MatchLeft" adjustment layers correct, create an action to do the Edit/Convert to Profile, then add each "MatchLeft" adjustment layer, and load the settings for each. You run this action as a final step for every print you make on a printer calibrated using this technique.

These saved settings are actually being used to edit the profiled image on-the-fly before making your print. I, Barry, do this all the time to "edit my profiles," and you can try it without having to buy an expensive profile editor. I find that it works great, and for small adjustments I can sometimes avoid step 6 and just guess at what my step 7 adjustments will be. I try them out and tweak them once or twice, and then I end up with a Curve, or some other adjustment, that I can use over and over again just to tweak the changes made by the profile so things look just right on the printer. You may need to make a set of these saved tweaks for each profile, but you can keep them in an appropriately named folder and just load them into adjustment layers with a print action when you need them.

I've used this technique to get the color prints from my Epson 2200 and 4000 to match those on the 7600 when using Bill Atkinson's profiles. That way I can print on any of the three printers and have those prints look 95% the same. Most people can't see the differences between them.

Color Management Systems and How They Fit into the Photoshop Environment

Color management systems, like ColorSync, take an image that you have corrected on your computer screen and remap that image based on the color gamut of the particular output device it is being printed on. The color gamut of an output device is the set of colors and brightness ranges that the output device can print. Each different output device, such as a digital printer, CMYK proofing system, transparency writer, and so on, has its own specific gamut. If you take the same digital file and print it, unmodified, on a number of different output devices, each print will look different from the next, and also probably different from the image on your screen. The purpose of a color management system is to adjust for these differences so that the same image will look as similar as possible on different computer monitors and will print as similarly as possible on different types of output devices.

A color management system measures the difference between various types of output devices and creates a device profile for each one. Photoshop and ColorSync use ICC profiles to characterize devices. When you send an image to a particular device, the color management system changes the image, using that image's device profile, to try to make it print in a standard way on that device. If you print the same picture on many devices, the color management system does its best to make all those pictures look as similar as possible to each other. I say "does its best" because you can't always get the same colors on one device that you can on another. Each device has its own color gamut—the range of colors that device can scan, display, or print.

Apple's ColorSync color management system is a generic one that allows many other third-party companies to contribute device profiles for their specific products. I have, for example, an Epson Stylus Photo 2400 inkjet printer. I love the photographic-quality prints it gives me, but if I took the digital file that produced a print on that Epson printer and printed the same file, unmodified, on someone else's model of Epson printer, you might see differences between the two prints. To solve this problem, a color management system needs to be able to measure the output from each particular device and create a custom ICC device profile for it. Color management systems and color profile-making software can characterize different types of scanners and film input types, different types of monitors, and other factors that affect color production along the way to final output. Given the great many variables involved in what can happen to the colors, it's no wonder color calibration and correction often prove so difficult.

Color management systems can help you deal with the differences in the gamuts and characteristics of different types of input and output devices, and they are improving all the time. Some color management system marketing implies that these systems can automatically scan, correct, and output images so that they print like originals. It's usually not that easy, and you need to do it carefully and correctly. Although color management systems can be adjusted to give you a high degree of calibration and control between devices, doing this correctly still requires a lot of measurement and control of every part of your color production system.

Calibrating Your Output Device

Many issues arise when you're trying to get quality output to a digital printer, film recorder, or imagesetter. First among them are calibration issues. You must calibrate the output device and keep it calibrated. When your output device is not calibrated and consistent, any calibration and correction you do on your computer will be less useful. The job of a digital printer, for example, is to print exactly the same

This is the ArtistryCalibColMatch.psd printer calibration image. You can use it as an RGB test image to check your screen calibration and your printer output to an Epson RGB printer, an HP RGB printer, and a variety of RGB devices. The Photoshop file is in ColorMatch RGB or Adobe RGB format and can be converted to a printer profile for print tests using Edit/Convert to Profile, as described earlier in this chapter. If your monitor is calibrated correctly and you have a monitor and print-viewing space with controlled lighting, then this image should match your prints when viewed onscreen using View/Proof Setup/Custom correctly set to your printer's profile, which was used to make your prints.

way every time. If you change the batch of ink or the type of ink or paper, that may change the results and require you to recalibrate. The supplier of your inks and papers must employ strict controls to keep them consistent, or else you will have to recalibrate every time you get new inks or papers even if you are using the same type of ink or paper. Epson printers, inks, and papers have become much more consistent over the years allowing you to use the same Epson profile for a particular model of printer, ink, and paper even though thousands of printers of that model exist. With earlier printers, you had to make a custom profile for each particular instance of the model, as there were too many production variations in the printers and sometimes even in the inks and papers. Luckily these problems have now mostly been solved.

When you scan or capture an image, or have it scanned, you need to be sure to get the best scan or capture—and having an ICC profile of your scanner or digital camera could be helpful. The Photoshop Camera Raw filter has built-in profiles for a variety of digital cameras. (You can read about how to use Camera Raw in Chapter 9.) If you are not doing the scanning yourself, you need to know how to check the scans that others have done to make sure that the maximum amount of information is available. And you need to understand how to make the most of the information that you have. We cover the scanning part of the process in Chapter 17, "Image Resolution and Scanning."

Trying to calibrate your monitor or perfect your process of making color corrections doesn't do any good unless the output device you are sending to (imagesetter, color printer, film recorder, or whatever) is consistent and calibrated. A good way to test this calibration is to send a group of neutral colors to your output device. I have created a file, called the StepWedgeFile, for testing the calibration of your output device. The StepWedgeFile consists of wedges of neutral gray that have a known value. Two issues are involved in calibrating your output device. The first is whether the device will print the correct density. If you send a 50% density value to the device, it should measure and look like 50% when it prints. All densities should print as expected. The second issue is getting colors to print correctly. If, using all its colors, the output device prints these neutral gray values correctly, it's a good sign that it will also print colors correctly. You want the densities on the gray wedges to be correct, and you also want each wedge to continue to look gray, because when you see a cast in your printed grays, that cast usually gets added to all color-correct images.

Checking Printer Output on Your RGB Printer

Barry has created a Photoshop printer test file from some of his prints and the StepWedgeFile. It is called ArtistryCalibColMatch.psd and is included in the Chapter 16 folder on the *Photoshop Artistry* DVD and also printed on the previous page. You can use this RGB file in the ColorMatch RGB space to test output to your RGB printer or other RGB output device. Before doing any tests, be sure to set up your Color Settings preferences as shown at the start of this chapter. In this edition of *Photoshop Artistry,* I've also included a version of this image, named ArtistryCalibAdRGB.psd, in the Adobe RGB space.

To make your own test image, create an 8.5x11 canvas in RGB mode, fill it with a neutral gray background, and save it as MyPrinterTest or something like that. Now use Image/Mode/RGB to convert the grayscale StepWedgeFile, in the Chapter 16 folder on the DVD, to your RGB working ppace, and then paste it into your test file. Next, find some color-corrected RGB images that are typical of your normal work. Copy and paste these images into your test file. Save the final RGB version of your RGB test file.

Use your test image, or ours, to output to your RGB printer or device in the way that you would normally use that device. If you have a profile for the printer, use Edit/Convert to Profile to convert a copy of the test image to that color space. Then print the image using printer settings that do no further color management or changes, because the profile should have done that for you. If you are not using a color profile, then use whatever settings you would normally use with your printer. The ArtistryCalibColMatch.psd image prints well on most Epson printers on an 8.5x11 sheet of Epson paper. If you have an Epson 2200, 2400, 4000, 7800, 9800, or similar Epson printer, use the print dialog recommendations shown earlier in this chapter.

When comparing your test print to the image on your monitor, make sure you view the test print in the lighting you have calibrated for and that you preview the image onscreen via View/Proof Setup using the profile you use for your printer and paper. If you are not using a profile, then just view the image onscreen using your normal RGB working space. I, Barry, view my art prints under halogen floods with a color temperature of around 2700K because that is the light source used in most galleries. When working on a book that will be printed on a press, I view proofs from the book's print shop using my Soft View D5000 Transparency/Print Viewer, which lights them at 5000K, the standard for most press rooms in the United States. The light you view your print under will make a big difference in the way it looks!

If converting the test file to CMYK for a CMYK printer or a press, make sure your CMYK Color Settings preferences are set correctly for the type of printer or paper and press you are using. If you normally use Image/Mode/CMYK to convert from RGB to CMYK, do just that with your separation test. If you use someone else's separation tables, do it that way. If you normally save your files as Photoshop EPS or DCS files and then put them into Quark, do the same thing in your test. Save your final CMYK version of the file under a different name than the RGB version. Whenever I'm going to print a new version of *Photoshop Artistry,* I always have the printer make a set of proofs using their current best color proofing system. Lately, the printer has been using Kodak Approval proofs, which are digital proofs that can be printed on the actual paper the book is being printed on. The type of paper you use for your proof can also affect the color.

When evaluating your test image, the densities should look correct in the gray stepwedge, and they should also look gray. If the stepwedge densities are not right, or if they have a cyan, magenta, or some combination of color casts, it's a sign that the RGB or CMYK output device, imagesetter, platemaker, or proofer isn't calibrated, or something's not right about the way you created the output. You should not have altered or color corrected the stepwedge file using your monitor, so it should be gray. If it doesn't look gray or the densities are not correct, you will have to calibrate your printer, edit your printer profile, or, for CMYK, adjust your separations to solve this problem. See the section titled "Editing Profiles with Photoshop Adjustment Layers," earlier in this chapter, for another idea about how to make your monitor color closer to your printer output. If the stepwedge looks good and this test prints with the correct densities and no color casts, you know your output device is calibrated.

Conclusion

If the techniques in this chapter and/or this book have not taught you everything you need to know to get the prints you want from your problem images, please check the Workshops or Videos pages of www.barryhaynes.com so we can help you get exactly the prints you want from your problem images—and all your photography.

The Fernwood Pier mask on the Remove Magenta layer.

The Fernwood Pier Darken and Desaturate Masks were both faint along the horizon.

Layers that were added to the Fernwood pier image after sharpening just to tweak the printout. The Remove Magenta layer used Hue/Saturation to desaturate Magentas by setting their saturation to −100. Blues were saturated by setting their saturation to +66. But notice the top mask at the top here, which applies this layer only slightly where the deep blues were. The Darken and Desaturate layers were also applied very faintly just along the horizon.

Special Printing Situations

The Fernwood Pier original image after scanning and initial correction in Levels in 16 bit. This image was created in Photoshop 7.

Images that have a lot of deep, saturated blue—or any really saturated color—in them can be difficult to print. Sometimes you need to make subtle tweaks at the final print stage to get just the color and mood that you want with a particular printer and profile. This can involve using View/Proof Setup/Custom to try out different rendering intents to see how they affect saturated colors and/or blacks. Barry has printed several saturated blue water images using the Saturation rendering intent, which is normally intended for presentation graphics. For this image, he added several adjustment layers after the final sharpening but applied them only very subtly to the deep blues and blacks to remove unwanted color casts. See the information about these to the left.

The final Fernwood Pier image after the tweaks shown to the left were applied.

17 ◆ Image Resolution and Scanning

When capturing digital images or scanning film, everyone must understand about resolution and how to relate digital file size and pixels per inch to output print size and printer dots per inch. Most photographers now attending our workshops shoot new images with digital cameras. They only need to scan those thousands of film images from photography they've done previously. Many people are discovering that with Photoshop they can print film images they would have rejected in the past due to scratches, spots, or difficult color correction problems. If you need to buy a scanner or produce better scans, then the tips in this chapter will be helpful.

Bytes, Bits, PPI, and DPI

When working with digital images, you need to understand resolution and the issues involved in determining what size to make a scan or digital capture. Because we're going to be talking about size in bytes, let's take a minute to talk about bytes, bits, and dpi. A *byte* (8 bits) is the most common unit of measurement of computer memory. All computer functionality is based on switches that can be turned on and off. A single switch is called a *bit*. When a bit is off, it has a value of 0. When a bit is on, it has a value of 1. With a single bit, you can count from 0 to 1. With two bits lined up next to each other, you can count from 0 to 3 because now there are four possibilities (00=0, 01=1, 10=2, and 11=3). Add a third bit, and you can count from 0 to 7 (000=0, 001=1, 010=2, 011=3, 100=4, 101=5, 110=6, and 111=7). With 8 bits, or a byte, you can count from 0 to 255, which is 256 possible values. With 12 bits you have 4096 possible values, and with 16 bits you have 65,536 possible values.

A grayscale 8-bit digital image has 1 byte of information for each value scanned from the film. A value of 0 is the darkest possible value—black—and a value of 255 is the brightest possible value—white. Values in between are different levels of gray, the lower numbers being darker and the higher numbers being lighter. You can think of these values the way you would think of individual pieces of grain within a piece of film: the more values you have per inch, the smaller the grain in the digital file. Also, the more of these values that you have per inch, the higher the resolution—also referred to as pixels per inch (ppi) or samples per inch when scanning film) in your file. An 8-bit-per-channel RGB color digital image has 3 bytes of information (24 bits, 1 byte for each channel of red, green, and blue) for each value scanned from the film. And CMYK files have 4 bytes per pixel. A 16-bit per channel grayscale file has 2 bytes and 32,769 (0 to 32,768 is 32769 values) possible tonal values per pixel or sample. A 16-bit-per-channel RGB file, 48 bits in all, contains 32,769 possible tonal values per color channel. With today's scanners, scanning 16-bit-per-channel images is something well worth considering. This 0 to 32,768 value range is what Photoshop's Info palette shows when you turn on the Show 16 Bit Values option in its Palette Options menu.

Digital Prints vs. Traditional Prints

If you have an enlarger in the traditional darkroom, you can make a 20x24 print from a 35mm original. Its quality will not be as good as if you made a 20x24 print on the same paper from a 4x5 original of the same type of film, because the 4x5 has more film area with which to define the image. If you were printing on different types of paper, the paper's grain would affect the look of the final print. It's the amount of

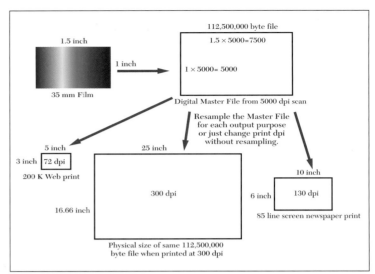

If you will use the scan for more than one purpose, make the original scan for the size of the biggest file you will need. Do your overall color correction, image enhancement, and spotting on this largest master file. You can then resample that corrected file down to whatever resolution and file size you need. Above you see some sample uses. When scanning most files on a high-end scanner, you will find that you don't get any more detail information from the film by scanning it at more than 5000 ppi (pixels per inch). If you scan at a higher ppi than this, you probably will not get any better data than you would by just resampling up the 5000-ppi file. A file of this ppi can certainly be resampled down using Image Size or the Cropping tool to 72 ppi for the Web, 300 ppi for a digital art print, 170 ppi for a newspaper print, or anything else you need.

grain in the original film that makes the difference when you project that film on the same paper to make a traditional darkroom print.

When you make a print on a digital printer, the dots-per-inch (dpi) rate of the printer is analogous to the grain in the photographic paper. The digital printer's dpi is the number of individual sensors, or inkjets, or laser spots that the particular printer can put down per inch. Each digital printer has its own maximum possible dpi rate, based on its specific physical limitations. The relationship between the ppi of a digital file and the dpi of a digital printer is analogous to the relationship between the grain size of film in the enlarger and the grain size of the paper you are printing on in a traditional darkroom. A digital

> **NOTE**
>
> If the image is to be published as a halftone on a printing press and you want the best quality, you need to scan it at a ppi of at least twice the line screen of the publication. For example, if you are printing a 6x7-inch photograph in a 150-line-screen publication, you should scan it at 300 dpi for the number of inches you're printing it. A higher dpi scan can always be downsampled in Photoshop to 300 dpi.

file at 100 ppi will print on a digital printer that can output at 720 dpi, but it won't look as good as a 300 ppi file of the same image printed on the same printer. A digital capture with 2000 pixels across the image area usually won't print with as much detail as a digital capture with 6000 pixels across the same image area. Similarly, a print on photographic paper from ASA 1600 (large grain) film will look grainier than a print from ASA 25 (small grain) film.

PPI and How It Affects Print Size

The ppi that you scan a file at is based on the size of the original piece of film you are scanning from. When you print that file, you will often lower the ppi used in making the print so that you can print at a larger size. For example, if you scan a 4x5 inch piece of film at 2400 ppi, you will get 4x2400=9600 pixels in one dimension and 5x2400=12000 pixels in the other dimension. If you used 480 pixels per inch when you printed that file, you have enough data for a 9600/480=20 by 12000/480=25 inch print. Printing that with 240 pixels per inch would allow for a 40x50 inch print! I could use either of these ppi settings when printing the same file with my Epson printers, and only the size of the print would change. The one printed at 480 ppi would look slightly more detailed, but most people would not be able to see the difference.

When you make a print on a printing press, the line screen of the halftone is analogous to the grain in the photographic paper.

How Big Should I Make a Scan or a Digital Capture?

When you are scanning an image, you should know the intended purpose of the scan ahead of time. If you have more than one purpose and image size, scan the image at the maximum size you expect to use, or, better yet, at the maximum optical ppi of your scanner.

I usually scan my 35mm or 120mm film at 4000 ppi because that my scanner's maximum optical ppi. Scanning at higher than the maximumoptical ppi of a scanner just means that the scanner software is upsampling your file. Photoshop can do as good a job or better of upsampling as your scanner software can, so there's no need to scan at higher than the scanner's optical resolution. With digital cameras, I usually shoot Raw files at the maximum resolution for the camera's sensor. For more info on shooting Raw files, see Chapter 9, "Camera Raw."

Calculating Scan Sizes

The formula for calculating the required byte size for a scan of, for example, a 6x7 image to be printed using 300 ppi is (6x300 ppi) x (7x300 ppi) x 3. This file would be 11,340,000 bytes in size. (The final factor represents the number of bytes for each pixel in the image; 3 is the number for an RGB color image.) If you were saving the complete file after scanning at either 12 or 16 bits per channel, or anything more than 8-bits per channel, you would end up with a 16-bit-per-channel file in Photoshop, which would double the above file size, making this final factor 6. For an 8-bit CMYK scan, the factor is 4 instead of 3, because there are 4 bytes for each pixel in a CMYK image. Although years ago CMYK was the norm for print publications, I wouldn't recommend scanning in CMYK these days, since scanners are RGB devices and RGB files have better image information. If you do a black-and-white scan, you can remove this factor because such scans require only 1 byte per pixel, 2 bytes for a 16-bit grayscale scan. Here's the general formula for the required byte size of final publication scans:

Scan Size = ((height of image) x (2 x line screen dpi)) x ((width of image) x (2 x line screen dpi)) x 3 (for 8-bit RGB) or x 6 (for 16-bit RGB)

If you scan a file for output to a digital printer, such as an Epson 2200, 2400, 4000, 4800, 7600, 7800, etc., or the LightJet 5000, you don't need to do the scan at the same dpi as the resolution of the printer you plan to use. After scanning the file, you can set the resolution to different values depending on the printer you're using for that print. For output to the LightJet 5000, which has a print resolution of 120 pixels per centimeter (304.8 dpi), the formula and byte size would be (6 x 304.8 dpi) x (7 x 304.8 dpi) x 3 = 11,705,783 bytes.

If you have trouble remembering formulas and don't want to bother with a calculator, there is an easy way to calculate the file size you'll need for a certain print size: Use the New command in Photoshop. Choose File/New, and then enter the width and height dimensions in inches for the largest size you expect to print the image you are scanning. Based on the current discussion, set the Resolution in pixels/inch to match what you will need for your line screen or printer resolution. Now set the mode to Grayscale, or RGB Color according to the type of scan. If the scan you are making will be 16 bits per channel, then change the bit depth pop-up to 16 bit. The Image Size that shows up at the right side of the New dialog is the size in megabytes that you should make your scan. Now you can cancel from this dialog; Photoshop has done the calculation for you.

If you scan small files, usually measured in pixel dimensions, for Web sites or multimedia applications, you often can get better results if

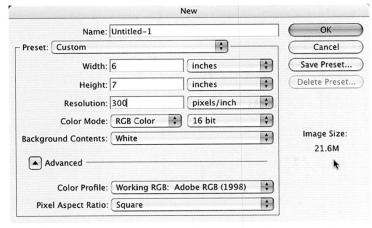

Use File/New to calculate the size of the scan you'll need. Notice that Photoshop has a Preset sizes pop-up in the New dialog, as well as an Advanced area allowing you to set the Profile and Pixel Aspect Ratio, usually Square, of the new file. Just to the right of Color Mode is the Bit Depth pop-up, which is set to 16 bit here.

you scan a simple factor larger in each dimension. I did some Web images where the final spec for the GIF file size was 180×144 pixels. I scanned the files at 720×576 and did all my color corrections and masking at that larger, more detailed size. One of the final steps before creating the GIF files was to scale the corrected and sharpened files to 25% of the larger size. This 25% scale factor is a simple ratio that allows for very accurate scaling.

If you need some digital files to prototype a project, you don't need to start with the large scans we describe here. I find that RGB scans of about 4 MB usually provide plenty of screen detail for prototyping. When you decide on the final dimensions for the images in your project or printed piece, you can do a final scan for the intended output device at those dimensions. Personally, I just do one big scan of each image, then make a downsampled copy of that for prototyping if needed. I find that scanning is time-consuming, so I only want to scan each image once. When you get a big final scan, archive that original file on DVD as it was scanned, and use copies of it to do color corrections, color separations, and crops, so that you can go back to the original if you make a mistake. Happy scanning!

For Epson Printers

The Epson 2200, 2400, 4800, and so on have printed dpi rates of 720 up to 2880. The way the Epson printers use dots, however, is different from the methods of digital printers like the dye-sublimation printers and the LightJet 5000. I have found that for these types of Epson printers, you get great results if you use a file of about 300 ppi or higher. For the 1440-dpi output setting I usually use for my Epson

printers, I'd set the ppi of the file to 360 or 480 for optimal prints; but most people won't see the difference so long as the ppi is over 240 on film scans, and some digital camera files look great when printed at 180 ppi. If you have really fine detail, like many small branches on a tree or bush, that detail will print a little bit more distinctly with the file set at 360 or 480 ppi.

If you need to upsample (add pixels) or downsample (take away pixels) an image, you want to do that before sharpening the image. With scans from film, you probably don't need to upsample your file if you have at least 240 ppi to use in your print. If you want to make a really large print, though, and if with Resample Image turned off in the Image Size dialog there is less than 240 ppi after setting your desired Width and Height, then turn Resample Image on and set the ppi to the resolution you want, such as 240. This will upsample, or add pixels to your image.

One File Fits All Print Sizes

I recommend scanning your film at your scanner's highest optical ppi, up to around 5000 ppi (4000 ppi with the Nikon 4000, 5000, 8000, or 9000). If you have the option of scanning or capturing at 12, 14, or 16 bits per channel and saving all that information in your file, you should do that. You can then color correct this large master file using adjustment layers. A flattened copy of this color-corrected master layers file gets sharpened—after upsampling if required for larger prints. Now you have a flattened, sharpened version of your master file. This can be the file you use to make all your prints, regardless of size. You could downsample this file for smaller prints, but I usually don't. In that case, I just increase the ppi.

Instead of downsampling my larger scans when doing letter-size test prints, for example, I turn off Resample Image in the Image Size dialog, then set the Resolution to a high-enough ppi so I can get a letter-size print. Referring to the top screen shot of the Image Size dialog on the next page, if Resample Image were off, we could set the Height to the maximum letter size of 10.3 inches, which would change the pixels/inch to 528.252 with that image. I don't like the fractional ppi values when making prints, so I would then change the pixels/inch to 530, which would give me a letter-size test print 10.266 inches high and 7.136 inches wide. This allows me to make a letter-size test print of my image without resampling it and maybe even without resharpening it, which one often has to do after resampling.

With some ink and paper combinations, you might find that printing using digital files that have a different ppi can affect the colors in the print, in which case you would always want to resample your images

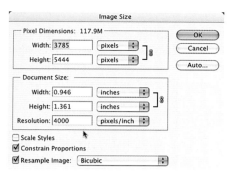

Going into Image/Image Size on a 35mm file that was just scanned using a Polaroid SprintScan 120 at 4000 pixels/inch. The Width and Height values in the Document Size area are still set to the size of the crop on the actual 35mm film. Notice the Pixel Dimensions values.

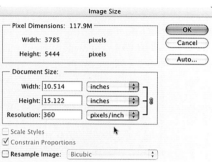

This is Image Size on the same file as above. Here we turned Resample Image off, then changed the Resolution to 360 pixels/inch. Now we see in the Width and Height values in the Document Size area how big a print we'd get from this file when printing at 360 ppi. Notice that the Pixel Dimensions and file size values, in the top area, have not changed since Resample Image was turned off.

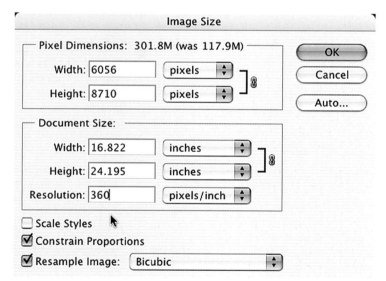

If we wanted to print the 16x24 Image Size shown to the right at 360 ppi, we'd turn on Resample Image, then type 360 in the pixels/inch box. Notice that the Pixels Dimensions values have changed because doing this with Resample Image on adds pixels to the file. Study the Image Size command and make sure you understand all of its possible variations. *Study the Image Size command and make sure you understand all its possible variations.* Yes, I said this twice because this dialog is the most misunderstood thing in Photoshop, but it is also the most important to understand! For best results when upsampling a digital capture file, read Chapter 9, first. Also look at the Sharpening section of Chapter 12, "Essential Photoshop Techniques for Photographers."

so that the ppi of the file you sent to the printer was a standard 360 or 480, or whatever works for you. I haven't found color shifts with different ppi rates to be a problem with my images.

Evaluating Histograms to Make Better Scans and Final Images

Now that you know how big to make a scan or capture, you need to know how to make a better scan or capture using histograms. The key to this technique is learning how to use the Histogram palette and the histogram displays in scanner software, in digital cameras, and Levels to evaluate initial scans and captures, as well as your image as you improve it during the color correction process.

A *histogram* is a bar graph of the samples of each possible setting in the 0-to-255 range in the image. This range, in the file itself, may actually be a 0-to-32,768 range when working with 16-bit images. The diagrams here show you some of the useful information that a histogram can provide. With normal subject material, the best possible circumstance is to have an original image, transparency, or negative that has a good exposure of the subject matter and shows a full range of values from very dark to very bright, with some detail in all areas. Chapter 14, "Digital Imaging and the Zone System," tells you how to create a high-quality exposure with a camera. If you have a good image that contains values in all zones and has been scanned or captured correctly, you'll often see a histogram like the one shown here. When you photograph a normal scene with a full brightness range, you should aim to get a scan or digital capture that has a full range of the values present in the original.

Scanning or Capturing All Parts of an Image

When you photograph or capture an image and then later scan it, there are several areas where you need to be careful what values you

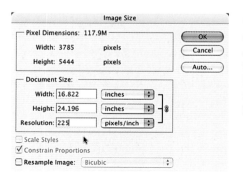

Here, on that same file, we have changed the pixels/inch to 225, allowing us to make a 16x24 print from this same file. Notice that the Pixel Dimensions values still have not changed since Resample Image is still turned off.

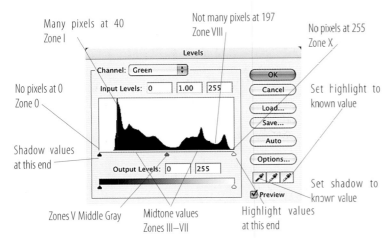

Many pixels at 40
Zone I

Not many pixels at 197
Zone VIII

No pixels at 255
Zone X

No pixels at 0
Zone 0

Set highlight to
known value

Shadow values
at this end

Set shadow to
known value

Zones V Middle Gray

Midtone values
Zones III–VII

Highlight values
at this end

A histogram, like the one in this Layers dialog above, is a bar graph you get of an image when you look at it in Photoshop's Levels dialog or the Histogram palette or in various scanner software interfaces. For more information on Levels and histograms, turn to Chapter 20, "Levels, Curves, Hue/Saturation, and the Histogram," where we furnish a detailed introduction to Levels. Also refer to Chapter 14, to see how histograms relate to traditional photography and light.

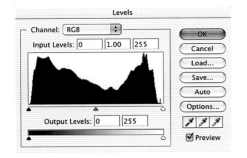

A histogram that has a full range of values. The shape of histograms in the midtone area, not the extreme highlights or shadows, is different for each image depending on the ranges of its tonal values.

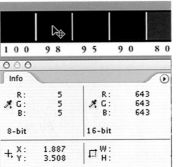

After converting my calibration image to 16-bit, this value that reads 5 in 8-bit now reads 643. Pure black is still 0!

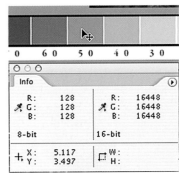

This 50% value that reads 128 in 8-bit now reads 16,448 in a 16-bit version of the file.

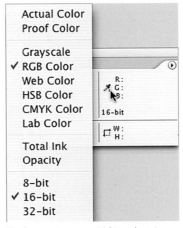

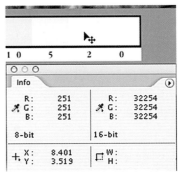

This 2% value that reads 251 in 8-bit now reads 32,254 in a 16-bit version of the file. Pure white is now 32,768 in a 16-bit Photoshop world!

Use these settings to get 16-bit readouts in your Info palette areas. You have to click the right-pointing arrow next to the eyedropper to bring up this menu.

obtain. There can be places within the image that are totally black. These should occur only if the original has areas that are totally black (*black shadows*, Zone 0). Then there are the regular shadows, which are the darkest places in the image that still show texture or detail when printed (Zones I and II). On the other end of the spectrum are specular highlights—areas in the original that are totally white, such as the reflection of the sun in the chrome bumper of a car (Zone X). Next, there are regular highlights, the brightest areas of the image where you still want to see some texture or detail (Zones VIII and IX). When you photograph the image, you need to be aware of the dynamic range of your film or digital camera, which is the amount of brightness variance it can capture. If your film or digital camera does not have enough dynamic range (also referred to as *latitude*) to capture all the highlights and shadows in a scene, it can sometimes help to bracket exposures. One exposure would get all the shadow information, and a second exposure would get all the highlight informa-

tion. With the camera on a tripod, it is possible to combine these two images using Photoshop to get a full range of values. See Chapter 27, "Compositing Bracketed Photos," for more info on how to do this.

To some extent, we can call everything between the regular highlight and shadow areas *midtones*. At the dark end of the midtones, are the *three-quarter tones* (shadow areas where you can see a fair amount of detail), and at the bright end of the midtones, the *quarter tones* (highlight areas where you should also be able to see a fair amount of detail).

Adjusting the Scanner to Get the Right Values

When you do a scan or correct a digital capture, the values that you want to obtain for the shadows and the highlights may depend on

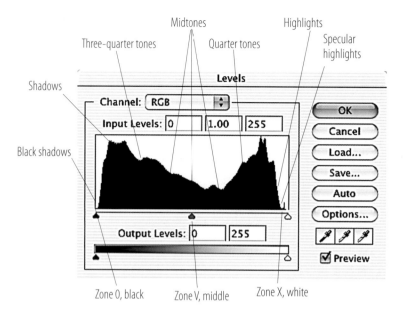

Labels on figure:
- Midtones
- Three-quarter tones
- Highlights
- Quarter tones
- Specular highlights
- Shadows
- Black shadows
- Levels
- Channel: RGB
- Input Levels: 0 1.00 255
- OK
- Cancel
- Load...
- Save...
- Auto
- Options...
- Output Levels: 0 255
- Preview
- Zone 0, black
- Zone V, middle
- Zone X, white

the type of output device you're directing the final image toward. If you are not sure of the output device, or if you might be using different output devices, the highlights (Zone IX) should have a value in the range of 245 to 250, and the shadows (Zone I) should have a value in the range of 5 to 10. With an original image that has a full range of colors in each of the Red, Green, and Blue channels, you need to adjust the scanner or Camera Raw filter to get these types of 8-bit highlight and shadow values. With 16-bit files, you can get 16-bit values in the readouts for the Info palette using the pop-up Eyedropper menu for that readout area. See the illustration on the previous page. The 5-to-10 range in 8-bit values would be about 643 to 1300 in 16-bit values.

See the illustrations on the previous page for a comparison of 8-bit and 16-bit values. If you get the highlight and shadow values correct, the values of the quarter tones, midtones, and three-quarter tones usually fall between these endpoint shadow and highlight values. With this complete scan, you can always adjust the image in Photoshop to get different highlight, midtone, and shadow values, as well as different brightness and contrast, and you will know that you started with all the information from the scanner or digital camera. This is why many digital cameras, and most scanner software, include a histogram display of the file. I usually start out doing my scans or Camera Raw adjustments with the normal default settings. Some scanners allow you to add a curve or histogram display that adjusts the image as you scan it. If the scanner preview is too light or dark, or the contrast is way off, I might use a curve or histogram in the scanner software to

fix this, although I usually leave those adjustments until I get the file in Photoshop; but then I'm always making 16-bit scans. My objective with most scanners, though, is to get all the information out of the film without throwing any of it away.

When the file you are saving is an 8-bit per channel file, the scanner software will then have to decide how to convert the 12 to 16 bits of information the scanner is actually getting down to 8 bits per channel in the file that will be saved. When you are doing 8-bit scans, it is very important to use the settings in the scanner software to optimize how the scanner converts from the higher bit depth down to 8 bits. With 16-bit scans, you can make most of these decisions later in Photoshop, which gives you more control.

Scanning up to 16 Bits Per Color Per Pixel

Scanners these days scan a lot more than 8 bits of information per color per pixel. The scanner gets this information out of the film

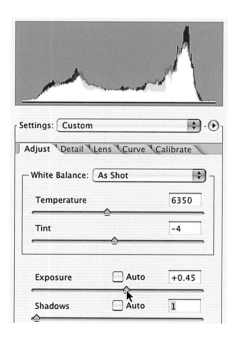

Figure controls:
- Settings: Custom
- Adjust Detail Lens Curve Calibrate
- White Balance: As Shot
- Temperature 6350
- Tint -4
- Exposure Auto +0.45
- Shadows Auto 1

The Photoshop Camera Raw filter allows you to adjust the histogram of a Raw digital camera file to optimize it before converting the file into a normal RGB format. You normally want to adjust this histogram so that you lose no shadow or highlight details. See Chapter 9, for more info.

and then, often by default, the scanner software uses a curve or other scanner settings to reduce this down to 8 bits per pixel when it gives it to you in Photoshop. If you later decide you are not happy with the 8 bits of information you got, you will have to rescan the image to get a different set of values. For example, the scanner may actually pull more shadow range information from the film, but, due to the fact that 8-bit files are limited to a total of 256 tones per color, the scanner software throws out a lot of this shadow info when it reduces the file to 8 bits. Because Photoshop now has full support for working with files that have more than 8 bits per color, it's much better to bring into Photoshop all the information the scanner gets from the film before the scanner software reduces it down to 8 bits. That way you can save this extra info on disk and modify it many different ways without having to rescan the image. Photoshop now allows you to work with up to 16 bits of information per channel using almost all of its tools, including layers and adjustment layers. Scanners these days allow for the saving of files with more than 8 bits per color channel. This is an important feature to check for when buying a scanner to use for high-end color work. I wouldn't purchase a scanner that didn't allow me to save the full information from the scanner's sensors.

My preference is to save the full bit depth from the scanner into a file and then use the Photoshop Levels, Curves, and Hue/Saturation adjustment layers, which usually give me more control than the scanner software, to do the adjustments on the 16-bit-per-channel file. Remember that in Photoshop any image of more than 8 bits per channel will open as 16 bits per channel. The hardware sensors on many scanners actually do whatever they do without allowing for much adjustment; however, the software controls in most scanners adjust how the data from the scanner's hardware sensors is converted from 12 bits up to 16 bits and down to 8 bits when the file is saved. Saving the data directly from the scanner's hardware sensors into a 16-bit-per-channel file allows you to use the more accurate Photoshop tools to readjust that scan as many times as you like without ever having to rescan the file. This is the strategy that makes the most sense for fine artists and people who want to tweak their images to the max. With many scanners, doing raw scans that don't have scanner software adjustments is actually a lot faster. If your raw scans are really dark or have other serious flaws, you may want to use the scanner software to do some adjustments before saving the scans and then working on them in Photoshop. I don't, though—I find it both more efficient and more effective to fix these things in Photoshop. If you are a service bureau or you're doing production scans for a magazine or newspaper, then you may want the scanner software to do as much of the work as possible and just give you an 8-bit file you can place

Accurate measurement of pixels, at Arrow cursor, within the preview scan.

Set the sharpening available in the scanner software to None, or don't sharpen. Do this in later Photoshop.

Very accurate histogram controls.

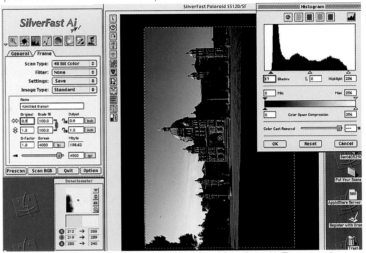

The scanner dialog from the SilverFast Ai with the Polaroid SprintScan 120. This is a good scanner interface because you can create the cropping box in the prescan window in the center, and set its dimensions and its ppi independent of each other. You can also see accurate histograms, like those shown here, and measure pixel values. SilverFast is quality scanner software that is available for a variety of scanners, allowing you to switch to a different scanner without relearning the scanner software. This is an older version of SilverFast, but it still works fine for me.

and print, or maybe even a CMYK file. But most artists will want the finer control Photoshop and 16-bit files can provide.

Scanning Step by Step

Whenever I scan, using any scanner, I always use the same, simple technique. First I set up the default brightness, contrast, and color balance controls on the scanner. I remove any preset curves that would change the contrast of the scan from the scanner setting. I make sure that I set the scanner for the correct type of film. I then do a prescan, which shows me the image in the scanner's preview window. Using the scanner software, I set the crop of the image to scan the area I want to scan—usually the full image. For evaluating the histogram of this scan, it is best if this crop does not include any black or white borders around the edges of the film. In the SilverFast scanner dialog at the top of this page, the prescan and crop are shown with the image preview in the center. If the scanner software doesn't have an accurate histogram display, I set the scanner to do about a 4 MB test scan. I usually don't have the scanner sharpen the image, because sharpening works best when customized to each final image size, and I can usually get better sharpening of images from film with the Photoshop

Unsharp Mask filter and the Sharpen Only Edges BH action. If I get a good, focused raw scan from the scanner, I know Photoshop sharpening can do a great job. Then, either I evaluate the histogram based on the scanner software preview or I do a 4 MB scan at the default settings and look at the histogram in Photoshop. If you have to preview the histogram in Photoshop, it helps to have a scanner that has a Photoshop plug-in allowing it to scan directly into Photoshop.

Next, I evaluate the histogram using the scanner software itself or using the 4 MB scan with Levels or the Histogram palette in Photoshop.

Keep on doing scanner previews or small 4 MB scans and adjusting scanner settings each time until you get the best histogram you can for your particular image. Once you get the histogram to look correct in the scanner software or on the small 4 MB scan, use the same scanner settings for exposure, and increase the size of the scan to get the final number of megabytes that you will need. I suggest doing the final scans at more than 8 bits of information per color channel and saving all that information to your file. The Imacon and the Polaroid SprintScan 120, which I have, do scans at 16 bits per channel; the Nikon 4000 and 8000 scanners do them at 14 bits. All of these scanners allow you to save all this scan info into your file. When doing 8-bit scans, it is best to get a good-looking histogram from the scanner before you make corrections to the histogram in Photoshop. On the other hand, if your scanner software doesn't have a histogram display, a 16-bit raw scan with no adjustments in the scanner software, other than for film type, is often all you need. That 16-bit file can be corrected quite nicely in Photoshop. If you aren't personally doing the scan, you at least now know how to evaluate the scans you get. The next step is to correct the histogram after the scan using Photoshop's color correction utilities and the overall color correction process described in Chapter 21, "Overall Color Correction."

Getting the Right Histogram

Time and again I am asked in classes, "What is a good histogram?" Let me ask a question in response. If you have three different photographers taking a picture of a basket of apples, which would be the "good" photograph? The one that is dark, moody, and mysterious; the one that is light, delicate, and ethereal; or the one that is an accurate representation of a basket of apples in the sunshine? In actuality, any or all of the three may be excellent photographs. Judging a histogram is similar, in that many different histograms could be the "right" histogram for a given photograph, depending on the artist's interpretation of the subject.

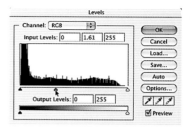

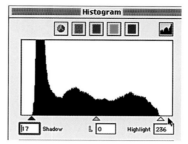

Here is the histogram of the British Columbian Parliament buildings image as set up in the SilverFast on the Polaroid SprintScan 120 with a Raw scan. As scanned, this image is dark and has dark shadows as shown below.

After running this Levels adjustment layer on the parliament image to open the shadows and the entire image, we have converted the histogram by moving the skinny shadow area to a wider, more spread-out shadow shown below. Look on the next page to see the final histogram and image.

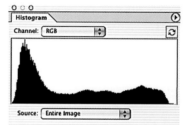

Comparing the Histogram to the Original

The histogram can't be evaluated separately from the original slide or photo. A good histogram of the original is one that accurately reflects the amount of information in the original. A good histogram of the final output accurately represents the artist's visualization. Never does the adage "garbage in, garbage out" apply more fully than in digital imaging. If you have an original piece of film with no highlight detail, there is absolutely zero possibility that even a high-end scanner can give you something to work with. A good scan of a good original gives you a full range of information that you can manipulate digitally, just as you would manipulate information in the darkroom.

If you start with a very low-contrast original, your histogram will have a shortened value scale; that is, the representation of the pixel values will not stretch across all the values from 0 to 255. Note that we are discussing 8 bit values here even though the files will hopefully be 16 bit. In general, as you color correct this scan, you force the values of the pixels in the scan to spread out along the luminosity axis all the way from deep shadows (between about 3 and 10) to bright highlights (around 245 to 250). Notice that we say "in general." If the effect you wish to achieve is a very low-contrast image—say, a photo that appears ghosted back—you may need to do very little adjustment to the histogram. Just as you use the Zone System to set where the values of the actual subject matter will fall

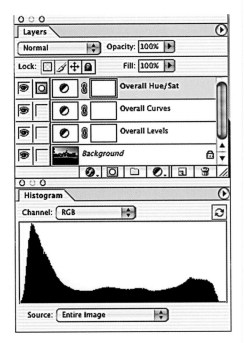

After adding a small S-curve to adjust the contrast and a Hue/Saturation adjustment, we see a final histogram showing what the overall color correction process has done to it. The image below shows how those adjustments, along with sharpening, have improved this image.

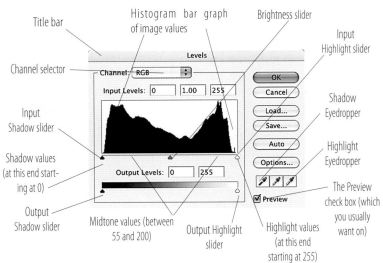

Study this diagram to learn the various controls of the Levels tool.

on the film, in digital imaging you choose (by manipulating the histogram) where the values of the scan or digital capture will fall in the final output. Therefore, you must view the histogram in the context of the original input and the desired output. You must ask yourself, "What is actually there?" and "What do I want the audience to see?"

Modifying with Levels and Curves

Once you get a good scan with a good histogram, you can modify it with Levels and Curves to get your visualization of that image for your final print. If you move the Levels Input Highlight slider to the left, you move your Zone VIII and IX values toward Zone X, brightening the highlights. If you move the Output Highlight slider to the left, you move your Zone X, IX, and VIII values toward Zone IX, VIII, and VII, respectively, dulling the highlights. Similarly, you can use the Shadow sliders to move the zone values around in the shadow parts of the histogram. If you move the Input Brightness slider to the right, you move Zone V values toward Zone IV or III, making the midtones darker and more contrasty. If you move the slider to the left, you move Zone V values toward Zone VI or VII, making the image lighter and brighter.

The Curves tool allows you to make even finer adjustments to values in specific zones. Read Chapter 20 and 21 as well as Chapter 22, "Correcting Problem Images" to try out these techniques and see how digital imaging gives you more power to realize your vision. As Ansel Adams says in his book *The Negative* (Little Brown, 1995), "Much of the creativity in photography lies in the infinite range of choices open to the photographer between attempting a nearly literal representation of the subject and freely interpreting it in highly subjective 'departures from reality.'" Many people think of Adams's prints as straight photos from nature. Actually, Adams did a lot of adjusting with his view camera and in the darkroom to create his visualization of the image that would bring forth his feelings and emotions from

Corrected Photographs and Their Good Histograms
(The shape of each histogram is quite different depending on the image.)

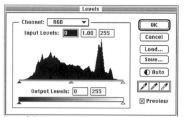

Santa Cruz sunset from the boardwalk.

Young Lakes.

Lots of three-quarter tones on the dark parts of the beach. The large number of quarter tones are probably in the sky and the waves. This page contains historical Photoshop Levels dialogs, but the histogram shapes have not changed.

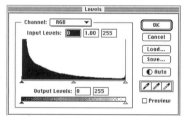

The Paris Cafe.

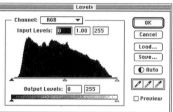

Lots of values everywhere across the full brightness range.

Lots of very dark areas show to the left of the histogram and a few very bright areas in the spike to the right. Even totally black and white areas are OK in this photo.

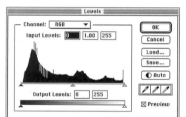

The Burnley church.

Shells in Costa Rica.

This histogram has lots of dark shadows in the trees and the fence. The spike at the far right is the white buildings.

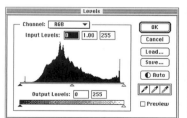

Man on the beach at sunset.

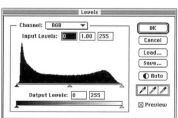

Notice the small spike for the dark shadow areas that are small but so important in the photograph.

This histogram probably is so smooth because all the objects have a similar range of colors and subtle tones.

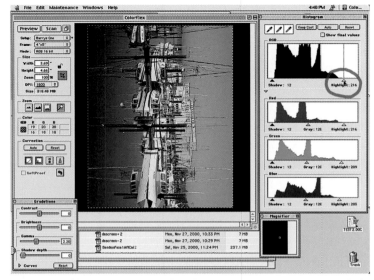

Here are some of the more important controls on the Imacon Precision II scanner using its ColorFlex software. In this 320 MB 16-bit scan of the Bandon 4x5 image, notice the very exact histograms within Imacon's Histogram dialog to the right. You can keep this dialog up all the time, and the histograms get updated every time you make a new Preview or a new crop. As you can see me doing with the cursor in the topmost RGB histogram, you can adjust the highlight and shadow points for RGB exactly, which adjusts all the settings, and you can also adjust each color separately.

the original scene. I believe he would enjoy digital imaging and all the extra control it would give him.

Some Scanners We Recommend

This section discusses various scanners we've used and would recommend, and compares their features.

I have been comparing scanners a lot over the years, though less so in the last two years, since I'm shooting mostly digital these days. I can now recommend many scanners I feel you'll be quite happy with. No doubt there are some newer models than the ones I mention here. But even so, the scanner market is starting to shrink, as many photographers move to digital cameras. Still, many of us have a large library of film that we plan to scan "one day." If you are not going to scan your film now, wait until you do to buy a scanner, and make sure at that point that the scanner's software works with your current computers. I have to either run my Polaroid SprintScan 120 scanner on OS 9 or buy new scanner software, which I don't really need since the old software still works fine. Don't wait too long to buy a film scanner, though, as manufacturers may stop making them at some point!

If you're just scanning 35mm film, I'd recommend the Nikon Super Coolscan 4000 or 5000. Both do great 8- and 16-bit scans of 35mm film at up to 4000 optical ppi. If you need to scan 35mm and 4.5x6, 6x6, 6x7, 6x8, or 6x9, then I'd recommend the Nikon Super Coolscan 8000 or 9000, both of which scan up to 4000 dpi optical with either format. The Imacon Flextight Photo, is also a great scanner for 35mm and 6x sizes. If you want to scan 35mm, 6x6 or 6x7 or 6x9, and also 4x5 or larger film, a less expensive solution would be to get a Nikon Super Coolscan 4000 or 5000 for the 35mm and then use the Epson Perfection 4990 flatbed scanner, or similar Epson flatbed scanner, for 6x6-cm and 4x5-inch scans at up to 4800 optical dpi. You could also get the Nikon 8000 and just use the Epson to scan 4x5s. Most flatbed scanners I've tested don't focus as sharply on film as dedicated film scanners do, but you may find the quality of scans fine for the larger 6x and 4x5 film formats. I use the Polaroid SprintScan 120 for 35mm and 120 film (an old but great scanner similar to the Nikon 8000), then scan 4x5s with my Epson Perfection 2450 (a really old model), which produces beautiful 20x30 prints when sharpened properly! The best desktop scanners I've tested that do all three formats of film are the Imacon Precision II, III, and 848. I have used many Imacon scanners and am very impressed with them. To find out about newer models of some of these scanners, go to the Links section of www.barryhaynes.com and click the links to the manufacturers' Web sites.

How to Compare Scanners

Scanner prices tend to drop quickly when something new and better comes out, you can buy all the scanners I mention here at great prices. Scanners are much cheaper than they were several years ago. For my scanner comparisons I've always scanned, among others, two particular images—both transparencies. The first one is a 35mm Kodachrome 25 photograph of the Santa Cruz beach and boardwalk that was shot from the Santa Cruz pier using a great Canon 50mm lens with my trusty old Canon F1 mounted on a tripod. This is a very sharp and low-grain photograph that I can print sharply at 25 inches wide on the LightJet 5000 when scanning with a Tango drum scanner at 5000 dpi. The second image I use for comparison is a 4x5-inch original of the harbor in Bandon, Oregon, shot on Kodak Ektachrome with a 4x5 camera using a 210mm Nikor lens. Both of these images are very sharp originals that have a broad range of values, from bright white down to dark black, and lots of sharp details.

When looking at scanners, I don't discuss the details and features of their software at great length. I've found over the years that scanner vendors try to sell their scanners by wowing people with all the software features or the bundle of toys that come with the scanner.

Scanned at 5000 dpi with the Lino Tango Drum scanner zoomed to 100% within Photoshop and color corrected within Photoshop.

A close-up of a section of the 35mm Santa Cruz boardwalk image scanned at 5760 dpi with the Imacon and zoomed to 100% within Photoshop.

Many of these features duplicate things that Photoshop can do just as well and often better. If you just get a reasonable raw scan from any scanner and are able to save this as a 16-bit-per-channel file, then you can use Photoshop's Levels, Curves, and Hue/Saturation tools, among others, in a standard way to get great results from many different scanners. If you are saving 8-bit-per-channel files from the scanner, then you need to rely on the scanner's software not to damage the data, and also to optimize that data as it transforms it from the 12, 14, or 16 bits per channel that the scanner hardware gets (down to 8 when saving the file). My main philosophy in scanning these days is to get 16 bits per channel of info from the scanner, then do most of my corrections in Photoshop. It certainly helps if you start with a scan that matches the original film fairly closely. Making a custom profile for your scanner using MonacoEZcolor, the GretagMacBeth Eye-One system, or other software, can often help simplify that step. People who are doing hundreds of batch scans daily may want to use their scanner's software or a custom scanner profile to automate this process.

Imacon Flextight Scanners

The Imacon Flextight Precision II, III, 848, and several newer model scanners are at the high end of the non-drum scanners. The Precision II can scan a 35mm at 5760 dpi, a 6x6cm at 3200 dpi, and a 4x5-inch at 1800 dpi maximum optical resolution. The newer models do even better. They use a unique mounting system where the film is placed and lined up on one of four thin metal backing holders, one for each film size. After you line up the film, a hinged magnetic flap drops down over the film to hold it in place. A hole is cut in the metal backing holder and also in the magnetic flap, allowing you, and the scanner, to see the film through this holder. After the film is mounted, one frame at a time, the holder is then placed on a light

table attached to the front of the scanner. The holder snaps into place and is held by magnets. After setting the correct preferences for the type of film you are using and the type of scan you want, you click the Preview button in the scanner's ColorFlex software to create a preview of the scan, which you then crop as you would like. To actually do the scan, the FlexTight film-carrying mechanism bends the holder, and the film within it, so they are wrapped around a drum as they are drawn into the scanner. The drum in this scanner is actually two metal bands that contact the holder on each side and bend the holder and the film into a position so that it doesn't buckle and is a consistent distance from the scanner's CCD sensor. It's like bending the film around a real drum scanner drum but with no actual drum surface, just air, where the film passes over the sensor. It is much easier to do than real drum scanning, and yet you get some of the same benefits in the way the film is bent into a known plane of focus. With a real, wet-mounted drum scan, there are some benefits to having the film surrounded by liquid, since the liquid will fill many scratches and imperfections that might be on the film's surface. The disadvantage to wet mounting, though, is that your film must be cleaned before and after the process. It is best to have clean and dusted film for any scans, but wet-mounted drum scans put your film through more torture, and are more work for the scanner operator, than most other scanning processes.

The Nikon Super Coolscan 4000, 5000, 8000, and 9000

The Nikon 8000 and 9000 scan both 35mm and 120 film formats at up to 4000 dpi optical resolution. With a scanning density range of 4.2, the 8000 or 9000 may be considered a more economical Imacon. The 35mm scans are very sharp, similar to the Imacon's, but maybe just a tad less sharp. They are certainly so close to the Imacon's that

The same area scanned at 4000 dpi with the Nikon 8000 and zoomed to 100% in Photoshop. All images on this page have been color corrected.

The same area scanned at 4000 dpi with the Polaroid SprintScan 120 and zoomed to 100% in Photoshop, then color corrected by me in Photoshop.

just a small sharpen on the Nikon 8000 or 9000 35mm scan will make it equal in sharpness to the Imacon's. The Imacon Precision II actually scans at 5760 dpi, a little bigger the the Nikon scanners. The software for Nikon 120 size supports 6x4.5, 6x6, 6x7, 6x8, and 6x9, but since it is a long, undivided holder, you can actually scan 6x17s by doing two scans and piecing them together later in Photoshop. The Nikon Scan software that comes with the 8000 and 9000 and the 4000 and 5000 is certainly the most versatile that I have tested and appears to be on a par with that of Imacon. The 9000 is the newer model of the original 8000 (for 35mm and 120) and the 5000 is the newer model of the 4000 for 35mm only. All these scanners actually allow the intensity of the lamps to be increased in the hope of getting more detail out of very dense film. This software shows updated histograms after all adjustments, has adjustments similar to the other, better packages I tested, and also has an additional LCH curve adjustment for doing Luminance, Chroma, and Hue adjustments. Very cool! Nikon Scan allows scanning in either 8-bit or 14-bit on either the 4000 or the 8000 scanner; you can also make more than one scan pass and average the results together for a more accurate scan. I used the four-pass setting for my scans. The 5000 and 9000 models do full 16-bit scans versus 14-bit on the older models. The 8000 comes with a 35mm slide holder that holds up to five mounted slides at a time, a 35mm strip film holder that can hold two 6-frame strips side by side, and a 120 holder that holds the 120 formats I mentioned.

Batch Scans and Making a Scanner Profile

Using MonacoEZcolor 2.5, Gretag Eye-One, or another profiling package to make a custom profile for the scanner will help you get scans that initially match your original slide. I've tested this with MonacoEZcolor and a Nikon 4000 using the optional 35mm IT8 film target, and it works quite well. Once you make a profile for your

film scanner, you want to assign this profile to your scans. If the scanner software won't allow you to attach the profile directly, save the file without a profile. When you open the file into Photoshop, use Edit/Assign Profile to assign the profile you made to the files you scan. If you then want to work in a specific color space, like Adobe RGB, choose Image/Mode/Convert to Profile and convert from the scanner profile you just assigned to Adobe RGB. The image on your screen should now look very similar to your original scan when that scan is viewed using a 5000 kelvin viewing box. Making and assigning profiles will help if you want to batch scan hundreds or thousands of well-exposed slides and you don't have time to color correct each one. The 4000 and 5000 have a batch-scan attachment that can automatically scan up to around 50 slides at a time. This is helpful if you have many scans to do. Many of my workshop students have these Nikon 4000 and 5000 batch scanning attachments and are generally happy with them.

I don't usually bother with scanner profiles for my personal work, as I've found all these scanners get me close enough that I can use Photoshop to get the colors I want within the Adobe RGB color space. When you don't have time to color correct the scans, a scanner profile may be helpful.

The Polaroid SprintScan 120

The Polaroid SprintScan 120 is a great scanner with functionality similar to the Nikon 8000's. The SprintScan 120 will scan 35mm and 120 film at up to 4000 ppi with either 8-bit or 16-bit-per-channel scans. The Sprintscan 120 comes with a 35mm mounted slide holder that holds up to four slides. It also has a 35mm strip film holder that holds up to a six-frame strip. The 120 holder and software supports 6x4.5, 6x6, 6x7, and 6x9 formats but doesn't have the mechanism to stretch the film tightly across the width as the Nikon 8000 holder does. Stretching the film is one way to keep it flat for uniform focus across the entire image. The scans I've made with the SprintScan 120 are very similar in sharpness to those of the Nikon 8000, with the Nikon being just a tad sharper. The difference between the two is minimal and could probably be made up with a small Unsharp Mask factor. I use the SprintScan 120 with the SilverFast scanning software, which is a fully featured package offering features similar to the Nikon 8000 and Imacon software. The SprintScan 120 is a very good scanner and compares better to the Nikon scanner in sharpness than the previous Polaroids have compared to their Nikon counterparts. If you have the SprintScan 120 and want scanning software with a lot of features, make sure you get it with the SilverFast software. Polaroid is no longer making this scanner; it's too bad because I'm very happy with the one I have.

If I were buying a scanner these days, I'd probably get the Nikon 5000 for just 35mm or the 9000 for 35mm and 120. If you have to scan a lot of 35mm images, the batch-scanning attachment for the 5000 is a great time-saver.

Epson Perfection 2450, 3200, 4990 and V700

These Epson flatbed scanners allow you to scan printed matter and film formats up to 4x5 in size. The Epson Perfection scanners have a color bit depth of 48 bits. That allows you to scan at an optical resolution of 2400 up to 6400 dpi (depending on the model). I've found that unbalanced scanner optical resolutions (2400 x 4800, for example) usually do their best job at the lower balanced number, which would be 2400x2400 up to 6400x6400 depending on the model.

Unbalanced Flatbed Resolutions

The reason for the imbalance in many flatbed scanners is that the scanner's CCD actually gives you only the lower resolution—say, 3200—in one direction, but the stepper motor moving the CCD over the image steps at the higher value, like 6400. You're getting 3200 dpi from the CCD and 6400 from the stepper motor.

Film Holders

One nice thing about the film holders that came with these Epson scanners was that they didn't cut much from the edges of the image area. I was able to scan the full frame of the 35mm shot and very close to the full frame of the 4x5.

Comparing Models

I actually have the 2450, but it looks and works very much like the 3200 and 4990. For the money—$450 to $600 for the 4990 and $550

to $800 for the V700 and V750—these scanners are a great deal. The 2450 and 3200 are older models. I wouldn't use the older ones for high-end scans of 35mm, but they would be great for Web scans or smaller prints for the 13-inch-wide or smaller Epson printers. I'd like to try the V700 for 35mm since it has a D-Max of 4.0 and a 6400 dpi resolution. The larger the D-Max, the better dark shadow details can be scanned. The V750 Pro model even allows for wet-mount film scanning. I have made beautiful 22x28 prints from 4x5 film originals scanned at 2400 dpi with my old 2450. These 2450 images require more color correction work and sharpening than if they were scanned with an Imacon, but the final prints are quite impressive. If you shoot 120 or 4x5 and can't afford an Imacon, $450 to $800 for the 4990 up to the V-750 may be money well spent.

Scanning Film with Flatbeds vs. Film Scanners

The problem I've always had when trying to scan film from a flatbed scanner is getting sharp scans. I have not yet found a flatbed scanner that gives scans as sharp as a film scanner with a good focus mechanism. The older Epson 2450 and 3200 scanners also fall into that category with the film scans not being as sharp compared to the ones on the Imacon, the Nikon scanners, or the Polaroid SprintScan 120. I haven't tried the 4990 or the V700 series, which may be better. If you scan a 4x5 piece of film, though, or maybe even a 6x6cm image, you can get prints that will appear quite sharp and acceptable to most people; just use the Sharpen Only Edges BH action script described in Chapter 12. Another difference between most flatbed scanners and the dedicated film scanners we discuss here is the scanning density range. If you have images that have really deep shadow detail that you need to capture in a scan, you'll find that the dedicated film scanners here generally do a better job. Again, the V700-to-V750 series may break that rule, as they have a D-Max of 4.0, meaning that they're supposed to be able to scan more-dense film. Seeing is believing, though, so "try before you buy" is my motto.

Some Black-and-White Scanning Ideas

Another way to use a flatbed scanner when working with 4x5 black-and-white negatives is as follows. Some of my friends in the Corvallis Photo Arts Guild are making beautiful black-and-white prints by first making a good 8x10 print in the darkroom from their 4x5 negative, then scanning that print on a flatbed scanner, like the two mentioned above. That scan of a print, which these scanners do so well, can be further improved in Photoshop. Let's say, for example, you shoot a 4x5 original on film and then make an 8x10 very sharp, high-quality black-and-white print from that film in the darkroom. Now you could scan that 8x10 print at 2400 dpi on on the above scanners

The image on the cover of this book, and at the start of this chapter, was taken with Barry's 6-megapixel Digital Rebel camera. That gives enough data to be printed to about 24 inches in width. The image above of the same ruin was shot with his Pentax 6x7 120 film camera. This image was scanned with the Polaroid SprintScan 120 to a 16-bit file size of over 500 MB. With that much data, it can be printed to a much larger size.

and get a great scan. After improving the digital file in Photoshop, you could then make a great Epson 9600 print with it, without resampling, and at 360 dpi this print would be 53x66 inches in size! If you wanted to output the image at 600 dpi to an imagesetter, this would give you a black-and-white digital negative at 32x40 inches in size, which you could then very easily contact-print back onto darkroom paper.

Conclusion

If you need a scanner, then I hope the tips here were helpful. Be sure to check out the Links section of www.barryhaynes.com, where you'll find links to the Nikon, Epson, and Imacon Web sites. These sites provide the lastest info about the companies' scanners. Also use Google, http://luminous-landscape.com, and other online resources to read the latest reviews about new scanner models. I'm betting new scanner models will become like new film cameras, fewer and farther between!

18 ◆ The Master Image Workflow

Despite all the hype and "buzzword" status attached to the subject of digital imaging workflow, the concepts behind it are fairly simple and accessible—far from the mysterious black art that some people perceive it to be. Simply put, a workflow is the order in which you perform certain procedures on your image during the editing process. The exact order you end up using, as well as the nature of the different techniques, will be influenced by several factors: the origin of the image (for example, whether it's a scan or digital capture, a Raw file, or a conventional file format), what you want to do to the image, and what the final output will be (say, fine art print, offset press reproduction, or Web site or multimedia usage). However, a few core concepts apply to most image editing scenarios.

Both Photoshop and photography (the ways in which we acquire images) have evolved over the years, and yet our basic workflow for preparing our fine art images has changed very little. In this chapter, we'll present an overview of our standard workflow for creating color-corrected master images that can be repurposed for various output scenarios, including fine Epson inkjet prints, LightJet photographic prints, CMYK press reproduction, and the Web. Along the way, we'll explain the key steps to give you a clearer understanding of this important part of the digital imaging process. You can experience many of these techniques firsthand by following the step-by-step tutorial exercises later in the book.

The Master Image

Throughout this book, we refer to the concept of the master image, which is integral to our workflow and editing process. Before we delve further into the procedural nuances of digital workflow, perhaps a definition of this term is in order.

A *master image* is the primary version of an image file; it's where we do most of our Photoshop editing work, and we do it with the aim of maximizing future editability. It contains the original scan or the optimized version of a Raw file; if we want to make any additional color or tonal corrections, we do it using adjustment layers for global corrections and adjustment layers combined with layer masks for more localized corrections to specific areas of the image. Whenever possible, we make edits this way so that we can easily undo or modify those changes. Similarly, we do all retouching or compositing on separate layers for maximum flexibility. The master image is

the source from which we prepare different, flattened versions of the file for specific sizes and output. We never apply resizing and primary image-sharpening changes to the master image, in order to preserve its integrity and flexibility to serve as a source for versions that can be repurposed for several different types and sizes of output. Once we've color corrected the image, it should not require further color correction for us to be able to print it with the same, or very similar, color on a number of different devices. In our digital workflow, the master image is the central concept around which all other editing is structured.

Choosing Your Color Working Space and Color Management Policies

The first step in implementing a workflow for your own digital darkroom is choosing a working space in Photoshop's Color Settings dialog (Edit/Color Settings). The chosen working space determines how Photoshop interprets the colors in images that have no embedded profiles, and it establishes the color profile of newly created documents. The Color Management Policies control how images with mismatched profiles, or no profiles at all, are treated. For most photographic work, we recommend using Adobe RGB (1998) as

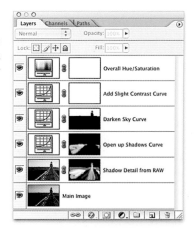

The Layers palette for a master image file. All tonal and color correction is done using adjustment layers with layer masks.

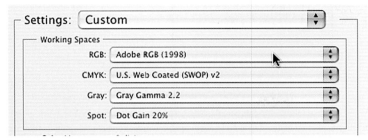

The Working Spaces section of the Color Settings dialog.

your RGB working space, though there are situations where another working space might be more appropriate. For work that is destined for reproduction on a printing press, for example (such as this book), one might use the ColorMatch RGB working space, since it represents colors that are closer to what the image will look like once it is converted to CMYK (however, we used Adobe RGB for this book). If you have configured the Color Settings as we recommend in Chapter 2, "Preferences and Color Settings," then your RGB working space should already be set to Adobe RGB (1998). For more in-depth information on choosing a working space, read Chapter 15, "Color Spaces, Device Characterization, and Color Management." The parts of the Color Settings and Preferences that affect color correction and the appearance of images onscreen are described in Chapter 16, "Color Preferences, Calibration, and Printing."

Digital Capture Workflow: Maximizing Quality in the Camera

The workflow outlined in this chapter is based on our standard approach for color correcting photographs. It was initially developed, and has evolved over the years, as a result of our working with scans from film originals. In recent years, the file size and quality of images produced by digital SLRs has improved to the point where digital cameras can produce prints of excellent quality, both in terms of sharpness and tonality. If you are relatively new to photography and Photoshop, it's conceivable that you create the majority, if not all, of your images using a digital camera. The color correction workflow we will discuss here is appropriate for both digital camera captures and scanned images. If you're using a digital camera that shoots in Raw, however, the process differs somewhat, most in the part before you do the main color correction work in Photoshop.

With a digital capture, the workflow really begins where the image does, in the camera, with the decisions you make regarding image size,

image quality, and file format. So before we get into the main color correction workflow, a few words about maximizing image and tonal quality in the camera. First, unless you have clear reasons for using a smaller image size (such as for posting shots of an esoteric collectible you're trying to sell on eBay), our recommendation is to always capture images at the largest size your camera offers. This allows you more flexibility in terms of how large you can print the image, as well as whether you can apply a creative crop without losing too many precious pixels. Hand in hand with image size is the issue of image quality settings; image quality settings are a factor only if you're shooting in JPEG format. If you decide to shoot JPEGs, then you should always have the quality set to the highest level available (a high level of quality means the least amount of file compression). Finally, for images saved by the camera in JPEG format, we recommend turning off additional camera settings such as sharpening, contrast, and color saturation. In our view, it is much better to apply such adjustments in Photoshop, where you have more control and can preview their effects first. The exception to this latter recommendation would be if you are a high-volume photographer and capture hundreds of images per day. As long as you have experimented with how your camera's settings affect the image and are comfortable with them, then having the camera handle some of those adjustments might be a possibility to reduce the postproduction workload.

If your camera offers the ability to shoot in Raw format, then we recommend using that for the images you really care about. With Raw

Shooting in Raw and processing the images with Adobe Camera Raw provides you with a great deal of control for improving less than optimal exposures, or simply allows you to explore different interpretations of an image.

you are always shooting at the largest pixel size possible; there is no destructive compression, and it is only by shooting in Raw that you have access to the high-bit data that most digital SLRs can capture. In situations where the exposure is less than ideal, Raw provides a large safety net and a means of easily correcting the bad exposure after the fact. Converting the image in Adobe Camera Raw gives you unprecedented control and flexibility for optimizing the tonal and color balance of the image, as well as for salvaging a less than optimal exposure, before you bring it into the main Photoshop program. For more detailed information on getting the most out of your Raw files, refer to Chapter 9, "Camera Raw."

8-Bit or 16-Bit?

Many scanners, and all digital cameras with Raw capabilities, offer the ability to capture an image using more than 8 bits per channel. Similarly, Photoshop CS2 supports the most important image editing functionality in 16-bit mode (any image that is more than 8 bits per channel is classified as a 16-bit image by Photoshop, even if it is really less than 16 bits). The ability to capture an image with more than 8 bits per channel is important, because an 8-bit image has only 256 levels of tonality per color channel. Since all color or tonal correction with digital images involves the discarding of some tonal information in order to get the histogram (and, therefore, the image) looking the way you want, working on an 8-bit image gives you less room to maneuver, especially with images that need drastic corrections. If too much information is thrown away in the tonal correction process, you'll notice gaps in the histogram where there is no longer a smooth transition from one tonal value to the next. If the number of gaps become excessive, this can lead to *posterization* (areas that have lost texture or tonality and become flat), or *banding* (an abrupt change in tone in what would normally be smooth tonal transitions), especially in the shadow tones, both when the image is viewed onscreen and when it's printed.

A Raw file from a current digital SLR camera offers 12 bits of information, which translates to a more generous 4096 levels of tonality per color channel. Many scanners let you scan at 14 bits per channel, which is 16,384 tonal values for each color channel. When you're performing color and tonal corrections, working on a high-bit image gives you more tonal "headroom" for making your adjustments. You may still lose some tonal information when making your corrections, but since you are starting out with so many more tonal values, the effect will be negligible, and you will be much more likely to end up with a histogram with no objectionable gapping.

This image of a boatyard was exposed so that the bright highlights on the boats were not blown out to a total white. As a result, the shadow areas in the lower part of the image are too dark.

A Curves adjustment layer with a layer mask is applied to lighten the underexposed shadow areas on the boatyard photo. The same adjustment was applied to both an 8-bit and a 16-bit version of the photo. The histograms (see below) show the impact on the tonal quality.

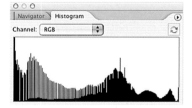

After the shadows were lightened on an 8-bit version of the boatyard image, the histogram shows significant gaps that indicate tonal loss and posterization in the shadows.

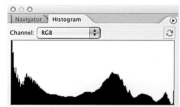

When the same shadow-lightening curve is applied to a 16-bit version of the boatyard image, the histogram does not show any significant tonal erosion.

Realities of a 16-Bit Workflow

Although a 16-bit image is highly advantageous from a tonal perspective, the downside to working with 16-bit files in Photoshop is that the file size is double that of an 8-bit file. When you add layers, adjustment layers, and layer masks, the file size can increase very quickly. When working on larger images, you can end up with files from several hundred megabytes to close to a gigabyte or more. Whether such file sizes are workable for you will depend on several factors, including the amount of RAM you have, how much free hard drive space you have available for Photoshop to use as a scratch disk, and how much storage space you have.

If such large file sizes are an issue for you, consider using a 16-bit file only for the overall tonal and color corrections, or for significant local adjustments. Apply these corrections to the 16-bit image using adjustment layers, and then save that version as a 16-bit master file. From this 16-bit master, you can choose File/Save As and create a copy file that you can then flatten and convert to 8 bits per channel in the Image/Mode menu. Since you made the initial global corrections to the 16-bit master, the histogram has been optimized using a more generous tonal range, and the histogram is better than if those same corrections had been applied to an 8-bit file (note that for this method to work, the copy file does need to be flattened before the conversion to 8 bits per channel is made). You can now do additional local color correction and/or compositing and retouching on the smaller 8-bit master file.

Scanner Workflow: Scanning for Print Size and Best Quality

Our philosophy when making scans is to make the best possible scan at a file size that is big enough to accommodate the largest print we can envision making from the photo. There are two main reasons for this. First, scanning requires a time investment. Instead of making a small initial scan, and then having to go back and do it again if we need a larger scan, we'd rather just do it once. Second, scanned images do not respond as well to upsampling (making the image larger) as do images from digital cameras. This is because scans from film always include some amount of film grain, and when you resample the scan, you are also resampling the grain, which can become very noticeable depending on the image in question and how much you are enlarging it. For this reason, it's best to try and scan your photos so they're big enough for the largest size print you might want to make.

Barry creates most of his master digital photographs from scans that are big enough to make large prints with minimal or no resampling.

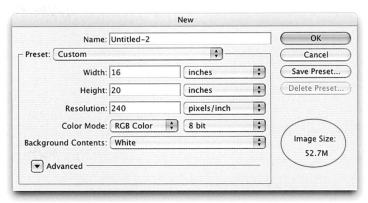

Using the New File dialog as a "calculator" to determine the required file size for a scan that will be used to make a 16x20-inch print.

In scanning 35mm color transparency film, his experiments have shown that a scan from a good drum scanner at around 5000 ppi (pixels per inch) will capture all the information from the film. High-quality scans that he has made using an Imacon scanner, a Nikon Coolscan 4000 and 8000, and a Polaroid Sprintscan 120 have resulted in images that make very fine prints. With 35mm and 120 film, Barry usually scans at his scanner's maximum optical resolution, which is 4000 ppi. For larger film formats, such as 4x5, a lower ppi will often give you as big a file as you will need.

An easy way to determine the necessary file size for the size print you want to make is to use Photoshop's New File dialog as a calculator. Just enter in the width and height of your desired print, and the resolution required for good quality (such as 240 or 360 ppi) and see what the file size is. Then, when you make your scan, just make sure that it's close to that file size.

The main objective when making a scan is to capture as full a range of tonal values as possible without clipping any values in either the shadows or the highlights. You should make tonal and color adjustments in Photoshop and not with the scanner software, because you have much more control both in evaluating the image and also in how you apply significant color and tonal adjustments.

We also recommend scanning at more than 8 bits per channel if your scanner offers it (and most do these days). This will give you thousands of tonal values to work with instead of the meager 256 you get with an 8-bit image, so any tonal loss created by adjustments you make in the scanning software is not noticeable. See Chapter 17, "Image Resolution and Scanning," for more detailed information about scanning, resolution, bit depth, file size, and capturing the best possible histogram.

Opening the Image: Working with Mismatched and Missing Profiles

When you open a new digital capture or scan into Photoshop, you should convert it to your RGB working space before you begin editing. Some images that you open may not have a profile already embedded in them and should have a profile assigned to them before converting to the working space. The exact sequence for assigning a profile and converting to your working space will vary depending on the source of your image. Here is an overview of a few different scenarios for image files from digital cameras and scans.

Opening a File with an Embedded Profile That Is Different from Your Working Space

If you open an image that has an embedded profile and that profile is different from your working space, you will see the Embedded Profile Mismatch dialog. As long as the image has an accurate profile attached to it, Photoshop can make a correct conversion from one space to another. If this is the case, simply choose the second radio button: Convert Document's Colors to the Working Space.

Opening a File with No Embedded Profile

If you open an image from either a scanner or a digital camera that has no profile associated with it, then the Missing Profile dialog will appear before the file opens in Photoshop. Your three choices are Leave As Is (Don't Color Manage), Assign Working RGB (1998), and Assign Profile. With the first two options, the image will look the same, since both choices will interpret the image according to the specifications of your chosen RGB working space. The only difference is that with the second choice (Assign Working RGB), the profile for your working space is formally assigned to the image. The third option lets you choose from a drop-down menu of different profiles that are installed on your system. If you know for a fact what the profile should be and it's available in the menu (for example, a profile for your model of scanner), go ahead and choose that, then click the check box for And Then Convert Document to Working RGB. This will assign the profile, giving Photoshop the information it needs to make a correct conversion and then convert the color data to your chosen working space (i.e., Adobe RGB) as the file is opened.

Using Assign Profile to Test-Drive Different Profiles

The one thing missing from the Missing Profile dialog, however, is a preview that displays how your choice will affect the colors in the

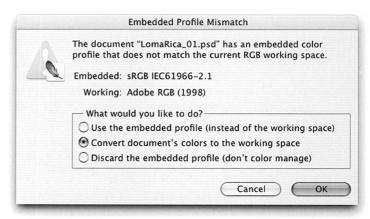

An Embedded Profile Mismatch dialog alerts you that the embedded profile does not match your working space.

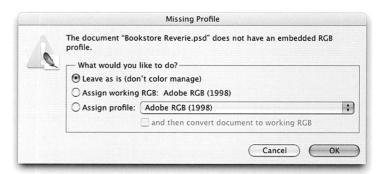

A Missing Profile dialog alerts you that the image you are opening has no embedded profile. Unless you know for a fact what the profile for the image should be, our advice is to choose Leave As Is."

image. Since the image is not actually open yet, of course, it is impossible to create a preview. Unless you know what the profile should be for an untagged image, our advice is to use the first option, Leave As Is (Don't Color Manage). When the file opens, the colors in the image will be displayed according to your working space. This may or may not be correct, but once the image is open in Photoshop, there is a way for you to preview how different profiles will affect the image.

To do this, go to the main menu and choose Edit/Assign Profile (if you are using Photoshop CS, 7, or 6, that menu option is found under Image/Mode/Assign Profile). Click the third radio button in the Assign Profile dialog, and open the menu to access the profiles. If you have a profile installed for your scanner, it should show up in this menu. If you are assigning a profile to a digital camera capture, then Adobe RGB, ColorMatch RGB, or sRGB will often provide good results (profiles for digital cameras are generally useful only if the lighting in the shot is exactly the same as it was for the source image that was used to generate the profile, such as might be the case for very controlled studio conditions). You can also try out other profiles, although most of them will not be appropriate, especially if they represent devices such as scanners, printers, or monitors, and some may make the image look downright ugly. Keep in mind that assigning a profile does not change the color numbers in the file; all it does is apply a different interpretation to the color numbers. The object here is to find an interpretation that you feel is most appropriate and accurate for the image. Once you've assigned an accurate profile, the image can then be converted to the working space. For untagged images from some of his digital cameras, for example, Seán uses the Assign Profile dialog to assign the sRGB profile, because test images he has made have shown that sRGB creates the most accurate interpretation for certain cameras.

Converting to the Working Space

Once you've assigned a profile, you can convert the image to your chosen working space by using the Convert to Profile dialog (Edit/ Convert to Profile). In previous versions of Photoshop this command is found under Image/Mode/Convert to Profile. In the Destination Space drop-down menu, select Adobe RGB (or whatever your working space is). Leave the Engine set to Adobe (ACE) and for the Intent, Perceptual is the best choice. In most cases, Use Black Point Compensation should be unchecked and the Use Dither option should be checked. Since the Convert to Profile dialog does have a preview option, you can see how different rendering intents or the use of black-point compensation actually affects the image.

Some scanners have color management settings that allow you to choose from several standard RGB working spaces, and will import the image directly into Photoshop with a color profile already embedded. Nikon's Coolscan scanners do this; and if your monitor is properly calibrated and profiled, once the Adobe RGB (1998) scans are opened in Photoshop, they are an exact match to the prescan in the NikonScan software. In the case of images created with this scanner, there's no need to use either Assign Profile or Convert to Profile.

Raw Captures and Profiles

Apart from metadata that includes exposure information and identifies the model of camera that created the image, Raw files do not have embedded color profiles such as those that are used elsewhere in Photoshop. When you use Adobe Camera Raw to process Raw files, the software applies a default "starting point" conversion based on the type of camera you have. In Photoshop CS2, some auto corrections are also applied (and these can be turned off if you wish). In addition

Choosing a profile in the Assign Profile dialog. The preview feature in this dialog allows you to test-drive different profiles on your image. The profiles you see in this menu will depend on your own particular system and what monitor, scanner, and printer software may have been installed.

Adobe RGB (1998)

ColorMatch RGB

sRGB

Epson 2200 Enhanced Matte profile

Above: An untagged test image is assigned different profiles using the Assign Profile dialog. The actual color numbers in the image have not changed, only the interpretation of what those numbers mean. The inclusion of the Epson printer profile is shown to illustrate that, with the possible exception of a scanner profile, device profiles are almost never acceptable to use on untagged images.

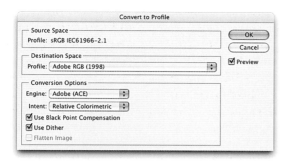

The Convert to Profile dialog.

to modifying several aspects that control exposure and color balance, you can also choose what RGB working space to use when the file is converted and opened in the main Photoshop program. Because the color profile is based on the working space you choose for the image in the Camera Raw dialog, you do not have to go into the Assign Profile or Convert to Profile dialogs. For a thorough overview of working with Adobe Camera Raw, refer to Chapter 9.

Color Correcting the Scan or Digital Camera Image

Even after capturing a great scan or digital camera image, you usually need to do some further color correction work. The first step in any color correction, either from a scanned image or a digital capture, is to optimize the histogram until you get it as close to perfect as you can given the data available. For most images, you should usually do your color correction in a specific order following the method we discuss in this chapter. If you are starting with a Raw capture from a digital camera, you can accomplish much of the initial histogram optimization in the Adobe Camera Raw dialog. Even after optimizing the Raw file, however, additional work may still be necessary, especially if you want to apply color or tonal correction to specific areas of the image; so much of the workflow discussed here still applies to Raw files. Refer to Chapter 9 for an in-depth look at workflow considerations within Adobe Camera Raw.

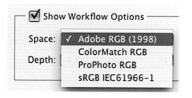

The working space options for assigning a profile in Adobe Camera Raw.

The rest of this chapter provides an overview of the steps you should use for creating a master image, making global and local color corrections, applying additional edits, and creating device-specific versions from the master file. Chapter 21, "Overall Color Correction," goes into much greater detail, offering a step-by-step tutorial for performing basic color correction on a photograph.

Using the Info and Histogram Palettes

We always have the Info and the Histogram palettes showing when we are making color corrections, simply because they provide useful information and feedback about the image. Bring up the Info palette by choosing Window/Info [F9]. In the default arrangement, the Histogram palette is grouped with the Info palette, so you will need to separate them by clicking the name tab for the Info palette and dragging it off by itself (if you have already created specific Photoshop workspaces, such as the color correction workspace mentioned in Chapter 3, "Navigating in Photoshop," then you can just recall that saved workspace). The Info palette will then show you the 8-bit and 16-bit RGB values at the cursor's current location. When you are working in a dialog such as Levels or Curves, the Info palette also shows you how any color correction is changing these values by displaying the "before" values on the left of the slash and the "after" values on the right. You can also place a Color Sampler point to keep track of values at specific locations (such as highlights and shadows). The Color Sampler tool is grouped with the Eyedropper tool flyout menu in the Tools palette. To add a point sample, just click the image using the Color Sampler tool or Shift-click when in the regular Eyedropper tool. The Color Sampler values, up to four per image, show up at the bottom of the Info palette. When you use a color correction tool, the color values at all the point sample locations are updated to reflect any changes in color.

The Histogram palette displays the histogram for the image and will update it as you work on the tonal range. This is valuable for seeing problems that might result from possible highlight or shadow clipping (forcing values to either a total white or a total black) or excessive gaps that appear if a drastic correction is made. While working in a dialog such as Levels or Curves, it can also display a before and after version so you can see how your corrections are affecting the histogram.

Creating the Initial Master Image

After you first open a file, whether a scanned image or a Raw capture that has already been processed in Camera Raw, you should save a copy of the original digital capture or scan as your master image (if you are working with a scanned image that has not been saved yet, you should first save the scan and name the file so it is clear to you

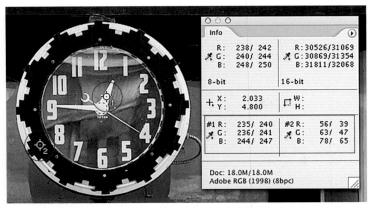

The Info palette during a color correction. The numbers on the left of the slash represent the color values before the adjustment, and the numbers to the right of the slash indicate the color values after the adjustment. Color Sampler points have been placed on the hour hand of the clock and on the dark border near the number 8.

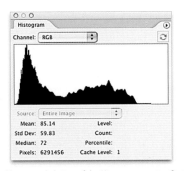 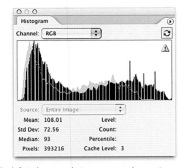

The expanded view of the Histogram palette. On the left is the normal view you see when an image is open in Photoshop. On the right is a "before and after" display that shows the original histogram in light gray, and the adjusted histogram in black. This view will display as you are making adjustments to the tonal range of an image.

that it is the original scan file). The easiest way to do this is to choose File/Save As and save the file with a new name. Choosing a naming convention that indicates that the file is a master image is helpful. In this book, we use the convention of appending "-layers" to the filename to designate it as a master file, but any naming system can work as long as it's consistent and the meaning is clear to you (for example, Seán uses a "-M" at the end of his filenames to denote a master image file).

Once you've saved a copy of the original as a master image in the PSD or TIFF format, you should do all your editing work on this file. This allows you to return to that original capture or scan if you make any major mistakes. As mentioned earlier, if you are working with a scan, you also want to make sure that the original scan is large

enough for the biggest-size output you intend for that image. For example, Barry makes 16x22-inch prints of his 35mm transparencies. For prints of this size, he scans at 16 bits per channel at 4000 dpi with the Polaroid SprintScan 120, which gives him about a 112MB file from 35mm film, and a 500MB file from 120 film. He does the color corrections on the master image version this file. Flattened copies of the large master image can then be resampled down for smaller prints, books, and for Web site usage.

Color Correction and Workflow Summary

Once we have created our master image file, the basic workflow we use for nearly all of our images can be summarized as follows.

First we tackle the overall (global) color and tonal correction issues. This includes neutralizing highlights and shadows, and adjusting overall brightness, contrast, and saturation. Then we move on to area-specific (local) color and tonal correction (for those familiar with darkroom terminology, this is the point in the workflow where we do our dodging and burning). After completing the color correction, we switch gears and address any additional edits the image may need (for example, retouching). Finally, we spot the master image file to remove any dust spots, and we save it with all layers intact.

Next, to prepare specific versions from the master image, we create a flattened copy of it, use the Image Size dialog to resample the image to the desired output size, and then apply sharpening. We make a final spotting pass to check for any dust specks we may have missed in the initial spotting and that sharpening may have accentuated. We then convert the file to the output profile for the printer and paper that will be used, or convert it to CMYK if it's destined for an offset press. If necessary, we make minor adjustments to the converted file.

That is just a brief summary of our basic workflow. Below is a more detailed outline of the workflow we use when starting with an RGB scan or a digital capture (as noted earlier, when you're working with a Raw capture, much of the initial histogram optimization can be achieved in the Camera Raw dialog). Not all image editing scenarios are the same, and not all situations may require this exact sequence; but for most images, we feel this is a good road map to follow.

Workflow Details

Camera Raw

When working with a Raw capture, our first step is to process the file in Adobe Camera Raw. Our aim here is to optimize the histogram and sometimes the overall color balance using the tools in the Camera Raw dialog. We open the image at a size (pixel dimension) that is appropriate for the largest-size print we may make from the file. Generally, we will open it as a 16-bit file to allow for maximum tonal quality for further editing in Photoshop. Please refer to Chapter 9 for more detailed information on making image adjustments in Adobe Camera Raw.

Cropping

If you are working with a scan, the first step is to crop off any unwanted black or white edges. For some images you may wish to apply additional cropping for aesthetic reasons, or simply to remove an unwanted section from the image; the big question in terms of workflow is "when to crop?" Some people prefer to crop at the beginning of the process, especially if they know exactly how they want the image to look. Others prefer to wait until later in the workflow, and never like to apply any cropping to the master image. We usually never crop a master image file, because different uses for the final image may require a different crop. If the master image is cropped, then we lose the flexibility to reinterpret the framing. We know other photographers, however, who feel the need to crop as the first step, because decisions they make in interpreting their image depend on seeing the scene displayed with the final crop. Either approach works, but just remember that cropping is generally irreversible once you've saved and closed the file.

If you turn the background layer into a regular layer by double-clicking it, you can use the Hide option for the Crop tool (found in the Options bar once you've drawn a cropping box) and simply hide the cropped area instead of actually deleting it. As long as you do not resize the image, you can restore the cropped areas by choosing Image/Reveal All.

If you do choose to crop early in the workflow, be very sure of your crop because, depending on what you do to the image in the editing

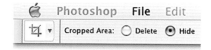

When cropping an image where the Background has been turned into a layer, you can choose to Hide the cropped areas after drawing the cropping box.

process, it might be impossible to revert your master image to the precropped version.

Save the Master File

After importing an image from Camera Raw or opening a scan, and after applying any preliminary cropping, you should save a copy of the file as your master image. Choose File/Save As and give the file a name to indicate that it's a master file. Now you are ready to begin with the main work on the image.

Overall (Global) Color Correction

The techniques for overall color correction outlined in this section, as well as some of the fundamental theory behind them, are covered in more detail in the step-by-step tutorials found in Chapters 21 and 22.

Add a Levels Adjustment Layer

For nearly all images, our first step is usually to add a Levels adjustment layer. This allows us to identify the brightest and darkest points in the image and adjust them to specific target values that will also neutralize them (remove color casts).

Using the clipping display in the Levels dialog (left) to locate the brightest point in the image. A Color Sampler point is then placed there so it can be targeted with the highlight Eyedropper tool.

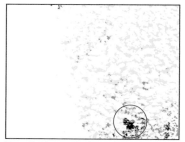

Using the clipping display in the Levels dialog (left) to locate the darkest point in the image. A Color Sampler point is then placed there so it can be targeted with the shadow Eyedropper tool.

- From the main menu, choose Layer/New Adjustment Layer/Levels [Command (Ctrl)-F2]. Option (Alt)-click the Highlight or Shadow slider to bring up the clipping display to identify the brightest and darkest points in the image; these points will serve as the highlight and shadow target areas. Shift-click to place a Color Sampler at each point (be sure to return the Shadow and Highlight sliders to the default starting positions of 0 and 255 before using the eyedroppers as described in the next step).

- Using the white- and black-point eyedroppers in the Levels dialog, set the Highlight and Shadow values for the image (this can also be done manually by observing the Color Sampler values in the Info palette and adjusting the endpoint sliders in each of the Levels color channels). Neutralizing the highlight and shadow points will often go a long way toward fixing any color casts in the image, but if color casts persist, proceed to the next step.

- If necessary, adjust the overall brightness of the image with the middle RGB slider.

- If any color casts remain after you've set the highlight and shadow points, go into the Red, Green, and/or Blue Levels channels and make corrections, being especially careful that neutral colors stay neutral and don't take on a new cast (the Info palette is useful for monitoring image color values).

> **NOTE**
>
> With the exception of using the clipping display to identify the brightest and darkest points in the image and seeing the detailed histogram of this image as you adjust the endpoints, you can also achieve many of the above steps using a Curves adjustment layer.

The Hue/Saturation dialog.

- Turn the Levels preview check box on and off as a final check. Since you've applied your Levels corrections with an adjustment layer, you can modify them later without degrading the image.

Add a Curves Adjustment Layer

For overall contrast adjustments or for more controlled tonal corrections to a specific area of the tonal range, Curves [Command (Ctrl)-F3] is the tool to use. You can also access the Red, Green, or Blue channel drop-down menu in Curves to adjust colors in specific tonal and color ranges.

Add a Hue/Saturation Adjustment Layer

To increase or decrease overall saturation, add a Hue/Saturation layer [Command (Ctrl)-F4]. Use the Edit menu at the top of the Hue/Saturation dialog to make adjustments to the hue, saturation, and lightness of specific colors.

Add Grayscale Effect for Black and White

If you want to convert a color image to black and white, add an adjustment layer to achieve this effect (see Chapter 25, "Black and

The Layers palette after the addition of the overall color correction adjustment layers of Levels, Curves, and Hue/Saturation.

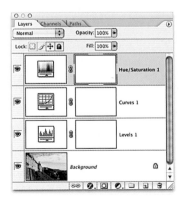

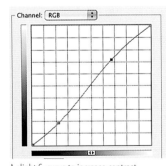

A slight S-curve to increase contrast.

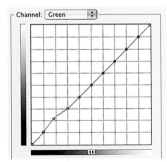

A curve targeting a very narrow range of darker tones in only the Green channel.

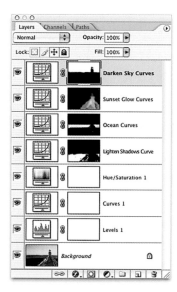

The layer stack for an image after local, area-specific corrections have been applied with adjustment layers and layer masks (top four layers). The bottom three layers are the initial, overall color, and tonal corrections.

White, and Duotones," for various methods to convert from color to black and white). Even if your goal from the beginning is to have a black-and-white image, we feel it is generally better to get the color version looking correct before converting to black and white.

Color Correction of Specific (Local) Areas Using Layer Masks

The techniques for area-specific (local) color correction outlined in this section are covered in more detail in the step-by-step tutorials in Chapters 21 and 22.

◆ Make color or tonal changes to specific image areas using Levels, Curves, Hue/Saturation, and other adjustment layers, using a layer mask with each to apply a correction to a defined area.

You can create a layer mask by having a selection active in the image when you add an adjustment layer, or by painting with black, white, or gray directly on the layer mask that is automatically added with each new adjustment layer. Although you can have many adjustment layers in an image, you should avoid changing the same image area too often, as excessive corrections could lead to tonal "erosion."

Retouching, Multi-Image Compositing, and Spotting

Spotting—the removal of dust spots or any other small flaws—can also be done before color correction, as the very first step in the process. Whether you do it first or at this point is largely a matter of personal preference. We generally prefer to work on the major issues first,

and since color correction is a more pressing matter than the removal of dust spots, we place spotting at this later point in the workflow. Also, after color correction, you may decide not to use this image, so why take the time to spot it before you're sure you'll use it?

◆ Spotting and minor touch-ups: Using the Spot Healing brush (Photoshop CS2), the Healing brush or the Clone Stamp, remove dust spots and small scratches from your master image *Background* layer.

◆ If you need to do any significant retouching or restoration (apart from simple spotting and scratch touch-ups), create a separate, empty layer, or use a copy of the *Background* layer in order to keep the retouching separate from the main image, so that you can modify it easily if necessary.

Retouching and restoration techniques are covered in Chapter 26, "Restoring Old Photos."

◆ If your project requires compositing multiple images together, use separate layers to do this, as well as layer masks to hide or reveal portions of each image layer. Using layer masks for compositing is nondestructive, giving you much more flexibility than if you erase image pixels.

Techniques for creating multiple image composites are covered in Chapter 27, "Compositing Bracketed Photos," and Chapter 30, "Product Compositing."

Saving and Archiving the Master Image

At this point you will have two separate files of your image: the original scan, the JPEG, or the Raw digital capture; and the layered master image file. Once you have made any necessary test prints and final adjustments to the master file, you should archive it and save a copy in an off-site location to protect against catastrophic data loss (say, a direct meteor hit on your digital darkroom). As described in the next section, you will create a flattened copy of the master image that you'll use to make prints for specific sizes and output devices, or to resize for Web or multimedia use.

◆ Save and archive your master image with all layers intact.

Resizing, Sharpening, Mode Conversions, and Final Adjustments

At this point, you have a color-corrected master RGB image that is saved with all its adjustment layers and/or retouching and compositing layers. The next series of steps entails creating a flattened copy of this master file, resizing it to a desired size, sharpening it, applying any mode and/or profile conversions, and making final adjustments and test prints as needed.

◆ Create a copy of the master image with the layers flattened.

To create a flattened copy of the layered master image, choose Image/Duplicate from the main menu. In the Image Duplicate dialog, click the check box for Merged Layers Only and add something to the filename to indicate it's a flattened version (for example, "-flat"). This will create a flattened copy of your master image. Your layered master image will still be open, in addition to the flattened copy.

◆ Using the Image Size dialog (Image/Image Size), resample the flattened copy of the image to the desired final output size. If you are making the image larger, choose Bicubic Smoother as the interpolation method. If you are making the image smaller, such as for a Web-size image, then Bicubic Sharper is the better method. We often resize in 10% increments using the Artist-Keys action ResUpBy10. More details about this can be found in Chapter 10.

◆ Sharpen the image (detailed coverage of sharpening techniques can be found in Chapter 12, "Essential Photoshop Techniques for Photographers").

Since sharpening often accentuates tiny flaws or spots you may have missed when you spotted the master image, you may also want to do a final spotting pass at 100% (choose View/Actual Pixels, or double-click the Zoom tool) after sharpening. The level of sharpening you apply is influenced by the size of the image as well as how it is being printed (for example, offset press, inkjet, glossy, matte, or watercolor paper), so for critical prints you might consider conducting a sharpening test in which you duplicate a representative section of the image several times on the same image canvas, and then apply different levels of sharpening to each one. After making a test print on the paper you'll be using for the final print, you can make a more informed decision about how much sharpening to apply.

◆ Inspect the image at 100% (View/Actual Pixels) and perform a final pass to retouch any sharpening-enhanced dust spots.

If your image will be reproduced on a printing press, this is the point where you would convert from RGB to CMYK. There are two ways to do this: If you've set the correct CMYK working space in the Photoshop Color Settings, you can use the Image/Mode menu and choose CMYK. You can also use the Convert to Profile dialog, which is found at the bottom of the Edit menu in CS2, or under the Image/Mode menu in prior versions of Photoshop. In the Convert to Profile dialog, choose the desired CMYK space from the Profile drop-down menu.

◆ Convert to CMYK (if necessary).

If you are going to have the file printed on an RGB printer at a photo lab or service provider, and you have downloaded the correct profile and installed it on your system, use Edit/Convert to Profile (in versions of Photoshop prior to CS2 you'll find this under the Image/Mode menu) to convert the colors into the profile for the printing device you'll use.

◆ For RGB output, convert to the correct output profile, or use the Print with Preview dialog if you're making the prints yourself.

If you are printing the file to your own printer, choose File/Print with Preview, and in the Color Handing options, choose Let Photoshop Determine Colors; then choose the correct printer profile from the Profile drop-down menu. See Chapter 16 for more on profiles and printing issues, and Chapter 21 for a tutorial-based tour of the Print with Preview dialog.

◆ After you have applied a color mode or profile conversion (or when using View/Proof Colors before the conversion), you can make minor color adjustments to specific color areas using adjustment layers and, if necessary, layer masks. These final adjustments should not be major revisions to the overall color or tonal balance of the image, but minor tweaks designed to compensate for subtle nuances created by converting to a different color mode such as CMYK, or to a device-specific profile. For major adjustments or reinterpretations of the image, you should return to the layered master file.

Saving Device-Specific Output Files

Once you have created, resized, and sharpened versions of a master image and are happy with the way they look when printed on a given output device and paper stock, you may want to save a version of the file for that specific device, or to print at a specific size.

For example, if you commonly sell prints that are 12x18 inches, you might want to save a sharpened version of a file to print at 12x18 inches that you will print on your own inkjet printer. You can already convert this file to the profile of your printer and paper, or you can use the Print with Preview dialog to let Photoshop handle the conversion as the data is sent to the printer. For larger prints, you might save a profiled version of the image that you will send to a service provider for printing on a LightJet 5000 photographic printer. With this approach, reorders of popular images can easily be routed to the proper vendor or on-site printer with confidence that they will print correctly and as expected.

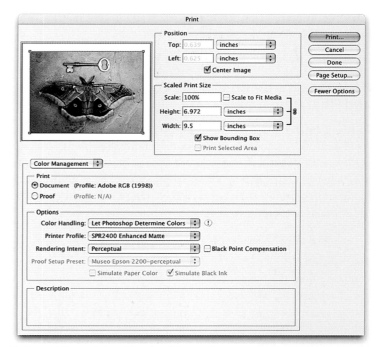

The Print with Preview dialog in Photoshop CS2, set up for printing to an Epson R2400 printer.

Portfolio

Seán Duggan

" About the image: "Along the Path"

This image, entitled, "Along the Path," is of Seán's daughter Fiona walking along a forest path near their home. Seán shot the photo with a Holga—a plastic toy camera with virtually no controls that uses medium format film and produces a square negative—then used multiple adjustment layers to adjust the contrast and apply two "flavors" of irregular sepia toning as well as faint blue tones to the image. Seán appreciates the serendipitous chance and low-tech approach that is a part of making images with toy cameras. While sharpness and clarity are not hallmarks of photos from these cameras, they are ideal for visually portraying the more intangible characteristics of memory and emotion.

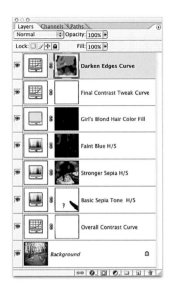

19 ◆ Making Selections

Choosing the appropriate methods and tools for making good selections is the basis for great composites and color.

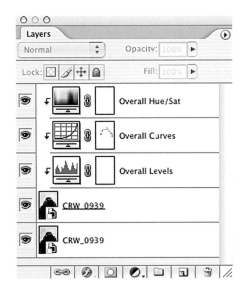

The file you will work with already has its initial color correction layers.

Most of the selections we make these days are simple. We create a rough outline of the area we need to work with, and create some sort of mask. Once we create the effect we want, we edit the mask with the Brush tool. This methodology allows you to finesse the edges of the mask while seeing the effect. You don't have to guess whether the edge will be sharp enough or soft enough, because you can see exactly how it looks as you work. This is true for both color correction and compositing.

This chapter will give you a chance to practice some often-used techniques for making selections. In some cases there are better methods for selecting certain areas, but we are going to start with easy methods. You'll be learning more advanced techniques as you go through the other chapters. If you are new to making selections, make sure you read Chapter 6, "Selections, Channels, Masks, and Paths," to get more information about how selections fit into your Photoshop workflow.

The file you'll be working with already has its initial color correction done for you. This particular image of Barry with his Pentax 6x7 camera is extremely contrasty. We've built the file with two versions of the Camera Raw image placed in the file as Smart Objects. This allows you to have one layer (the bottom one) that has detail in the sky and a second layer that has the detail for the body, hands, and camera.

In subsequent steps you'll be building several other layer masks on adjustment layers. Don't stress over making choices on the adjustments for these layers. We'll tell you what settings we used, and you can also open our final image from the DVD to see what our changes look like. For now, the emphasis is on making the selections. The next three chapters will explain how we go about making our initial color corrections.

Create a Layer Mask

Your first task is to make a selection that can be used as a layer mask on the second layer so that the sky of the lower layer can show through.

Use the Magic Wand

1a Because the sky on the bottom layer is a fairly homogenous blue, we can begin with one of the simplest tools that uses color values to create a selection, the Magic Wand. The most important setting for this tool is Tolerance. The value that you input controls how many levels of color are selected when you click the tool on a specific pixel. We'll use a tolerance value lower than 32 (the default), then use the Shift key with the tool to add areas to our selection. When you press Return (or Enter if you have an extended keyboard), you are taken to the first input areas of the Options bar. Pressing Return (Enter) a second time accepts the value that you input and returns you to the image.

◆ Open the file BarryOriginal.psd from the folder Ch19.Making-Selections on the *Photoshop Artistry* DVD. Type F to put the image in Full Screen mode.

◆ Go to Window/Layers [F10] to show the Layers palette.

◆ Turn off the Eye icon for the next-to-the-bottom layer. This also turns off the visibility for the color correction layers.

◆ Type W for the Magic Wand tool. Set the Tolerance on the Options bar to 20. You can either type directly into the input

1a The first click of the Wand will give you a selection that looks something like this.

1a By the third click of the Wand, you should have all the sky other than the small section between the handle and body of the camera selected.

area or press Return (Enter), then type 20, and press Return (Enter) again. Make sure that Contiguous is checked. Contiguous limits the selection of pixels to adjacent pixels that fall within the tolerance range.

◆ Click with the Wand somewhere in the upper-left portion of the sky. This will not select the entire sky.

◆ Hold down the Shift key as you click with the Wand in the upper-right section of the sky to add to the selection. Depending on where you click, you may need to do this one or more times to get all of the sky except for the area showing through the camera between the body and the handle. That's the next step.

Use Similar

1b Rather than use the Wand with the Shift key again for the small section between the handle and the body of the camera, we'll use the Similar command. This looks at the current selection of colors and then uses the Magic Wand's current Tolerance setting to select pixels in other areas of the image that fall within the tolerance range.

◆ Use Select/Similar to add pixels to your selection.

The Magic Wand and the Grow and Similar commands don't have to use a constant value for each new addition. You can start with a high value on the Wand to make the major portion of the selection, then lower the value before you Shift-click or use Similar or Grow to capture a smaller set of pixel values. Sometimes, you can zero in on just the colors you want this way.

Inverse the Selection and Create the Mask

1c We now have the basic selection of the sky, so we need to make the second layer active again (turn on its Eye icon) and add the selection as a layer mask. Unfortunately, the selection we just made is of

1b Your selection after using the Similar command looks like this.

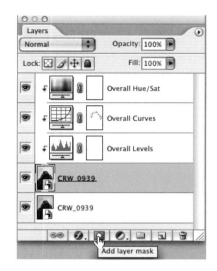

1c Click this icon to add the layer mask.

the sky, and if we create the layer mask now, the sky from the lighter, top layer will be visible and the body and camera on this layer will be masked out—exactly the opposite of what we want. So before we create the layer mask, we'll invert the selection. This is an important point to remember about making selections: Always make the selection that gives you the best and fastest results. Then, if you need the opposite selection, you can simply invert the selection or mask.

◆ Use Select/Inverse to invert the selection. The lower portion of the image is now selected.

◆ Click the next-to-the-bottom layer to make it the active layer, and turn on its Eye icon by clicking it.

◆ Click the third icon from the left on the bottom of the Layers palette. This will create a layer mask for this Camera Raw layer.

◆ Go to Filter/Blur/Gaussian Blur [Shift-F4] and blur the mask by 3.5 pixels.

You've probably already noticed some areas that don't look too good with this mask, most notably the tuft of hair just under the left side of the visor. We might have created a better mask using a channel—a technique we show you in both Chapter 21, "Overall Color Correction," and Chapter 22, "Correcting Problem Images." Sometimes, especially where hair is an issue, the Extract command does a good job of creating the initial selection. That technique is explored in Chapter 29, "Portrait Compositing." Blurring the mask by 3 or 4 pixels helps some areas, but is detrimental to others. For the final version of this file, which you can open from the DVD, we used the Brush tool to paint on this layer mask to blend the two layers together.

Darken the Top of the Camera

There are several other changes we want to make to this image. Notice how the triangular top of the camera has caught the light and really stands out as if it is the center of attention in this photo. We need to tone it down a bit. To do this, we'll make a selection with the Lasso, then clean up our selection with Quick Mask.

Use the Lasso and Polygonal Lasso

2a The area that needs to be selected here has both straight edges and curved areas. The Lasso tool can handle both types of selections. We begin with the regular Lasso, then add the Option (Alt) key to access the Polygonal Lasso. Before we begin to draw this selection, we put a small feather on our Lasso, so the edge of the selection we make is not hard but just a bit soft. This helps with blending the effect between the area being adjusted and the area that is not.

◆ Type L to access the Lasso. On the Options bar, change the feather value to 2. You can type directly into the input area or press Return (Enter), 2, Return (Enter).

◆ Begin drawing your selection in one of the curved areas to be adjusted. You can look at the illustrations to see where we started. Draw freehand until you come to a section that has a fairly straight edge.

◆ Hold down the Option (Alt) key and let go of the mouse button. Now, when you move the mouse around, you'll see a straight line from the point where you released the mouse to the point where the mouse is now stationed. Wherever you click the mouse, your selection will be anchored. You can continue to click this way connecting straight lines to straight lines, or, if you keep the mouse button down and drag, you can draw freehand again. There is no need to release the Option (Alt) key when you do this.

◆ Continue working your way around the area to be selected. When you come back to the beginning point, click to close the selection and let go of the mouse to create the selection marquee.

If you let go of the mouse before you get back to the beginning, Photoshop automatically closes the selection for you, joining the starting point and the last click. If that happens you may need to type Command (Ctrl)-D to deselect everything and start again. If your selection looks almost correct, that's good enough. We're going to finesse the selection in Quick Mask.

Use Quick Mask

2b We don't use Quick Mask a lot in the work that we do, but when you only need to make a small adjustment to a selection, it can be a quick solution. Working with Quick Mask will also help prepare you for working with mask channel overlays. The default color for the Quick Mask overlay is red, which is not the best color for this image, so we'll change the color. We'll also show you how to change whether the Quick Mask covers the masked areas or the selected areas.

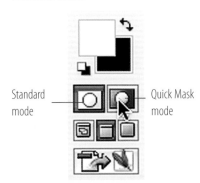

Standard mode — Quick Mask mode

2b Normal Quick Mask mode has the dark rectangle and a light circle.

2b Your initial Quick Mask will look something like this.

2a Most of the selection of this area was done by clicking with the Polygonal Lasso. It's not a perfect selection, but it leaves only a little work to be done in Quick Mask.

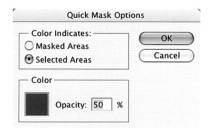

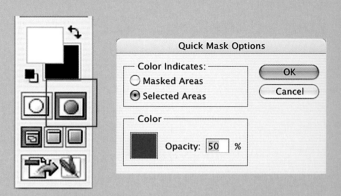

2b Set Color Indicates to Selected Areas rather than the default Masked Areas.

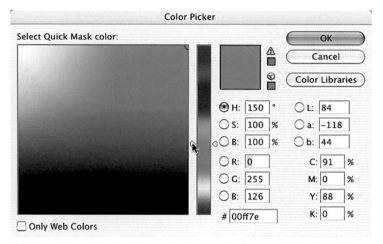

2b Slide the Hue slider to pick a different color for your overlay. Once you click OK in this dialog, you will return to the Quick Mask Options dialog, where you'll need to click OK again.

2b A green overlay makes it easier to see the edge of the camera against the orange visor.

◆ While the selection you made is still active, click the Quick Mask icon on the bottom of the Toolbox. A red overlay will cover everything except the selection you made with the Lasso. The red color is masking out areas that you do not want to alter.

◆ Double-click the Quick Mask icon on the Toolbox. A dialog appears that allows you to change whether the red color covers the masked areas (the default) or the selected areas. Click on Selected, then click OK to close this dialog.

Only the top of the camera is now covered with the overlay, and it's a little easier to determine where you need to edit the Quick Mask. However, it's confusing up at the top of this red overlay where the

Quick Mask No-No

We can't say it enough. If you use Quick Mask, do not leave it in this state with the dark circle on the inside and the light rectangle on the outside. Double-clicking the Quick Mask icon will show you that you have the overlay color indicating the selected areas. Even though Quick Mask continues to do what you expect, any mask channels that you create while in this state will show black for the selected areas and white for the masked areas—exactly the opposite of the way we normally work.

visor stops and the camera begins. Choosing a different color would make it easier to see the edges of the overlay.

◆ Double-click the Quick Mask icon again, then click once on the color square in the dialog. The Adobe Color Picker appears. Drag the slider on the vertical hue bar down until you have a bright green color. Click OK in the Color Picker, and then click OK in the Quick Mask dialog.

◆ Type B for the Brush tool and choose a soft, round 5-pixel brush from the Brush pop-up on the Options bar. If you've loaded BarrysPhotoBrushes.abr from the Ch02.Preferences folder on the DVD and opened the palette as we suggested in Chapter 3, "Navigating in Photoshop," this will be the 5-pixel brush in the third row.

◆ Type D for the default colors. When you paint with black, you'll be adding to the green overlay—painting with white removes the overlay. Clean up the edges of the overlay by painting. Type X to quickly switch from the foreground color to the background color.

If you click the Standard Mode icon at this point, you will get a selection of the top of the camera, just as you hoped. Unfortunately, you leave Quick Mask in a state that will invert any mask channel you create from this point. So we need to return Quick Mask to its

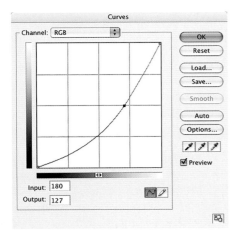

2c Here is the curve we used to darken the top of the camera. Your curve may be steeper or less steep.

3a Here's the progression of the three clicks we made with the Magic Wand. Your three clicks may give you a slightly different selection. We've highlighted the area where we clicked because it's difficult to see the cursor in these screen shots.

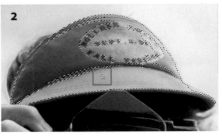

default state. Before, we double-clicked the icon to change the state of the Quick Mask mode. Here, we'll do it the easy way.

◆ Option (Alt)-click the Quick Mask icon to return it to the default of having the overlay cover the masked areas of the image. If you notice areas that need to be painted when you invert the mask, paint them now.

◆ Click the Standard Mode icon to return to the selection marquee rather than the mask.

Use Curves to Tone Down the Top of the Camera

2c Now that we have the selection we want, we'll add a Curves adjustment layer to darken the area.

◆ Go to Layer/New Adjustment Layer/Curves.

◆ Click the middle of the curve and drag it downward until the top of the camera is a middle gray rather than light gray. See the illustration or check the BarryFinal.psd file to see the curve we used.

Recolor the Visor

We'd like the visor to match the colors on the vest logo better, so we need to make a selection of the visor and use a Hue/Saturation adjustment layer to move the color more toward red.

Use the Magic Wand

3a Again, we'll start our selection with the Magic Wand.

◆ Type W for the Wand. Press Return (Enter), then type 40, and press Return (Enter) again to set the tolerance value for the tool to 40 pixels.

◆ Click a spot on the visor that you feel represents the overall color. The illustrations show where we made our clicks.

◆ Hold down the Shift key and click on any large area that has not already been selected.

◆ Make a third click in the light area on the visor above the handle of the camera.

We found that clicking the small area in the third illustration was particularly important in being able to isolate the edge of the visor correctly.

Use the Grow Command

3b The Similar command that we used earlier in this example uses the tolerance value of the Magic Wand to select nonadjacent pixels throughout the image. The Grow command uses the tolerance value to select only those pixels adjacent to the selected area that fall within the tolerance range. If we use 40 as the tolerance for the Grow command, we'll take parts of the fingers into the selection border, which we don't want, so we'll reduce the value before using the command. When you are working on an image on your own, you'll find that

3b After you use the Grow command, the selection looks something like this.

3c It's easy to add this area and the logo into the selection by using the Lasso with the Shift key.

3c Adding this area using both the Shift key and the Option (Alt) key is much trickier. Here we are just about ready to move the mouse back to the starting point and add this portion to the selection.

you often guess at a value to begin with, then make the value higher or lower after you see how much of the image is selected when you click. It's trial and error, but usually you can get a good value within about three tries. If you take too much or too little, use Command (Ctrl)-Z to undo the last selection without deselecting the area from the Magic Wand.

◆ Press Return (Enter), then type 20 and press Return (Enter) again to set the Tolerance to 20.

◆ Use Select/Grow to add pixels to your selection. You may need to use the command a second time as well. You won't have all of the visor, but you won't take much, if any, of the fingers holding the camera.

Add Areas to the Selection with the Lasso

3c Now we'll use the Lasso with modifier keys to add or subtract sections of the visor to or from the selection. You use the Shift key to add to the selection, just as you did with the Magic Wand. However, because the bottom edge of the visor still needs to be added to the selection and that edge is fairly straight, we want to add to the selection while using the Polygonal Lasso. If you remember from step 2a in this exercise, you use the Option (Alt) key to access the Polygonal Lasso from the regular Lasso tool. But once you have an active selection, holding down the Option (Alt) key also means that you want to subtract areas from the current selection. So, it's very important that you use the modifier keys in the proper order, or you'll change your selection in unintended ways. We'll walk you through it.

◆ Type L for the Lasso. You should still have a 2-pixel feather set, which is fine.

◆ Hold down the Shift key and add in the section in the crease of the visor by drawing a loose circle around it. Release the mouse to add this area to the selection.

◆ Hold down the Shift key again and add the portions of the visor's logo that were not selected.

◆ Now, hold down the Shift key and begin to draw around the lower edge of the visor. Once you've started drawing, hold down the Option (Alt) key, then release the mouse and move it to draw a straight line, clicking several times along the edge of the visor to follow the curve. We clicked three or four short sections, including one up the edge of the top of the camera.

◆ When you get back to your starting point, release the mouse first, then all modifier keys.

◆ If you need to add areas of the visor's rim on the other side of the camera, do that now.

Subtract Areas from the Selection with the Lasso

3d There may be a few areas like the top of Barry's right forefinger and some of the hair at the top of the visor that are currently in the selecton and need to be removed. Again, we use the Lasso and the

3d Draw simple loops with the Lasso and the Option (Alt) key to subtract unneeded areas from the selection.

Option (Alt) key. This time the modifier key is telling the Lasso to subtract areas from the selection. We can accomplish what we need with only two or three small selections.

◆ Hold down the Option (Alt) key and lasso any small areas that need to be removed from the selection. If you take too much away, press Command (Ctrl)-Z and try again.

You can also switch back to Shift plus the Lasso to add back in areas if you subtract too much.

Use Hue/Saturation

3e Now we'll change the color of the visor with a Hue/Saturation adjustment layer. Because we already have a selection, the adjustment layer's mask will restrict the changes that we make to only our selected area.

◆ Use Layer/New Adjustment Layer and choose Hue/Saturation. Move the Master slider to the left to about −12 to make the visor more red.

Darken the Camera Lens

4 Some selections are easy to make with the right tool and a little know-how. To darken the lens of the camera, we can use the Elliptical Marquee. To draw it and position it correctly, we use the Option (Alt) key to tell Photoshop to draw the selection from the center. In addition, we'll use the Spacebar to help us place the selection marquee as we draw it.

◆ Type M for the Marquee tool, then Shift-M for the Elliptical Marquee.

◆ Set the Feather to 2 pixels.

4 Drawing from the center out is often easier.

Subtracting with the Polygonal Lasso

If you need to subtract from a selection and you want to use the Polygonal Lasso to do it, you need to hold down the Option (Alt) key and start drawing; then, with the mouse still down release the Option (Alt) key, and press it again. After this you can draw with the Polygonal Lasso.

You can also use the Selection interaction icons on the Options bar to tell any of the selection tools that you want to add to, subtract from, or intersect with an active selection. In this case you would choose the third icon (subtract), start to draw, then add the Option (Alt) key to access the Polygonal Lasso. Using the Selection interaction icons is great if you have to do a lot of manual adding or subtracting from a selection. Using the icons also protects against inadvertently clicking with a selection tool and losing the active selection. So why do we prefer using the keyboard modifiers? If you forget to reset your Selection interaction icons to the default Create New Selection icon, you can have difficulty making your new selections. So use the icons if you need them, but remember to reset them.

◆ Hold down the Option (Alt) key, place the cursor in what you think is the middle of the lens, and drag down and out to start drawing the ellipse.

◆ When you are close to the right size and shape for the selection, keep one finger on the Option (Alt) key, and use another finger or your thumb to hold down the Spacebar. With the Spacebar down you can move the left edge of the selection border to the left edge of the lens. If you need to resize the ellipse, release the Spacebar but not the Option (Alt) key, and continue drawing. When you have the selection drawn and placed as you want it, let go of the mouse button first, then let go of both the modifier keys.

◆ Go to Layer/New Adjustment Layer/Curves [Command (Ctrl)-F4] and move the lower portion of the curve downward to darken the camera lens. Click OK to create the adjustment layer.

We often use the technique of holding down the Spacebar as we draw selections to move the selection boundary. However, you could simply draw the selection as accurately as you can, then use Select/Transform Selection to adjust the selection to fit. You can find out more about transforming in Chapter 8, "Transformation of Images, Layers, Paths, and Selections."

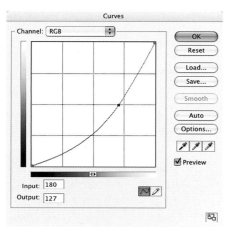

4 This is the curve we used to darken the camera lens.

Recolor the Sunshine Coast Logo

5 There are times when you don't really need to make a precise selection, because the changes that you need to make are confined to a particular color. If you plan on using Hue/Saturation to change the color of an object, look at whether that object is primarily one color and whether that color is present in the area surrounding the object to be adjusted. In the case of the Sunshine Coast logo on Barry's vest, we can change both the blue and the the yellow sun without having to make exacting selections.

◆ Type L for the Lasso and make a loose selection around the blue area of the logo.

◆ Create a Hue/Saturation adjustment layer [Command (Ctrl)-F3], and, rather than moving the Master Hue slider, use the Color pop-up to switch to Blue.

◆ Move the Blue Hue slider to the right to +10.

◆ Switch to the Cyan pop-up and move the Cyan Hue slider to the right to +10 as well. Then click OK to create the adjustment.

◆ Make a loose selection of the yellow sun in the logo, then create another Hue/Saturation adjustment layer.

◆ This time, use the Color pop-up to switch to Yellow.

◆ Move the Yellow Hue slider to +8 and the Saturation slider to +12.

In both these cases we did not need a tight selection, because the pixels adjacent to the colors we were shifting were neutral, and the portions of the image we were adjusting were primarily the color we were adjusting. Try this same technique with the visor—it works there as well if you only adjust the red colors, because neither the sky

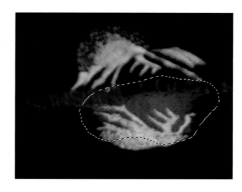

5 This is the selection we made of the blue areas of the logo.

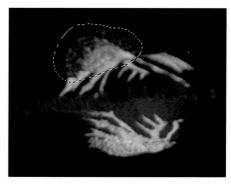

5 This is the selection we made of the sun in the logo.

nor the hair are primarily red. However, you do need to be careful with the fingers in this image. If you include them in the selection, there's enough red in them to show a difference if the adjustment is dramatic. If it's only a minor adjustment, you might get away with using this technique.

Portfolio

James Weiss

James takes pictures of Africa, and also leads photographers on photographic expeditions each year. James wanted his prints to match his photographs, and Barry's class gave him that and more. Check out James' work at www.eyesonafrica.net. You might also see pictures of the new baby.

20 ◆ Levels, Curves, and Hue/Saturation

Although Photoshop provides a wealth of tools with which to adjust your images, for much of the overall color correction in our own workflow, we use Levels, Curves and Hue/Saturation most often. After applying overall, global corrections, we also use these tools, along with layer masks, for addressing specific areas of the image. In this chapter, we'll provide an overview of the controls, features, and functionality of each of these essential color and tonal correction tools. The material in this chapter will serve as a foundation for many of the subsequent tutorials in the book.

Introduction to Levels

We'll be using Levels in the color correction tutorial in the next chapter, but before we apply it to a real world editing situation, let's take a tour of the Levels dialog and explain the different controls and how they affect the tonal range of an image.

◆ From the Ch20.Levels Curves HueSaturation folder on the *Photoshop Artistry* DVD, open the file called Paper Mill Bridge. psd. This image was taken in southwestern Vermont and contains a broad range of tonal values, including deep shadows and bright highlights. In addition, we have already added some Color Sampler points to the image so that you can track the highlight and shadow values and see how the adjustments are affecting the image.

◆ Once the image is open, make sure you can clearly see both the Info and the Histogram palettes (we'll cover the Histogram palette in more detail shortly). With these palettes clearly in view, go to the main menu and choose Layer/New Adjustment Layer/Levels. In the New Layer dialog, click OK to bring up the Levels dialog.

> **NOTE**
>
> Levels, Curves, and Hue/Saturation are used to manipulate an image's tonal (brightness) and color values. For further information on the underlying tonal and color structure of a digital image, as well as bit depth, histograms, and color management, we recommend that you read Chapters 15, 16, 17, and 18 before beginning this chapter.

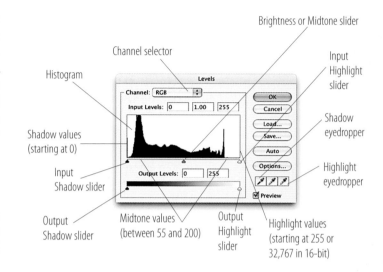

The Levels dialog.

The primary Levels controls consist of two sets of sliders, the Input Levels and Output Levels, numeric fields for these settings, and three Eyedropper tools. In the initial RGB section of the dialog, these controls let you set the value for the brightest and darkest points in the image, as well as control overall brightness. Depending on the adjustments you make, the controls can also increase or decrease contrast. The Eyedropper tools, too, can affect the color balance in the image, and we will cover them a bit later in this chapter. We'll start by taking a closer look at the Input Levels.

Input Levels

The Input Levels include a histogram display, numeric fields for the input values, and three sliders that control the shadow (black point), the highlight (white point), and the midtone.

The Input Shadow Levels (Black Point)

The location of the Input Shadow slider, on the left, sets the black point (level 0) for the image. As you move it to the right, the darkest shadows will become a solid black, and the rest of the image will also become darker. If you look closely, you will see that as you move the Input Shadow slider, the Midtone slider also moves.

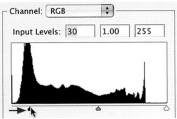

Original image

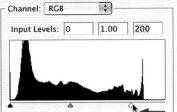

Moving the Shadow slider to the right will darken the image by remapping the black value in the image, causing the shadows and midtones to become darker. In this example, any tone at level 30 or below is being remapped to a total black (level 0). Detail is being lost in the darker areas of the photo, such as inside the covered bridge.

Original image

Moving the Input Highlight slider to the left will lighten the image by remapping the white value, causing the highlights and midtones to become brighter. In this example, any tone at level 200 or above is being chnaged to a total white (level 255). Detail is lost in the brightest areas of the photo, such as the light areas around the bridge entry.

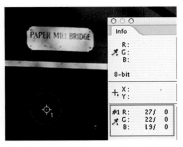

After the example adjustments above, Color Sampler points in the Info palette show clipping in the shadows (left) and the highlights (right). Numbers to the left of the slash are "before" values, while numbers on the right are "after" values.

◆ Move the Input Shadow slider to the right until the numeric value on the left reads 30. You will notice that, although the contrast and color saturation of the image have improved, detail has been lost in the darkest shadows.

◆ In the Info palette check the values for Color Sampler point #1 at the lower left. Numbers on the left of the slash represent the values before any modification, and numbers on the right show the tonal values after the adjustments. In the case of the roof beams inside the bridge—the location of Color Sampler #1—subtle shadow detail has been lost and forced to a total black.

It's important to realize that when you move the Input Shadow slider to the right, any tonal values on the histogram to the left of the slider will be changed to level 0, a total black with no detail. This means that if any subtle shadow details exist in those areas, you will be throwing that tonal detail away. If you care about that detail in the shadows, this would not be a good move to make. When tonal detail is remapped to either a total black or a total white, this is called *clipping*. In the case of this adjustment, we have clipped the shadow values below level 30.

◆ Return the Input Shadow slider to the far left side of the histogram.

The Input Highlight Levels (White Point)

The Input Highlight slider, on the right, sets the white point (level 255) for the image. As you move it to the left, bright highlights will start to turn total white, and the rest of the image will brighten. Just as with the Shadow slider, moving the Highlight slider also causes the Midtone slider to move.

◆ Move the Input Highlight slider to the left until the highlight number above it reads 200. While the overall increase in image brightness may look appealing, it is important to notice that detail has been lost in the brightest areas of the image—the parts of the bridge entry that are painted white.

◆ In the Info palette check the values for Color Sampler #2 in the lower right. The numbers to the right of the slash show that the tones of the white stripe where Color Sampler #2 is placed have been clipped to 255, a total white with no detail.

When you adjust the Input Highlight slider, any tonal values on the histogram to the right of the slider will be clipped to level 255, which is total white.

◆ Return the Input Highlight slider to the far right side of the histogram.

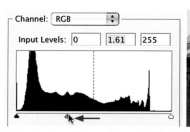

Moving the Input Midtone slider to the left will lighten the image, because a darker tone is being remapped to be the new midtone point of level 128 (the original midtone is indicated by the red dashed line). When viewing the Levels histogram, you can see that the image is becoming lighter because more of the tonal levels are being moved to the bright side of the midtone.

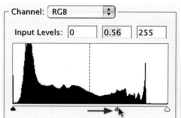

Moving the Input Midtone slider to the right will darken the image, because a brighter tone is being remapped to be the new midtone point of level 128 (the original midtone is indicated by the red dashed line). When viewing the Levels histogram, you can see that the image is becoming darker because more of the tonal levels are being moved to the dark side of the midtone.

The Midtone Slider

The Midtone slider (also known the Gamma slider), in the middle of the histogram, adjusts the brightness of the image by determining where the exact middle tonal value is (50% gray, level 128, or Zone V). Because the slider adjusts overall image brightness without affecting either the black point or the white point, we also sometimes refer to this as the Brightness slider. Moving it to the left will lighten the image, because that sets a current value that is darker than 128 to be the new level 128. Moving it to the right will darken the image, because you are choosing a current tone that is lighter than 128 to be the new level 128.

◆ Move the Midtone Brightness slider to the left and right to see how it affects the image.

Output Levels

Underneath the Input Levels are the controls for the Output Levels. These consist of two numeric fields and sliders for the shadow/black point on the left and the highlight/white point on the right. These

sliders do the opposite of the corresponding sliders in the Input Levels. Moving the Shadow slider to the right lightens the shadow tones, while moving the Highlight slider to the left will darken the highlights and make them duller.

When you set the shadow Output Levels to 10, for example, Photoshop will take any tone that is currently level 0 (black) and make it level 10. All other tonal values will be adjusted proportionately, with the end result being a lightening of the image and a decrease in contrast, especially in the shadow areas. If you were to move the Output highlight slider until the number above it read 245, any current tone with a value of 255 (white) would be darkened to level 245. This will darken the highlights slightly and reduce contrast.

◆ Move the sliders for both the black and white Output Levels and see how they affect the shadows and highlights in the image. Move your cursor over areas that used to be either very dark or very bright and see what the before and after values in the Info palette are (whenever you are working in a color or tonal correction tool, your cursor will always function as the Eyedropper tool when you move it over an image area).

Output Levels are most useful when you're making final endpoint adjustments to compensate for the limitations of a specific type of output, such as you might run into if you were printing grayscale images on newsprint. You can also use it to darken a blown-out highlight that you do not wish to print as paper-white. When we do find ourselves in need of such adjustments, however, we tend to use Curves, which can easily replicate what the Output Levels can do, but which also allows for more control over how the rest of the tonal range is affected. We'll cover this further in the Curves section later in this chapter.

◆ Press the Option (Alt) key to turn the Cancel button into a Reset button (this works in many Photoshop dialogs). Click the Reset button to return the image to its unaltered state, and click OK.

Input/Output Values in Levels and Curves: Same Dance, Different Partner

The input and output values in Levels are exactly the same as the corresponding functions in the Curves dialog; you can make the same adjustments using either command.

The actual meanings of the terms input and output are much clearer in Curves than it is in Levels. In Curves *input* refers to the original, unaltered value (before), and *output* is the modified value (after). In Levels, the input values for the endpoints (black and white) allow for darkening of the shadows or brightening of the highlights. The output values do exactly the opposite, lightening the shadows and darkening the highlights. Using the shadow tones as an example, the illustrations below show how you can apply the same adjustment using either Levels or Curves.

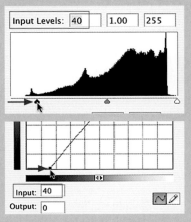

This illustration shows the same adjustment applied to the Input value in Levels (top) and Curves (below). In each case a shadow value of level 40 is being remapped to level 0 (total black). The Input (before) and Output (after) values fields in Curves make it much clearer what is happening.

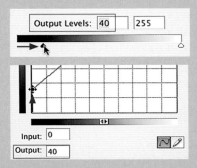

This illustration shows the same adjustment applied to the Output values in Levels (top) and Curves (bottom). In each case a shadow value of level 0 (total black) is being remapped to level 40, resulting in a lightening of the shadows.

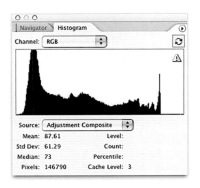

The Histogram palette shown here in expanded view. To see a before and after histogram as you are making changes to the image, open the Source menu and choose Adjustment Composite.

The Histogram Palette

Before we continue with our exploration of the Levels dialog, we'll take a short detour to consider the different types of information the Histogram palette displays, and how you can use this as you are making adjustments in Levels, Curves, or any of the color and tonal correction tools.

◆ Click the submenu button in the upper-right corner of the Histogram palette, and choose Expanded View. Set the Source menu under the histogram graphic to Adjustment Composite if it isn't already.

Using Adjustment Composite as the source allows you to see both before and after histograms as you are making changes. The original histogram is shown in gray, while the current histogram that reflects your changes is shown in black.

If you see a small exclamation mark in a triangle, this means that the histogram is currently being created from the cached image data. The image cache enables Photoshop to speed up its performance by caching different sizes of the image.

◆ To refresh the histogram so it is created from the actual image data and not the cached data (and thus is more accurate), click the exclamation mark symbol, or the refresh button just above it (the circular arrows icon).

◆ Double-click on the thumbnail for the Levels adjustment layer you added earlier to re-open the Levels dialog. Lighten the image by moving the Midtone slider to the left until the midtone values read 1.75. Release the mouse button and watch how this affects the display in the Histogram palette.

By specifying that a value in the darker part of the tonal range should be the new midtone, the shadow values to the left of the Levels Midtone slider, which range from 0 to approximately 76, are mapped

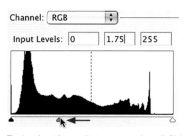

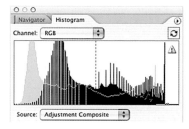

The Levels midtone adjustment seen here (left) lightens the image, and results in the altered histogram seen at right. The red dashed line represents the midtone point, and in the image on the right the original histogram is shown in gray. The adjusted histogram (displayed in black) shows that more tonal values are now on the brighter side of the midtone point.

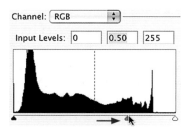

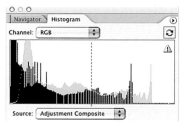

The Levels midtone adjustment seen here (left) darkens the image, and results in the altered histogram seen at right. The red dashed line represents the midtone point, and in the image on the right the original histogram is shown in gray. The adjusted histogram (displayed in black) shows that more tonal values are now on the darker side of the midtone point.

to new values and stretched across a larger area from 0 to 128. This results in the gaps that can be seen between some values. Large gaps such as these can be problematic, as they can cause uneven banding between tonal gradations, also known as posterization, that can be noticeable when an image is printed.

◆ Now darken the image by moving the Midtone slider to the right until the middle value reads 0.50. Take a look at the Histogram palette to see how the histogram has changed.

In the Histogram palette, you can see that by moving the Midtone slider to the right and specifying a lighter area as the new midtone point has stretched the highlight values over a larger area, producing some gapping on the highlight side. More image pixels have been assigned tonal values on the darker side of the midtone point, which results in more tonal values being compressed together on that side of the histogram. In the case of this adjustment, it has also resulted in some shadow clipping (tonal values forced to black), as can be seen by the tonal bars running up against the left side.

◆ Press Option (Alt) and click the Reset button in Levels to return the controls to the original, unchanged settings.

Adjusting Color with Levels

In addition to allowing corrections that can be applied to the overall brightness values, Levels also provides the means to adjust the tonal range of the individual color channels in your image. At the top of the Levels dialog is a channel selector that gives you access to the color channels. The names of the available channels will depend on the color mode you've specified for your image (for example, Grayscale, RGB, CMYK, or Lab). For the purposes of this introductory overview, we will continue working with the RGB image of the Paper Mill Bridge.

When you first enter Levels, the RGB composite channel is selected and any adjustments you make will be applied to all three color channels, resulting in changes to the overall brightness and, in some cases, the contrast of the image. You will not see shifts in color balance until you start working with the individual color channels. Let's try this out now so you can get a sense of how it works.

Modifying Color with the Midtone Slider

◆ You should still have the Levels dialog open from the previous section. If not, double-click the Levels adjustment layer thumbnail to call up the dialog. At the top of the dialog, set the Channel menu to Red.

◆ Move the Midtone slider for the Red channel to the left and then to the right. Moving the slider to the left will add red while moving it to the right will add the complement, or opposite, of red, which is cyan.

◆ Return the Midtone slider to its original postion (1.00). Then select the Green channel from the drop-down menu, and move the middle slider to the left and right. Return the slider to the starting position, and then do the same with the Blue channel.

As you can see from these quick experiments, the Green channel controls green and its opposite of magenta, and the Blue channel controls blue and its opposite of yellow. Familiarizing yourself with the relationships of these colors is important for learning and applying color correction. For example, you might need to color correct

> **NOTE**
>
> When adjusting any of the color channels in Levels, moving the Midtone slider to the left will add more of the color whose name appears in the channel selector menu, and moving it to the right will add that color's opposite.

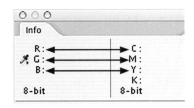

When you are working on an RGB file, the default setup for the top two panes of the Info palette provide a handy cheat sheet to help you remember the basic color relationships: Simply draw a line between the letters to see a color's opposite.

an RGB image that has a strong cyan cast to it. If you look for the Cyan channel in Levels or Curves you won't find it, but if you know the basic color relationships (red-cyan, green-magenta, blue-yellow), you will know that the Red channel is the best place to start to try and fix that color cast.

Modifying Color with the Input and Output Endpoint Sliders

As we saw in the previous section, moving the Midtone sliders for the different color channels will affect the midtone color balance in an image, by shifting the colors between the selected color and its opposite. The Input and Output sliders do the same thing, but their primary effect is on the highlights and shadows.

◆ Press the Option (Alt) key and press the Reset button in the Levels dialog to reset the sliders, and try experimenting with the

Input and Output Shadow and Highlight sliders for the different color channels.

In the Red Levels, the colors you work with are either red or its opposite of cyan. Adjusting the Input and Output endpoint sliders will have the following effects: Moving the Input Highlight slider to the left will add red to the highlights, and moving the Input Shadow slider to the right will add cyan to the shadows. Since the Midtone slider always moves whenever either endpoint slider is adjusted, you will also see changes throughout the entire image. Moving the Output Shadow slider to the right will add red to the shadows, and moving the Output Highlight slider to the left will add cyan to the highlights.

In the Green Levels, the colors you work with are green or its opposite of magenta. Moving the Input Highight slider to the left will add green to the highlights, and moving the Input Shadow slider to the right will add magenta to the shadows. Moving the Output Shadow slider to the right will add green to the shadows, and moving the Output Highlight slider to the left will add magenta to the highlights.

In the Blue Levels, the colors you control are blue or its opposite of yellow. Moving the Input Highlight slider to the left will add blue to

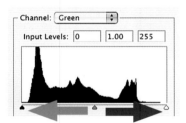

The Red Levels control red and its opposite color, cyan.

The Green Levels control green and its opposite color, magenta.

The Blue Levels control blue and its opposite color, yellow.

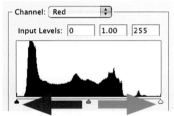

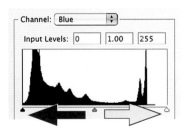

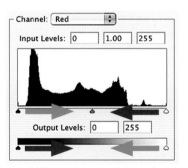

In the Red Levels, the Input and Output Shadow and Highlight sliders allow you to add red or cyan to the shadows or highlights.

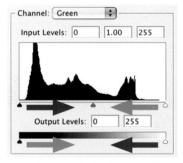

In the Green Levels, the Input and Output Shadow and Highlight sliders allow you to add green or magenta to the shadows or highlights.

In the Blue Levels, the Input and Output Shadow and Highlight sliders allow you to add blue or yellow to the shadows or highlights.

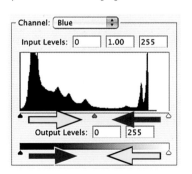

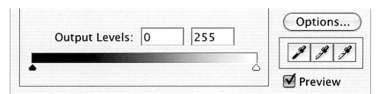

The Levels Eyedropper tools.

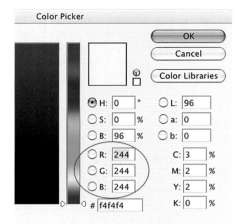

The Color Picker showing the target values for the highlight eyedropper.

the highlights, and moving the Input Shadow slider to the right will add yellow to the shadows. Moving the Output Shadow slider to the right will add blue to the shadows, and moving the Output Highlight slider to the left will add yellow to the highlights.

The Levels Eyedropper Tools

The final area of the Levels dialog we will cover are the Eyedropper tools that are in the lower-right corner above the preview check box. You use these tools to set target values in the image for the shadows (black point) and the highlight (white point), and to specify that a tone should be a neutral gray. We will not go into these in depth here, since we'll explore how to use them in the tutorial in the next chapter.

The Highlight (White Point) Eyedropper

This eyedropper remaps any pixel you click on to the target value that has been set for the tool. Clicking the eyedropper once will turn it on; it will appear darker gray and slightly recessed. Clicking twice brings up the Color Picker, where you can either inspect or set the target values (more on that in a bit).

Just as moving the Input Levels Highlight slider will remap the midtone point as well as the highlight values, clicking in the image with this eyedropper will have a similar effect on both areas of the tonal range. The default value for this eyedropper is 255 for red, green, and blue. This, of course, is a total white, with no detail and, in general, is not really appropriate for photographic images.

In Chapter 2, "Preferences and Color Settings," we directed you to change the target values for this eyedropper to ones more appropriate for photographic use. To access and change the target values you

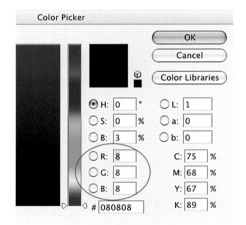

The Color Picker showing the target values for the shadow eyedropper.

double-click the highlight or white-point eyedropper, which will bring up the Color Picker. The values for red, green, and blue should each be set to 244. As we shall see in the next chapter, using this eyedropper tool properly not only can help to set a specified target value as the brightest point in the image with highlight detail, but can also ensure that the highlight is neutral (without any color cast).

The Shadow (Black Point) Eyedropper

This eyedropper is used for setting a precise target value for the shadows or black point. Double-clicking the eyedropper will open the Color Picker. The default is 0, which is a total black with no detail. If you have set the values as recommended in Chapter 2, the values for red, green, and blue should each be set to 8.

Just as with the highlight eyedropper, this tool not only allows you to set a precise shadow value for the darkest pixel in your image, it also ensures that those shadows are neutral. Having highlights and shad-

> **NOTE**
>
> In most photographs, the only time a white tone should have a value of 255 for all three color channels is if it is a specular highlight—a very bright tone such as that produced by reflections off of metal, glass, or water.

ows that are neutral is one of the central tenets of color correction, and on some images, the use of just these two eyedroppers can go a long way toward fixing color cast problems.

The Gray-Point Eyedropper

In addition to the white- and black-point eyedroppers for targeting the values of the highlights and shadows, Levels also offers a gray-point eyedropper. The default target values for this eyedropper are 128, 128, 128, which is an exact neutral gray tone. In some situations you can use this to help neutralize a color cast that is primarily affecting the midtone values. The caveat here is that the image needs to contain a tonal area that should be neutral (such as gray concrete or metal).

Unlike the highlight and shadow eyedroppers, which change the brightness and the color balance, this tool changes only the color balance and does not really alter the overall brightness values. So even though the default value is set to 128 for all three channels, you can click a very dark area and it will still remain dark, and you can use it on a bright highlight without altering the basic brightness of that area. Some brightness changes take place on a per-channel basis in order to create a neutral tone, but in most cases the overall brightness level is not affected.

We don't use the gray-point eyedropper very often for several reasons. First, the highlight and shadow eyedroppers, properly used, often do much of the color cast removal for us. Second, we generally prefer to adjust the color balance ourselves, using the sliders in the Levels color channels or in Curves. Finally, this tool also tends to be more picky in terms of the tone you choose to use it on than the white-balance eyedropper in the Camera Raw dialog, which performs a very similar function but is generally much more effective. Still, in some instances and with the right image, it may help you remove a troublesome color cast. The main thing to remember is that you have to use it on a tone that should be neutral.

The Levels Clipping Display

Before you use the highlight and shadow eyedroppers to set a specific black- and white-point value, you need to determine where the brightest and darkest points in the image are. The Levels dialog provides an easy way to do this through its clipping display. We will cover exactly how to do this in greater detail in the next chapter when we take you through a basic color correction exercise, but we want to introduce the concept here and explain some of the display's nuances.

◆ From the Chapter 20 folder on the DVD, open the file called Protest.psd. This is an image that we have prepared specifically for this discussion by adding colored bars to demonstrate how to interpret the clipping display.

◆ Bring up the Levels dialog using Image/Adjustments/Levels. Hold down the Option (Alt) key, and click and hold down the Input Highlight slider. Most of the image will turn black. Apart from the colored gradient bars at the lower right, which we will discuss shortly, you will see some red areas on the banner and two small white specks from the white helmets of the two police officers in the background.

When the highlight clipping display is shown, white areas indicate places where the tonal value is 255 in all three color channels. Areas that are red, green, or blue, such as the red spots on the banner, indi-

The Protest image. We have added the gradient color bars to this image to illustrate how the clipping displays work in Levels.

Option (Alt)-clicking the Input Highlight slider in Levels results in this highlight clipping display for the Protest image. White areas indicate clipping in all three color channels. Colored areas indicate clipping in one or two color channels. Black indicates no clipping.

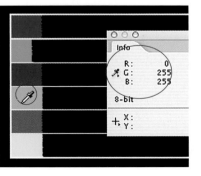

Color analysis of a highlight clipping display in an RGB file: Red, green, and blue indicate highlight clipping (level 255) in those colors. Cyan indicates clipping in the Green and Blue channels (as shown by the eyedropper and Info readout in this illustration); magenta shows clipping in the Red and Blue channels; and yellow reveals clipping in the Red and Green channels. White shows clipping in all three channels.

Option (Alt)-clicking the Input Shadow slider in Levels results in this shadow clipping display for the Protest image. Black areas indicate clipping in all three color channels. Colored areas indicate clipping in one or two color channels. White indicates no clipping.

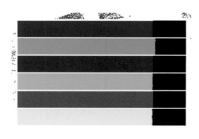

Color analysis of a shadow clipping display in an RGB file: Red, green and blue indicate shadow clipping (level 0) in the other two channels (red = clipping in Green and Blue; green = clipping in Red and Blue; blue = clipping in Red and Green). Cyan indicates clipping in the Red channel; magenta shows clipping in the Green channel; and yellow reveals clipping in the Blue channel. Black shows clipping in all three channels.

cate that the value is 255 in that color channel. Areas that show up as cyan, magenta, or yellow indicate that the value is clipped to 255 in two of the color channels. Cyan represents blue and green, magenta represents blue and red, and yellow represents red and green.

◆ Move the Input Highlight slider to the left (still holding down the Option (Alt) key), and you will see more areas begin to appear as bright, flat tones of color, and then turn to white.

The more you move the slider to the left, the more tones get clipped to 255, either in individual color channels, or in all three channels. It is important to stress that this is not an adjustment that you will actually apply to the image; it is simply a way to identify where in an image clipping is occurring, and in which color channels. In a typical photo with bright highlights, finding the areas that turn white first is also a handy way of identifying the brightest points in the image in all three color channels.

◆ Now return the slider to the right side, and try the same thing with the shadows. Hold down Option (Alt), and click and hold the Input Shadow slider. Most of the image will turn white, which indicates no shadow clipping, but there are large areas of magenta, cyan, blue and red. Wherever you see a color, it means there is shadow clipping in that part of the image. In the deep shadows

in the background, some areas are totally black. This indicates that those areas are already clipped to level 0 in all three channels.

To decipher the meaning of the colors in the shadow clipping display, let's look at the collection of color gradient bars we have placed in this image. These gradients transition from a fully saturated red, green, blue, cyan, magenta, or yellow to black. Whenever you see red, green, or blue in a shadow clipping display, it means that the tones are clipped in the other two channels. You can see a numerical representation of this by placing your cursor on the left side of the red bar and looking at the values in the Info palette. You'll see that red is 255 (fully saturated), while green and blue are both at 0 (no detail). So when you see red in the shadow clipping display, it means that the details are clipped to black—no tonal detail—in the Green and Blue channels. Green means that detail is clipped in the Red and Blue channels, and blue means that detail is clipped in the Green and Red channels.

To understand what the colors of cyan, magenta, and yellow mean in a shadow clipping display, you need to know what that color's opposite, or complementary, color is. When you see cyan it means the red shadow detail is clipped; if you see magenta it means there is shadow clipping in the Green channel; and if you see yellow, it means that there is no shadow detail in the Blue channel. In the woman's red sweater, for instance, you can see a lot of magenta tones in the shadow clipping display. This simply means that the Green channel is contributing no detail to those parts of the image. All of the detail is coming from the Red and Blue channels (red + blue = magenta).

How the Clipping Display Fits into the Overall Color Correction Process

Knowing how to show the clipping displays, as well understanding what they mean, is an important part of the overall color correction process that we cover in this book and teach in our workshops. Apart from the most basic function of alerting you to where clipping might be occurring in certain channels, it is also highly useful for identifying the brightest and darkest points in an image, as you will see in the next chapter. In addition, as you saw in Chapter 9, "Camera Raw," these basic colors also show up in the clipping display in Adobe Camera Raw.

Familiarizing yourself with the basic color component relationships (green and blue = cyan; red and blue = magenta; red and green = yellow) is also important for deciphering what the histogram is telling you in the Camera Raw dialog, or in the Histogram palette if you choose to view the full color histogram.

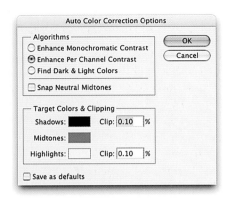

You can access the Auto Color Correction Options by clicking the Options button in the Levels or Curves dialog.

The original Hoover Dam image is too dark, a bit too blue, and lacking in contrast.

Auto Color Correction Options

Photoshop does offer some automatic color correction options in the form of Auto Levels, Auto Contrast, and Auto Color, which can be found in the Image/Adjustments menu. We generally do not favor the autocorrections, simply because we prefer to make critical color correction decisions for ourselves. Additionally, a big part of this book has always been to help our readers and students learn these essentials themselves rather than relying on a canned auto correction formula. Still, we recognize the strong temptation to click anything in Photoshop labeled "auto" that promises to do the job for you. So in this section, we'll give you an overview of just what the autocorrections are doing to your image and, more important, show you a way to take advantage of these corrections and still have the ability to further adjust or fine-tune the initial correction.

Unfortunately, the place where the autocorrections are most visible to users is also the worst way to apply them. When accessed from the Image/Adjustments menu, Auto Levels, Auto Contrast, or Auto Color simply applies a formula correction directly to the pixels, offering no dialog where you can change the settings or preview to see whether you like the effect (if you're using the custom *Photoshop Artistry* menus, you'll need to click Show All Menu Items to see these choices). So our advice here is firm: Stay away from the autocorrections in the Image/Adjustments menu!

The best way to see if the autocorrections improve your image is to add a Levels or Curves adjustment layer and apply the corrections using the Options button in those dialogs. When you click that button, the Auto Color Correction Options dialog appears (the Auto button in Levels or Curves simply applies the default settings of this dialog). At the top are three algorithms that perform the same corrections as the three auto options in the Image/Adjustments menu. Enhance Monochromatic Contrast is the same as Auto Contrast;

Enhance Monochromatic Contrast (Auto Contrast) has improved the contrast, but the image is still too blue.

Enhance Per Channel Contrast (Auto Levels) does a much better job with both contrast and color adjustment in this image.

Find Dark & Light Colors (Auto Color) with Snap Neutral Midtones checked is very similar to Enhance Per Channel Contrast, though not quite as bright.

Are the Auto Color Corrections Worth Your Time?

The answer to this is the same as the answer to many questions regarding digital imaging: It depends. It depends on the image and the color problems it may have; how successful the initial autocorrections are; and your own experience with color correction.

If you're comfortable working with Levels and Curves and know how to tinker "under the hood" to make adjustments to an image's color balance and contrast, then we suspect you'll find the autocorrections to be a bit too clunky and imprecise. In most cases, we think it's easier to use the color correction approaches that we will show you in the next two chapters.

But if you are new to Photoshop and to color correction, then this feature might help you to make the initial adjustments that will get your image "in the ballpark" of where it needs to be. Then you can fine-tune it with further corrections in Levels or Curves.

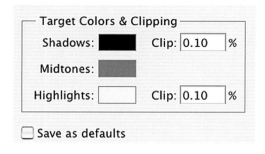

In the lower half of the Auto Color Correction Options dialog, you can specify the target colors for the shadows, midtones, and highlights, as well as the percentage by which the shadow and highlight endpoints are clipped by the adjustments.

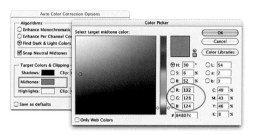

With Find Dark and Light Colors (Auto Color) and Snap Neutral Midtones checked, we clicked the midtone color swatch and changed the value of the midtone for this image, increasing the red value and slightly lowering the blue to create a warmer look.

Enhance Per Channel Contrast is the same as Auto Levels; and Find Light & Dark Colors is the same as Auto Color. There is also an option called Snap Neutral Midtones. Let's take a look at what each adjustment does to the image.

What the Autocorrections Do

Enhance Monochromatic Contrast (Auto Contrast), increases contrast by applying the same adjustment to the endpoint sliders for each color channel. While this choice is sometimes useful for making a quick contrast adjustment, it will do nothing to fix a color cast, which makes it the least useful of the three options in this dialog.

Enhance Per Channel Contrast (Auto Levels) adjusts the sliders in each color channel individually with the aim of increasing contrast and fixing color casts. This is somewhat more useful, but the results are very image-dependent: Sometimes you get a correction that works well, but just as often it makes the image look worse.

Find Dark & Light Colors (Auto Color) is the most promising option of the three. It identifies the darkest and brightest tones in the image and remaps them to be a neutral highlight and shadow using the target values for the Levels eyedroppers as a guide. When the Snap Neutral Midtones box is checked, it locates any midtone value that is close to neutral and adjusts it so it becomes neutral.

The result of using Find Dark & Light Colors (Auto Color) and Snap Neutral Midtones with the custom, warmer midtone balance described in the illustration above.

Fine-Tuning the Autocorrections

For both Enhance Per Channel Contrast and Find Dark & Light Colors, the result is usually better if you click the Snap Neutral Midtones button. This is not always the case, however, and until you understand how the autocorrections are evaluating and then adjusting an image, the success or failure rate may seem very arbitrary.

If after applying these corrections the overall feel of the color in the image is still not quite right, or if you notice that bright highlights are in danger of blowing out to a total white, you can fine-tune the correction in the lower part of the dialog. The default shadow and highlight clipping values of 0.10% are a good starting point, but if you measure the bright highlights in your image and feel they are too bright, you can reduce this value.

A dinner table display on the *Queen Mary*. The strong color cast is caused by the lighting.

Enhance Monochromatic Contrast (Auto Contrast) shows no perceptible improvement.

Enhance Per Channel Contrast (Auto Levels) does not address the color problem, and causes the contrast to become flatter.

Find Dark & Light Colors (Auto Color) attempts to fix the color, but the result is still pretty ugly.

Find Dark and Light Colors (Auto Color) with Snap Neutral Midtones checked is the best yet, but it is still much too blue and too flat.

Manual corrections applied in Levels.

For the overall color balance, click the midtone color swatch and change the values for R, G, or B in the Color Picker to shift the color balance to something more acceptable (make these adjustments in small increments). The important thing to remember is that you should not try to make everything perfect with this one adjustment. If you decide to use the auto corrections at all, they should be used as an initial step to get the overall state of the image in the proverbial ballpark. You should do your real fine-tuning in Levels or, for the most control, in Curves.

The best thing about test-driving the autocorrections with this dialog is that once you click OK, you are still in the Levels or Curves adjustment layer dialog and are free to make additional corrections. On the rare occasions when we do use this feature, we always follow up the initial corrections with fine-tuning in either Levels or Curves.

When the Autocorrections Fail

The primary Achilles' heel of the autocorrections is that they rely on a formulaic approach in evaluating and adjusting the tonal values of an image, and with some images the formula just doesn't work. A prime example is a photo that has a strong color cast but also a pure black and a pure white. The presence of those white and black points will confuse the autocorrections just enough so that they will do nothing to fix the color cast, or they will attempt to fix it but with unacceptable results.

The failure of the autocorrections can be seen in the photograph of the dinner table aboard the *Queen Mary*. None of the autocorrections address the ugly color cast caused by the interior lighting, because they're confused by the presence of a black point in the shadows under the table and a white point in the form of a specular highlight on the covered serving dish by the flowers. We were able to get a much better correction simply by adjusting the Levels sliders manually. This illustrates the importance of knowing how to make these adjustments yourself rather than relying on the automatic color corrections.

Introduction to Curves

The Curves dialog, one of Photoshop's most essential features, offers powerful and precise capabilities that make it the tonal and color correction tool of choice for many professionals and amateurs alike. Although new users may find it intimidating at first, it's definitely worth your while to learn it if you want to do serious work in Photoshop. In this section, we'll take a look at the dialog and explore some Curves essentials.

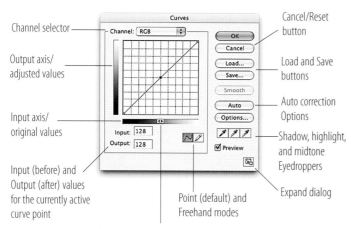

Channel selector

Output axis/
adjusted values

Input axis/
original values

Input (before) and
Output (after) values
for the currently active
curve point

Cancel/Reset
button

Load and Save
buttons

Auto correction
Options

Shadow, highlight,
and midtone
Eyedroppers

Expand dialog

Point (default) and
Freehand modes

Click here to switch between black on the
left with levels values (0 to 255), or black on
the right with the readout given in ink dot
percentages (0% to 100%).

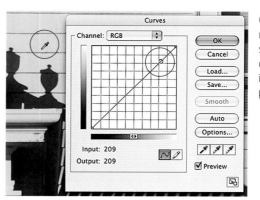

Click and hold down the
mouse button in the image to
see where that tone lies on the
curve. Command (Ctrl)-click
in the image to place a control
point there.

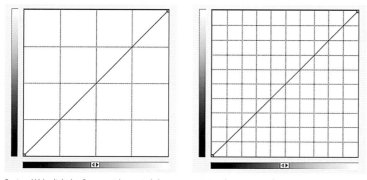

Option (Alt)-click the Curves grid to switch between a 4x4 and a 10x10 grid.

Most adjustments that you can make with Levels (with the exception of the black- and white-point clipping display) you can also make with Curves, but the latter tool provides much more control over specific areas of the tonal range and more ways to modify them. Where Levels lets you adjust the white point, black point, and midtone point, Curves allows you to adjust individual points anywhere along the tonal scale. In Levels you have five sliders that essentially allow you to adjust only three areas of the tonal range: the endpoints (black and white) and the midtone. With Curves, you can place as many as 16 points on the curve and adjust each one separately.

Deconstructing the Curves Dialog

Levels shows you the graphic display of the histogram when you enter the dialog, but Curves is somewhat enigmatic, presenting you

only with a grid of squares bisected by a diagonal line running from the lower-left corner to the upper-right corner. Once you know how it operates, however, it's not so mysterious.

Changing the Grid Size

The default configuration for Curves shows a 4x4 grid. By Option (Alt)-clicking anywhere inside the grid, you can toggle between the 4x4 grid and a 10x10 grid. For photographers who are familiar with the Zone System, working with the 10x10 grid may help demystify Curves a bit, since it divides the tonal range into 10 steps (the Zone System actually uses 11 steps, from Zone 0 (black) to Zone X (white), but the 10x10 grid is a close approximation of this). The exact middle point on the curve grid, level 128, would represent Zone V. The 4x4 grid is useful for those who are used to working with press reproduction and like to divide the image into shadow, three-quarter-tone, midtone, quarter-tone, and highlight.

Finding a Tone on the Curve

If you move the cursor over your image while holding down the mouse button, you will see a ball appear on the line, indicating where that image tone can be manipulated on the curve. Command (Ctrl)-click to place a control point on the curve that corresponds to the area in the image where you clicked. To remove points from the curve, simply click them and drag them out of the curve grid.

How to Interpret the Curve

In the default configuration for an RGB image, black (level 0) is in the lower-left corner, the midtone point (level 128 or Zone V) is in the exact center of the graph, and white (level 255) is in the upper-right corner. The horizontal axis of the grid and the gray ramp under the grid represent the input, or unaltered, values, as does the default diagonal curve line. The vertical axis and the gray ramp on the left

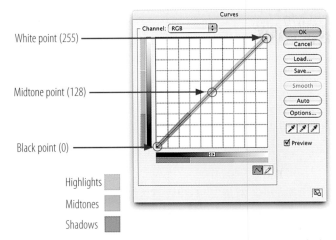

White point (255)

Midtone point (128)

Black point (0)

Highlights

Midtones

Shadows

The horizontal gray ramp underneath the grid represents the input, or existing, tonal values, and the vertical gray ramp on the left side of the grid represents the output, or modified, tonal values. The colors in this illustration indicate the placement of shadows, midtones, and highlights on both the curve and the input and output gray ramps.

side represent the output, or altered, values. You can change the orientation of the lower gray ramp, and the values used to describe your adjustments, by clicking anywhere inside it. Black on the left side of the lower gray ramp will display digital values (0 to 255), and white on the left will display ink dot percentages (0% to 100%).

To see how the grid lines and the gray ramps can help you understand how Curves is modifying the tonal range of an image, try the following:

◆ From the Chapter 20 folder on the DVD, open the file Marshall Point House.psd.

◆ Add a new Curves adjustment layer (Layer/New Adjustment Layer/Curves). Click OK in the New Layer dialog to bring up the Curves dialog. Make sure that you have a 10x10 grid to work in (Option (Alt)-click in the grid to change it), and ensure that black is on the left side of the horizontal gray ramp under the grid (click inside it if you need to change it).

◆ In the Marshall Point House image, click and hold the mouse button down in the lowest middle glass pane of the window on the right. In the Curves dialog, an indicator should appear in the vicinity of the graph's center intersection.

◆ Place a point directly in the center of the graph by clicking there. This point represents a middle gray tone. If you follow the vertical grid line down from the point, it will end at the corresponding tone in the lower gray ramp (in this case, that tone is hidden by the arrow buttons). If you follow the horizontal line out to the

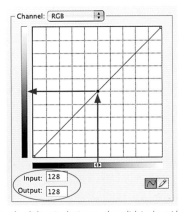

Find the tonal value for the lower part of the window by clicking in the image, then click in the grid to place a point there. The window tonal value is approximately at the midtone point. The lower gray ramp represents unaltered values, and the vertical gray ramp represents adjusted values. At this point no changes have been made, so the indicated gray tones and the input and output values are the same.

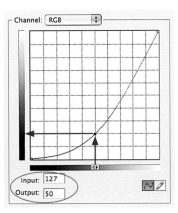

The midpoint of 128 is lowered to 50, remapping that tone to a much darker value.

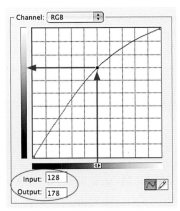

The midpoint of 128 is raised to 178, remapping that tone to a much brighter value.

Before and after versions of the image showing the effects of the S-curve shown below. The red circles in the image on the right indicate where Color Sampler points have been placed to track the changes in highlight and shadow values (see the Info palette below).

left, you see it end in the middle gray tone on the vertical gray ramp. You've made no changes yet, so the input and output values are the same.

◆ Now, change the output value to 50 using the Output field in the lower-left corner (you can also just drag straight down to the point shown in the illustration). The curve moves downward, and the image becomes darker. Follow the horizontal grid line from the adjusted point on the curve to the left side, and it will end at the corresponding tone in the side gray ramp that represents the new, darker tone. Of course, since the entire curve moved, the entire image becomes darker, not just that one point.

◆ Change the output value to 178. The curve moves upward, and the image becomes much lighter. Follow the horizontal grid line from the adjusted point on the curve to the left side, and it will end at the corresponding tone in the side gray ramp that represents the new, brighter tone.

As you can see from these example moves, dragging the curve down darkens the image, and dragging it up lightens it. It might help to remember that in the digital tonal scale, higher numbers represent brighter tones, while lower numbers indicate darker tones. By dragging the curve up, you are adjusting the value of the point you clicked (as well as other parts of the curve) upward, increasing the numeric value of the tones and making them lighter. To use a photographic analogy, you are increasing the exposure and giving the image more light. Dragging the curve downward does just the opposite, decreasing the value and darkening the image. This would be akin to giving a scene less exposure to make it darker.

Using Curves to Adjust Contrast

In photographs, contrast typically refers to the relationship between the light and dark tones in an image. When they differ significantly, that gives definition and separation to the various tonal regions. We describe such an image as having good contrast. If there is too much difference, we tend to think of the image as being high contrast, and when the difference between the highlights and shadow tones is

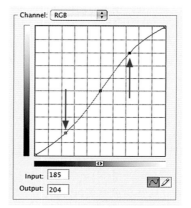

The S-curve adjustment to increase contrast in the Marshall Point House image. At right is the Info palette showing the how the numbers for the shadow (#1) and highlight (#2) Color Sampler points have changed (original values are to the left of the slash and modified values to the right).

minimal, we describe the image as being low contrast, or "flat." You modify the contrast by making separate adjustments to the bright tones and the dark tones of an image.

Curves is the primary tool for applying precision contrast adjustments in Photoshop. Once you get the hang of working with it, you'll never again go back to the crude, blunt instrument that is the Brightness/Contrast command.

Increasing Contrast

To illustrate a few contrast concepts, we'll use the Marshall Point House image from the previous example. We'll begin with a simple S-curve to increase contrast.

Before (left) and after versions of the image showing the effects of the reverse S-curve shown below.

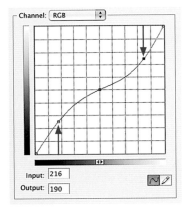

A reverse S-curve to decrease contrast. This type of curve will reduce contrast by lightening shadow values and darkening highlight values.

◆ Bring up the Curves dialog either by adding a Curves adjustment layer (Layer/New Adjustment Layer/Cuves) or by choosing Image/Adjustments/Curves.

◆ Click in the middle of the grid on the exact center intersection of horizontal and vertical grid lines to place a control point.

◆ Now click and place a point in the middle of the upper curve section between the center point and the top-right corner. Click and place a point in the middle of the lower section, between the center point and the bottom-left corner.

◆ Click the point on the highlight section of the curve, and drag upward a bit. Click the point on the shadow section of the curve and drag downward a bit. The result is an increase in contrast; the lighter tones have become brighter and the darker tones have become darker. This type of curve is called an S-curve, because of its subtle S shape.

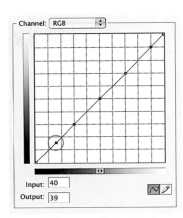
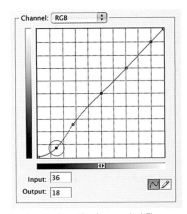

Using a lockdown curve: On the left is the curve before the adjustment has been applied. The target point that will be adjusted is circled in red. On the right is the adjusted curve showing how the lockdown points have kept the upper part of the curve from moving. A slight downward adjustment has also been made to the point immediately above the lowest point.

Before (left) and after views of the image after only the shadows have been darkened by adjusting a specific area on the curve using lockdown points to control the rest of the curve.

NOTE

For fine adjustments, you can use the arrow keys on the keyboard to move an active control point on the curve. The up and down arrow keys move the point vertically and change the Output (after) value, and the left and right arrow keys move the point horizontally, changing the Input (before) value. Using the Shift key with the arrow keys will move the point in increments of 10 tonal levels.

Decreasing Contrast

If you have an image that you feel has too much contrast, you can decrease the contrast by making an adjustment that is essentially a reverse S-curve: Raise the shadow part of the curve and lower the highlight part of the curve. By bringing the brightness values of the highlight and shadow tones closer together, you are making them less different, and so the contrast in the image is decreased. You can use this technique to tame the highlights in scenes with extreme contrast. Keep in mind that it won't magically bring back detail if such detail was never recorded by the camera, but it can temper the bright highlights so they are less harsh and glaring.

Adjusting Specific Areas

One of the areas where Curves is more powerful than Levels is the ability it gives you to make precise adjustments that affect only specific areas of the tonal range. As we have seen, when you click the image and hold the mouse button down, a small circle appears on the curve to show you where on the curve that specific image tone is located. This allows you to identify exactly what part of the curve needs to be changed. Although the entire curve will move if you are working with just a single point, by placing additional points to keep the rest of the curve in control, you can apply precise and targeted modifications to the tonal range. This technique is known as using a "lockdown curve," and we'll explore it with the Marshall Point House image.

◆ Bring up the Curves dialog or add a Curves adjustment layer, as we did in previous examples with this image. Move your cursor over the shaded window panes of the lower window and click and hold down the mouse button to find that tone on the curve.

If you Command (Ctrl)-click in the image it will automatically place a point at that location on the curve.

◆ Next, click every other intersection on the diagonal curve to place lockdown points. These will keep those areas of the curve from moving as you make adjustments to the lower part where the darker window tones are.

◆ Click back on the original point in the lower left that represents the tonal area you want to adjust (the shadows). Start to drag the point down a bit to darken the shadows, You can also click the point to make it active, and then use the up or down arrow keys on the keyboard to adjust it. Notice that the points you placed along the middle and upper parts of the curves are keeping those areas "locked down," so the adjustment is affecting only the darkest parts of the image.

Creating and Saving Lockdown Curves

Lockdown curves can be very useful for making controlled adjustments to specific areas of the tonal range. Sometimes you may need to create a more precise lockdown curve with more control points. To save yourself the repetitive work of placing points every time you need to use a lockdown curve, you should consider saving the curve

Luminosity Blending with Curves

In RGB images, brightness, contrast, and color are controlled by the three color channels, and sometimes a Curves adjustment can introduce an unwanted color shift. You can see this in the Marshall Point House image. In the step where the shadows were darkened, those tones have taken on a slight bluish color cast. To remove the cast while also making sure the adjustment is applied to only the brightness, or luminosity, of the image, change the Blend mode for the Curves adjustment layer to Luminosity.

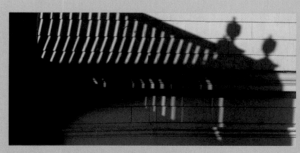

The Curves layer set to Normal.

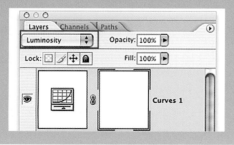

The Luminosity Blend mode selected in the Layers palette.

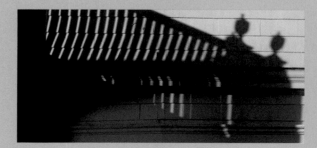

The Curves layer set to Luminosity.

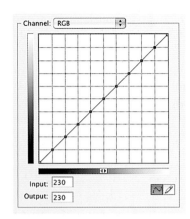

Input: 230
Output: 230

A lockdown curve with a control point at each intersection (left) and a group of saved lockdown curves (above).

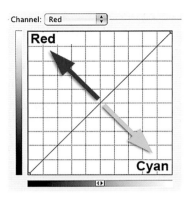

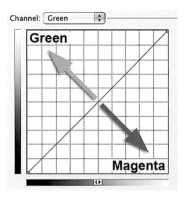

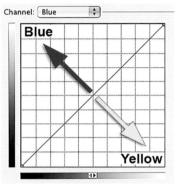

How color balance is affected when making adjustments in the Red, Green, and Blue curves.

after you create it. This will allow you to use it on other images without having to set new control points every time.

For a lockdown curve to use on the main RGB curve, click to place a point at every intersection along the diagonal line. (To make the grid larger and the intersection lines easier to see, click the Grow button in the lower-right corner of the Curves dialog.) Then press the Save button, name the curve "RGB_Lockdown_Curve," and save it to your hard drive (we suggest creating a specific folder for your custom Photoshop settings). You might also choose to open the Channel menu at the top of the Curves dialog and create a lockdown curve for each of the three color channels. These would be named "RED_Lockdown_Curve," GREEN_Lockdown_Curve," and "BLUE_Lockdown_Curve." You can also create a curve where all three color channel curves and the RGB curve are locked down.

Color Adjustments with Curves

With Curves, as with Levels, not only can you make adjustments to brightness and contrast, but you can also access the individual Red, Green, and Blue color channels in an RGB image, or the Cyan, Magenta, Yellow, and Black channels in a CMYK image.

The color relationships are the same as we saw in the section on Levels earlier in this chapter. In an RGB image, modifications to the Red curve will affect red and its opposite, cyan; adjustments to the Green curve will affect green and its opposite, magenta; and changes to the Blue curve will affect blue and its opposite, yellow. Having a good understanding of the basic color relationships is essential for color correction work in Photoshop.

The shadow, midtone, and highlight sections of the curve function the same as in the main RGB curve, but they affect only the color channel you're working in. If you wanted to remove a reddish cast from the highlights, for example, you would work on the upper-

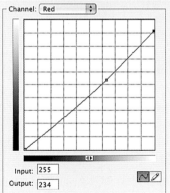

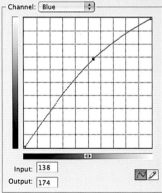

Input: 255
Output: 234

Input: 138
Output: 174

The *Queen Mary* dinner table image above left has a strong reddish/yellow color cast due to the tungsten display lighting that illuminated the scene. The color cast was corrected (above right) by adjusting the Red and Blue curves as shown above.

right portion of the curve in the Red channel, pulling it to slightly to subtract red by adding its complement, cyan. Although lockdown curves can come in handy when you're making subtle adjustments to the color channels to control the areas you do not want affected, in some cases you may need to rely on the precision of applying your color corrections using layer masks. We will cover using Curves and layer masks in Chapter 21, "Overall Color Correction," and Chapter 22, "Correcting Problem Images."

A sepia tone was added to this grayscale image by first converting to RGB mode and then adding red with the Red curve and yellow by pulling down on the Blue curve. The red and yellow combine to create a brown tone.

In addition to correcting color images, Curves (and Levels) can also be used to create toning effects for black-and-white images. To add a sepia tone, for example, you first convert the image to RGB mode (Image/Mode/RGB Color), then simply increase red and yellow. You can do this with adjustments to the Red and Blue channels in either Levels or Curves. When you apply the change as an adjustment layer, you have the added flexibility of modifying the effect using the Opacity slider for the layer. For more on working with black-and-white images, including creating toning effects, see Chapter 25, "Black & White, and Duotones."

Dangerous Curves

The diagonal line of a curve when you first enter the dialog represents a smooth, gradual progression from one tone to the next. One thing to keep in mind when working with Curves is that, in most cases, you want your adjustments to produce a smooth, subtle curve without the abrupt changes in direction that cause steep slopes, obvious bumps, or a plateau or shelf effect. Drastic rearrangements that change the curve in these ways can have unwanted tonal repercussions in your image, such as a range of different tones becoming a single tonal value, or extreme contrast (see the illustrations below). If the top of the curve flattens out against the top edge of the grid,

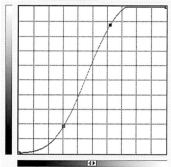

When two tonal points that used to occupy different places on the curve are adjusted to the same tonal level; the result is a "shelf" that causes different colors and values in the image to merge together into an ugly flat tone. The unaltered version is seen on the left, and the "shelved" version is shown on the right.

If the curve is too steep, as seen here, the contrast in the image will become extreme. In addition, beware of the curve flattening out along the top of the grid, as this may indicate that you are clipping highlights to a total white (seen on the "o" above right). Having the lower part of the curve snap to the bottom part of the grid means that shadow tones may be clipped to a total black. This type of curve can be useful, however, for adding contrast to really flat, low-contrast images.

some highlight values are being clipped to a total white. Similarly, if the bottom part of the curve flattens out along the lower part of the grid, then shadow values are being forced to a total black. When you are working with Curves, if the tonal or color values in the image appear to be "freaking out" (that's a technical term), the likely cause is that your adjustments are too extreme.

Introduction to Hue/Saturation

The Hue/Saturation command is one of Photoshop's most useful tools for altering the character of colors in an image. It contains three sliders for modifying the Hue (color), the Saturation (intensity or purity), and the Lightness. Let's take a tour through this dialog and see how it works.

◆ From the Chapter 20 folder on the DVD, open the file called Teacup Ride. psd. This is a good image with which to explore the capabilities of Hue/Saturation, because it has several distinct colors. Add a Hue/Saturation adjustment layer by clicking the Add Adjustment Layer button at the bottom of the Layers palette, or via the main menu (Layer/New Adjustment Layer).

Detail view of original Teacup Ride image (left) and the adjusted version (right) after moving the Hue slider to +50.

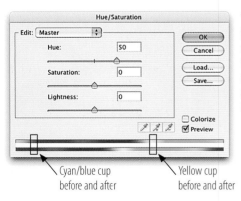

The Hue/Saturation adjustment for the above example. The spectrum bars on the bottom show how the colors have changed. Original colors are in the top bar, and the altered colors are in the lower bar.

Cyan/blue cup before and after

Yellow cup before and after

◆ When you first enter the dialog, the Edit menu at the top is set to Master, which means that any changes you make will affect all colors in the image. First experiment by sliding the Hue slider back and forth. As you can see, the colors in the image change dramatically. What this adjustment does is shift the existing hues to a different location on the color wheel. If you look at the spectrum bars at the bottom of the dialog, you can see that the lower bar is changing in relation to the upper bar. The upper bar represents the original colors in the image, and the lower bar represents how they are changing.

◆ Return the Hue slider to zero, then move the Saturation slider back and forth. Positive values on the right will increase color

Moving the Saturation slider to the right hypersaturates the colors.

The colors are desaturated by moving the Saturation slider to the left.

Moving the Saturation slider all the way to the left removes all color from the image.

The effect of Lightness settings of +50 (left) and −50 (right) in the Master channel.

saturation, while negative values on the left will reduce saturation. Desaturating an image slightly will produce a soft, muted color palette. When you move the slider all the way to the left, all the color values are removed from the image, resulting in a grayscale effect.

◆ Return the slider to the middle point, and now experiment with the Lightness slider. For adjustments that affect all the colors, this is the least useful of the three because it alters the brightness values in a way that looks unnatural. Moving the Lightness slider to positive values creates the effect of a translucent white overlay. Though this can be useful for creating a ghosted-back effect that works for overlaying type on top of images, it's not very useful for photographs. Moving the Lightness slider into negative values darkens the image, but again, the result is not very convincing. Using Levels or Curves is a much better way to darken an image.

Editing Specific Colors with Hue/Saturation

Of the controls available in the Master section of the dialog, we tend to use the Saturation slider the most. The reason for this is that the majority of our work involves images where we are interested in working with the natural colors as photographed. The Hue slider creates unnatural (though sometimes oddly fascinating) shifts in color that are usually not appropriate for what we want to do and the

Lightness slider, as previously mentioned, makes changes to the luminosity (brightness) values that are unconvincing.

Once you start to edit the individual colors, however, both the Hue and the Lightness sliders can be very useful. To explore this, we'll make one final adjustment to the teacups image, and then move on to another photo.

◆ If you have changed the value of the Lightness slider, return it to the starting postion in the middle (or simply enter a "0" in the numeric field). Open the Edit menu at the top of the dialog, and choose Yellows. Enter −30 for the Hue value.

This adjustment turns the yellow teacup in the background orange. Other tones that have some yellow in them are affected, as well, including the tan teacup in the foreground and the brown stripes around the cyan cup and the purple cup in the background.

◆ Next, move the Saturation slider for the Yellows all the way to the right to fully saturate those colors. This is not an adjustment that we are recommending, but it is a useful strategy for seeing just which colors in the image will be affected by moving the Hue

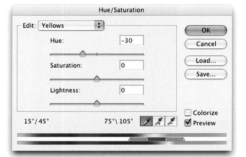

The yellows changed to a −30 Hue value.

The original Teacup Ride image.

The result of the change to the Yellows Hue setting. The yellow cup in the background, as well as the tan cup in the foreground and the brown stripes on some of the other cups, have been changed.

Increasing the Saturation for a given color to the maximum value is useful for revealing which areas of the image will be affected by any change you make. Here, the saturation for the yellows has been set to +100.

The original Yellow Wall image.

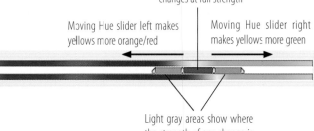

Dark gray area receives
changes at full strength

Moving Hue slider left makes
yellows more orange/red

Moving Hue slider right
makes yellows more green

Light gray areas show where
the strength of any change is
gradually feathered to zero

Saturating the yellows at full strength to see which areas of the image will be affected.

slider for a specific color. In the case of this photo, it reveals the areas we already mentioned, as well as the fake stone wall in the background. Return the Saturation slider to 0.

Notice the spectrum bars at the bottom of the dialog. A range of yellows is indicated by the markers and areas of dark and light gray. The dark gray area in the center of these makers shows the range of yellow tones that will be fully affected by any adjustment you make. The lighter gray areas on either side represent the range of yellow tones where the effect will be feathered and gradually reduced to zero. The degree numbers above the spectrum bars indicate the locations on the circular color wheel that will be affected by any change. In this case, areas that fall between 45° and 75° will receive the full effect of the adjustment. The area where the change will be gradually faded to nothing are between 15° and 45° in the orange-red range and 75° and 105° in the yellow-green range.

To see an important indicator of how the color you are adjusting will change, look at the range of yellows that are being changed. To the left of this area, the yellows transition to orange and then red. On the right they change to green and eventually cyan. So moving the Hue slider to the left will shift them to orange and then red, and moving the slider to the right will change them to green and then cyan.

Fine-Tuning the Color Range

The teacups image contains obvious and distinct separations between the different colors. Next we'll show you how to fine-tune the affected range of colors using the +Eyedropper and the −Eyedropper. For these further explorations, we will use an image with a bit more subtlety than the teacups have to offer.

◆ Close the teacups image and from the Chapter 20 folder on the DVD, open up the file called Yellow Wall.psd. Add a Hue/Saturation adjustment layer, and in the dialog open the Edit menu and choose Yellows. Our goal is to make some changes to the yellow in the wall without affecting the red brick or the wooden door.

> **NOTE**
>
> The green grass is also receiving a noticeable saturation boost after we set the saturation for the yellows to maximum. In many cases, if you want to saturate the color of green grass, you'll find that you need to adjust the yellows, and sometimes the cyans, more than the greens

With the Hue/Saturation dialog open, your cursor will automatically be in the Eyedropper tool. Click in the area shown to sample the yellow color in the wall.

When to Use Hue/Saturation and When to Use a Layer Mask

The controls in the Hue/Saturation dialog are very powerful for making subtle corrections and adjustments to the overall color saturation in an image, as well as to specific ranges of color. The ability to create a custom range of sampled colors and to add to that range or subtract from it using the eyedroppers make this one of Photoshop's most essential color correction tools.

But there will be times when you will need to apply your corrections with more control than even the Hue/Saturation command can offer. Any time when there is not enough tonal or color separation between the areas you want to adjust and those you don't, you will need to use a layer mask on an adjustment layer to precisely apply color or tonal changes exactly where you need them. For more information on the use of adjustment layers with layer masks for making precise adjustments to color and tone, see Chapters 21 and 22.

The default yellows range (top) and the custom yellows range after we sampled the wall in the image with the regular Eyedropper tool.

The narrowed yellows range after using the −Eyedropper tool to subtract the red brick arch and the wooden door from the sampled range.

The saturated yellows before subtracting the bricks and the door from the affected range.

The saturated yellows after subtracting the bricks and the door from the affected range.

◆ The first thing to do is to try the 100% saturation trick by moving that slider all the way to the right. As you can see, the wall, the bricks, and the door all have traces of yellow. Return the Saturation slider to 0. Take a moment to notice the range of yellows that are being affected in the spectrum bars at the bottom of the dialog.

◆ When you are working in a color or tonal correction dialog such as Hue/Saturation, the regular Eyedropper tool is selected by default, allowing you to easily sample tones and colors in the file. Move your cursor into the image, and click the area of the wall just to the right side of the window (make sure to click only the yellow wall and not any areas where the paint has fallen off). Notice that the range of yellows that will be affected has now changed to include more oranges and fewer greens. You have just selected a custom range of yellows.

◆ Increase the Saturation to +32. This creates a rich, saturated yellow in the wall, but the red brick arch over the door and the wooden door itself are also being affected.

◆ Click the −Eyedropper to make it active. This will allow you to subtract areas from the previously sampled colors. Click and drag the −Eyedropper across the red brick arch over the door. Then drag it across the wooden surface of the door. The colors that you sample with the –Eyedropper are removed from the range that is being affected by the adjustment. If you look at the range indicator at the bottom of the dialog, you'll see that it is now very narrow.

◆ To add the brick and door colors back into the range of affected colors, simply click the +Eyedropper to make it active, and click and drag back over those areas.

◆ As a final exploration, you can try moving the Hue slider and the Lightness slider.

Since some of the red brick and wooden door is still being affected, you can't move the Hue too drastically or the new color will show up in those areas (try moving it far to the right to make the wall green, and you'll see what we mean).

The Lightness slider will make the affected colors either darker or lighter. Unlike the Master controls, which create unconvincing effects as noted earlier with the teacups image, moderate adjustments with the Lightness slider can sometimes be effective when you're working on specific colors. This can work well, for instance, when you're trying to darken the blues in a sky.

Starting with a Good Foundation

Levels, Curves, and Hue/Saturation are three of Photoshop's most powerful and versatile tools for applying foundation tonal and color corrections. When we say "foundation," we are referring to the concept of performing all of your global corrections first to create a good foundation from which you can then make more detailed corrections and enhancements in specific areas of the image.

After reading this chapter and working through the exercises, you should have a good understanding of the basic functionality of each dialog. In the following two chapters, and in many of the subsequent chapters, we will present hands-on exercises that make use of these tools to apply color and tonal correction to a variety of images, both "normal" images and those that present more challenging problems.

21 ◆ Overall Color Correction

The final, corrected version of the Mount Chicon image.

Performing overall color correction using Levels, Curves, and Hue/Saturation adjustment layers; adjusting specific areas with layer masks; sharpening; and preparing to print.

The original Mount Chicon image.

Photoshop is an amazing program that provides us with a wide array of tools to correct and enhance our images. But even with all of this transformational power at our fingertips, our primary technical goal when taking a photograph (apart from the aesthetics of composition) is to get the image "right" in the camera. This means making sure we have a good exposure with a range of tonal values that is appropriate for the scene we are photographing. It also means using a shutter speed that will yield a sharp image, or if necessary, using a tripod to stabilize the camera, and choosing an aperture (f-stop) that will give us the depth of field (areas of the image in sharp focus) that we want the photograph to have. The more you can do to get a good exposure in the camera (or a good scan from a good exposure), the less you will have to correct in Photoshop. You'll also be starting off with much better image data, which will make your corrections easier to apply and the results more satisfying.

Even images that are well exposed, however, generally need some amount of basic color and tonal correction. In this chapter, we'll take you through our workflow for overall color correction on a normal image (by "normal" we mean that the photo is well exposed and has no major problems). We'll begin by creating a master file and evaluating the image to determine what corrections it may need. Next we'll move on to finding the brightest and darkest points in the image, placing Color Sampler points to track those values, using Levels to neutralize the highlights and shadows, and making overall adjustments to brightness, contrast, and saturation. After the overall adjustments, we'll introduce the concept of making simple adjustments to specific areas using basic techniques that will provide a good foundation for some of the more advanced procedures that will follow later in the book. We'll finish up by checking for and removing any dust spots,

resizing to a specific print size, applying basic sharpening, and exploring the Print with Preview dialog in Photoshop CS2.

Evaluating the Image

The image that we'll use for this tutorial is a photograph of Mount Chicon, a 5500-meter peak (18,044 feet) in the Andes of Peru. This was taken with a digital SLR, but the steps we will use to evaluate, color correct, and prepare it for printing also apply to images that are scanned from slides or negatives. When working with Raw files from digital cameras, some of the overall tonal and color correction would normally take place in the Adobe Camera Raw dialog (see Chapter 9, "Camera Raw," for more on working with RAW files). This photo was originally captured as a Raw file but has been converted into the Photoshop format without corrections in order to serve as an example for this tutorial. From a Raw file (or from a high-bit-depth scan), you also have the opportunity to import the image into Photoshop as a 16-bit file, which we recommend since it gives you more tonal "overhead" if you need to make significant modifications to the tonal scale. This version of the Mount Chicon image is a 16-bit file.

◆ From the Ch21.Overall Color Correction folder on the *Photoshop Artistry* DVD, open the Mount Chicon.psd file in Photoshop.

Activate Full Screen Mode

1 Begin evaluating an image by putting the image into Full Screen mode to remove any desktop distractions. More important, using the Full Screen gray viewing mode surrounds the image with neutral gray. This is very important when you're trying to see if there are any color casts that need to be corrected, since any other colors surrounding the image might interfere with your ability to accurately see subtle color issues.

◆ Press F to put the image into Full Screen mode (you can also press the center Screen View icon just under the Quick Mask icons near the bottom of the Tools palette). Press the Tab key to hide all of the Photoshop palettes.

1 The image in Full Screen mode with the palettes hidden.

1a Unless you have prior experience at evaluating images, you might not know where to start. To help you out, we'll describe our impressions of this image. At first glance, it might seem as if it has no significant problems. The main issue we noticed initially is that it seems a bit too light and perhaps in need of a boost in contrast. There are some darker shadows in the donkeys and the bull, but the far mountain seems a bit flat. Though there appear to be no major color cast problems in this image, if you look closer at the mountain, you may see that it appears slightly blue. This was probably caused by the fact that that photo was taken at a high altitude (approximately 10,000 feet), and the color of the light at higher altitudes is cooler and bluer than at lower elevations.

◆ From the Window menu, choose Histogram to bring up the Histogram palette.

If you take a moment to look at the Histogram palette, you can see that the shape of the histogram confirms the initial impression that the image is a bit too light. Most of the tonal data is grouped on the right hand side of the histogram, which is where the brighter tones

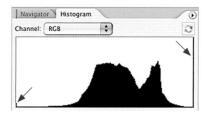

1a The initial histogram for the Mount Chicon image. The tall thin "spike" on the highlight side is the white area that contains the copyright notice. The small bump at the far left is the actual black text of the copyright notice. These will disappear once we crop off the copyright banner in the next step.

in the image are located. Hardly any tones are located on the left side of the scale, which is where the darker shadows are. This lack of deep shadow detail is responsible for an overall flatness or lack of contrast in the image.

Initial Cropping and Creating a Master File

2a Before we get started with the color correction, we need to crop off the copyright notice on the bottom of the image. Cropping off the notice here (or in any image included on the DVD) does not cancel the copyright, it just gives us a cleaner image to work with and will ensure a more accurate histogram display in terms of the black- and white-point.

◆ With the image in Full Screen mode, choose the Crop tool (C) from the Tools palette. Make sure there are no preset crop dimensions in the Options bar (if there are, press the Clear button on the right side). Position the tool cursor outside the image, above the top-left corner, click down in the gray area, and drag diagonally across the image toward the lower-right corner until you have a crop box surrounding the entire image. Release the mouse button, then click on the center bottom "handle" and move it up until the white area containing the copyright notice is not included in the crop box. Press the Enter key, double-click inside the crop box, or click the check mark button on the right side of the Options bar to apply the crop.

2b Now that the initial crop is applied, it's time to save a master-file version of the image. By doing this we are preserving the unaltered original image in case we ever need to return to this source file.

◆ From the File menu, choose Save As. Change the name of the file to indicate that it is a master file (for example, add "-layers" to the filename, or something similar) and choose the Photoshop (PSD) format in the drop-down file format menu. Since the original file is on the DVD, you will need to choose a new location on your hard drive in which to save the image. Make sure that the option to embed a color profile is enabled, and click the Save button. All further editing will now be applied to this master file.

Add a Levels Adjustment Layer

3 Now that we have evaluated the image and have some idea of what might help it, it's time to roll up our sleeves and get to work! Our first steps will be to add a Levels adjustment layer, determine where

3 Add a Levels adjustment layer by using the menu at the bottom of the Layers palette, or by choosing Layer/New Adjustment Layer/Levels.

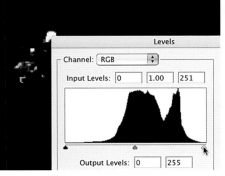

4 The Levels clipping display (lower image), shows the brightest point in the image as the area that turns white first. In the case of this image, the brightest point is in the snowfield on the mountain. The lower image also shows the technique of using a corner of the Levels dialog as a "pointer" to mark the spot until a ColorSsampler can be placed.

the brightest and darkest points in the image are, and then neutralize those points (remove any color casts from them).

◆ Press the Tab key to bring back the palettes. Make sure that you can see the Layers, Info and Histogram palettes (the Info and Histogram palettes, normally grouped together, should be separated so you can see both at the same time). Leave the image in Full Screen mode. If you need to reposition the image so it's not covered by any palettes, you can press the Spacebar and click and drag to move it over to the left side of the screen.

◆ From the main menu, choose Layer/New Adjustment Layer/Levels. You can also access this choice from the adjustment layer button at the bottom of the Layers palette. If you access the option from the main Layers menu, name this layer "Overall Levels" and click OK. Accessing an adjustment layer from the button at the bottom of the Layers palette will not give you the ability to name the layer as you create it unless you press the Option (Alt) key before you click the button.

Finding the Brightest Point

4 With the Levels dialog open, the next step is to locate the brightest and darkest points in the image and mark them with Color Sampler points. We'll start with the highlights. Since the brightest points in this particular image are probably somewhere in the snow on the mountain, make sure you can see that area of the image.

◆ Hold down the Option (Alt) key and click and hold down the mouse button on the Highlight slider on the right side under the histogram. The image will turn black, but as you slowly move the slider to the left, you will see parts of the snow begin to turn white. The place where you first see a patch turn white is the brightest spot in the image.

◆ Let go of the Option (Alt) key, hold down the Command (Ctrl) key, and click and drag a zoom marquee around that part of the image to zoom in for a closer view on that area. To help you

locate the brightest spot again, you can move the Levels dialog and use one corner of it as a "pointer" to that spot. Now hold down the Option (Alt) key, and click and hold the Highlight slider until you have located the brightest point again. Release the Option (Alt) key and move the Highlight slider back to the far right side. It is important to return the Highlight slider to the starting position, since this movement of the slider is not an adjustment, but only a means of helping us identify the brightest point in the image.

◆ Position your cursor over the area where the brightest point is, hold down the Shift key and click once to place a Color Sampler point there. If you look in the Info palette, you will see that a new info readout has been added at the bottom.

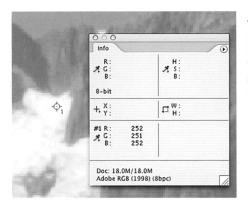

4 The first Color Sampler point is placed on the snow to mark the brightest point in the image. The values for this point sample are displayed at the bottom of the Info palette.

Finding the Darkest Point

5 Now we'll move on to locate the darkest point in the image. Since this is likely to be somewhere in the lower half, where the donkeys and bull are grazing, make sure that you can clearly see that area.

◆ Press Command (Ctrl)-0 (zero) to zoom out so you can see the entire image.

◆ Hold down the Option (Alt) key, and click and hold on the Shadow slider on the left side under the histogram. The image will turn white, but as you slowly move the slider to the right, you will see areas of the donkeys begin to turn black. The place where you first see a patch turn black (the neck of the donkey in the back) is the darkest spot in the image.

◆ Let go of the Option (Alt) key, hold down the Command (Ctrl) key, and click and drag a zoom marquee around the donkeys to zoom in for a closer view on that area. To help you locate the darkest spot again, you can use the trick of using a corner of the Levels dialog as a pointer to that spot. After you have repositioned the Levels dialog, hold down the Option (Alt) key, and click and hold the Shadow slider until you have located the darkest point again. Release the Option (Alt) key and move the Shadow slider back to the far left side.

◆ Position your cursor over the area on the donkey's neck where the darkest point is, hold down the Shift key, and click once to

5 The Levels clipping display (lower image), shows the darkest point in the image as the area that turns black first. In the case of this image, the darkest point is on the neck of the donkey in the background.

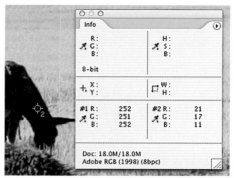

5 The second point sample is placed on the background donkey's neck to mark the darkest point in the image. The values for this point sample are displayed at the bottom of the Info palette.

place a Color Sampler point there. In the lower part of the Info palette, you will see that a new info readout has been added for Color Sampler #2.

Neutralizing the Highlights

6a With the Color Sampler points marking the brightest and darkest points in the image, the next step is to neutralize those endpoints using the Eyedropper tools in the Levels dialog. We'll start with the highlights.

◆ Go to the main menu and zoom the image to 100% by choosing View/Actual Pixels (while you're there, take note of the keyboard shortcut listed for that command in the menu). Then press the Spacebar down, and click and drag to scroll the image until you can see the snowy part of the mountain where the first Color Sampler is.

◆ Double-click the highlight eyedropper in the lower-right corner of the Levels dialog to bring up the Color Picker. If you set the Preferences as recommended in Chapter 2, "Preferences and Color Settings," then the correct highlight target values should already be set, but it's always good to double-check. The R, G, and B values should be 244, 244, 244. If they are not already set to those numbers, change them now, then click OK to exit the Color Picker.

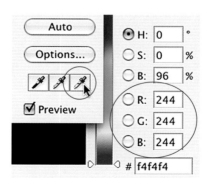

6a Double-click the highlight eyedropper in the lower-right corner of the Levels dialog, and double-check that the highlight target values are set correctly in the Color Picker.

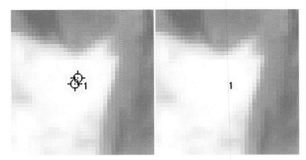

6b When you line up the precise cursor (Caps Lock key enabled) of the highlight eyedropper with the Color Sampler point, both crosshairs will disappear or dim when they are perfectly aligned (right).

6b The highlight eyedropper is now active, so you have to be careful about accidentally clicking the image. Your preferences should be set up so the eyedropper cursor is a precise crosshairs as shown in the 6b illustration. If you don't have this precise eyedropper cursor, you can temporarily press the Caps Lock key to show the crosshairs cursor.

◆ Zoom in closer on the Color Sampler on the snowy mountain. Position your cursor so it overlaps with the Color Sampler point. When they are exactly lined up, both should either disappear or dim a bit. Click once to remap this point to the specified highlight target color of 244, 244, 244.

◆ Once the highlight has been set, click the highlight eyedropper to turn it off. If you check the Info palette values for Color Sampler #1, you should see that the numbers on the right side of the slash have been adjusted to 244, 244, 244.

This adjustment does two things: It establishes the value for the brightest point in the image, and it ensures that the tone is neutral, with no color casts. It's important to note here that this technique is designed for an image that has a bright white area with detail that should be neutral. Not all images fall into this category, but a surprising number of them do.

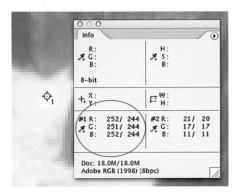

6b The Info palette after the highlights have been targeted to the specified values for the highlight eyedropper. The numbers on the left of the slash are "before" values and the numbers on the right are "after" values.

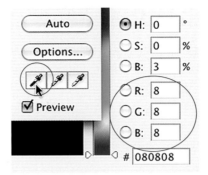

7a Double-click the shadow eyedropper in the lower-right corner of the Levels dialog, and double-check that the shadow target values are set correctly in the Color Picker.

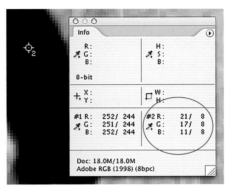

7b The Info palette after the shadows have been targeted to the specified values for the shadow eyedropper. The numbers on the left of the slash are "before" values and the numbers on the right are "after" values.

Neutralizing the Shadows

7a Next, we'll set the black point and neutralize the shadows. As we did in the last step, we'll verify that the target values are correct.

◆ Double-click the shadow eyedropper in the lower-right corner of the Levels dialog to bring up the Color Picker. The R, G, and B values should be 8, 8, 8. If they are not already set to those numbers, change them now, then click OK to exit the Color Picker.

7b With the shadow eyedropper active, we will now set the shadow point to the specified values.

◆ Press the Spacebar, and click and drag to scroll the image so you can see the Color Sampler point #2 on the donkey's neck. Zoom in if necessary for a closer view—Command (Ctrl)-+ (plus). The cursor should still be set to precise (Caps Lock key enabled). Position your cursor so it overlaps with the Color Sampler point. When they are exactly lined up, both should either disappear or dim a bit. Click once to remap this point to the specified shadow target color of 8, 8, 8.

◆ Once the shadow values have been set, click the shadow eyedropper to turn it off. If you check the Info palette values for Color Sampler #2, you should see that the numbers on the right side of the slash have been adjusted to 8, 8, 8.

Overall Brightness Adjustments

8 With the highlight and the shadow tones neutralized, we can move on to addressing overall brightness and specific color adjustments for the individual color channels.

◆ Move the middle slider in the Levels dialog a little to the right, to about 0.92. This will darken the overall midtone brightness in the image. This same adjustment could be made using Curves.

◆ The mountain still looks a bit too blue. From the drop-down Channel menu at the top of the Levels dialog, select the Blue channel. Move the Midtone slider to the right until the numeric readout is 0.95. This reduces blue and adds a bit of yellow.

◆ The mountain still doesn't look quite right, and a trace of cyan seems to be lingering there. To fix that, select the Red channel from the drop-down Channel menu (red is the opposite of cyan). Move the red Midtone slider slightly to the left until the numeric value is at 1.04. This adds a bit of red to the midtones and makes the tones in the mountain look more earthy and natural.

◆ Click OK to close the Levels dialog and apply the corrections.

The Levels adjustments we made addressed the overall tonal balance of the image by targeting the highlight and shadow points to a precise neutral value. Additionally, we darkened the midtones slightly and made some minor adjustments to the color balance in the Red

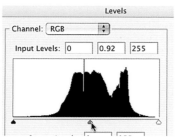

8 The midtone Levels adjustments.

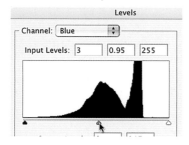

8 The Blue Levels adjustments.   **8** The Red Levels adjustments.

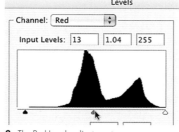

8 Moving the Midtone slider to the right slightly darkens the image. In the Blue channel (below left), moving the middle slider to the right subtracts blue and adds yellow. In the Red channel (below right), moving the middle slider to the left adds red and subtracts cyan.

When to Use the Levels Eyedropper Technique

Using the eyedroppers in Levels (or Curves) to neutralize the highlights and shadows in an image can be a very effective way to apply basic color and tonal correction on many types of images. If the image has a color cast, the simple act of making the highlights and shadows neutral can often go a long way toward fixing a lot of the color problems. Even images that you think look fine can be improved by using this technique.

The main thing to remember, however, is that an image needs to have a bright highlight (and to a lesser extent) a dark shadow that should be neutral. The photo of Mount Chicon has both of these (although the case could be made that the shadows on the side of the donkey's neck might not necessarily be strictly neutral). If an image does not have these tonal areas, such as a photo of a foggy morning at dawn, or a stage shot lit with colored lights taken inside a jazz club, then this technique should not be used. For photos that do not have obvious highlight and shadow points that should be neutral, or images that have a color cast that is an integral part of the scene (such as a sunset or the previously mentioned jazz club), manual adjustments to the individual Levels channels can be made.

and Blue channels. In the next part of this exercise, we'll improve the overall contrast and color saturation.

Improving Contrast with Curves

9 After we have used Levels to set the endpoints, which neutralizes the highlight and shadows in the image, and made any necessary adjustments to overall brightness and color balance, we usually move on to fine-tuning the contrast in the image. For this, Curves is the best tool to use.

◆ Add a Curves adjustment layer, either from the Layer/New Adjustment Layer menu, or by clicking the Create a New Fill or Adjustment Layer icon at the bottom of the Layers palette.

◆ We're going to add a slight S-curve to increase the contrast a bit. Place your cursor over the center intersection in the grid, and click to set a point. This will serve as a pivot point for the S-curve.

Curves, Contrast and Color Saturation

In an RGB image, the individual color channels control both the color values and the brightness values. In some cases, an increase in contrast can also increase the color saturation, and if the contrast increase is significant, there can sometimes be unwanted changes in color as well. For the S-curve contrast adjustment we have added to the Mount Chicon image, a slight increase in color saturation is taking place. This is particularly noticeable in the yellow grass of the field. Although this is not a problem for this image (it actually helps it), there may be times when you want to apply a contrast boost and not affect the color in an image.

Fortunately, there is an easy way to do this: At the top of the Layers palette, change the Blend mode for the Curves adjustment layer to Luminosity. If you turn the layer on and off by clicking the Eye icon, you can see that there is an increase in contrast but the colors and color saturation are unaffected. The Luminosity Blend mode tells Photoshop to apply the tonal change only to the brightness values in the image and to leave the color values alone. It is one of the most useful Blend modes for tonal correction. For more on Blend modes, see Chapter 31, "Blend Modes, Calculations, and Apply Image."

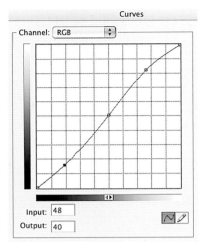

9 An S-curve to boost contrast. The active curve point, indicated by a solid black node, is in the lower left portion of the grid and is controlling the shadows. The Input and Output values show that the active tone is being darkened from 48 to 40.

9 Before increasing contrast with Curves.

9 After increasing contrast with Curves.

Next, click in the middle of the upper half of the diagonal curve line to set a point. Drag up slightly on this point to brighten the highlights. Our input (before) value was 195, and the output (after) value was 210. Pay attention to the Color Sampler #1 values in the Info palette to make sure that you're not making the snow too bright. In ours, we raised the values for that area from 244 to 247 with this adjustment.

◆ Next, place a point in the middle of the lower half of the diagonal curve line and drag down a bit to darken the shadows. Our input value here was 48 and the output value was 40.

Adjusting Color Saturation

10 Our work up to this point has addressed the target values and neutrality of the black and white endpoints, and some slight midtone brightness and color adjustments; and the most recent adjustment increased the contrast. Next we will explore how to adjust overall

NOTE

An S-curve is a useful way to boost the contrast in an image, but it doesn't take much to overdo it. Curve adjustments should be subtle, with smooth, gradual changes in the curve. The steeper the curve becomes, the more pronounced the effect on the image. For fine movements of the control points on the curve, you can also use the arrow keys on the keyboard.

10 The overall Saturation adjustment.

10 The Hue/Saturation adjustment for the Blues.

color saturation, as well as the saturation of specific colors. To do this we'll use the Hue/Saturation command.

◆ Add a new Hue/Saturation adjustment layer above the previous Curves layer. You can do this by clicking the Create a New Fill or Adjustment Layer icon at the bottom of the Layers palette, or by choosing Layer/New Adjustment Layer/Hue/Saturation from the main menu.

◆ Increase the overall saturation slightly by raising it to +10.

◆ Next, we'll make some adjustments to the sky. Click the Edit menu at the top of the dialog, and choose Blues from the drop-down menu. Increase the Saturation to +8.

◆ Move the Blue Hue slider to +3. Moving the Hue slider will add a bit more magenta to the blues, which makes the blue in the sky appear deeper and richer. If you want the sky to have more of a soft, powder blue color, move the Hue slider to the left to add cyan to the blues.

◆ Now select Reds from the drop-down Edit menu. If you increase the red saturation all the way, you'll see that there is a lot of red in the field. Return the red saturation to 0, then move the Hue slider slightly to the right until the value reads +5. This will make the red a bit more yellow.

Using Oversaturation to Find Colors

You have to be careful when adjusting individual colors with Hue/Saturation, because sometimes the color you are trying to modify can be present in other areas of the image that you might not want to adjust. To see where in the image a color is present, simply increase the saturation for that color to the maximum by moving the slider all the way to the right.

In this photo you can see that the shadows on the mountain contain significant amounts of blue. This lets us know to be cautious when adjusting the Blues or we might emphasize blue in the mountains that we tried to remove earlier in the exercise.

Increasing the Blue saturation to the maximum amount shows that there is a significant amount of blue in the mountain.

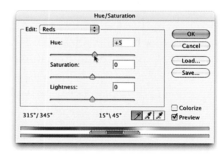

10 The Hue/Saturation adjustment for the Reds.

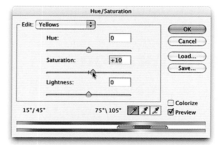

10 The Hue/Saturation adjustment for the Yellows.

◆ Finally, choose Yellows from the Edit menu and increase the saturation to +10. Click OK to apply the Hue/Saturation adjustments.

Fine-Tuning Specific Areas

11 At this point we have taken the image as far as we can go in terms of "global" adjustments that affect the entire image, or that affect certain colors, as with the Hue/Saturation layer. If we want to affect only portions of the image, we have to start using layer masks in our adjustment layers to target where the adjustments will be visible. To explore the concept of making corrections to specific areas, we'll use a couple of additional adjustment layers to do some fine-tuning and show you some simple ways to apply those corrections to certain parts of the photo.

The Hue/Saturation adjustment we made to enhance the blue in the sky has caused the blues in the mountain to become a bit too pronounced for our tastes. The easiest way to fix this is to edit the layer mask that is already present (the "empty" white thumbnail next to the Hue/Saturation thumbnail for that layer), changing it so that the adjustment is not applied to the mountain.

◆ Select the Brush tool in the Tools palette. In the Options bar, make sure the Mode is set to Normal and the Opacity is 100%. Click the Brush icon in the Options bar to open the Brush Picker. We used a 300-pixel brush tip. Next, press D on the keyboard to set the default colors, then press X to exchange them and make black the foreground color.

◆ Making sure that the Hue/Saturation layer is active in the Layers palette, brush over the mountain to mask it from being affected

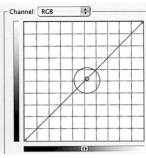

12 Click down in the image to see where that tone is located on the curve.

by the Hue/Saturation adjustment. If you look at the Layers palette, you will see a black area appear in the layer mask thumbnail. Wherever you paint with black, you are "masking" the adjustment so it doesn't affect that part of the image.

Color Correcting the Mountain

12 Now that we have removed the faint blue cast from the mountain, we'll do a little more to make it look even better.

◆ Add a new Curves adjustment layer above the Hue/Saturation layer. The adjustments we make here will initially affect the entire image, but we will fix that in the next step. First, open the Channel menu at the top of the Curves dialog and select the Red channel. In the image, click on the darker area of the mountain just below the snow and hold the mouse button down. A small indicator circle will appear on the curve to show you where that tone is located; it should be somewhere just below the center point. In the Curves grid, drag that part of the curve up slightly to increase the amount of red (our input and output numbers were 105 and 119).

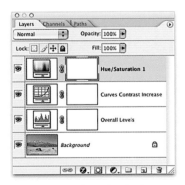 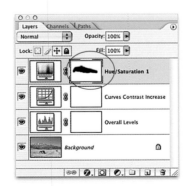

11 The Layers palette after the three overall adjustment layers have been added, and before the layer mask for the Hue/Saturation layer has been modified.

11 The Layers palette after painting on the layer mask for the Hue/Saturation layer to prevent it from affecting the mountain.

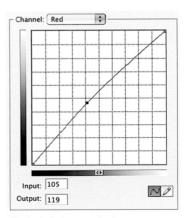 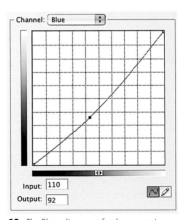

12 The Red adjustment for the mountain.

12 The Blue adjustment for the mountain.

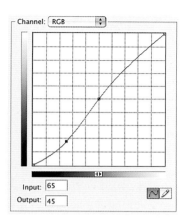

12 The RGB curve adjustment for the mountain darkens the shadow portions.

Input: 65
Output: 45

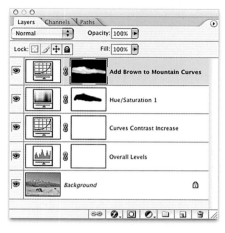

13 The top adjustment layer and its layer mask add earth tones to only the mountain.

◆ Now select Blue from the Channels menu in Curves and place a point in approximately the same area. Drag down to decrease blue and add yellow. The combination of adding red and yellow will create a brownish, earth tone color that works well for the slopes of Mount Chicon.

◆ Finally, return to the main RGB curve. Click to place a point in the center of the grid, then click in the middle of the lower half of the curve and drag down to darken the mountain. Click OK in Curves to apply the adjustment.

Editing the Curves Layer Mask

13 While this change looks good on the mountain, we do not want this adjustment to affect the rest of the image. Here is how we will change that and apply it only to the mountain.

◆ From the Image menu, choose Adjustments/Invert (Command (Ctrl)-I). This will invert the tones of the layer mask from white to black. The black areas in a layer mask will hide what that layer does to the image. In this case, it will hide the Curves adjustment we just added.

◆ Select the Brush tool in the Tools palette. Press D on the keyboard to set the default colors. When you are working on a layer mask, the defaults are white in the foreground and black in the background. In the Options bar, set the brush opacity to 50%. Using the same size brush as when we edited the Hue/Saturation layer mask (a 300-pixel brush), paint with white over the mountain to modify the layer mask and allow some of the Curves adjustment to show through. If you accidentally reveal too much of the correction on the field, simply press X on the keyboard to switch your colors, making black the foreground color, and paint on the area to mask it out again.

13 The mountain before color correction.

13 The mountain after color correction.

> **NOTE**
>
> When a brush tool is active, you can change the brush opacity by using the number keys; for example, pressing 5 will give you a brush with 50% opacity, 3 will set it to 30% opacity and so on. Pressing two numbers in quick succession, such as 2 and 7, will set the opacity to an amount that is in between the standard 10% increments (in this case, 27%). Pressing 0 (zero) will set the brush opacity to 100%.
>
> You can also change the size of the brush tip by pressing the left or right Bracket keys on the keyboard. The left bracket key ([) will make the brush smaller and the right bracket key (]) will make it larger.

Opening Up the Shadows

14 The final adjustment we'll make is to open up (lighten) some of the darker shadows on the donkeys and the bull. They have become darker as a result of our other adjustments. We'll use the same basic technique that we used to fine-tune the color on the mountain: Add an adjustment layer, invert the mask to black, and paint with white where we want the adjustment to show.

◆ Add a new curves adjustment layer. Click and hold on one of the donkeys to see where that tone can be found on the curve. If you Command (Ctrl)-click the image, a point will be placed on the curve for you. Raise this point upward until you bring back some of the shadow detail on the donkeys. Click OK when you're pleased with the result.

◆ Choose Image/Adjustments/Invert to change the layer mask from white to black. With the Brush tool active, use the left Bracket key to make the brush size smaller until it is an appropriate size for brushing in detail on the donkeys. Press X on the keyboard to make white the foreground color. Change the brush opacity in the Options bar to 50%, and begin painting over the donkeys

to gradually bring back some shadow detail. When you are done lightening the shadows, save the file.

At this point we are finished with the overall and area-specific corrections to the image. If you want to see a quick before-and-after view, hold down the Option (Alt) key and click the Eye icon for the *Background* layer. This will turn off all of the layers except for the Background layer. Option (Alt)-click it again to turn all the layers back on.

For the rest of the chapter, we'll use this image as an example to illustrate some of the steps that occur later in the workflow, after corrections have been made to the master file, and we'll show you what we would do next if we wanted to make a print from this file. The steps include spotting the master file, creating a copy with the layers flattened, resizing the copy, sharpening, and printing via the Print with Preview dialog.

Spotting the Master File

15a Before we create a flattened copy of the image to prepare for printing, we need to do one more thing to the master file; check for dust spots or other small flaws and remove any that we find. Since this image was taken with a digital camera, we don't need to worry about the many dust specks and tiny hairs that often show up with a scanned image; but we do need to take care of a few dust spots from the image sensor.

◆ If you are still in Full Screen mode, press the keyboard's F key twice to return to the Normal Screen mode. Arrange the document window so that it fills a good section of your monitor while still allowing you access to the vertical and horizontal scroll bars. Arrange the Navigator palette so that you can see it on screen.

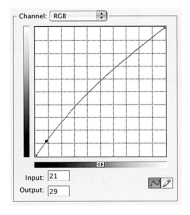

14 A curve to lighten the darker shadows.

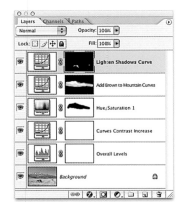

14 The Layers palette after lightening the donkeys and bull.

> **NOTE**
>
> In terms of where it fits in the workflow, spotting the image can also be done as the first step, before any color correction work is done. When working with scans from film images, for example, Seán likes to spot the scan file before creating a master-image file. That way the archived scan never has to be spotted again. For digital camera images, especially if you shoot Raw, it makes more sense to spot the master file. Whether you choose to spot it as the first step or after the overall color correction is up to you.

14 Donkeys before lightening the shadows.

14 Donkeys after lightening the shadows.

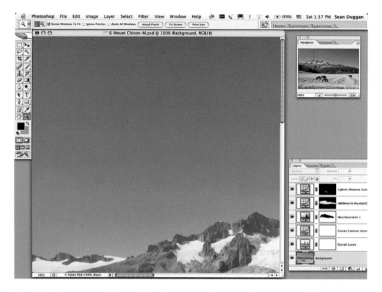

15a The document window and the Navigator and Layers palettes arranged for spotting the image.

15a Viewing the image at 100%, and arranging the Navigator palette view the top-left corner of the image.

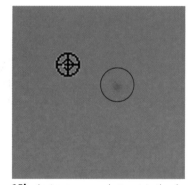

15b An image sensor dust spot in the sky (circled in red) and the cursor for the Spot Healing brush.

15b Clicking the dust spot with the Spot Healing brush will remove it.

15b The dust spot removed.

◆ Click the *Background* layer to make it active, then select the Spot Healing brush in the Tools palette. In the Options bar, choose Proximity Match and make sure that Sample All Layers is not checked.

◆ Double-click the Zoom tool to zoom the image to 100%, or actual-pixels view. In the Navigator palette, drag the red box to the upper-left corner of the small preview thumbnail.

15b In the upper-left corner of the image, you should see a few dark spots in the sky.

◆ Use the Bracket keys to make the brush smaller until you have a good size for retouching the dust spots in the sky (we used a 20-pixel brush tip). Place the brush cursor over one of the dust spots and click once to remove it. The Spot Healing brush looks at the area surrounding the spot to determine what colors to use to retouch the spot. Retouch all the spots you find in that first window view.

15c Now we'll move the image view over one exact window view. This ensures that we won't miss any areas.

◆ Move your cursor to the empty track of the horizontal scroll bar and click in the empty track. This will move the image over one exact window view.

◆ Retouch any spots in the second window view, then click in the empty horizontal scroll track to move the image over a third time. Proceed until you reach the right side of the photo, then click in the vertical scroll track to move the view down one. Retouch that area and click in the horizontal track to start making your way back across the image to the left side. We call this pattern "mowing the lawn." Continue back and forth through the image until you have checked the entire photo for dust spots or small flaws you may want to remove. When you are finished spotting, save the file.

NOTE

For minor dust spotting such as we have in this image, using the Spot Healing brush directly on the *Background* layer is generally fine. If you have an image that requires more intricate retouching or restoration of missing or damaged areas, or if there is any question whether something should be retouched (such as a portrait restoration job for a client), then it is best to create a separate layer, or a copy of the *Background* layer, for all the retouching.

15c After spotting the first window view of the image at 100%, click in the empty track for the horizontal scroll bar to move the image over one exact window view.

15c After clicking in the empty space in the horizontal scroll bar, the image is moved over one window view—which the Navigator palette shows.

15c Click in the vertical track of the scroll bar to move the image view down one row.

15c Tha Navigator palette after the top row has been spotted.

15c After clicking in the vertical scroll bar, the window view is moved down one row.

15c Moving the window view back toward the right side of the image.

Creating a Suggested Crop Guide

16a For most photographs, we never like to crop our master image, but some people like to see how the image will look in its cropped form before they start applying color and tonal correction. To see the image with the final crop you know you want and still preserve the flexibility to change your mind at a later date, you can use this cool technique (this can be applied either in the beginning of the process or after you have made color and tonal corrections to the image).

◆ Make sure the top layer is active. Choose the Rectangular Marquee tool. If you want the crop to conform to a specific proportion or aspect ratio, you can open the Style menu in the Options bar and choose Fixed Aspect Ratio. For this image, we'll use 11 for the width and 8 for the height.

◆ Click in the image where you'd like to have the upper-left corner of the crop be, and drag diagonally across the image toward the lower-right corner. With the mouse button still held down, you can also press the Spacebar and reposition the selection marquee as you are creating it. Release the mouse button when the selection/crop guide is the way you want it.

◆ If you need to adjust the selection after you have released the mouse button, choose Select/Transform Selection. A bounding box will appear around the selection. By holding down the Shift key, you can drag the corner handles to resize the box while preserving the original aspect ratio (proportions). Or, if you don't

16a The Fixed Aspect Ratio options for the Rectangular Marquee.

16a The selection marquee created with an aspect ratio of 11x8.

16b The selection marquee inverted.

16c The Color Fill layer creates an overlay that frames the image with the suggested crop.

care about the exact aspect ratio, you can grab any of the handles to resize the selection. Press the Enter key or click the check mark button at the top right of the Options bar to apply the transformation.

16b This sets up the selection marquee to define the area we want to see, but to actually use it to create a cropping overlay, we need to invert it to select the areas that are currently not selected.

◆ With the selection active, go to the main menu and choose Select/Inverse.

16c With the selection marquee inverted, you can now add a Color Fill layer to create an overlay that indicates a suggested crop.

◆ Next, choose Layer/New Fill Layer/Solid Color. In the New Layer dialog, name this layer "suggested crop overlay" and click OK. In the Color Picker that appears next, move the circle in the color box all the way over to the middle of the left side to choose a neutral gray tone, and click OK. The inversed selection marquee is turned into a cropping overlay that can always be changed or deleted.

17 The last step is to create an alpha channel for the suggested crop that can be easily accessed for applying this crop to a flattened copy of the file.

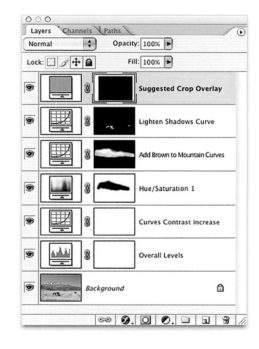

16c The Layers palette with the Color Fill layer at the top, which is used to indicate a suggested crop.

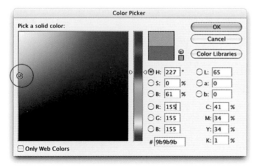

16c Choosing a neutral color for the suggested crop Color Fill layer.

> **NOTE**
>
> If you are working with images from a digital camera, you should always try to compose the image using as much of the viewfinder as possible. The reason for this is that any cropping you do essentially reduces the megapixel resolution for that shot by discarding pixels. Fewer pixels in the image mean that you cannot enlarge it as much, especially if you are cropping off a significant amount of image area.

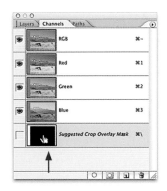

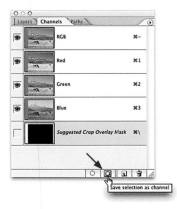

18 The Duplicate Image dialog. Choosing to duplicate merged layers only will flatten the layers of the duplicate image.

17 Command (Ctrl)-click the thumbnail for the crop overlay layer mask to load it as a selection.

17 Saving the inversed selection of the overlay layer mask as a new alpha channel.

18 In the Channels palette, Command (Ctrl)-click the thumbnail of the channel to load it as a selection.

17 The new alpha channel at the bottom of the Channels palette.

◆ Hold down the Command (Ctrl) key and click the thumbnail for the layer mask on the suggested crop layer. This will load a selection of the white areas of the layer mask. Choose Select/Inverse to inverse the selection. Now, hold down the Option (Alt) key and click the Save Selection as Channel icon at the bottom of the Channels palette. In the New Channel dialog, name the channel Suggested Crop, and click OK.

◆ Save the changes you've made to the master file.

Check the box for duplicating the merged layers only, which will create a copy with all the layers flattened. Click OK.

◆ In the new duplicate file, go to the Channels palette, hold down the Command (Ctrl) key, and click the thumbnail for the Suggested Crop alpha channel to load it as a selection. Then choose Image/Crop to create a crop of only the selected areas.

Create a Flattened Copy Using the Suggested Crop

18 Our master image file now includes all the color and tonal correction layers, it has been spotted, we have added a solid-color fill layer to indicate a suggested crop, and the file has been saved. The next step is to create a flattened copy of the file, resize it to the desired print size, and apply some sharpening. If you want to use the cropped version to print, follow the steps below. If you don't want to use the suggested crop version, proceed to the next section.

◆ From the main menu, choose Image/Duplicate. In the Duplicate Image dialog, give the file a different name (perhaps "Mount Chicon_13x" to indicate that we will make a print on 13-inch paper).

Create a Flattened Copy with No Suggested Crop

19 If you have no suggested crop layer, or you don't want to use it for printing, these are the steps to follow (for the rest of this example, we'll be using the full-frame image):

◆ If you do have a suggested crop layer but you don't want to use it, turn its Eye icon off.

◆ From the main menu, choose Image/Duplicate. In the Duplicate Image dialog, give the file a different name that indicates it will be a print version (we used "Mount Chicon_13x") and click the check box for Duplicate Merged Layers Only. This will create a copy with all the layers flattened. Your layered master file will also still be open in Photoshop.

◆ Once the flattened copy of the master file has been created and is open in Photoshop, you can close the layered master file.

◆ Choose File/Save As and save the duplicate, flattened file.

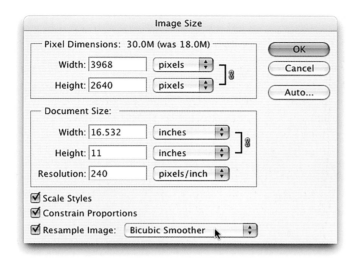

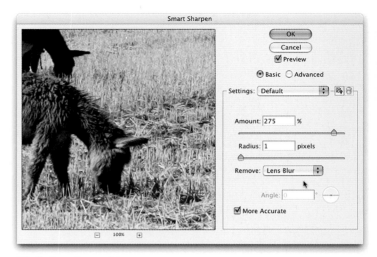

20 The Image Size dialog with the values for resizing the uncropped Mount Chicon image.

21 The Smart Sharpen dialog.

Resize for Print

20 Now it's time to resize the file for the specific print size that we will make. In the case of this example, we're going to make a print on 13x19-inch paper. As mentioned earlier, we'll be using the full-frame uncropped version of the image.

◆ From the main menu, choose Image/Image Size. With the Constrain Proportions and the Resample Image check boxes enabled, enter 11 inches for Height. When the image is centered on 13x19-inch paper, this will leave a 1-inch border on the top and bottom, which not only looks good, but also is useful for handling the print. The Resolution should be set to 240 pixels per inch. Finally, open the drop-down menu to the right of Resample Image, and choose Bicubic Smoother. This choice is best to use when making an image larger (as we are here). Bicubic Sharper is best to use when making an image smaller. Click OK to resize the image.

Sharpening with Smart Sharpen

21 Next we will sharpen the image. Before we bring up the Sharpening filter, however, zoom your image to a 100% view. Having the image at 100% is important to accurately judge how the sharpening is affecting the image.

◆ To apply the sharpening in a nondestructive way, make a copy of the *Background* layer by choosing Layer/Duplicate Layer.

21 The donkey before sharpening.   **21** The donkey after sharpening.

21 The mountain before sharpening.   **21** The mountain after sharpening.

◆ Double-click the Zoom tool icon to zoom the image to 100% view. You can also use the keyboard shortcut, Command-Option (Ctrl-Alt)-0. Next, press the Spacebar, and click and drag so that you view an area that has good detail for evaluating the sharpening effect. In this image, we will be examining the area in the foreground where the donkeys are grazing, as well as the mountain. Arrange the display so you can see the donkeys. Press the Tab key to hide all of the palettes.

◆ From the main menu, choose Filter/Sharpen/Smart Sharpen.

In Basic mode, the Smart Sharpen filter only has two sliders, Amount and Radius, as well as a Remove Blur feature. As with the old standby

When the Radius setting is too high in either Smart Sharpen or Unsharp Mask (in this example it was set to 6 in Smart Sharpen), it can result in glowing edges or "halos," as can be seen here along the edge of the mountain. Detail in the snow has also been lost to the exaggerated edge contrast.

The radius in this example was set to 1.0.

of the Unsharp Mask filter, the Amount value controls how much sharpening is applied ,and the Radius determines how far out from a contrast edge the effect is visible. If the Radius setting is too high, the result can be unwanted "halos" or glow effects along contrast edges. The Gaussian setting for Remove Blur causes Smart Sharpen to behave similarly to the Unsharp Mask command; the Lens Blur setting is the best for most images, as it tries to compensate for slight deficiencies caused by optical lens blurring; the Motion Blur setting attempts to compensate for blurring caused by camera or subject motion (don't expect any miracles with this setting, however).

The Smart Sharpen filter is also good for sharpening images with noticeable noise. By clicking the Advanced radio button, you can access controls that let you sharpen the shadows and highlights separately, thus minimizing the effect of sharpening in the shadows, where

NOTE

A printed image will never look as sharp as the image on the monitor, so for precise sharpening of fine art prints, you may want to make sharpening test strips where a representative section of the image is sharpened at different amounts (take notes as to what the sharpening values are). These test strips would then be combined into a single file, output onto the chosen fine art paper and evaluated to see how sharp the image looks when it is printed.

it might make the noise more visible. Since this image doesn't have any noise issues, we won't be exploring the advanced options of Smart Sharpen in this chapter.

Although we really like the Smart Sharpen filter, we still use the Unsharp Mask filter sometimes, especially if we need the extra option of the Threshold slider. The Threshold control can be useful for restricting the sharpening to certain areas based on tonal values (if, say, you don't want to sharpen a sky, or the smooth skin on a person's face). For more detailed coverage of Photoshop's sharpening features, see Chapter 12, "Essential Photoshop Techniques."

◆ In the Smart Sharpen dialog, set the Remove pop-up to Lens Blur. Set the amount to 275, the Radius to 1 and select the More Accurate check box. The preview will take longer with More Accurate checked, but at this stage, it's worth taking a little extra time to ensure that the sharpening effect is what you want.

◆ Click the preview box on and off and evaluate how the sharpening is affecting the donkeys. Press the scrollbar to get the Hand tool and click and drag in the image to scroll up to the moutain peak.

(In some versions of Windows, we have noticed that pressing the Spacebar will normally activate the highlighted button in the dialog, such as OK, Cancel, or Preview, so click inside a numeric field box in the dialog before using the Spacebar to scroll).

◆ Turn the preview on and off to see how the mountain looks with and without sharpening. Click OK to apply the Smart Sharpen filter.

Final Spotting Check

22 After sharpening a file, we usually do a final spotting check at 100% view just to make sure that the sharpening process has not enhanced any dust specks we may have missed in the initial spotting pass. You can use the "mowing the lawn" method with the Spot Healing brush that we covered earlier in this chapter. Save the file when you are done. Leaving the sharpening layer in the file will allow you to return and redo the sharpening if needed.

The Print with Preview Dialog

In the last part of this tutorial, we will take a look at Photoshop's Print with Preview dialog. We use this for all of our printing from Photoshop, and we strongly recommend that you take advantage of it, too. For the purposes of this tutorial, you don't have to actually make a print of this image (though you can if you want to); our goal

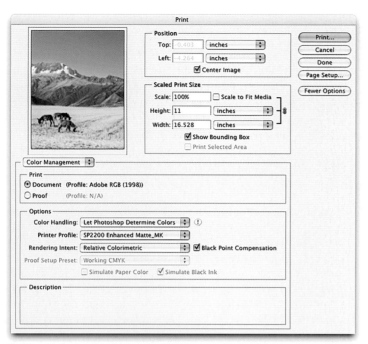

The Print with Preview dialog in Photoshop CS2. The size and layout of the image seen in the upper left is wrong because our Page Setup dialog is set to letter-size paper and this image has been sized to print on 13x19-inch paper.

The Page Setup dialog on a Macintosh.

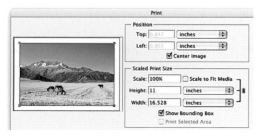

The size and layout of the image preview is corrected after the correct paper size and orientation options are set in the Print with Preview dialog.

here is to discuss the options in the Print with Preview dialog and explain how you should configure the color management settings featured there.

◆ From the main menu, choose File/Print with Preview. If you see a much smaller dialog than the one pictured here, simply click the More Options button to expand it to the full size.

Checking Image Orientation and Paper Size

The first thing you should check is that the small preview of the image looks OK in terms of how it will fit on the paper. As you can see from the illustration on the left, our preview is vertical and the image is cropped. The problem is that our printer is still set up to use letter-size paper and to print in a vertical orientation.

◆ If the the image preview is different than you expect, press the Page Setup button, choose the correct printer and paper size that you will be using, and click OK. When you return to the Print with Preview dialog, the preview will be corrected.

Our illustration here shows the Mac Page Setup dialog. The Windows version will look a bit different but will contain similar choices for choosing page size and orientation.

◆ Once you've set the correct page size and the layout preview of the image looks good, make sure that the drop-down menu immediately under the preview image is set to Color Management.

Print with Preview Color Management Options

If you are familiar with earlier versions of Photoshop, you'll notice that this section of the Print with Preview dialog has been remod-

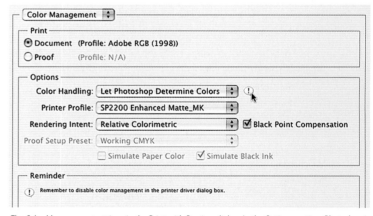

The Color Management settings in the Print with Preview dialog. In the Options section, Photoshop is set to handle the color conversion to the specified output profile, using the chosen rendering intent.

eled in Photoshop CS2. The Color Management options have two primary sections: Print and Options. At the bottom, another section offers a description of what a certain choice does, or a reminder if you move your mouse cursor over an exclamation point icon.

The Print section lets you specify whether Photoshop should print the open document (the choice you would use in most cases), or should print a proof on your inkjet printer that will represent how the image would look when printed on a commercial CMYK printing press or another device (for this latter choice you would need to specify the desired proofing space earlier in Photoshop; see Chapter 16, "Color Preferences, Calibration, and Printing," for more on proofing images). For the purposes of this tutorial, we're going to be exploring making a print on our own inkjet printer.

◆ In the Print section, choose Document. The profile listed to the right should be Adobe RGB (1998).

◆ In the Options section, open the menu for Color Handling and select "Let Photoshop Determine Colors." This will enable the Printer Profile menu so you can choose a profile that represents your printer and the type of paper you will be using. If you have an inkjet printer with profiles that appear in this list, you should choose the one that matches your printer and the paper you'll be using. In this example, we are printing to an Epson Stylus Photo 2200 on Enhanced Matte paper using matte black ink.

◆ The Rendering Intent determines exactly how the color information from the source space (in this case, the Adobe RGB working space) is converted to the printer space. For photographic purposes, there are only two choices that make any sense for most users: Relative Colorimetric or Perceptual.

There are ways that you can use Photoshop's soft-proofing features to visually test-drive how a different rendering intent might affect the image, and whether there is any difference between having Black Point Compensation on and leaving it off. Of course, the ultimate way to evaluate the differences would be to make test prints to see the actual results created by ink on paper. Refer to Chapter 16 for in-depth information on these subjects.

— Reminder —————————————————————

(!) Remember to disable color management in the printer driver dialog box.

When you choose "Let Photoshop Determine Colors," this reminder will appear at the bottom of the dialog when your cursor is over the exclamation icon near that choice.

◆ Next to the menu choice for "Let Photoshop Determine Colors," there is a small exclamation mark icon. Hover your mouse over this and you'll see that the reminder tells you to "Remember to disable color management in the printer driver dialog box." This is a very important step, because these settings are directing Photoshop to perform the necessary color conversion to the printer profile. Any additional color adjustments that are subsequently made in the printer driver will interfere with this and most likely will produce a print with inaccurate color. This is one of the most common mistakes people make, even if they have configured the Print with Preview dialog correctly. We will cover how to disable printer color management in the next section.

Printer Driver Considerations

At this point, we have done all that we can do in the Print with Preview dialog. The next step would be to press the Print button, which would take you into the printer driver software for your particular printer.

Since printers have different software (even in different models made by the same manufacturer), and new ones are coming out all the time, we can't show you every possible combination of choices that you might find in your own printer software. Apart from the different options and buttons that are available in your printer driver, following some basic concepts will ensure that the profile conversion you made in the Photoshop Print with Preview dialog is honored when the ink finally meets the paper.

To illustrate these concepts, we will use the printer driver for the Epson Stylus Photo 2200 and point out what settings to look for in your own printer driver. The design for these printer dialogs differs depending on the operating system you're using, so we will cover the Mac and Windows versions separately.

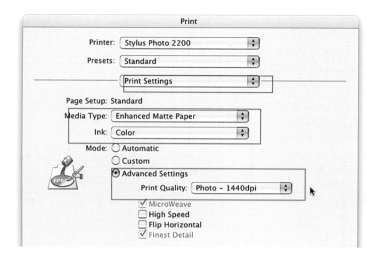

The Print Settings for the Epson 2200 driver for the Mac.

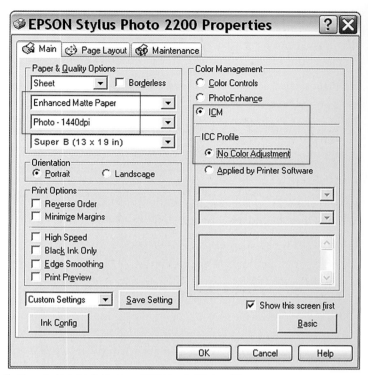

The Properties Main tab for the Epson 2200 driver for Windows XP.

The Color Management settings for the Epson 2200 driver for the Mac. This is where the all-important No Color Adjustment option is found.

The Epson 2200 Driver for Mac

In the Mac version, we first select Print Settings and make sure that the correct paper type is selected. When the Advanced option is selected, it allows us to choose a printer dots per inch setting. Next, we choose Color Management and select No Color Adjustment. If you are using the Photoshop Print with Preview dialog to convert to the printer profile, then this is perhaps the most important setting to make in the Epson 2200 driver in terms of color management.

The Epson 2200 Driver for Windows XP

In the Epson 2200 driver for Windows XP, clicking the Properties button in the initial dialog will expand the dialog. All of the important choices pertaining to paper type, printer dpi, and color management are grouped together under the Main tab. One important thing to be aware of is that the critical color management options

are not even visible until you click the ICM button in the Color Management section in the upper-right corner. Then, under ICC Profile, you can choose No Color Adjustment.

The most important concept to take away from this section is that no matter what printer you have, you need to figure out how to turn color management options off in the printer driver dialog in order for the Photoshop color management workflow described here to function correctly. The exact appearance of printer driver dialogs, the location of buttons, and even the nomenclature, may vary with each printer, but understanding the basic concepts behind these choices remains constant.

Portfolio

Seán Duggan

This image, "Where the Sea Comes In", was photographed along the coast of Maine while Seán was teaching at the Maine Photographic Workshops in June 2006. It shows an inlet channel under a small rock bridge that allows the sea flow through into a narrow bay. The image was made from two tripod-mounted exposures designed to capture both the detail in the dark rock and the seaweed and the brooding dark clouds of the approaching storm. The original files were processed in Camera Raw and then composited together and re-interpreted using several adjustment layers and layer masks.

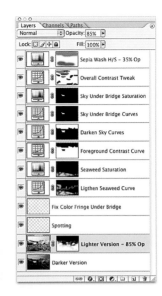

22 ◆ Correcting Problem Images

All that stands between my (Barry's) original Mono Lake problem image on the left and the final fine print on the right is a large Layers palette full of adjustment layers and masks. Problem images are ones that don't have a good place to set the highlights and/or shadows. They may have a color cast you want to keep, or several conflicting casts you need to get rid of. They often contain one or more difficult color or contrast issues. Your normal color correction workflow may appear not to work for problem images. But when you turn one into that print you dreamed about, it sure feels good! In this exercise I'll be talking about choices I've made in color correcting some difficult images, and we'll work together on one of those images.

Play Color Correction Like Music

Color correction is a process where you follow a workflow strategy to evolve an image to the point where you are happy with its colors and contrast, the highlight and shadow details, the crop, and the overall mood of the image. Chapter 18, "The Master Image Workflow," and Chapter 21, "Overall Color Correction," have given you the general recipe for our views on the color correction process. Make sure you have studied those chapters before going through this one. Following our workflow will get you started in this process, but you need to learn to play this workflow like a musical instrument. Not all images have a white highlight or a black shadow or even a place you can neutralize with the Eyedroppers to start bringing the image into color harmony.

Our color correction workflow is not always followed by "first do Levels, then do Curves, then do Hue/Saturation…." You often have to go back and forth between the steps. Go back to Levels and tweak the shadow or highlight values after you've done the Curve, the Hue/Sat, brought out shadow values, and so on. Increase the curve a bit, saturate the colors a bit more, and then go back to Levels to add just a touch of magenta or maybe take out a subtle green cast you didn't notice before. Each of these tools—the order they are applied in, their masks, the opacities of their layers—are all keys to play on the piano of getting a final master image and print.

Eventually you'll learn to look at an image's histogram and see how changes in the histogram's shape affect subtleties and relationships within that image. Is there a gap in the highlight end of one or more color channels, and what does this do to the image? How does the histogram of a subtle sunset or a foggy day differ from that of a contrasty afternoon at the harbor? How will the image change if the black end of its histogram tapers off slowly versus ending in a vertical bar at 0? Do you want pure blacks and/or whites in this image, and on this print, on this particular paper? Is your particular eye for color contrasty and saturated, or more flat and subtle? How do you see color, and can you think in black and white?

What Is a Problem Image?

A generic "normal image" is something that has a good black value—say, the shadow in the shade under a car tire—where you can set your shadow Color Sampler. A normal image also has, for example, a person with a white shirt on, or a white cloud or some white snow, where you can set your highlight. These shadow and highlight values then represent the extreme ends of brightness values in this "normal image"; neither one of them has any color cast, and all you have to do is adjust the contrast and colors of the values between these two endpoints so that they have the kind of contrast and saturation you'd see on a good, sunny day.

A "problem image" is not a normal image for any of a number of reasons. There may be no good highlight and/or shadow values. The highlight and/or shadow values may be in a location that has a color cast, like a sunrise or sunset, and you want to keep that color cast as part of your final image. The image might be abnormally bright or flat or contrasty and that is the way you want the print to be. You might want the print to look the opposite of what the camera captured, which is often the case. These are just some examples of problem images. In our workshops over the past 16 years, we've helped thousands of photographers make the best of their particular problem images so that they become beautiful prints. This chapter shows you some of the techniques we've learned.

Gibsons Morning, Our First Problem Image

Open the GibsonsTownMorningLayers.psd file from the folder Ch22. Correcting Problem Images on your *Photoshop Artistry* DVD. This is the final image we are going to create in this section. This backlit image of Gibsons, B.C., was shot as a Raw file with Barry's Canon Digital Rebel. In printing this, we want to bring out the details of the town and harbor while also enhancing the colors in the sky and the silhouette of the trees we're looking through. First we'll show you how to embed the Raw file into the Photoshop layers.

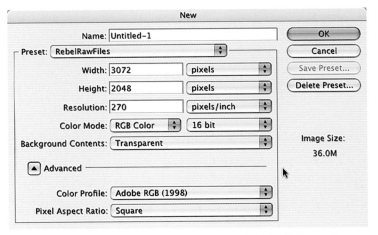

1 These are the settings you would use to prepare to accept a placed Raw file. These settings were created using the Save Preset button to the right. When creating one for your camera, just make sure you set the width and height of your camera's Raw files in pixels, the Background Contents to Transparent, the Color Profile to Adobe RGB, and the Color Mode to RGB Color 16 bit.

Creating a Raw Smart Object

1 We want to bring this image into Photoshop as a Raw file Smart Object. That way the Raw file will be embedded in the Photoshop layers, allowing us to go back anytime to the Camera Raw filter to change its settings by just double-clicking that layer. This way, after building a group of adjustment layers on top of the image in the bottom layer, we don't have to go and find that Raw file again if we decide we need to change the initial Camera Raw settings.

◆ Choose File/New in Photoshop to create a new 16-bit file the size of your digital camera Raw files. We've set up a predefined file type named RebelRawFiles whose settings are shown on the previous page. Since this image is vertical, choose Image/Rotate Canvas/90° CW.

◆ Choose File/Place and Navigate to the Chapter 22 folder on the DVD, then double-click the file named CRW_1090.CRW to open it into Camera Raw. The XMP file for this image is also in the Chapter 22 folder, so Camera Raw should already be set up with my settings of a Linear curve, Chromatic Aberration adjustments, my default Detail settings, and you can see my Adjust setting on this page. The goal here is to get all the information from the histogram into Photoshop. Click the Open button to open this file into Photoshop.

1 The original Gibsons morning image after opening it from Camera Raw but before any color correction in Photoshop.

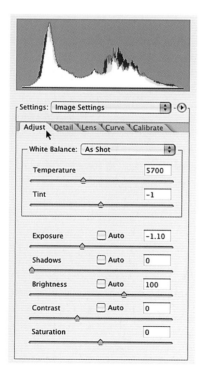

1 The Adjust settings for the 1090 image. I usually leave the White Balance set to As Shot unless I'm just trying to make my corrections in Camera Raw without going into Photoshop. Notice that we have a nice histogram here without losing anything from either end.

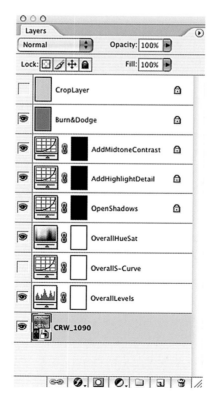

2 This is the CRW 1090 file as it would look after running the action BarrysColor-CorrectionTemplate on it. These adjustment layers are not yet doing anything, but they are set up for you in the proper order to save time and help you remember the color correction workflow. When you open the GibsonsTownMorningTemplate file, this is the Layers palette you'll now have.

In Photoshop you'll see an X across the image allowing you to scale the placed image. Just press the Return (Enter) key, as you don't want to do any scaling at this point.

Automatically Creating Your Workflow

2 At the bottom of your Layers palette, you'll see a Smart Object layer named CRW_1090. This is the Raw file actually embedded in this initial Photoshop layer. We're now going to build up a set of adjustment layers on top of this file as we go through correcting it. We could create these layers one at a time like we did in the previous chapter, but there's a faster way! Barry has created a set of actions to speed up the color correction workflow. These actions automatically create a blank set of adjustment layers to speed up color correction projects. We'll now open a file created with the action named BarrysColorCorrectionTemplate. This is one of these new actions.

◆ Choose File/Open and open the file named GibsonsTownMorningTemplate.psd. Type an F to put this image into Full Screen mode, then choose Window/Workspace/Color Correction to bring up your color correction palettes (Info, Navigator, and Histogram). Since this is a vertical image, you can move your Info palette to the left side. You don't need your Tools palette up—[F2] will close it. If your Layers palette is not up, use [F10] to bring it up, open it so you can see all the layers, and move it to the right side. These four palettes, along with the Options bar, are all you need on screen for now. Your Zoom Factor, which you can see in the Navigator palette, should be about 25% so that you can see the entire image without palettes being on top of it.

This file is the same as the CRW_1090 file you just opened, but it has a group of default adjustment layers on top of the same Raw file in the bottom layer. These new adjustment layers give you a template to follow as you color correct this image.

◆ Use the Window menu to switch back to the file named Untitled-1. Now choose File/Close and don't save any changes. We'll use the GibsonsTownMorningTemplate.psd file instead.

Finding the Highlight and Shadow with Threshold

3 Instead of trying to find the Highlight and Shadow values in an image from within Levels, I find doing this in Threshold to be easier and more precise, because you don't need to do it with the Option key held down as you'd have to within Levels.

◆ You should now be working on the GibsonsTownMorningTemplate image, and the bottom layer, CRW_1090, should be active. Otherwise, click the word *CRW_1090* to activate that layer. If

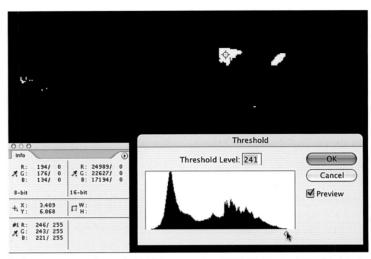

3 Here we are zoomed in on the highlight area at about 200%. We have just Shift-clicked on the highlight spot to create a new highlight Color Sampler, #1, and we are about to move the slider to the left to look for the shadows. We have to use Command (Ctrl)-0 to zoom out, though, before looking for the shadows.

you were to double-click that layer, this would bring you back into Camera Raw and allow you to change the Raw setting for this file. No need to do that now.

◆ Use Layer/New Adjustment Layer/Threshold to bring up a Threshold adjustment layer that we will use temporarily. Click OK to close the New Layer dialog.

You can't use Image/Adjustments/Threshold because you are not allowed to directly modify a Raw Smart Object layer. We are going to cancel this Threshold adjustment layer when we're finished with it, as we are just using it to find the Highlight and Shadow.

◆ With the Preview button on, move the Threshold slider to the right until just the brightest highlight areas in the middle of the image are white and everything else is black. Use Command (Ctrl)-Spacebar-click to zoom in on those areas, and measure the values by putting the cursor over each area and looking at the RGB numbers—the original numbers to the left of the slash—at the top left of the Info palette. When you find the highest set of numbers, Shift-click on top of them to set a Color Sampler there. See the illustration on this page of what this looks like.

◆ Type Command (Ctrl)-0 or use View/Fit On Screen to zoom back out, then move the Threshold slider to the far left so you are looking at the shadow areas. The darkest shadows in this image are at the bottom right underneath the cars. Zoom in on that area, then move the cursor around over these shadows to see what the pattern is. Shadows often have a pattern, and if they do, you want to put your Color Sampler on a point that follows that pattern. The pattern in this image is that the Red values are less than the Green values, and those are less than the Blue values. This actually gives these shadow areas a greenish-blue cast, which we will remove in the next step. When you find the darkest values that fit the pattern, Shift-click to create your shadow Color Sampler.

◆ Use Command (Ctrl)-0 to zoom back out, then click the Cancel button to get out of Theshold. All we wanted to do there was set these two Color Samplers. Zoom in or out to get the image back to 25%, or to where you can see the entire image.

Overall Color Correction Steps Starting with Levels

4 Now we'll show you how to quickly go through the Levels, Curves, and Hue/Saturation overall color correction steps we covered in more detail in Chapter 21.

◆ Click the leftmost layer thumbnail of the Overall Levels layer to activate it, then double-click on this thumbnail to open the now-blank Levels settings.

◆ Click the rightmost Highlight eyedropper within the Levels dialog. Zoom in on Color Sampler 1, the highlight area, and notice that it has a yellow-red cast. This was the morning sun behind this thin layer of clouds. If we click on this with the Highlight eyedropper to set it to white (the 244, 244, 244 value you should have set up in Chapter 2, "Preferences and Color Settings"), you will lose that yellow-red cast that can give this image an interesting mood. Try it by clicking once with this Highlight eyedropper exactly on that highlight Color Sampler point. Notice that this sky area now becomes neutral white and the numbers to the right of the slash in Color Sampler #1 are now 244, 244, 244. Use the Channel pop-up at the top of the Levels dialog to see how clicking with the Highlight eyedropper changed the values on the right side (the Highlight side) of each of the Red, Green, and Blue channels. The initial values to the right, before our click, are 255 and 0. The Blue channel changed the most. The gap on the right side of this channel is what gives the image its yellow cast.

◆ Use Command (Ctrl)-Z—or Option (Alt)-Cancel—to undo this step and return the cast that will help us here in the highlights area of this particular image. Command (Ctrl)-Z changes the last thing you did within a color correction tool. Holding the Option (Alt) key down changes the Cancel button to Reset, and clicking Reset will undo all the changes you've made with this tool. All the color correction tools work in this same way, so this is a useful thing to remember.

◆ Click on the leftmost Shadow eyedropper in the Levels dialog; then, using this eyedropper, zoom into the place below the car where you set the shadow Color Sampler #2, and click on this, which should change the values to the right of the slash on that Color Sampler to 8, 8, 8 and neutralize the shadows. Zoom back out—Command (Ctrl)-0—and turn the Preview button off, then on again, so you can see how the removal of this cast from the shadow areas improves this image.

The color cast in the highlights is helpful to this image, but color casts in the shadows are less likely to be desirable in a print. Now we'll set the middle Brightness slider, then see if the overall cast needs to be adjusted.

◆ Move the middle Brightness slider to the left to open up this dark image. I often open an image up more than one would initially think is needed. After you add the S-curve above and then come back to Levels to darken the shadows, you'll see that opening this image is good. Go into each of the Red, Green, and Blue channels, and if the bottom-left Output slider is not zero, set that to zero. Now move the top-left Shadow slider to the right until the Shadow Color Sampler #2 in the Info palette reads about 6 or 7 again for that color.

Since we brightened all the values at the start of this step, we are just darkening down the shadows again. Muddy shadows generally don't look good in a print. You usually want your deepest shadows to be neutral and black.

◆ Now choose the Green channel and move the middle slider to the right 4 to 5 points. This adds some magenta. Do the same thing with the Blue channel, which will add some yellow. Click OK in the Levels dialog.

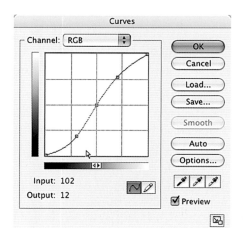

5 My final S-curve for this image, which you load in step 5. This curve increases the contrast of the mid-tone areas by making the slope of that middle part of the curve steeper. It also makes the shadows darker and the highlights brighter.

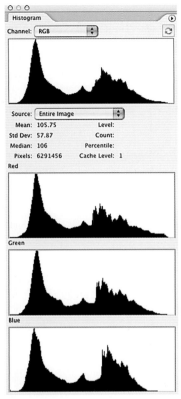

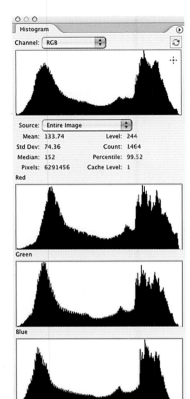

5 Here is the histogram of this image as it looks when we first bring it into Photoshop from Camera Raw. Notice the gaps on either end of the Red, Green, and Blue channels. Also note the shape of the shadow part of the RGB histogram on the left. It is steep and pointed, meaning all the shadow values are crunched together. This non-spread-out histogram is characteristic of a dark, flat image. To get this histogram display, choose All Channels View from the Histogram palette menu.

5 The histogram after the Levels and Curves settings. See how the gaps on the left of the Red, Green, and Blue channels are mostly gone, and notice how the shadow part of the histogram is now spread out more, with a rounded top. Notice also on the rightmost highlight side that values have been spread out and are closer to the right. These changes give the image more contrast and detail.

Adjusting the S-Curve Template

5 This image will still look flat, but we'll add an S-curve and saturate the colors before we go back and finalize our Levels settings.

◆ Click the leftmost layer thumbnail on the next adjustment layer named OverallS-Curve. Click the Eye icon for that layer so it's now active and visible. You'll notice that your image increases in contrast a bit. Double-click the leftmost layer thumbnail to bring up the Curves dialog, and reveal the subtle S-curve I initially placed in this template layer. Click the bottom-left point and drag it down and to the right. Click the top-right point and drag

it up and to the left. These adjustments increase the contrast of this curve. Now Shift-click the middle point and the bottom-left point till all three points are selected. You can now click and drag any of the three points to move the entire curve at once. Moving it up and to the left lightens the image and moving it down and to the right darkens it.

◆ Click the Load button and browse to the file MyFinalGibsonsS-Curve.acv in the Chapter 22 folder on the DVD. Load this curve and notice how it makes the image more dramatic but probably too dark. Choose OK in the Curves dialog, then double-click the leftmost Levels layer thumbnail to reopen your Levels dialog. Move the middle Brightness slider to the left till it reaches 1.66. Now the image should look better. Go into each of the Red, Green, and Blue channels and move the Top Shadow slider until the shadow Color Sampler, in the Info palette, reads about 2 for that color. Remember that once you click on the Shadow slider, you can use the up and down arrows on your keyboard to move its value by just one number at a time. This is often easier and more exact than trying to get a specific value using a click-and-drag in a Levels slider with the mouse.

We've adjusted the histogram of this image to spread out the many shadow values and we've also increased the contrast in the shadows by brightening the midtones and darkening the deep shadows. You are massaging the histogram to correct it as you color correct this image. See the illustrations of the histograms at the top of this page.

Saturating the Colors

6 Now we'll set the values in the Hue/Saturation adjustment layer template.

◆ Click the Hue/Saturation layer above the S-Curve layer, then double-click its layer thumbnail to open the Hue/Saturation dialog. Move the Master Saturation slider to the right to saturate all the colors. I set mine to 22. Now change the Edit pop-up to Reds. Move the Hue and Saturation sliders here to see how they influence the image, especially the sun colors in the sky. I set the Hue to −4 and the Saturation to +8. This further saturates things that have red in them. Now switch to Yellows and see how adjusting the Hue and Saturation of yellows affects this image. I set the Yellow Hue to −3 and the Saturation to +12.

◆ If your color looks a bit off here, click the Load button in the Hue/Saturation dialog and load MyFinalGibsonsHueSat.ahu from the Chapter 22 folder on the DVD, then click OK for Hue/Saturation. Now double-click back on the Levels thumbnail and load

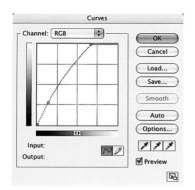

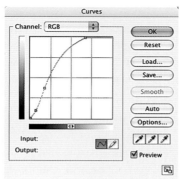

7 This is the default shadow curve in my color correction template.

7 Here is the shadow curve as I adjusted it for this image. This curve is steeper in the middle, which adds more contrast to the shadows and midtones.

MyFinalGibsonsLevels.alv, and you should be where I was at this point in the correction process. If the color still looks off, well, we're not done yet!

Opening the Shadows

7 The next three steps adjust the Shadows, Highlights, and Midtones. You can do this kind of adjustment with the semiautomatic Shadow/Highlight tool, but I think you'll see here how doing it with Curves adjustment layers and masks gives you so much more control than the Shadow/Highlight tool, which we seldom use.

Eventually the top and bottom parts of this image will be cropped off, so we want to focus on the areas above the cars and below those branches at the very top that come in from the sides. Let's open some shadow details in those areas that will remain in the final image.

◆ Click the next layer—called OpenShadows—in the color correction template. It's not doing anything to the image right now because its layer mask is all black. Shift-click its rightmost Layer Mask thumbnail to temporarily turn off this mask, and you'll see that this curve opens up the town of Gibsons and the houses and trees on the point behind the town. Shift-click the mask again to turn it back on.

◆ Type B for Paintbrush, choose the Airbrush 7% option from the Tool presets, and type D for default colors, and you'll be painting with a white soft brush. Zoom in to 100%, use the left or right bracket key to adjust your brush size, and paint over the image where you want to see more shadow details. With the Airbrush option, the longer you hold the brush down, even in one location, the more paint you get. It's like applying shadow detail with a can of spray paint! When you paint on any adjustment layer, the paint

8 The setup for creating your gradient with white as the foreground color, black as the background color, and the top-left Foreground to Background gradient chosen. You also want Linear Gradient to be set as the Gradient type, the Mode to be set to Normal, and the Opacity to be set to 100%.

automatically gets applied to the layer mask. You paint directly over the areas of the image that you want to change, but it's the whiteness or blackness of the mask that changes. If you get too much shadow detail in a particular spot, type X for Exchange, which will change your painting color to black. Now paint over the mask in that area with black, and you can lower the shadow detail until you are happy with it.

◆ Open the image named GibsonsTownMorningLayers.psd, which is our master layers file of this image. Type F to put it into Full Screen mode. Turn off the Eye icons for all the layers above the OpenShadows layer. Now you see where I was at this point. You

8 To create our gradient, we clicked down just about where we had set our highlight; then, while holding the mouse button down, we dragged downward with the Shift key also held down and then released the mouse button just above the horizon—or actually at the horizon. This created a gradient that was white everywhere above where we clicked down and black everywhere below where we released. This makes the highlight adjustment layer turn on in most of the sky but slowly blend off as it approaches the horizon.

can turn the Eye icon for this layer off and then on again to see how it influences our version of this image. You can look at the mask we made by Option (Alt)-clicking on the Layer Mask thumbnail. Notice how the white areas of the mask are pretty subtle and no areas are totally white. You don't want to open these shadows too much or they will look too noisy or blown out.

◆ Now you can go back to your version of this image, called GibsonsTownMorningTemplate, by choosing it from the Window menu or by using Control (Ctrl)-Tab to switch back and forth between the two open documents.

◆ Another thing you can do once you get your shadow mask started is to double-click the layer thumbnail to bring up my default shadow curve. You can then adjust this curve, making it steeper for more shadow contrast or less steep if the shadows are looking too blown out.

Improving the Highlights

8 Now we'll see what we can do with the sky and trees in this image. Remember that we are planning to eventually crop the upper part of the sky where the branches come in from either side.

◆ When you are happy with the shadows, click the layer thumbnail for the next adjustment layer, which is AddHighlightDetail. The process here is the same as with the shadows. You can Shift-click on the mask for this adjustment layer to see what it would do if it were all white. Another Shift-click turns the mask back on again. Now press B for Brush and D for default colors, and paint in the areas where you want highlight details.

◆ Another way to handle the highlight mask, which is what we did with this image, is to use the Gradient tool to make the mask white in just the highlight areas and black everywhere else. Type G for Gradient, then D for default colors. See the illustrations to the left for help with all your settings.

◆ Click down an inch or so above the horizon, then drag downward toward the horizon and release when you reach it. Holding the Shift key down will force the line to be vertical and the gradient to be horizontal. The mask will now be on in the sky and off below the horizon. You can redo the gradient by just dragging another one until it looks right. You'll probably find that the contrast this gradient has created is too much. Type H for the Hand tool, then type a number between 0 and 9 to change the opacity of this layer: 0 is 100%, 1 is 10%, and 5 is 50%, which is what we set our opacity to. If you type the numbers while still in the Gradient tool, this changes the opacity of future gradients—that's

why we had you type H for the Hand tool! When you get the overall opacity right and most of the sky looks good, then type B to go back to the Brush and paint along the horizon in black, where you want to lessen the effects of this layer, and white where you want more of this layer. You want to be painting using the Airbrush 7% Tool preset. If you double-click the layer thumbnail of the AddHighlightDetail layer, you can bring up the Curves dialog and adjust the default curve that the template set up for this layer.

◆ Use Control (Ctrl)-Tab to switch to my version of the image, and turn my AddHighlightDetail adjustment layer's Eye icon on and off to compare what you did to what I did. Notice that I added a Hue/Saturation adjustment layer above this one to tweak just the parts affected by my AddHighlightDetail mask. Turn that layer on and off too, so you can understand what it does. Double-click this Hue/Saturation layer thumbnail to see what adjustments I made. Double-click the AddHighlightDetail layer thumbnail to see what adjustments I also made to this curve.

◆ Use Control (Ctrl)-Tab to switch back to your version of the image, then choose Layer/New Adjustment Layer/Hue/Saturation and make sure the check box is on for the Use Previous Layer to Create Clipping Mask option. This will cause this new layer to be indented, which means it will also share the gradient mask you made for the previous layer. Now, if you want to match what we did, Saturate Master by 20%, set Yellows to +2 on Hue and +17 on Saturation, and set Blues to −16 on Hue and +40 on Saturation. You should play with these settings to get the combination that you like best in your version of this image.

Adjusting the Midtone Contrast

9 You may find that the area above the cars in the foreground, and the horizon in the middle, looks a bit flat. This next layer will solve that problem, we hope.

◆ Click the next AddMidtoneContrast adjustment layer to activate it. Paint white in its mask using a soft brush with the Airbrush 7% option over any areas where the image is too flat. We painted over the houses, the boats in the harbor, and many locations within the town. I also painted over the water in some areas to add contrast there too. As with the Shadows and Highlights, you can also change my default midtone contrast curve and/or the opacity of any of these adjustment layers.

◆ Use Control (Ctrl)-Tab to switch to my version of the image, and turn the Eye icon off and on again for my AddMidtoneContrast adjustment layer so you can compare your results to mine.

Making a Channel Mask to Enhance the Water

10 Now we'll change the color and contrast of the water, but we first need to make a mask that is white just in the areas where the water is. This is a complex mask due to the silhouette of the trees that you can see the water through. We'll look at the Red, Green, and Blue channels and see if one of them will help in making this mask.

◆ Notice that above my AddMidtoneContrast adjustment layer, I've added a Curves adjustment layer named TweakWater. The purpose

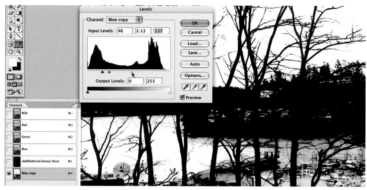

10 In Image/Adjustments/Levels, making the mask of the water area from the Blue copy channel. Notice that the sky above is white, as are some of the boats. We have a nice silhouette of the trees, though, which would be hard to do by hand. We can now easily paint around the water to create the final mask, where all but the water is black.

10 The final water mask after painting the surrounding areas black. Once I carefully went around the edges of the water with a smaller, black 80% brush, I then used the right bracket key to increase the brush size a lot so I could quickly paint the rest of the mask black.

of this layer is to change the contrast and color of the water. Click the TweakWater layer to activate it, then Option (Alt)-click on its mask and you'll see that this mask is quite detailed. I made it by copying the Blue channel and using Levels to isolate the areas of the water from its surroundings. Let's make a similar mask in your version of this image.

◆ Use Control (Ctrl)-Tab to switch back to your version of this image, which needs to be finished through the AddMidtoneContrast step with that top AddMidtoneContrast layer being active and all the layers under it active with their Eye icons on. Bring up the Channels palette [Shift-F10] and click the word *Red* to look at the Red channel. Make sure the Eye icons are off for RGB and the other channels. Zoom into 50% and look at the area where the water can be seen through the trees. You want to find the channel that has the most contrast between the water, trees, and the waters surroundings. Click on Green to check the Green channel, then on Blue to look at the Blue channel. In my version of this image, the Blue channel has the most contrast.

◆ Click the word *Blue* and drag this on top of the New Channel icon just to the left of the Trash icon at the bottom of the Channels palette. This will make a copy of the Blue channel named Blue copy. Choose Image/Adjustments/Levels and move the rightmost Highlight slider to the left and the leftmost Shadow slider to the right until the water area is white with a good sil-

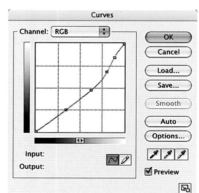

10 This is my main TweakWater curve adjustment, although I did make minor color changes in the Green and Blue curves, too. You can load my curve and check out all the channels by using the Load button and choosing TweakWaterCurve.acv in the Chapter 22 folder on the DVD.

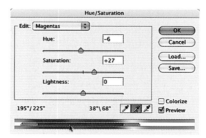

10 The water Hue/Saturation adjustment. Notice the wide range of colors being adjusted, shown at the bottom around the arrow cursor.

houette of the trees and a dark outline around most of the water. Click OK in the Levels dialog, then type B for the Paintbrush and choose the PaintBrush Opacity 100% Flow 100% option from the Tool presets pop-up in the Options bar. Now pick a fairly large brush from the second row of brushes. These all have their hardness set to 80% so the edge is a little soft, but they are much more precise than the soft brushes. Type D for default colors, then X for exchange, and you'll be painting with black. Make an outline around the edges of the water, then paint in the rest of the mask so only the water is left white. Remember that you can use the left and right bracket keys to change the size of your brush.

◆ Command (Ctrl)-click on the Blue copy channel, which will load the white areas as a selection. Click on the word *RGB* at the top of the Channels palette. Now choose Layer/New Adjustment Layer/Curves—[Command (Ctrl)-F3]—to add a new curve for adjusting the water. Click the Load button and load TweakWater-Curve.acv from the Chapter 22 folder on the DVD. Notice that we also made small changes to the Green and Blue channels. If our curve doesn't seem to do the right thing to your image, you can adjust our curve or make your own.

◆ Use [Command (Ctrl)-F4] to add a Hue/Saturation adjustment layer, and be sure to check the Use Previous Layer to Create Clipping Mask option in the New Layer dialog. You can use this adjustment layer to make subtle changes to the water's color. I started out adjusting Blues but wasn't able to get the change I wanted. I then dragged the +Eyedropper tool across the water to include the range of blues that were there in that water area. You can use the middle +Eyedropper tool to add colors to the default range of color Photoshop assigns each of Red, Green, Blue, Cyan, Magenta, or Yellow. The area I dragged across included so many colors that the color range got renamed from Blues to Magentas. When you start with a particular color range and then drastically change it using the −Eyedropper tool, Photoshop will sometimes change the range's name to reflect its predominant color. I then adjusted this range with a Hue adjustment of −6 and a Saturation adjustment of +27.

Using the Burn&Dodge and Crop Layers

11 The next layer in the template is called Burn&Dodge. To create one of these layers from scratch, choose Layer/New/Layer, and in the New Layer dialog set the Blend mode (just called Mode in the dialog) to Soft Light. You then get the choice to Fill with Soft-Light Neutral Color (50% gray). If you turn this choice on and click OK,

you get a layer that is filled with 50% gray, but you can't see any difference in your image from before. That's because in Soft Light mode 50% gray doesn't do anything. Areas that are darker than 50% gray will darken your image, and areas that are brighter make your image lighter. In this case "your image" is the cumulative effect of all the layers underneath this current layer.

I usually end my image adjustments with a Burn&Dodge layer, but if I'm going to crop the image, the Crop layer will be at the top of my Layers palette.

◆ Make sure the Eye icon is on for the Burn&Dodge layer and click it to activate it. Leave the Eye icon off for the Crop layer at the top of the Layers palette.

◆ We're going to set the crop of that Crop layer now, before we do the final burning and dodging. Type M to switch to the Rectangular Marquee tool. Click in the gray area at the top left around

11 Here we made this Marquee selection by first clicking down in the gray area to the left of the image, just at the top of the trees. We released the mouse when we got to the gray area just to the right of the image, next to the white truck. By starting and ending your selections in the gray areas, you make sure you get all the pixels along the edge of the image without having to worry about exactly selecting that edge. Now we've clicked on the CropLayer to activate it and we're about to Option (Alt)-click the icon at the bottom of the Layers palette; that will add a layer mask to the CropLayer with this selection inverted so that all we see of this layer are the nonselected parts. Those parts will then be the same gray color as the gray background in Photoshop, so it will look like we cropped the image. After adding the layer mask, we just need to turn the CropLayer's Eye icon on to see the effect.

The original image after opening it from Camera Raw but before any color correction in Photoshop.

The image after the Levels, Curves, and Hue/Saturation overall color correction steps, and also after the Shadow, Highlight, and Midtone adjustment layers were added.

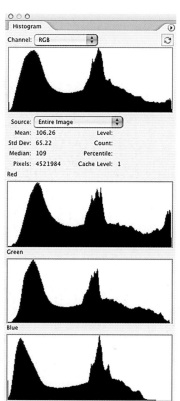

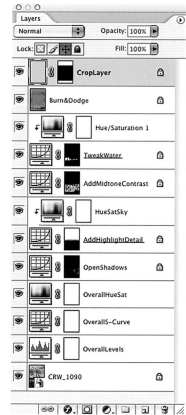

Here we see the final histogram after all the layers have been added. Notice how much fuller and spread out it is than the histogram at the beginning of this example.

This is the final Layers palette for the adjusted image you see to the right.

The final cropped image after tweaking the water color, adding the Burn and Dodge layer, and sharpening using Smart Sharpen. Sharpening techniques and the various sharpening options are explained in detail in Chapter 12.

the edge of the image, just above the tops of the tree limbs whose trunks you can actually see, and drag to the bottom-right gray area so the horizontal line at the bottom just cuts off the leftmost car. If you were in the Oval Marquee by mistake, do Command (Ctrl)-Z to ditch your selection, then use Shift-M to switch to the Rectangular Marquee. If the starting position of your selection was incorrect, hold down the Spacebar before releasing the mouse button and you'll find that, while the Spacebar is held down, you can move the top-left corner of the marquee till you get it in the right place. Releasing the Spacebar puts you back into normal drawing mode so you can complete your Marquee selection. See the selection illustration on page 281 if you are having trouble visualizing what we are talking about.

◆ Once you have your selection made, you then want to click the word *CropLayer* to activate that layer, then Option (Alt)-click on the Add Layer Mask icon at the bottom of the Layers palette. Another way to add the mask is to choose Layer/Layer Mask/Hide Selection. Now just turn on the Eye icon for CropLayer to see the effect.

◆ Now that you can see the part of the image that you are planning to actually print, click back on the word *Burn&Dodge* to activate the Burn&Dodge layer. Type B for the Brush, choose Airbrush 7% from the Tool presets to the left of the Options bar, then type D for default colors. When you type D while working on a mask, you get white as the foreground color and black as the background color. Since this layer is actually a normal layer, and not a mask, typing D gives you black as the foreground color and white as the background color. You are now set to Burn, or darken, an area that you paint with black on top of this layer. Try it for areas around the edges of the image, like the light car and truck at the bottom. If you make things too dark, instead of Undo just type an X to "exchange" to white and paint over the too-dark area with white till it lightens up some. You're creating the image interactively, the way a painter would. To lighten areas of the image, just paint over those areas with white.

◆ In Soft Light mode you can only lighten or darken the existing image—you can't make it pure white or black. If you use the Blend Mode menu, just under the Layers tab at the top of the palette, to switch the Blend mode of this layer to Overlay, you'll notice that the changes become more contrasty. With Hard Light they are even more contrasty and probably unusable. I've found that Soft Light works the best for this technique because the changes look the most natural with photographs. Burning and Dodging your image in this way is a nondestructive process. You

can change it as many times as you want without degrading the pixels in your original image layer. We don't use the Burn, Dodge, and Sponge tools in the Tools palette because they would actually change the image pixels.

If you like the time savings of having your color correction workflow set up in a template like it was in this image, you can create your own set of actions to make your own color correction templates. See Chapter 10, "Automating Photoshop," to learn more about doing this. You can also get BarrysPhotoshopActions, which include BarrysColorCorrectionTemplate, used here, along with others, in the Actions area of www.barryhaynes.com.

Other Problem Images

In this section we'll open the final Layers palettes of several images I have worked on that required more than the normal amount of

12 This image of the Boat and Sunset on Howe Sound waterway in Gibsons was taken during very low light at the last minute, without a tripod. I saw the light on the mountains and ran two blocks down the road to capture what my eyes were amazed at. What the camera actually saw was quite different, but since I shot in Raw mode, I was able to put things back, maybe even better than what my eyes originally saw, in the print. This image is great for showing you what can be done with both highlight and shadow color casts.

effort to create a fine print. I will talk about various choices I made in correcting those images and compare their Layers palettes to the Layers palette of the image we just worked with in the first part of this chapter.

Sunset and Water Color Casts in Boat and Sunset on Howe Sound

12 Looking at the final Layers palette for this image, on this page, we see a lot of similarities and some differences compared with the previous image. The Howe Sound image starts with the normal Levels, Curves, and Hue/Saturation. As in the previous image, there was no good place to set the highlight because I wanted to preserve the red and yellow sunset colors. This image also has the blue water in the foreground shadows, then the transition between these two extremes of light. We also had to remove color casts from the boat dock and the white boat surrounded by blue water.

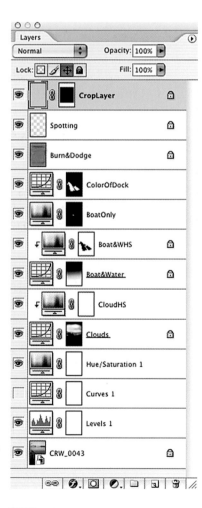

12 Here is the final Layers palette for the BoatSunsetHoweSound image. Note the traditional Levels, Curves, Hue/Saturation start, followed by a couple of layers to adjust the clouds, and a gradient curve to adjust the color and contrast of the blue water in the foreground and separate it from the sunset clouds. The Hue/Saturation adjustment layer connected to this gradient has a mask that is black where the boat dock is, so the Hue and Saturation changes do not affect the dock. Above that we have a tweak for the boat, another dock color adjustment, then our Burn&Dodge layer, a little spotting, and finally the crop.

Setup to Work with This Image

◆ Close all other images you were working with and save your version of the previous image if you want to. Open the file Boat-SunsetHoweSoundLayers.psd from the Chapter 22 folder on your DVD, and type F to put it in Full Screen mode. Bring up the Layers palette and resize it so you can see all the layers. It should look like the palette pictured on this page. Arrange your screen so you can see all of the image and all of the Layers palette. Close other palettes that might clutter your workspace.

Looking at the Levels Settings and Color Casts

◆ Double-click the leftmost Levels layer thumbnail to bring up the Levels adjustment again. This is the second layer from the bottom. Notice that the histogram for this image has quite a gap on the right side. This is often the case with sunset images especially if the light is low and we are moving into dusk.

◆ Switch to the Red channel and click the Input Highlight slider. This is the rightmost slider in the top group. Slide it to the left and notice how the reds in the sky become more brilliant. Hold the Option (Alt) key down as you slide to the left, and see how that the increasing solid red area is showing you how this adjustment will throw away subtle highlight details in those clouds. Now slide it to the right, without the Option (Alt) key depressed, and notice the move toward cyan in these highlight areas of the image. There was no good place to set a neutral highlight point here, so I just had to adjust the sliders until it looked right on the screen and in my prints. Move this slider back to 245, where it started.

◆ Move the Red shadow slider, the top-left one, to the left and notice how the dark blue water and dock in the foreground get a red cast. If you move this too far to the right, the cast goes cyan. Now hold the Option (Alt) key down and see how shadow details get lost (go to black) as you move it to the right. Move it back to 9, where it started.

◆ Switch to the Green channel and try similar experiments with the Highlight and Shadow sliders there, too. Notice how radical the change in dark blue water color is, and the color of the dock, too, if I move the Green leftmost Shadow slider from 5 up to 8. This is why I emphasize control of shadow and highlight colors and values so much in this book and in my digital printmaking workshops. People often make muddy-looking prints. To avoid this problem, we check to see if the shadows are black and if they have a cast in them. One of those issues is often the cause of muddy prints. Even though there are no values in the highlight side of the Green histogram, notice how dramatic a color change happens when we move the Green highlight slider to the right or left just a few points.

◆ Move on to the Blue channel. Some subtle moves with the endpoints of Blue along with the endpoints of Green can give me a much deeper blue water color if that is what I'm looking for. Play with these colors and have some fun! When you are done playing, use the Cancel button to return Levels to where it started.

A Dormant Curves Layer

Notice that my overall Curves adjustment layer, named Curves 1, has its Eye icon turned off so it is not currently affecting this image.

◆ If you turn its Eye icon back on, then double-click its layer thumbnail, you'll notice that it is a reverse S-curve, which I used to initially reduce the contrast on this image. After making the other adjustments to this image, above this one, I decided the image looked better with this curve off. Click Cancel in the Curve dialog and turn this layer's Eye icon off again.

Adjusting the Clouds

◆ Turn the Clouds curve layer's Eye icon off and then on again to see what this curve does to the contrast and mood of this image. Double-click this curve's layer thumbnail to actually bring up the curve. Hold the mouse button down over different parts of the image and notice the circle on the curve that shows you where that mouse location shows up on the curve. Notice that I also changed the Green channel in this curve to increase the amount of magenta in the sky. Zoom into 100% while looking at the parts of the sky where the mask for this layer is whitest. Change different parts of the RGB and/or the Green curve to learn how it can affect this image. Think how you might apply these techniques to your own images! Use Cancel when you close this Curves dialog so that the rest of the discussion about this image is still valid. You might want to turn the Eye icon off for my curve, then use the step I mention next to create a similar curve of your own.

◆ Click the Hue/Saturation 1 layer below my curve before you create your own. That will put your curve in the correct location. To initially make the Clouds curve, choose Layer/New Adjustment Layer/Curves, and, while looking at the clouds and other areas you want to modify, adjust the curve to get those areas to the color and contrast that you want. Now click OK in the Curves dialog and use Image/Adjustments/Invert to invert the Curves layer mask to black. At this point typing B, for Paintbrush, choos-

ing the Airbrush 7% preset, and typing D for default colors will allow you to paint white in the mask where you want to apply the effect of this curve most. When you are done with your curve, turn its Eye icon off and my curve's Eye icon back on so we can talk about the rest of this image.

◆ Turn the CloudHS Eye icon off and then on again to see what this layer does. It is sharing the same mask as the Clouds layer below. If you double-click the CloudHS layer thumbnail, you'll see that all the adjustments were made to the Reds, Yellows, and Blues. In sunset scenes I often modify the Reds and the Yellows to help separate the two from each other and also to get the exact intensity and color that I want. For this adjustment, the Blues setting is tweaking the area that is a transition between the deep blues at the bottom of the image and the water at the top that has the red-green reflections in it. Modify these Red, Yellow, and Blue Hue and Saturation sliders to get an understanding of how they affect the sky and also interact with each other and the water.

Curve Subtleties, Clipping Masks, and Groups of Layers

◆ Turn the Eye icon off and then on again for the Boat&Water curve, which is applied using a gradient as we did in step 7 with the previous image. Notice that I also made subtle changes to the Green and Blue channels of this curve.

Even though this curve removes many of the brightest highlights, as shown in the illustration here, those highlights in the image are protected by the Curves mask.

Notice that the mask for the Boat&WHS Hue/Saturation adjustment is black in the areas of the dock and boat. Since this layer is indented, it shares the gradient mask from the Boat&Water curve below but it also has its own mask. By making its mask black in the

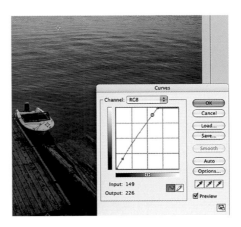

12 Even though this curve on the Boat&Water layer has removed all the highlight detail in the top third of the dynamic range, it's OK because no values in the areas where its mask is nonblack are in that dynamic range. You can see that, because I've got the cursor down toward the top of this layer's range and the circle on the curve is still not all the way to the top of the diagram. The gradient mask in this area is also fairly dark gray, so this curve is not being applied anywhere near 100% in that brighter area.

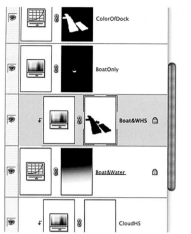

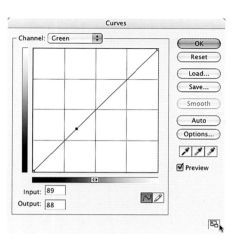

12 Here you see a section of the Layers palette with the active layer containing the mask shown to the right. The mask on the Boat&Water layer, directly below, is also part of the mask for this layer.

12 This mask on the Boat&WHS Hue/Saturation layer shares the gradient mask in the underlined Boat&Water layer below it.

12 When you need to place a point on a curve and just move it a small amount, click the icon at the bottom right of the Curves dialog to get the bigger Curves dialog. You can place a point on the curve that corresponds to a certain color in an image by Command (Ctrl)-clicking on that part of the image while the Curves dialog is up and you are in the channel you want. Then to move that point by just one number value, use the arrow keys on the keyboard or type the new value you want. When you are in the smaller curve diagram, the arrow moves a point by two number values.

areas of the dock and boat, those areas are excluded from the effects of this layer. Where this layer's mask is white, those corresponding areas of the image get some of the effects of this mask if the mask of the Boat&Water layer below is not black in those areas. This is a very useful technique: using the main mask at the bottom of an indented group, yet allowing each layer in the group to have its own mask tweaks.

Removing a Color Cast from Bright Neutrals

The next Hue/Saturation layer, named BoatOnly, has a mask that is only white in the areas where the boat is white.

◆ Double-click the layer thumbnail to bring up the Hue/Saturation dialog, and you'll notice that I moved the Master Saturation slider to −51.

This removes, or reduces anyhow, the blue cast that is on the white parts of the boat. I use this local desaturation technique a lot to remove color casts in rushing water scenes or anywhere that something white or close to white has a cast that I want to remove. This works better than trying to fix the cast with a Levels or Curves adjustment because those types of adjustments, to fix local casts, often cause an opposite cast somewhere else. They also cause a change in brightness or contrast, which I didn't want here.

Really Minor Curve Tweaks Can Have Big Impacts

◆ Turn the Eye icon off and then on again for the next ColorOf-Dock layer. This will allow you to see what this layer does.

The mask just affects the dock area, which had too much of a green cast for my eye. This dock actually is greenish because it is treated wood and also has some moss growing on it.

◆ Double-click the layer thumbnail to look at the curve for this ColorOfDock layer, and you'll be surprised how much such a subtle curve change affected the color of the dock.

When changing between green and magenta, moving a curve just one point can often make the needed difference. That's what I did here: I moved the Green curve one point, from Input of 89 to Output of 88, and moved the Blue curve two points, from Input of 114 to Output of 112.

Burn&Dodge and the Crop Layer

Above this ColorOfDock layer is my Burn&Dodge layer for this image.

◆ Turn its Eye icon off and on to see how I used it in this image.

Above that is a Spotting layer, which just removes a dark cloud from the top-left corner of the part of this image we are using, after the crop is applied. I normally do my simple spotting on the Background layer, but since this image has a Raw smart object as the bottom layer, and also since I might change my crop at a later time, doing the spotting on a separate layer gives me more options.

To create this Spotting layer, while the Burn&Dodge layer was active, I chose Layer/New/Layer and named it Spotting in the New Layer dialog. This gave me a new layer filled with transparency. I then typed S to put myself in the Clone Stamp tool and turned on the Sample All Layers option in the Options bar for Clone Stamp. While still on my Spotting layer, I then Option (Alt)-clicked on the part of the sky I wanted to use to copy over this small dark cloud. I then painted over the cloud to copy the lighter sky area over the dark cloud until everything matched and looked the way I wanted it to.

To actually use the top CropLayer to make a crop, try this!

◆ Click the word *CropLayer* to activate that layer. Use [Shift-F10] to bring up the Channels palette where you'll see the CropLayer Mask at the bottom. Click the words *CropLayer Mask* and drag the mask to the New Channel/Copy Channel icon at the bottom of the Channels palette just to the left of the Trash icon. This will make a copy of the Crop Layer mask named CropLayer mask Copy. Now choose Image/Adjustments/Invert to invert this mask.

You'll see why in a minute. You want to use the crop at the point when you want to make a print of this image.

◆ To make a print of this image, choose Image/Duplicate and turn on the Duplicate Merged Layers Only check box. Do this now.

This will give you a flattened copy of this layers document, which you'll want to sharpen before making the print. Notice though that in the Channels palette of that copy, you still have the channel named CropLayer mask Copy. All your other layer masks and layers are now gone, since this is a flattened copy.

◆ Command (Ctrl)-click on this CropLayer mask Copy, then choose Image/Crop to crop your image. Finally you can press Command (Ctrl)-D to get rid of your selection, and then you can drag the CropLayer mask Copy channel to the trash.

Doing the crop this way, after the Image/Duplicate step, is safer because you don't risk accidentally doing a save of the flattened image over the top of your master layers file. Cropping a flattened copy is also much faster because all the other layers, and their masks, don't also have to be cropped! To learn how to sharpen the flattened copy of a master layers file, look at Chapter 12, "Essential Photoshop Techniques for Photographers."

Looking at the Mono Lake Image

13 Let's spend a few minutes here talking about one of my favorite images—Mono Lake Dried Bush. This image was taken while I was at California's Mono Lake teaching Digital Printmaking for the Ansel Adams Digital Workshops. Mono Lake is just east of Yosemite, at 6000 feet. In a half-hour drive from Mono lake, you can be at 10,000 feet in Yosemite's Tuolomne Meadows, also a great place to shoot. The town of Lee Vining, at Mono Lake, is a wonderful place to stay when doing photography. TI took this image with my Pentax 6x7 camera and its wonderful 45mm wide-angle lens. The amount of information I get with this camera on 120 film, when scanned at 4000 dpi, gives me more detail than most digital cameras.

◆ Close all the other images you have open, then use File/Open to open the file named MonoLakeDriedBushLayersSm.psd from the Chapter 22 folder on your DVD. Type F to put this image into Full Screen mode, and arrange the Layers palette to the right of your image so you can see all the layers; then open your Histogram palette to the left of the image. With the image zoomed to 50% on your screen, you can see all these things at once and all of the image in the middle of your screen.

Comparing Histograms to Images

Over the next three pages, I have three versions of the Mono Lake image—13a, 13c, and 13e—comparing it before color correction to halfway through color correction to the final corrected image. I also have five versions of the histogram palette, 13a–13e. Three of those histogram palettes correspond to the three images, and the other two are intermediate steps. One way of thinking about color correction is that when we color correct, we are massaging the image's histogram

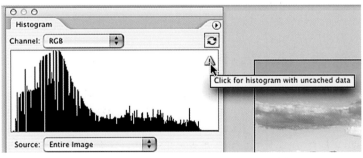

13 When you are looking at a histogram display in the Histogram palette and it looks full of gaps like this one, click the yellow exclamation point icon and the histogram will be recalculated from all the data available for the image instead of from the small image cache version, which is the way the histogram initially gets calculated. If the yellow exclamation point is not there, then the histogram you are seeing has been calculated from all the data. The other screen shots of histograms in this chapter were made using the images' complete data.

13a This is the original Mono Lake image as I scanned it. See the histogram for this image in histogram illustration 13a to the right of this image. I generally scan without doing adjustments in the scanner software because I want to do all my color adjustments in Photoshop and make sure I don't lose any highlight or shadow information during the scan. With 16-bit scans, there is no reason to do color adjustments with the scanner software since the 16-bit file gives Photoshop everything that the scanner gets from the film.

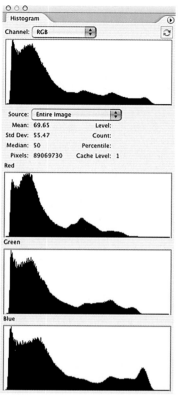

13a Original Mono Lake Histogram with no adjustments. Notice how the shadow values, to the left side, are all crunched together, and the large gaps to the right on each of the Red, Green, and Blue channels. This is why the original image is so flat.

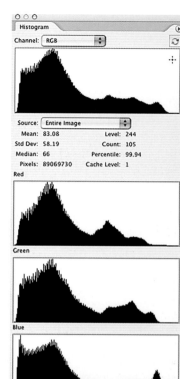

13b Here is the histogram of this image after just the levels adjustments are made. Notice that we spread the histogram out some across the possible range of image values.

to get the effect we want. With this image, we want it to have a full range of values, with black shadows and bright highlights, even white in the brightest parts of the clouds. Look at the three images and the five histograms; reading the captions under each will show you how to relate some of the changes in the histograms with the changes in the images and vice versa.

While color correcting, look at the Histogram palette from time to time to make sure you haven't lost some detail that you wanted to keep. The histogram can also tell you if your shadows are flat, if there is a cast in the image, and if the camera or scanner lost some information when capturing the image.

The Dust and Scratches Filter

With this photograph, I used the Dust and Scratches filter to help spot the image. This process is further explained in Chapter 12.

◆ Option (Alt)-click the Eye icon of the Background layer of this image to turn off all the other layers. Click the D&S 3,12 layer and turn on its Eye icon. This is just a copy of the Background layer that I ran Filter/Noise/Dust and Scratches (with a Radius of 3 and a Threshold of 12) on to remove crud that is in the lake and sky areas. I'm only using this layer in those areas, as they don't contain sharp details, which D&S will blur. Remember that what you are looking at here is a greatly downsampled version of my original scan and master layers file. That is a 1.6-gigabyte file. Still, if you zoom in to 400%, then look at the difference between the D&S layer and the original, in the areas where the mask is white you can see some of the spots and noise that the D&S layer

13c This is the state of the Mono Lake image after the Levels plus Open Up and Drama Highlights adjustments were completed on it. Now we have an image, and histogram, that looks more like a normal photograph than a problem image. The rest of the adjustments are more typical than the curve I created to open up the dried bush in the foreground of this image. This bush was flat in the film, because the light on it was low and I had to expose so that I also got the bright clouds and highlights on the film. What I'm doing with the Open Up adjustment curve is returning that bush to the way I visualized it being in the print, and also more closely to the way my eyes saw it.

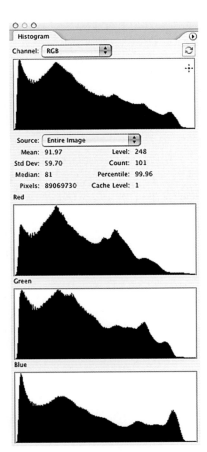

13c The Mono Lake Histogram after the Levels and Open Up and Drama Highlights adjustments. The Open Up adjustment layer curve greatly brightened the dried bush in the foreground of this image, which is a main part of the photograph. Notice how the shadow and midtone parts of this histogram moved to the right and spread out during this adjustment.

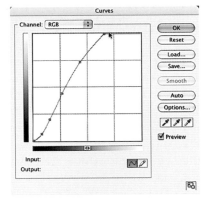

13c Here is the curve used to bring that dull, dried bush back to life. If there were any original values in the range from where my cursor is at the right, this curve would force them to pure white. The mask stops that from happening. Turn the curve's Eye icon off and then on again to see the far-reaching effect on the foreground bush and other parts of this image.

removed. A good place to use the Dust and Scratches filter is on skies from film where there is a lot of spotting and no detail in the skies.

The Open Up Curve and Drama Highlights Curve

The Open Up curve brings the dried bush in the foreground back to life, as it does other, less dark areas of the image.

◆ After turning the Levels layer and its Eye icon on, you'll see that this layer improves the image to some degree. Now turn the Open Up Curve layer and the Drama Highlights Curve layer on, and you'll see a dramatic improvement to the image. Double-click the curve's layer thumbnail so you can take a look at the curve. Notice how the top-right highlight side has values turned completely to white. Doing this is one thing that adds such contrast

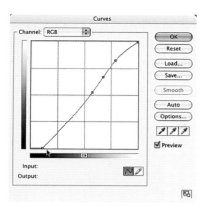

13c This is the Drama Highlights curve. Notice that this curve forces dark areas to pure black to the left of where my cursor is at the bottom left of the diagram. Look at the whitish areas in the mask for this layer, and you'll see that some of those areas in the image become much more dramatic when this curve is applied. Turn the curve's Eye icon off and then on again to see its effect in the background areas of this image.

to the bush area of the image. Increasing the steepness of the curve and moving it to the left are the other factors. Because the bush's values were originally so dark, they are not forced to pure white, so we are not losing any highlight detail, even with such a dramatic curve. Curves are amazing! Now open up the Drama Highlights curve and notice that the bottom-left shadow end of this curve is also potentially forcing values to pure black. Pure black in small areas gives a print drama. Look at the bright whites and dark blacks in some of Ansel Adams prints. I've looked at the originals up close, and they are definately dramatic. That steep drop-off at the left end of the 13e histogram hints at some of the drama in this image too.

The Hue Saturation 1 and Desat Layers

◆ With all Eye icons on for all layers, turn the Eye icon off and then on again for the Hue/Saturation 1 adjustment layer. You can see that this adjustment has a big impact on the image. Double-click its layer thumbnail and bring up the Hue/Saturation dialog. In Master all the colors were saturated by +16. I also saturated the Yellows by +25 and took a little magenta out of their hue with the +3 setting. Switch the Edit pop-up to Yellows, and move the Yellow Hue slider back and forth a bit between + and − so you can see what this does to Yellows. Notice how this changes the sunlit tufas in the background. Switch to Blues now and

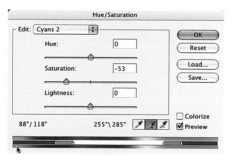

13 The Hue/Saturation dialog for the Desat layer. We used the +Eyedropper tool, which is selected in this dialog, to drag across the colored area on the rocks that we wanted to desaturate. This is what caused the wider range of colors in the color bar at the bottom of the dialog and also what caused Blues to be changed to Cyans 2.

notice how moving the Hue slider to the left makes the blue lake and sky more cyan. We moved it to the right a bit to add some magenta to these blue areas, which makes them a bit deeper. You have to be careful not to go too far in that direction or things start looking purple. Cancel out of Hue/Saturation.

◆ If you zoom into the lower-right corner of the image, then turn the Eye icon off and then on again for the Desat layer, you'll notice that it takes the blue-green cast out of the whitish rocks in that corner and at the bottom of the image. Looking at the Hue/Saturation dialog for this layer, you'll see a Cyans 2. This started out as blue, but I dragged the +Eyedropper icon over these

13 Without the Desat Bush and Bush Contrast2 adjustment layers, the white parts of the bush have a subtle reddish-blue cast. I wanted them to be bright white.

13 With the addition of those two adjustment layers, the white parts of the bush had the bright, stark look that I wanted in my prints, which I made with my Epson 7600, 4000, and 2400 printers.

13 Here we see the Desat Bush mask. Notice how lightly I painted in the white areas. Workshop students often have to learn to paint more slowly with the Airbrush tool so that the mask doesn't get too white, which would make the effect it's controlling too intense.

blue-green rocks to get their full range of colors, and this added a lot of cyan, and even greens and purples, which you can see in the color bar at the bottom. This is different from the normal definition of blues.

The Sky Color and WaterColor Tweak Layers

Both these Hue/Saturation adjustment layers are using masks to increase the saturation and deepen the color of Blues in the water and sky areas. I used two different layers so that I had separate control of the sky verses the water.

◆ Turn their Eye icons off and then on again so you can see what they do.

Desat Bush and Bush Contrast 2

◆ Zoom in to the bush area at 100%. Turn off the Eye icon for the Desat Bush adjustment layer. Notice that this also turns off Blush Contrast 2, which is using the same mask as Desat Bush. Desat Bush is desaturating the Reds and Blues. This removes the reddish-blue cast from the bright white areas in this dried-out old bush. In reality these are a very bleached white color, so I needed to remove that cast. Option (Alt)-click the Desat Bush layer mask to take a look at it. Notice that this is applied in a subtle way. The whites here are not really bright.

When I make these I'm looking at the areas of the bush that I want to change and overdoing the desaturation adjustments in the Hue/Saturation dialog. Then when I click OK and use Command (Ctrl)-I to invert the mask, I can paint just enough white in the mask to remove the amount of color I want to. I'm painting with the Airbrush 7% Tool preset we showed you how to load in Chapter 2, "Preferences and Color Settings."

◆ Bush Contrast 2 is just an S-curve that increases the contrast of these bright-white areas in the bush. I made a test print and found that in the print these didn't have the stark, bright white that I remembered. Adding this curve, which is set up to use the previous layer as a Clipping Mask, just increases the contrast in those areas we worked on in the previous layer.

Crop and Burn&Dodge

The Crop and B&D layers on this image are similar to those in the other images. As we did in the other images, it's better to put the Crop layer above the Burn and Dodge layer. That way you don't see any Burn or Dodge along the edges changing the gray background of the Crop layer, which is supposed to match the Photoshop gray

around the edge of images. I didn't do that in this image because I hadn't refined that part of my workflow yet. The final illustrations for this example about the Mono Lake image are on the next page. Turn there to compare the final histograms to earlier versions and also to look at a final version of this image.

Sharpening the Image and Sending It to the Printer

Whenever you're finished with your master layers file and want to make a test print, you first want to archive your master layers file. You should always save these, along with all the layers, so you can make subtle changes to the image after you've made some prints. Sometimes the print will be on your wall for several months before youl realize that you'd like to make a change. You don't want to have to go through all this work again! After archiving your master layers file, use Image/Duplicate to make a flattened copy of your layers file, which you'll sharpen and then print from. Go to Chapter 12, where we show you how to use Image/Duplicate to make the flattened copy, then go through special techniques to optimally sharpen the file. In Chapter 16, "Color Preferences, Calibration, and Printing," we also go through the print dialogs for the Epson 2200, 4000, 7600, 9600, 2400, 4800, 7800, and 9800 printers. These are all great printers that we highly recommend for your photographic prints!

Conclusion

If the techniques in this chapter and/or this book have not taught you everything you need to know to get the prints you want from your problem images, please check the Workshops or Videos pages at www.barryhaynes.com and come take a printmaking workshop in wonderful British Colombia, Canada, or try our QuickTime training videos so we can help you get exactly the prints you want from your problem images and all your photography.

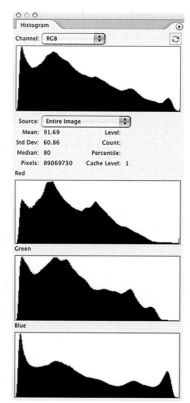

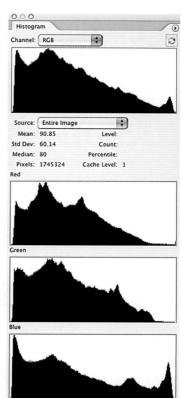

13d Mono Lake histogram after the Levels, Open Up, Drama Highlights, and Hue/Saturation 1 adjustments. Adding the Hue/Saturation adjustment to the previous histogram stretched out the Blue channel a bit to the right and also moved Red and RGB to the right some more. In that Hue/Saturation adjustment, we saturated blues and yellows a lot (this accounts for the Blue channel change), and we also saturated the Master channel (which accounts for the RGB histogram change). When you saturate a particular color, you need to be careful that you don't lose highlight details in that color.

13e Here's the final Mono Lake Dried Bush image after all the adjustments—it corresponds to the histogram 13e display to the right. These three images are actually after the crop has been done, but the histograms are without the Crop layer. When you turn the Crop layer on in the master layers file, it messes up the histogram because that Crop layer has all those values that are equal to the Photoshop gray background. If you ever go to Mono Lake, it's a wonderful place to photograph; but be careful not to damage any of the tufa, which are the mineral growths that you see around Mono Lake. You can see some Tufa lit by the sun in the background of this image.

13e Mono Lake histogram after all the final adjustments but without the Crop layer's Eye icon on. The Sky Color and Water Color Hue/Sat adjustment layers both were focused on blues and cyans, and they pushed the blue highlights all the way to the edge. Pretty dramatic difference between this histogram and the original one. The colors are far better in the final image, eh?

Portfolio

Jeff Blewett

Jeff (jblewett@frontiernet.net) worked on these images during Barry's Digital Printmaking workshop in Gibsons. Jeff lives in Garden Valley, Idaho, and shoots with 4x5 and 6x8 film cameras, as well as a Nikon D70, which he used to make the Old Farm House image below. For this final print, Jeff added layers and masks using the techniques we covered in this chapter. Miner's Cabin was shot as a grayscale with his 4x5 film camera. We scanned this on our older Epson 2450 flatbed scanner at 2400 dpi. We could have made a beautiful 30-inch-wide print from this scan.

23 ◆ Replace Color, Color Range, and Selective Color

This is our converted, adjusted, and cropped CMYK version of the AutumnLeaves file.

Use Replace Color and Color Range to create a selection for a Hue/Saturation adjustment layer.
Enhance colors using Selective Color and Hue/Saturation to improve the CMYK version.

The original AutumnLeaves image has primarily orange and red leaves.

In this book we talk a lot about selections, how important they are, and how to make them, save them, and use them. In this hands-on session, we have a rather difficult selection to make based on color. Normally, when you think of a color-based selection, you head directly for the Magic Wand. It's a good tool and is often all you need. And, previous to this example, you used channels to isolate areas of your image for editing. In this example, we'll call on two other selection tools you may be less familiar with: Replace Color and Color Range. The tools are similar but with some important differences that often make using them together best practice. After we make the selection we need, we'll use it as a layer mask for a Hue/Saturation adjustment layer. Once we change the color of the leaves, we'll convert our image to CMYK, then use Selective Color to perk up colors dulled by the conversion.

Replace Color

We're going to use Image/Adjustments/Replace Color to make our initial selection of the red and orange leaves. This tool gives you the capability to make a selection and, at the same time, use Hue/Saturation sliders to change the color. For minor color tweaks and quick turnarounds, this may be the only tool you use. However, we like to keep our options open so that we're able to adjust the image at many points during the workflow—something that isn't possible using only Replace Color. Instead, we're going to save the range of colors we choose using Replace Color and then load them into Color Range. We'll make the initial selection with Replace Color because this tool's Hue slider gives us a better preview of which colors to choose than do the masks in Color Range.

Make the Initial Selection

1a One of the issues confronting a photographer who needs to make color changes is the amazing number of hues, shades, and tones that make up what we perceive as color. In this instance, red and orange are the primary hues you need, but there are many variations of those hues in the highlights and shadows of the leaves. Using the various eyedroppers in Replace Color allows you to select them all.

◆ Open the RGB file, AutumnLeaves.psd, from the Ch23.Replace-Col ColRange SelCol folder on the *Photoshop Artistry* DVD. Type F to put the image in Full Screen mode.

◆ Type I to get the Eyedropper tool, and change the Sample Size setting to Point Sample.

◆ Choose Image/Adjustments/Replace Color. Use the Eyedropper to choose a representative red from the leaves. Leave the Fuzziness value set at 40.

◆ Use the +Eyedropper to add colors by clicking on not-yet-selected colors in the image while looking at the mask in the preview window.

Change the Hue and Finesse the Selection

1b Even though you won't be using such an extreme change when you create a Hue/Saturation adjustment layer, moving the Hue slider

1a For your initial click, choose a spot that you feel represents the most-often-seen color in the image.

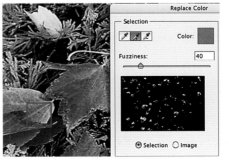

1a Subsequent clicks in the image with the +Eyedropper add white to the mask.

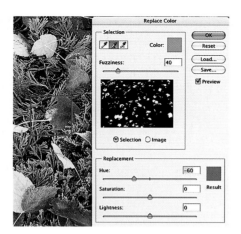

1b After you change the hue of the leaves, you'll see additional colors that you'll want to add to the selection criteria.

to a radically different hue helps you see which colors to add or subtract.

◆ Use the Hue slider to move the colors toward purple—about –50 or –60.

◆ Use the +Eyedropper to add more colors. If you select portions of the background, type Command (Ctrl)-Z to undo the last Eyedropper click or use the –Eyedropper to subtract colors from the selection.

At some point, you'll have to decide how much of the overturned leaves you want to select. You'll also find shadows under or between leaves that you may want to add, but make sure you view the image at 100% and scroll around to check various areas. If you notice that you've taken stems from the juniper bush, you'll want to use the –Eyedropper to remove those colors. If you are not viewing the image at 100%, remember that you can use Command-Option (Ctrl-Alt)-0 to magnify to 100%. Feel free to change the Fuzziness setting at this point to get a better selection as well.

Save the Replace Color Settings

1c Because we need a selection to create a mask for a Hue/Saturation adjustment layer, and Replace Color doesn't return a selection,

we need to save the settings for the colors we've just selected so we can load them into Color Range.

◆ Click the Save button in this dialog, and in the subsequent dialog name your settings "reds" and choose where to save the settings. We saved to the desktop for easy reference.

◆ Once you save, you are taken back to the Replace Color dialog. Click the Cancel button so that no changes are made to the file at this point. Even though you cancel here, your settings are saved.

Color Range

Color Range doesn't have the ability to show you how a color change will affect the file like Replace Color does, but it returns the "marching ants" selection we need to create a mask. In addition, Color Range has a couple of features that Replace Color lacks. When you use the Select pop-up at the top of the Color Range dialog, you have some "automatic" ranges that Color Range can choose for you. It can select out the six primary colors, the highlights, the midtones, the shadows, and the out-of-gamut color; however, you can't access the Eyedropper to add or delete colors from these automatic ranges. In the case of the AutumnLeaves file, the colors of the leaves are orange as well as red and yellow, so the color choices won't give us the selection we need. In another file, one of those primary colors might work perfectly. Seán uses the Highlights, Midtones, or Shadows choices to select tonal ranges in order to create split-toning effects on images that will eventually be a combination of grayscale and toning; and we sometimes use the Out Of Gamut range to tweak colors before printing.

Color Range also has several different viewing modes that help you see exactly what you have selected. These are: Grayscale, Black Matte, White Matte, and Quick Mask. All of these modes overlay the image itself, so your preview is much larger than the small preview in the dialog. Grayscale makes your image look exactly like the dialog preview and is not all that helpful except for looking at edges. Black

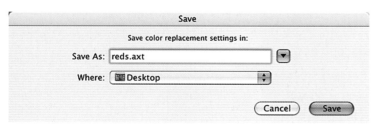

1c You don't actually make any changes to the file with Replace Color—you simply save your settings for later use.

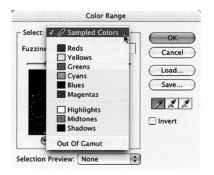

Color Range has selection "ranges" that you can choose from for automatic selections. If you choose one of these ranges, the Eyedropper tools are disabled, so you can't add or delete from the range.

Matte and White Matte show you a bit more of what information is being selected; these are the previews we use most often. Quick Mask viewing mode looks exactly like the overlay used in the Quick Mask mode that you access from the Toolbox (and will appear in the current color of that Quick Mask); it can be useful especially if you are used to working with that type of overlay. But unlike with Quick Mask, rather than editing the mask with painting tools, you change the parameters of your selection with the Eyedropper tools.

Most of the time, we do not make further adjustments to the Color Range settings because we feel that seeing the settings in action in Replace Color is a better indication of how the selection will work than simply seeing an overlay in Color Range. If we do make a change in Color Range, we're usually removing extraneous pixels with the −Eyedropper. Be careful how you use the Eyedropper, though. If you are viewing the file at 100% (which we recommend) and you take out some portions of a twig, you need to watch the small preview in the dialog to make sure you're not removing large amounts of that same color from something else, like the leaves.

Load the Settings and Check the Preview

2 We're going to load the settings we created in Replace Color. If you make changes to the selection here in Color Range, you might want to save your Color Range settings, and then load them into Replace Color and use the Hue slider to check any modifications you made. Of course, you'd have to reload your final settings in Color Range at the end of the process to create the selection marquee, but switching between these two tools is painless and quick.

◆ Go to Select/Color Range, click the Load button, and load the reds.axt file you created earlier in this example.

◆ Click the Selection Preview pop-up and choose Black Matte. Scroll around the image and look at what you have selected.

2 This is how your file looks when you preview in Black Matte mode. It's a good idea to check White Matte mode as well, because some problems with your selection show up better against white.

◆ Switch the preview to White Matte and again check your selection criteria.

◆ Click OK to accept these settings and create the selection.

You may have noticed areas where the edges of your selection seem a bit rough, but don't worry. We'll deal with those issues after we've created the Hue/Saturation adjustment layer. Creating a mask gives us the flexibility to alter the selection later.

Create a Hue/Saturation Adjustment Layer

3 You now have the selection you need. Creating this particular selection would have been difficult any other way. When you create the adjustment layer, the layer mask is automatically created from the active selection.

◆ Go to Layer/New Adjustment Layer and choose Hue/Saturation, or choose Hue/Saturation from the Create New Fill or Adjustment Layer icon at the bottom of the Layers palette. Name your adjustment layer ChangeLeaves.

◆ Move the Hue slider to −15 to move the selected colors toward red, and move the Saturation slider to +15 to brighten them.

Blur the Mask

4 Adding a small blur to the ChangeLeaves mask can smooth the transition from unaltered pixels to those you've manipulated, making the two blend seamlessly. The mask for this adjustment layer has very sharp edges on some of the leaves, and we don't want the edges to "pop," since we upped the saturation of those colors. The blur helps. On most images, 0.5 to 1 pixel is enough. We used 1.5 pixels on this file because that was where the edges became soft enough.

◆ Look at the Layers palette and make sure the layer mask for the Hue/Saturation layer is active.

3 After the Hue/Saturation changes, your file will look something like this. Yours will be more vibrant, though, because the bright, saturated colors we've chosen are not printable in CMYK. Later we'll regain a bit of the lost intensity.

4 Before you blur the ChangeLeaves mask, the edges around some of the leaves and stems are hard.

4 The result of a 1.5-pixel blur.

6 When you first use Window/Arrange/Tile Vertical, your screen may look like this.

◆ Use Filter/Blur/Gaussian Blur to blur the ChangeLeaves mask. Scroll around to find a sharp edge, and raise the blur amount until the edge is not so dramatic. We chose 1.5 pixels.

◆ Save this file as AutumnLeavesLayers in Photoshop format.

Duplicate the File and Convert to CMYK

5 If you were going to print this image to a digital printer—say, an Epson 7600—all you'd need to do now is crop the photo, resize, sharpen, and print. However, this image is going to be printed on a press with CMYK inks, so we have to convert it and deal with the color shifts that sometimes happen in CMYK, especially with bright colors. It's important to keep the layered RGB file as our master image, so we need to make a duplicate first.

◆ Go to Image/Duplicate [F5] and create a copy of this image. Click the Duplicate Merged Layers Only option to flatten the file as you duplicate it.

◆ Use Image/Mode/CMYK Color to convert the image to CMYK. In a real-world situation, you'd want to make sure were using conversion settings provided by your printer, but for this exercise we're using our default CMYK setting, U.S. Sheetfed Coated v2.

Compare the Images

6 You probably noticed how your beautiful, bright colors dulled considerably when you converted. This is a limitation of CMYK inks. Many bright colors can't be reproduced with only those four inks. This is why art directors often specify special inks such as PANTONE to be used when certain colors have to reproduce exactly. If this particular image were going to be printed in a high-end brochure or art

6 After selecting Match Zoom and Location, you get a really good side-by-side comparison. By setting your Hand and Zoom tools to move all the windows at once, you can then zoom or scroll while keeping the same relationship in both images. You will not see as much color difference in this illustration as you will see on your screen because everything here has been converted to CMYK.

book, we would create a *bump* plate—a film separation in addition to the basic CMYK separation plates that would control where special inks would print to ensure we got the colors we needed. That's an expensive, time-consuming process, so instead we'll compare the images, try to discern which colors are causing our problems, then use Selective Color to restore some of the pizzazz of the master file. For the rest of this exercise, you will want to show or hide your Layers palette as needed. We suggest using ArtistKeys [F10]. If you do not have ArtistKeys loaded, you will need to access the Layers palette via either the Window menu or the default shortcut key F7.

◆ Save your CMYK version as AutumnLeavesCMYK in Photoshop format.

◆ Type H for the Hand tool, and on the Options bar click Scroll All Windows if it's not already on.

◆ Type Z for the Zoom tool, and on the Options bar click Zoom All Windows if it's not already on.

◆ Press the Tab key to hide all the palettes except the Menu bar.

◆ Use Window/Arrange/Tile Vertically to tile the two files. If any other files are open in Photoshop, they will tile as well, so make sure only AutumnLeavesLayers and AutumnLeavesCMYK are open.

- Click the title bar for the AutumnLeavesCMYK image to make it active.

- Use Command (Ctrl)-Spacebar-click or Option (Alt)-Spacebar-click to zoom in or out, respectively, until your file is at 50%. Now use Window/Arrange/Match Zoom and Location.

- Hold down the Spacebar so both images scroll simultaneously, and scroll around the active image until you find an area that has a wide variety of colors. Compare the colors of the two images.

Use Selective Color

7 As you scroll around the image, notice which colors seem not to match. Also notice colors that do seem to match well—especially the more delicate colors of the overturned leaves and leaves that were not brightly colored in the beginning. You don't want to do anything that skews colors that match well in both versions; you only want to adjust colors that don't currently match. The most serious problems occur where the original image is bright red or bright orange. Both these colors are composed of differing amounts of magenta and yellow inks, so our primary focus is adding oomph to those colors, warming or cooling them to match our original as closely as possible. Selective Color uses the CMYK color model as its basis, giving us some options that we might not have with Hue/Saturation. In Selective Color, rather than just moving the reds more toward magenta *or* yellow as you would with Hue/Saturation, you can adjust the percentages of the component inks to increase the amount of *both* magenta

7 The areas marked in Cyan are some of the places to check each time you adjust color in the image. The small yellow and orange leaf in the top, right rectangle is the most difficult to match.

and yellow. You can even change the amount of cyan and black ink that makes up the areas that Photoshop considers red.

The illustration on this page shows you areas that we looked at as we corrected. You won't be able to get all areas of the CMYK image to exactly match the RGB image, and when you adjust for one area, you may find that you shift another unintentionally. You need to find a balance where all the colors look a bit better and you don't sacrifice one color for another. Also, while you want to look at the image at 100%, to judge your color changes, you also should zoom out to see the entire image, to adjust for overall impact. Color is not just a bunch of numbers to be matched, but also an intention and an intensity. Your colors may never match exactly, so work to match the feeling of the piece as well. You may want to turn on View/Gamut Warning as you adjust, to see what colors are not printable.

- Make sure AutumnLeavesCMYK is the active file, then use the Create New Fill or Adjustment Layer icon on the Layers palette to choose a Selective Color adjustment layer.

- Red is the first color that appears in the Colors pop-up and it's the most important color to adjust here. Check the Absolute check box, which adds the amount of ink you specify in absolute amounts, giving you a stronger result than Relative. Add 10% Magenta to the Reds and 50% yellow. This will push a few small

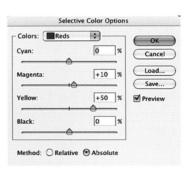

7 The Selective Color adjustment for Reds.   **7** The Selective Color adjustment for Yellows.

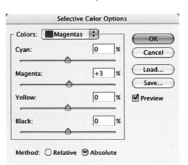

7 We've already added magenta to everything that Photoshop considers Reds, but here we are asking for just a little more magenta ink where Photoshop considers a color Magenta. Depending on how you have selected colors, you may find that you want to take out a bit of magenta in the Magentas. Try it both ways.

areas out of the gamut of the printer, but the overall result is so much better that it's worth it.

◆ Click the Colors pop-up and switch to Yellows. We added 20% more yellow ink to all the colors that Photoshop considers to be yellow.

◆ Switch the Colors pop-up to Magenta. We added a mere 3% more magenta ink to the Magentas in this image. Depending on how you made your selection earlier, you may find you want to add more or even take away a bit of magenta ink.

Add a Hue/Saturation Adjustment Layer

8 Selective Color definitely helped punch up the color, but we can do more. Now, we'll add a Hue/Saturation adjustment layer to saturate the colors, and shift them a bit to try to regain some brightness. We want the reds, oranges, and yellows to be brighter and more intense; we'll do that by adding yellow and decreasing the magenta.

◆ Use the Create New Fill or Adjustment Layer" icon at the bottom of the Layers palette to create a new Hue/Saturation adjustment layer.

◆ Saturate all the colors 10% by moving the Master to +10.

◆ Use the Edit pop-up and switch to Reds. The reds need to be a bit more orange, so move the red colors in the image toward yellow by moving the Hue slider to the right to about +7. Now saturate the reds by +15 to give them more intensity.

◆ Use the Edit pop-up again and switch to Yellows. The yellows need to be brighter, as they've gotten too warm and have too much red in them. Move the yellows in the image toward green by moving the Hue slider to the right to about +11. Saturate the yellows by +15.

◆ Finally, switch the Edit pop-up to Magentas. We're going to move the magenta toward blue by moving the Hue slider to about −3, to better match the leaves that are primarily magenta. Also desaturate all the magentas by −8.

You may find after making your hue and saturation adjustments that you want to go back to the Selective Color adjustment and change it a little. When you are doing color correction, it's not unusual to make one adjustment and then go back to something you did previously and tweak it. This is one of the reasons we do almost everything we can with adjustment layers.

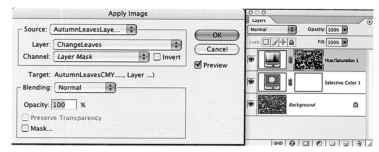

9 You can preview how the Apply Image command will affect the Layers palette, as well as see the effect on your image.

Add a Layer Mask with Apply Image

9 In this image, we found that there were parts of the image underlying the leaves that were affected negatively by the Hue/Saturation adjustments. We want to take those areas out of the adjustment completely. We could click the Paintbrush and paint those areas out of the adjustment layer's layer mask, but in the original RGB file we have just the mask we need; we used it for the RGB ChangeLeaves adjustment layer. Because the RGB and CMYK files are exactly the same size in pixel dimensions, we can use Apply Image to bring information from the RGB version over to the CMYK Hue/Saturation adjustment layer. When using Apply Image it's important to make sure that you are on the layer or layer mask where you want the change to occur. This will be your target. You can't change the target in the Apply Image dialog, so if you are on the wrong layer before you start the process, you'll need to cancel Apply Image, choose the correct layer or layer mask, then start again.

◆ Make sure the AutumnLeavesCMYK Hue/Saturation adjustment layer is active in the Layers palette.

◆ Go to Image/Apply Image. The target is the layer mask for your CMYK Hue/Saturation adjustment layer. For the Source, you want the AutumnLeavesLayer file. The Layer should be the ChangeLeaves layer, and the Channel should be the Layer Mask. Set the Blending to Normal, with Opacity at 100%.

◆ Click OK to apply the mask.

In some images, you may want to use a Curves adjustment in addition to or instead of the Hue/Saturation adjustment layer to brighten, lighten, or intensify colors. Each image presents its own problems and opportunities. Don't be afraid to try something new—you may discover a great technique.

Portfolio

Curt Fischbach

Curt came to Wendy's intro class with a broken neck and a whole lot of images of Africa. In the N.D. Chair image, below, he learned to use two versions of the same Camera Raw file to increase the available range of tonalities. In the African Girl image, he used a channel mixer adjustment layer with a layer mask to selectively use both black and white and color in the same photo.

24 ◆ Color Matching Images

Measure and adjust the color of objects so that differently colored items can be changed to match.
Make subtle color adjustments after CMYK conversion to deal with faded CMYK hues.

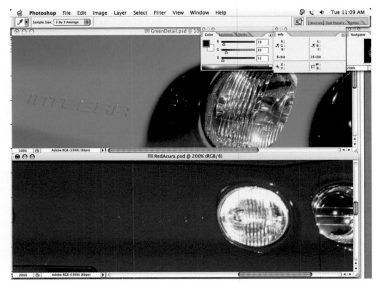

1 Your workspace should look like this after the first step. Both the Color palette and Info palette are critical in this lesson.

Imagine that you need to create an advertisement using two photos of an Acura Integra. One photo is of a red Integra and the other is of a green one. You need to convert the green car photo so that its color matches that of the red one. You also need to convert both cars to CMYK and do some final color matching in CMYK.

Set Up the Screen and Palettes

1 You need to set up your workspace and palettes in such a way that you can quickly access the information as you compare the two photos. If you did not set up a Color Correction workspace in Chapter 3, "Navigating in Photoshop," look at the illustration for this step and arrange your palettes accordingly.

◆ Go to Window/Workspace and choose Color Correction. Close the Histogram palette and move the Info palette up beside the Navigation palette.

◆ Open the Color palette [Command (Ctrl)-Shift-F9] and move it to the left of the Info palette. Click the palette pop-up and change the display to HSB.

◆ Type H for the Hand tool, and on the Options bar turn off Scroll All Windows if it is on. Type Z for the Zoom tool, and turn off Zoom All Windows if it is on.

◆ Open the RedAcura.psd and GreenDetail.psd files in the Ch24. Color Matching Images folder on the *Photoshop Artistry* DVD. Go to Window/Arrange/Tile Horizontally so you'll be able to see both images.

◆ Type I to choose the Eyedropper tool, then press Return (Enter) to bring up the Eyedropper's Options bar if it's *not* already visible. Make sure Sample Size is set to 3x3 average.

Choose the Color Match Spots

2 Both of these photos have highlight and shadow areas that you want to match. Usually, if you can locate a good midtone area in both images and get those midtone areas to match, the rest of the image will also match fairly well. Find a spot on the red car where the color appears to be an average, intermediate color that could represent the color you want for the whole car. We call this location the color match spot. Put the Eyedropper over the color match spot and click to take a measurement in the Info palette. Hold the mouse button down and measure around a bit to make sure the spot you're using as this first measurement is an average measurement for this area. We used the area on the front of the car to the right of the chrome Acura emblem, just above the word *Integra* embossed on the red bumper. Because this spot exists—and the lighting on it is similar—in both photos, you can use this location on both cars to get the colors to match. Choose an exact location to place Color Samplers in both images. When you place a Color Sampler, the Info palette will remember values for that location.

◆ Click the RedAcura file to make it active.

◆ Shift-click with the Eyedropper tool just above the *T* in *Integra* to place a color sampler at that location.

◆ Change the current display of those values for Color Sampler #1 in the Info palette to HSB by clicking the pop-up beside the #1 Eyedropper.

◆ Switch to the green car and find the same location right above the embossed *T*. Shift-click to create a Color Sampler in this image, too. Change the Color Sampler display of this spot in the Info palette to HSB.

If you ever have trouble seeing the Color Sampler part of the Info palette at the bottom, you can always choose Hide Color Samplers

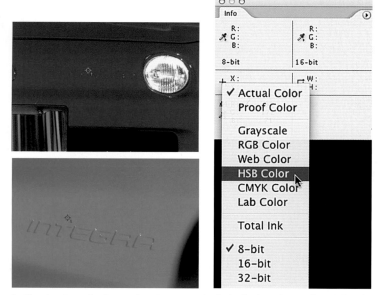

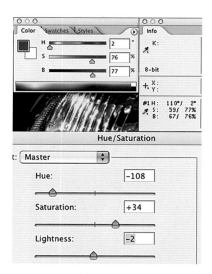

4 These were the values we used for moving the green colors to match the RedAcura image as closely as possible. Depending on where you click, your numbers may vary slightly.

2 After choosing each color sampler point, convert the display for that color sampler to HSB in the Info palette.

followed by Show Color Samplers from the Info palette's options; this will bring all your Color Sampler values back into view.

Sample Color from the RedAcura

3 Now you are going to sample color from the RedAcura image to get a reading for the Color palette. The Color palette remembers the last place you clicked with the Eyedropper tool, whether in the active image or a previously active image. This is particularly important in this instance because it keeps a record of the hue, saturation, and brightness values at the color sampler location in the RedAcura image as we adjust the GreenDetail image to match.

◆ Click the title bar for the RedAcura image or Command (Ctrl)-click the image itself to make the RedAcura file active.

◆ Move the Eyedropper over the sample point, and when the samplers line up and disappear, click the mouse. The color from the sample point will now appear in the Color palette.

◆ Use the Color palette pop-up to change the display to HSB.

Adjust Hue/Saturation in the GreenDetail Image

4 Now we'll add a Hue/Saturation adjustment layer to the Green-Detail image in order to change the color of the image to the red we need to match. We use Hue/Saturation rather than Levels or

Curves, because using the Hue slider will not change the brightness or contrast of the image. The Color Sampler in the Info palette will continue to show you how the color match spot, where you set it in the green car, changes based on the Hue/Saturation slider movements. The Color palette, on the other hand, will show you the values of the RedAcura that you are trying to match. Try to get all three numbers to match exactly, but don't worry if one of them is off by a point in either direction. The Saturation and Lightness settings influence each other as you move them. As you change one, the other also changes, so you must tweak both of them until you get as close as possible to the values you had in the red car. Working in Adobe RGB, we didn't need to move the Lightness slider much, if at all, to match the colors. When we used this same example in the ColorMatch RGB color space, we had to move the Lightness slider quite a bit. So remember, when you are working in the real world, the relationship between these sliders may be different. The important issue is to match the values as closely as you can. You can use the Tab key to move quickly between the input areas; and when a number is highlighted, you can use the up and down arrow keys to increase or decrease the values by 1.

◆ Switch back to the GreenDetail image.

◆ Choose Layer/New Adjustment Layer and choose Hue/Saturation [Command (Ctrl)-F4] to create a new Hue/Saturation adjustment layer.

◆ Move the Hue slider so that the Hue value in the Info palette for the green image's color match spot matches the value in the red image.

- Now move the Saturation and Lightness sliders back and forth until saturation and lightness values in the Color Sampler match the numbers in the Color palette.

- Click OK to accept the adjustment.

Adjust RGB Values with Levels

5 Now you'll cross-check the color in the GreenDetail image by changing the displays of both the Color Sampler and the Color palette to RGB. Because you haven't clicked anywhere with the Eyedropper since step 3, the color from the RedAcura image is still the current color in the Color palette. However, when you are in the GreenDetail file, the Color palette will show a grayscale slider. Don't freak out. The Color Sampler is reading the value on the adjustment layer mask. As soon as you enter the Levels dialog, the color will return to the Color palette. You'll use the midtone sliders in a Levels adjustment layer to make any further changes required to match the colors exactly. You don't need to go back to the RedAcura image and change that sampler to RGB, as the Color palette will not have changed as long as you haven't clicked a new point with the Eyedropper.

- Go to Layer/New Adjustment Layer/Levels [Command (Ctrl)-F2] to create a new Levels adjustment layer.

- Use the Color palette pop-up to change the display to RGB.

- Use the Color Sampler pop-up for Color Sampler #1 in the Info palette to change its readout to RGB.

Where Did My Number Go?

When you adjust the Hue slider in a Hue/Saturation dialog, you may notice that the value in your Info palette goes down to 0° and then goes to 359°. This is because hue is measured as a position on the color wheel. (See Chapter 5, "Picking and Using Color," for more on this.) This sometimes confuses our students because they can't move the Hue slider down far enough to get the number they need. The solution? Move the slider in the other direction.

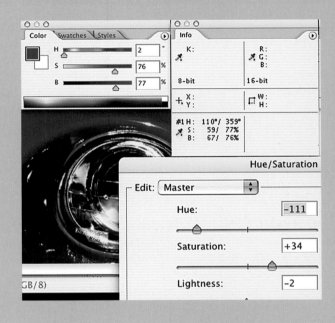

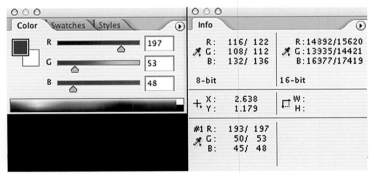

5 When you are in the GreenDetail image at this point, before you create the Levels adjustment layer, your Color palette reflects the values of the adjustment layer mask. The color sampler in the Info palette is the RGB readout with the Hue/Saturation adjustment applied.

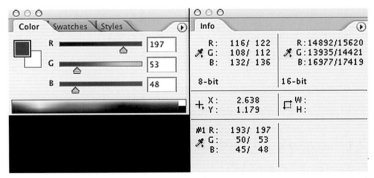

5 Once you are in the Levels adjustment layer, the Color palette reflects the last spot you clicked with the Eyedropper tool—still the Color Sampler #1 point on the RedAcura image. The Color Sampler #1 values here in the GreenDetail image are on the left side of the slash and the adjusted values from Levels are on the right. When you click OK on the Levels adjustment, there will be only one set of values for the color sampler.

- Move the midtone sliders of the Red, Green, and Blue channels until the Info palette's readout matches the values in the Color palette.

- Click OK when the values match.

It didn't take a lot of adjustment in Levels to make our RGB values match exactly. We moved the Red midtone slider to 1.07, the Green midtone slider to 1.04, and the Blue midtone slider to 1.04. Your values may differ from ours—and that's fine as long as the values from the two images on your screen match.

Convert to CMYK Mode

6 If you are going to print this ad on a four-color press, you now have to convert the colors to CMYK and deal with any color shifts. As you saw in Chapter 23, "Replace Color, Color Range, and Selective Color," when colors are bright, you'll often have problems matching the press to the original photo. Make sure your color settings are correct, as described in Chapter 2, "Preferences and Color Settings," before you do this step.

- Click the title bar for the RedAcura image to make it active.

- Using the Color palette menu, switch the palette to CMYK display. Also, convert your #1 Sampler readout to CMYK.

- Use Image/Mode/CMYK Color to convert the file to CMYK.

- Switch to the GreenDetail image and convert that file to CMYK as well. Flatten the file when prompted. In the Info palette, change the Color Sampler #1 readout to CMYK.

Use Selective Color

7 Once again we turn to Selective Color to help us restore some of the spark of the original. And we'll keep the Color palette onscreen because its sliders help us choose how we want to shift the colors. As you move each slider, the color bars in the palette shift to show you what any other adjustment will do to the color.

- Switch to the RedAcura image and go to Layer/New Adjustment Layer/Selective Color. Make sure that Colors is set to Reds because you're going to be adjusting the car's red colors.

- Set the Method to Absolute so that you can make the color adjustments more quickly.

- Move the cursor exactly on top of the color match spot; at that point the circle and crosshairs will disappear. Click to take another

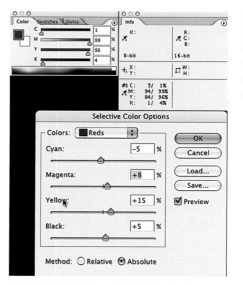

7 Because you clicked on the color match spot with the Eyedropper while you were in Selective Color, the values in the Color palette change as you adjust the CMYK sliders.

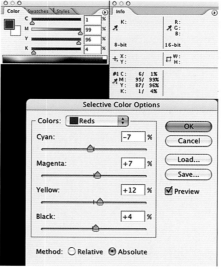

7 Because you did *not* click with the Eyedropper on the GreenDetail file, the colors in the Color palette remain static as you adjust the CMYK sliders, giving you a reference for the colors you are trying to match.

measurement at the color match spot, and notice that when you click, the new values come up in the Color palette.

The values in the Color palette should now match the color match spot's values in the Info palette—although the match may not be exact. Values change in the Color palette only when you click or take a reading with the mouse button held down. The values in the top-left area of the Info palette change whenever you move the mouse, and the values of the color sampler for your color match spot in the Info palette will change only when you change that spot's color. Earlier, we didn't need to click more than once on the color match spot to set the color in the Color palette, but once we changed to CMYK mode, we needed to reestablish the color in the Color palette.

7 This is how the RedAcura file prints to CMYK without the Selective Color adjustment.

7 Compare this version of the file after the Selective Color adjustment to the one above. Although the color is not significantly different, this version has more pizzazz.

Notice that the color consists mostly of magenta and yellow. The colors of the sliders in the Color palette show you how the color at the color match spot will change if you add or subtract more cyan, magenta, yellow, or black ink.

◆ If the Cyan value is greater than 0, subtract cyan using the Selective Color slider until the Cyan value reads 0 in the Color palette; if you find that 1 or 2 is as low as it will go, use the cursor keys to move your adjustment back to the first place you get that low value. Trying to move below the lowest value will merely degrade your file. Once you reach the lowest Cyan value, you should see that same value in your Info palette Color Sampler reading. This maneuver adds red to the car color.

◆ Add magenta with Selective Color until the Magenta value in the Color palette is about 98 or 99, to make the car a deeper, richer color.

◆ Adjust the yellow until the Yellow value in the Color palette reads about 96. To get a slightly darker, richer color, add some black until the Black value reads about 4.

The colors in the Color palette's sliders will give you hints about what to do to improve the CMYK color of the spot you are reading in your image. You don't have to use the exact same numbers that we have; just adjust the cyan, magenta, yellow, and black percentages on the color match spot until you like the car's shade of red.

◆ Click the title bar for the GreenDetail image to activate it.

◆ Use the Info palette Color Sampler #1 pop-up to display those values in CMYK.

◆ Use Layer/New Adjustment Layer/Selective Color to create your new adjustment layer. Then use the Selective Color sliders to adjust the cyan, magenta, yellow, and black inks, until the percentages in the Info palette color sampler match the other image's final adjusted percentages as displayed in the Color palette.

We used Cyan = 1, Magenta = 99, Yellow = 96, and Black = 4, but your values can be different. You just want the two red colors to match to your satisfaction.. This method is a good way to match the colors of objects that start out differently but have to end up the same.

The final version of the GreenDetail file.

The final version of the RedAcura file.

25 ◆ Black and White, and Duotones

Delve into the world of digital black and white. Photoshop offers many possibilities, but which are great and which are merely adequate?

Digital black and white, like its counterpart in the film world, is a large area of photography with its own set of issues, problems, and solutions. There are probably as many digital techniques for working with black and white as there are photographers trying to achieve results. In this chapter we will talk a bit about various methods of working with black-and-white imagery, but we will focus on techniques we've found to be flexible and expansive enough to satisfy even the most discriminating artist.

Getting the Best Input

If you have a collection of black-and-white negatives or positives that you need to scan, you'll want to follow the directions for getting the best scan presented in Chapter 17, "Image Resolution and Scanning." Just as when scanning color, you want to get the most information from your image with the least amount of scanner software interference. Learning to read the histogram of your scan and compare it with the original is a great technique for ensuring that your scanner has captured all of the tonal variations in your film. And in black and white, tonal variation is a key issue. Without color to lead the eye or add detail to the image, we must rely on delicate tonalities to convey the richness of the scene.

Shoot Color

If you are shooting digitally, shoot in Raw mode to capture the most detail in the camera. This allows you to use Camera Raw to interpret data and give you the widest range of tonal values. In some cases, as in the image we use in the first part of the chapter, this means opening

This is the color-corrected version of the file that we'll be using.

two different versions of the same image to give good definition in the highlights as well as the midtones and shadows.

Color Correct First

You'll save yourself a lot of time working with black and white if you do your regular color correction procedures before you create your black-and-white version. This should set your highlights and shadows appropriately, and give definition to specific areas of your photo. In addition, this gives you some time to work with the photo and analyze it, deciding where you want to focus the viewer's attention. As you'll see later in this chapter, though, a color-correct original does not automatically ensure that the values in your black and white will match your visualization. Gray values of differently colored areas can sometimes be maddeningly close to each other.

Methods for Conversion

We are going to give you a brief overview of some of the more commonly used techniques for converting a color file to black and white. We'll be working with the River image you see here, and we'll build a layered file that gives you lots of options for creating your print. We will use different conversion methods and put the results back into the original file for comparison.

Desaturate

We've seen people use either the Desaturate command or a Hue/Saturation adjustment layer with the Master Saturation slider moved all the way to the left to create black and white. Neither of these methods produces a result worthy of a good black-and-white print. The results are flat, so we recommend against using this technique.

Image/Mode/Grayscale

1 If you have an image that has been color corrected well and has good tonal range to begin with, simply converting to grayscale can sometimes give you a good, basic black-and-white image for your starting point in creating a great print. It's a good idea to save your color-corrected RGB file in case you want to try other techniques later.

◆ Open the file RiverColor.psd from the folder Ch25.Blackand-White Duotones on the *Photoshop Artistry* DVD. This is Barry's flattened color-corrected version of the original Raw image.

◆ Use Image/Duplicate [F5] to make a copy of your image. We'll use this image to help us create the layers for the final layered file. This file is named RiverCclor copy by default.

1 Our grayscale version of the image.

2 Our Lightness Channel version of the image.

◆ Go to File/Save As and save this image as RiverWorkCopy.

◆ Bring up the History palette [F8], which we will use for returning RiverWorkCopy to RGB after conversion.

◆ Use Image/Mode/Grayscale to convert RiverWorkCopy to grayscale. If you get a dialog asking if you want to discard the color information, click OK.

◆ Type Command (Ctrl)-A to select the entire image, then Command (Ctrl)-C to copy it.

◆ Switch to the RiverColor image and type Command (Ctrl)-V to paste this grayscale version as a new layer. Double-click the name of this layer and rename it Grayscale.

The Lab Channel

2 The grayscale version you just made is is not a bad place to start. However, we often find that converting to Lab and using the Lightness channel produces an image with more variation to work with.

◆ Switch to the RiverWorkCopy file and in the History palette, click on the Duplicate state to take you back to the color version of the file.

NOTE

If you have only two files open, you can switch between them by typing Control (Ctrl)-Tab. If you have more than two images open, this command cycles through the images.

◆ Use Image/Mode/Lab and convert to Lab color.

◆ Open the Channels palette [Shift-F10] and click on the Lightness channel.

◆ Type Command (Ctrl)-A to select all of the Lightness channel, then Command (Ctrl)-C to copy the information.

◆ Switch to the RiverColor image, and type Command (Ctrl)-V to paste the Lightness channel information as a new layer.

◆ In the Layers palette, turn the Eye icon on and off for the Lightness Channel layer. This compares the Lightness channel version to the Grayscale version. We liked the Lightness channel version best.

A Single RGB Channel

3 Occasionally, you have an image where one of the RGB channels on its own is closer to the values you want in your print than either the Grayscale or Lab version of the file. In this image, that is not the case. However, we often find that each channel has areas of interest that we might like to use in our final print, so we like to make a copy of each channel to include as a layer with a layer mask that can be painted to reveal those details. Because we want only a small portion of each channel in the final print, we add a layer mask that hides the entire layer, then paint with white on the mask where we want the details from that layer to show. If you were going to use information from only one channel, you would choose the one that had the best information. Because we are going to use all three channels in this image, we'll start with the Red channel and copy them in order. When you add a layer mask that hides the layer, you'll have to turn

3 and 4 From top to bottom, the Red. Green, and Blue channels of the image.

the mask on and off by Shift-clicking it to determine which portions of the layer you want to use.

◆ Switch to the RiverWorkCopy version and click back on the Duplicate state in the History palette to go back to the RGB color version of the file.

◆ In the Channels palette, click the Red channel to activate it. Use Command (Ctrl)-A to select all of the channel, then type Command (Ctrl)-C to copy the information.

◆ Switch to the RiverColor image and type Command (Ctrl)-V to paste the Red channel as a new layer above the Lightness channel layer.

◆ Use Layer/Layer Mask/Hide All to create a layer mask that is completely black and hides this layer.

All Three RGB Channels

4 If you had decided to use one of the three color channels as your main black-and-white image, you might be done now. If you look at the illustrations to the left and compare them to the Lightness channel image on the preceding page, you'll see that no single RGB channel is as interesting as the Lightness channel layer. But we are going to make copies of the Green and Blue channels as well, in case we want to use portions of them.

◆ Switch to the RiverWorkCopy version, and in the Channels palette, click the Green channel to activate it. Use Command (Ctrl)-A to select all of the channel, then type Command (Ctrl)-C to copy the information.

◆ Switch to the RiverColor image and type Command (Ctrl)-V to paste the Green channel as a new layer above the Red Channel layer. Name the layer Green Channel.

◆ Option (Alt)-click the Add Layer Mask icon at the bottom of the Layers palette to create a layer mask that is completely black.

◆ Follow this same procedure to create a new layer from the Blue channel of the RiverWorkCopy image.

◆ As long as the masks on these three channel layers are all black, they are not adding to the cumulative effect of this image. If you want to use any portion of any channel layer as part of the final image, all you have to do is paint white in the mask of that layer in the area you wanted to use. That is what Barry did in his more complex version of this image, whose Layers palette is shown on page 366.

◆ Save this file as RiverLayers.

The Channel Mixer

5 Many people use the Channel Mixer (or the Channel Mixer with variations) to create their black-and-white images. While you can create some very nice photos this way, we don't generally use this method for our fine black-and-white prints, as we prefer to have more control over exactly which areas of the separate channels we use for an image. We'll show you how this technique works and point out some of its advantages and limitations.

◆ Turn off the Eye icons for all the layers except the *Background* layer. You need to start with an RGB or CMYK image to blend the channels together.

◆ In the Channels palette, click each of the three color channels to determine which one has the detail you'd like to start with. We chose the Green channel, which is often the one with the best tonal variation. That does depend on the content of the image, though.

◆ Make sure the Blue Channel layer is active in the Layers palette, because you want the Channel Mixer layer to be the top layer at this point. Click RGB in the Channels palette, then click the Create New Fill or Adjustment Layer icon on the bottom of the Layers palette and choose Channel Mixer from the pop-up menu.

◆ In the Channel Mixer dialog, choose Green in the Output Channel pop-up. This sets the Green channel as the primary source of your information.

◆ Click the Monochrome check box at the bottom of the dialog, and make sure the Preview box is checked as well. Your image switches to black and white with the Green channel at 100% and both the Red and Blue channels at 0%.

◆ Move the Green Source Channel slider to the left until it reaches about 85, then move both the Red and Blue sliders up to about 10. Watch as you move the sliders to see how the black-and-white tonal values change. In general you want the sum of the sliders to be 100%, but sometimes being a little over or under that creates a nicer black and white. To lighten or darken the overall image, use the Constant slider—but only a little, or you'll blow out your highlights or flatten your shadow detail.

◆ When you've manipulated the sliders to get what you think is the best black-and-white image, click OK to close the dialog. If you love your result and want to use the same settings for other images, click the Save button before you exit the dialog to save the setting for later use.

◆ Compare the Channel Mixer version to the Lightness channel version by turning the Eye icons on and off for those layers. If you have trouble deciding which is best, use Image/Duplicate with Duplicate Merged Layers Only checked to compare the versions side by side. Our Lightness Channel layer was still the best.

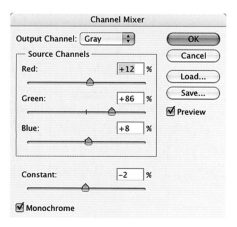

5 Here's how we adjusted the Channel Mixer for this image.

5 Here's how the image looks with the Channel Mixer settings from the previous illustration. It's nice, but it still doesn't have the snap of the Lightness channel version.

You can combine different Channel Mixer adjustments, as we do in Chapter 26, "Restoring Old Photos," by using layer masks to conceal or reveal the portions of each that you like. You can also add a curve above a Channel Mixer adjustment layer to increase or decrease the contrast of the adjustment. The main reason we don't generally use Channel Mixer is that getting a version that you like is a trial-and-error process—you just have to move sliders until it looks about right. By using individual RGB or CMYK channels, you can target the exact areas from each that you want to use with layer masks.

Channel Mixer with Variations

6 You can use a Curves adjustment layer above the Channel Mixer adjustment as we mentioned in the last step, but you can also modify the effect of the Channel Mixer adjustment by using one or more adjustment layers beneath the Channel Mixer. You can use Hue/Saturation, Color Balance, Levels, or Curves to modify your image. But be careful how you use them. Depending on the original image, it's very easy to blow out highlights or flatten areas of color, creating a posterized effect. Make sure you view your image at 100% and scroll around to check the tonal values if you use adjustment layers beneath your Channel Mixer layer.

◆ In the Layers palette, turn off the Eye icon for the Lightness layer. Click the Blue Channel layer, because you want your Curves adjustment layer to be created above this layer and below the Channel Mixer layer.

◆ Click the Create New Fill or Adjutment Layer icon at the bottom of the Layers palette, and choose the Curves type.

◆ Look at the values in the image you want to adjust. Use the RGB curve to adjust the overall image, but then switch to individual channels to adjust the values—say, in the green undergrowth or the blue cast on the water. You may need to click OK to accept the curve, then go back to the original RGB image to decide which color curves to adjust. You can see how we adjusted our curves in the illustrations on this page.

Burn and Dodge Layer

7 Finally, on the top of this stack of layers we use a Burn and Dodge layer. This is for the final details. If you found that one of the layers, or some combination of layers that you've built so far, gives you most of what you want, you can use this final layer to airbrush only those areas that still have problems to be corrected. We use a layer in Soft Light Blend mode filled with 50% gray for this.

◆ Click the Channel Mixer layer to make it the active layer.

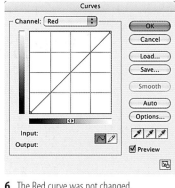

6 The RGB curve we used brightens the midtones of the image.

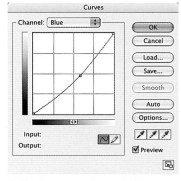

6 The Red curve was not changed.

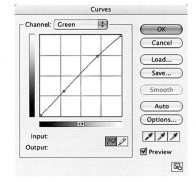

6 These Green curve changes brighten the vegetation areas of the image.

6 This Blue curve darkens and adds contrast to areas where the white water mixes with the dark water.

6 After adding the Curves adjustment layer under the Channel Mixer layer, the image is more in line with what we want for a final version.

- Option (Alt)-click the Create a New Layer icon at the bottom of the Layers palette, and change the Mode to Soft Light. Once you've changed the mode, you can click the Fill with Soft Light Neutral Gray button. You can also name this layer Burn and Dodge before you click OK.

- Type B for the Brush tool and use Airbrush 7% from the Tool presets pop-up at the top-left of the Options bar to dodge or burn areas of the image. Type D for the default colors, and, remember, white lightens or dodges the areas, black burns or darkens. Type X to switch between the two colors.

- Use Command (Ctrl)-S to save the file.

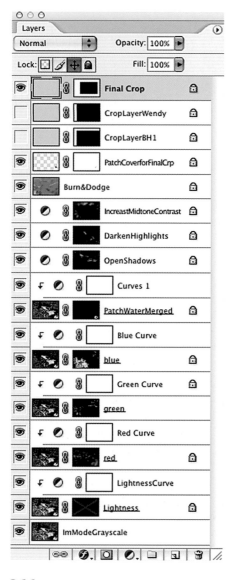

This is Barry's final layered file, named River6521ColUSMBW. psd on the DVD. You can see the amount of work he puts into creating an image. It starts with a black and white action to set up the workflow and adjustment layers similar to these. To get the action he uses for black and white, along with a video explaining how to use it, see the Videos section of www.barryhaynes.com.

A Curve for Every Layer

Although we are not going to take the time to add a Curves adjustment layer to every layer in this file, you might find that you need curves on several of the layers just to tweak values. Included in the Chapter 25 folder of the DVD is Barry's final layered version of this image. Barry uses an action he created to set up the adjustment layer workflow he normally uses to make a black-and-white print. If you open the file called River6521ColUSMBW.psd you can see that the action creates a Curves adjustment layer grouped with each layer that we normally create for black and white. In addition there are three curves adjustment layers that we have not built in this example, one each for adjusting highlights, midtones, and shadows. Note that Barry's version contains no Channel Mixer adjustment layer. He uses separate Red, Green, and Blue channels, like those you made earlier, each having its own layer mask for controlling which parts of the image come from that channel. In this image, these masks are not all black. Turn each layer's Eye icon off and then on again to see how that layer contributes to the final image.

Cropping

In our River image, we found that cropping was not easy. Barry and Wendy each saw something different in the image they wanted to emphasize. It took several versions (the crop layers at the top of the layered file) before we agreed on how to crop this image, and then our preferred crop brought attention to an area of the image we felt was distracting. If you turn off the Eye icon for the PatchCoverforFinalCrp layer, you can see the area that we patched for the final version of the image shown at the beginning of the chapter.

Toning

Not only can you create the black-and-white version of your image in numerous ways, but you can also tone areas of the image to alter the effect of the artwork in many different ways. Just as you will discover which method of converting to black and white works best for your workflow, you will need to experiment with different toning options to find which works for you. You may, for example, need simple formulas that are repeatable and that you can implement by setting up an action. Our technical editor, Wayne Palmer, uses Variations for that very reason. He needs the effect to be simple, quick, and formulaic.

Here in the second half of this chapter, we will cover some of the different ways you can introduce tones into a black-and-white image. Some of the techniques we'll cover briefly; others we'll describe in more detail, particularly those we feel give you the most flexibility and power.

For this part of the exercise, we will use a flattened file. You can either use a flattened version of the RiverLayers file you created earlier, or open our RiverCropped file from the Chapter 25 folder on the DVD.

The first type of toning we'll discuss is simple: We will shift all of the tonal variations in the image toward a single color.

Hue/Saturation Adjustment Layer

8 The technique you will probably see most often for single-toned images is to use a Hue/Saturation adjustment layer to colorize the image.

◆ Either use Image/Duplicate and check the Duplicate Merged Layers Only check box to create a new, flattened version of your file, or open RiverCropped from the Chapter 25 folder on the DVD.

◆ Add a Hue/Saturation adjustment layer [Command (Ctrl)-F4] and click the Colorize button.

◆ Adjust the Hue slider to the right until you get a blue tone for the image. We used 235. We also lowered the saturation to 15. Click OK to create the adjustment.

◆ In the Layers palette, lower the opacity of this layer at least 50%.

The advantages of using this technique are its simplicity and the fact that you can save your Hue/Saturation settings to use later. The disadvantage is that you don't have a visual reference in the Hue slider to tell you what color you are moving toward. So unless you've done it a lot and know which direction to go, you will probably spend some time fiddling around trying to find the color you want.

Color Fill Layer

9 A better method than Hue/Saturation is to use a solid color fill layer in Color Blend mode. This allows you to actually see the colors you are choosing, and it also includes access to custom color libraries such as PANTONE and TruMatch.

◆ Turn off the Eye icon for the Hue/Saturation adjustment layer you just created.

◆ Option (Alt)-click the Create New Fill or Adjustment Layer icon at the bottom of the Layers palette, choose Solid Color, and then

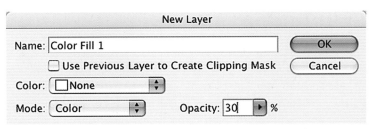

9 Change the Blend mode and Opacity *before* you begin to choose the color, or the color will completely cover the image, making it difficult to tell how the image will be affected.

9 This is how the cropped image looks with a single-tone color fill adjustment layer.

change the Mode pop-up to Color. This will allow you to see how the fill layer is affecting the underlying tones as you are choosing the color you want to use. Lower the opacity to about 30% as well, then click OK.

◆ Use the Color Picker to choose a deep blue for this image. If you get the Out of Gamut for Printer warning icon (the tiny triangle with an exclamation point), don't worry about it at this point. Although the color might be out of the printer's range if printed at full opacity, here we are using a reduced opacity, as well as blending the color with the blacks in the image. If you want a lot of color, however, be aware that raising the opacity of an out-of-gamut color increases the possibility of your image printing incorrectly. So if you're going for some wild effect, make sure you choose appropriate colors.

Split Toning

Split toning takes the process of color shifting one step further. In a split-toned image, the highlights are generally one color, while the shadows are another. The colors might blend in the midtones, or a separate color might be chosen for the midtones as well. This color mixing reaches its zenith in quadtone prints—four separate inks laid down for an image, with curves controlling exactly which tones accept which ink. We'll talk about duotones, tritones, and quadtones in a while, but for now let's focus on simpler techniques.

Adjustment Layers with Layer Masks

10 You can achieve split-toning effects with either of the adjustment layers used in the previous two steps by adding a mask to limit the color to only one area. By duplicating the layer, choosing a new color, and inverting the mask, you have a second color adjusting the other area. We'll do this by loading a luminosity mask and adding it to the Color Fill adjustment layer.

◆ Click the Color Fill adjustment layer to make it active.

◆ Show the Channels palette [Shift-F10] if it's not currently open.

◆ Command (Ctrl)-click the RGB channel in the Channels palette to load that composite channel as a selection. This will select all the pixels that are 50% gray or lighter.

◆ Type D for the default colors, which makes black the background color. Because you want to conceal this adjustment in the high-

10 This image uses dark blue for the shadows and bright orange for the highlights.

lights, you want the layer mask to be black in the highlight areas. Press the Delete (Backspace) key, which will fill the currently selected highlight areas to the background color, black.

◆ Drag this layer to the Create a New Layer icon at the bottom of the Layers palette to make a copy. Use Command (Ctrl)-D to deselect the selection.

◆ Double-click the Color thumbnail for the copy to bring up the Color Picker, and choose a new color for your highlights. We clicked the Color Libraries button and chose a PANTONE orange for our highlight color. Click OK to the Color Picker.

◆ Type Command (Ctrl)-I to invert the mask for this layer and apply the color only to the highlights.

◆ Rename the Color Fill 1 layer as Color Fill Shadows. Rename the Color Fill 1 copy layer as Color Fill Highlights.

◆ Save your image as RiverToned.

Keep your image open if you want to experiment further with the following techniques. If not, you can close the image and simply read on. If you look in the folder for Chapter 25 on the DVD, you'll see our RiverToned image, which includes additional layers as well as a Layer Comps palette you can use to compare the toned versions we created.

Color Balance

We've seen tutorials that use Color Balance to create tones in an image. The Color Balance dialog allows you to specify the highlights, shadows, or midtones as the tones you want to adjust, and you can adjust all three in the same layer. Our main complaint with Color

10 If you set up your window so that the Layers palette and the Color Picker are on one side of the screen, you can see how your image is affected as you change colors. It's great to get this sort of instant feedback on your color choices.

Color Range to Select Tones

If you need to select the midtones only, or you want shadows or highlights with no midtones included, you can use Select/Color Range to select each of those three tonal values individually. Color Range returns a selection, so you can use that selection to create a mask for your adjustment.

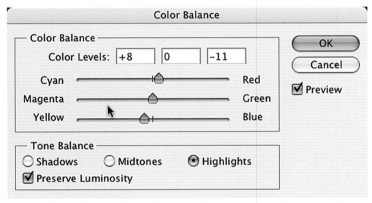

The Color Balance tool gives you buttons for choosing Shadows, Midtones, or Highlights to adjust.

This is the image with a single Color Balance adjustment layer controlling the tones of both the Shadows and the Highlights. We lowered the opacity of the layer to 50% and changed the Blend mode to Color.

Balance is that you have to guess at how to mix the color you want. Will adding magenta make your blue too purple, will adding cyan make it too wimpy? Also, using the Color Balance tool in Normal Blend mode, even at a lowered opacity, seems to add contrast to the image—not what you want if you've carefully crafted your image. If you use Color Balance to tone, we suggest using it in Color mode rather than Normal and using separate Color Balance layers for each tone you want to introduce, because you can then paint the layer mask for each tone.

Gradient Map

A final technique for toning that we'll discuss briefly before we show you how to create real duotones is the Gradient Map tool. While we don't use this tool very often, it does produce interesting results. A gradient map takes the colors of a gradient and "maps" them to the tones of a grayscale image. The color at one end of the gradient represents the shadows and the opposite end of the gradient will replace the highlight colors. The intermediate blend of the gradient will handle the midtones. The effect of the Gradient Map adjustment layer is rather dramatic and probably not what you want for a fine black-and-white print. However, if you change the Blend mode to Soft Light and lower the opacity to 30% or so, the effect is pleasing. Again, if you want to try creating a Gradient Map adjustment layer, we suggest you

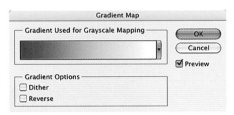

This is the first dialog you see when you create the Gradient Map. Click the color band itself to go to the Gradient Editor.

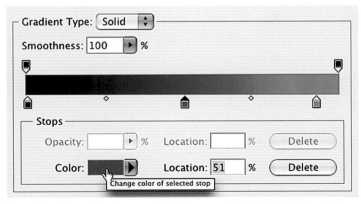

If you click a color stop, the color appears in the lower area of the dialog. Clicking the color brings up the Color Picker.

This Gradient Map adjustment layer uses the colors of the three-tone gradient on the previous page in Soft Light Blend mode at 30% opacity.

11 The BurnleyGraveyard image printed as black and white using only black ink.

Option (Alt)-click the Create a New Fill or Adjustment layer icon on the Layers palette so you can change the Blend mode and opacity of the layer before you begin choosing colors for your gradient. Once the Gradient Map dialog appears, you can click on the gradient itself to go into the Gradient Editor, where you can select the colors you want to use. You can move the color stops for the gradient and watch how that affects the image, and you can move the midpoint diamond between two color stops to have the gradient map to more or fewer tones.

Duotones, Tritones, and Quadtones

Duotones are used to get more tonal range when you're printing black-and-white photos on a press. Black-and-white digital images can have up to 256 tones in digital format, but you can't get those 256 tones on a printing press with just the single black ink. If you use two or more inks to print black-and-white images, part of the tonal range can be printed by the first ink and part of it by the second ink. Many of Ansel Adams's well-known black-and-white posters are actually duotones. Besides giving you a larger tonal range, duotones allow you to add rich, subtle color to your black-and-white images.

Typically, you use black ink for the dark shadows and a second color, a brown or gray, for the midtones. You can add a third and even a fourth color to enhance the highlights or some other part of the tonal range. Many books are printed with two colors, black for the text and a second color, such as red or blue, for text section titles, underlining, and other special colored areas. If this type of book has photographs,

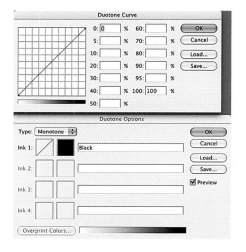

11 The default settings when you convert to Duotone mode are a monotone print with black ink in a straight curve.

you can often make them more interesting by using duotones instead of just black and white.

Creating a Duotone

11 The photo we use in this section was originally a color transparency, but Barry felt a black-and-white or duotone printing of it would better convey the feelings he had about this stark graveyard where his grandfather and uncle are buried. Before using Image/Mode/Grayscale to convert the image to black and white, he did the overall color correction to get the best version of the RGB image he had scanned. After converting to grayscale (your image must be in grayscale for Duotone to be available), Barry edited the contrast of the sky and the foreground separately to bring out the drama of

11 The BurnleyGraveyard image created in Duotone mode as a duotone with black and PANTONE Warm Gray10 C inks, both with straight curves, and later converted to CMYK for this final output.

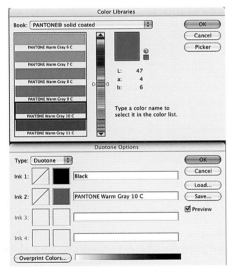

11 Pick the second color by clicking the rightmost color square for Ink 2.

the scene. He also fixed a section of the sky that was blown out due to the high dynamic range of the original photo.

◆ Open and crop the BurnleyGraveyard image from the folder for Chapter 25 on the DVD.

◆ Choose Image/Mode/Duotone to start working with the Duotone options. Start with the Type set to Monotone and the curve for Ink 1 straight. If the curve is not already straight, click the Curve box (the leftmost one) for Ink 1 and bring up the curve. Click and drag any extra points in the middle of the curve

to outside the dialog box to remove them, or hold down Option (Alt) and click the Reset button to remove all the points.

The horizontal axis of the curve diagrams in the Duotone Options dialog has the highlights on the left and the shadows on the right—the opposite of the default for Levels and Curves. The numbers in the boxes represent a percentage of black. Box 0, for the brightest highlight, should read 0, and box 100, for the darkest shadow, should read 100. All the other boxes should be blank when you have a straight curve.

◆ Click OK in the Duotone Curve dialog. The Ink box for Ink 1 should be black, and Black should be its name.

◆ Change the Type pop-up to Duotone to activate Ink 2 with a straight curve. To pick the color of Ink 2, click the Color box (the rightmost one) for Ink 2 to bring up the Color Libraries Picker, then select a PANTONE, Focoltone, Toyo, TruMatch, or other color from one of the custom color systems.

Look in Chapter 5, "Picking and Using Color," if you need help using the Color Libraries Picker. If you were going to print your duotone on a two-color book job or a job with a spot color, you would probably use one of these color systems.

◆ We selected PANTONE Warm Gray 10 C for Ink 2. You now have a black ink and a medium gray ink, both with straight curves. Make sure the Preview box is checked in the Duotone Options dialog to give you a preview of what it should look like with the current inks and curves.

Printing two inks, both with straight curves, is like printing the image in black and then printing the exact same image again with the second ink color. When printing with halftone screens, the second ink will be printed with a different screen angle to add some additional tonality. Printing the two inks using the same curve will cause the image to have too much density and seem very dark. This is not taking advantage of the possibilities for duotone improvements.

Adjusting Your Duotone Curves

12 You want to adjust the black ink to make it prevalent in the shadows, but less prevalent in the midtones and highlights.

◆ Click the Curve box (the leftmost box) for Ink 1.

◆ Click a point in the middle of the curve and drag that point downward to remove black from the midtones and highlights.

◆ Click the shadow end of the curve (to the middle right) and drag it up to add a little more black to this area of the image. See the

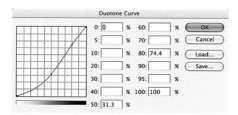

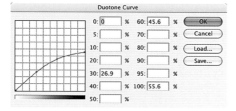

12 The black curve emphasizing the shadows.

12 The midtone curve for Ink 2, lowering this color in the shadow areas.

check box in Duotone Options is selected, you should be able to see these changes as you make them.

You have now made the basic adjustments for your duotone curves. Now change each curve just a little bit, one curve at a time. Tweak these curves until you are happy with your duotone.

◆ Click OK in the Duotone Options dialog, and use File/Save As to save the image as BurnleyGraveyardDuo.

Creating a Tritone

13 To further enhance this image, you can add a third ink for the highlight areas to alter them in subtle ways. Before doing so, however, take time to make a copy of the two-ink version of the image so you can compare the two onscreen.

◆ Choose Image/Duplicate [F5] and name it BurnleyGraveyardTri.

◆ Choose Image/Mode/Duotone, and select Tritone from the Type menu in Duotone Options so a choice for Ink 3 will be added.

◆ Click the Ink Color box and choose a lighter gray for the highlights. (For Ink 3 we chose PANTONE 422 C.) Adjust the curve for this highlight color so that it has ink only in the brightest part of the image. The illustration at the top of the next page shows the curve we chose for the third ink. Notice how we moved the 0 position of the curve up to 6.3 instead of leaving it at 0.

This strategy actually adds some density to the brightest parts of the image—that is, in the clouds and where the sun reflects off the gravestones, two areas that previously were pure white. Here, we are using a third ink to subtly fine-tune the main image created by the first two main inks.

12 The BurnleyGraveyard image created in Duotone mode as a duotone with black for the shadows and PANTONE Warm Gray 10 C for the midtones and highlights, after adjusting the curves for those two colors, and then converting to CMYK.

You may want to measure some values on the screen using the Eyedropper tool. When working with duotones, you want to set the top-left area in the Info palette to Actual Color, so that it will give you measurements of the ink density percentage of each color. If you measure one of the highlight areas in the clouds, you can see that there is no density there from Inks 1 and 2, but that Ink 3 has 6% density in that area. If you measure a shadow area, the maximum density there will be from Ink 1, black. There will be some density from Ink 2, and no density from Ink 3 because its curve specifies no ink in the shadow areas.

illustration of the black curve above. Click on the OK button for black.

Because we want the dark areas of the image to be represented mostly by black, we need to remove the gray from the shadows.

◆ Click the Curve button for Ink 2 (warm gray) so you can work on its curve. Click at the top right of the curve and drag it down to about 55.

◆ Now you need to put the gray back in the highlights and midtones, so click a couple of points in the middle of the curve to pull it up so it looks like the curve to the left. When the Preview

You have added a third color specifically for the highlights; therefore, you may want to go back to Ink 2 and remove some of the midtone ink from the highlight areas.

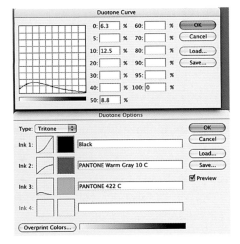

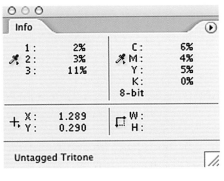

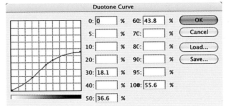

13 Final tritone values with details of the highlight curve. Notice how this curve actually starts above 0 on the Y axis. This adds density in the very brightest areas.

13 The Info palette measuring a highlight in Tritone mode.

13 The midtone (Ink 2) curve for the tritone with a small dip in the highlight area and a bigger dip in the shadows.

◆ Click the Curve box for Ink 2 and lower its curve in the highlight areas by clicking a point there and dragging it downward. Above is the final curve we used for Ink 2 in the tritone. Our final tritone image appears on the next page.

◆ Go back and try some different colors and different curves for this duotone or tritone. Try some blues, greens, purples, magentas, and yellows—lots of rich colors. Experiment with some radical inverted curves to discover the great range of effects you can achieve with the Duotone options.

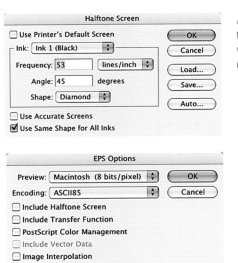

After you click the Screen button in the Output section of the the Print with Preview dialog, you get this dialog.

The dialog and settings for saving the file as EPS Duotone.

Calibrating and Printing Your Duotones

If you are not having any particular calibration problems, especially if you are converting duotones to CMYK for final output, we recommend that you leave your calibration settings and preferences set up the same as those for your CMYK workspace as described in Chapter 2, "Preferences and Color Settings."

When you output your duotones, you have several choices to make. If you actually print with PANTONE or some other custom spot color, you need to save the file as a duotone in Photoshop EPS format. You can set your screen angles for the duotone in Photoshop using File/Print With Preview with the More Options check box on. Use the pop-up to select Output, then click the Screen button. You can also set your screen angles in QuarkXPress or InDesign if you are placing your duotone into one of those page layout applications. Talk to your service bureau about how and where to set your screens and what screen angles and frequencies to use. One important issue is to make sure the name of each color is exactly the same (including upper- and lowercase letters) in your page layout application; otherwise, your duotone may be output as CMYK.

To save from Photoshop as a duotone, leave the Mode menu set to Duotone, choose File/Save As, and then set the Format to Photoshop EPS. In the EPS dialog box, set Preview to Macintosh (8 bits/pixel) and Encoding to Binary, and then click the Include Halftone Screen check box only if you have set your screens and frequencies using Print with Preview in Photoshop. In Windows, you may want to set the Encoding to ASCII, depending on the page layout application you're placing the duotone into. Check that application's manual.

If you want to convert the duotone to CMYK to output it with process colors, use the Image/Mode menu to convert the image to CMYK color. For more information on the options for saving CMYK files, see Chapter 18, "The Master Image Workflow." You can also convert your duotones to RGB format if you want to composite them with other images for Web or multimedia use, or for output to a film recorder or some other RGB device, like an Epson printer. To do the conversion to RGB, just select Image/Mode/RGB.

When you work on a duotone or tritone, the Channels palette displays a single channel—your original black-and-white image. When you print the tritone, this same black-and-white channel prints three times, and each time the separate curve for the particular tritone color is used to modify it before it goes to the printer. If you want to see each of these three-color tritone channels as they will look after the curves are applied, switch the Image/Mode menu to Multichannel. The Channels palette will now show you three channels: Channel 1 for black, Channel 2 for PANTONE 10, and Channel 3 for PANTONE 422. You can then click each channel in the Channels palette to see how that channel will look on film. If you wanted to edit each of these channels separately, you could do so now, but after doing that, you could not convert them back to Duotone mode. From Multichannel mode these three channels would have to be output as three separate black-and-white files. If you were just looking at the three channels and not editing them, you would choose Edit/Undo Multichannel to undo the mode change and put the image back into Duotone mode.

The final BurnleyGraveyard image created in Duotone mode as a tritone with black shadows, PANTONE Warm Gray 10 C midtones, and PANTONE 422 C highlights, then converted to CMYK for final output.

Portfolio

Barry Haynes

This image of Gibsons harbor to the right was converted from Raw to corrected color and then to grayscale by using a combination of the Lightness, Red, Green, and Blue channels. The color image of Howe Sound in Gibsons, British Columbia, below was created as a composite of three shots from Barry's Canon Digital Rebel. The grayscale version of the image was created using the Red channel as the main image, parts of the Green and Blue channels in certain areas, and then four different curves and masks to change the contrast of various parts of the image.

26 ◆ Restoring Old Photos

The original, badly damaged version of Doc as a child.

Your completed exercise should look something like this.

Increase density, heal, clone, and filter an old and damaged photograph to make a new version with better tonal range.

All of us have memories we want to hold on to forever. Our old photographs are links to our past, to our heritage. And now it's possible for us to restore those images to some measure of their former dignity. In this example, we take a very badly damaged and discolored print of Wendy's father, Dr. Warren Crumpler, and use a variety of Photoshop tools to restore and re-create his childhood sweetness.

Prepare the File

1 This image was scanned at 800 dots per inch and was a 56 MB file. For purposes of this example, we've resampled it to about 5.5 MB. We scanned it in RGB because we thought we might get more out of the information by using three channels rather than just black.

◆ Open DocAsChild.tif from the folder Ch26.Restoring Old Photos on the *Photoshop Artistry* DVD. Type C for the Crop tool. Make sure there are no previous settings by clicking the Clear button on the Options bar. Crop the image, leaving part of the darker band on the left side because we need to re-create part of the finger on the right hand. Use File/Save As and save the file as DocLayers in PSD format.

Increase the Density

2 Like most old photos, this one has lost density over the years. In the darker areas of the image, this is particularly unfortunate as much detail has been lost. In the first few steps of correction here, we're simply going to try to discern as much detail as possible. There will be places where we have to use our imagination and "paint" details back in.

◆ Drag the Background layer to the New Layer icon at the bottom of the Layers palette to duplicate the layer.

◆ Change the Blend mode of the layer to Multiply and change the opacity of the layer to 50%.

For some images you restore, you'll want to keep the second layer at 100% opacity, and you may even need a third layer in Multiply mode.

Use Levels to Bring Back Detail

3 Normally you use Levels to color balance your RGB image. In this instance, we use Levels to bring out detail and show us what exactly needs to be retouched. Once we get as much detail as possible, we'll retouch and then complete the normal steps for making a good print.

Set the Highlights

3a We use the same basic approach as setting the highlight for an image that does not have a good white point. You'll need to switch between a close-up view of the face and fitting the image onscreen to choose where to set your Levels.

◆ Go to Layer/New Adjustment Layer/Levels or choose a Levels adjustment layer from the Create Fill and Adjustment Layers icon at the bottom of the Layers palette.

◆ Type Command (Ctrl)-1 to go the Red Channel. Type Command (Ctrl)-0 to fit the image onscreen. Now hold the Option (Alt) key as you slide the Red Highlight Input slider to the left. The first areas that turn red are scratches and tears on the picture.

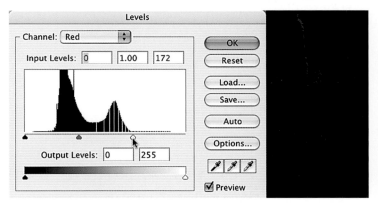

1 Leave some space on the left edge of the photo to re-create the finger. We've changed the color of the Crop tool overlay to give you a better idea of how much to crop.

2 Change the opacity and the Blend mode of the Background Copy layer.

3a If you start to see pixels of the face turning red, you've moved the slider too far.

◆ Release the Option (Alt) key, then hold down the Spacebar and drag a marquee around the face to zoom in. Once again, hold down the Option (Alt) key and click the Input Highlight slider to see what pixels you are affecting on the face. The scratch should be red; the pixels of the skin should not. We set the highlight for red at 175.

◆ Follow this same procedure for the Green and Blue channels. We set highlights for Green at 157 and Blue at 127.

Set the Shadows

3b Generally, when you set the shadows, you want to force the deepest shadows to black. But because so much of this image has faded to deep gray already, we'll only move the Shadow sliders in a bit to give the file a little definition. If you use the same technique on the Input Shadow sliders as in step 3a where you move the sliders until you start to clip detail information, you'll lose even more of the edges that tell you where the body ends and the furniture begins.

◆ Move each Input Shadow slider just to the point where the information starts. For the Red channel we used 12, for Green we used 10, and for Blue, 7.

Set the Midtones

3c Again, look for a setting that brings out details. Look around the left knee, the right foot, and the button on the right knee before you choose a setting.

◆ Move the Midtone slider to somewhere between 1.05 and 1.15. We chose 1.08.

4 This is the Channel Mixer of 86, 12, −4. **4** The Channel Mixer of 100, −10, 10.

Use the Channel Mixer

4 The print had yellowed a great deal when we got it and scanned it in RGB. You'll notice that there are scratches and water stains, but it also looks like something red was spilled in a couple of places.

We're going to use the channel mixer via an adjustment layer to bring the color back to black and white, which will make those red splotches easier to retouch. We'll also make some choices about tonal values here.

◆ Use Window/Channels [Shift-F10] to show the Channels palette. Click first on the RGB Composite channel, then click the Red channel, the Green channel, and the Blue channel in turn to see which has the most useful information. That will be the channel we use for the base of the mix. We chose Red.

◆ Go to Layer/New Adjustment Layer/Channel Mixer or choose Channel Mixer from the Create New Fill and Adjustment Layer icon at the bottom of the Layers palette. Make sure Red is the Output Channel, then click the Monochrome check box at the bottom of the dialog. Your image now looks like a grayscale image and you can move the sliders for each channel to try to bring out detail and also to choose some tonal values. For this mix, we chose 86, 12, and -4 for the RGB values, respectively. Double-click the name of the layer to rename it Mix 86, 12, -4.

◆ Now, turn off the icon for the Mix 86 layer and set up another Channel Mixer adjustment layer. Use 100, -10, 10 for the values in this layer. Rename this layer Mix 100, -10, 10. It's important

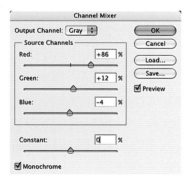 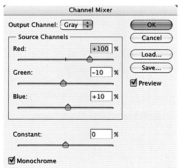

4 The settings for the first Channel Mixer adjustment layer. **4** The settings we used for the second Channel Mixer layer.

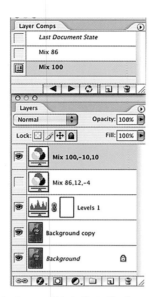

5 On the left is the way your Layers palette should look when you click the Create New Layer Comp button on the Layer Comps palette. On the right is the Layers palette set up when you create the Mix 100 comp.

- Use Window/Layer Comps to open the Layer Comps palette.

- Turn off the Eye icon for the Mix 100, -10, 10 layer and leave all the other Layer icons on. Click the Create New Layer Comp icon at the bottom of the Layer Comps palette and name this comp Mix 86. You only need to turn on Visibility under the options.

- Turn on the Eye icon for the Mix 100, -10, 10 layer and turn off the Eye icon for the Mix 86, 12, -4 layer. Click the Create New Layer Comp icon and name this comp Mix 100. Only Visibility needs to be on.

- Click the Apply Layer Comp box to the left of the comp view you want to see, or use the Previous or Next button or the Cycle button to move through the comps.

Once we were able to quickly see the difference between the two Channel Mixer adjustments, we decided that we liked the upper portion of the Mix 86 comp but the lower portion of the Mix 100 comp. By adding a graduated masks to the Mix 86 layer, we can have the portions of both that we like best. Wow, all this before we even retouch.

Add a Graduated Mask

Set Up the Gradient

6a We'll work with the Mix 86, 12, -4 layer first. We want a mask that's completely white over the face, but completely black by the time it reaches the left knee. Our first step is to set up a gradient that will paint the mask.

- Type G for the Gradient tool (if you get the Paint Bucket instead of the Gradient tool, type Shift-G.) Now type D for the default colors of white foreground and black background.

to remember to turn off the Mix 86 layer before you create the second Channel Mixer adjustment, because Channel Mixer uses all the visible information on layers below it when making its adjustments.

- Turn the Eye icons off and on for the two Channel Mixer layers to decide which you like better.

Create Layer Comps

5 You may have noticed in the previous step that it's a bit difficult to catch the subtle differences in the two Channel Mixer layers when you have to take the time to turn one Eye icon off and the other on. In those seconds, your eye adjusts to the screen and your brain can't remember what was there before. You could turn on the appropriate Eye icons and use Image/Duplicate with Merged Layers Only checked to make a couple of duplicates of the image to compare side-by-side, but what we like about using the Layer Comps palette is that both versions reside in the same file. As you make changes to the image, you can update the Layer Comps palette to reflect your new idea of what the image should be. The Layer Comps palette can remember visibility (as in which layers were on and off), the position of the layers, and the appearance of the layers. Appearance includes what Blend modes, opacities, and layer effects are used. So if you need a side-by-side comparison, use Image/Duplicate. For more flexibility, use Layer Comps.

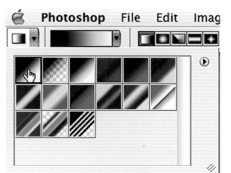

6a The first swatch in the Gradients presets is the Foreground to Background gradient.

6b The drag for the Mix 86 gradient should be about this long.

6b You image should look something like this after you add the mask to the Mix 86, 12, –4 layer.

6c When you turn the Mix 100, –10, 10 adjustment layer back on, your image looks like this.

◆ Click the Gradient Swatch pop-up on the Options bar and make sure the first gradient in the palette is chosen. If you have tool tips turned on and hold the mouse over the swatch, you'll see that it says Foreground to Background. If you clicked the swatch itself, you got the Gradient Editor, and the swatch will be named in the Name input area. When you've chosen the swatch in either place, you can press Return (Enter) to close the Presets palette.

Add a Gradient to the Mix 86, 12, -4 Layer Mask

6b When you are drawing or redrawing the gradient, make sure you are on the mask and not the layer. The double black border will be around the layer mask thumbnail when the layer mask is active.

◆ Click the Mix 86 Apply Layer Comp icon, which turns off the Mix 100, -10, 10 adjustment layer. Click the Mix 86, 12, -4 adjustment layer to make it active, then click the Add Layer Mask icon at the bottom of the Layers palette (it's the third from the left) to add a new, white layer mask.

◆ Because white is the foreground color, you want to start your drag to create the mask below the neckline so that everything above that is completely white on the mask and the adjustment will show through. We started our gradient at the top of the knot on the bow. Let go of the mouse when you get to the white bands on the left sleeve. If you hold the Shift key down as you drag, your drag will be constrained to a vertical line.

When you've completed the gradient on the mask, the top portion of the image will be black and white, and the bottom will still look brown because you're seeing through to the Background copy.

Turn on the Mix 100, -10, 10 Layer

6c When you turn the second Channel Mixer adjustment layer back on, you'll be seeing the bottom portion from this layer only because

the layer mask on the Mix, 86, 12, -4 layer keeps the Mix 86 layer from affecting the result of the Mix 100 layer. In the upper portion of the image you see the results of the Mix 86 layer because the Channel Mixer uses all underlying layers in its computation and the Mix 86 adjustment layer has turned the upper portion of the image to black and white. This means that in the upper portion of the image all three channels are exactly the same, so the adjustment has no effect.

◆ Turn on the Eye icon for the Mix 100, –10, 10 layer. The image should be completely black and white with no brown showing through.

Add a New Comp and Update Previous Layer Comps

At this point you may want to use the Layer Comps palette to check the three versions of your file so far. However, if you click the Apply Layer Comp button for the Mix 86 comp now, you'll see that the comp is influenced by the new mask that you built. This is not helpful for checking your work. We'll need to update those comps.

Add a New Layer Comp

7a First, because our image is in a state that we want to save, we'll create a new layer comp.

7b You can use the forward and back arrows to cycle through all the layer comps or only ones that you've selected by Shift- or Command (Ctrl)-clicking.

◆ Once your masks are accurate and both Eye icons are turned on for your Channel Mixer adjustment layers, click the Create New Layer Comp icon at the bottom of the Layer Comps palette. Save only the visibility of the layers, and name this comp Both Channel Mixers.

Update Previous Layer Comps

7b For the Mix 86 comp, you have to turn off the layer mask and resave the comp to have it behave as it did when you created it.

◆ Click the Mix 86 layer comp to make it active, and also click the Apply Layer Comp button next to its name to put your file back in that state.

◆ Shift-click the layer mask to turn it off, then click the Update Layer Comp button on the Layer Comps palette. It's the one in the center that looks like two arrows in a circle.

◆ Cycle through the comps by using the arrow buttons at the bottom of the palette.

A Little More on Layer Comps

We had you save only the visibility of your layers in the Layer Comps palette, but you might find it easier to go ahead and turn on all of the options until you understand exactly what the Layer Comps palette does and does not save. In step 7b above, for instance, Photoshop did not know that we wanted to see the Mix 86 layer without its mask, even though when we created the comp the mask did not exist. If you paint on a layer after you've created the comp, the same thing will happen. Photoshop will know which layers to turn on and off but it will not reflect some history state where there was no paint on the layer. So if you plan to do retouching, say, you'd want to create a new layer for the retouching if maintaining the original information is important to you.

If you change the state of layers in a way that causes Photoshop not to be able to re-create the layer comp that you created, you'll see a triangle with an exclamation point to warn you. In this example, if you delete your Levels adjustment layer, all three comps will show you the warning. However, you can add layers—they simply won't be turned on when you go back to one of the comp states.

If you change the order of the layers in your document, that order will be reflected in all of the previous layer comps you created, so try to have all the layers in the order that you want before you create comps. The Position option remembers the position of the layer in the window, right-left or up-down. It does not remember the position of the layer within the Layers palette.

Use the Apply Layer Comp icon for the Last Document State to help you create comps and compare states of the document.

Create a New Layer and Merge

You're finally at the point where you can begin retouching the file. We'll be using a variety of tools for this, the Spot Healing brush, the Patch tool, and the Clone Stamp, as well as simply copying portions of the file from one place to the other. There are different ways you could set up your file for retouching. Normally, you could simply use a new blank layer and turn on Sample All Layers for the retouching tools. One advantage to this technique is that you can change the opacity of your retouch layer. However, the Patch tool is really useful on badly damaged areas, and it does not have the Sample All Layers option.

8 You're going to merge all the work you've done so far into one layer and use that as the retouch layer.

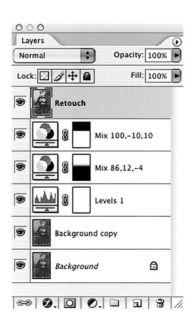

8 Your Layers palette looks like this after you created the merged layer in step 8.

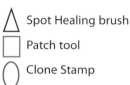

You can use this as a rough map of where to apply the different retouching tools we use in this example.

△ Spot Healing brush

▢ Patch tool

◯ Clone Stamp

◆ Make sure the Mix 100, −10, 10 layer is active.

◆ Hold down the Option (Alt) key and use the Layers palette pop-up menu to Merge Visible Layers. You can also do this by pressing Command-Shift-Option (Ctrl-Shift-Alt)-E. In earlier versions of Photoshop, you needed to make a new blank layer to use this technique.

◆ Double-click the name of this layer to rename it Retouch.

Retouch and Repair

One of the first things you need to do in retouching is really look at the image and try to get a sense of which tools you think will work and where. We're giving you our "map" of where we used most of the tools, and in this portion of the example, we've laid out the tools in a certain order. In reality, we generally work with the tool that we think can accomplish the most work first and switch when it doesn't do what we need. So we may be in the Clone Stamp for quite some

9 I was able to do all this retouching using the Spot Healing brush.

10 The background area at the top right side of the head is a particular problem.

10 I dragged the patch to this area. It looked like a good match.

10 The completed patch was darker than I had expected, but the texture is good. I can fix the color later with a curve or the Clone Stamp.

10 This is the right sleeve before patching.

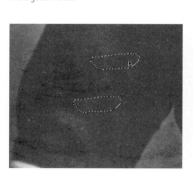

10 I used 10 or 12 small patches to match texture on the sleeve.

10 You'll notice that I didn't try to do the edges of the shirt with the Patch tool. That's a job better suited to the Clone tool.

time, switch to the Healing Brush for a few strokes, go back to the Clone Stamp, then make a selection and copy it. The main thing is to experiment with the tools. Learn what they do, use them with different brushes and angles, change directions, and redo a stroke. Play.

The Spot Healing Brush

9 Start with the amazing Spot Healing brush. While this tool doesn't do everything, what it does it does so well that it cuts your retouching time dramatically. If you're doing this as a class assignment, you're going to be really grateful that this tool exists. Like the Healing brush, the Spot Healing brush uses a complex blending algorithm to match the texture from one area of the image to another while keeping the luminosity and color of the original area. Unlike the Healing brush or the Clone Stamp, you do not need to Option (Alt)-click to specify the source for the healing. Photoshop averages the information from around the brush. In general, use a brush just large enough to cover the area that you want healed. The direction of the stroke you use, where you start, and where you end are all clues to Photoshop about where you want to take the information from. So if you use the brush and you don't get the desired result, Command (Ctrl)-Z and try the stroke from a different direction. Small strokes or dabs work better than long strokes, and for wrinkles heal from the outside of the wrinkle to the inside. You can make a selection before healing to restrict the results of the tool to certain areas.

◆ Use the Spot Healing brush at between 20 and 30 pixels in Proximity Match mode. This brush worked well on the large white spots on the bottom of the image, on water spots that were over background areas or areas of flat color, small facial imperfections, and the large scratch at the upper left of the photo. It does not work well whenever you are in an area that has an edge of the clothing or furniture, or in the hair.

Use the Patch Tool

This is a tool we've grown to love for retouching. Most of the time we use it in Source mode, because you get a preview of the area from which you'll sample information in the place where the blending will happen. This allows you to do some matching of color and texture as you drag. When you reach a spot that you think might match well, release the mouse and the patch happens. If you switch to Destination mode, you make a selection of an area that has the texture you want and drag it to the position that needs to be patched. If you need that same texture in several areas, you needn't make another selection—it stays active, so you can simply drag to another location to perform another patch. You can make a selection with any of the selection tools and then switch to the Patch tool to make the drag and patch, so you can be very particular with your selections if need be. As with the Healing brush, you need to be careful near the edges of objects. If you get too close, you'll soften the edges or cause unwanted color or brightness values to bleed into the area you are trying to patch.

10 We often use the Patch tool to bring texture back to blown-out skin tones in portraits, but here most of the patching will be on areas of the background or the clothing.

◆ Use the Patch tool in Source mode to correct some of the areas marked on the "map" on the previous page. Switch to Destination mode and try that out as well. The right sleeve would be a good place for that. Sometimes it helps to use Command (Ctrl)-H to hide the edges of the selection before you make your drag for the patch. It gives you a better idea of how the edges of your selection match.

Use the Clone Stamp

Almost everyone who uses Photoshop uses this tool—for good reason. It's a real powerhouse when it comes to correcting imperfections in an image. Clone out power lines, clone in flowers, you name it, it's been done. Think of it as the detail fix-up tool. Use it when you need to precisely control the effect of repair.

11 In this image, use the Clone Stamp to correct major imperfections as well as clean up some edges. As you clone, you'll find some areas

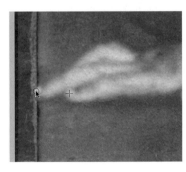

11 We re-created the tip of one finger by sampling another.

that work better with the Healing brush or Spot Healing brush. Feel free to switch to those tools and back to the Clone Stamp. Around the shoes and the right leg, there's not enough information to know exactly what to clone, so don't bother with those areas now.

◆ Type S for the Clone Stamp and make sure the Aligned option is checked. Use a soft-edge brush of about 8 to 10 pixels. Change the size of the brush using the left and right bracket keys as you work.

◆ Clone the major tear in the hair. Don't try to make one pass with the Clone Stamp to do this. You'll need to sample first from one side of the tear, then the other, and use short strokes to make this work. There is also a big scratch on the right leg that requires similar treatment. Be careful not to clone portions of the pants or stockings that have edges or color differences that will cause a repeating pattern as you clone. Also, be aware of the button on the rim of the pants. Don't clone over it.

◆ There are two small scratches under the chin. You'll want to clone the edge of the chin in some areas and just the skin in others.

◆ Remember using the Patch tool on the right sleeve? Now's the time to clone the edge of the sleeve to make the outline crisp. Check the right edge of the jacket as well.

◆ Finally, clone areas of the fingers that are missing. There's a tiny area on the left index finger and the larger problem of the tip of the finger on the right hand. We used the tip of the index finger to clone the problem area.

Don't try to use the Clone Stamp to re-create the left edge of the photo; it's too big, and the following technique works well and quickly.

Make Feathered Copies

12 This is one of the oldest retouching methods, and it still works well for large areas like the black tape mark down the left edge of the photo. Start working from the top; you'll have to use smaller selections as the background gets darker. Feel free once again to Clone or Heal to make the edges of your selection fit better.

◆ Type M to switch to the Marquee tool. Press Return (Enter), then 10, then Return (Enter) again to set a feather value of 10.

◆ Marquee a section to the right and below the first area that you want to patch. Be careful not to take an area with too much pattern. See the illustrations to get an idea of what to choose.

◆ Type V to switch to the Move tool. Type Command (Ctrl)-H to hide the edges of the selection, then hold down the Option (Alt) key and drag your selection to the top-left edge of the image. You'll see a pair of tiny arrows that let you know your selection is being copied as it is moved.

◆ If the selection you made works well, type Command (Ctrl)-D to deselect the area, and drop it into place. If it doesn't, you can type Command (Ctrl)-T to Free Transform the selection, stretching,

12 This is the area where we made the initial selection to heal the upper portion of the black band.

12 Even though you don't see the edges of the selection, you can tell that you are making a copy when you have the little double-arrow icon.

12 Here is our selection in place. We'll darken this area a bit layer using a Curves adjustment layer.

13 Actually drawing the shapes of the legs and shoes helped locate other areas to heal, as well as guide the dodging and burning.

skewing, or rotating it for a better fit. Be careful, though. With so much grain, you can only stretch a little bit before the grain pattern becomes noticeable. If all else fails, press Delete, get rid of the selection, and make a new one.

Sketch in Details

At this point you may be fretting about all the garbage around the shoes. But there's not enough information left in the original image, especially in the area of the left shoe and the edge of the right leg, to tell us what should stay and what needs to go. We've been known to steal information from a totally different picture, so if we had another shoe that we could clone and transform, we would do it. We don't. The only alternative is to make something out of nothing, to draw it in. This happens all the time in portrait retouching, where camera angles or incomplete preparation leaves a little hole in the hair that has to be filled in. In the case of this image, actually drawing in details would most likely overwhelm the rest of the information and look unreal unless you are a very good artist and your layer is very transparent. So we are going to create what we believe to be the shapes of the shoes, legs, and knees, then use dodge and burn layers to suggest the edges. First we draw.

13 You don't have to be a great artist here. Just sketch in the shapes the best you can. You can follow our sketch in the illustration for this step, or open our DocLayers.psd file from the DVD. As you start drawing the lines, you'll find more areas to heal or clone as well. Switch to the appropriate tool when necessary; S for the Clone Stamp, J (or Shift-J) for the Spot Healing brush or Healing brush.

◆ Make a new, blank layer by clicking the Create New Layer Icon on the Layers palette, using Layer/New Layer, or typing Command (Ctrl)-Shift-N.

◆ Type B for the Brush tool and D for the default colors of black foreground and white background. Click the Brush Tip icon and choose a brush of about 8 to 10 pixels with a medium-soft edge.

◆ Draw the outline of both shoes, the right leg, and the left knee.

Use Curves to Burn and Dodge

In some of the other examples in this book, you create a new, Soft Light layer where you do both the burning and dodging on an image. For this image, we wanted the flexibility of being able to adjust the highlight and shadow areas separately, so we'll use two separate Curves adjustment layers, one to burn and one to dodge.

14a After the Darken layer.   **14b** After the Lighten layer.

The Darken Curve

14a First we'll burn in (darken) areas around the legs and shoes. Subtlety is the name of the game here.

◆ Go to Layer/New Adjustment Layer/Curves, or Option (Alt)-click the Create New Fill or Adjustment Layer icon at the bottom of the Layers palette and choose Curves. Name the layer Darken. When the dialog appears, grab the center of the curve and pull down to darken the image overall. We used 134 for the input value, 109 for output. Your numbers do not need to match exactly. Click OK to close the dialog.

◆ Type Command (Ctrl)-I to invert the mask for this adjustment. The mask is now black, and none of the adjustment shows.

◆ Type B for the Brush tool and click the Tool Presets icon at the far left of the Options bar. Use the Airbrush 7% preset, then use the left bracket key to resize the brush to between 10 and 20 pixels. If you are using a mouse, this brush will probably work fine for you. If you are using a pressure-sensitive tablet, lower the opacity to about 80%. Type D for the default colors.

◆ Burn on the outside edge of the left arm and left leg. Burn up from the top edge of the band at the bottom of the knickers on the right leg and down below the bottom edge. Use your sketch to determine where to burn around the shoes and the right leg. We also modeled the right knee a bit.

◆ Turn the Drawing layer off, then turn the Darken layer on and off to judge the effect of your work.

◆ When you feel you have burned in all the areas you wanted to change, lower the opacity on this layer. We used 70%.

14b Fewer areas need to be lightened in this image, but this step cleans up the area around the hair left over from the Patch tool. It gives definition to the bottom of the piano bench as well.

◆ Create a new Curves adjustment layer and name this layer Lighten. Pull up on the center of the curve to lighten the image overall. We used 98 for the input value, 149 for the output.

◆ Type Command (Ctrl)-I to invert the mask.

◆ Use the same brush as in step 14a, and airbrush the areas you want to lighten. We drew in some areas of the left shoe, just to give the impression of the top of the shoe. We highlighted a few creases at the left elbow, and lightened the area around the hair plus a few other minor annoyances on the lighter part of the background.

◆ Using a smaller, medium-soft brush, we highlighted under the edge of the piano bench. A technique that works well here is to click one end of the area you want to paint, then Shift-click the other end to create a straight line. You may need to do this several times to create a nice, clean line. After you've lightened the line, you may want to switch to a larger, softer brush, perhaps lower the opacity a bit more, and brush down from the line to soften its effect.

◆ We used a very small brush at a higher opacity with a fairly hard edge to bring out the outline of the button and the buttonhole on the knickers.

◆ Once again, experiment with the Opacity setting for the layer. We used 80% for this layer.

Create a Curves Adjustment Layer for Contrast

15 Finally, we've come to a step that's actually akin to the first steps you normally take on an image. We'll add a contrast curve. Notice that the curve we used is not particularly dramatic. We were not trying to bump up the contrast to "brand-new photo" status. We wanted a softness that worked with the age of the photo. You may make different choices.

◆ Click the Create New Fill or Adjustment Layer icon at the bottom of the Layers palette, and choose a Curves adjustment layer. Use a slight S-curve to increase the contrast of the image.

Use Dust and Scratches on Selected Areas

As you've noticed, there's a lot of dust in certain areas of the image, notably around the right shoe and also in the top-right background area. Rather than try to get all of that with the Healing brush, we'll create a new composite layer and use the Dust and Scratches filter. Once you've run Dust and Scratches, you should be able to finish the retouching for this master file.

16 Although we could run this filter on the Retouch layer itself, creating the composite layer allows us to incorporate all the changes thus far, as well as have the possibility of adding a mask later if we want to lessen the effect of the filter selectively.

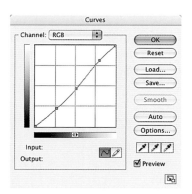

15 This is the curve we used for contrast on the image. Yours may differ slightly.

16 The Dust and Scratches filter does a good job on areas like this around the shoe that would take a long time to clean up.

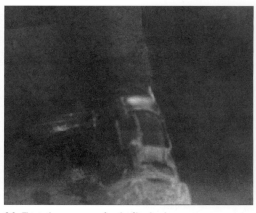

16 This is the same area after the filter has been run.

◆ Make sure the Drawing layer is not visible, then hold down the Option (Alt) key and choose Merge Visible from the Layers palette menu. You can also use Command-Option-Shift (Ctrl-Alt-Shift)-E to do this step. Double-click the name and rename this layer Dust and Scratches.

◆ Go to Filter/Noise/Dust and Scratches and experiment with settings to reduce the noise throughout the image. We used 2 for the Radius and 20 for the Threshold.

The filter softened the eyes more than we liked and also added some artifacts in the teeth that need to be removed. We'll add a layer mask to this layer and correct those areas.

◆ Use Layer/Layer Mask/Reveal All or click the Add Layer Mask icon at the bottom of the Layers palette to create a new, all-white mask.

◆ Make sure the double black border is around the thumbnail for the Dust and Scratches layer mask. If not, click the layer mask thumbnail to make it active.

◆ Type B for the Brush tool, D for the default colors, then X to paint with black and mask out the effect of the filter. Use an 8-pixel brush at 100% opacity, 100% Flow. Use a medium-hard to hard-edge brush and brush out the irises and the teeth.

Make a Duplicate to Print

17 At this point you're back in the regular workflow of the print-making process. This is now your master file. Make sure to save it and archive it. From here we use the steps you've followed in other examples.

◆ Use Image/Duplicate [F5] and be sure to check Duplicate Merged Layers Only to create a flattened version of the file.

◆ Go to Image/Image Size [F7] to resize the image if necessary for the print you want to make. We did not make any change to the print size for this image.

◆ Run Unsharp Mask. We used Barry's SharpenOnlyEdgesBH action from the Actions palette. We used 145, .8, and 5 for our settings. You may find that different settings work for you depending on how you have resized the image.

◆ Print the file.

In reality, it usually doesn't stop there, and this image was no different. We printed a version on a glossy paper and it looked good, but we wanted to use a matte paper. We changed the mode of the image to Grayscale and then Duotone (see Chapter 25, "Black and White, and Duotones," for how to do this). We used one of Adobe's canned duotone curves. We liked most of the print, but the burned-in areas that looked fine on glossy paper plugged up on the matte paper. So we went back to the Darken layer in the master file, and softened what we had done there. We had to re-create the Dust and Scratches composite layer and mask, then duplicate the image and the adjustments that we had done. The second print was better. Finally, we went back to the duotone curve and adjusted the curve for the second color ink (in this case, a PANTONE Orange) and made a third print. That's the version you see here.

27 ◆ Compositing Bracketed Photos

Barry's Ship Rock Fire Sunset image, which was on the cover of *Photoshop CS Artistry* and has also been on the cover of the Santa Fe Photographic Workshops catalog, is a composite of two bracketed photos created from one original 16-bit film scan. We'll show you how the Ship Rock image was created later in this chapter.

Bracketing Your Exposures

When you are shooting a high-contrast scene where either your film or digital camera can't capture the full brightness range of the scene, you can put the camera on a tripod and shoot two or three exposures of the image. One exposure gets highlight detail and the second gets the rest of the midtone and shadow detail. You could also shoot three exposures, one for highlights, one for midtones, and one for shadows. This is called *bracketing* your exposures. When you do this, you want the camera on a tripod so that all the exposures you shoot line up once you get them onto the computer.

Sometimes you may have one exposure that is highly contrasty on film or in a digital Raw file, and you might decide to open that one exposure two different ways from the Raw filter, scan it two different ways with a scanner, or even process different parts of that same file in different ways within Photoshop. The procedure for doing this, and for working with the resulting layers, is very similar to the procedure for bracketing the original exposures and then working with them to get exactly what you want from each part of the image.

A third option, now available with Photoshop CS2 and later, is to take many exposures over the full dynamic range of a very high-contrast scene, then combine those photos into one High Dynamic Range (HDR) image. This new format allows you to produce one image that can capture the full dynamic range in some of the most contrasty scenes that occur in nature. Before HDR this could not be done with film or digital cameras. The tricky part now, though, is seeing that image on your monitor and also making a great print from it on your printer.

Out in the field, when you're shooting a scene, you need to have all these techniques available in your bag of tricks, and then know which one to use in which situation.

Digital Capture

With digital cameras, you can use the histogram display in the camera to see if you lost highlight or shadow detail when you made the initial shot. If you see a vertical bar on the right side of the histogram and/or flashing bright areas in your picture preview area, then you lost highlight detail—the more common situation. In this case, shoot another exposure with your camera set to underexpose by one f-stop. If the vertical bar is still there after that, underexpose by two stops, etc. If you have a vertical bar on the left side of your histogram display, this means you lost shadow detail and you need to overexpose by a stop or two until the shadow detail returns. Losing shadow detail happens less often than losing highlight detail.

A digital camera histogram display that looks like this shows that the camera did not capture all the shadow details. There also may be dark flashing areas in the camera's picture display that show you which shadow details were lost.

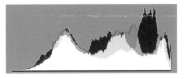

Here we have the opposite situation, where some highlight details are lost. Many camera image displays will show the lost areas with bright blinking or flashing areas. In this case, take another exposure that is underexposed a stop or so until you don't have the vertical line on the right of the histogram.

Film Capture

With film cameras, you need to know the dynamic range of your film, then set the middle exposure range—the Zone V exposure—so that your highlight details are not so much brighter than this setting that they aren't captured by the film. Having a spot meter and knowing how to use it helps in these high-contrast situations. You can then read the darkest spot and the brightest spot where you want details, then set your exposure(s) so you get it all. If the range is too great for your film, you may need a second exposure to capture highlight or shadow details. See Chapter 14, "Digital Imaging and the Zone System," for more info on how exposure calculations work and how they relate to both film and digital capture.

Other Issues When Capturing the Images

Using a tripod usually allows you to get sharper images, and if you're making multiple exposures that you want to combine later, it makes combining much easier and more accurate.

One thing we like about digital cameras is that the histogram display shows you right away if you captured all the information or if you need a second shot. The most difficult type of situation I've encountered in the last few years was shooting in a riverbed canyon. The canyon was partly in the shadows, and there were a variety of dark areas under bushes and other greenery. The water had dark areas between rocks, but also bright highlights where sunlit water was running over rocks. The bright blue sky above this shadowy canyon contained bright white clouds lit by the sun high above the canyon. Even underexposing by two stops—my camera's autobracket limit—did not capture the brightest highlights. Time for the camera's manual exposure controls! I, Barry, usually don't use the autobracket feature on the camera, because I seldom need the overexposed shot to get shadow detail. With the camera on a tripod, you can set aperture priority, then change the shutter speed to adjust your exposure. When you change the aperture setting, this changes the focus and depth of field of the scene. That's why it's better to leave the aperture the same and to vary the shutter speed between each shot. Having a tripod is a big help here and also makes combining the images later in Photoshop much easier—or, in some cases, even simply possible. Sometimes, if you can't get the range of focus you need in a scene to make everything sharp, you can purposely bracket the focus as well, then combine several images where one has the front objects in focus and the other has the distant objects in focus. Depending on the subject matter in your scene, this could get tricky in the places where you blend these images together.

Shooting for HDR (High Dynamic Range) Images

Another instance where exposure bracketing can now be used is when you're creating an image in the new HDR 32-bit file format. In the sidebar below, we captured the Photoshop Help screen, which describes the steps for shooting in HDR. Capturing for HDR is different than regular bracketing, but you can get very interesting results with an extended dynamic range. I, Barry, did some experiments

---

Keep the following tips in mind when creating photos to combine using the Merge To HDR command:

- Secure the camera to a tripod.
- Take enough photos to cover the full dynamic range of the scene. It's recommended that you take at least five to seven photos, although you can take more exposures depending on the dynamic range of the scene. The minimum number of photos should be three.
- Vary the shutter speed to create different exposures. Changing the ISO or aperture may cause noise or vignetting in the image.
- In general, don't use your camera's auto-bracket feature because the exposure changes is usually too small.
- The exposure differences between the photos should be one or two EV (Exposure Value) steps apart (equivalent to about one or two f-stops apart).
- Don't vary the lighting, such as using a flash in one exposure but not the next.
- Make sure nothing is moving in the scene. Exposure Merge only works with differently-exposed images of the identical scene.
- When converting camera raw images for use in Exposure Merge, make sure the Adobe Camera Raw Exposure, Shadow, Brightness, and Contrast settings are at "zero." Making camera raw exposure adjustments throws off the computations for creating the 32-bits-per-channel file. You can make color adjustments if they are consistent throughout all the camera raw images.

Exposing for HDR

Important Issues: You need to take at least 3 but preferably 5 to 7 shots, with each shot being one or two exposure values apart. Do not vary the f-stop, but vary the shutter speed! Also note that when you bring these through Camera Raw, the Exposure, Shadow, Brightness, and Contrast settings need to all be set to 0.

---

bracketing as I normally would with two exposures versus shooting up to ten exposures and combining them via HDR.

I usually shoot in shutter-speed priority (TV mode on a Canon), because many of my images are wide-angle shots with everything in focus anyway. Deciding on the shutter speed is quick and allows me to pan for motion if I want, to use high speed to stop the motion of either the subject or my hand-held camera shots, or to know when I need to attach a tripod because I'm shooting at less than a 60th or 30th of a second. When you are shooting for HDR images, though, it is recommended that you leave the f-stop the same and vary the shutter speed. If you use the camera's autobracketing features and you also have the camera set to shutter priority, as I usually do, the aperture will change when you autobracket exposures. For HDR you need to change the camera to aperture priority—AV on a Canon—so that the autobracket will change the shutter speed and not the aperture. The autobracket on my camera only does a maximum of plus or minus two exposure values. I've found that HDR works better with even more exposures. For the image we'll be using here to try out HDR, I shot +3.5 to –3.5 exposure values, which is probably more than you need. I set the camera to Manual at f11 and put it on a tripod. I then varied the shutter speed from 1/25 to 1/3200 as I made multiple exposures of the scene. If anything is moving, this can cause a problem. The three-exposure autobracket on the camera is better at making the exposures quickly, so slow movements are not a problem. I shot lots of images of boats in the Gibsons harbor, like those in the illustration below, but the slow movement of the boats in the water caused some blurring when the images were combined using HDR. In the image we're going to use here, an extremely contrasty picture shot from my balcony, the clouds were moving; you'll notice that they are stretched more in the ten-exposure HDR

With everything in the Adjust section of Raw set to 0, the image can look pretty flat. Sometimes it looks blown out or very dark, too. You are not adjusting each of these images in the Raw plug-in; you are leaving them alone so that the Merge To HDR filter can combine them and get the best parts of each image. I did go into the Lens section and adjust the Chromatic Aberration for the image in the middle of my exposure range, then used these same settings for all the images in my dynamic range.

image. You might get away with stretched clouds, but another HDR image I took had a truck going by in the far background. My final HDR version of that image had three blurry trucks blending together. Movement during the many exposures is a serious problem when you're shooting more than the three exposures most cameras can automatically fire off.

Once you've moved the images to your computer, you can select them all in Bridge, then open them into Camera Raw. There, all the images should have the same settings of 0 in the Adjust section. If you want to set the Chromatic Aberration, adjust this on your middle-exposure image, then do Select All and Synchronize to set all the images to these same settings.

When to Use HDR and When to Shoot Just One or Two Exposures

You might think you'd benefit by shooting for HDR with every exposure. This is not the case! If your digital or film camera can capture the entire dynamic range of the scene without losing info from either end of the histogram, you will probably get the sharpest results by making just one exposure. This is especially true when the entire scene is one type of lighting. The boats in the harbor at the bottom of the previous page didn't really benefit from my shooting for HDR. I compared an eight-exposure HDR version of that image to one where I captured the entire image in one shot. Since everything in that image was brightly lit, I didn't need the extra shadow detail or have the blown-out highlights that HDR could improve on. Also, things like the moving truck in the background cause problems in the HDR version that were not there in the single shot. If I really wanted to make sure I got all the highlight details in this scene, I could shoot a second exposure that was underexposed by a stop or two. The camera histogram would tell me how much to underexpose. If you have important shadow and highlight details— even if the histogram seems to span the entire range—it doesn't hurt to shoot a second exposure for highlights and a third for shadows. You might not need them, but it's better than having to reshoot.

HDR really pays off when you have an extremely contrasty scene like the one shot into the sun from my deck, which we use in the last eight pages of this chapter. In that scene the sky and clouds above the horizon were extremely bright, and the items below the horizon, including the distant harbor and my neighbors' homes and yards, were quite dark compared to that bright sky. Even when I shot two images, one underexposed to get the sky and the other a normal exposure letting the sky blow out a bit, the information in

the areas below the horizon was grainy and had poor shadow details and color. The HDR image did much better in this case.

Combining Two Versions of the Same Image

The following steps are common to many bracketing processes. You get two versions of the same image by doing two different scans of it, two different Raw interpretations of it, or several initial adjustments to it to get different main sections of the image ready for final compositing and adjustment.

Opening the Ship Rock Image

1 Let's take a look at the Ship Rock image that you see on the first page of this chapter. We'll open a small version of my final layered file for this image.

◆ Copy the Ch27.Compositing Bracketed Photos folder from the *Photoshop Artistry* DVD onto your hard disk. Open files from the copy as you work through this chapter. That way, Bridge and Camera Raw can update their files on the copy, which they can't do on the DVD.

◆ From that copy in the ShipRockFiles folder, open the files ShipRockLayers.psd, ShipRockForeGround, and ShipRockSky. Use the Window menu to bring ShipRockLayers to the front, then type an F to put this in Full Screen mode. Close all your palettes except for the Options bar at the top of the screen. Choose Window/Layers [F10] to bring up the Layers palette, and move

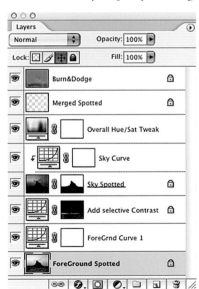

1 Here is the Layers palette for the Ship Rock image. The bottom Foreground layer gives detail to all but the sky, which comes from the Sky layer. Both layers are named Spotted, which indicates that we've spotted each layer. The ForeGrnd Curve and the Add Selective Contrast curve only affect the Foreground layer because they are below the Sky layer. The layer mask on the Sky layer only shows that layer in the sky area where this mask is white. Since the Sky Curve is indented, it also uses the Sky layer mask so it only affects the Sky area. The three layers above the Sky Curve layer affect the entire composite image under them.

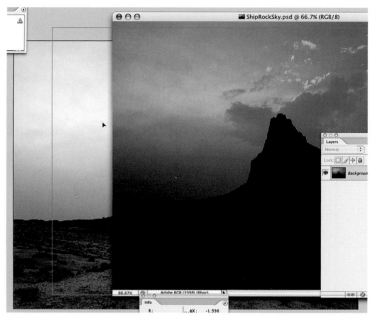

2 Use the Move tool (V) while pressing the Shift key to click the topmost ShipRockSky image. Hold down the mouse button and drag the image to the ShipRockForeGround image. When you see the outline of the ShipRockSky image on top of the ShipRockForeGround image, release the mouse button (before you release the Shift key) to create the new Sky layer centered on top of the *Background* layer of the Foreground image.

it to the right side of your screen. Open up the Layers palette so that you can see all the layers in this document.

The layers named Foreground Spotted and Sky Spotted originally came from the same 16-bit scan from Fuji Velvia film and a 6x4.5 Mamiya 120 camera. This image was originally created using Photoshop 7, which supported 16-bit files but not 16-bit layers. What I had to do in Photoshop 7 to create Foreground Spotted and Sky Spotted (let's just call them Foreground and Sky) was to open two copies of the original scan, then process each of those copies using a Levels adjustment followed by a Curves adjustment. The adjustments to the Foreground image were done to open up the details in front of the rock and on the rock itself. The adjustments to the Sky image focused on getting the optimal sky values from that original scan and didn't worry about what those adjustments would do to the details in the foreground. Those foreground details were going to come from the foreground image. After making the adjustments, I then converted each of those images to 8 bits per channel using Image/Mode/8 Bits/ Channel. I then combined them into one Photoshop layered file, and added the adjustment layers you see in the ShipRockLayers file. If I were to create this image using Photoshop CS, CS2, or beyond, the Levels and Curves adjustments I made to the original 16-bit image

would be done as 16-bit adjustment layers, and the ShipRockLayers file would still be in 16-bit mode, preserving all the information. In any case, right now we'll show you the process for moving several versions of an image into one file as different layers. You'll be using a similar process regardless of whether you're combining several bracketed scanned images, several bracketed digital Raw images, or even several versions of the same image, as we are doing here.

Combining the Two Files

2 We need to move both the Foreground and Sky images into one file, with one on top of the other. Either one could actually be on top, so in this case we'll put the Sky image on top.

◆ Use the Window menu to select the ShipRockForeGround image. Type an F to put this in Full Screen mode. Now use the Window menu to select the ShipRockSky image. It should not be in Full Screen mode. Make its window small enough so you can see the ShipRockForeGround image behind it.

◆ Type a V to switch to the Move tool. Hold down the Shift key while you click in the Sky image area; then drag the cursor, with the mouse button still down, so it's on top of some part of the Foreground image area. Now release the mouse button first and leave the Shift key down for a moment.

The Sky image should now be copied on top of the Foreground image as a new layer in that Foreground image. Holding the Shift key down as you drag and drop this layer forces the layer to be centered in the new document. Since both these documents are exactly the same size in pixels, the two layers are lined up exactly. Doing this without holding the Shift key down or letting up on the Shift key before the mouse button could cause the Sky layer not to be centered over the Background layer.

◆ Double-click the word *Layer 1* on that new layer, and type the word *Sky* to rename that layer. Now click the Layer Lock Position icon to make sure that this layer is not accidentally moved.

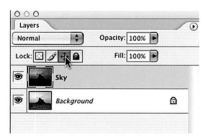

2 Naming and locking the Sky layer.

3 The Layers and Channels palettes set up to see the Blue channel of the Sky layer. This is the one we chose to copy for creating the mask.

3 The Layers and Channels palettes set up to see the Red channel of the Background layer.

◆ Use the Window menu to switch back to the ShipRockSky image, then close it. You should now be back in the ShipRock-ForeGround image.

Creating the Mask Separating Sky from Foreground

3 When you composite bracketed photos, a mask usually determines which portion of each photo is visible in the composited image. When there are only two images, you want only one mask because that simplifies the editing needed to get the two images to fit together seamlessly. This type of mask is difficult to do seamlessly because the sky has a considerably different adjustment than the rest of the image, and the edge between the two is very contrasty. We are going to make a copy of one of the channels and use it to make this mask. We want to find the channel that has the most contrast between the sky and the rest of the image. In this case we have six channels to choose from—three from the Sky and three from the Background layer.

◆ Use Window/Channels [Shift-F10] to bring up the Channels palette. The Sky layer should still be active so click right on top of the word *Red* in the Channels palette. Turn off the Eye icons for the Green and Blue palettes if necessary. See how much contrast this channel has between the sky and everything else. Now look at the Green channel by clicking the word *Green,* and look finally at the Blue channel by clicking the word *Blue.* The Blue channel is the best candidate in this layer.

◆ Now click back on the letters *RGB* in the Channels palette, then click the word *Background* in the Layers palette and turn off the Eye icon for the Sky layer. You are now just looking at the Background layer. Click the word *Red* in the Channels palette, then *Green,* then *Blue,* and you'll see that the Red channel is the best candidate in this layer, because it has the most distinct contrast between sky and foreground along the horizon. You could probably use this channel, but let's go back to the Blue channel in the Sky layer.

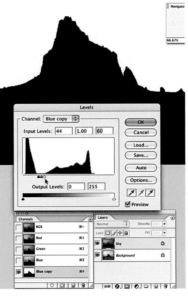

4 Here we are making the adjustments to the top three sliders in Levels to create the mask. Notice how the Channels and Layers palettes are set up and how the mask looks at this point. Scrolling around to look at different parts of the mask as you turn the Preview button off and then on again will help you make a mask that matches the horizon as closely as possible.

◆ Click the word *Sky* in the Layers palette, then turn the Eye icon back on for the Sky layer and click the word *Blue* in the Channels palette. Now click-and-drag the word *Blue* down to the Copy icon, just to the left of the Trash icon, at the bottom of the Channels palette. This will make a copy of the Blue channel, called Blue copy, which we'll turn into a mask.

◆ Choose Image/Adjustments/Levels (Command-L) to run Levels on this Blue copy channel.

Using Levels Adjustments to Make the Mask

4 I chose this particular channel, over the Red one from the Background layer, because there's a gap between the darker and lighter areas of the histogram. This is usually a sign that the mask will be easier to create.

◆ Within Levels, using the top set of sliders, move the rightmost Highlight slider to the left and the leftmost Shadow slider to the right until you get a mask that has a clean separation between the sky and the rest of the image. When you get the basic mask, notice how subtle adjustments in each of the three sliders affect the edge of the mask. Getting this edge just right is the key to saving yourself hours of work later tweaking the mask by hand. One helpful technique is to turn the Preview check box off and then on again to compare the mask to the original channel to make sure you have the best match. You'll often have to adjust a few areas with a brush after you leave Levels.

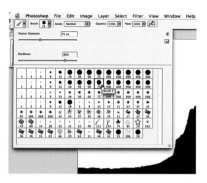

4 Here you see the Brushes palette accessed from the Options bar as I choose a middle-row brush. Photoshop has a bug, which it's had for a long time, that causes this pop-up Brushes palette to intermittently return to Stroke Thumbnail view and also to change the size of this box. When this bug happens to you, use the pop-up at the top right of this Brush dialog to return the dialog to Small Thumbnail view. Then use the grow box at the bottom right of the dialog so that the 500-pixel brush is the rightmost brush in each of the top three rows of brushes. Then call Adobe, report the bug, and mention that the Brushes bug Barry Haynes has been reporting over the years really does exist.

◆ Choose OK from Levels, then type B for the Paintbrush and choose "Paintbrush Op100% Flow100%" from the Tool presets drop-down menu to the left of the Options bar. Choose about a 75-pixel brush from the middle row of round brushes in the BarrysPhotoBrushes palette that you loaded in Preferences. Now type a D, followed by an X, to set your color to Black. Press Tab to get rid of your palettes. Paint in any white holes in the black part of the mask. Type X to switch back to White, and fix any areas on either end of the horizon where some nonwhite pixels extend into the sky area. To be more exact here, use Command (Ctrl)-Spacebar-click to zoom into those areas on either side of the horizon, then use the left or right bracket keys to change the size of your brush. Don't worry about doing a perfect job now, as you'll have to do final horizon cleanup once you put the two images together.

◆ Press the Tab key to bring your palettes back, then Command (Ctrl)-click the words *Blue copy* in the Channels palette to load this mask as a selection. Now click the letters *RGB* at the top of

the Channels palette, and you're ready to add this mask to the Sky layer.

◆ Choose Layer/Layer Mask/Reveal Selection to add to the Sky layer a layer mask that shows only the sky parts of this layer. The rest of this now-composite image is coming from the Background layer.

Fine-Tuning the Two Parts of the Image

5 Now that the initial mask is made, it's better to fine-tune the color and contrast of the rest of the image before trying to make this mask perfect. I've found that it's usually best to first make a rough mask, then go back and perfect it after correcting the parts. When you add contrast, saturation, burn and dodge, etc., this may change how well the mask blends the parts. You don't want to have to do difficult edits to the mask more than once.

◆ Use [Shift-F10] to close the Channels palette. Double-click the *Background* layer and rename it Foreground, since this layer does represent the foreground of the Ship Rock image. Click the Lock Position icon to stop this layer from accidentally being moved.

◆ If you choose Layer/New Adjustment Layer, you are now in the correct position to start adding adjustment layers that will just modify the way the Foreground of this image looks.

Instead of actually doing the changes to this image, we're going to study the changes I did to the original image. That way we can cover several different types of images and masking situations while we go through this chapter.

◆ Go to the Window menu to get, or the File menu to reopen, the original ShipRockLayers image from the *Photoshop Artistry* DVD. If you are not already there, use Command-Option (Ctrl-Alt)-0 to zoom into 100%, and press F for Full Screen mode. Turn off the Eye icons for the ForeGrnd Curve 1, and Add Selective

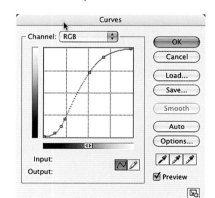

5 The Add Selective Contrast curve is radical because it dramatically increases the brightness and contrast of everything except the darker values at the bottom left of the curve. This is why it needs to be applied sparingly using an adjustment layer mask.

4 How your workspace should look with your selection and the Layers and Channels palettes when you choose Layer/Layer Mask/Reveal Selection.

Contrast layers in that image, and you'll see what they did to the original Foreground layer. One at a time, starting with ForeGrnd Curve 1, turn on its Eye icon, then double-click its leftmost layer thumbnail and bring up the curve I created.

This will help you understand how that curve is influencing this image. The first ForeGrnd Curve 1 just makes all the foreground values brighter and more contrasty.

◆ Close the ForeGrnd Curve 1 curve dialog using the Cancel button, then double-click the Add Selective Contrast layer thumbnail so you can look at that curve. Add Selective Contrast does more of the same, but notice how the bottom left of that curve is pulled down sharply. This makes the dark areas even darker, which adds dramatically to the contrast. Shift-click the rightmost layer mask thumbnail for this layer, and you'll see what it would have done to the image if the mask had been all white. It's a pretty radical curve! Option (Alt)-click the layer mask thumbnail to look at the mask, and notice how subtly I applied it using faint white brush strokes with the Airbrush 7% Paintbrush Tool preset. Option (Alt)-click again to see the image.

This is why after I created this mask I used Command (Ctr))-I to invert it, then just airbrushed a little white in the areas where I wanted to apply it.

◆ Click the Sky Spotted layer, then choose Layer/New Adjustment Layer/Curves but stay in the New Layer dialog. Notice that Use New Layer to Create Clipping Mask is checked. This is what I chose in the above Sky Curve layer to make it indented in the Layers palette. This indention means that this curve will use the mask in the Sky Spotted layer as its mask too. Whatever I do with this curve will not affect the foreground area, since that area is black in the Sky mask. Click Cancel in the New Layer dialog, then turn the Sky Curve layer's Eye icon off and then on again so you can see what it does. Double-click the Sky Curve's leftmost layer thumbnail to open the Curve dialog and study this curve. It's just a subtle S-curve to add more drama to the sky.

◆ The next Overall Hue/Sat Tweak layer is just a 12% Master Saturation boost, so turn its Eye icon off and then on again to see what it does. Notice that since this layer is not indented and its mask is white, it affects both parts of the image below it.

Tweaking the Mask

6 Now comes the trickiest part of this image, where we have to tweak this hard-edge mask between a contrasty foreground and sky.

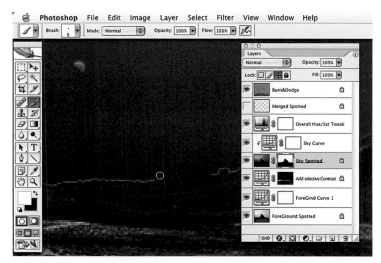

6 Here we see the setup for editing the edge of the mask. Notice that the rightmost layer mask thumbnail is activated, showing up as a highlight around that rightmost thumbnail. We are painting with white using a 5-pixel 80% brush, but we are actually using the edge of the brush. You'll notice that if you paint too far toward the bottom, you get a black line on the edge and then the foreground area turns black. That is because you are actually painting white in the mask at that area, which reveals that area from the sky image.

◆ Turn the Eye icon for the Merged Spotted layer off, then turn it back on again until you notice the white line appearing along some parts of the horizon between the Sky layer and the Foreground layer. This white line is showing you defects in the Sky mask. Leave the Eye icon for the Merged Spotted layer off, then click on the Sky Spotted layer to activate it. Now click the rightmost Layer Mask thumbnail of that layer so that when you paint you'll be painting on the mask, not the layer itself.

◆ Use Command (Ctrl)-Spacebar-click to zoom into exactly 300% at the horizon area below the sun. If the Navigator palette is up, you can tell that your zoom factor is 300%. You want to be at exactly 300%, because, as I've explained before, the image is sharper at even multiples of 100%.

◆ Type B for the Brush, choose Paintbrush Op100% Flow100% from the leftmost Tool presets area of the Options bar, then choose a 5-pixel brush from the middle row of brushes in the Brush area of the Options bar. These have their hardness set to 80%, so when you paint with them the edge is a little softer than with a 100% hard-edge brush. Type D for Default Colors, which will set your foreground color to white.

◆ Start painting using the edge of the brush just above and touching the white line you see. That white line is actually coming from the mask, revealing the brighter sky from the fore-ground image

7 The Ship Rock image after the border selection has been pruned by the Lasso tool.

below. If you paint too far to the bottom, the foreground area of the image will become too dark because it will now be coming from the Sky layer. To see the current mask, Option (Alt)-click the mask thumbnail in the Sky layer. It would take hours and could well be impossible to make the horizon look perfect by just editing the mask. Even if the mask were perfect, differences in how the Foreground layer color adjustments and the Sky layer color adjustments affected pixels along that horizon could leave you with a dark or bright line in some places along the edge.

Creating a Merged Edge

7 Instead of editing this mask forever, we can create a new layer, just along this edge, where we can set all the pixels just the way we want. That is what the Merged Spotted layer is. This type of solution is only required when you have a really sharp and contrasty edge where either side of that edge has been adjusted quite differently.

◆ Command-click the Sky mask thumbnail to load its mask as a selection. Now choose Select/Modify/Border and use a value of 10. When you click OK, you'll see a selection that spans both sides of the horizon.

◆ Choose View/Fit on Screen, or Command (Ctrl)-0, so you can see your entire image, and you'll notice that this border extends around the top of the sky. Type L for the Lasso tool, then hold the Option key down because you're going to delete from this selection. You want only the part of the selection that spans the horizon. Click down in the middle of the sky, then hold the

mouse button down while you move the mouse to one end of the horizon, all the way around the top edges of the image, back to the other side of the horizon, then back to where you started. Finally, release the mouse button followed by the Option (Alt) key.

See the illustration here of what this finished selection should look like.

◆ Use [Shift-F10] to bring up the Channels palette, then click the Save Selection icon—the second icon from the left, at the bottom of this palette—to save this selection in a new channel named Alpha 1. Click the Alpha 1 channel, and you'll see that the selected area there is now white. Choose Select/Deselect, or Command (Ctrl)-D, to get rid of the selection, then choose Image/Adjustments/Invert, Command (Ctrl)-I, to invert the mask. The edges of it are not smooth, so choose Filter/Blur/Gaussian Blur [Shift-F4] and do a 2-pixel Gaussian blur on this.

◆ Now click back on the letters *RGB* at the top of the Channels palette, then turn off the Eye icon for the Burn&Dodge layer. Click the Overall Hue/Sat Tweak layer to activate it. While holding down the Option (Alt) key, choose Merge Visible from the Layers palette pop-up menu. Leave the Option (Alt) key down until Photoshop has finished creating the new layer. This will create a new layer named Layer 1; you want to double-click that name and change it to Merged.

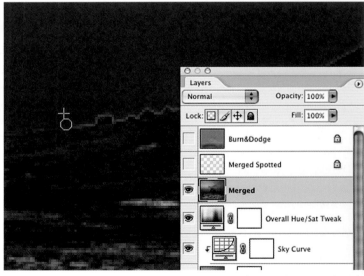

7 Cloning out the edge with the Clone Stamp tool. We are copying from the + location just above the circle, which is where the brush is painting.

We have now merged everything from the layers below up into this new layer. CS2 automatically creates a new layer when you do Option (Alt)-Merge Visible. If you were doing this in CS or another Photoshop version, you'd have to first use Layer/New Layer to create the new layer above the Overall Hue/Sat Tweak layer, and then, while that new layer was active, choose Option (Alt)-Merge Visible. We are now going to use the Clone Stamp tool to clean up the edge on that new layer, but we are only going to keep that thin part of it along the horizon as defined by the Alpha 1 channel selection we just saved.

◆ Type S to get the Clone Stamp tool, set the Opacity and Flow to 100%, and pick that same 5-pixel middle-row brush you were using before with the Brush tool. This time we're using the Clone Stamp tool, though. To remove the white line along the horizon, Option (Alt)-click in the sky directly above where you want to remove the white, then just click (without the Option (Alt) key) over the white area you want to remove. Again, you are just using the edge of the brush. When you get a feel for this, move along the line until all of the white edge is removed. If you go too far or mess up, that is what the History palette is for, so use it to go back a few steps. If you have areas where there is a black line toward the bottom, Option (Alt)-click in the Foreground area just below that, and copy from there over the black line. This will take a while but it will work!

◆ You can actually speed up this process by clicking in one spot with Clone Stamp and then Shift-clicking a little further along the Horizon line. This will do the same thing as if you had held the mouse button down and dragged it along a line between those two spots. Only do this in small segments so it's not obvious that you've done a straight-line segment.

◆ When the Horizon is finished, use File/Save As and save this as ShipRockLayersTemp. Now bring up your Channels palette, and Command (Ctrl)-click the Alpha 1 channel you made earlier. Since you inverted this, the selection you see will be a selection of everything except the area along the horizon. Now press the Delete key (Backspace on the PC), or choose Edit/Clear, and the majority of this Merged layer will now be gone. The part that remains is the part that fixes the horizon. Type Command (Ctrl)-D to delete the selection.

This solution allows you to later make small tweaks in the layers below this horizon-fixing Merged layer; you probably won't have to redo this tedious layer.

◆ Click the Burn&Dodge layer to activate it, then turn its Eye icon off and then on again so you can see what it does for this image. We explain how to make and use these layers in Chapter 22, "Correcting Problem Images."

8 This is how the two images would look when lined up. This is a perfect case, since these two images actually came from the same piece of film. With a real two-scan situation, there will still usually be a small amount of embossing because the two images may not be exactly rotated the same in the scanner. If your scanner has a ridge that you can line an edge of the film up on, this helps avoid a situation where the two pieces of film are rotated slightly differently. That is the hardest situation to fix. To try to fix it, you have to use Edit/Transform/Rotate or sometimes even Free Transform on the top layer while viewing the two layers together as shown here, and try to minimize the embossed effect with the Rotate or Free Transform.

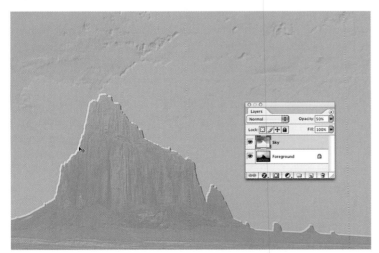

8 Here we see the two images when they are not lined up. Note that we have inverted the Sky layer and set its Opacity to 50%. Also note that the Sky layer is no longer set for Locked Position.

Combining Two or Three Shots

If the two parts of the Ship Rock image were actually made from two separate exposures, then we'd have to line them up in Photoshop. Two separate digital camera exposures automatically line up if they were shot using a steady tripod. If you hand-held them, then they'd also have to be lined up. Two film exposures always need to be lined up, even when shot from a tripod, unless there is a way to line up the two pieces of film in the scanner the exact way they were lined up in the camera. Most scanners can't do this.

Lining Up Two Shots

8 In this step/section, we'll describe a generic technique for lining up two shots. We are not actually going to do it with the next two images we'll be using, since they were shot with a digital camera on a tripod.

◆ Move both shots into the same Photoshop layers file similar to the way we moved the two Ship Rock images into the same file in step 2 earlier in this chapter.

◆ With the Shift key down, move the second image on top of the first. This will probably get you 95% to 99% of the way there, as your intention when you shot these was for them to be lined up. To help line up the two images, choose Image/Adjustments/Invert (Command-I) to invert the top of the two images each of which are now layers. Now type a 5 to set the Opacity of this top layer to 50%.

◆ Type a V to switch to the Move tool. Do not lock the position of the top layer until we line up the two images. If the two images were exactly the same and they were lined up exactly, at 50% inverted, all you'd see now would be solid gray. If the images were not lined up quite right, you'd see an embossed pattern formed by the pixels that were off. You could then use the arrow keys to move that top image 1 pixel at a time until this embossed pattern disappeared and the images lined up.

◆ We took the two images from Ship Rock and purposely set them up here in step 8 as described above; then we put them out of alignment. Since these two images are not exactly the same, you see the embossed pattern and you also see a strange ghost of these two images. Using the arrow keys to nudge the top image, it will be most closely lined up when this embossed pattern is gone or as small as possible.

◆ Once the embossed pattern is removed, use Command (Ctrl)-I to reinvert the top layer, and type a 0 (zero) to return its Opacity

to 100%. Now click the Lock Position icon in the Lock area of the Layers palette to lock this newly aligned layer.

Combining Three Lined-Up Digital Camera Shots

9 I've been out shooting scenes to get some images that will illustrate the trade-offs between just bracketing exposures versus using the new HDR feature. Many of the scenes I shot had a low enough brightness range to capture everything in one Raw image. Other ones I shot in the field had everything in one Raw file with the exception of just a few highlight details that I had to get from a second exposure. For something to really require HDR, it needs to have a very large dynamic range. Even then, shooting two or three exposures is often a viable alternative, too. The image I've decided to use for this example is certainly not what I'd call one of my best photographs, but it does have the necessary elements available in it so you can learn the issues and trade-offs between bracketing and shooting HDR.

The first exposures I made of this image were one exposure to capture everything, then a second exposure to capture the highlights. Looking at the in-camera histograms when I took these exposures, it appeared that I had captured all the details. Later in Photoshop, you'll see that the shadow details in this two-exposure sequence left much to be desired. See the comparison on the next page. With the camera still on the tripod, I set it to manual operation with aperture priority, then I set the Aperture to f11. I made 11 exposures ranging from 1/25 at f11 up to 1/3200 at f11. I used all of these to create the HDR image, then I used three of them to create the composite we'll make next.

◆ Go into Bridge and choose Command (Ctrl)-F9 to go into your FoldersBig workspace. Click the Chapter 27 folder on your *Photoshop Artistry* DVD, then click the DeckShotFiles folder within that. Choose Show 5 Stars from the Filtered pop-up at the top right of your screen. The files CRW_0780, 0782, and 0785 all have 5 stars, so you now see them.

◆ Click CRW_0780, and Shift-click CRW_0785 to select the three images. Then choose Open With/Adobe Photoshop CS2. This will bring you into Camera Raw from Photoshop. Click the icon for each image within Camera Raw, and you'll notice that the adjustments are already set. This is because I included the XMP files for these images within the DeckShotFiles folder.

Looking at the Exposure settings that I adjusted, the adjustments for file 780 would give us shadow details, 782 would be the main foreground image, and 785 would be used for sky detail. To do this in Camera Raw, I first clicked on image 782 and did all the adjustments

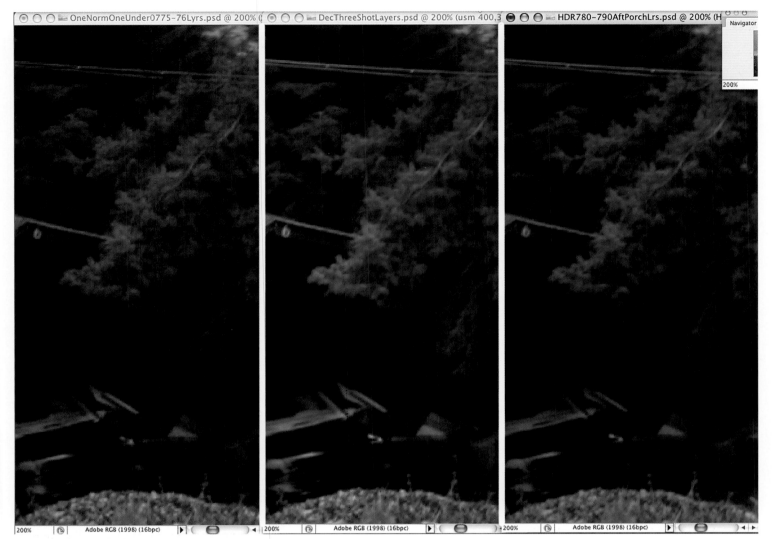

9 LEFT: The left image shows shadow details from a composite made of two exposures. The first one was an overall exposure that captured the foreground information but the sky was blown out. Even though the sky was blown out, the scene was so bright that the overall exposure had most of the shadow details crunched into a small area of the histogram on the left side. The second exposure captured the sky, and I put these together to create a complete image. Looking at the deep shadow details on this left image, though, you'll see that the car's taillights have no color in them and the dark shadows in the carport are grainy and lack much color. The tree details are also not as nice as those in the two images to the right. **MIDDLE:** The middle image is a composite of three exposures, two used for the foreground and shadow info and the third used for the sky. The three exposures used were: 1/25 at f11 for deep shadows, 1/60 at f11 for overall foreground, and 1/250 at f11 for the sky. They were then composited together, as shown in steps 9 through 12, to form the final image. **RIGHT:** The right image was created from 11 exposures, then combined with Merge to HDR, then color corrected after that. It generally has the most color depth and has nice colors in the shadows. The details in the middle image may be slightly sharper, since most of them are created from one or two exposures. The HDR image didn't require the creation of the difficult sky mask that the middle image required. Read the example starting with step 9 for all the details.

for that image, including the Lens adjustments to fix any Chromatic Aberration. I then clicked Select All, in the upper-left corner, and then I clicked Synchronize so that all three images were set the same way. After doing this, I went back to the Adjust settings and changed the Shadows for image 780 and the Exposure and Brightness for 785. These adjustments have already been made for you here. See Chapter

11, "Image Processing with Bridge," for more detailed info on using Bridge and Camera Raw to speed up your processing of multiple images. After these steps I was finished with Camera Raw, now you can follow along with the next few steps.

◆ Click Select All in the top-left corner. Now click on Open Three Images to the bottom right and all three of these files will open

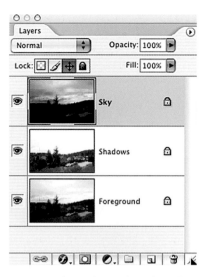

9 The basic layer setup for this composite of three digital files. The 785 Sky image is on top, then there's the 780 Shadows image, and finally the 782 Foreground image is on the bottom. For each layer, we have clicked the Lock Position icon so this layer can't be accidentally moved in relationship to the other layers.

into Photoshop after the adjustments we made are applied to them.

◆ Use the Window menu to bring image 782 to the top, then type F to put this image into Full Screen mode. I usually put the main image of a composite at the bottom, then add the more peripheral images on top of that one. Now switch to image 780, type V for the Move tool, and use the techniques we learned in step 2 to drag and drop, with the Shift key down, this image on top of image 782. Now switch to image 785 and drag and drop that one on top of the other two.

◆ Double-click 785, Layer 2, and rename it to Sky, then click the Lock Position icon for this layer. Double-click 780, Layer 1, and rename it to Deep Shadows, then set Lock Position for this layer. Finally double-click the Background layer and name it Foreground, then click the Lock Position icon for this layer. Now you have your basic layer setup for this composite. Choose File/Save As and save this file as DeckLayers.psd. You can now close the other two files.

Separating Sky from Foreground

10 With this image, the main Sky details are going to come from the Sky layer, and the foreground and shadow details are going to come from the other two layers. Since the Sky layer is on the top, it will need to have a layer mask on it that is white where we want to see the sky from that layer and black where we want to see the foreground details from the two layers underneath the sky layer. Since this image has a contrasty horizon, we can try to use a copy of one of the Red, Green, or Blue channels to help us make that mask. This

is similar to the technique we used earlier for the Ship Rock image, except this time we choose from three possible layers to find a starting channel to copy from.

◆ Click the Sky layer to make it active; then use [Shift-F10] to bring up the Channels palette, and click the word *Red* to look at the Red channel. The Eye icons for the other two channels should be off so that we just see the Red channel. Compare its horizon contrast to that of the Green and Blue channels. Turn off the Eye icon for the Sky layer, click the Deep Shadows layer, then look at its Red, Green, and Blue channels too. Now turn the Deep Shadows layer Eye icon off, click the Foreground layer, then look at its Red, Green, and Blue channels. You can use Command (Ctrl)-1 as a shortcut to see just the Red channel, Command (Ctrl)-2 for the Green channel, and Command (Ctrl)-3 for the Blue channel. Command (Ctrl)-~ gets you back to RGB.

You have to decide which of these nine channels will make the best template for a mask to separate the sky from the foreground in this image. How the details in the trees and other objects along the horizon are handled by each channel will determine if this will be a good mask or not. If it is not a good mask, then you'll have to do a lot of work by hand to fix this edge, as we did in the Ship Rock image. This image will be much more difficult, however, since we have so many tree branches and fine detail along the horizon. I originally tried a copy of the Red channel from the Foreground layer to make the mask, but after I added the color and contrast changes to all the layers, I realized that this mask was not the best fit along the horizon. There was a white halo around the tree branches, especially toward the left half of the image. I made a new mask from the Red channel of the Sky layer, which worked much better. To save some time here, we'll just start with the Red channel of the Sky layer.

◆ In the Channels palette, click the word *Red,* then drag this down to the Copy icon, just to the left of the Trash icon. This new channel will be called Red copy. You are now working on that copy in the Channels palette. Use Image/Adjustments/Levels on that channel—Command (Ctrl)-L—to adjust the edge between the sky and the foreground.

◆ Move the rightmost Highlight slider to the left, which makes the highlights brighter. Move the leftmost Shadow slider to the right, which makes the shadows and midtones darker. The middle slider effects midtones and often the thickness of the edge if you adjust the middle slider after you've got the right and left sliders in about the correct locations. Play with these on this channel to see how they work to create the mask.

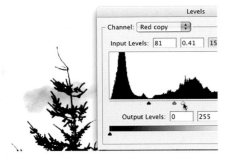

10 This set of Levels adjustments makes the branches more substantial than the set of adjustments you see to the right. Which set will work and how much to apply a Gaussian blur to the final edge is all a matter of experimentation and experience.

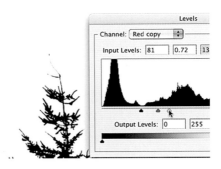

10 This set of Levels adjustments makes the tree here have thinner branches. This might cause a bright halo around the edges of the branches due to the bright sky there; on the other hand, the darker edges of the tree from the sky image might blend in just fine. It depends on the two images you are dealing with.

10 Here we see a piece of the mask I got when I started with the Red channel from the Foreground image. The edges on the trees didn't blend into the new sky as well as the one to the right.

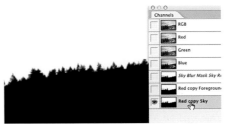

10 This worked better, starting with the Red channel from the Sky image. The Levels adjustments I did to each channel were different because the brightness values along the horizon were different. I prefer making masks this way than by using the Extract filter because I can control what I'm doing more.

Sometimes you have to compromise between one set of adjustments that make one part of the mask look best and another set that make a different part look best. In a perfect world you'd get it white above the horizon and black below. The nature of that edge will determine how well the mask works. What is in the subject matter of the image and also how the exposures were made will also determine how easy your job will be. Some masks work perfectly just from the Levels adjustments, while others require lots of tweaks to get them right.

◆ Once you think you have the sliders positioned optimally, choose OK to Levels, then type B for the Paintbrush, pick PaintBrush Op100% Flow100% from the Tool presets, then type D for default colors. You're now painting with white, so pick the brush you need and fill in any black or white areas that need to be 100% part of either the foreground or the sky part of the mask.

◆ To try this mask out, Command (Ctrl)-click the words *RGB Copy* in the Channels palette, click the letters *RGB* at the top of the Channels palette, then Click the Sky layer to activate it. Choose Layer/Layer Mask/Reveal Selection to create a layer mask from the channel you just edited.

◆ This mask can now be further edited by another iteration of Levels or Curves, or by using the techniques discussed earlier in steps 6 and 7. Remember, though, that it is often better at this point to do your other color and contrast corrections to the overall image, as well as to each different layer that makes up this image, before doing final tweaks to the masks.

Basic Adjustments to the Foreground and Sky

11 Before we can create the mask for the Shadows layer, we should probably do some basic adjustments to the Foreground and Sky layers.

◆ Click the Shadows layer to activate it, then choose Layer/Layer Mask/Hide All to add a black layer mask to this layer. Now all you are seeing is the Foreground layer where the Sky mask is black, and the Sky layer where the Sky mask is white.

◆ At this point I found the entire image to be dark and the Foreground to be dark and flat. Click the Foreground layer, then use [Command (Ctrl)-F3] to bring up a new Curves adjustment layer. Click the Load button and load a curve named ForegroundCurve from the DeckShotFiles folder in the Chapter 27 folder on the *Photoshop Artistry* DVD. Adjust this curve if you don't like what it does to the foreground.

◆ Now click the Sky layer to activate it, and use [Command (Ctrl)-F3] again to create another curve; but this time in the New Layer dialog check the Use Previous Layer to Create Clipping Mask check box. This will use the layer mask on the Sky layer for this layer as well, so this curve will only affect the sky. When you enter the Curve dialog, click the Load button, then load SkyCurve and edit this curve if you don't like what it does to the sky.

◆ Now use [Command (Ctrl)-F4] to add a Hue/Saturation adjustment layer, and also check the Use Previous Layer to Create

Clipping Mask box; then use Load in the Hue/Saturation dialog to load the SkyHueSat settings from the DVD.

Adding Shadow Detail with the Shadows Layer

12 The mask for the Shadows layer is a different type of mask. You will just paint in more detail where you need it.

◆ Click the Shadows layer to activate it. You've already added a layer mask hiding this entire layer; now click this mask—which is the rightmost thumbnail for this layer. Choose Command-Option (Ctrl-Alt)-0 to zoom into 100%, then type H for the Hand tool. You can now scroll around in the Foreground part of the image until you find an area where you'd like to see more shadow detail. Now type B for the Paintbrush, choose Airbrush 7% from the Options bar's leftmost Tool presets pop-up and type a D for default colors, giving you white. Paint anywhere with white if you want more shadow detail. Remember to use the left and right bracket keys to lower or increase your brush size and hold the Spacebar down when you want the Hand tool to scroll. Move around the foreground area of the image and add shadow detail anywhere it's needed. If you add too much, remember that you can type X to exchange the colors and switch to black, then paint some with that in the mask to lessen the shadow detail you've added.

The shadow detail you're adding may still seem dark and a bit flat. That brings us to the next curve we are going to add.

◆ Type [Command (Ctrl)-F3] to bring up another curve and again check the Use Previous Layer to Create Clipping Mask option. When you check this option, this new adjustment layer is indented, which means it's using the mask on the previous layer as its starting mask. In the Curve dialog use the Load button and load the file named ShadowsCurve.acv in the DeckShotFiles folder of Chapter 27 on the DVD. Once the curve is loaded, notice how you can adjust the brightness and contrast of the shadow areas you've already painted white in the Shadow layer mask by tweaking this curve. Making the slope of the curve steeper increases the contrast; moving the curve further to the left increases its brightness. Remember that you can hold the cursor over the image and then press the mouse button down to see where those particular values are on the curve. A small circle will show up on the curve as long as the mouse button is down. Try these things and have fun with your shadows!

You'll now probably notice that your mask edge has some white noise around it. This is where you can go back to the techniques of

steps 6 and 7 to try to improve this mask. To see my final layers for this version of this composite, open the file DeckThreeShotLayers. psd from this same folder on the DVD. We'll talk about the remaining layers at the top of this file at the end of this example when we compare this image to the HDR version.

13 Here we see the correct Adjust settings for HDR images. Leave the White Balance as the camera shot it. Later when you synchronize all images, don't synchronize the white balance. Exposure through Saturation should all be set to 0.

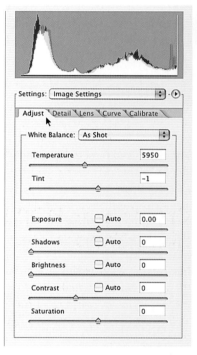

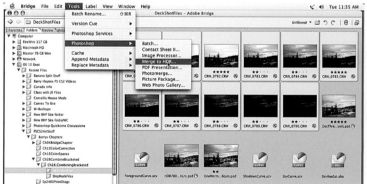

13 Here we clicked image 780, then Shift-clicked image 790 to select the range of images within. We then go to Tools/Photoshop/Merge to HDR to open these images into the Photoshop Merge to HDR filter.

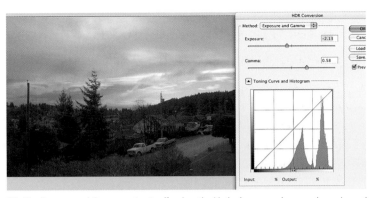

14 The Exposure and Gamma option is offered on the Method pop-up when you choose Image/Mode/16-Bits/Channel while working on an HDR image. The histogram display shows the brightness range of this image. Each red mark is similar to an f-stop or exposure value. With this option, you can't modify the curve or histogram associated with this display. To convert such a high-range image as this, you must move the Exposure to the left to see the highlight details and move the Gamma to the right so the shadows don't get too dark. The resulting image looks flat but has values for every part of the image. You can adjust it in Photoshop to regain local contrast.

13 The Merge to HDR dialog displays the 11 exposures selected. The histogram shows that the image really does have a wide dynamic range, from a +3.36 to −3.64 exposure value. Moving the slider on the histogram changes the way the image looks, but the HDR image created when you click OK actually has the full range of tones from all the exposures until you convert the HDR image to a 16-bit image. Use the new Image/Adjustments/Exposure command to look at the range in a different way.

Creating an HDR Image from Many Exposures

Now we'll compare the image we just created with 3 exposures to the HDR image created with 11 exposures. What we gain from the HDR process of merging all these images together is that we'll be able to compress a very large dynamic range image into one file without having to make a mask separating the sky from the foreground and without having to make a mask for the deep shadow details. This HDR image will have lots of color detail and depth in both the shadow and highlight areas.

Combining the Images into a 32-Bit HDR File

13 The first thing we need to do is select all 11 images in Bridge and open them using Merge to HDR within Photoshop.

◆ Go back to Bridge and click the DeckShotFiles folder inside the Chapter 27 folder. Click image 780, then Shift-click image 790 and choose File/Open in Camera Raw (Command (Ctrl)-R) to open all these images into Camera Raw.

◆ In the Adjust area, set all the values to 0 but leave the White Balance as is. In the Detail area, set the Sharpening to 0 and the

Color Noise Reduction to 12 (usually). In the Lens area do your normal adjustments for Chromatic Aberration. See Chapter 9, "Camera Raw," for more information about making those adjustments. Finally, just use a Linear curve on this image.

◆ When you've made all these adjustments, click Select All in the top-left corner, then click Synchronize, also in the top-left corner. When the Synchronize dialog comes up, synchronize all the settings except for White Balance and Crop. Now click the Done button in the bottom-right corner of the Camera Raw dialog to apply these changes to all the images and then return to Bridge. From Bridge, with all these same images still selected, choose Tools/Photoshop/Merge to HDR.

The only option you have, just before you get to the above dialog, is a check box to Attempt to Automatically Align Source Images. You'd only want to turn this option on if you hand-held the camera while you made the exposures. I *strongly* recommend putting the camera on a tripod. After the computer chugs along for a while in Photoshop, you will get the Merge to HDR dialog.

◆ Once you see the dialog, the only other option is to uncheck the check box below certain images, which will exclude them from the calculations to create the merged image. Try unchecking the top three images, and you'll notice that the shadow part of the histogram changes. Recheck those three images. You can also move the histogram slider around, but this only affects the way the image looks when it first comes up in Photoshop. HDR

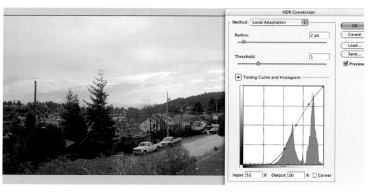

14 The bottom Method option you are looking at here is called Local Adaptation. It is quite useful but more tricky to use than the Exposure and Gamma option. The cool thing about this option is that you can move the points in the curve, and when you hold the mouse button down on your image, the position of the values in the mouse location show up on the curve. Notice that I've moved the top highlight and bottom shadow endpoints of the curve to be close to where the right and left endpoints of the histogram are. I've also adjusted the curve slightly. Note that this Local Adaptation option also has Radius and Threshold sliders. Lots of toys to play with, but they were initially confusing for me. We'll discuss them in depth within this example.

images, like this one, will have a much larger dynamic range than you can display on your monitor or print on your printer. No matter where you leave the slider, the actual HDR image data will be the same. The slider just controls what you are seeing initially on your low-dynamic-range monitor, so move the slider so that you can see as much of the image as possible without losing too much highlight detail and without the shadows going too dark. Don't worry, you're not throwing anything away. Click OK to finish creating the HDR image.

After the new HDR image comes up in Photoshop, you should use File/Save As to save it in PBM (portable bitmat) format. This is the new 32-bit image format. Saving this archives all 32 bits of information about this image.

Converting the HDR Image to 16 Bits

14 To actually color correct the image within Photoshop now, you have to use Image/Mode/16 Bits/Channel to convert this image into a 16-bit image, which allows you to add adjustment layers, masks, and so on.

◆ Choose Image/Mode/16 Bits/Channel, and you'll see the dialog shown above. To see the histogram display, you have to click the down arrow to the left of the words *Toning Curve and Histogram*. There are four Method options for the ways you can use this HDR Conversion dialog. The first Exposure and Gamma option is what you initially get. This option doesn't actually allow you to adjust the curve or histogram. See the illustration above for how

to adjust this choice, then try out the Exposure and Gamma sliders to get a feel for how they influence the image.

◆ The next option from the Method pop-up is Highlight Compression. Choose this option to reduce the brightness of the highlights until they fit within the 16-bit range. With this option, the entire sky looks really flat and you have no control. The shadows also looked really dark with this one. If you first go into Image/Adjustments/Exposure and change the Gamma and Exposure settings of this 32-bit image, then go back into Highlight Compression, you will get a different result. I tried this, using Exposure to open up the shadow values in the image, but when I went back to Highlight Compression, the highlights looked even flatter. Give it a try!

◆ Now choose the Equalize Histogram from the Method pop-up. This option creates very strange contrast in the foreground of the image. I don't like what either one of these options does.

◆ The last option—Local Adaptation, shown in the figure here—appears to offer the most control of all four. This is the only option where you can actually adjust the curve diagram and make useful changes. Still, the names of the controls seem a bit strange for what we are doing here. First, let's play with the curve. The histogram that is fixed on the curve diagram just shows you where the values for this image are in relation to the curve controls. Move the shadow point in the bottom-left corner over to just to the left of the leftmost end of the histogram. The highlight point at the top right of the curve is already at the right end of this histogram. Now click where the middle horizontal line meets the curve, to place a center point. You can then create an S-curve to increase the contrast by placing points on the line one-quarter of the way down where it meets the curve and moving that point up and to the left. Finally, place a point three-quarters of the way down where the line meets the curve, and move this point down and to the right. Adjusting these three points allows you to add more contrast to the image.

◆ Use Command (Ctrl)-Spacebar-click to zoom into 100%, and look at the image along the horizon. Notice how changing the Radius adjusts how the treetops blend into the sky and how the horizon and sky blend together. These settings also influence the details within the image. I found that a Radius of 2 and a Threshold of 1 worked best for this image. Click OK, and you'll have a 16-bit version of your HDR image. Save this under a different name so that you keep both the 16-bit and 32-bit versions of this file. If this 16-bit version doesn't color correct well, you can always go back to the 32-bit HDR file and create a different

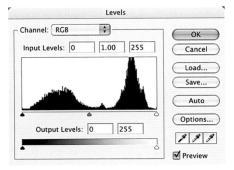

15 The idea when converting an HDR image to 16 bit is to get a histogram that represents the full range of values in the image spread across the full area of Levels without losing highlight or shadow details. The 16-bit HDR image may start out looking flat, but you can fix that with appropriate adjustment layers above it and you probably won't require as complicated a mask set as you would doing the traditional composite of several layers.

interpretation of it using the Local Adaptation or Exposure and Gamma method.

Finalizing the 16-Bit Version of the Merged Image

15 Now that we can add adjustment layers, we just want to go through the overall color correction steps on this 16-bit image. What we've gained from this process of merging all these images together is that we compressed a very large dynamic range image into one file and we did that without having to make a mask separating the sky from the foreground and without having to make a mask for the deep shadow details. You'll see that this image has lots of color detail and depth in both the shadow and highlight areas.

◆ Now you want to proceed through the Overall Color Correction steps outlined in Chapter 21, "Overall Color Correction," and Chapter 22, "Correcting Problem Images," and follow those steps for this 16-bit version of the HDR image. First do the Levels adjustment, then the Curves, then the Hue/Saturation, and so on. Remember to set your highlight and shadow points using Threshold before entering Levels.

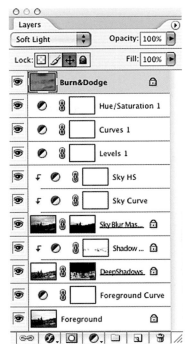

15 The final Layers palette for the image made from a composite of three exposures. This Layers palette is more complicated since each image layer component requires its own mask and also its own specific adjustments to get the three layers to work well together. Above all those are the overall Levels, Curves, and Hue/Saturation adjustments as well. This solution is more work but may ultimately give you more control.

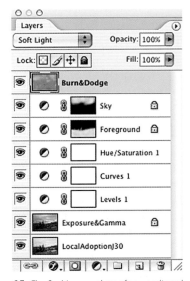

15 The final Layers palette after we adjusted the converted HDR image as a 16-bit image with adjustment layers. At the bottom of this layers stack you can either have the conversion from HDR using the Exposure&Gamma setting or the LocalAdaptation setting. In either case, the number of layers and complicated masks will probably be less than for the image made from a composite of three exposures, where each exposure requires its own mask. If you put the camera on a tripod and bracket the entire dynamic range of the scene, then you could make an HDR image if you wanted to. In that case, you'd also have the option of just using two or three of those exposures to create a bracketed image similar to the one whose Layers palette is to the left.

Tree, car, and color details from the three-shot bracketed composite image.

Tree, car, and color details from the 16-bit HDR image.

The final three-shot bracketed image after Smart Sharpen of 150, 1,1, 1-20.

The final 16-bit HDR image after Smart Sharpen of 150, 1,1, 1-20.

- If you find after doing these initial color correction steps that the shadows are too flat and not detailed enough, create a Shadow Curve as we showed you in Chapters 21 and 22. Do a similar thing for the highlights if they are too flat. You create each of these curves while looking at the part of the image you want to adjust and with only those parts of the image in mind. After clicking OK in the Curves dialog, you use Image/Adjustments/Invert to make the mask for this curve black. You then use the Airbrush 7% option with a soft, white brush to paint on the mask in the shadow or highlight areas where you need the effect of that specific curve.

- Bring up the final version of this image, DeckThreeShotLayers, and study the layers and masks I created. The final Layers palette is shown to the far right.

- Compare this to the final version of the three-shot bracket image—HDR780-790AftPorchLrs. That image's Layers palette actually has a similar structure, but the overall Levels, Curves, and Hue/Saturation adjustments are applied after the specific adjustments to get the three layers to work together properly.

Conclusion

Bracketing your exposures on a tripod to make sure you have both good shadow and highlight detail is great when you have the time. That gives you the option of creating an HDR image or using two or three of your bracketed images to create a final piece of art that will have nice colors in the dark areas and also fine details in the highlights. The particular option that you choose will depend on the stillness and dynamic range of the image you shot, and also on the types of masks you might have to create. Now you have several choices and some new techniques to use with your bracketed exposures. Have fun!

Portfolio

Carl Marcus

When we were thinking of photographers who understand transformations, one name leapt to mind. Carl Marcus has made an art of the process, presenting images of nature that are provocative, humorous, penetrating, and powerful. See more of his images at www.kaleidophoto.com.

28 ◆ Compositing Multiple Images

Use the Pen tool and a variety of selection and masking techniques to create a composite of four images, giving us a rainy street scene in San Jose, Costa Rica.

In this session, we will use the Pen tool and other selection and masking techniques to create a composite of a rainy scene using photographs from San Jose, Costa Rica. We want this scene to appear as though you are looking at it through the front window of a bus that is coming onto this street.

Set Up the Four Files

1 The first thing you need to do is get all four images that you want to use in one file. We are going to move the other three images into the Blue Bus file, each as a separate layer. Moving layers from one document to another with the Shift key held down causes the composited image to be centered on top of the main image.

◆ Open the PSD files, Blue Bus.psd, Bus Window.psd, Red Car.psd, and Woman.psd in the Ch28.Compositing Multiple Images folder on the *Photoshop Artistry* DVD. Press the Tab key to remove your palettes from the screen.

◆ Click the Blue Bus file to make it active, then type F to put it in Full Screen mode, followed by Command (Ctrl)-0 to fill the screen with this file.

◆ Type V to switch to the Move tool, and activate the Red Car file from the Window menu. You should now see the Blue Bus file behind in Full Screen mode and the Red Car file in front, but within a window.

◆ Hold the Shift key down, click within the Red Car window, and drag the Red Car image until the cursor has moved on top of the Blue Bus image. Release the mouse and Shift key at that point, and you should have dragged and dropped the Red Car image as a new layer on top of the Blue Bus image. Close the Red Car image.

◆ Use the Window menu to make the Woman file active, Shift-drag her image on top of the Blue Bus file in the same way you moved the Red Car over, then close the Woman file.

◆ Again, use the Window menu to activate the Bus Window file and Shift-drag it onto the Blue Bus file. Close the Bus Window file.

◆ Use Window/Layers [F10] to bring back the Layers palette. Your Blue Bus file should now have a Layers palette with Blue Bus on the bottom, then Red Car, then Woman, and finally Bus Window on top.

◆ Choose File/Save As and save this as RainInCostaRicaLayers.psd.

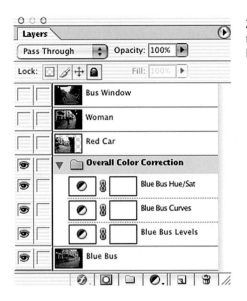

2 The Layers palette after doing the overall color correction on the Blue Bus image.

Crop, Color Correct, and Group

2 We need to crop out some of the Blue Bus layer. Crop the black borders from the left, bottom, and right side, but be careful not to crop off any more than is needed to remove the non-image black border from around the edge. This example is mostly about compositing, not color correction, so we're not spending a lot of time on the color correction aspects. At any time, though, you can also open and look at our final version of this composite, called RainInCostaRica-FinalCC.psd, from the Chapter 28 folder on the DVD. Go through the process covered in Chapter 21, "Overall Color Correction," to do the Levels corrections on this image. We left the highlights on this image as they were to keep the dull and rainy look the image has. If you'd like, you can load our Levels adjustments, called BlueBusLevels.alv, from the Chapter 28 folder on the DVD.

◆ Turn off the Eye icons for the top three layers so you are viewing only the Blue Bus layer at the bottom of the Layers palette. Click on the words Blue Bus to activate that layer.

◆ Type a C to get the Crop tool and crop the black borders.

◆ Choose Layer/New Adjustment Layer/Levels [Command (Ctrl)-F2] to create the Levels adjustment layer and do Overall Color Correction on the Blue Bus image. Click OK when you are happy with your Levels adjustments.

◆ Use [Command (Ctrl)-F3] to create a new Curves adjustment layer. Create an S-curve or load the one from the DVD, called

BlueBusCurves.acv, to increase the contrast a bit. Click OK to accept this adjustment.

◆ Use [Command (Ctrl)-F4] to create a Hue/Saturation adjustment layer. Load the settings called BlueBusHueSat.ahu from the DVD.

◆ Choose Layer/New/Group and name the group Overall Color Correction. Drag the layer thumbnail for each of the Levels, Curves, and Hue/Sat adjustment layers, and drop it on the Overall Color Correction group thumbnail. Make sure they are still in the same order within the set, with Levels on the bottom, Curves in the middle, and Hue/Sat on the top.

◆ Close the group to make your Layers palette smaller.

Paths and the Pen Tool

If you already know how to use the Pen tool and Paths, you can skip to step 3. But if you want to brush up on your skills, the next few sections discuss how to use the Pen tool and Paths in detail. The Pen tool's primary use for photographers is to make selections, called paths, by clicking to create points between either straight or curved lines. These paths can be used to create a selection for a layer mask or, if sharp edges at varying resolutions are needed, a vector mask.

Points, Segments, and Curves

The Pen tool works by placing points and connecting those points with line segments. A segment can be either straight or curved. Each segment has two points associated with it, a beginning point and an endpoint. The points that control the segments can have handles. Notice that we say "can." A corner point (that is, a point that connects two straight-line segments) has no handles. A smooth point connecting segments in a continuous curve has two handles that are dependent on each other. If you adjust the direction of one of the handles, you affect the other handle in an equal and opposite manner. However, a corner point can also join two curve segments that are noncontinuous and abut sharply, as in the two curves forming the top of this lowercase *m*. In that case, the anchor point would have two handles that work independently of each other. And finally, a straight-line segment that joins a curve segment does so by an anchor point that has only one handle, which controls the direction and height of the curve. This type of point is sometimes referred to as a cusp.

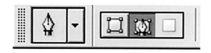
Use the middle icon to draw paths.

If you click a point and immediately release the mouse, you create an anchor point. To draw straight-line segments with the Pen, click where you want to place anchor points. To draw a curved segment, click and drag before releasing the mouse, and that point becomes a curve point. When you create or move a curve point, you get two lines coming out of the curve point; Adobe calls these direction lines, we call them handles. The handles control the shape of the curve. To make a corner point with handles that work independently, click and drag out a handle, but after you drag, hold down the Option (Alt) key to access the Convert tool. Use the tool to drag the handle in a different direction. The handle that controls the previous segment will not change, but when you place a new anchor point, you'll have a corner rather than a smooth curve.

Open and Closed Paths

Paths can be either open or closed. An open path is one that has a start point and endpoint that do not join. You might draw such a path if you need to make a stroke of a precise shape and position on your image. If you need the path to create a selection, you would use a closed path, where the start point and the endpoint are the same point.

The Path Selection and Direct Selection Tools

When you work with paths, you not only need to build them, but you will want to manipulate them. This is done by use of the black arrow, the Path Selection tool, which selects the entire path to be moved or copied, and the white arrow, the Direct Selection tool, which selects only points or segments to be modified. So, if you wanted to move only one anchor point a little higher, you would select it with the Direct Selection tool and drag it or nudge it. You can also grab a segment or a curve with the Direct Selection tool to move it. If you wanted to move the entire path a little higher, you would select it with the Selection tool.

Pen Tool Practice

Unlike many of Photoshop's tool, the Pen tool is not particularly intuitive. It requires a bit of practice. But the time spent is worthwhile. It's not a tool that the three of us use often, but we all know how to use it fairly well. For selecting and masking chores where a crisp, sharp edge is needed, it is simply the very best tool available. We encourage you to take these few moments to familiarize yourself with the tool before you begin the next part of the exercise.

We've created a simple file for you to practice with. Each type of path you'll have to deal with is represented in this practice session.

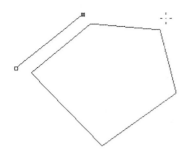

To create the trapezoid, you only need to click.

Constraining your drag with the Shift key assures you a smooth curve and also places the second anchor point on a horizontal line with the first anchor point.

There is a different path in the Paths palette for each one. We suggest you redraw each path, but also play around a bit with handles and segments.

Create a Trapezoid

Let's start with the simplest type of path you can make—a trapezoid of some variety.

◆ Open the Pen Tool Practice.psd file from the Chapter 28 folder on the DVD.

◆ Type [Shift-F8] to bring up the Paths palette. Click the Trapezoid path to make it active.

◆ Type a P for the Pen tool. On the Options bar, click the Make Path icon, the middle one.

◆ Click outside any vertex of the trapezoid to place the first point. Release the mouse, move to the next vertex, and click outside that vertex to place another anchor point. Continue around the trapezoid.

◆ Put the last anchor point on top of the first. A little circle appears next to the arrow, indicating that you are closing the path.

You now have two subpaths on the trapezoid path. After you name a path, any changes you make to it are automatically saved as part of that path.

Create an Oval Closed Path

When you create an oval or curved path, you want to use the fewest possible points to create the curve. This keeps the path very smooth. It takes a while before you know how many points to use or where, but here we're being absolutely minimalist. To create a circle or an oval, you only need two points. This time rather than just clicking, you must click and drag. We're also holding down the Shift key as we drag to constrain the handles that the Pen tool creates. Wherever

you click is the location of the anchor point, and dragging out the handlebar beyond the point affects the shape of the line segment between that point and the previous point, as well as between that point and the next point.

◆ Click the Oval path in the Paths palette.

◆ Type A or Shift-A for the Direct Selection tool (the white arrow, not the black one). Click the activated path to see where the anchor points have been placed.

◆ Type P for the Pen tool. Click outside the left anchor point, hold down the Shift key, and drag upward. With the Shift key still down, lift your mouse and click-drag downward somewhere outside the right side of the oval.

◆ Let go of the Shift key, lift the mouse, and position it over the initial anchor point. When you see the little circle indicating the close of the path, click without dragging.

You should have an oval, very similar to the first one. If your path got all twisted up, you dragged on the final click rather than just clicking. In that case, type Shift-A to get the Selection tool (the black arrow), click your path, and hit the Delete (Backspace) key. This should delete the entire path, then you can try this again.

Create an Open Curved Path

To create a curved path, you click and drag. The click should place an anchor point at the beginning of the curve, and the drag denotes the direction the curve will move in. The next anchor point designates the end of the first curve and the beginning of the next. We're going to ask you to draw this curve twice, once with the Rubber Band option turned on. For those who use Illustrator or another vector drawing program, you might find the Rubber Band option annoying.

Click the middle anchor point to see how the handles work for this curve.

Once you start drawing another curve, the handles for the first will disappear. Now you have to guesstimate where to drag the handles and where to place the points to re-create the curve.

When it's time to turn on the Rubber Band option, this is where you'll find it.

But for those who do not, you might find the option very useful for placing points and handles.

◆ Type A or Shift-A for the Direct Selection tool, and click the Curve path in the Paths palette. If you click the middle anchor point, you'll see the handles for all three points, indicating the direction of the curves.

◆ Type P for the Pen tool.

◆ Click above the left point and drag upward. Lift the mouse, click where you think the second point should be, and drag down. Lift the mouse again, click where you think the third point should go, and drag upward.

◆ Hold down the Command (Ctrl) key and click outside the path you just drew to deactivate it.

◆ On the Options bar, click the pop-up arrow beside the Custom Shape icon and turn on the Rubber Band option. This will give you a sort of preview of what your curve will look like before you place the next point.

◆ Redraw the curve with this option turned on.

Whether you found drawing easier with or without the Rubber Band option, you'll want to use those settings for knocking out the bus window later in this example.

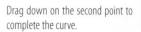

Drag down on the second point to complete the curve.

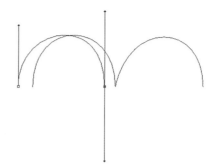

Hold down Option (Alt) and drag the lower handle up to create the beginning of the next curve.

Click the third point and drag down to complete the second curve.

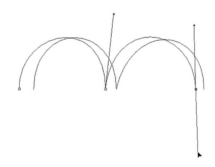

Create a Corner Point

There are times when you'll need two curves to meet in a point, one curve going in to it and another going out in the same direction, so rather than a wave pattern, you have humps. To create such a point, you have to create the first anchor and curved segment, but after you click and drag on the second anchor point, you do not click a third point. Rather, you release the mouse, hold down the Option (Alt) key, then drag the second handle of the curve out in the direction you want to curve to flow. After that you can set the third anchor point. To re-create this path, draw your path to the left of the original.

◆ Click the Corner Point path in the Paths palette.

◆ Type P for the Pen tool.

- Hold down the Shift key to constrain your drag, then click and drag up.

- With the Shift key still down, click to the right of the first point (and to the left of the original path) and drag down to set your second anchor point and complete the first curve.

- Let go of the mouse, hold down your Option (Alt) key, then move the mouse over the second handle for the second anchor point. When you get the inverted V, you are in the Convert tool and can drag this handle up near the point's first handle.

- Let go of the mouse.

- Hold the Shift key down and click and drag down to create the third anchor point and the second curve.

Create a Cusp Point

The last type of point and curve you'll encounter is sometimes called a cusp. It's where a straight line meets a curve. You might need to start with the straight-line, or you might need to start with the curve. Here, you'll do both.

- Click on the Cusp Point path in the Paths palette.

- Type P for the Pen tool.

- Click above the left point, then (without dragging) click to the right to complete the straight line portion of the path.

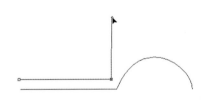

Click twice without dragging, then Option (Alt)-click the second anchor point and drag out a handle for a curve.

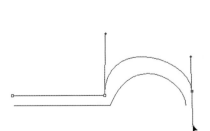

Clicking and dragging down completes this curve.

- Hold down the Option (Alt) key, click directly on the point you just created, and drag upward to begin the curve.

- Click and drag downward at the right to complete the curve.

- Press the Delete (Backspace) key twice to delete this new path.

- Now, draw the path in the other direction. Click and drag upward above the right point to begin the curve.

- Click and drag down to complete the curve.

- Option (Alt)-click the second point to delete the second handle for this point.

- Click (without dragging) above the left point.

Adding and Deleting Points

You can add points to a path with the Pen+ tool (the Add Anchor Point tool) and delete points with the Pen− tool (the Delete Anchor Point tool). To add a point, click using the Pen+ tool along the line segment where no point currently exists. Over an existing point the Pen+ tool turns into the Direct Selection tool because you can't add a point where one already exists. With the Pen− tool, you can click any existing point to remove it, but you will be in the Direct Selection tool when you are not over an existing point. When you add a point with the Pen+ tool, it's a curve point. You can then change the shape of the curve by adjusting that point's handles with the Direct Selection tool.

- Click any path in the Paths palette.

- Choose the Pen+ tool and click the path to add a point.

- Choose the Pen− tool and click a point to delete it.

Converting a Point

If you want to change a curve point to a corner point, or vice versa, click it with the Convert Point tool. To change an anchor point with no handles to a curve, you click and drag the corner point to define the length and angle of your handles. You can also use the Convert Point tool to decouple a curve point's handles. Clicking either handle and moving it slightly with this tool allows you to later use the Direct Selection tool to drag each end of the handle to change its curve segment shape without changing the one on the opposite side of the handle's point. A point like this with two handles that work independently of each other is a corner point where two curves meet but move out from the point in the same direction, causing a sharp angle. To recouple the handles again for a smooth curve, click and drag on the point between the handles using the Convert Point tool. You can access the Convert Point tool from the Direct Selection (white arrow) tool by holding down Command-Option (Ctrl-Alt) and placing the cursor over an existing point or handle end. Access the Convert Point tool from the Pen tool using only the Option key.

◆ Click the Trapezoid path in the Paths palette.

◆ Choose the Convert Point tool and click the path to activate it.

◆ Click and drag one of the anchor points to turn it into a curve point.

◆ Click the Oval path in the Paths palette.

◆ Click the bottom curve segment. With the Convert Point tool, drag one of the bottom handles out and up.

◆ Next, use the Convert Point tool to click the anchor point of the handle you just moved.

Copying a Path

In the chart below are several ways to copy an entire path.

Use	Do This
Path Selection tool	Option (Alt)-drag the path
Direct Selection tool	Option (Alt)-click the path, then keep the modifier key down as you drag
Pen tool	Command-Option (Ctrl-Alt)-click and drag
Pen+ tool	Click and drag when not over a point
Pen– tool	Hold down Option (Alt), and drag when not over a point

Now you give it a try.

◆ Choose the Direct Selection tool.

◆ Hold down the Option (Alt) key and click the path.

◆ Option (Alt)-drag the path to copy it.

Turning a Path into a Selection

There are several ways to turn a path into a selection: Choose Make Selection from the pop-up menu in the Paths palette, drag the path to the Load Path as a Selection icon (the third one) at the bottom of the palette, highlight the name of the path and click the icon, or Command (Ctrl)-click the name of the path.

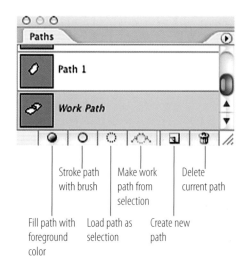

Stroke path with brush
Make work path from selection
Delete current path
Fill path with foreground color
Load path as selection
Create new path

Saving Paths

If you start to draw with the Pen tool when no path is active, you create a work path and it immediately shows up in the Paths palette. This is a temporary path and unless you save it by choosing Save Path from the Paths palette menu, it can be overwritten. You can keep this from happening by clicking the Create New Path icon at the bottom of the Paths palette before you begin to draw the path or by making sure you save the path once you've begun drawing it. The other icons on the Paths palette allow you to fill a path, stroke a path, turn the currently active path into a selection, or turn a currently active selection into a path. And, of course, the Trash icon lets you delete unwanted paths.

Knock Out the Bus Window

3 We're going to use the Pen tool now to do the knockout of the bus window. It's the perfect tool to use here because we have a hard-edge object, the window, with both straight lines and curves. We are going to use the tool's Rubber Band. If you found it easier to determine where to place points without this option during the Pen tool tutorial, feel free to work without it. Once you've created subpaths for both windows, you'll turn the path into a selection to use as a layer mask.

◆ Type P for the Pen tool. Click the pop-up arrow beside the Custom Shape icon, and click the Rubber Band option.

◆ Press Tab to get rid of all your palettes, and use Command (Ctrl)-0 to fit the image onscreen. If Tab doesn't get rid of your palettes,

3 Start your path at the top left of the bigger bus window. Click to make the first point, then click and drag on each additional point to make the direction that you drag in parallel with the window edge at that point.

3 Once you have worked your way all around the window, place the cursor back on top of the first point you clicked and you will see a small circle next to the arrow at the lower right. When you see this circle, click once to complete the path.

3 While working on a path in Photoshop, the History palette [F8] keeps track of each point that you enter. If you want to go back to redo several points, just click a few steps back in the History palette. The hand here is showing us the place where we closed the path on the big window.

try Return (Enter) and then Tab a few times until the palettes disappear.

◆ Make sure the Bus Window layer is active and visible.

◆ Click at the top of the larger window to place the first point, then trace around the window clockwise, placing points as you go. See the illustrations on this page for comments about drawing this path.

◆ When you've traced all the way around, again click the point that started the path, which completes and closes this path.

◆ Trace a similar path around the smaller window on the left side. Close the path.

◆ Use [Shift-F11] to bring up your Paths palette. Double-click the work path and name it Bus Windows.

◆ Choose Make Selection from the pop-up menu on the Paths palette. Set the Feather to 0, turn on Anti-aliased, and choose New Selection if it's not already checked.

Create a Layer Mask

4 You are now going to remove the area of the window from view in this layer.

◆ Choose Layer/Layer Mask/Hide Selection to mask out the area of the selection.

◆ Type B for the Brush and D for the default colors.

◆ Select a small, hard-edge brush, zoom in to 200%, and slowly look around the edge of the bus window for selection edges that don't look correct. Paint with black to remove more from the window frame edge and paint with white to bring some window edge back.

Use Channels to Correct the Mask

When you added the layer mask from the Pen tool selection, it removed the windshield wipers from the bus windows. We'd probably like to keep them in the picture since the bus is going out into the rain. We could have selected those with the Pen tool also, but to give you some other selection skills, we'll select the wipers using Levels on a channel mask.

4 A window edge that has an ugly black line showing. Using the Paintbrush and painting in the mask with black along this edge, we removed it below. Where the line is straight, you can click at one end of the part you want to remove, then Shift-click on the other end to paint in a straight line.

5a Here is the Layer and Channel setup for choosing the Green channel as the one to create our mask. Dragging it to the New Channel icon to the left of the Trash icon in the Channels palette will make a copy of this Green channel.

Choose the Best Channel

5a We'll look at each of the Red, Green, and Blue channels separately to determine which has the best contrast, then make a copy of that channel.

◆ Temporarily turn off the mask you just created by Shift-clicking the layer mask thumbnail, the rightmost one, for this Bus Window layer.

◆ Use [Shift-F10] to bring up the Channels palette. Click first on the letters *RGB*, then click each channel to see which has the most contrast between the wipers and the background street scene.

◆ Drag the Green channel to the Create New Channel icon at the bottom of the Channels palette.

Adjust Levels for the Best Mask

5b The right wiper separates easily, so zoom in on it and get the settings that separate it as exact as possible. Move the Levels Shadow, Brightness, and Highlight sliders as you are doing this to see what they do to the mask.

◆ Choose Image/Adjustments/Levels to go into the Levels dialog for that channel. Move the Highlight and Shadow sliders in toward the center left as you try to separate the wipers from all the noise in the window scene.

◆ Turn the Preview button off and then on again in the Levels dialog to make sure the mask you are creating correctly gets the edges of the wiper.

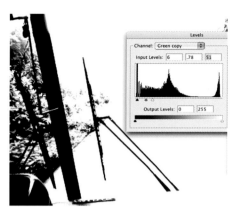

5b Here we are using Levels to separate the wipers from the rest of the image in this copy of the Green channel. These are the settings we used to separate the wipers.

◆ Now look at the leftmost wiper and the metal bar that comes down into the window area on the left side. Select them as well as you can, but know that you will have to use the Paintbrush to clean up this mask.

◆ When the mask looks as good as you can get it, choose OK in Levels.

Paint the Channel Mask Where Needed

5c Remember that you can get a straight line with the brush by clicking at one end of a line and then Shift-clicking at the other end, which draws the brush in a straight line between those two points.

◆ Now type a B for the Paintbrush and a D for the default colors, which will give you white as the foreground color. Paint with white at 100% to remove all the other parts of this mask that are not the wipers and that metal bar.

Load the Channel Mask and Add to the Layer Mask

5d You are actually loading everything but the wipers, since the wipers were black in this channel.

◆ When you are finished editing this mask, Command (Ctrl)-click this Green copy channel to load the white parts of it as a selection.

◆ Choose Select/Inverse to invert the selection so that the wipers are actually selected.

◆ Click back on the letters *RGB* in the Channels palette, and you will again be working on the Bus Window layer. Shift-click the Bus Window Layer Mask thumbnail to turn the mask on again.

◆ Choose Select/Save Selection and set the Channel pop-up in the Save Selection dialog to Bus Window Mask. Choose the Add to Channel option, then click OK to add in the wipers.

5c After clicking OK to Levels, we are using the Paintbrush to paint with white in the Green copy channel to cleanly cut out the wipers.

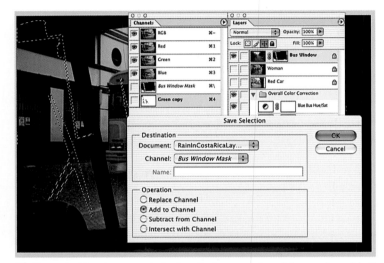

5d Here we load the wipers as a selection from the Green copy channel, then we choose Select/ Save Selection, and add the wipers to the Bus Window mask using the Add to Channel option.

Paint the Layer Mask

5e We had to paint a little more white in the layer mask so that the wipers looked connected to the dashboard.

◆ Click the Bus Window Layer Mask thumbnail to make sure you are editing the Bus Window Mask, then use the Brush again to do any final mask cleanup on the ends of the wipers where they connect to the bottom of the dashboard.

Lock the Layers

6 You now have two layers in position, and you don't want them to be accidentally moved.

◆ Click the Lock Position check box to lock the position of the Bus Window layer.

◆ Click the words *Blue Bus* to activate that layer, then lock its position.

Position the Red Car and Add a Layer Mask

7 You will see the red car and the blue bus superimposed on each other when you turn on the Red Car layer. When you use the Lasso tool and press Return (Enter), 3, Return (Enter), the first Return (Enter) selects the Feather text box, the 3 sets the Feather, and the second Return (Enter) deselects that feather text box so that the next time you type a number it refers to the Opacity of the Red Car layer.

If you hold down the Command (Ctrl) key to activate the Move tool, you can inadvertently move a layer if you click and drag by accident. That's one reason to lock the position of layers that are already in place. The correct position for the red car is within the left front window of the bus as you look out. Getting the yellow curbs in the two images to line up is a good way to position the car on the road. You don't want to move the Blue Bus layer, though; it should already be in the correct position, and you locked it in the last step to keep it from moving.

◆ Click the Eye icon for the Red Car layer in the Layers palette.

◆ Type 5, which sets the Opacity of this Red Car layer to 50%.

◆ Hold down the Command (Ctrl) key while you click and drag the red car to the left so it looks like it is driving down the road in front of the bus.

◆ When the red car is approximately in the right place, type 0 to set the Opacity of the Red Car layer back to 100%.

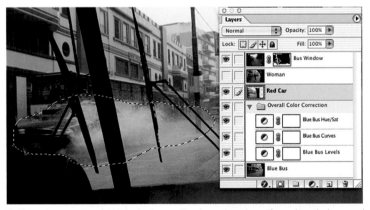

7 This is the approximate initial selection you'll make on the red car. After making the layer mask from this selection, you will paint white or black with the Paintbrush in that mask to add to or subtract from this selection.

◆ Type L to switch to the Lasso tool, then press Return (Enter), 3, and Return (Enter) to set the Feather of the Lasso to 3.

◆ With the Lasso tool, make a very loose selection around the red car. Make sure you include all of the red car's splash.

◆ Choose Layer/Add Layer Mask/Reveal Selection, or click the Add Layer Mask icon at the bottom of the Layers palette.

This adds a layer mask that removes the rest of the Red Car layer from this composite. You'll notice that the color correction on the Red Car layer doesn't match, but that can actually be an asset at this point, making it easier to see what is on each layer.

Increase the History States

8 Before you begin to do all the blending needed, be sure to increase the number of history states. That way, if you don't like the way the image is looking, you can back up along the way. It's amazing how quickly you can do more than 20 history states when retouching or blending a mask.

◆ Use Command (Ctrl)-K to bring up the General Preferences and set the History States to 99. This takes quite a bit of RAM, so if you don't have a lot of memory, or you are working on a really large file, you'll need to user fewer states or suffer poor performance from your computer.

Paint the Red Car Mask

9 We're assuming here that you have BarrysPhotoBrushes loaded as explained in Chapter 2, "Preferences and Color Settings." If not, you may want to load those brushes from the Preferences folder on the DVD. In front of the red car, you want to keep most of the car's splash. If you're using a tablet, the splash is a good spot to use a brush with Shape Dynamics.

◆ Turn the Eye icon off for the Bus Window layer so you can concentrate on cleanly integrating the red car.

◆ Type B for the Brush to paint the Red Car layer mask in order to blend the red car and its splash into the Blue Bus scene.

◆ Use one of the brushes from the middle set, which have 80% hardness, painting with black to cleanly remove the original background from behind the roof of the red car.

◆ Set the Opacity of your brush to about 30%.

◆ Use a soft brush, from the third row of brushes, to blend the splash and underside of the front of the car with the road in the Blue Bus layer.

Color Correct the Red Car

10 When you have made some progress blending the car and its splash, color correct the car to match the rest of the scene.

◆ Click the Overall Color Correction Group thumbnail and drag this up until the line above the Red Car layer is highlighted.

◆ Release the mouse at this point, and the color corrections you made to the Blue Bus layer are applied to the Red Car layer as well.

The two layers should now look good together, but if not, continue to work on the Red Car layer mask. If you are having trouble getting it to work, check out the version in the file called RainInCostRicaFinalCC.psd in the folder for this chapter on your DVD.

Resize the Car

11 The red car may now look a little small because we have moved it in front of the blue bus and closer to your point of view, so it needs to be a bit bigger in relationship to the bus. Once you begin to Free Transform the car, if you can't see the corner handles to do the transform, press the Escape key to get out of Free Transform, then close palettes, put your window in Full Screen mode, or do whatever you need to do to have room to scale this layer. You will want to hold down the Shift key in Free Transform while scaling the car so that the scaling stays proportional. We held the Shift key down, then clicked and dragged the top-right handle up and to the right to increase

11 Here is the red car in relationship to the blue bus before we scale the car.

11 Here is how the car and bus look after the car is scaled up by 145% and also moved to this new location further to the left and front of the bus.

typing a new value into either the horizontal or vertical scale text box. For a review of what Free Transform can do, see Chapter 8, "Transformation of Images, Layers, Paths, and Selections." When you are happy with the Free Transform, press Return (Enter) to see it in full resolution. You will probably now want to click the Layer Mask thumbnail in this Red Car layer so you can go back and edit this mask a bit more using black and white with the Brush. To get our red car to look right, we scaled it up by 145% in width and height, and moved it further to the left and front until part of it was no longer visible. We also used [Command (Ctrl)-F3] at this point to add a Grouped Curves adjustment layer to the Red Car layer and then used this to darken the car a bit in relationship to the Blue Bus scene. You can load our DarkenCarCurve.acv curve settings from the Chapter 28 folder on the DVD.

Add the Running Woman

12 The last element of this composite is the running woman.

◆ Click the word *Woman* in the Layers palette to activate that layer.

◆ Type L to go back to your Lasso tool, and make sure the Feather is still set to 3. Make a very loose selection around the edge of the woman and the shadow of her feet and legs on the pavement. Make sure this selection is wide enough to be considerably more than the 3-pixel feather away from the edges of the woman.

◆ Click the Add Layer Mask icon at the bottom of the Layers palette to remove the parts of the Woman layer you are sure you won't be using.

11 The red car and blue bus after our final edits on the mask for the red car to tone down the splash a little. At this point, we have not yet added the Grouped Darken Car curve to the Red Car layer.

the size of the car. You can then release the mouse from the corner handle and move the red car's position by clicking and dragging in the center area of the scaling box.

◆ Click the Red Car Layer thumbnail to be sure that layer is active, then press Command (Ctrl)-T to use Free Transform so you can scale and move the red car.

◆ Scale the car and reposition it until you are happy with its size and location.

◆ Lock the position of the Red Car layer when you finish scaling and moving it.

The Options bar at the top of the screen gives you the amount of scaling you have done so far; you can change this amount by just

12 The initial Lasso selection for the woman.

13 The tighter selection of the woman made with the Wand and then the Lasso.

13 After saving the above selection to the Woman mask channel, and then deselecting that selection, we Gaussian Blur the mask by 1 to soften the edges. The final step is to blend the woman's hair and foot shadow with the Blue Bus layer's background.

13 Here's the Woman layer mask as it is on the final version of this example on the DVD.

13 Here's that same mask finessed with brushes that use Shape Dynamics.

Refine the Woman Mask

13 Now you are going to refine the mask, then reposition and resize the woman if necessary. When you move or scale a layer that has a linked layer mask attached, the mask also moves and scales in the same ways. When you normally add a layer mask using the Add layer Mask icon or the Layer/Layer Mask menu, that mask is linked to the layer. You can see the small Link icon between the layer's Layer thumbnail and its layer mask thumbnail.

◆ Type a W to switch to the Magic Wand. Make sure the Tolerance is set to 32 and that Contiguous is checked.

◆ Click the Layer thumbnail for the Woman layer and make a tighter selection on the woman by Shift-clicking several times in the black areas of her clothes.

◆ After selecting what you can this way with the Wand, type L to switch to the Lasso tool, then press Return (Enter), 2, and Return (Enter) again to set the Feather to 2.

◆ Now with the Shift key down, add in the areas that were not selected by the Wand. I've set the Feather to 2 because in the original image the woman is a bit soft along the edges since she is running.

◆ Choose Select/Save Selection and save to the Woman Mask channel using the Replace Selection option.

◆ Choose Select/Deselect to get rid of your selection, since it already has been saved to a mask and we now are going to want to blur that mask.

◆ Choose Filter/Blur/Gaussian Blur and do a blur of 1 to make her edges a bit softer than the Magic Wand did.

◆ Type B for the brush and click the Airbrush icon on the Options bar. Use soft brushes with a Flow of about 10% to blend the woman's flopping black hair and foot shadow into the Blue Bus layer's background. If you are using a tablet, select a brush with Shape Dynamics on, raise the Flow to about 20%, and turn off the Airbrush setting.

13 Here we see the composite with the running woman added into the original Blue Bus scene.

14 Your final Layers palette should look like this.

As you can see from the illustration above, hair is a good place to use a pressure-sensitive tablet and a stylus for masking. You should also drag the Overall Color Correction layer set up above the Woman layer so it's color corrected in the same way as the other two. Since all three of the Blue Bus, Red Car, and Woman shots were taken at the same time with the same roll of film and only seconds apart, it is possible and even beneficial to use the same color corrections on all three layers. Keep working on the Woman layer mask until she blends in well.

Finish the Composite

14 Now your composite should be almost complete. We liked the location of the woman where she was, but if you don't, you can click the word *Woman* in the Woman layer to reactivate it, then use the Move tool to move that layer around, as you did the other layers earlier.

◆ Turn the Eye icon back on for the top Bus Window layer.

◆ When the location is final, lock the position of the Woman layer.

◆ Drag the Overall Color Correction layer set to the very top of the Layers palette; the composite should now look complete.

For a more realistic composite, you'd want to add some rain on the bus windshield and maybe blur the wipers. The more realistic details you add, the better your composite will look.

29 ◆ Portrait Compositing

Composite faces or portions of faces to create a pleasing family portrait. Retouch faces with a variety of methods, then use the Extract tool to replace the background.

From left to right we have Wolf, Justin, Denise, and Zach; the Wagman/Saunders family. This is the best overall portrait, taken in Barry and Wendy's carport at the end of a family vacation.

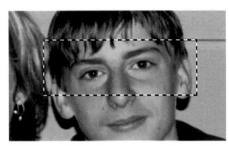

2 Take about this much of Zach.

As is often the case when you take family portraits, this image has a couple of faces that start out right about where you want them, one that has some minor issues, and one that needs to be replaced completely. In this example, we'll replace Justin's head and Zach's eyes, do some retouching, primarily on Denise and Wolf, then use the Extract tool to knock out the background and replace it with something more pleasant.

Decide Which Images to Use

1 The first thing we have to do is look at the different images we shot and decide which parts of each to use. The best overall image is the one in which Denise and Wolf look good, Zach looks good except he's looking in the wrong direction, and Justin looks, well, not very good; so we'll work with that image since it's the best one. Two other images have much better pictures of Justin, but not great of anyone else, and a fourth has a good picture of Zach. We'll use the Arrange command to look at everything.

◆ Open BestOverall.psd, BestJustin1.psd, BestJustin2.psd, and BestZach.psd from the Ch29.Portrait Compositing folder on the *Photoshop Artistry* DVD.

2 Take about this much of Justin from BestJustin1.

◆ Close any other files that you currently have open, press Tab to hide all your palettes, then use Window/Arrange/Tile Horizontally to tile the images.

◆ Choose Window/Arrange/Match Zoom and Location to show the same area of each image onscreen and at the same zoom percentage.

◆ Scroll and zoom the images to decide how much of each to take to replace the areas in the BestOverall.psd image that need replacing. If your Zoom and Hand tools are not set up to adjust all windows, hold down the Shift key as you zoom or scroll.

Let's use the face from BestJustin1.psd.

Copy to the Overall Best Image

2 We're going to copy Justin's head but only Zach's eyes to the composite image. Make sure you take some of the area around Justin's head including a bit of both his parents' shoulders, to make lining up the images easier.

◆ Close BestJustin2.psd. and click BestOverall.psd to make it the active image. Type F to put the image in Full Screen mode.

◆ Use the Window menu to bring BestJustin1.psd to the foreground, making it the active image.

◆ Type M for the Marquee tool and select Justin's head and neck.

◆ Type V for the Move tool and move this portion of the image to the BestOverall.psd image, then close BestJustin1.psd.

◆ Double-click the name, Layer 1, and rename this layer Justin.

◆ Use the Window menu to bring BestZach.psd to the foreground and make it the active image.

◆ Type M for the Marquee tool and select Zach's eyes, then type V for the Move tool and move that section to the BestOverall.psd image.

◆ Close the BestZach.psd image. Double-click the name for the new layer you created and rename it Zach.

Adjust Composited Portions and Create Masks

It's not enough to simply stick a head in place. You need to match size, color, contrast, and lighting. We generally create a group of layers to color correct each separate composited image to match the background; then we do the overall color correction for the entire image. That way, if any individual piece does not match, we can go back to the color correction layers for that particular piece and tweak its adjustments. In this portrait, we're lucky because the lighting on Zach matches well, so that leaves only Justin for us to color correct; a simple curve will take care of that. Both composited images need to be transformed to fit better.

Adjust Justin

3a These were originally Camera Raw images, but this image of Justin was opened at a different time than the others and the settings were slightly different. You might have this same issue if you open different versions of the same file in order to change the Camera Raw settings to bring out details in a particular area. We'll match him to the background and reposition his face. Matching the color and contrast on the shirt color is more important than on the outer areas of the image. You'll need more of Justin's shirt than his jacket from the overlaid image. When trying to decide how to resize a composited piece, it's a good idea to try to line up any static points in the two images; we often use the eyes. While that won't work in this case, because Justin's eyes are in such different places in each image, you do have the line of the wood above Justin's head, and you'll need somehow to match up areas of Justin's jacket.

3b Lower the opacity of the layer to see how things are lining up and where you want to mask out the layer.

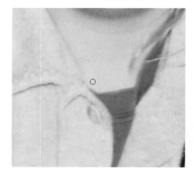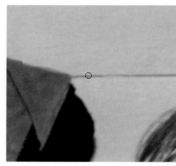

3a The two areas that I found were the most difficult to match were Justin's collar and neck, and the edge of Wolf's jacket and the line on the wall.

◆ Click the Justin layer to make it the active layer.

◆ Create a new Curves adjustment layer [Command (Ctrl)-F3], group it with the previous layer, and name the layer Adjust Justin.

◆ Use an S-curve to increase the contrast on Justin's composited head.

◆ Lower the opacity of the Justin layer to about 50% so you can see which areas you want to use from this image.

◆ Type Command (Ctrl)-T to free transform the Justin image. Click the Link icon between the width and height adjustment input areas to constrain the adjustment to proportional. We used 101.9%. Try to line up the line on the wall above Justin's head, as well as the bottom of his collar. Press the Return (Enter) key when you're happy with the free transform.

◆ Reset the Opacity of the Justin layer to 100%, and lock its position so you don't accidentally move it.

◆ Type B for the Brush tool, and from the Tool presets pop-up choose the Airbrush 7%. Type D for the default colors, then X to exchange the colors.

◆ Use Layer/Add Layer Mask/Reveal All, or click the Create a New Layer Mask icon on the Layers palette to add a layer mask to the Justin layer. Paint the edges of the Justin layer until it matches the background.

You'll need to pay particular attention to Justin's collar, and you'll have to decide which image to use for Denise's shoulder and scarf and Wolf's shoulder. Luckily, the clothes they're wearing have lots of folds and layers, which will make disguising the seams a bit easier. Make sure you don't have disappearing collars, buttons, or zippers. Use the Move tool and the arrow keys to reposition the layer if necessary

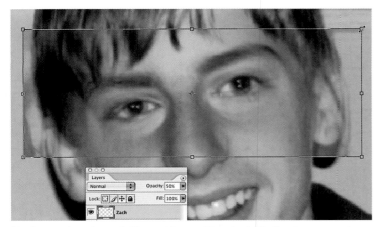

3b You can resize and rotate Zach's eyes at the same time using the Free Transform command.

to get a better composite. Raise or lower the flow of the brush, and change its size to make finer adjustments where necessary.

Adjust Zach

3b Zach is a much easier compositing job than his brother, but he still requires several adjustments. The eyes need to be resized, rotated, and masked. You'll need to decide which set of eyebrows you want to use. We used the right eyebrow from the Zach layer and the left eyebrow from the Background layer.

◆ Lower the opacity of the Zach layer to about 50%.

◆ Type V for the Move tool, and move the eyes basically into position.

◆ Type Command (Ctrl)-T for Free Transform, make sure the Link icon is on, and scale and rotate the eyes. We scaled down to 94.4% and rotated −1.3°. Press Return (Enter) to accept the transformation.

◆ Bring the opacity of the layer back to 100% and lock the position of the layer by clicking the third icon (it looks like a cross) in the lock section at the top of the Layers palette.

◆ Click the Create New Layer Mask icon at the bottom of the Layers palette to create a new mask for Zach's layer.

◆ Type B for the Brush tool. You should still have the Airbrush preset, but if not, click the Tool Preset pop-up and choose the Airbrush 7%.

◆ Paint the layer mask to blend the edges of the Zach layer with the Background layer.

◆ If you have not already done so, save the file.

Do Overall Color Corrections

4 You are now ready to create the overall adjustment layers for the image. This image does have both a good highlight and a good shadow point. The highlight is in Zach's T-shirt, and the shadow is in the creases of the right arm of Wolf's jacket. The image also has a bit of a green cast. If you've been working through the examples in this book, you've done a lot of color correction, so give this a try. If you have questions or want to see what choices we made, open BestOverallBuild.psd from the Chapter 29 folder on the DVD. Here are the basic steps, without the settings, for these corrections.

◆ Create a new Levels adjustment layer [Command (Ctrl)-F2]. Set the highlight, shadow, and contrast, then correct for color casts. Name the layer Overall Levels.

◆ Create a new Curves adjustment layer [Command (Ctrl)-F3]. Adjust the contrast. Name the layer Overall Curves.

◆ Create a new Hue/Saturation adjustment layer [Command (Ctrl)-F4]. Saturate the colors. Name the layer Overall Hue/Sat.

◆ Shift-click the three adjustment layers, and type Command (Ctrl)-G to group the layers. Name the group Overall Corrections.

Retouch Denise

5 This is a fairly good picture of Denise, but we can remove minor imperfections, give better color balance to the face, and do a little modeling with light and shadow to make the overall effect a little more pleasing. We're going to make a copy of Denise's face above the Background layer, then make several adjustment layers on top of

5 Denise, before the retouch, on the left, and after the retouch, on the right. A little less shiny, a little less red. Just a little brighter. And a little is usually all you want.

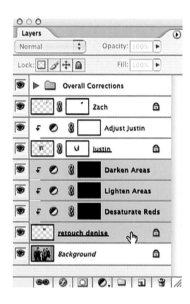

5 Shift-click contiguous layers, then type Command (Ctrl)-G to group them. If the layers are not right above each other, you can Command (Ctrl)-click them to highlight them for grouping. Groups are a great way to keep track of numerous layers and keep your palette organized.

that and group them all together. See Chapter 26, "Restoring Old Photos," for tips on the retouching elements of this step.

◆ Click the *Background* layer to make it the active layer.

◆ Type M and marquee Denise's face. Type Command (Ctrl)-J to jump this selection to a new layer, then lock the position of the layer.

◆ Type J or Shift-J until you get the Spot Healing brush. Correct minor blemishes and shiny spots. Type Shift-J again until you have the Patch tool for the large shiny spot on her left cheek. Name the layer Retouch Denise.

◆ Type B for the Brush tool, lower the opacity to 20%, then Option (Alt)-click her lips to choose a red color to lightly paint areas of the lips that are burned out.

◆ Create a Hue/Saturation adjustment layer to desaturate the reds of her face and make them a bit more yellow than magenta. Add a layer mask, invert it, and use the Brush tool to use the adjustment only where you need it.

◆ Create a Curves adjustment layer to lighten areas, invert it, and paint with the Brush tool to gently lighten portions of the skin. Name this layer Lighten Areas.

◆ Create a Curves adjustment layer to darken the light strip under the chin and on the left cheek. Invert the mask, paint it, and name the layer Darken Areas.

◆ Shift-click the four layers you just created, and type Command (Ctrl)-G to group the layers. Name the group Denise's Face.

Correct Five-O'Clock Shadow

6 Wolf's face is also basically good, except for the five-o'clock shadow. That definitely needs to be taken care of. We do this via a Gaussian Blur layer, a useful technique for correcting skin in a lot of portrait retouching. However, you'll see that the technique can quickly get out of hand, making your subject look like plastic, so use it sparingly.

◆ Click the Background layer to make it active.

◆ Type M and marquee Wolf's face, then type Command (Ctrl)-J to jump his face to a new layer. Name the layer Retouch Wolf and lock its position.

◆ Go to Filter/Blur/Gaussian Blur, and blur this entire layer by about 4.5 to 5 pixels.

◆ Add a layer mask, invert it, and use the Brush tool to paint out Wolf's beard. Use a smaller brush around the sharper edges of the nose, cheek, and lips. You can also use this same layer to soften the lines around the eyes and on the forehead.

◆ Change the Opacity of this layer to about 85%.

◆ Create a new Curves adjustment layer, and group it with the previous layer to use the Retouch Wolf mask as the mask for this adjustment. Lighten the area of the beard in the RGB channel, then use the individual channels to match the color of this area

6 At first glance, the blurred version of Wolf looks pretty good. But when you lower the opacity of that layer to 85% and add a Curves adjustment layer and Hue/Saturation adjustment layer, you can see how much more realistic and natural the second version is.

of the face a bit better to the forehead. It won't match exactly, but get as close as you can. Name this layer Correct Beard.

◆ Create a new Hue/Saturation adjustment layer and group it with the previous layer as well. Saturate the Master slider by about 5% or 6%. This brings the color of the skin back to the same intensity as the rest of the face. Name this layer Resaturate, then save the file.

Liquify

The Liquify command or filter is a really useful tool for making facial corrections. It is, however, a destructive tool; that is, it actually changes the pixels of your image. So make sure you use it on a copy of the file. We use Liquify to open eyes; to slim noses, cheeks, and other body parts; and to rectify aberrations that have been caused by camera angles. Although it is not a difficult tool to use, it does require some practice, and you need to know what each tool is good for. We're going to take a break from the exercise for a moment to explain how to best use Liquify.

Choose Only What You Need

One key to successful operation within the Liquify dialog is to use a selection to isolate the portion of the face or body you want to work with. Liquify is very memory intensive and the larger the area you open, the longer your processing time. Also, it's a good idea to do each bit of retouching in a separate Liquify session. That is if you have to do an eye and a cheek, do one first, exit Liquify, check your work, reenter Liquify, then do the other area. That way if you don't like the result of one part of the retouch, you don't have to do it all over again.

Learn the Tools

There are a lot of tools in the Liquify toolbox. The default settings for the tool seem far too heavy-handed for most photographic uses, so lower the Brush Rate and Brush Pressure to 30% or less for more control. Keep the Brush Density at a very low number for realistic retouching. For most retouch jobs, we use several small motions or clicks to achieve the effect we want, even if the brush is one that can accumulate an effect when you hold in one position. The tools Wendy uses most often are Pucker, Bloat, Push, Freeze, and Reconstruct. From top to bottom the tools are:

Warp This tool pushes pixels forward as you drag. When you use it, be very careful of the direction of your drag. It's easy to create unsightly lines as you drag. If this happens, you can often use the Reconstruct tool to modify your result.

Reconstruct This tool brings back the original image detail in specific areas. The Reconstruct mode in the Reconstruct Options section of the dialog controls how this tool makes its corrections.

Twirl This tool twirls pixels clockwise from the center of the brush. Using Option (Alt) along with the tool twirls in a counterclockwise direction. The tool is useful for creating whirlpools and eddies in water and some special effects.

Pucker This tool is akin to the Pinch filter because it pulls pixels in toward the center of the brush. It's useful for slimming the bridge of the nose, for moving or changing folds in clothing, and sometimes for dealing with flyaway hair.

Bloat This tool pushes pixels out from the center of the brush in a spherical fashion. It is usually a good tool for opening eyes, and can also be used to widen the bridge of a too-thin nose or straighten a nose that has a crook in it.

Push This tool pushes pixels to the left when you drag straight up or to the right as you drag straight down. This is Wendy's favorite tool for slimming cheeks, jowls, hips, thighs, and anything else that needs it.

Mirror This tool copies pixels from the side of the stroke to where you make the stroke. None of us has ever been able to make this tool do anything that we couldn't do much easier and better another way.

Turbulence As the name implies, this tool pushes the pixels around in a chaotic but smooth fashion when held in one place. If you move the tool, it acts much like the Warp tool but with more finesse. Adobe lists it as being good for creating fire, clouds, and waves. None of us creates effects, but I'm sure if Adobe says it, it must be true.

Freeze This tools allows you to paint a mask over areas that you want to leave unaffected by whatever tool you're using. This is most helpful. Use it to freeze keylights in the eyes when you use the Bloat tool or to freeze the pupil if you don't want it to dilate. Freeze nostrils if you don't want them to pinch, or any folds or creases that need to stay in place. Most helpful.

Thaw If you find you've painted too much with the Freeze tool, use this "eraser" to unfreeze portions.

Learn the Settings

The Tool options control how the all the brushes in Liquify will behave. Unlike with Photoshop itself, the settings do not change from tool to tool. Density controls how much feather is on a brush. The

Diane's pupil is very close to her bottom lid, so you'll need to freeze more of it than we did here. We made three or four clicks with the Bloat tool here rather than holding in one spot. We also had to use the Reconstruct tool on a bit of the iris.

Use smooth strokes on the jaw and shave a bit at a time.

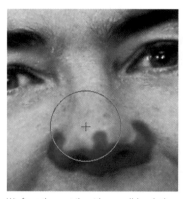

We froze the nostrils with a small brush then switched to a larger brush for the Pucker tool. Once again, we made several quick clicks rather than holding down the mouse and pinching the nose.

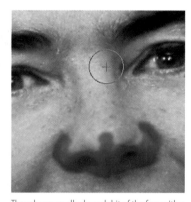

Though we usually do each bit of the face with a different iteration of Liquify, here we have done the upper portion of the nose with the Bloat tool after having done the lower portion.

Diane before retouching.

Diane after retouching. We've used the Healing brush, the Patch tool, and Liquify.

lower the density, the softer the brush. Set this high and you create a real sledgehammer that makes changes with little or no subtlety. Pressure controls how quickly changes are made when you drag a brush, whereas Rate controls how quickly changes occur when a brush is in a stationary position, such as with Twirl, Pucker, and Bloat. Jitter applies only to the Turbulence brush and controls how shaky the turbulence is when you use the tool. At a low setting, it's like stirring paint together. At a very high rate, it's like a cocktail shaker. Reconstruction Mode applies only to the Reconstruct tool. Although we use Revert almost exclusively, other options may give you a smoother or more interesting transition from the Liquified state back to the original. The Stylus Pressure check box applies if you are using a tablet and want to use its pressure sensitivity to control the brush. Sometimes we use Stylus Pressure, sometimes we don't.

Practice, Practice, Practice

Liquify is not a tool you'll learn to use well in a single session. Its rewards are great if you do a lot of retouching, but it's going to take some time to learn to use it well. To that end, we have a few practice situations for you to try.

◆ Open the Diane.psd file from the Chapter 29 folder on the DVD.

◆ Use the Freeze tool to freeze portions of the right eye, then use the Bloat tool to open the eye a bit.

◆ Use the Push tool in a downward path to slim Diane's jawline on the right side.

◆ Freeze the nostrils, then use the Pucker tool to narrow the bottom of the nose a bit, and use the Bloat tool to straighten the upper-left portion of the nose, near the eye.

Use Liquify to Open the Eye

7 Now that you know more about how Liquify works, let's use it to open Wolf's right eye just a bit. Remember, with Liquify, do a little at a time, even if you have to re-enter Liquify several times.

◆ Once again, return to the Background layer. Use the Marquee tool to select only Wolf's right eye and jump the selection to a new layer. Lock the position of the layer and name it Eye Only.

◆ Move this layer in the Layers palette above the Resaturate adjustment layer. Don't worry if you brought back some eye wrinkles—you can mask those out or delete them later.

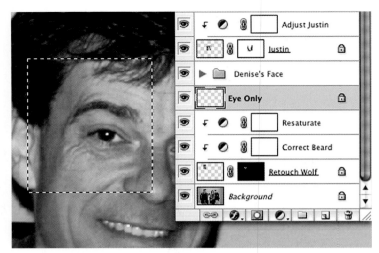

7 When you move the Eye Only layer above the other Wolf layers, you may reintroduce some lines around the eye because you are copying information from the unretouched layer, but they can be removed with a layer mask.

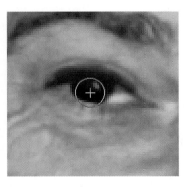

7 Freeze the upper portion of the eye before using the Bloat tool.

◆ Use the Marquee tool on the Eye Only layer to select the eye. Hide the marquee by typing Command (Ctrl)-H, then go to Filter/Liquify to enter the Liquify dialog.

◆ With the Freeze tool, paint over the top portion of the iris and over the pupil. Then use the Bloat tool at about the size of the iris. Keep the settings low and open the eye only a bit at the bottom. If you go too far, click the Restore All button in the Reconstruct options section of the dialog and try again.

◆ When you think you've made a good adjustment, click OK.

◆ Type Command (Ctrl)-Z several times to see if you like your correction.

◆ If you need to, add a layer mask to this Eye Only layer, and paint with black on the mask to hide portions of this layer that cover the work you did with other three Wolf layers.

◆ Select the four Wolf layers by Shift-clicking them, and use Command (Ctrl)-G to group them. Name the group Correct Wolf.

Correct Justin Again

Now that we've done all the corrections to the rest of the family, Justin looks a bit washed out.

Add a Photo Filter Layer

8a There are many ways to add a little color to an image, but when no other problems such as contrast or color casts need attention, Wendy sometimes uses a Photo Filter adjustment layer—and that's what we're going to do here. If there's absolutely no information on the film at all, if it's completely blown out, turn off Preserve Luminosity. That way, color will cover the blown-out areas. In Justin's case, we just want to add a bit of oomph, so we kept Preserve Luminosity checked. Because the filter layer comes in above the Adjust Justin layer, it's grouped with Justin's head. You'll need to add a layer mask to take out portions of the face like the eyes that should not be part of this adjustment. We're simply adding warmth to the cheeks, neck, and a bit to the hair.

◆ Click the Adjust Justin layer to make it active.

◆ Choose Photo Filter from the Create a New Fill or Adjustment Layer icon at the bottom of the Layers palette.

◆ Choose the Warming 85 filter. Leave Preserve Luminosity on and use the default value of 25%. Click OK to create the adjustment layer.

◆ Add a layer mask to the Photo Filter layer, invert it, and paint with white where you want the adjustment.

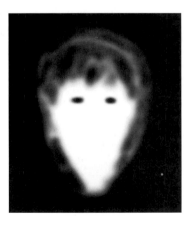

8a This is the mask we created for the Photo Filter layer.

Use the Red Eye Tool

8b Although Justin's red eye problem is minimal, we might as well take care of it while we're here. It's simple enough with Photoshop's Red Eye tool.

◆ Click the Justin Layer to make it active.

◆ Type Shift-J until you are in the Red Eye tool. Set both the Pupil Size and Darken Amount to 30%.

◆ Click with the tool on the red area of one eye and then the other. It will take Photoshop a few seconds to process the Red Eye change, so be patient.

If you like, you can use the Red Eye tool on Denise and Zach as well. You'll want to change the settings on the tool, especially for Zach. For him, we used 15% for pupil size and only 10% for darkening.

Brighten Teeth

9 Again, this portrait is in good condition, but we usually do a little eye and teeth brightening on most portraits before printing. We're only going to do a little to the teeth here, and we'll be quick about it. We add blue to the image via the curve, because white that contains blue is perceived as being brighter than white that contains yellow.

◆ Click the Overall Corrections group to make it active, then create a new Curves adjustment layer.

◆ Lighten the image by clicking the middle of the RGB curve and moving it upward, then switch to the Blue curve and add blue to the image by moving the midpoint of that curve upward as well. Click OK to accept the adjustment and name this layer Brighten Teeth.

◆ Type Command (Ctrl)-I to invert the layer mask.

◆ Type B for the brush tool, D for the default colors, then X to exchange the colors. Use the Airbrush 7% tool preset, but make the brush about 10 to 15 pixels.

◆ Airbrush the mask to brighten the teeth on Zach, Denise, and Wolf.

◆ Save the file.

Sharpen

10 At this point our file is starting to be a bit bulky, so we're going to create a flattened duplicate to sharpen and extract. Because we

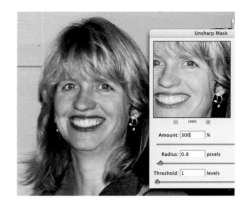

10 Keep an eye on Denise's face as you sharpen. Hers is the most critical face. It's fairly soft, but over-sharpened—you can see how the eyes start to pop too much. Here we like the overall effect, but we'll need to soften the effect of the flash on her eyes.

are dealing with faces, we're going to use Barry's SharpenOnly EdgesBH action. This constrains the sharpening filter to only the edges of objects, and for faces it works really well. It sharpens the eyes, lips, and edges of features without sharpening the pores of the skin. It also gives you a mask to work with, so if an area is oversharpened or undersharpened, you can paint the mask to make further corrections. This action does, however, convert your file to Lab color space. You'll probably want to convert back to RGB to composite and print.

◆ Go to Image/Duplicate [F5] and click Duplicate Merged Layers Only to create a flattened duplicate of the file.

◆ Type F to put the image in Full Screen mode, then type Command-Option (Ctrl-Alt)-0 to view the image at 100%.

◆ Type [Command (Ctrl)-F5] to run the SharpenOnlyEdgesBH action. When the Unsharp Mask dialog appears, move the sliders until you feel the image is appropriately sharpened. Turn the Preview check box on and off to help you choose your settings. We used 300, .8, and 2. Click OK to create the Sharpen layer and mask.

◆ Make sure you are on the mask for the sharpened layer. Type B for the Brush tool, D for the default colors, then X to exchange the colors. Using the Airbrush 7% tool preset, gently paint the mask for each person's eyes to lessen the effect of the sharpening.

◆ Save this file as Wagman/SharpExtract.

The Extract Filter

Unless you find the interior of carports attractive, you'll probably want to put a different background behind your carefully crafted portrait. Depending on the complexity of the image you work on, you may not need to make a detailed selection of the person or persons before you superimpose them on another image. Often a loose selection with the Lasso suffices if you are adept at painting on a layer mask. This also allows you to choose the amount of softness between the two images. But there are times when you need a more detailed selection, and, especially when wisps of hair are involved, the Extract tool can do a lot of the masking work for you.

As with most of the "automatic" selection tools, Extract is rarely perfect. With some photos you'll have no additional work to do to make your composition look seamless, but most of the time you'll want to do some additional masking. For this reason, it's better to use your extracted layer as a guide for the layer mask rather than using the extracted layer itself. Then you can still add a layer mask and delete portions of the image. If you take too much away with Extract and you haven't saved a copy of the layer, there's nothing you can do but go back and do the whole extraction over again. You can't create information where there is none, unless you're an incredibly good painter. And then, you'd be doing things the hard way.

With Extract, you always want to make a copy of the layer and work on the copy. Yes, we mean always. Extract deletes all the pixels it does not use and that's always dangerous. So even if you think you don't need it, make a copy. Also, Extract does not currently work with 16-bit images, so you'll have to convert 16-bit images to 8 bits per channel to use the Extract command.

Once you are in the Extract window, you must take several steps to make a good extraction.

Highlight the Edges

First you need to completely highlight the edges of the items you want to extract. Use the smallest brush you can manage that overlaps both the background and the edge that you want to keep. Turn on Smart Highlighting for edges that are sharp. For areas that are blurry and soft, such as wisps of hair, you need to highlight the wisps as well, so it's easier if you turn off Smart Highlighting in these areas. Try not to add highlight over the holes in the hair. You may even need to choose a very small eraser to erase highlighting in those areas. If you are lucky, the new background will match up reasonably well with what the Extract command does, and there won't be too much touch-up to do. But don't expect Extract to be perfect.

Fill the Interior

The second task in the Extract process is to fill the highlighted area. To do this you use the Paint Bucket tool in the Extract toolbox. Simply click inside the highlighted area. If the highlight spills over into the background, your highlight was incomplete somewhere; it needs to be a closed loop. Click the Highlight tool again and scroll around the image to find the missing areas. Once you complete the highlight, use the Paint Bucket again.

Cleanup and Edge

Once you've done the highlight and fill, you can preview the extraction by clicking the Preview button. Check first for any major mistakes you've made, and correct them through rehighlighting and refilling. Then the real fun begins. The fifth tool in the toolbox is the Cleanup tool. If your extracted image has pixels from the background still clinging to it, brushing over with the Cleanup tool will get rid of them. If the extraction has bitten into the area you want to keep, Option (Alt)-dragging with the tool will bring those areas back from the original image. Make sure you try your images with different backgrounds in the Preview section of the dialog. You can use a white, gray, or black mask, a Quick Mask red overlay, or choose a color for the matte. We suggest that you try at least black, white, and gray once each. Some pixels will look artificial against white, but perfectly fine against gray or black. Or good against black and terrible against white. In the Preview section, you can also switch back to the original image to see what has been removed.

If you need a sharper edge in some areas, you can drag over your image with the Edge Touchup tool, the sixth tool in the toolbox. This tool will discard or push pixels that do not appear to be part of the edge, leaving you with a very sharp outline.

Extract

Only when you have the best preview you can possibly get do you want to click OK to perform the extraction. You can't go back into the Extract dialog and reload the settings you just made; you have to start the highlighting process all over again. And getting a good extraction is not a fast process on an image like the one we're going to use here. Expect to spend some time to get it right.

Extract the Family

11 In this particular extraction, you have hard edges around the clothing and soft edges around the hair. Once inside the Extract dialog, you'll need to turn Smart Highlighting on and off as you move around the image. Keep it on where you have sharp edges. The most difficult areas of this extraction are the places where dark clothing is in front of dark shadows (plan to do cleanup here) and the tiny wisps of hair on the right side of Denise's face.

◆ Type Command-Option (Ctrl-Alt)-E to merge the lower two layers into one layer. Name this layer Merged. Drag this layer to

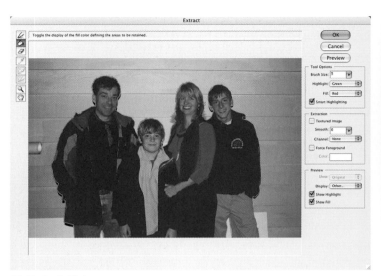

11 Use Smart Highligting on the clothing. **11** Turn Smart Highlighting off for wispy hair.

11 The family filled.

11 The family highlighted.

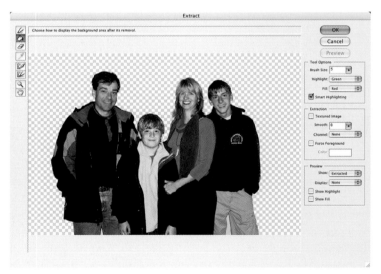

11 The initial extraction.

the Create a New Layer icon on the bottom of the Layers palette to make a copy of the layer. Name this copy Extract. Turn off the Eye icon for the Merged layer.

◆ Go to Image/Mode and convert to 8 bits per channel.

◆ Use Filter/Extract to enter the Extract dialog.

◆ Click the Highlighter tool, turn on Smart Highlighting and start the highlight at the lower right of Wolf's pant. Work in a clockwise fashion, turning off Smart Highlighting when you reach

an area with hair. Go all the way around the family. If you need to erase highlighting, hold down the Option (Alt) key with the Highlighter tool and it will become an eraser.

◆ Click the Paint Bucket tool and fill the area you want to keep with color. We changed the fill color to red to make it easier to see against all the blue clothing and background.

◆ Click the Preview button to see the initial extraction.

◆ Zoom in and inspect the edges of the extraction.

11 Wolf's jacket against the White matte shows some definite problems.

11 Denise's hair doesn't look great against the Black matte. Photoshop had a lot of difficulty deciding what was hair and what was background. Part of the problem is the ambient blue light cast on her hair from the flash against the wall. We'll have to deal with that down the line.

11 Wolf's hair looks good on the White matte.

- Click the Cleanup tool (the fifth one) and drag over areas that need to be removed from the extract. Option (Alt)-drag over areas where you need to reinstate portions of the original image.

- In the Preview area, change the Display to White matte, Black matte, then Gray matte, and inspect the edges each time, making corrections as necessary.

- Click OK when you have the best extraction you can get.

Use the Extract Layer for a Layer Mask

12 If you need to work fast and you don't have to be completely accurate, you can drop the Extract layer on top of a new background. Or if you had an image with really good edges and Extract did a great job—well, then, you're done. But trust us on this, most of the time you'll want to use your extracted version as the basis for a layer mask. That's what we'll do here.

- Command (Ctrl)-click the layer thumbnail for the Extract layer to load that layer as a selection.

- Click the Merged layer to make it active, then click the Add a Layer Mask icon at the bottom of the Layers palette to create a layer mask from the selection.

Add a New Background

13 We're going to bring the background over to this image rather than bringing this layer over to the background. You could do it either way.

- Click the Sharpen layer to make it the active layer.

- Open the MollysReach.psd image from the folder for chapter 29 on the DVD.

- Type V for the Move tool, click the Background layer, and Shift-drag it over to the WagmanSharpExtract image. It should fit perfectly.

Finesse the Mask

14 There was a bit of a halo on our subjects when we added the new background on our image. Depending on how tightly you did your extract, you may or may not have a halo on your image. To correct this, we threw away our layer mask for the Merged layer and created a new one, again using the Extracted layer as the starting point.

14 You can see a bit of a halo around everyone's hair and Denise's shoulder when we used the Extracted layer without modification to create the layer mask.

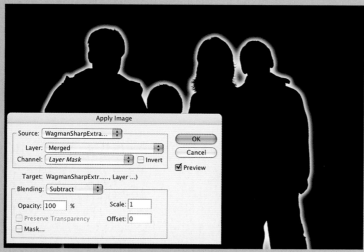

15 After contracting the selection to create the layer mask and adding a photo filter on Denise's hair, you can see how much better the transition is.

◆ Go to Select/Modify/Contract and contract this selection by one or two pixels, then again click the Add a Layer Mask icon at the bottom of the Layers palette.

You may find that you still need to paint on the layer mask to bring back detail or smooth rough edges. Remember that painting white on the mask will return portions of the Wagman/Saunders family, while painting black will show more areas of the MollysReach image.

And Finally

15 Remember when we mentioned the blue ambient light on Denise's hair? We took care of that by making a loose lasso selection and adding a Photo Filter layer. We also added a curve to increase contrast in the portrait, a curves layer above the Molly's Reach layer to open up and warm up the background, and another curve to add a few lighter, red highlights to everyone's hair to suggest reflections from the many red lights in the room. For the version at the beginning of this exercise, we linked all the layers that adjust the Merged layer and then used the Move tool to move the family into a more natural position. Then we cropped the image.

◆ Take a look at the final WagmanSharpExtract image on the DVD. Look at the layers, adjustment layers, and layer masks. Double-click the adjustment layer icons to see what settings we used for each of the layers.

Happy compositing!

How'd They Build That Mask?

On the Shadow layer, this is the how the layer mask controls where the shadow falls. To build it we once again loaded the Extract layer as a selection. This time we expanded the selection by 15 pixels using Select/Modify/Expand and then used Select/Feather and feathered the selection by an additional 15 pixels. At that point we created a Curves adjustment layer, and the top illustration became the mask for that layer. Next, we used Image/Apply Image and subtracted the Merged layer's layer mask from the one for the Curves adjustment layer. Apply Image is really useful for complex masks.

◆ Click the layer mask thumbnail (not the layer thumbnail) on the Merged layer, and drag it to the Trash icon at the bottom of the Layers palette. Discard it—do not Apply it.

◆ Command (Ctrl)-click again on the Extracted layer to load that layer as a selection. This does not make the layer visible or active—the Merged layer is still the active layer.

Portfolio

Barry Haynes

Barry had the honor in June 2006 of shooting pictures of the Pulling Together journey of British Columbia First Nations tribes and various Royal Canadian Mounted Police groups. This is an annual weeklong traditional First Nations Canoe event, which this year traveled the Sunshine Coast, where Barry and Wendy now live. Long days of paddling are followed in the evenings by greetings from local First Nations elders, traditional storytelling, drumming, and gift giving. Here a canoe is paddling about 6 a.m. up Sechelt Inlet after passing through world-famous Skookumchuck rapids.

30 ◆ Product Compositing

Create an image from components for a specified canvas size, like a magazine ad. Work with drop shadows, knockouts, the Pen tool, and linked layers for high-quality output. Use the Layer Comps palette to show three versions of the ad.

The PowerBookOrig.psd image.

The HeronOrig.psd image.

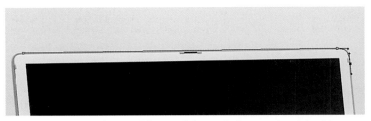

1 We started the path in the upper-left corner. Click to set the first point, then click and drag to set the next two points. Once you've set the third point, you can retract its handle to make a straight segment to the fourth point.

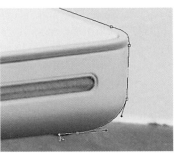

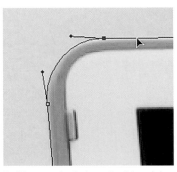

1 When you get ready to outline the computer's foot, you'll need to convert this handle so you have a corner point here.

1 When you finish the path, click and drag the point so that you have a curve with two handles.

In this exercise, you are going to create an ad for a computer brochure. The ad needs to be 7 inches wide by 5 inches high for a 150-line-screen print job. That means you need to have an image that is at least 2100 pixels wide by 1500 pixels high, because you need 300 dpi to print at 150 line screen. The image we are using is just slightly larger than that. You'll use the images above to build a new background with the computer sitting on the rock.

To complete the ad, you'll need to create an image to display on the screen of the PowerBook. Because you need a computer screen showing several images, and they need to fit the angle of the computer screen here, you'll composite all of the requisite images in another file, then bring them into this image as a group.

Create a Knockout Path

1 First, let's work on getting rid of all the extraneous clutter around the PowerBook. You want the edges of the computer to look sharp even if you resize or transform the computer to fit the background. So you will use a vector mask that can be edited at any time without affecting the pixels of the image. Fortunately, this PowerBook is a simple shape to draw. If you need practice with the Pen tool, you can go back to Chapter 28, "Compositing Multiple Images," and do the tutorial within that example. The long, straight edges of the computer need only 1 point at the beginning and 1 point at the edge. The curved edges need only 1 point before the curve and 1 point after the curve. We drew the path with just 17 points. We mention this

because the fewer points you use, the smoother the path will be. Use as many points as you need but no more. And remember, the Pen is not the most intuitive tool—it may take some practice.

◆ Open the file OrigPB.tif from the Ch30.Product Compositing folder on the DVD.

◆ Double-click the only layer in the Layers palette and name it PowerBook.

◆ Type P for the Pen tool and choose the middle Paths option at the top left of the Options bar. Make a path around the outside edge of the PowerBook. Start at the top-left edge of the Power-Book and click and drag curve points as you work your way around the computer, being careful to draw your path as close to the actual edge of the computer as possible.

◆ When you've drawn points all the way around the edge of the computer, click back on the original point to complete the path. Bring up the Paths palette [Shift-F11] and double-click the work path, renaming it Portable Outline. Click in the empty area of the Paths palette, toward the bottom, to deselect this path.

We have created a path called PowerBook in the Paths palette. You can use our path for guidance, or, if you get really frustrated with this step, you can use our path to create the vector mask in the next step. If you use our path, though, be sure to come back and work on your Pen tool technique until you're comfortable. It's worth the time and effort.

Create and Edit the PowerBook Vector Mask

2 In Chapter 28 we showed you how to use the Pen tool to make a layer mask by creating a path and turning it into a selection. Sometimes, however, you want to create a vector mask from the path. A vector mask, like a layer mask, hides portions of the file and reveals others. Unlike a layer mask, a vector mask always has a crisp, sharp edge, so it's not appropriate when you need gradual blending. However, an advantage of the vector mask is that you can activate the path that comprises the mask and edit it with great specificity. As you are editing the path by moving points or their handles, you may want to hide the path to see how the image has been affected. Use Command (Ctrl)-H to hide the path but still keep it active. Using the same command a second time will show the path again.

◆ In the Paths palette, click your Portable Outline path to activate it. Now click in the Layers palette on the PowerBook layer to activate the layer. Choose Layer/Add Vector Mask/Current Path. Adding this vector mask to the PowerBook layer should remove the background from around the PowerBook image.

◆ Type A for the Arrow tool, then press Shift-A until you get the white Arrow tool—the Direct Selection tool.

◆ Click the path once with this tool to bring up the path points; then to edit a point, click and drag it to a new position.

◆ If you see a white line on the edge of the PowerBook, then you need to move the path in a bit until the white edge disappears. Scroll around the entire edge of the PowerBook, editing the path until you see no white borders and the path is smooth and clean.

◆ Save this file to your hard drive. Press Command (Ctrl)-Shift-S, name the file PowerBook, and save it as a .psd file. You probably won't need it again, but if you do, you'll have a copy with your path and vector mask saved.

Move the PowerBook and Mask to the Background File

3 Now that you have a layer with a vector mask, you are going to move the layer and mask to an image that's going to be the background for your ad.

◆ Open the HeronOrig.psd file from the DVD and type F to put this image in Full Screen mode.

◆ Use the Window menu or Control (Ctrl)-Tab to bring the PowerBook image to the front.

◆ Type V for the Move tool and drag the PowerBook layer over to the HeronOrig.psd file. Move the image into position above the rock.

◆ You can now close the PowerBook file.

You'll notice that all you see is the PowerBook, but you've actually brought over the whole layer. We prefer to work this way, because if you delete portions of the image trying to get a nice tight knockout, you may find that you've deleted too much and have to redo the knockout.

Transform the PowerBook

4 You need to make the PowerBook look as if it's sitting on the rock more than it does now. It needs to be a bit smaller, rotated a little, and perhaps skewed to make it fit better. All of the transformations can be accomplished by using Free Transform. When we use this command

3 When you first place the PowerBook, it looks something like this.

4 Here, we've rotated the PowerBook. Notice how the point of transformation is now at the corner of the computer.

4 Our PowerBook at the end of step 4.

to rotate and skew, we're going to move the point of transformation from the center to the corner of the computer.

◆ Type Command (Ctrl)-T to invoke the Free Transform command.

◆ To scale the PowerBook proportionally, hold down the Shift key and pull one of the corner handles of the transform bounding box toward the center of the box. Notice the scaling percentages in the Options bar. Scale the computer to 97%.

◆ Now move the Point of Transformation icon from the center to the lower-left corner of the computer by clicking and dragging it. All transformations you do now will originate at this point.

◆ Rotate the PowerBook until the bottom of the computer is roughly parallel to the rock on which it sits.

This looks good, but you want the computer screen to angle back a little more. To do this, we need to distort the computer. You can do this by holding down the Command (Ctrl) key and moving one of the corner handles. You'll see that they now can move independently of each other. Alternatively, you can go back up to the Edit menu and choose Distort from the Transform options; with this method, you don't need to hold down any modifier key. You may also want to try Skew to achieve the look you want. For more information on Transform, be sure to read Chapter 8, "Transformation of Images, Layers, Paths, and Selections."

◆ Go to Edit/Transform and choose Distort, or hold down the Command (Ctrl) key and move the upper corners of the transform bounding box.

◆ When you complete all the transformations you want to make, press Return or Enter to accept the transformation.

Correct the Vector Mask

5 Depending on what transformations you made, you may or may not need to reedit the vector mask. In general, the vector mask is transformed with the layer, but sometimes when you change the point of transformation during the free transform, the vector mask will be just a little off. Luckily, because you are working with vectors, only a few tweaks usually need to be made.

5 You may need to tweak the vector mask after you make your transformation.

6 Here's the portable before and after neutralizing the color cast.

◆ Use the Direct Selection tool to edit the vector mask if needed.

Neutralize the Color Cast

6 Notice the brown color around the bottom of the computer and to a lesser extent on the upper-right side. This color cast is reflected light from the brown background of the original image. There's no reason for it to be in this image, so we need to get rid of it. We'll use a Hue/Saturation adjustment layer.

◆ Create a new Hue/Saturation adjustment layer [Command (Ctrl)-F3] and group it with the PowerBook layer by clicking Use Previous Layer to Create Clipping Mask.

◆ Completely desaturate the Master Saturation slider by moving it all the way to the left, then click OK. The adjustment layer is grouped with the PowerBook layer, so that vector mask keeps the adjustment from happening to the background. This works for the PowerBook because it's primarily neutral gray. In another image, you might want to just sample the offending color and desaturate that.

◆ As an optional step, you can create a blue color cast in the same areas by creating another grouped Hue/Saturation adjustment layer, clicking the Colorize button, and moving the sliders until you get a blue that looks like the water. After creating the adjustment layer, invert the mask and paint the blue color cast on areas

that might be affected by the water. See our final version for the settings and opacity we used.

◆ Shift-click the PowerBook layer and the color cast layer or layers, and use the Link icon at the bottom of the Layers palette to link them together in case you need to reposition the computer.

Add a Drop Shadow on the Computer

7 To give the computer more weight on the rock, you need to add a drop shadow. The drop shadow layer style is not exactly what you need, but you can start with that and modify it. When you are in the Drop Shadow areas of the Layer Style dialog, you can move the cursor over the image and notice that it becomes the Move tool. If you click and drag your drop shadow, you can easily move it to the position you want, relative to the object you're adding the shadow to. This will change the Distance and Angle values in the Drop Shadow subdialog. You can use the Opacity slider to change the darkness of the shadow, and you can use the Size slider to soften the shadow's edge. The Spread controls how quickly the shadow blends into the background. You can also change the Blend mode of the shadow, although Multiply usually works quite well. Finally, if you click the color to the right of the Blend Mode pop-up, you can bring up the Color Picker and change the hue of the shadow. We'll need to turn this shadow into a regular layer because we want to use Edit/Free Transform to make it match the lighting of this image.

◆ Click the layer thumbnail of the PowerBook layer, then double-click to the right of the word *PowerBook* to bring up the Layer Style dialog for this layer.

◆ Click the words *Drop Shadow* toward the top left of the dialog to create a drop shadow. This not only turns on the effect (which is

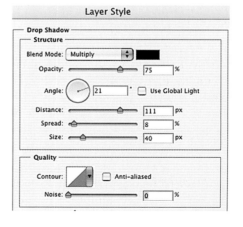

7 Here are the settings we used for the drop shadow layer style.

what happens when you click the check box), but also brings up the settings for the effect so you can modify them. See the settings in the illustration for this step to see our choices for the shadow.

After adjusting your shadow as much as you can in the dialog, click OK to add it to this layer as an effect. If you are not sure how dark to make it, it's better to make it darker than you think, because you can always make it lighter later by lowering the opacity of the future Shadow layer.

Nevertheless, no matter how you adjust the shadow in the Layer Styles dialog, you'll see that it simply doesn't look right in this instance. If you position the shadow so that the rock to the left of the computer is shaded, you have a shadow that falls in the air off the back of the computer screen. Clearly the water is too far away for this shadow to affect it. We need to manipulate the shadow further by applying a mask. That's not possible when using a layer style, so we must turn this effect into its own layer.

8 Dragging the Gradient tool about like this will give you a good start on a mask for the Portable's Drop Shadow layer.

Create a Shadow Layer

8 As we mentioned above, to manipulate the shadow further, you have to turn it into a regular layer. Once you create the layer, you'll add a layer mask and use a gradient to edit the mask. You'll need to do some touch-up with the Brush, so don't worry about getting the mask perfect with the Gradient tool. However, if you don't like the first gradient you build, you can simply redraw the gradient until you get one you like.

◆ Choose Layer/Layer Style/Create Layer to turn this drop shadow effect into a real layer. If you get a message saying "Some Aspects of the Effects Cannot be Reproduced with Layers," just click OK. Now you will have a new layer underneath your PowerBook layer named PowerBook's Drop Shadow.

◆ Click the Add Layer Mask icon at the bottom of the Layers palette to create a new blank layer mask.

◆ Type G for the Gradient tool and make sure that the default Foreground to Background gradient and Linear are chosen on the Options bar. If you're unsure whether you've got the right gradient selected, click the gradient swatch and check the Gradient Editor dialog.

◆ Type D for the default colors, then X to switch Black to the foreground color.

◆ Make sure you are on the mask for the Portable's drop shadow layer, and drag a short gradient at an angle from just above the

portable's hinge on the left side. See the illustration here for the drag we used.

◆ Type B for the Brush tool. From the Tool Presets icon at the left of the Options bar, choose Airbrush 7%. Paint with black to remove the drop shadow where it's not appropriate to the illustration. If you remove too much, type X and paint with white to bring portions back.

◆ Shift-click the PowerBook layer, then click the Link icon at the bottom of the Layers palette so these two layers move together if you shift their position or transform them.

Using the slider at the top of the Layers palette, you can lower the opacity of this layer. If you want to change the color of the shadow at this point, you use the Color Picker to pick a new foreground color and choose Edit/Fill (Shift-Delete on the Mac and Shift-Backspace on Windows). Fill with the Preserve Transparency check box turned on in the Fill dialog; after the Fill you may want to readjust the opacity again.

Make a Path for the Computer Screen

9 We'll be adding a layer mask to the screen images that we're going to create in the next step. As we've been using the Pen tool in this exercise, we'll create a quick path (it's only four points) to use as the basis for the layer mask. You could create a channel mask instead by using the Wand and saving a selection. Be careful to create the path accurately around the edge of the PowerBook's viewing area.

◆ Type P to switch to the Pen tool, and create a path around the edge of the screen area on the PowerBook. Go to Window/Paths to bring up the Paths palette [Shift-F11] and double-click on the words *Work Path*, naming it Screen.

Assemble the Screen's Images

10 Because we need to distort whatever we put on the PowerBook's screen, it's easier to create another composite image in a different file and bring all those images over to the PowerBook Layers file as a group.

◆ Open the following files from the DVD: HeronOrig.psd, SailboatCamp.psd, toolbox300.tif, and menubarCS2.tif. You'll notice that the MenuBar image is wider than the canvas width of the HeronOrig and SailboatCamp images.

◆ Use the Window menu to bring the HeronOrig image to the front, then type F to put this file into Full Screen mode. Save this file as ScreenLayers.

◆ Now use the Window menu to bring the SailboatCamp image to the front inside a normal window. Move the SailboatCamp window to the side so you can see part of the HeronOrig image underneath.

◆ Type V to switch to the Move tool; then, while holding the Shift key down, drag and drop the SailboatCamp image on top of the HeronOrig image. Having the Shift key down will center the SailboatCamp image on top of the HeronOrig image. Double-click each layer in the Layers palette and name them with the correct names for each image. The bottom layer will be named Heron, and the next layer Sailboats.

◆ Use the Window menu to choose the MenuBar image, then drag and drop it so it's the layer on top of the Sailboats image. Double-click this layer and name it Menu.

◆ Use Free Transform to scale the MenuBar layer until it spans the image. About 72% should work. You can either hold the Shift key as you scale or click the Link icon between the W and H input areas on the Options bar to keep the scale proportional.

Now you are going to move the Toolbox image into this file. You want to maintain the actual relationship of the Toolbox to the MenuBar, and the Toolbox is definitely too large. It should line up with the edge of the Options bar (not the Menu bar itself) on the

10 As you move one image on top of the other, you get a gray outline to show you the move. When you get a black outline around the destination file, you can let go of the mouse. Holding the Shift key down as you do this constrains the file to the center of the background image. Because these two images are the same size, the Sailboats image will completely cover the Heron image.

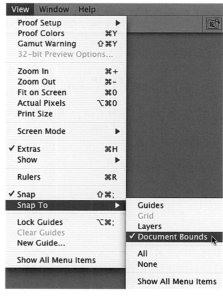

10 If you are having trouble positioning the Toolbox, the Snap-to options might be the problem.

left side and the line that separates the Tool presets from the rest of the Menu bar on the right. If you have Snap to Document Bounds turned on under the View menu, you'll find it's very difficult to drag the Toolbox just a pixel or two without having it snap to the edge of the screen. You can either turn off the Snap feature or simply use the Move tool in conjunction with the arrow keys to position the left edge of the Toolbox.

Line up the Toolbox
between these two lines.

10 Scale the Toolbox so it fits here.

11 Select the small area to the left of the Options bar, then create a layer mask and invert it.

◆ Use the Window menu to switch to the Toolbox image, then drag and drop it on top of the others. Use the Move tool to line up the Toolbox below the MenuBar.

◆ Type Command (Ctrl)-T to free transform the Toolbox to 77% of its original size.

◆ Double-click the Toolbox layer and name it Toolbox.

Add a Layer Mask to the Menu

11 It's a little thing, but on the Mac whatever image is showing onscreen should show in the small space to the left of the Options bar. A quick layer mask solves the issue.

◆ Click the Menu layer to activate it.

◆ Type M for the Rectangular Marquee, make sure there is no feather set, and drag the tool to select the rectangle to the left of the Options bar.

◆ Click the Add Layer Mask icon on the bottom of the Layers palette to create the mask, then type Command (Ctrl)-I to invert the mask.

Create Drop Shadows

12 Because you're working on a Mac image and a Mac PowerBook, you need to make the Menu and Toolbox look more like they do under OS X by adding drop shadows. On all three drop shadows in this example, you need to make sure Use Global Light is unchecked,

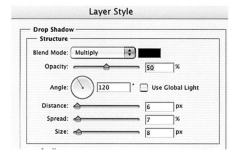

12 Here are our settings for the Menu drop shadow.

as all three shadows are slightly different. To add the drop shadow to the Toolbox layer, we'll simply copy the effect from the MenuBar layer and see how it works.

◆ Double-click the Menu layer thumbnail to bring up the Layer Style dialog, then click the words *Drop Shadow* on the left of the dialog. We used 50% for the opacity, 125° for the Angle, 6 for Distance, 7 for Spread, and 8 for Size.

◆ Click the F symbol on the far right of the Menu layer, then hold down the Option (Alt) key and drag the symbol down to the Toolbox layer. When you see the double black line, you can release the mouse and drop the effect.

◆ Click the triangle beside the Layer Effects icon (the F) to open the Effects area for this layer.

◆ Double-click the Drop Shadow sublayer itself to bring up the Layer Style dialog, opened to the Drop Shadow effect settings.

◆ Change the settings to those in the illustration on the next page.

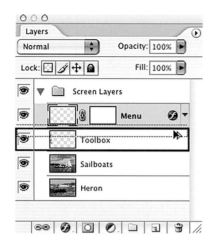

12 Option (Alt)-drag the Layer Effect icon on the right side of the Menu layer to copy the drop shadow to the Toolbox layer.

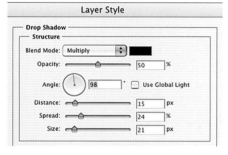

12 The settings for the Toolbox drop shadow.

Group the Layers

13 To bring all the images in this file over to the PowerBook Layers file in one step, you'll create a group. As an alternative, you could create a Smart Object to place. The sidebar here gives you more information on that.

◆ Shift-click the four layers of this file and use the Layers palette pop-up to create a New Group from Layers. Name your group Screen Layers.

◆ You can now use the Window menu to switch to each of the Sailboats, Toolbox, and MenuBar images and close them. Your PowerBookLayers and ScreenLayers files should still be open.

Copy the Screen Layers to the PowerBook File

14 The top layer on the PowerBookLayers file should be active, and this file should be in Full Screen mode before you bring the Screen Layers group over.

Placing a Smart Object

If you are doing a composite and have built an "outside" file as we have in the ScreenLayers file, you could also place the file as a Smart Object, so you could continue to change the appearance of the file and have it update in the composite. Unfortunately, you can't currently distort a Smart Object, although you can scale, rotate, skew, or warp it. And as in the case of this composite, you can't make layer comps as easily if you need to turn on or off the visibility of layers in the "outside" file. So whether you place a Smart Object or simply copy the layers will depend on several factors. Think ahead. What are the most likely changes you'll need, and where will they be more easily accomplished? In this example, we chose to copy layers because we want layer comps, we'd like to use Distort to transform our layers, and we're sure that the two computer screen images we're using are the two the client wants. Our final version has a Smart Object layer, placed and Warped. Here's a picture of it below.

◆ Use the Window menu to activate the ScreenLayers file, and type F until it is no longer in Full Screen mode. Move this file over to the left until you can see the PowerBookLayers file underneath.

◆ With the Move tool (V), click the Screen Layers group, and drag and drop it on top of the PowerBookLayers file. All four layers of the ScreenLayers image move over to the PowerBookLayers file and remain in the group called Screen Layers.

15 Begin the distort while zoomed out, then zoom in to 100% to more accurately place the corner points. We've also reduced the opacity here to help.

15 The first step in the transform is to make the images smaller by 50%. We did this by double-clicking the W input area, typing 50, then clicking the Link icon to scale the height by the same percentage.

Distort the Screen Layers Group

15 To make the Screen Layers group fit the computer, you have to scale it down. However, scaling alone won't create the illusion that this image is actually on the screen because the screen on the computer is tilted and angled away from us. Distort works well in this case. When you distort this group of layers to make it fit within the screen area of the portable, you want to try to place it accurately on the first try. This is because once you accept the transformation, the bounding box of any subsequent transformations will become a rectangle parallel to the edges of your computer screen. This will make it more difficult to see exactly where your edges of image information will be. It might be easier to step back through the history states and perform the transformation again from the beginning than to alter it with a second transformation.

◆ Make sure you're on the Screen Layers group layer, then type Command (Ctrl)-T for Free Transform.

◆ Double-click the W input area on the Options bar. This controls the width of the transform. Type 50 to scale the width by 50%.

◆ Click the Link icon beside this input area. This will scale the height proportionally to the width.

◆ Choose Edit/Transform/Distort. The cursor will change into a gray arrow. While zoomed out so that you can see the entire computer, you want to drag each of the four corner handles until they line up with the four corners of the actual computer screen. If it helps, you can lower the opacity of the Screen Layers group layer at any point during the transform or distort.

◆ Type Command-Option-(Ctrl-Alt)-0 to zoom to 100% and look more closely at the top-left corner. Move the handle for that corner inward for a moment so you can clearly see the top-left corner of the PowerBook's screen area. Place each corner point of the transform just slightly inside the edge of the screen.

◆ After getting all four corners where you want them, press Return (Enter) to complete the distort.

While within Transform/Distort, you can move each of these corners as many times as you want until you are happy with the results. The Screen Layers group may from time to time seem to revert to a rectangle as you make changes, but give the screen a moment and it will redraw properly. You will notice that the image details are sharper once you accept the changes than they are in the preview you saw using the Distort tool.

Add a Layer Mask

16 To soften any edges of pixel information that might be near the edge of the computer screen, you need to add a layer mask. Depending on how closely you've placed the images to the edge of the screen, you may or may not see much difference when you add the mask. To soften the transition between the edge of the screen and the images that will be displayed inside it, you'll also put a blur on the mask. This will look like a shadow you might see around the edge of a computer screen.

◆ Use the Window menu to bring up the Paths palette [Shift-F11]. Click the Screen path you made earlier to bring it up on your screen.

◆ From the pop-up menu of the Paths palette, choose Make Selection to turn this path into a selection with a Feather value of 0 and Anti-aliased turned on.

◆ Choose Layer/Add Layer Mask/Reveal Selection to add this selection to the Screen Layers group as a layer mask.

◆ Choose Filter/Blur/Gaussian Blur and put a 2-pixel blur on the layer mask you just added to the Screen Layers group layer.

◆ Command (Ctrl)-click the PowerBook layer, then click the Link icon at the bottom left of the Layers palette to link this grouped layer to the other layers.

Only the Background layer is not linked now. This means if you need to move the Portable, all the other layers will move as well, maintaining their relationship to one another. If you decide to further transform the PowerBook at this point, your screen preview of the transform may not work because there are too many layers for Photoshop to display on the fly. Once you accept the transformation, you'll see that all the layers transformed. However, without the onscreen preview, it's very difficult to adjust the image. So try to have everything the way you want it before this point.

Use the Layer Comps Palette

17 At the end of a project, when everything you need has been added to the file, it is nice to save versions to show the client with different layers visible, in slightly altered positions, or with different Blend modes and effects. Before Photoshop CS you had to save each different version of the file. If you were working with a large image, this took quite a bit of disk space. If you saved flattened versions to save disk space, any minor adjustments to a proof would require you to go back and remember exactly what you had in the version you needed to work with. With the Layer Comps palette you simply save a comp for each version and turn on that comp to quickly switch between versions. You can even make changes to a comp and update it. To learn more about the features of the Layer Comps palette, see

Chapter 26, "Restoring Old Photos." Here, we'll show you a few other features.

◆ Go to Window/Layer Comps to bring up the palette. Currently, the sailboats are showing on the screen and it looks really good, so you definitely want to save this version of your file as a comp. Click the Create New Layer Comp button at the bottom of the palette.

◆ For maximum safety, check all three boxes. Name this comp Sailboats.

◆ Click the Eye icon for the Sailboats layer to turn this layer off. The Heron image is now visible with the Toolbox and Menu. Click the Create New Layer Comp button again and name this comp Heron.

If you look at our version of this image in the file called PowerBook-Layers.psd inside the folder for this chapter, you'll see we added a note to the Sailboats comp as well. The note says, "John likes the Toolbox with less shadow. See other comp." When you look at the difference between the Heron comp and the Sailboats comp, the shadow seems to look heavier on the Sailboats image even though you haven't made any changes. Luckily, you can edit the layer effect, then update the Sailboats comp or save a different comp. For this example, save a different comp.

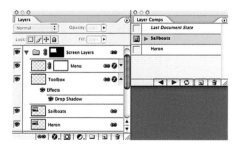

17 This is how the Layers and Layer Comps palettes look for the Sailboats comp. The triangle beside the Sailboats comp tells you there is a comment about this comp.

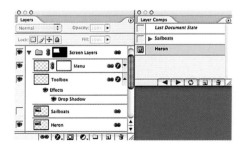

17 The Layers and Layer Comps palettes for the Heron comp.

- Click the visibility box for the Sailboats comp. This takes you back to having the Sailboats on the computer screen.

- Double-click the Drop Shadow effect for the Toolbox layer. This brings up the settings that you originally used for the shadow. You can click and drag the shadow so that it looks right to you. If you're using a Mac, just look at your own screen and try to match it. Once you're happy with the shadow, click OK.

- Click the New Comp icon and name this comp Sailboats Less Shadow.

- Click the visibility box for the Heron comp, then drag this comp to the New Comp icon to make a copy of this one. Double-click the name and call this comp Heron No Menu. Turn off the Toolbox and Menu layers, and show a full-screen version of the Heron.

- Click the Update Layer Comp button at the bottom of the palette to update this comp to show the changes you just made.

Click the icons for each state to see which one you like best, or use the Apply Previous or Apply Next Selected Layer Comp button at the bottom of the palette to scroll through the comps. These buttons don't show you the Last Document State, so you'll have to click that icon if you've made adjustments that you want to check. Photoshop is an incredibly powerful compositing tool, and the Layer Comps palette is one more addition to your digital tool set. Have fun!

17 The Heron comp.

17 The Sailboats Less Shadow comp.

17 The Sailboat comp.

17 The Heron No Menu comp.

31 ◆ Blend Modes, Calculations, and Apply Image

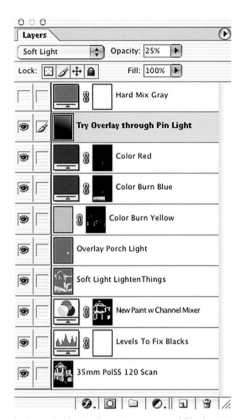

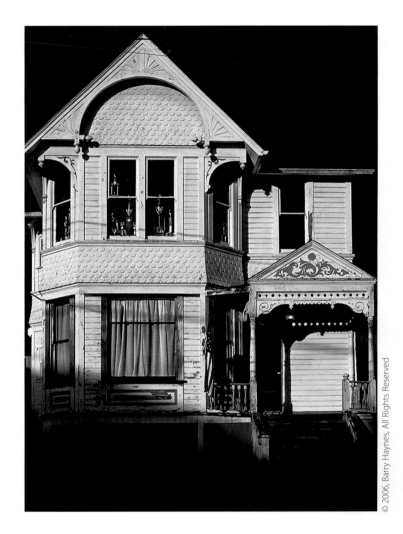

In the trophy Victorian house image, we used Blend modes in various ways to enhance the early morning light. Open the TrophyHouseatSunrise.psd file from the Chapter 31 folder on the *Photoshop Artistry* DVD, click each layer to activate it, then see how the Blend mode for that layer affects the results. Try some different Blend modes and learn what they do to the image.

Learning to blend images, masks, channels, and effects in Photoshop gives you a great deal of power to create not only composite images but also better color adjustments for all types of images. In addition, specialized Blend modes and applications make some types of tedious production work absolutely painless. Calculations and Apply Image are two commands that use Blend modes to determine their results, but the commands are, in their own right, methods for blending layers, masks, channels, and images together. Calculations and Apply Image seem fairly complex at first glance—and indeed, they can be complex—but most usages of the commands that you'll need are fairly straightforward. Complex masks and channels that would take many times longer to accomplish using other methods can sometimes be created with ease with knowledge of these tools. This chapter is both a tour of the Blend modes and a brief introduction to Calculations and Apply Image.

The Blend Modes

Blend modes (or Blending modes as Adobe calls them) work in conjunction with layers, painting tools, and some commands to merge two pixels into one color that you view onscreen. You'll use some of the Blend modes, such as Multiply, Overlay, and Soft Light, all the time. Others are more for design or production work, and you may rarely, if ever, use them. The Blend modes are used to determine how two sets of image information combine. The two sets of image information can be of various types, such as an image, an adjustment layer, a fill layer, an effect, or paint. The Adobe Photoshop manual calls the first set of information (usually on the bottom) the base color, and the second set of information the blend color. You can combine the base and blend colors using layers, one of the painting tools, or the Fill command. If you create a layer that is a solid color—the blend color—then you can combine this layer with a photographic image on an underlying layer (or layers) by using a Blend mode in that solid-color layer via the Layers palette. The cumulative effect of all underlying layers before the addition of the solid-color layer would then be the base color. Blend modes also appear in a variety of places within the Photoshop Layer Styles palette. In that palette the blend modes are usually affecting the way a shadow or effect looks. You

can use the Apply Image command with different Blend modes to combine two-color photographic images that are in separate documents and have the exact same pixel dimensions. You can use the Calculations command with Blend modes to combine two images of the same size when you want a black-and-white mask channel as a result. The Blend modes appear in the painting tools, the Fill tool, the Layers palette, the Layer Styles palette, the Apply Image command, the Calculations command, and the Stroke command. Not all of the Blend mode options are offered in each of these areas. As we explain each Blend mode, you'll see why some of them make more sense in one area or another. Many of these options also give you a way to use a mask as you combine the two sets of image information. The mask will affect the parts of the two groups that are combined.

The Tools for Blending

First, we'll discuss the different tools and methods for blending, and when it makes the most sense to use each of them. Later, we'll discuss each Blend mode and its unique applications within each of the different blending tools. You can find many of the images we use in this chapter in the folder for this chapter on the *Photoshop Artistry* DVD. Although this chapter is not a step-by-step hands-on session, we encourage you to play with and explore these techniques. By experimenting on your own, you'll learn new things and have fun, too.

The Blend modes for the Layers palette, which we call the standard set of Blend modes. These are also the Blend modes that appear in Layer Styles.

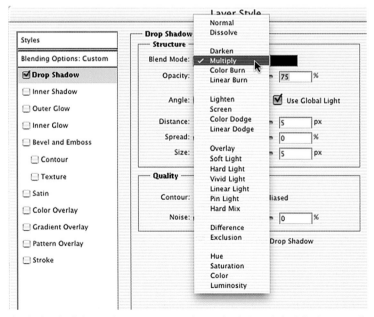

The Blend modes for layer styles appear in various places within the Layer Styles dialog but are usually the same set of Blend modes that you get in the Layers palette.

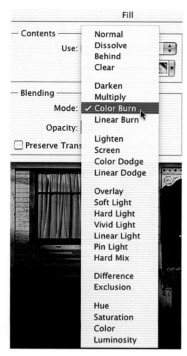

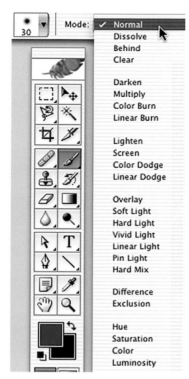

The Blend modes for the Fill command, which also include Behind and Clear.

The Blend modes for the painting tools. Notice the addition of Behind, which paints only in the transparent areas, and Clear, which paints only in the nontransparent areas.

The Fill Command

The Edit/Fill command, which you access by typing Shift-Delete (Backspace), is used to fill a selection, or the entire layer if there is no selection, with color (the foreground or background color, or a color you choose from the Color Picker), black, white, 50% gray, a pattern, or information from the History brush location. The Blend mode and Opacity setting in the Fill command just determine how this fill image will combine with what was there previously. Normal, at 100% Opacity, completely covers what was there before with the new color, pattern, or image. We mention "image," because you can change the "Use" pop-up to fill from the current History brush setting or from a pattern. An Opacity setting of 50% will give half what was there before and half the new filled image or color. We usually use Fill to completely cover a selection or the entire image with a solid color or a tint. We sometimes use Fill to revert the selected area to a Snapshot or other location in the History palette. When you use Fill, you need to pick a Source, Opacity, and Blend mode before you do the operation, and then you have to undo the Fill if you want to change it. If you need to experiment with the Opacity or Blend mode of your

Fill, use the layer techniques we show you in this book, because it's quicker to make variations in the Layers palette than it is to fill an area, undo it, and try again.

The Painting Tools

You use a painting tool when you want to apply an effect by hand and softly blend it in and out, as you would do with an airbrush or paintbrush. Brushes in Photoshop have a lot more power, however, due to the magic of digital imaging and the Blend modes. Read Chapter 4, "The Toolbox," and Chapter 32, "Digital Paint," to learn about the subtleties of each painting tool. With the Blend mode options in the painting tools, you don't just lay down paint, or even a previous version of the image. Instead, you can control how this paint or image combines with what is already there. Although we might add a small touch-up here and there using a brush in Blend mode, we are more likely to use paint on a layer that has a particular Blend mode. That way we have more options to change what we've done by erasing, repainting, changing Blend modes, or changing opacity.

Combining Images Using Layers and Blend Modes

Layers and adjustment layers are the most powerful ways to combine two or more images while keeping the most options open for making further variations and creating many versions of your composite. With layers, you can always change the content of the layer, move the layer, or change the opacity or Blend mode without having to totally redo your image. Unlike the contents of the History palette, which go away when you close the file, layers stay around as long as you want. You can try an effect and turn it on and off at will. Layers gives you the most sophisticated control over the Blend modes as well as many other abilities. If you don't understand layers, read Chapter 7, "Layers, Layer Masks, and Layer Comps," before you continue.

Combining Images, Layers, and Channels Using Apply Image

The basic function of Apply Image is to copy one image, layer, or channel, called the *source,* and use it to replace, another image, layer, or channel of exactly the same pixel resolution, called the *target.* To combine two items with Apply Image, they must be exactly the same width and height in pixels. The two images are combined using a Blend mode and opacity that you choose from the Apply Image dialog. You can optionally choose a mask, which will combine the images only where the mask is white. Apply Image is useful when you're copying a channel or layer from one place to another, especially when you want to put it on top of an existing channel or layer and combine the two with a Blend mode.

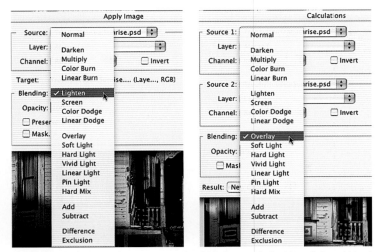

The Blend modes for the Apply Image command and Calculations, which additionally have Add and Subtract but don't have Dissolve, Hue, Saturation, Color, or Luminosity.

Before you enter Apply Image, the image, layer, or channel you want to target should be active. It will be modified when you click OK and exit Apply Image, so you may want to first make a copy of that target item.

If the Preview button is on, you can see the results of the operation in the Target window. In choosing the source, you can pick any open document, layer, or channel, as long as it's the same exact pixel dimensions as the target. Like the source, the mask can be any open document, layer, or channel that has the same pixel dimensions as the target. The Preserve Transparency option, which is enabled if the target has transparent areas, will stop the Apply Image command from changing any transparent areas within a layer. Both the source and the mask have an Invert check box that you can select to turn that channel or layer to its negative.

In this chapter, we use three images that we have cropped to be exactly the same pixel size. They are the Las Vegas Night image, the CenturyPlant image, and the Times Square Lights image. The Las Vegas Night image has a mask, called VegasLights, that is white

where the neon lights are. If you want to get a result that is in color rather than black and white, you need to use Apply Image instead of Calculations. Many of the effects you can create with Apply Image you can also achieve with layers, by first copying each different image into a separate layer within the same document. Layers give you more flexibility because the different layers don't have to start out being the exact same size, and you can move them around within the image window as well as change their stacking order relationship to each other. You can also try and undo effects within layers in multiple combinations by turning the Eye icons on and off.

Generally, you should use Apply Image in cases where you already know the spatial relationship between the objects being combined, and you have to do the operation quickly for some production purpose. Motion picture and multimedia work (where you are compositing many frames of two sequences together that have been preshot in registration, to be lined up exactly) is a good example of how you would use Apply Image. You could automate this process over hundreds of frames by using actions with a batch or by using another application-automation tool like AppleScript.

We use Apply Image in Chapter 23, "Replace Color, Color Range, and Selective Color," to apply a layer mask from one image to another image of the same size. We also use Apply Image in Chapter 29, "Portrait Compositing," to create a complex layer mask.

Combining Channels Using Calculations

The main purpose of the Calculations command is to use the Blend modes to combine images, layers, or channels and end up with a single black-and-white channel as the result. When you need a color result, use Layers or Apply Image; when you need a mask channel result, use Calculations. Calculations provides for two source files, Source 1 and Source 2, and a Result that can be either a New Document, a New Channel, or a Selection. When you enter Calculations, the two source files are set to the active window within Photoshop. You can use the pop-up menus to change any of these source files to any other open file that has the same pixel dimensions. The source files are the two

Apply Image to Create a Special Printing Ink Plate

In this example, the red fireworks dulled a lot when we proofed the colors in CMYK. Luckily, there's very good color differentiation in the RGB channels here. We used the Channels menu to choose New Spot Color and chose PANTONE Orange 021 C as the "bump plate" color. The channel is automatically named and is created as a completely white channel. With the new Spot Color channel active in the Channels palette, we used Image/Apply Image to apply an inverted version of the Red channel to the Spot Color channel. This covered the Red areas, but it added the PANTONE ink over the greens as well as the reds, so we needed to take those colors out of the Spot Color channel.

The solution was to run the Apply Image through an inverted mask of the Green channel. This took out most of the greens. We also lowered the Opacity of the Apply Image to 50%. Once we clicked OK to accept this operation, we had to do only a little manual work on the channel with the Brush to take out areas of yellow in the original image that were in danger of being covered with the PANTONE ink.

This same type of Apply Image could be done after conversion to CMYK by choosing other channels to work with.

 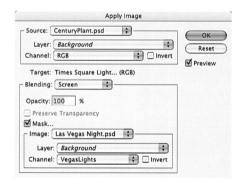 

In the center, you see most of the possible options of Apply Image. Before we entered Image/Apply Image, we made Times Square Lights the active document in Photoshop. The active document or layer is always selected as the Target of Apply Image, so you will be changing that document, channel, or layer. The Source pop-up window shows you only open documents that are the same pixel size and dimensions as the target document. Here, we chose the Century Plant as the Source. The Blending pop-up is where you choose the Blend mode. There is an optional mask, selected here, that causes the blending to happen only within the areas of the mask that are white. If the Preview button is on, you see the results of the Apply Image in the Target window. This lets you try different options and see what they do. On the left, here is the VegasLights mask we used. On the right, you can see the results of this Apply Image command. The Century Plant image is brought into the Times Square Lights image where the VegasLights mask was white. In that area, it is blended using the Screen Blend mode.

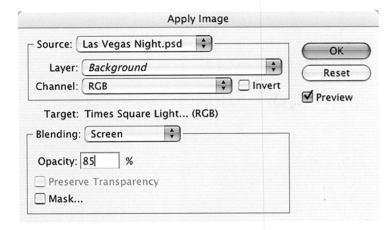

Apply Image

Source: Las Vegas Night.psd

Layer: Background

Channel: RGB ☐ Invert

OK Reset ☑ Preview

Target: Times Square Light... (RGB)

Blending: Screen

Opacity: 85 %

☐ Preserve Transparency

☐ Mask...

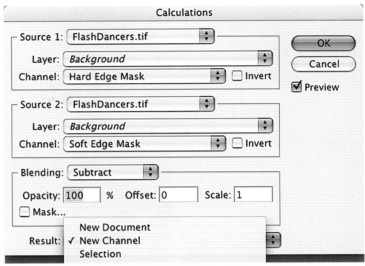

Calculations

Source 1: FlashDancers.tif

Layer: Background

Channel: Hard Edge Mask ☐ Invert

OK Cancel ☑ Preview

Source 2: FlashDancers.tif

Layer: Background

Channel: Soft Edge Mask ☐ Invert

Blending: Subtract

Opacity: 100 % Offset: 0 Scale: 1

☐ Mask...

Result: New Document ✓ New Channel Selection

Here's a simpler application of Apply Image. The resulting image is shown here. The light areas of the images are emphasized by using Screen as the Blend mode. Setting the Opacity to 85% made the Las Vegas Lights a little less bright in the composite image. We did not use a mask in this composite.

Here are the Calculations settings to produce the mask of the glow without the sign. When doing a Subtract, the item that you want to subtract should be in Source 1. The item you are subtracting from should be in Source 2. In this case, the result was a new channel. Depending on the choice we make for Result, it could be a new channel in the existing file, a new file itself, or a selection in the existing file.

that will be combined using the Blend mode that you choose. The Layer pop-up on each of these files is available for layered documents and allows you to choose the merged layer, which is the composite of all layers that currently have their Eye icons on or any other layer in the document.

The Channel pop-up allows you to choose any channel in the chosen file or layer. To access a layer mask in the channel pop-up, you need to first choose the layer that owns that layer mask in the Layer pop-up. You can also choose the Transparency channel, which is a mask of any transparent areas in the chosen layer. This interface allows you to blend any two documents, layers, or channels that are open by using the Blend modes, and to then put the result into a new channel, document, or selection. These open items must have the same pixel dimensions as the active window. The blending interface also allows an optional mask, which will force the blending to happen only in the areas that are white in the mask. Both source items and the mask have an Invert check box to optionally invert any of them before doing the composite. You will learn more about Apply Image and Calculations as you go through this chapter.

The Flashdancers sign, where we want to make a mask of just the glow without the sign so we can have control over each separately. We have a hard-edge mask of just the sign. We put this into Source 1. We have a soft-edge mask of the glow, including the area of the sign. We put this into Source 2. Here is the resulting glow mask where we subtracted the hard-edge mask from the soft-edge mask. To move the sign to another background, we used the hard-edge mask to copy the text into one layer and the glow mask to copy the glow into another layer. We then had separate color, blending, and blur control over each item in the sign that allowed us to get the result we wanted on the new background.

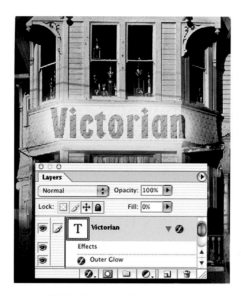

We added an Outer Glow effect to the type layer, then lowered the Fill Opacity to 0%. At this point, changing the Blend mode of the layer will have no effect on the appearance of the image. If you want to change the way the glow interacts with the rest of the image, you can do so in the Outer Glow Layer Styles dialog.

Blend Modes and Opacity in Layer Styles

Each layer style has its own Blend mode options. That means if you've applied several different styles to a layer, and you want to change the Blend modes, you need to go into each style and change the pop-up there. The Blend mode of the layer does not affect the look of the layer style.

The opacity of a layer style has two controls. The opacity for the layer affects the style, as does as any opacity setting within the Style dialog. The Fill opacity setting applies only to pixels of the layer containing the style. If the regular Opacity is set to 100% and you then set the Fill to 0%, you will no longer see the objects in the layer but you'll still see the layer style, as in the illustration above.

Understanding Each Blend Mode

We'll go through the Blend modes in the order they appear in the Layers palette Blend mode pop-up and also according to the way they are grouped. We'll cover the five Blend modes that occur in other parts of Photoshop (Behind, Clear, Add, Subtract, and Pass Through) at the end of this chapter.

Normal

When painting or filling in Normal mode, you are filling the selected or painted area with the foreground or background color, a History state, or a pattern. Specifying Normal mode at 100% Opacity and 100% Fill for a top layer, or any layer, in the Layers palette means that the layer will be opaque—you will not see any of the layers below.

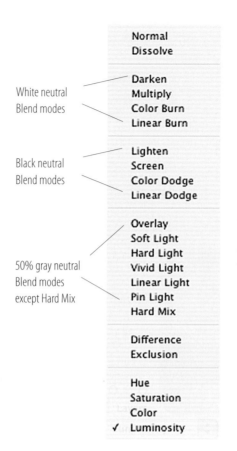

The Blend modes are organized according to their neutral colors. The neutral color is the color that causes a particular Blend mode to have no effect on underlying layers. The Darken, Multiply, Color Burn, and Linear Burn modes are grouped together because they all have white as their neutral color. The Lighten, Screen, Color Dodge, and Linear Dodge group all have black as their neutral color. The group starting with Overlay and ending with Pin Light all have 50% gray as their neutral color. Though Hard Mix is grouped here, it has no true neutral color—50% gray is the most neutral color with this mode.

You use Normal mode and 100% Opacity in Calculations or Apply Image to copy the source layer or channel to the target, layer or channel, without any blending. This totally replaces the target with the source.

Dissolve

Depending on the Opacity setting you specify for the dissolve, this mode takes the opacity as a percentage of the pixels from the blend color and place those pixels on top of the base color. Try this with two layers, setting the mode between them to Dissolve. If you set the Opacity to 100%, you will see all of the top layer and none of the bottom layer. The same thing happens if you use a Fill of 100% or paint at 100% in Dissolve mode. When you set the Opacity to 50% and look at the pixels up close, you will see that about 50% of the pixels are from the top layer and 50% are from the bottom. If you set the Opacity to 10%, only 10% of the pixels are from the top layer or blend color.

With Dissolve, the pixels are entirely from one image or the other; there aren't any blended pixels. If you want to achieve this type of Dissolve effect between two images but also have more control over

The Las Vegas Lights layer at 30% opacity in Dissolve mode on top of the Century Plant image.

Here, we've created a layer mask for the Las Vegas Night layer, then used Filter/Noise/Add Noise at 100 pixels, and blurred the mask by about half a pixel. The layer is in Normal Blend mode and the Opacity is at 70%. Not only is this result more delicate than what the Dissolve Blend mode would offer, but also the mask is editable, giving you more flexibility.

the pattern used to create the dissolve, create a layer mask on the top layer filled with solid white. Then, go into Filter/Noise/Add Noise and add Gaussian noise to the layer mask. Where the noise is black, the bottom layer will show through and you will get an effect similar to Dissolve. This way you can use Levels or Curves or even a filter to change the pattern in the layer mask and thus change how the two images are combined. The more noise you add, the more you will see of the bottom layer. Also, by using noise in a mask, some of the pixels can actually be blended between the layers, especially if you use Gaussian Blur to blur your layer mask, too. Dissolve is not an option

with Apply Image or Calculations, but you can get a similar effect here by using a Gaussian noise mask as you combine images, layers, and channels.

The White Neutral Blend Modes

The Blend modes in the first group, below Dissolve, all have white as their neutral color. This means that wherever the blend color is white, these particular Blend modes will have no effect on the base color. When you choose Layer/New/Layer and select a Blend mode from this group in the New Layer dialog, you will be asked if you want to fill that layer with the white neutral color. You can then paint in this area with colors or patterns that are darker than white to influence what this layer will do to your overall composite. Depending on the Blend mode chosen from this group, your results will vary.

Darken

The Darken Blend mode is easy to understand. In the Darken mode, each of the corresponding pixels from the original image and the blend color, pattern, or image are compared, and the darker of the two is chosen for the result. If the blend color is white, this Blend mode's neutral color, you can easily see that the base color will then always be darker or the same, so nothing will change. This Blend mode and its opposite, Lighten, are most useful in combining masks to create new masks. An example of this, shown on the next page, would be a situation in which you have pasted two objects into a composite scene. You have a mask for each object, because when you paste an object in Photoshop, the transparency of the object's layer can be used as a mask. You have a mask of each separate object, and now you need one mask that contains both objects at the same time.

Here, we used Calculations to set the Blend mode to Lighten between the two masks, creating the mask of both the objects. You can then use the inverse of this mask to create a mask of the background. To do this in one step, select the Invert check boxes on both the Source channels in Calculations. Because both Source masks have now been inverted, you would have to use Darken to combine the two masks and get the final inverted mask with the white background.

Multiply

Multiply is a very useful Blend mode that is available within all the Blend mode pop-ups. When you multiply two images together, what you get is analogous to what you would see if both the images were transparencies that you sandwiched together and placed on a light table or projected onto the same screen: Anything that was black in either image would be black in the resulting composite image;

The shoes and the glasses have each been placed here separately.

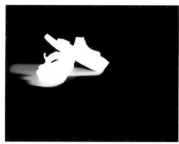

You have one mask for the shoes.

Another mask for the glasses.

anything that was white or clear in either image would let you see through to the other image in that area. When you multiply two images together, the 0 to 255 values of the corresponding pixels in each image are actually multiplied together using the following formula:

(Source 1) x (Source 2) / 255 = destination

Just like with multiplication in mathematics, the order of the Source 1 and Source 2 images doesn't matter. Dividing by 255 at the end forces all the values to be in the 0 to 255 range. You can see that when either Source value is 0—black—you are going to get 0 as the result. When either Source value is 255—white—you are going to get the other Source value as the result, because 255/255 = 1, so you end up multiplying the other Source value by 1. Multiply is the default Blend mode for layer styles that create a shadow effect.

A powerful use for Multiply is to seamlessly add a gradient to an existing selection. Let's say we wanted to use the Glow mask from the FlashDancers sign image to create a glow that was bright at the left side and fading toward the right. To do this, we would want to drop a gradient into this mask. If you did a Load Selection on the mask and then created the gradient within that selection, you would get a light halo around the edge of the gradient toward the right side. This unwanted effect is caused by the loaded selection. To avoid getting

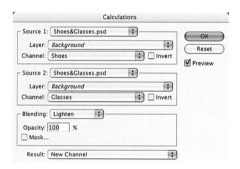

These Calculations settings using Lighten Blend mode will create the new mask below to the left.

Unwanted halo effect

The original Glow mask we want to drop a gradient into.

Doing a Load Selection on the glow, left, and dropping the gradient into the selected area, produces the halo around the glow at the right side.

This mask of both shoes and glasses was created with Calculations using Lighten.

To create this background mask with a single calculation, invert both the source masks and use Darken instead of Lighten.

Create the gradient in a separate mask channel and use Calculations to Multiply for the effect at right.

A Calculations Multiply of the Gradient and Glow mask channels drops the gradient into the glow area without a halo.

this halo, just create the gradient in a separate channel and then multiply the two channels together to produce a better fade.

Multiply is often used to create more density in an image whose color is thin. Simply make a copy of the layer, set the Blend mode to Multiply, and lower the opacity of the layer until the image has enough information to work with. We use this technique in Chapter 26, "Restoring Old Photos."

Color Burn

Color Burn darkens and adds contrast to the original image, the base color, as the blend color goes further toward black. Because white is the neutral color, a Color Burn with white does nothing; then as the blend color gets darker, the original image increasingly picks up darkness and color from the blend color. See the examples of how to use Color Burn in the images below.

Linear Burn

With Linear Burn, the base color will be darkened as the blend color gets darker and darker. White is the neutral color for this Blend mode and black will completely blacken the base color. Where Color Burn works with contrast, Linear Burn works more with the lightness values, producing a darker, less constrasty result.

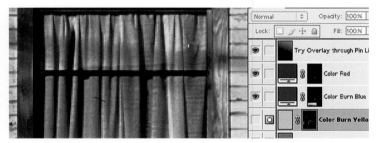

This is the original window frame without the Color Burn effect on.

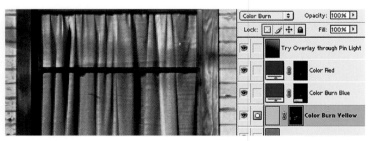

In this window frame, we have intensified the warm lighting by doing a Color Burn of the solid yellow color. Notice that the Blend mode of the active layer is set to Color Burn. Its layer mask is painted white in the window frame areas where we wanted the warm color effect.

The Black Neutral Blend Modes

The Blend modes in the second group, starting with Lighten, all have black as their neutral color. This means that wherever the blend color is black, these particular Blend modes will have no effect on the base color. When you choose Layer/New/Layer and select a Blend mode from this second group in the New Layer dialog, you will be asked if you want to fill that layer with the black neutral color. You can then paint in this area with colors or patterns that are lighter than black to influence what this layer will do to your overall composite. Depending on the Blend mode chosen from this group, your results will vary.

Lighten

In the Lighten mode, each of the corresponding pixels from the original image and the blend color, pattern, or image are compared, and the lighter of the two is chosen for the result. This Blend mode is most useful in combining masks to create new masks. See the example of doing this, using Lighten and Darken, in the previous section, "The White Neutral Blend Modes." Comparing Lighten mode to Screen mode, if you use Screen the two images will appear to be blended together more. Because of this blending effect, screen often looks better when you're working with photographs. However, Lighten can be a very useful Blend mode for retouching, especially on faces. If you shoot digitally, you may sometimes get red artifacting around the nose, jaw, or hairline of a subject. If this happens, you can sometimes use a new layer in Lighten mode, then sample color from near the area to be retouched and use a soft brush to paint out the artifacts. Because Lighten does not pop the contrast, you can successfully cover some areas that might be more difficult to retouch with the regular retouching tools. However, unless you use some sort of textured brush, you may lose the grain, so this method is not appropriate for large jobs.

Screen

Screen mode is sort of the opposite of Multiply, in that when you do a Screen between two images, anything that is white in either image will be white in the resulting image. Anything that is black in either image will show the other image in that black area. Screen, like Multiply, is also available in all the different Blend mode pop-ups. What you get when you Screen two images together it is analogous to what you would see if both the images were projected from two different slide projectors onto the same screen. Here is the formula for Screen:

255 − ((255 − Source 1) x (255 − Source 2) / 255) = Destination

You can simulate the Screen command using the Multiply command if you first invert both of the Source images and then multiply them together, and, finally, invert the result of that Multiply operation. That is exactly what this formula for Screen does: (255 − Source1) does an Invert of Source 1. With the Screen formula then: The Invert of Source 1 is multiplied by the Invert of Source 2 and then is divided by 255. That part of the formula does the Multiply of the two inverted images. Finally, subtracting that result from 255 at the end does the Invert of the result of that Multiply, giving you a Screen. The important thing to remember about Screen and Multiply is that a Screen of two images will emphasize the lighter areas and a Multiply will emphasize the darker areas.

Screen is the default Blend mode for layer styles that create a glow effect. Along with Color Dodge and Linear Dodge, Screen can be used to dodge areas of your image. Look at the illustrations here to see how different modes affect the image.

Color Dodge

Color Dodge brightens the original image, changing its contrast as the blending color goes further toward white. Black is the neutral color, so a Color Dodge with black does nothing; then, as the blending color gets lighter, the original image increasingly picks up brightness and color from the blending color.

The Original Century Plant image.

Here's the same layer with the Blend mode set to Color Dodge.

Here, we made a copy of the Century Plant layer and set the Blend mode to Screen and the Opacity to 50%. We added a layer mask that hid the screened layer, then painted the mask to reveal the screen only in the areas of brush on the right side of the path.

Here's the same layer with the Blend mode set to Linear Dodge.

Linear Dodge

With Linear Dodge, the base color will be lightened as the blend color gets lighter and lighter. Black is the neutral color for this Blend mode and white will completely whiten the base color. Linear Dodge appears to pick up less of the blend color and more of the blend lightness values than Color Dodge, so it is less contrasty than Color Dodge.

The 50% Gray Neutral Blend Modes

The Blend modes in the third group, starting with Overlay and ending with Pin Light, all have 50% gray as their neutral color. This means that wherever the blend color is 50% gray, these particular Blend modes will have no affect on the base color. (Hard Mix is included in this grouping although it actually has no neutral color, possibly because 50% gray is the most neutral color for this Blend mode.) When you choose Layer/New/Layer and select a Blend mode from this group in the New Layer dialog, you will be asked if you want to fill that layer with the 50% gray neutral color. You can then paint in this area with colors or patterns that are lighter than 50% gray and your image, your base colors, will be lightened or brightened in some way. Painting or blending with colors that are darker than 50% gray will darken your image in some way. Depending on the Blend mode you choose from this group, the appearance and mood of your composite will change.

Open the image named TrophyHouseatSunrise.psd from the Chapter 31 folder on the DVD, and try out various Blend modes from this group, and the other groups, on the layers in this file. Don't forget that you can use Shift-+ (plus) and Shift-− (minus) to cycle through the different Blend modes. This experientation will help you to get a feel for what each of the modes does. These effects can be only somewhat described with words. This is a case where a picture is indeed worth a thousand words.

Overlay

Overlay is a sort of combination of the Multiply and Screen modes. The dark areas of an original image are multiplied and the light areas are screened. The highlights and shadows are somewhat preserved, because dark areas of the image will not be as dark as if you were doing a Multiply and light areas will not be as bright as if you were doing a Screen. The tonal values and details of the original are preserved to some extent, but this mode produces a more contrasty transition than Soft Light, though not as radical as Hard Light.

Soft Light

In Soft Light mode, the original image is blended with the blend color, pattern, or image by making the original image either lighter or darker, depending on the blend image. If the blend image is lighter than 50% gray, the original image is lightened in a subtle way. Even where the blend color is pure white, the resulting image will just be lighter than before, not pure white. If the blend color is darker than 50% gray, the original image is darkened in a subtle way. Even where the blend image is pure black, the resulting image will just be darker than before, not pure black. The tonal values and details of the original are fairly well preserved—just subtly modified by the blend image. If you add a 50% gray layer above an original image and set the Blend mode to Soft Light, you can then use a soft brush and paint or airbrush with white or black to dodge or burn the image by lightening or darkening this gray layer. Use less than 100% Opacity on your brush to get more subtle effects. This technique is better than using the dodging or burning tool because it's infinitely adjustable—you're not actually changing the original image, though you are increasing file size more than with an adjustment layer.

Hard Light

In Hard Light mode, the original image is blended with the blend color, pattern, or image by making the original image either lighter or darker depending on the blend image. If the blend image is lighter than 50% gray, the original image is lightened with a high-contrast Screen-type effect. If the blend image is pure white, the resulting image will be pure white. If the blend image is darker than 50% gray, the original image is darkened with a high-contrast Multiply-type effect. If the blend image is pure black, the resulting image will be pure black. In Hard Light mode, the resulting image takes its luminosity from the blend color, pattern, or image. Because the tonal values of the original are not preserved very well, the adjustment is a radical one. Using Hard Light will produce a radical, contrasty dodge and burn effect. Use less than 100% Opacity on your brush if you are painting in this Blend mode, or you will get pure white or black. If you find the effect you create using this Blend mode too harsh, try lowering the opacity of its layer or switching the Blend mode to Overlay or Soft Light.

Vivid Light

Vivid Light burns or dodges the image by changing the contrast depending on whether the blend color is lighter or darker. In general, this technique tends to have a much more contrasty and radical effect than most of the other Blend modes in this group. It is similar

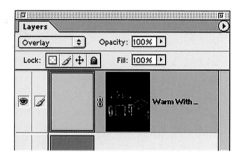

In the Illustrations on this page and the next, we used a layer filled with a solid color that has a layer mask that is white where we want to apply that color as a warming effect. Changing the Blend mode of this layer modifies the mood and intensity of the effect. This could have also been done using a Solid Color Fill layer instead of a regular layer.

Applying the warming using Soft Light.

The original Victorian before any effects are applied.

Applying the warming using Hard Light.

The mask showing where effects will be applied.

Applying the warming using Vivid Light.

Applying the warming using Overlay.

Applying the warming using Linear Light.

Applying the warming using Pin Light. Color Burn is another Blend mode that looks good with this image and is the one we used in the final version.

This is the effect of using a 50% gray layer in Hard Mix mode on the Trophy House image with its color correction layers turned on.

to doing a Color Burn in the areas darker than 50% gray and a Color Dodge in the areas lighter than 50% gray, though it may not be quite as radical a move on either extreme.

Linear Light

Linear Light is similar to Vivid Light except it changes the base color's brightness instead of the contrast, depending on how different the blend color is from 50% gray in either the light or dark direction. Using Linear Light is like doing both a Linear Burn and a Linear Dodge on either side of 50% gray.

Pin Light

Pin Light is like doing a Lighten when the blend colors are lighter than 50% gray and doing a Darken when the blend colors are darker than 50% gray. This may be useful in some mask and effects operations.

Hard Mix

Hard Mix gives you a posterized effect. A pure white layer will return white, and pure black will return black. At 100% Opacity, all other col-

ors are forced to pure values and will therefore be Red, Green, Blue, Cyan, Magenta, or Yellow.

Blend Modes for Sharpening and Contrast

Overlay, Soft Light, and Hard Light can be used to increase local contrast in an image and make the image appear sharper. Occasionally, you have a photo that's a nice shot, but for some reason, the focus is just too soft to be usable. If you try to run Unsharp Mask on it, you can only make it a little better before Unsharp Mask starts to introduce too much grain. If you try to run the ArtistKeys action, Sharpen Only Edges, the focus may be too soft for the action to determine the edges. Here's a technique that might save the image.

Radical Sharpening with Unsharp Mask

Open the file WendyAndStig.psd from the Chapter 31 folder on the DVD. There are several layers in this file, and they are all about alternative ways to sharpen your image. The first layer above the *Background* is called USM 250, 20, 0. To make this layer, we made a copy of the *Background*, changed the Blend mode to Soft Light, then ran the Unsharp Mask filter with settings of 250 for the Amount, 20 for the Radius, and 0 for the Threshold. When you first run Unsharp Mask at such at such a high amount, you may think you've made a terrible mistake. Changing the Blend mode and opacity modify the effect greatly, so be fearless. You'll need to experiment with the opacity of the layer but we usually start out with about 25%.

High Pass Sharpening

High Pass Sharpening is another technique that you might use by itself with an image or in addition to the Unsharp Mask technique for a photo that still needs sharpening. High Pass sharpening does tend to change the image's contrast, so we don't use this technique as a basic sharpening technique for images, but using this in conjunction with the Unsharp Mask technique with an especially blurry image can be very helpful. On the other hand, Wayne Palmer, our technical editor, uses this as his primary sharpening technique because it's nondestructive and fully editable if you lower the opacity or double the layer.

To create the High Pass layer you can either make a copy of the Background (that's what we did with WendyAndStig), or, if you are using it in conjunction with the Unsharp Mask technique, you can merge the visible layers into a new layer by typing Command-Option (Ctrl-Alt)-Shift-E.

The original picture of Wendy and her mother.

Here's the USM 250, 20, 0 layer in Soft Light mode at 100%0 opacity.

When you initially run the Unsharp Mask with the large radius, your image will look like this.

Lowering the opacity of the USM 250, 30. 0 layer to 35% gives you this version.

Although we don't use this technique often, if you need to process images quickly and they don't have to be museum quality, this is a good technique to remember.

Merge and Resharpen

If you've used both the Radical Sharpening technique and the High Pass sharpening on an image and it still isn't quite sharp enough, you can merge all the layers to that point using Command-Option (Ctrl-Alt)-Shift-E. You can also do this by holding down the Option (Alt) key and choosing Merge Visible from the Layers palette menu. Once you've merged, you can run the Unsharp Mask filter with more normal settings and usually get a reasonably sharp image.

You may need to take out areas of both the High Pass layer and the final Unsharp Mask layers to keep highlights from popping and skin from becoming too pixelated.

The Rest of the Blend Modes

Of the remaining Blend modes, Difference and Exclusion appear in most of the Blend mode menus; Hue, Saturation, Color, and Luminosity do not appear in Apply Image or Calculations; Behind and Clear appear only in the PaintBrush, Fill, and Stroke Blend mode menus; Add and Subtract are exclusively in Apply Image and Calculations; and Pass Through is a Blend mode that is used only in layer sets. Here we go!

Difference and Exclusion

Difference is one of the most useful Blend modes. Difference compares two images and gives you a result that is black where each of the two images are exactly the same and is nonblack and closer to white the more the images are different from each other. Here is the formula for Difference:

| Source 1 - Source 2 | = Destination

Difference is similar to Subtract but the results are never inverted; they are always positive because the two vertical bars stand for absolute value and therefore make the result positive. With a little photographic planning, you can use Difference in conjunction with Calculations to automatically separate an image from its background. Pick a background that is quite different in color and brightness from the objects to be shot. Place the objects, adjust your lighting, and then shoot them. Without moving the tripod or changing the lighting, shoot the background without the objects. If these two photographs are shot in register, doing a Difference between them can often automatically give you a mask of just the objects. If you shoot film, you'll need to make sure your photographs are scanned in register. When using a digital camera, you should have no problem with registration as long as you don't move your tripod between shots. In this shoot of the shoes, bag, and glasses, we had the computer in the studio, so we could try Difference between the two images and then adjust the lighting and exposure to make sure we'd get the best knockout. Actually, to create the final mask of the objects in this case, first we used Calculations to do a Difference between the Red channels of the two images; then we used Calculations again to Screen the results of the Difference with itself. Screening an image (or mask) with itself brings out the brighter parts of the image. We then brought this Screened mask into Levels and increased its brightness and contrast slightly again to darken the blacks and brighten the whites. Finally,

The objects as originally shot.

The background shot with the same lighting and camera position.

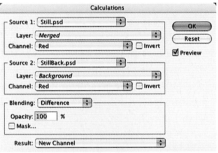

These Calculations settings using Difference will create the mask below.

Difference between the Red channels of the background and the object shots. Try each channel and see which does the best job.

we did some quick editing of the masks of the actual objects. Still, this process was faster using Difference and Screen than if we had done the knockout by hand. Using Difference to do knockouts works even better for objects that have no shadows or where the shadow is not needed in the knockout.

A digital camera hooked up to a computer is the norm for many photographers today, especially those who do a lot of repetitive catalog work. Also, consider the motion picture industry or multimedia

Above mask after some quick edits and a brightness adjustment with Levels. Sometimes using Calculations to Screen a mask with itself will bring out the bright values even more. After that, you can use Levels to redarken the shadows, adjust the shadow midtones, and further brighten the highlights that represent the objects you are knocking out.

New background placed behind the objects using an inverted version of the mask to the left. Check out these images on the DVD for Chapter 31 in a folder named Still, StillBk Difference Stuff. The Channels palette in the Still.psd file has these channels, along with hints about how we made them. Try it yourself and have some fun!

applications where artists or technicians might have to knock out hundreds or even thousands of frames to composite two sequences together. With Difference and a little computer-controlled camera work, you can automate this situation. Say you're shooting some guys on horses riding across a field and you will later want to superimpose that scene on another scene. Have a computer remember all the frame-by-frame motion of the camera while shooting the scene. Now immediately, while the lighting is still the same, use the computer to move the camera back to the original position at the beginning of the scene. With computer control, reshoot all those frames without the horses to get just the backgrounds. Now, using Difference and an Actions Batch, to automate hundreds of frames, you can quickly create a knockout of all those frames.

Exclusion is similar to Difference but not as intense. Both an Exclusion and a Difference with black will do nothing to the image. An Exclusion or Difference with white will invert the image completely. An Exclusion with 50% gray leaves you with 50% gray, whereas a Difference with 50% gray still changes the image to make it appear partially negative. A Difference from black blending toward white is a slow transition from a positive image to a negative image with no gray section in the middle. In an Exclusion from black blending toward white, the portion from black to 50% gray is actually a transition from the positive image toward 50% gray. From 50% gray,

the image turns more negative as you proceed toward white, where the image is totally negative.

Hue, Saturation, Color, and Luminosity

These Blend modes will affect the original image by using either the hue, saturation, color, or luminosity of the blend color, pattern, or image as the hue, saturation, color, or luminosity of the original image, the base color. Open the sunriseLayers.psd image to see some of the variations shown on this page and the next.

Hue and Color

Hue uses the luminosity and saturation values of the underlying image and only the Hue values of the blend color. With a solid-color layer on top of an image, this gives you a sort of split-toned image. Color uses the luminosity of the base image but the hue and saturation of the blend color. For this reason, Color mode gives a more homogenous color over the image, a sort of duotone effect but using RGB.

Saturation

Normally when we want to saturate an image, we use a Hue/Saturation adjustment layer and move the Master slider to saturate all the colors. If you look at the image on this page, you'll see a very predictable result. However, if you add a Solid Color adjustment layer, use a color that is 100% saturated and change the Blend mode of the

Hue mode gives more of a split-toned effect.

Color mode gives a sort of duotone effect, like using the Colorize button in the Hue/Saturation dialog.

The original Gibsons Sunrise image.

When you turn on the Hue/Saturation adjustment layer, you get this.

Here's the Solid Color adjustment layer at 15% opacity. The color we used was 50% bright and 100% saturated.

Luminosity

If you've ever had an image in which you wanted to adjust the reds to make them a little brighter, you might have thought, "Well, I'll just use a curve." But in Normal mode the Red curve moves the red colors from red to cyan. The solution is to set your Curves adjustment layer to Luminosity mode. That way, the RGB curve does not introduce color casts into shadows or highlights, and the color curves control how light or dark the Reds, Greens, and Blues are in the image.

Behind

The Behind Blend mode is used to paint into the transparent part of a layer. It is available only from Fill and the painting tools, and only if the layer has a transparent area. It's not available if Lock Transparent Pixels is on for that layer. Behind allows you to paint a shadow or color behind an object (like a circle) in the layer, using a painting tool or the Fill command. The existing pixels in the layer won't be affected because Behind only paints into the transparent area. Once you have laid down paint, however, it becomes a permanent part of the layer and cannot be turned off like a layer style. Painting in Behind mode is like painting on the back of the acetate. Here we see a glow that was added to a circle using the Brush tool in Behind mode with a large soft brush.

Clear

The Clear mode is available only when you're in a layered document and only from the Fill command, the Paint Bucket, the Brush, and the Pencil tool. It will fill the selected area with transparency. This is the

layer to Saturation, you'll see that you saturate the colors in a different way than if you use the Hue/Saturation command. In this particular image, less saturated colors in both the clouds and the island gained saturation, becoming more colorful. We were using a color that had 50% Brightness as well as the 100% Saturation. The brighter the color, the more the image tended toward posterization. It doesn't matter what color you use when you employ this technique. Because you are in Saturation mode, only the saturation of the blend color is being used to manipulate the image, so the Hue doesn't affect the image at all.

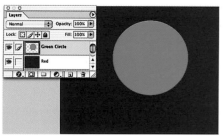

The green circle is in the top layer, with red in the bottom layer. Now both layers' Eye icons are on.

Here we see the circle and its shadow without the background color. When painting in Behind mode, we didn't have to worry about painting on top of the green. It is automatically masked out because it's not transparent.

Here is just the circle with the Red layer turned off. The transparent area shows up as a checkered pattern.

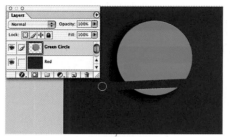

Here we used a hard-edge brush to create the red line going across the circle by painting the line in Clear mode.

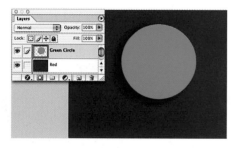

We have painted black into this transparent area using Behind mode with a large soft brush.

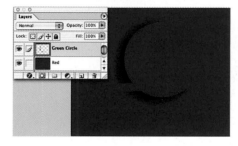

Here we clicked the green circle with the Paint Bucket in Clear mode, leaving only the shadow with this nice effect.

little checkerboard pattern that means you can see the layers below through the transparent areas. Clear is also available as a menu item from the Edit menu, although Edit/Clear behaves a little differently depending on whether you are in a normal layer or a *Background* layer. When you are in a normal layer, Edit/Clear fills the selected area with transparency. When in a *Background* layer, Edit/Clear fills the selected area with the background color.

Add and Subtract

Add and Subtract are available only in Apply Image and Calculations. Add takes the corresponding pixels of the original and the blend image, and adds them together using the following formula:

Add = (Source 2 + Source 1) / Scale) + Offset = Destination

Subtract takes the corresponding pixels of the original and the blend image, and subtracts them using this formula:

Subtract = (Source 2 − Source 1) / Scale) + Offset = Destination

Scale and Offset are additional parameters that you use with these Blend modes in Apply Image or Calculations. The normal values for

Scale and Offset for both Add and Subtract are 1 and 0. The order of the Source 1 and Source 2 parameters doesn't matter with Add, but it definitely does with Subtract. The Source 1 parameter is always subtracted from the Source 2 parameter, and the result has to be in the 0 to 255 range. When Source 1 is white (255), which represents a selection, the result of the Subtract will always be black. The effect of the Subtract is then to remove the selected areas of the Source 1 mask from the selected areas of the Source 2 mask. This is a very useful function. Of the two, Subtract is the Blend mode we use more often, and we usually do Subtracts between masks. See the example of Subtract with Calculations earlier in this chapter.

When doing either an Add or a Subtract, the Offset value will make the resulting mask lighter if the offset is positive, and darker if the offset is negative. The offset is a number, in the 0 to 255 range, that will be added to the result of each corresponding pixel's calculations. If we do an Add of two images and set the scale to 2, we are getting an average of the two. This would give us the same result: having one image in a layer on top of the other, with the top image having a Normal Blend mode and 50% Opacity.

Pass Through

Pass Through is a Blend mode that was created to describe the behavior of layer groups. When you create a layer group, its default Blend mode is set to Pass Through. This means that the layers inside the group will appear in exactly the same way as they would if they were not grouped. You can also set a group to a different Blend mode, though this may dramatically change the total image appearance since this will cause all the layers in the layer set to be composited with themselves, almost as if they were a separate image. Once the layers in the group are composited with themselves, the result of that composite is then composited, using the chosen Blend mode for the group, with the rest of the image as though the layers in the layer group were just a single layer. Choosing a Blend mode other than Pass Through stops the Blend modes of any of the layers inside the group from influencing any layers outside the group. It can produce a big change.

Blending Options

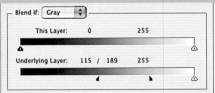

There are times in compositing images when it would be nice to be able to magically elimimate portions of a photo. The Blending options, accessed by double-clicking a layer in the Layers palette, gives you an oportunity to do something like that. Above are the two images we want to blend together. You can open the file BlendOptions.psd to see how we blended these. In the dialog above, which is a small part of the Blending Options dialog, you can see that we told Photoshop to push the darker portions of the underlying image (the one on the left above) through the layer above it. You can hold down the Option (Alt) key and drag a slider to split the slider and have the effect fade out gradually rather than all at once. In realistic photography, it's unusual to find two images that composite perfectly using this method. However, if you shoot a still life against a white background, you can sometimes make a really good knockout using only this tool. Most of the time, though, Blend If gives you interesting effects that might be useful for surrealist imagery.

32 ◆ Digital Paint

Explore Photoshop's brush capabilities. Learn to build, use, and save custom brushes, then employ custom brushes to create naturalistic artwork.

If you've come to this chapter to explore a personal impulse to express something other than the strictly photographic, you are in the right place. Although we cannot, in one chapter, tell you all there is to know about digital paint, we can begin to point the way for some of you. And we encourage you, whether you consider yourself an artist or not, to explore what's available to you in Photoshop and other applications in order to stretch yourself creatively.

Most pundits will tell you to write what you know. To draw, you must forget what you know about objects and simply draw what's there, what your eyes report to you. Painting is the point where you must do both. You must use everything you know about value, light, shadow, and color; at the same time, you must let go of all you know and be guided by internal impulse and by the paint itself. Only through exploration of the medium will you begin to know what you have to say.

We'll be re-painting a couple of different photographs in this chapter. It's not necessary to work from a photograph if you want to simply pick up your pen and paint. By pen, we mean a pressure-sensitive tablet you can really make use of and control the brush capacities. Wendy uses the Wacom Intuos 3 tablet with the grip pen, and in the section entitled "Photoshop's Limitations," she will show you some of the things you can do with Corel Painter that are beyond what Photoshop can do. If you really get the painting bug, you might want to try that application as well. Using the two in conjunction with each other gives you the most power and control, as each application has strengths the other lacks.

Why Paint Digitally?

There are several good reasons to work digitally, such as less mess, no drying time, and the ability to work in layers that allow you more flexibility in how elements work together. In addition, when you work on the computer, you can mix media that would be difficult or impossible to combine with traditional methods.

For commercial illustrators, the reasons are clear. Increasingly short deadlines and more-computer-savvy clients require faster turnaround than ever. Digital has the advantage, here. But for fine artists? Our feeling is that digital is neither the greatest nor the worst that art has to offer. It's simply another tool. In the hands of an artist, great art is possible. And for some of us, it is the perfect venue to begin to explore our artistic leanings. We already have the computer, an imaging program, and maybe even a pressure-sensitive tablet. We're ready to begin to paint.

But, before we start, we need to explore Photoshop's brushes.

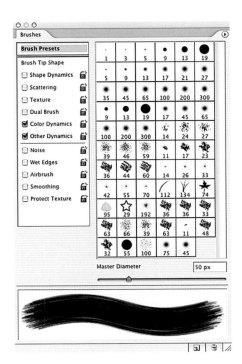

Here are the default Photoshop CS2 brushes in Small Thumbnail view. We'll be working with a smaller set than this for painting. The preview stroke at the bottom is for the current brush.

The Brushes Palette

The Brushes palette can be scary at first glance. There are so many options and so many brushes. You might think that you need a lot of brushes to accomplish work in Photoshop, but just as with traditional media, this is not true. A few good brushes are all you need for most jobs. However, also like with traditional media, knowing what each brush is good at and being able to make a brush do what you want are skills that you need to develop. Be patient with yourself as you experiment—and experiment a lot. Here, you'll get a little hands-on practice before you start painting.

When you look at the Brushes palette, you'll notice that it is divided into two sections. On the left side are the available options. On the right are the controls or icons for that set of options. Just as in the Layer Styles dialog that is the model for this dialog, clicking the check box on the left side of the dialog will turn on the options, but to actually see what settings are available with the options you have, you need to click the name of each of the options, such as *Shape Dynamics*, themselves.

Our first task is to develop a palette that gives us a few good brushes to work with.

13	Hard Round 13 pixels
59	Spatter 59 pixels
36	Chalk 36 pixels
63	Oil Pastel Large
39	Dry Brush
100	Rough Round Bristle

Keep these brushes and any others that you find interesting.

Reset the Brushes

We're going to assume that you have Barry's Photo Brushes loaded from the DVD. Barry set these up for working with realistic photography, but there are too many to really be effective for use in painting. So we'll load a special Tool presets library for the painting part of this exercise and bypass the Brushes palette for the most part. But you may want to modify brushes that we use in this chapter, so it's important to know your options. Also, although you'll notice that throughout most of the book we show you the Brushes palette in Small Thumbnail view, as shown in the illustration above, in this chapter we'll switch between Thumbnail and Small List view. You'll want to reload Barry's Photo Brushes when you finish this chapter in order to continue work on other exercises, but first, let's take a look at the default Brushes library that Adobe ships with Photoshop CS2. This is a big palette (far more than we need), but we're going to start with it because it has some nice brush tips to work with.

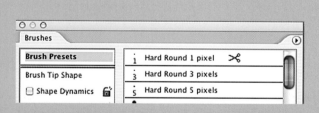

Delete a Brush via the Brushes Palette

If you have only a few brushes to delete, you may find it faster to delete via the palette rather than the Preset Manager. Simply hold down the Option (Alt) key as you move the cursor over a brush. When you see the scissors, click to delete that brush.

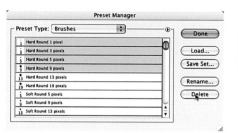

You can Shift-click adjacent brushes or Command (Ctrl)-click nonadjacent brushes to select multiple brushes before you delete.

◆ Type B to access the Brush tool (make sure you're in the Brush and not the Pencil, or all your brushes will be hard-edged), and use Window/Brushes [Shift-F12] to bring up the Brushes palette.

◆ If your Brushes palette is in the Palette Well, move it out of the well and onto the screen.

◆ Use the palette pop-up to reset the brushes to the default brushes. Click OK to completely replace the brushes instead of appending them.

◆ Click the pop-up again and switch to the Small List view.

Use the Preset Manager to Delete Brushes

We're going to work with the six brushes pictured in the illustration at the upper left of this page. We'll delete the brushes that we do not want for experimentation by using the Preset Manager. When you have a lot of changes to make to a library, this method is often faster than using the palette. Keep at least the six brushes shown above, but you can also keep others if you find them interesting. A quick way to see which brushes you might want to keep is to look at the Stroke preview for each brush in the Brushes palette. You can click each brush to see the stroke, or you can simply pause your cursor over one of the brushes. Once the Stroke thumbnail at the bottom of the palette updates, you can move fairly quickly over each brush to preview the stroke it makes. Write down the names of any that you want to keep before you go into the Preset Manager. Once you're in the Preset Manager, you can delete the brushes in groups to stay organized.

◆ Click the Brush Presets area of the Brushes palette to activate it.

◆ Click the palette pop-up and choose Preset Manager.

◆ Shift-click adjacent brushes to select them, then click the Delete button to delete them.

◆ After you delete all the brushes you want to delete, click Done.

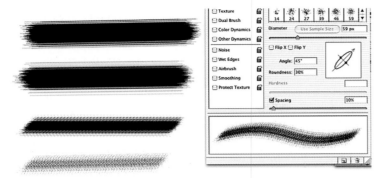

The top stroke is the default 59-pixel Spatter brush. In the second stroke, only the angle has changed. In the third stroke, Angle and Roundness have changed, and in the fourth stroke, Spacing has also changed.

◆ Use the Brushes palette pop-up, and choose Save Set to save these brushes as a preset library.

Brush Tip Shape Options

Now that you have a small set of brushes to work with, we'll create a new document as a sort of "scratch pad" and test out some of the options available. The Brush Tip Shape options were the first options that Photoshop had for brushes. Diameter is the size of the brush in pixels; Angle controls the angle of the brush; Roundness controls whether the brush is "squeezed" or used at full size; Hardness is the amount of blur applied to the edge of the brush, with 100% being sharply defined and 0% being soft and blurry; Spacing is how often a dab of paint is placed along a stroke—at 100% each dab will be tangent to, or just touching, the next, and at 25% they overlap to create a relatively smooth stroke depending on the brush tip. We are going to make progressive changes to one brush and mark our scratch sheet to see what those changes do to the stroke. Because we are using a brush shape that was captured as specific dots of paint for this first step, the Hardness setting is not available. For completely circular brushes, the Angle setting will not make a difference unless the Roundness setting is less than 100%.

◆ Go to File/New and click the Preset Sizes pop-up for a 5x7 document with a white background. Type Command-Option (Ctrl-Alt)-0 to make sure you view your document at 100%.

◆ Click the icon for the 59-pixel Spatter brush in the Brush Presets area of the Brushes palette.

◆ Click the palette's Brush Tip Shape tab and notice that the default Angle on this brush is 0°, Roundness is 100%, and Spacing is 2%.

Opacity and Flow

Get used to typing the keyboard shortcuts to adjust Opacity and Flow. For brushes that do not use the Airbrush option, type a number from 1 to 9 for 10% to 90% Opacity. Type 0 (zero) for 100%. Add the Shift key to set the Flow amount. If Airbrush is turned on, it's just the opposite.

Think of Opacity as the transparency of the medium itself. You'll find that thick oil paint is very opaque and a watercolor wash may have only 10% to 20% Opacity. Flow is more analogous to the amount of paint on the brush, with 0% being a dry brush and 100% being fully loaded.

◆ Type D for the default colors, and type 0 to make sure the Opacity of the brush is 100%. Type Shift-3 to set the Flow to 30%.

◆ Make a stroke on your new, blank canvas.

◆ Grab the arrowhead in the square to the right of the Angle and Roundness settings. Drag the arrow to the left until the Angle is 45°, and make another stroke.

◆ Now, grab one of the dots on the circle and push toward the center until the Roundness is 30%. If you have trouble doing this manually, you can double-click on any of the input areas to type in a value. Once again, paint a stroke on the canvas.

◆ Finally, change the Spacing to 10% and lay down a stroke.

Shape Dynamics

In the Shape Dynamics section you'll see several words that will be repeated over and over in different options in this dialog—Jitter, Control, and Minimum. Though each option is relatively simple, when you put all of them together, the possible iterations are overwhelming, so take it slowly.

First, let's talk about Control. This means how does Photoshop know what you want it to do? If you turn Control to Off, Photoshop makes the decisions for you. Use Fade if you want the effect or jitter to fade out after a certain number of dabs. With Pen Pressure, less pressure produces a smaller value, and heavier pressure gives you a higher value; so where Shape Dynamics are concerned, less pressure gives you a smaller brush, and more pressure gives you a larger brush. Pen Tilt is available only on tablets that support tilt, and when you use it, you have an additional slider for Tilt Scale—how far from the pen nib the paint will spray out. Stylus Wheel works when you have an

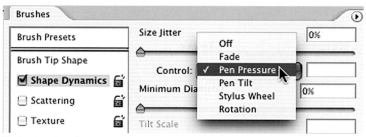

The Size Jitter Control options in the Shape Dynamics area of the Brushes palette.

Airbrush device with a wheel. Rotation works according to the rotation of the pen and is available only with the Wacom 6D Art Pen for the Intuos 3 tablet or the 4D mouse for the Intuos 2 tablet.

Size Jitter

Jitter means the amount of randomness. You are able to change the Jitter value for Size, Angle, and Roundness in this one little area of the Brush Options palette. In other areas, you can change the jitter setting for Hue, Saturation, Lightness, Opacity, and Flow, among others. This is a good brush for demonstrating what Jitter means.

◆ Change the Spacing back to 2%, and turn Shape Dynamics on by clicking the check box.

◆ Click the words *Shape Dynamics*.

◆ Turn the Control for Angle Jitter to Off, and turn the Control for Size Jitter to Pen Pressure. Set the Minimum Diameter for the brush all the way to 0%, then move the Size Jitter slider to the right and watch the Brush preview. Bring the Size Jitter slider up to 100% and make a stroke with the brush.

◆ Click back on the Brush Tip Shape area of the Brushes palette, set the Spacing of this brush to 100%, and make a stroke.

Setting the spacing to 100% means that the dabs of paint set down by the brush do not overlap. You can now see that there is variation in the size of the dabs. When you move the Size Jitter slider to

100%, Photoshop will apply maximum randomness to the size of the dab during the course of the stroke. Turning Control to Off means that Photoshop decides how the jitter will be applied to the stroke. When you choose Pen Pressure (the default on many brushes), the pressure of the stroke will control the amount of jitter. In this case, a light touch will produce small dabs, and more pressure will produce larger dabs.

Minimum Diameter

Another setting that contributes to the size of the dab that your brush lays down is the Minimum Diameter setting. In this case we're talking about the minimum size of the dab. With the slider all the way to the left, the dab can be so small as to be barely visible. The higher the value, the larger the dab must be. This setting can make a big difference when you're building brushes that behave like bristle brushes. With a watercolor brush, you'll want to be able to make a fine point; a flat hard-bristle brush will always have more width and will splay very little.

◆ Go back to Brush Tip Shapes and change the Spacing setting to 1%.

◆ Return to the Shape Dynamics area, use Pen Pressure as the Control method, and set Size Jitter to 0%. Notice how the beginning and end of the stroke preview are pointed?

◆ Now move the Minimum Diameter slider to the right, and you'll see that the beginning and end of the strokes enlarge.

◆ Set the Minimum Diameter back to 0%.

Angle Jitter

Like the Size Jitter setting, Angle Jitter controls how Photoshop will angle the brush as you stroke. If you look at the Controls for Angle,

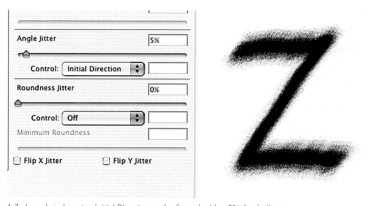

A Z-shaped stroke using Initial Direction as the Control with a 5% Angle Jitter.

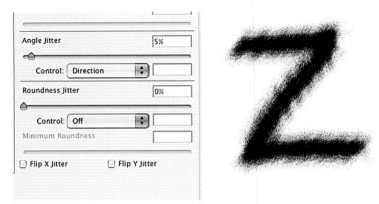

A Z-shaped stroke using Direction as the Control with a 5% Angle Jitter.

you'll see two extra Controls: Initial Direction and Direction. These are very important if you're using a flat brush. Initial Direction means that the angle of the brush will be consistent with the stroke of the stylus. Start a flat stroke horizontally and it will be large in the horizontal direction and thin in the vertical. Direction, on the other hand, will rotate the angle of the brush as the direction of painting changes.

◆ Set the Control for Size Jitter to Off.

◆ Set the Angle Jitter to 5%. Set the Control to Initial Direction, and make a Z-shaped stroke on the page.

◆ Set the Control to Direction and make a stroke on the page.

◆ Set the Angle Jitter back to 0% and turn the Control to Off.

Roundness Jitter

To experiment with the Roundness Jitter setting, you'll want to reset the Roundness of the brush in the Brush Tip Shape area to 100%, because the roundness percentage in the Shape Dynamics section is based on the current roundness of the brush in the Brush Tip Shape area. At only 30% Roundness, your brush doesn't have a lot of jitter space available to it.

◆ In the Brush Tip Shape area of the Brushes palette, change the Roundness setting to 100%. Change the Spacing setting to 100%.

◆ In the Shape Dynamics section of the Brushes palette, set the Roundness Jitter to 100%. Set the Control to Pen Pressure.

◆ Make a stroke, going from light pressure to heavy pressure.

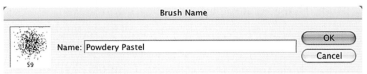

When you select New Brush from the Brushes Palette pop-up, you are prompted to name your new Brush preset. The default name will use the name of the original preset and append a number, but it's better to give your brushes more meaningful names.

◆ Set the Roundness Jitter Control to Off, and in the Brush Tip Shape section of the palette, change the Spacing back to 1% and the Roundness back to 30%

Save a Brush Preset

Let's review the brush that we've built so far. First, in the Brush Tip Shape section, you can see that the brush is 59 pixels and uses a custom brush tip. The Angle is 45°, the Roundness is 30%, and the Spacing is 1%. In the Shape Dynamics tab, the Size Jitter Control is set to Off. The Angle Jitter is set to 0% and its Control is Off. The Roundness Jitter is set to 100% and its Control is also Off. Because we've specified several different options from the original preset, it would be difficult to remember exactly what we set if we wanted

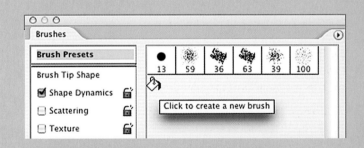

"Pouring" a New Preset

Rather than clicking the Brushes palette pop-up and choosing New Brush Preset, you can change the settings on a brush, and then "pour" your new brush into the palette. When you click an empty space, you get the Brush Name dialog shown at the top right of this page. If you Option (Alt)-click, you bypass the dialog and the brush assumes the default name of the original brush plus a number. You can pour a brush in any view. Here, we see the Small Thumbnail view.

to return to this brush (and the minute we click back on a different brush preset, we'll lose these changes). So we'll save this brush as a new preset.

By default when you save, you get the name of the preset that you used to create the brush, with a number appended. To me, this is not particularly helpful, so I always try to give my brush a name that means something to me. Alternatively, if you move your cursor over an empty area in the Brushes section of the palette, you get a paint bucket that allows you to "pour" your brush into a new preset. You can use either method—just be sure to save your presets. As we explore more of the capabilities of the brushes, you'll see how frustrating it is to lose settings.

◆ Click the Brushes palette pop-up and select New Brush Preset. Type in the name—Powdery Pastel—and click OK.

◆ In the Brush Tip Shape area, set the Roundness back to 30%.

Scattering

The next section of the palette, Scattering, scatters the dabs of paint away from the stroke—vertically for a horizontal stroke, horizontally if the stroke itself is vertical. When you click Both Axis, the dabs scatter in both directions.

◆ Click back on the Brush Presets tab and choose the Hard Round 13-pixel brush.

◆ In the Brush Tip Shape section, make the spacing 100% so you can see each individual dab of paint.

◆ Turn off Shape Dynamics by clicking the check box beside those words—no need to change any settings if you're not using them at all.

◆ Click the word *Scattering* to access that section of the palette. Set the Scattering Control to Off, and raise the amount to 200%.

◆ Make a stroke on the page.

◆ Move the Count slider up to 2.

◆ Make a stroke on the page.

Notice that instead of one dab at each location, you now have two. You can move this slider all the way up to 16, but at some point you'll see the dots overlap. You can also set a Jitter value here, which means that you could have 1 dot in some locations and up to 16 in others.

Texture

For Texture, let's use the Powdery Pastel preset that we saved earlier. In the Texture section of the palette, the Blend modes control how the brush tip and the texture interact. If you find a look you want to use again, save a preset for it. The Texture Each Tip check box will cause the texture to interact with each dab of the brush rather than the stroke as a whole. If you try this out using the 100% as the Depth setting, you won't notice much difference in the Blend modes. However, if you lower the Depth setting to about 50%, you'll see that

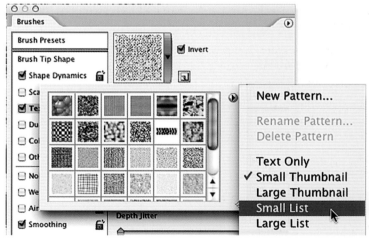

Once you have loaded the Artist Surfaces textures, switch to Small List view to make it easier to find the correct texture.

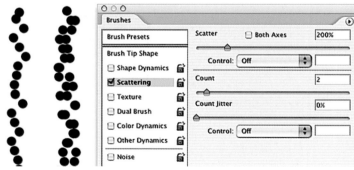

The stroke on the left was made with a Count setting of 1. The stroke on the right was made with the Count setting of 2. Though Spacing in the Brush Tip Shape section is set to 100%, that controls the spacing on the axis of the stroke, so vertically these dots do not overlap, but in the second stroke they overlap horizontally. To constrain the stroke to vertical hold down the Shift key; the placement of the dots is controlled by the Scatter setting.

Here is the Texture with the eight different Blend modes.

there are differences. The Depth setting controls how much paint is laid down on the texture. At 100%, no paint permeates the low points of the texture. As you lower the Depth setting, less paint is applied to the high sections of the texture until, at 0%, no paint is laid down at all. If you want to vary the depth, you can set a Jitter value and Minimum Depth (these settings are available only when you texture each tip). The Invert check box inverts the texture. Without it, the light parts of a texture receive the most paint. When Invert is on, the dark parts of the texture are high and receive the most paint.

◆ Click the Brush Presets tab, and click Powdery Pastel (or the last icon if you are in Small Thumbnail view).

◆ Click the word *Texture* on the Brushes palette to access this section.

◆ Click the Texture icon pop-up, and load the Artist Surfaces if you haven't loaded them already. Use the pop-up to view by Small List, and choose the Extra Heavy Canvas texture.

◆ Turn on Invert if it is not already on.

◆ Make a stroke using each of the eight Blend modes.

Dual Brush

Photoshop allows you to use two brush tips together to create effects and texture. We'll be using the Oil Pastel Large brush (it's the 63-pixel brush if you're viewing by thumbnail) to explore this option. We've chosen it because Dual Brush is the only option that is currently turned on for this brush. The Controls you see in this section are the Controls for the second brush. At the top, Mode determines how the second brush tip will blend with the first, or primary, brush tip. Next

are the icons for the secondary brush tips—in this case, the Brush preset uses a 90-pixel sampled brush for its second tip. The Controls below the icon allow you to change the characteristics of the second tip: its size, spacing, scatter, and count. This is another area where the options are so numerous, it's difficult to imagine all the possibilities. If you find a look you like (or even think you like), save a preset.

◆ Go to the Brush Presets area, and click the Oil Pastel Large brush.

◆ Click the words *Dual Brush* to activate those Controls.

◆ Change the Blend mode of this tip to Linear Burn and increase the Spacing to 100%.

◆ Move the sliders on the Scatter and Count Controls to get a better idea of how the two tips interact.

◆ Change the Brush Tip, then move the sliders for Spacing, Scatter, and Count.

◆ When you find an effect you like, make a stroke on the page.

Color Dynamics

Color Dynamics is used to build brushes that combine the foreground and background colors in each stroke. The Jitter setting Controls how much of each color is used, so you can skew the blend toward one of the two colors. In this same area of the palette, you have sliders for Hue, Saturation, and Brightness Jitter. If you use them, we recommend

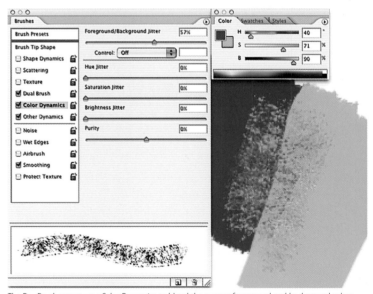

The Dry Brush preset uses Color Dynamics to blend the current foreground and background colors.

keeping the values low unless you are trying to achieve some special effect. There's also a Purity slider, which mimics the effect of adding white to your colors when you use a negative number, or using very pure pigments as you use higher positive numbers.

◆ Click the Color Dynamics area to see the settings.

◆ Choose two contrasting colors for your foreground and background.

◆ In the Brush Presets tab, choose the 36-pixel Chalk brush. Paint an area with one color, then press X and paint an adjacent area with the second color.

◆ In the Brush Presets area, choose the Dry Brush preset and color an area that overlaps both colors.

Other Dynamics

The Other Dynamics options Control the Opacity and Flow Jitter of brushes. We're going to paint with a version of the Rough Round Bristle brush and experiment with the Opacity and Flow settings, as well as the Other Dynamics settings. This brush has nice, feathery edges.

It's a good idea to switch your Color palette to HSB mode when you're choosing color for painting. You can click in any of the input areas and then use the up- and down-arrow keys to move the values. For example, if you've chosen yellow and want to warm it up by moving it toward red, click in the H input area and use the down arrow to move one degree at a time. Once you have a hue you like, you can do the same thing with saturation and brightness.

◆ Click the Brush Presets area and choose the Rough Round Bristle brush.

◆ Click the Shape Dynamics and the Dual Brush check boxes to turn off those settings.

◆ Click Other Dynamics to view the current settings. Both Opacity and Flow have a Jitter setting, and both Controls are Off.

◆ Set your Option bar Opacity to 100% by typing 0 (zero) and your Flow to 100% by pressing Shift-0. Click the Brush Presets area again and use the Master Diameter slider to make the diameter 50 pixels.

◆ Use Window/Color to show the Color palette if it's not onscreen. Use the palette pop-up to set the sliders to HSB.

◆ Choose a nice bright yellow and make some strokes.

Using this version of the Rough Round Bristle brush at 100% Opacity and 100% Flow gives you a nice stroke but very little depth.

Lower the Flow setting to 50% and the look is much more interesting.

The second set of red strokes is the same color as above, but the Flow has been lowered to 20%.

The third set of red strokes were made using 50% Opacity and 20% Flow.

◆ Now choose a yellow orange and make some strokes on top of the ones you just made.

◆ Lower the Flow to 50% by typing Shift-5, choose a nice red, and paint a few more strokes.

◆ Lower the Flow to 20% by typing Shift-2 to mix in even more of the underlying color.

◆ Lower the Opacity to 50% by typing 5 and make a few more strokes.

◆ Raise the Opacity and Flow Jitter values for an even "drier" brush and make several more strokes.

Now portions of the underlying paint show through and the color is richer. This brush is very delicate and allows quite a bit of underlying color to show through. Once again, you'll have even more control over how the color is laid down if you change the Control setting for Opacity and/or Flow Jitter to Pressure, Tilt, or Wheel.

Save a Tool Preset

If we save this brush as a Brush preset now, it will save the size of the brush, the brush tip shape, and the settings for the Opacity and Flow Jitter that we set in Other Dynamics. Unfortunately, it will not save the Opacity and Flow settings in the Options bar. To save those options along with the brush style, you need to save a Tool Preset. When you save a tool preset with the correct Blend mode, opacity, and flow, you have a much more complete brush. The caveat is that when you change the Options bar settings, choosing a mere Brush preset does not clear the Options bar but maintains the last settings that were used. You'll find yourself switching between Tool presets that you've saved and the Brushes palette, where you finesse the brush tips and dynamic settings to extend the versatility of a brush. Before you make a bunch of strokes, check the Options bar to avoid having to redo a lot of work because you're in an incorrect Blend mode. And keep that History palette handy (with a lot more than the default 20 steps available).

All of these strokes were made using the Acrylic Blend brush tool preset. We continued to lower to Opacity as we blended.

A bunch of flowers is sometimes just a single flower with adjustments.

◆ Set the Opacity Jitter back to 26% and the Flow Jitter back to 21%, and make sure Opacity is set to 50% and Flow is set to 20%.

◆ Click the Tool presets pop-up on the far left of the Options bar, and select New Tool Preset from the menu. Name this brush Acrylic Blend brush. Do not include the Brush Color.

We used this brush to complete the flower petals, adding a tiny bit of Hue Jitter in the Color Dynamics section. Lower the opacity as you blend in more color to keep the blend smooth. We made a selection of the flower, duplicated it twice, added stems, and did a couple of minor free transforms and Hue/Sat adjustments. Quick bouquet.

Other Brush Settings

In the lower section of the Brush options are five additional check boxes that have no settings associated with them. You can either click them on or off, but there are no sliders to slide or numbers to input.

The first three—Noise, Wet Edges, and Airbrush—turn on or off depending on the preset you use. The lower two options, Smoothing and Protect Texture, do not change from preset to preset but remain on or off until you manually change them.

Noise

Noise adds a bit more randomness to a brush and (according to the Photoshop manual) is primarily useful for brushes that are built with gray values. It's certainly a good idea, but this setting really needs a slider. Try it out with the Rough Round Bristle preset. Bring the opacity of the brush down to about 50%, and make strokes with Noise on and off. You may need to zoom in to see what's actually happening.

Wet Edges

Wet Edges has been around for a long time. It causes the color of the stroke to be weighted to the outside of the stroke, which gives you a watercolor effect. The Water Color Small Round Tip and Wet Sponge presets both use this option.

Airbrush

Next is the Airbrush option, which also appears on the Options bar. You can turn this on for any of the presets, and it will continue to build up the application of paint in one location if you hold the mouse or stylus down up to the maximum opacity you have set in the Options bar.

Smoothing

Smoothing helps to create a smoother stroke if you're using a stylus, but its computation sometimes lags behind the actual completion of the stroke, meaning that you have to slow the speed of your stroke if you want to see the paint you've just laid down. That can feel very unnatural.

Protect Texture

Protect Texture will use the texture that was active when you turned on the option for all brushes that use Texture. This is great because if you've built a brush using, say, the Burlap texture and you've got a portion of your painting done with that texture, you don't want to switch Brush presets to a brush that uses Granite.

Finally, we're ready to paint.

Acrylic Landscape

1 We're going to repaint a photo Barry took with a 3.3-megapixel digital camera when he was in Aspen teaching at Andersen Ranch. This version of the image has not been color corrected, but as you'll see, we're not going to be a slave to color, so this version will do. Lock the position of each layer you create to avoid accidentally moving the layer as you draw or paint.

Load Tool Presets

1a You are not constrained to using the techniques or tools presented here, but we've created a set of tools for use in this part of the exercise. You can use these as the start of your artistic exploration.

◆ Click the Tool Presets icon on the Options bar, then click the pop-up menu and choose Load Tool Presets. Choose the Red-MountainTools.tpl preset from the Ch32.Digital Paint folder on the *Photoshop Artsitry* DVD.

◆ Open the Red Mountain.psd file from the DVD.

1a The original Red Mountain image.

1b Use as much or as little detail as you need to decide where to block in colors.

1b Bring the opacity of the Sketch layer down to about 50% so you can see the underlying image as you draw.

Create the Initial Sketch

1b If you're used to sketching on paper, you may find this step disconcerting because the feel of the stylus on the tablet is very smooth; the surface has no bite as paper would. Some artists tape a sheet of paper over the tablet at this step to make the feel more familiar. We'll be using a very soft, large pencil, but notice that it has a low flow and moderately low opacity setting. You may need to move the Opacity slider on the Sketch layer up and down to check your work.

◆ Bring up the Layers palette [F10] and make a new blank layer. Type D for the default colors, and then Command (Ctrl)-delete to fill the layer with white.

◆ Double-click the layer name and rename this layer Sketch layer.

◆ Lock the position of this layer by clicking the third Lock icon on the top of the Layers palette, and lower the Opacity of the layer to about 50%.

◆ Type B to access the Brush tool. From the Tool presets, choose the Pencil Soft 20px brush. Trace over the major shapes and areas that you want to block in color in the next step.

Rough in the Color

1c We've created a basic palette for this step that you can load from the DVD called RedMountainSwatches.aco. When you paint, it's a good idea to build a Color palette that contains the basic colors you want to use often. You can choose colors from the *Background* layer, if you like, or use the Color palette to mix your own. Either choose all your colors first, or add them as you paint. Most often you'll have a set of colors that you start with, and you'll add colors as the image becomes more complete and more complex. Once again, setting the Color palette to HSB allows you to choose a basic hue for your colors and then move the sliders to warm or cool the color (Hue), change the tint (Saturation), or the tone (Brightness).

◆ Set your Color palette to HSB if you have not already done so.

1c Here is our blocked-in color version of the image. In some areas we've used large chunks of unbroken colors; in other areas, such as the rocks on the hill on the right, we've been more specific.

♦ Show the Swatches palette, then use the pop-up to load the Red-MountainSwatches.aco swatch set if you want to use it.

♦ Drag the Sketch layer to the Create a New Layer icon at the bottom of the Layers palette to make a copy of this layer, and rename the layer Block in Color. Turn off the Eye icon for the Sketch layer.

♦ Paint flat blocks of color into the shapes you've drawn.

You can be very precise with your edges, or you can be very loose. We liked leaving white canvas showing through in the sky and mountain, where the added luminosity works well. In the painting's darker areas, we were more particular about covering the canvas. We used the Oil Pastel CS brush for much of the work here, using the bracket keys to change the size of the brush as needed. We began by choosing colors from the Background layer and adding them to the Swatches palette, but we quickly found that turning the Eye icon on and off for the Block in Color layer and merely using the Background layer as a reference was preferable. This allowed us to interpret the color we were seeing rather than being completely literal. You don't need to strictly adhere to the color in the photograph; in fact, if you do, you'll probably end up with something stilted and lifeless. This is a good place to start to move away from the photo, and to paint what you feel, what comes to you. Remember, this is digital, so you can undo what you've done, or (like many a great painter) paint over your mistakes. Continue to add color to your palette and build Tool presets as you experiment with brushes. Save your file.

Add Detail

1d At this point, you need to decide what direction you're headed with this piece. For the look of flat acrylics with opaque colors, you can continue to work with the same brush you've been using to block in the color. Simply change the size of the brush as you become more detailed in your painting. Or you may work differently, preferring to use very clean and precise areas of pure color.

1d The Dry Brush 70% Hue Jitter brush has a bit of variation in the hue of the paint. In places like the sky this effect worked well.

1d In the areas where you layer a lighter color over a darker color, increase the Opacity of the brush to 100%.

Which technique do you want to mimic? Dry or wet? We're going to work on a Dry Brush version, which will add texture as we paint with a Brush preset. If you want to try a wet-into-wet version, you'll need to use the Smudge tool to blend your colors. With the Smudge tool, you'll want to block in the initial colors fairly completely over the canvas, unless you want to smudge the white of the canvas along with the paint colors. And if you really want to work wet into wet, Corel Painter offers you better tools and more options. We'll talk more about that application at the end of the chapter.

♦ Drag the Block in Color layer to the Create a New Layer icon to make a copy of the layer. Rename the layer Dry Brush.

♦ Click the Tool Presets icon on the Options bar to choose the Dry Brush 70% Hue Jitter brush.

♦ Hold down the Option (Alt) key and click to pick up colors from the roughed-in version and to spread paint into adjacent areas. Go back and forth, choosing color in first one area, then another.

♦ Notice that the brush you are using has only a 70% opacity and 40% flow. Raise or lower the Opacity setting to have more or

1d Here's our final dry-brushed version of the image. This version can be found in the RedMountain-Final.psd file on the *Photoshop Artistry* DVD.

less coverage in certain areas. This brush has a bit of Hue Jitter, which will give you some variation in the color of the paint. For areas where you don't want this, click the Color Dynamics check box on the Brushes palette to turn Hue Jitter off. Also, there may be times when you want to choose a color fresh from the Color palette rather than from the painting if you're working over an area that has become muddied from the mixture of paint.

Some areas, such as the trees, have a lot of very dark colors. You may need to increase the opacity all the way to 100% to get the coverage if you are layering lighter colors over the dark ones. We also decreased the brush size several times to get almost a pencil effect. Another Dry Brush preset we use on occasion is the Dry Brush Scattered 200% preset. We narrowed this down to about 9 pixels, again for small detail at 100% opacity. And for the trunks of trees and sharp edges of rocks or logs, we used the Pencil #2 preset.

This brings us to an important issue about digital paint. To create this piece, we used five Brush presets, though we could have used only three. You don't need a lot of brushes to paint. Use three or four and explore what their capabilities are. Get to know them well. Start with something that you think will work for you, then refine your brushes until they work the way you do. Don't get bogged down in the thousands of choices available to you.

Pastel Landscape

2 In this section, we offer another method for working with photos: cloning. We'll use the Clone Stamp tool with a special preset to create a pastel version of this same image. You can do just the first three steps of this section, or you can complete the whole exercise and use the result as the basis for doing more extensive work with a different Brush preset. Instructions here are minimal, but you'll figure it out quickly.

Create the Ground

2a Pastel artists often choose a color paper other than white to impart a certain feel to the image. So rather than working on a white canvas or ground, this time we will fill our lowest layer with color. The color you choose depends on the effect you want. We chose a light gray, but you could try a warm ivory, a cool blue, lavender, or even a darker gray or brown tone. Remember, this color is going to show through in places because we are using a lot of texture here.

◆ Turn off the Eye icons for all layers but the *Background*. Create a new, blank layer above the *Background* layer and name it Pastel.

◆ Use the Color palette to choose a color for your ground, then type Shift-Delete (Backspace) to fill this layer with the Foreground color you picked.

Set Up the Clone Relationship

2b We've created a Clone Stamp tool preset for you to use for this example. The Large Chalk Dissolve 20% stamp uses dissolve mode to clone color from the image, in this case the Background layer. The Opacity setting controls how dense the application of color will be, but the setting must be below 100% for the colored ground to show through. Before you use the Clone Stamp, you have to tell Photoshop the pickup location for the art you want to use.

◆ If you are not already in Full Screen mode, type F now to do so. Turn off the Eye Icon for the Pastel layer.

◆ Type I for the Eyedropper tool, then Shift-click a spot where you want to start cloning. A Color Sampler will be set at that point.

◆ Type S to use the Clone Stamp tool, then click the Tool Presets icon on the Options bar to choose the Large Chalk Dissolve 20% preset.

◆ Hold down the Option (Alt) key and click the center of the Color Sampler on the Background layer. This sets the tool's pickup location.

2b Hold the Option (Alt) key and click the Color Sampler on the Background layer. When you are exactly aligned, the crosshairs disappear.

2b Click the point sample on the Pastel layer without the Option (Alt) key to establish the clone relationship. If you are using the Large Chalk Dissolve 20% Stamp, your cursor will look like this.

◆ Now turn the Eye icon back on for the Pastel layer, and, without the Option key, click the center of the Color Sampler on this layer. This sets the putdown location for the Clone Stamp.

Now, whenever you paint, the Clone Stamp will pick up the color from the Background layer directly below the spot where the cursor is on the Pastel layer.

Clone the Image

2c As you go over an area with the Clone Stamp, the color will build up. If you use the Clone Stamp too much, your painting will start to look like a photograph again. Keep your touch light if you want a lot of the ground to show through. When you get as much of the underlying picture showing as you want, stop. You can decide you're done at this point, or you can use the Brush tool to fill in color where you want.

◆ Follow the basic flow of the scene and clone the underlying image. Lower the Opacity setting of the Pastel layer as needed to decide which direction to stroke the color.

Add Color and Detail

2d If what you wanted was a quick pastel, you can skip this step. However, if you want to add color and depth, you might try the Brush tool using the Oil Pastel Light Small Dissolve preset. This is currently set to a very low opacity; but feel free to switch from 40% to 70% or 90%, also changing the size of your brush when necessary to make fine marks. We used mostly colors from the image or the palette, but now and then we chose pure black to add detail and depth. In some areas, we used the ground color to add texture to areas that were too photographic. If you need to "repair" an area, you

2c Here, we've begun to clone the underlying image. With this preset, every time you move over an area again, the paint builds up—quickly. In our original try at this technique, we didn't follow the natural patterns of the image; that is, we didn't use horizontal strokes for the sky and diagonal strokes for the mountains, which gave a very unnatural look. Though you can cover a lot with pure pigment later on, every step is important.

2d Our final pastel.

can paint in solid areas of the ground color you used, then switch back to the Large Chalk Dissolve 20% preset of the Clone Stamp tool and reclone from the photograph. Make sure you've reestablished the clone relationship if you've closed the image before returning to the Clone Stamp.

This final pastel was completed using only two brushes. You don't need a complex set of tools.

◆ Type B for the Brush tool and click the Tool presets pop-up to choose the Oil Pastel Light Small Dissolve preset.

◆ Lower the Pastel layer's Opacity setting, and choose colors from the Swatches palette to fill in details in the image.

A Digital Watercolor

3 Rich Harris, former Creative Director at Wacom, originally showed us this quick technique for producing a watercolor or colored pencil drawing. Since it first appeared in a previous edition of this book, we've had several students bring in work they've done using the technique—both portraits and landscapes. And they've taken it further, using different brushes and filters to create ever more interesting artwork. We've updated the technique here to take advantage of more of Photoshop's features.

Create a Grayscale Version of the Image

3a You first need a grayscale version of the image. This version will give you the "lines" of the drawing, a sort of ink pen effect that helps give the image its shape. We're going to use a Channel Mixer adjustment layer and the Merge Down command to accomplish this.

◆ Open Painted Boat Orig.psd from the DVD. Drag the Background layer to the Create a New Layer icon at the bottom of the Layers palette to make a copy of the Background.

◆ Show the Channels palette [Shift-F10] and click each channel thumbnail to see which channel has the detail you want to use for your grayscale version. In this image, we like the Blue channel.

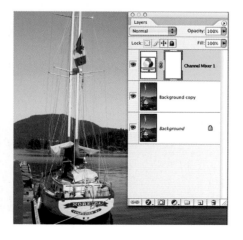

3a After you create the Channel Mixer adjustment layer, your Layers palette will look like this.

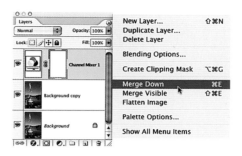

3a You can choose Merge Down from the Layers palette pop-up, or merely type Command (Ctrl)-E to merge the adjustment layer with the layer below it.

3b When you duplicate the layer and invert it, your image will look like this.

◆ From the Create a New Fill or Adjustment Layer icon, click Channel Mixer to create a new adjustment layer. For the Output Channel, choose Blue and click the Monochrome button at the bottom of the palette. Adjust the sliders to get your best black-and-white version. We used Red 12%, Green 8%, and Blue 80%. Click OK to close this dialog.

◆ Type Command (Ctrl)-E to merge this layer down. This creates your grayscale version.

Duplicate, Invert, and Blend

3b At the end of this step your canvas will go completely blank, but don't worry. We'll retrieve the detail in the next step.

◆ Make a copy of the layer by dragging it to the Create a New Layer icon at the bottom of the Layers palette.

◆ Invert this layer by typing Command (Ctrl)-I, and change the Blend mode to Color Dodge.

Gaussian Blur for Details

3c Once you do a Gaussian Blur, the details emerge again. You can use a different value for more or less detail. You can also use a Levels

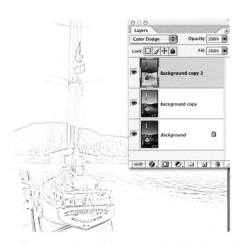

3c Once you Gaussian Blur the inverted grayscale layer, you have a sort of sketch effect to work with.

adjustment layer later to make this layer darker or lighter, as well as change the opacity of the layer itself.

◆ Go to Filter/Blur/Gaussian Blur and use about 7.5 pixels on this layer.

◆ Merge this layer with the one below it by typing Command (Ctrl)-E, and change the Blend mode to Multiply.

◆ Rename this layer Sketch. Lock the layer so it doesn't move or receive paint.

Create a Paint Layer

3d We'll create a separate layer under the Sketch layer on which we'll paint or clone. We do this rather than painting directly on the Sketch layer so that if we make a mistake, we can erase or paint over it without disturbing the lines of the sketch.

◆ Command (Ctrl)-click the Create a New Layer icon on the Layers palette to create a layer beneath the Sketch layer. Rename this layer Paint.

◆ Type Shift-Delete (Backspace) and fill this layer with white.

Clone or Paint

3e You can now choose a brush to lay down the color of the painting, letting the upper layer supply the detail; or you can use the cloning technique we just practiced in the "Pastel Landscape" section. Many of the Tool presets you have loaded currently will give you interesting results. Try different layers of color that use different brushes, some textured, some softer. Don't forget to experiment with Opacity and Flow as you paint. You can also make a copy of the Background layer and filter it, then use this version as the source for your clone. For the book, we've included a file with a filtered layer

Painter can smear underlying color as you work, even on a bristle-by-bristle basis. The Resaturation and Bleed settings let you control how much paint is picked up by your brush as you stroke.

that was cloned using the Giant Mop and Gentle Water tool presets for the Clone Stamp. If you clone using these tools, use a very light touch in the large, flat areas of color—the sky and the water. Getting a smooth look there requires some work.

If you create a clone version, try working on a watercolor version that is strictly painted rather than cloned, and use your own artistic judgement in choosing colors. To us, these versions, good or on the way to being good, always have more life to them.

Photoshop's Limitations

Photoshop has made great leaps toward letting users work naturalistically, but it still has limitations when you compare it to Corel Painter, or ask it to do some things that you could do with real paint.

Photoshop can do a pretty good job of simulating wet-on-dry methods of painting, or dry media such as chalk or pastel. You can't get realistic wet-on-wet results, however. There is no way to get underlying colors to spread or bleed as you paint a new color on top. Painter

Here are some of Painter's watercolor brushes. I've painted strokes with just a few so you can see the variety.

You can build a brush that blends the colors together in Painter without destroying the underlying texture.

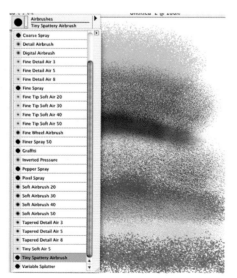

I've airbrushed with five of the default variants in Painter. The sprays from these brushes behave much more like a real airbrush than Photoshop's Airbrush option.

Painter's Impasto brushes simulate depth.

can do this, and it's one of the major reasons you might choose Painter over Photoshop for some situations.

Painter also works with paper grain better than Photoshop does. In Painter, you choose a texture for your canvas, and any brush that uses texture will know to use that paper grain. You can ask Photoshop's brushes to remember a texture by turning on Protect Texture in the Brushes palette, and that's a good feature. But when you switch to the Smudge tool to blend your colors, your texture is quickly obliterated. In Painter, you can build tools that smudge the colors together but recognize the underlying texture.

If you work in Watercolor or Airbrush, Painter is also a better choice for you. The tools in Painter are far superior to Photoshop's, and really, all the brushes are more responsive in Painter.

And finally, there's Impasto. Painter allows you to paint a brushstroke that has depth. If it's the look of thick oils or acrylics you're after, Photoshop will only frustrate you.

So, if you merely want a painterly effect, Photoshop probably has all the power and flexibility you'll need. If you want to feel like you're actually using paint, try out Painter now, or watch for future versions of Photoshop.

Choosing a Tablet

One-fifth of photographers who are using the computer to process their photographs are using a tablet as their input device, and one-third of all Photoshop users have a tablet. Wendy has used a tablet for over ten years and refuses to travel without hers. There are a lot of good reasons to use a pressure-sensitive tablet for your work on the computer. First, it's ergonomically easier to make strokes with a pen than it is holding onto a mouse. When your work includes lots of small, fine strokes, as it often does in retouching and color correcting, the pen causes less cramping and soreness. Second, you can vary your stroke with pressure. If you've ever drawn or painted, this will feel more natural to you. As you lighten the pressure on the pen, the stroke gets smaller or lighter. With many brushes you simply can't do what the brush is designed to do if you don't have pressure sensitivity. Third, for a precision input device, tablets are an exceptional value. We still sometimes use Wendy's first tablet in classes if we need an extra device. It's over ten years old, it's still supported, and it still works fine. Do you have any other computer equipment you can say that about? Wendy uses the smallest tablet because it saves desk space and arm movement. The less-sensitive tablets (which is all most photographers will need) cost under $100. As we said, an exceptional value.

Wet Paint

This version of Red Mountain was painted using Corel Painter and the Smeary Bristle Cloner brush. Where either of the two Photoshop versions took about eight hours to complete in a way that we liked, this version was accomplished in just half an hour. It has the look and feel of alla prima painting, with colors worked quickly and pigments mixing on the canvas. It was a lot of fun.

33 ◆ Contact Sheets, Picture Packages, Slide Shows, and Web Photo Galleries

Use Photoshop's automated features for generating contact sheets, picture packages, PDF presentations, and Web photo galleries.

One thing most photographers must contend with is the need to collect, arrange, and present groups of images, whether for clients, family, or just yourself. In addition, sometimes you need to reproduce many images at specific yet different sizes, and manually producing these picture package layouts can take a lot of time. Fortunately, Photoshop offers several features—Contact Sheets, Picture Packages, PDF Presentations, and Web Photo Galleries—that automate the production of photos into different types of collections or presentations. In this chapter we'll take a look at these features and show you how to use them.

Contact Sheets

Automating the creation of contact sheets is a great time-saver that any photographer will appreciate. All you need to do is gather the images for your contact sheet together in a folder, or select a group of images in Bridge. To explore the Contact Sheet feature, you can use your own images, or the images in this example, which we have provided in a folder called Fencing Class in the Ch33.Contact Shts Pic Pac Web Galleries folder on the *Photoshop Artistry* DVD. If you will be using your own images, they all need to be in the same folder. If you access the Contact Sheet command from within Photoshop, you can't pick and choose which images will be used; the contact sheet will be generated from all the images in the folder. If you will be accessing the images from Bridge (which is really the best way to do it, and the method that we will use), then you can select a range of images from a much larger collection of photos, and only the images you select will be processed into the contact sheet.

◆ To initiate the process from within Bridge, select the thumbnails you want to process for the contact sheet. To select a range of images, click the first one and then Shift-click the last one, and every thumbnail from the first to the last one you clicked will be selected. To select noncontiguous images, use the Command (Ctrl) key to add images to the selected files.

◆ Once you have selected the thumbnails you want to use in Bridge, go to the main menu and choose Tools/Photoshop/Contact Sheet II.

◆ Specify which images you want to use in the first section of the dialog. If you have accessed the Contact Sheet dialog from Photoshop, choose Folder and then click the Choose button to navigate to your source folder. If you launched the automation from within Bridge, the dialog will already say that Selected Images from Bridge will be used. You can also use any images that are currently open in Photoshop.

Launching the Contact Sheet automation for a group of selected images in Bridge.

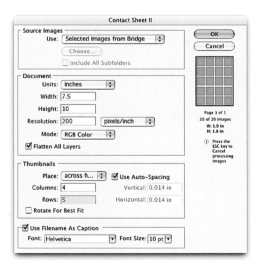

The Contact Sheet II dialog.

Using the Automated Presentation Features with Raw Images

When you specify a selection of Raw files in Bridge to be used for any of the automated processes covered in this chapter (Contact Sheets, Picture Packages, PDF Presentations, or Web Photo Galleries) you do not have the ability to change the Camera Raw settings for each image as a part of that process. Given the nature of an automated feature (that it does most everything for you), this is to be expected.

If you have previously made adjustments to the images in Camera Raw, then the last adjustment applied will be used. If you have never adjusted the image, then the Camera Raw default settings for that particular camera will be used. If you do need to generate an automated collection or presentation from Raw files and you want them to look as good as possible, then you should make your initial Camera Raw adjustments before running the automation.

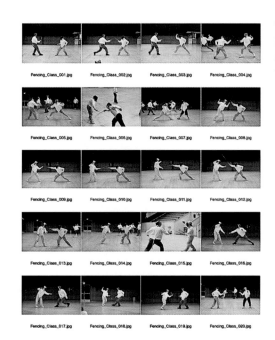

The contact sheet of the Fencing Class images generated using the settings in this example.

◆ Enter the size and resolution of the contact sheet in the Document section. These settings will usually be governed by the size of the paper you want to print on. For sheets on letter-sized paper, we usually make the contact sheets 7.5x10 inches to allow a little extra room on all sides for handling purposes or for scribbling notes. The resolution should be set to whatever you typically use for your printer. Since these are just contact sheets and not final prints, a slightly lower resolution, such as 180 pixels per inch, usually works fine and will yield a smaller file size. The mode should be set to whatever is appropriate for the images being used. In this case, even though the fencing class photos are grayscale, we're leaving Mode set to RGB since that is how we would normally print it. The Flatten All Layers option will flatten all the separate layers that are used to lay out the thumbnails and captions. If you uncheck this, all of the layers, including the type layers, are preserved. This is useful if you want to further customize things like the captions, or even rearrange the thumbnails in a way that is not provided by the program.

◆ Configure the layout of the image thumbnails on the page in the Thumbnails section. You can specify whether they are arranged across, left to right, or in vertical rows. You can also choose the number of rows and columns. The layout is generally determined by how many images you want to fit on a page. In this example, we are placing 20 images on a page, since that is the total num-

NOTE

If you have more images than will fit on a single page using the layout parameters you have chosen, Photoshop will keep generating new contact sheet pages until all images have been processed.

ber of files for the Fencing Class folder. For now, go ahead and enter the same values as shown in the illustration on the previous page. The Auto-Spacing option will determine the best spacing between the thumbnails, and the Rotate for Best Fit feature will rotate all images so they are in the same orientation.

◆ Check Use Filename As Caption, which is self-explanatory. You have a limited choice as to the fonts and font size that can be used. Note that if you uncheck this option, the size of the thumbnails in the preview grid will increase slightly.

◆ Click OK to start the Contact Sheet automation.

Picture Package

The Picture Package feature lets you create image layouts that include different print size combinations of the same or different images. The page sizes offered conform to standard paper sizes used in the photo lab industry and also used by most desktop printers. In addition to these preset print size configurations, you also get the ability to customize

The Picture Package dialog.

Click a thumbnail to add a different image file to that location in the layout.

layouts. To explore Photoshop's Picture Package feature, you can use any of your own images.

Picture Package can be launched either from within Photoshop or by selecting an image in Bridge. If you already have an image open when you launch from Photoshop, the frontmost image will be selected by default. If you have no images open in Photoshop, you will have to specify an image to use in the top part of the Picture Package dialog. When you launch it from Bridge, the first image selected will be used, even if you've selected more than one file.

◆ Choose File/Automate/Picture Package if you are accessing Picture Package from within Photoshop. If you are launching it from Bridge, choose a file to use and go to Tools/Photoshop/Picture Package.

The state of the Source Images menu at the top of the Picture Package dialog will vary depending on how you have accessed the command. Because in this example we started off with an image selected in Bridge, that is shown in the menu.

◆ Choose the paper size you will be printing the package on, the layout configuration (the default is two 5x7s), the resolution, and the image mode in the Document section. As with the Contact Sheet feature, you can also choose to have the layers flattened. Select 8x10 for the page size and (4)4x5s for the layout. For most proof-type prints, or for small snapshot images, 200 ppi generally works just fine. As with everything, however, you should test out

different resolutions to identify where your own quality threshold lies.

◆ Move the mouse cursor over one of the thumbnails, and click to select a new image file for that location of the layout. A dialog will open allowing you to navigate to where the other file is stored on your computer.

◆ Choose a label. You can use a variety of information for the label, including your copyright notice or an image title (both of these need to have been added previously to the image in the File Info dialog). You can also choose to add your own custom text. This might be useful for placing the word "PROOF" over the image in semitransparent text. If you are unsure if the chosen color or opacity of the text will work for all of the images on the page, you probably should uncheck the box for flattening the layers. This will allow you the flexibility to change the text to a more visible color or opacity after the automation is finished.

◆ Click OK the start the Picture Package automation.

It was not apparent until after the picture package was finished that 12-point type was too large to show the entire copyright notice. If the layers have been preserved, then you can simply change the type size on each layer. If you have chosen to flatten the layers for the package, however, then you will have to run the automation all over again with a different point size. After we changed the size to 8-point type, the entire copyright notice fit over the lower part of the image.

You may need to do some tests to determine what the correct size is for any text you add to the images. For the (4)4x5s layout with the vertical images in this example, 12-point Helvetica was too large to fit the entire copyright notice along the bottom of the image. Had these been horizontal, landscape-oriented images, this would not have been a problem. With the vertical images, however, we had to use 8-point type to comfortably fit all of the copyright notice over the image. Another way around this would be to place the copyright notice vertically along the long side of the images.

Customizing a Watermark

There are limited options in the Label section of the Picture Package dialog for customizing the watermarks or copyright notices you add to a layout. Fortunately, you can do a few simple things to modify the results into something that looks a bit better.

◆ Choose an image and bring up the Picture Package dialog again using the steps outlined previously.

◆ Use the same page size and layout settings as in the previous example (8x10 page and (4)4x5s). Make sure that the Flatten All Layers option is *not* checked.

◆ In the Label section, choose Custom Text for the content and in the text field, type the copyright symbol (Option-G on a Mac; Alt-0169 on the numeric keypad in Windows). Set the Font Size to 72, the Opacity to 25%, and the Position to Bottom Right. The

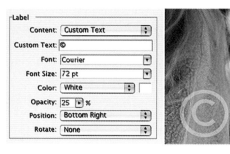

Typing in the copyright symbol for custom text and using the largest font size available with an Opacity of 25% and specifying the lower-right part of the image produces this watermark.

color you choose should be one that will show up well against the colors in your image. For the image in our example, we used white. Click OK to start the automation and generate the picture package.

When the package is finished, take a look at the Layers palette. You'll see that each copyright symbol is on its own layer above the corresponding image for that location. If you click one of these layers, you see that the two are linked together (the Link icon to the right of the layer thumbnail.

◆ Make the top copyright symbol type layer active by clicking it once. At the bottom of the Layers palette, click the small, italicized *f* icon to open the menu for Layer Style. Choose Bevel and Emboss.

◆ Change the Direction from Up to Down in the Layer Style dialog. This will make the symbol look as if it's embossed into the surface of the image. Click OK to apply the style.

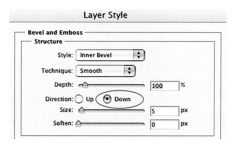

The only part of the default Bevel and Emboss settings that we changed was the Direction. The default is Up, and we used Down.

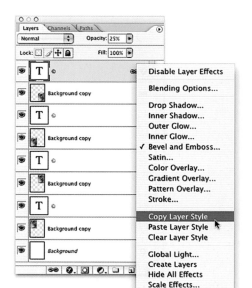

Right-click the Layer Style icon for a layer (Control-click on a one-button Mac mouse) to access a contextual menu with options related to layer styles.

- To apply the bevel and emboss style to all of the copyright symbol layers, right-click (Control-click with a Mac one-button mouse) the Layer Styles symbol for the layer you just modified (the italicized *f* on the right side of the layers palette). In the contextual menu that appears, choose Copy Layer Style near the bottom.

- Click one of the other symbol layers, and then Command (Ctrl)-click the other two symbol layers to select them. Right-click one of those selected layers in the palette, and in the contextual menu choose Paste Layer Style.

As a final customization for this example, we decided to increase the type size. To do this we selected all of the type layers using the same

method as when we pasted the layer style, then we made the Type tool active in the Tools palette, and on the Options bar we changed the size to 200 points. If you decide to move the symbols around a bit, remember that each one is linked to the corresponding picture layer. To unlink them, you will need to select each pair of layers and click the Link icon at the bottom of the Layers palette.

Editing Picture Package Layouts

One print size that is still missing from the list of default package layouts is one that is common to anyone who has ever had their photos processed at a 1-hour lab: 4x6. Since many photo albums, frames, and even greeting cards are formatted to fit 4x6 prints, it remains a mystery why Adobe has not added this most common of print sizes to the list of available packages. Fortunately, you can edit the existing layouts and create your own custom settings. In this section we'll show you how to edit an exisitng layout and create a new one.

- Open the Picture Package feature and choose 8x10 for the page size. Then choose a package layout that is the closest to what you want to create. Since our goal is 4x6 prints, we'll start off by selecting the (4)4x5 layout. In the lower-right corner of the dialog, click the Edit Layout button. In the top section of the Edit Layout dialog, set the Units to inches.

Photoshop refers to each image position as a zone. You can edit an image zone visually by dragging the handles around the image, or numerically by typing in values in the fields on the left side of the dialog. We'll give both methods a try.

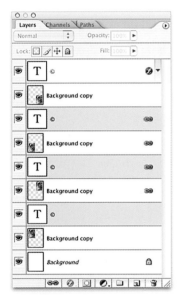

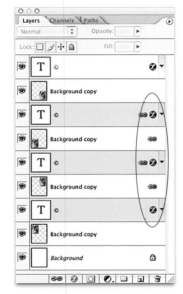

The three layers without a layer style applied are selected by clicking on one and then Command (Ctrl)-clicking on the others.

After the layer style has been pasted onto the selected layers, the Layer Style icon appears.

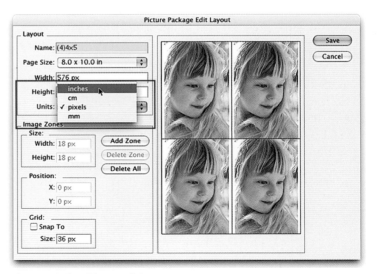

The Picture Package Edit Layout dialog.

The copyright symbol with no bevel (left) and with a bevel added (right). The size is 200-point type.

◆ Click the lower-left image, then click the Delete Zone button to remove it. Click the lower-right image, and delete that zone, too. Next, click the top-left image position. First, change the height of the upper-left zone to 6.0 inches by typing that value into the Height field. Now click the upper-right zone. Use the bottom center square "handle" and drag straight down while watching the Height value. Stop when you reach 6.0 inches. If you can't get it to be exactly 6 inches, just get it as close as you can and then type in the precise value.

◆ To add the third zone, Option (Alt)-click the top-right zone and choose Duplicate from the contextual menu. The duplicate zone appears in the top-left corner by default, so click and drag on that area to move the copy down to the lower part of the layout. Type in 6.0 inches for Width and 4.0 inches for Height to convert this zone to horizontal orientation. Carefully place this zone so that it butts up against the lower edge of the top two zones.

◆ Change the name at the top of the dialog to (3)4x6s and click the Save button to save the edited layout. By default, the file will be saved in the correct location in the Photoshop application folder. Once the new layout is saved, it will appear as a choice in the Layout menu of the main Picture Package dialog.

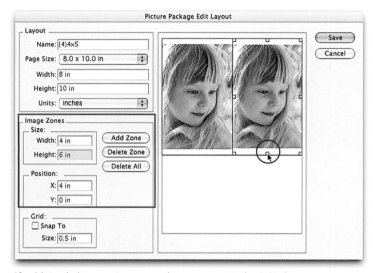

After deleting the lower two image zones, the top two are resized to 4x6 inches.

Edited layouts are saved in the Adobe Photoshop CS2 application folder in Presets\Layouts.

The saved layout for (3)4x6s in the Layout menu of the main Picture Package dialog.

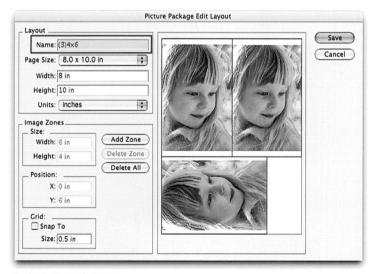

The finished layout for (3)4x6s.

PDF Presentations

Each new version of Photoshop provides more integration with the PDF format. For photographers who want to share a collection of their best shots, one of the most useful features is the ability to quickly create a PDF presentation that can run as a slide show when opened in the free Adobe Reader, or in Adobe Acrobat. You can also choose to create a regular PDF document instead of a slide show. To explore this feature, use any collection of your own images, or use the Fencing Class photos we used earlier in this chapter.

◆ In Bridge, navigate to a folder that contains the images you want to use. From the Window menu, choose Workspace/Lightbox to see just a view of the thumbnails. Use the slider at the bottom right to increase the size of the thumbnails if needed.

◆ Arrange the thumbnails in the order in which you want them to appear in the slide show. You can drag thumbnails around to create a custom order. If you want to preserve the order that you choose at this point, you can rename the files by adding a sequential number to the beginning of the existing filename, such as "01_Fencing_Class_003.jpg." Then when you choose View/Sort/By Name, the images will sort according to the number at the beginning of the filenames.

◆ Once you've chosen the images chose and placed them in order, choose Tools/Photoshop/PDF Presentation.

Images selected and arranged in the order in which they will appear in the PDF presentation.

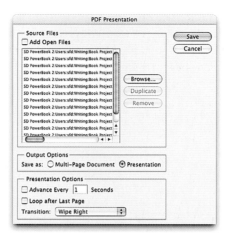

The initial PDF Presentation dialog.

NOTE

If you want the ability to advance the slides yourself during a presentation, either with a remote or from the keyboard, then leave the Advance Every option unchecked. This will allow you to manually advance the images using the Spacebar. The up and down arrow keys on the keyboard will let you move forward or backward through the images.

◆ In the PDF Presentation dialog, choose Presentation in the Output Options. Under the Presentation Options, you can select the duration that each slide will appear before transitioning to the next slide, as well as the type of transition effect. With the Loop option, you can also specify whether or not the presentation runs in a continuous loop.

◆ Click Save and you will be prompted to choose a location to save the file. Once that is done, you will be presented with a dialog containing several save options for the PDF.

The top section of the first panel of the save options lets you choose from a list of presets geared for specific purposes, such as Press Quality, High-Quality Print, or Smallest File Size, which is usually the best choice for onscreen display (the PDF/X presets are all prepress oriented). You can also specify the basic compatibility of the file in terms of which versions of Adobe Acrobat or Adobe Reader can open the file.

◆ Choose the Smallest File Size preset in the top menu, set Standard to None, and set Compatibility to Acrobat 5. The Options in the middle part of this first panel are self-explanatory and, for the purposes of an onscreen slide show, are not that important.

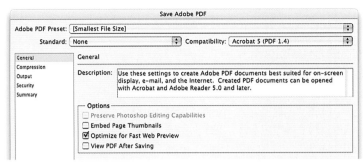

The General options of the Save Adobe PDF dialog.

The Compression options of the Save Adobe PDF dialog.

The Output options of the Save Adobe PDF dialog.

◆ On the left side of the dialog, click on Compression to move to the next section. The default Image Quality for the Smallest File Size preset is Medium Low. Since we are not concerned about file size for presentations that will be delivered from our laptops, we usually set this to High. If the presentation is not being delivered over the Web, then compressing to keep it at a low file size is not an issue. We usually leave the default resolutions for the Downsampling To settings unless we are using files that have already been prepared for a specific screen size, in which case we would not downsample the files.

◆ On the left side of the dialog, click Output to move to the next section. This covers whether to convert the images to a destination profile, what that profile is, and whether to include it in the final file. For screen displays, sRGB is fine, and we do include the

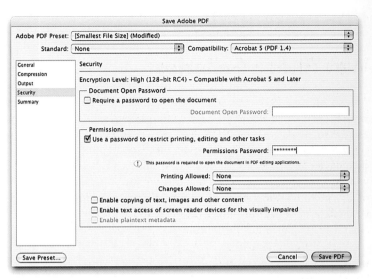

The Security options of the Save Adobe PDF dialog.

profile so that there is some reference for how the images should be displayed.

◆ On the left side of the dialog, click Security. This allows you to specify whether a password is required to open the file, or to edit or print it. For a document containing just photographs, most of these options, with the possible exception of allowing printing, are not that pertinent. Choose whatever you think best fits the needs of the presentation you are creating.

◆ The final Summary section is just a summary of the settings you have chosen. Click Save PDF to start the creation of the presentation.

If you had chosen View PDF After Saving (in the first section of the Save Options,) it will open up in Acrobat or Adobe Reader when it is finished. If not, then you'll have to find the file and open it (you specify the location where the file is saved after you set the initial options in the first dialog).

If your presentation has a manual advance (say, no timed advance was specified in the first dialog), you can use the Spacebar or the down arrow key to advance to the next image. The up arrow key will move backward through the images. The Escape key will exit the slide show.

In the first dialog that appears after launching this automation, you can also choose to create a Multi-Page Document. This will allow a person to click through the images manually using the page advance buttons in Acrobat or Adobe Reader. All the subsequent Save Options panels are the same as described earlier. If the file is intended for onscreen display, then the settings shown here will work just as well.

Web Photo Galleries

The choice of built-in gallery styles in Photoshop CS2 now numbers 20 (up from 11 in the previous version). With each version of the program, the galleries are becoming more sophisticated in how they allow visitors to your Web site to interact with your image galleries. In addition to a gallery style that automatically plays a slide show of your images, there are galleries that include image metadata, and that offer a place for the viewer to post feedback or approval of images that will be automatically emailed to you. You can use captions, copyright notices, and other items from the File Info dialog in the Web pages that display your images. Also available are two galleries that use Flash technology for thumbnail scrolling and image rendering. Thanks to Adobe's acquisition of Macromedia in late 2005, it's likely that more Flash galleries are in store in future versions of Photoshop.

In this section we'll go over the basics for creating Web Photo Galleries, point out some useful tips for getting the galleries looking

The Horizontal Feedback style.

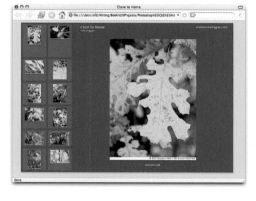

The Gray Thumbnails style.

Flash Gallery 1 style. When you roll your mouse over the thumbnails, they magnify to a larger view.

Dotted White on Black style.

The Horizontal Neutral style.

Flash Gallery 1 style. When you mouse over the larger image, your copyright notice (pulled from the File Info area) appears over the image.

the way you want them, and show you some basic gallery customization techniques you can use on some styles.

File Preparation

Before you rush right into churning out Web galleries, there are some basic things to do to prepare your images that will speed up the process. The following section is not a step-by-step exercise, but rather some suggested strategies for preparing the soil for a smoother and more efficient Web Photo Gallery process.

Adding Data to the File Info

To begin with, you should think about what type of data you can add to the File Info dialog that can be used by Photoshop as it creates the Web Photo Galleries. As you can see from the copyright notice in the Flash Gallery 1 style shown on the previous page, some information that you add to the File Info dialog can be extracted and put to good use. Ideally, adding metadata (information about the image) to the File Info dialog is something that should happen early in the process as you import your images into Bridge and, later, Photoshop. But you can still add info after you've created and perfected the master image.

Your master layered files are arguably your most valuable images, since you have already identified them as your best images and have put so much work into perfecting them. If you have not already added information to the File Info, you should do this before you spin off flattened copies for Web Galleries or other purposes. With the information added to the master files, any new copies you generate from them will already include this information as a part of the file.

You can add the information while the image is open in Photoshop by going to File/File Info, or you can also select the image in Bridge and go to the same menu location.

In terms of the Web Photo Gallery feature and what it can use, document title and copyright notice are probably the most important items to add. In the Web Photo Gallery dialog, you can specify that the title from the File Info be used both for thumbnails in some styles and for the main image page. The copyright notice is important because any image that you send out into the world should have your copyright notice. If image descriptions are important to how you market your images, then you might consider adding one here. Descriptions can also be extracted by the Web Photo Gallery automation, and, as we'll see later, they can be used for other information. While you're in this dialog, you may also choose to add keywords if any come to mind. The Web Photo Gallery feature doesn't use keywords, but they do

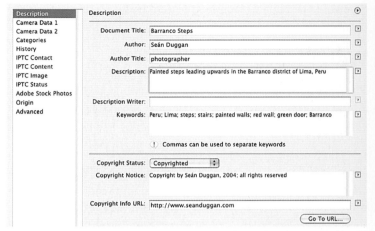

The File Info dialog, which you can access from Photoshop or from Bridge, allows you to add useful information to your file that can be used by the Web Photo Gallery automation and included on the Web pages it generates. Apart from Web gallery pages, however, it's just good image management practice to take advantage of the ability to add important metadata to your files.

Options from the Web Photo Gallery controls show data from the File Info area that can be extracted and displayed on the Web pages it creates.

come in handy. If you are already using an image cataloging program, then you are probably already aware of the importance keywords to your images and your ability to manage them.

Using Actions to Prepare Web Photo Gallery Images

Actions are covered in detail in Chapter 10, "Automating Photoshop," so the goal here is not to go over them again, but just to point out some suggested steps that can be appiled with actions that can help you prepare your images for a Web gallery. Although the Web Photo Gallery automation can take a large, layered master file and process it to use in a gallery, the larger and more complicated the file, the longer it will take and the more system resources it will gobble up.

Seán uses actions to create a flattened copy of the master file, resize it to a more manageable size, convert it to the sRGB profile, and place it in a Web Photo Gallery "drop folder." If he knows the specific size he will use for the Web gallery images, then he resizes them to those pixel dimensions. For images where the final size is not yet known, they are just resized smaller so that the gallery automation can process them faster. The files are saved in the Photoshop format to allow for further tweaking, especially if the final images for the Web page need sharpening (the Web Photo Gallery command does not apply sharpening to the images).

Here's a rundown of some of the basic steps used to prep a layered master file for a Web gallery. Wherever possible, we run these steps as actions to save time and ensure consistency.

◆ Double-check the File Info dialog for important data that can be used by the Web Photo Gallery command.

◆ Use Image/Duplicate to spin off a flattened copy (use the Merged Layers Only option in Duplicate Image dialog).

◆ Use File/Automate/Fit Image to resize to a specific size. This command is great for an action step because it works for both horizontal and vertical images. Just specify the same size in pixels for both width and height. If you desire more control, especially over the resampling method used, then you should do this step using the Image Size dialog; in that case, though, you would need to create two separate actions, for horizontal and vertical images.

◆ Use Edit/Convert to Profile to convert the image to sRGB (this is the best profile to use for images displayed on the Web). In Photoshop CS and earlier, this command is found under Image/Mode/Convert to Profile.

◆ Save in Photoshop format to a specified "drop folder" for images that will be used in Web galleries.

The Web Photo Gallery Controls

Once you've prepared your images for the gallery automation, it's time to choose the order in which you would like them to appear on the thumbnails page, or in a thumbnails row or column if that's the style you choose. By far the easiest way to do this is from Bridge. In the following section, we will take a tour of the different panels of the Web Photo Gallery dialog and explain the various settings and how they affect the final gallery pages. You can use a selection of your

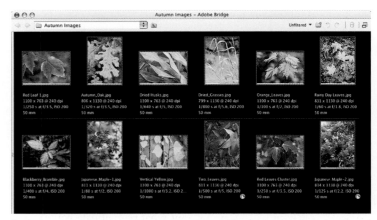

For the Autumn Details images in this example, we arranged them so that the horizontal and vertical images would alternate. In the gallery style that we will use, this will result in a visually interesting arrangement of thumbnails .

own images or you can use the Autumn Details folder of images in the Chapter 33 folder on the DVD.

◆ In Bridge, target the folder of images you want to use. From the Window menu, choose Workspace/Lightbox to show just the thumbnails. Use the slider at the lower right of the Bridge window to adjust the size of the thumbnails as needed.

◆ Drag the thumbnails around to rearrange them into the order in which you want them to appear on the thumbnails Web page. With the Autumn Details images, we arranged them so that the horizontal and vertical images would alternate. If you want to use all of the images in the folder, then Select All using Command (Ctrl)-A. If you want to use only certain images, Command (Ctrl)-click to select the ones you want to use.

◆ From the Tools menu, choose Photoshop/Web Photo Gallery.

The General Settings

The first panel of settings in the Web Photo Gallery dialog lets you choose from 20 preset styles. Although there is a small thumbnail sample of the style on the right, keep in mind that you can change the color scheme on most of the styles. The best way to get a sense of how the different styles look and work as a Web page is to try them out.

◆ For this exercise, choose the Horizontal Neutral style.

In this section you also specify the source images (because we started the process from Bridge, the Source Images setting should automatically indicate that it is using the selected Bridge images) and the

The Banner Options.

In the first panel of settings for the Web Photo Gallery, you choose a style, add your email address, specify the source files and destination folder for the final files, and configure a few General options.

The Banner area for the Centered Frame 2 - Feedback style. In this instance, the current date is not appropriate since the images were taken over a year earlier.

destination for the completed Web gallery files. It's best to specify a folder just for the gallery files.

♦ Click the Destination button and navigate to where you want the files to be placed. If you have not already created a folder for them, do so now using the New Folder button in the dialog. Name the folder with the name of the gallery style so you can keep track of them if you want to try different styles.

♦ Under the Style menu, add your email address if you want this to appear as a clickable link on the main thumbnails Web page.

In the lower part of the dialog is the Options section. The available choices will change depending on what is selected in the Options menu, and this is where we will be making the rest of the settings for the gallery (the top part of the dialog will stay the same). The first menu item is for the General Options. These deal mainly with under-the-hood HTML or encoding issues and do not affect the look of the gallery.

The Extension setting is not that critical. Either one will work fine, so use whichever format you prefer. We recommend that you check Use UTF 8 Encoding for URL and Add Width and Height Attributes for Images. The last choice, Preserve All Metadata, should be used only if you want images on the Web gallery pages to have all their metadata. This can be useful if you want your copyright notice to travel with the files, but keep in mind that other info, such as camera exposure data and date-created markers, may also go along for the ride.

♦ Open the Options menu and choose Banner.

The Banner Options

The Banner area on the Web page contains basic information such as the title of the gallery or site, the name of the photographer, contact info, and the date. Obviously, what you enter here will be determined by the images you are posting. For Contact Info, you might consider including your phone number if you want prospective clients to reach you by phone (your email address is taken care of in the very top section of the Web Photo Gallery dialog).

The one thing to be aware of here is the Date field. By default it automatically resets to show the current day's date, even if you never use it (we find this somewhat annoying and wish this setting were more "sticky," meaning that the values you last used, in this case no date, remain until you change it). For most of what we use the galleries for, the date is not important, so we leave it blank. Just keep in

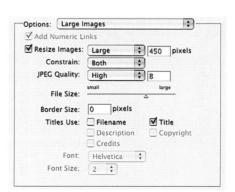

The options for size, quality, border, and titles for the large images.

mind that every time you use the Web Photo Gallery feature, you will have to delete the current date from the date field.

◆ Open the Options menu and choose Large Images.

Large Images Options

In this section you determine the size of the main display version of the images. In some cases these will be featured on their own page, while in others they may share the main page along with a row or column of thumbnails. The primary settings here affect the image size and the quality (the level of JPEG compression). If you have already sized your images to a specific size for the Web Photo Gallery and saved them as JPEGs, then you should uncheck the Resize Images check box. This turns off not only the resizing, but also the JPEG recompression. Unchecking the Resize Images option is useful if you want to prepare each image individually to ensure the highest quality in terms of size, sharpening, and compression.

◆ For this example, go ahead and choose Large for the Image Size. The Constrain option should be set to Both. Set the JPEG Quality to 8.

The Border feature can serve two purposes. First, in some gallery styles, through the use of the link color, the active link color, and visited link color (specified later in the Custom Colors section), a border can show which images have been visited. The problem with this is that in some styles, the images themselves are links; if you click them, you will move on to the next image. This means that if you choose the standard link color of blue, and you decide to use a border, you will have a garish blue frame around your image. Probably not what you had in mind. Using a visited link color of red only makes matters worse. We don't think link colors are appropriate with the artful display of photographs, as they compete with the image and are very distracting. The only time when they might conceivably make sense is

A 30-pixel border with all link colors set to white results in a classic "matted" look when used with the Gray Thumbnails Web gallery style.

NOTE

If a particular option is dimmed in the Web Photo Gallery dialog, that means it's not available for the gallery style you are using, or that its parameters cannot be changed.

if you have a lot of thumbnails on a page and want to provide a clue as to which images have already been looked at.

The other purpose for the border is that you can use it to create a "matted" look for the large images. This can look very cool, especially when used with a black or dark gray background. The caveat, however, is that it will work only if you set all the link colors to white.

◆ Leave the Border setting at 0.

Titles

If you have previously added infomation to the File Info dialog for an image, then you can specify that certain items be used as titles for the large display images.

◆ If you are using the Autumn Details photos for this exercise, check the box for Titles. Then open the Options menu, and choose Thumbnails to move on to the next section.

Thumbnails Options

In this section you choose the size of the thumbnails, the layout of columns and rows (if applicable to the style you have chosen), whether the thumbnails have a border, and whether a title will appear with the thumbnail. We generally do not use titles with thumbnails, because with most designs it looks too cluttered. There are some gallery styles, however, most notably the ones that allow client feedback, where extra room around the thumbnail makes using a title or other info more acceptable. The only way to tell what will work for you is to try out the various styles and configurations and see for yourself.

In the Simple style, a 30-pixel border with a link color of blue results in this visual travesty.

A visited-link color of red combined with a 30-pixel border produces this, a grievous offense against good design.

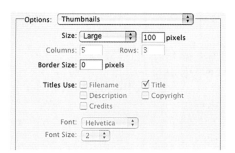

The Thumbnails options for the Horizontal Neutral style. Options that are dimmed are either unavailable, or can't be changed for the chosen style.

For the Horizontal Neutral style that we are using, you'll see no options for controlling the layout of the thumbnails in columns or rows. This is because, for this style, the thumbnails are automatically arranged in a horizontal row under the main image, and there is no way to change this.

◆ Set the size to Large, and use 0 for the border. Open the Options menu and choose Custom Colors to move on to the next section.

Custom Colors Options

In most cases, we are pretty conservative in our choice of colors for Web galleries. Our primary goal is to create a display environment that does not detract from the image or compete with it. So we use neutral colors such as white, black, and varying shades of gray for most of our Web galleries.

As we mentioned earlier in this chapter in the "Large Image Options" section, you have to be very careful about the link colors since they will show up in places where you may not expect them, like the borders around images and thumbnails.

For certain gallery styles, some of the colors may be fixed, as is the case with the Background color in the Horizontal Neutral style we are using in this example. Don't be concerned what color is set for the background here, as it will be ignored by the gallery style.

◆ Click the Banner swatch to open the Color Picker, and choose a dark gray. A value of approximately 100 for R, G, and B, or, if you click the Only Web Colors check box at the lower left of the Color Picker, you can click the third gray swatch from the bottom (#666666).

◆ Set the Text and all of the Link colors to white (255, 255, 255, or #FFFFFF in Web colors).

◆ Open the Options menu and choose Security to move on to the next section.

Security Options

The Security options are misnamed because they do not allow you to attach any type of security encryption or passwords to the gallery to control who can access them. This section should really be renamed "Watermark Options," since all it does is allow you to overlay information on top of the images. This information can be pulled from the metadata that has been added to the File Info, or you can enter your own custom text. Using lower Opacity settings can result in a "ghosted back" effect, which might work if you want to overlay the copyright symbol or your studio name, or even the word "PROOF" over the images. For this example we'll leave the so-called Security options set to None.

If you want to experiment with placing the copyright symbol over the images, set the Content to Custom, type in the copyright symbol, set the font size to 72 pt, the color to white, the opacity to 20% and the postion to Centered.

◆ Click OK to start the automation process. When it is finished, it will display the gallery in your default Web browser.

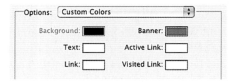

The Custom Colors options. The Background color is unavailable for the Horizontal Neutral style.

The Security options should really be renamed the "Watermark" options.

A copyright symbol placed over a Web gallery image at 15% Opacity using the Security options.

The finished Autumn Details gallery using the Horizontal Neutral style and the settings outlined on the previous pages. Note the alternating horizontal and vertical thumbnails that were set up in Bridge before launching the Web gallery automation. With this particular style, some scrolling may be required to see all of a vertical image. Be sure to test-drive different gallery styles with a variety of images, both horizontal and vertical, before deciding on a particular style.

Customizing a Gallery Style

If you are familiar with editing Web pages, either by tinkering with the HTML and CSS, or using a Web editor such as Adobe GoLive or Adobe (formerly Macromedia) Dreamweaver, you can use one of the existing gallery templates as the starting point for creating your own custom gallery style. This can be quite useful if you want to present images to your clients in a gallery that includes your studio logo.

We won't go into great detail on the ins and outs of editing the templates, since this is not a Web book. If you already know a modest amount about how Web pages are created at the code level (which describes our level of experience in this area), you will probably be able to figure out a lot of this on your own through a little trial and error. What we will be doing here is showing you the basic steps to get started, using the fairly simple example of adding a custom image in the banner area of one of the styles. What follows is not a step-by-step exercise, but a recounting of how we went about customizing a particular template. Not all Web editing programs are created equal, however, so your mileage may vary.

Making a Copy of an Existing Template

The first thing to do is to create a copy of the folder that contains all of the template elements for the style you wish to customize. You can find the Web gallery templates inside the Photoshop CS2 applica-

tion folder in the Presets folder. For this example, we're using Simple - Vertical Thumbnails. We copied the entire folder and renamed it "_Customized-Gray Vertical."

Deciding What to Change

It helps if you know what you want to customize before you start remodeling, so before we began tinkering under the hood, we used the automation feature to create a gallery from this style. We evaluated it in a Web browser to see what we wanted to change and what would have a visual impact without being too much trouble in terms of having to rewire the underlying structure of the design. In the end we decided to place a custom logo image in the top banner area.

The first thing we needed to know was the pixel dimensions of that area. To determine this, we made a screen capture of the gallery as it looked in the Web browser, then we opened that screen capture in Photoshop. We set our ruler units to pixels and used the Rectangular

Before modifying a copy of the Simple - Vertical Thumbnails style, we created a gallery with it and reviewed it to see what we wanted to change. We decided to add a custom logo image to the top banner area.

In Photoshop, we opened a screen capture of how the gallery looked in a Web browser and used a rectangular selection of the banner area to determine the pixel dimensions for our logo image.

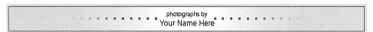

The namebanner.psd file that we created to customize the banner area of the Simple Vertical Thumbnails gallery style. This layered file is in the Chapter 33 folder on the DVD.

Marquee tool to carefully make a selection of just the top banner. In the lower-right section of the Info palette, we saw that the selection was 822x55 pixels.

Creating the New Logo Image

In Photoshop, we made a new file (File/New) that was 822x55 pixels. We filled this with the same gray as the background of the gallery template (RGB = 204, 204, 204, or #CCCCCC in hexidecimal values). We created a new layer and added a white-to-transparent radial gradient in the center of the file. Then we added some basic logo type and customized it by adding some small gray squares that faded out on either end. If you want to see what we did to make this file, we have included it in the folder called Custom Elements, which is in the Chapter 33 folder on the DVD. The file is called namebanner. psd and can easily be customized with your own name (we used the Frutiger typeface; if you don't have that font installed on your computer, you will have to substitute another one).

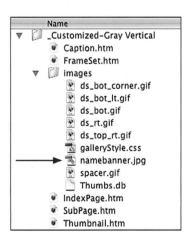

The new logo image is placed inside the "images" folder that is inside the copied gallery template folder.

The top portion of Frameset.htm opened in a Web browser confirmed that this was the file we needed to work on.

When the logo file was finished, we used File/Save for Web to save a JPEG version. We will be going over the many nuances of preparing image files for the Web, including the Save for Web dialog, in the next chapter.

Once we saved the file namebanner.jpg, we placed it inside the images folder that was inside the gallery template folder that we had copied.

Editing the HTML Pages

Several HTML pages are used in creating most of the gallery styles. On designs that use frame sets, such as this one, figuring out which frame you need to edit may entail opening each one in a Web browser. In this example, that is exactly what we did. We soon found out that the file we needed to edit was called Frameset.htm.

Next, we opened this file into Adobe GoLive CS2. You can use any capable Web editor for this part of the process; or, if you are comfortable at hand-coding, a text editor will also suffice (of course, if you are savvy about hand-coding, then you already knew that!). Using GoLive, we identified the code that defined the top banner section of the page. By selecting the HTML table that made up the banner, we then used GoLive's Inspector palette to specify a background image

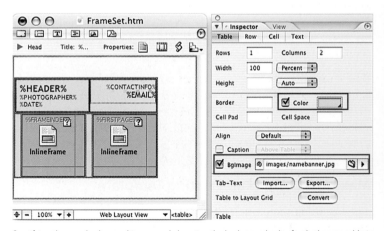

Specifying the new background image and changing the background color for the banner table in Adobe GoLive CS2.

```
61  <td valign=top valign=middle align=middle style="border:1pt solid #999999">
62  <table cellpadding=0 cellspacing=0 bgcolor="#CCCCCC">
63  <tr bgcolor="%BANNERCOLOR%">
64  <td colspan=4>
65  <table width=100% bgcolor="%BANNERCOLOR%">
66  <tr>
67  <td align=left valign=top>
68  <div id="titleframe">
```

The original code line that specifies the table width and background color. %BANNERCOLOR% indicates a value specified in the Web Photo Gallery custom color options.

```
61  <td valign=top valign=middle align=middle style="border:1pt solid #999999">
62  <table cellpadding=0 cellspacing=0 bgcolor="#CCCCCC">
63  <tr bgcolor="%BANNERCOLOR%">
64  <td colspan=4>
65  <table width=100% bgcolor="#CCCCCC" background="images/namebanner.jpg">
66  <tr>
67  <td align=left valign=top>
68  <div id="titleframe">
```

The edited code line with a defined value for the background color and the new namebanner image specified as the background image.

The customized template in the Styles menu of the Web Photo Gallery dialog.

to be used inside this table. The cool thing about a background image in an HTML table is that you can code text so that it displays on top of the image. This will allow us to still take advantage of the ability to choose a name for the gallery and add an email link, both of which will show up on top of the new logo image. We also changed the background color of the table to a light gray (#CCCCCC) to match that of the main section of the page.

Testing the Results and Fixing Glitches

After making our edits and saving the file, we opened it in a Web browser to double-check our work. Everything looked good, but when we took it for a real test drive by creating an actual Web gallery with it, the logo image was cropped a bit.

To fix this, we made another screen capture of the gallery in a Web browser that showed the slight cropping of the name image. Then we opened this into Photoshop and measured the banner area again using a rectangular selection marquee and consulting the width/height readout in the Info palette. This time we found that a height of 46 pixels represented the actual space taken up by the banner section of the table. We returned to the layered file for the namebanner image and changed the height and made the type a bit more compact to fit better in the narrower file, then saved a new JPEG using File/Save for Web. We then replaced the older namebanner.jpg file in the

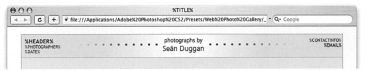

The initial test of the edited Frameset.htm file in a Web browser looked OK.

Creating an actual Web gallery using the new template showed that the namebanner image was being cropped a bit.

Resizing the namebanner image to 46 pixels high and making the type a bit more compact fixed the cropping problem. The final customized template is shown here in the Safari browser on a Mac.

template's images folder with the newer one. Tests with the new 46-pixel-high image worked fine.

Browser/Platform Differences and Other Disclaimers

One of the challenges with developing Web sites is that there are often differences in how the same Web page looks in different browsers, different versions of the same browser, and on different computer platforms. Sometimes these differences are minor and of little consequence, but sometimes they can be major enough to send you deep into the labyrinth of code to try and track down the problem. A good

Compared to Safari (previous page), the Firefox browser devotes too much space to the thumbnail column.

illustration of this is to compare how the customized gallery looks in Safari versus how it displays in Firefox (both on the Mac). In the Safari version the thumbnail column looks proportionately the right size, given the size of the thumbnails and the column's relation to the rest of the page. In Firefox, however, the area devoted to the thumbnails seems much too large. We have no idea why this is the case. We do know, however, that it has nothing to do with our customized version, because the default Simple - Vertical Thumbnails style looks the same when viewed in Firefox. The whole reason for this comparison is to point out that you may run into these differences and glitches. Whether you will be able to do anything about them will depend on your level of Web coding expertise.

Another thing to be aware of is that even seemingly minor changes to a Web page's code can cause the page to "break." The accidental deletion of a semicolon, a quotation mark, or an angled bracket can create glitches that can take a while to track down. If you do venture into tweaking the default templates, just be sure that you do so on a copy of the folder that contains the original style. And make sure that you give the copied folder a completely new name. We found out the hard way that just adding the word "customized" or "modified" to an existing style name caused Photoshop to generate error messages and refuse to use the style. Only after spending a lot of time troubleshooting other, seemingly more likely causes did we try a totally different folder name, which solved the problem.

Using Customized Gallery Styles

We have placed the modified template used in this example in the Chapter 33 folder on the DVD. Look in the folder called Custom Elements. In there you will find a file called namebanner.psd, which is the 46-pixel-high layered file ready for you to customize with your own name. There is also a folder called _Customized-Gray Vertical If you copy this folder to the Photoshop CS2/Presets/Web Photo

Gallery folder, it will appear in the Styles menu of the Web Photo Gallery dialog. The namebanner.jpg file currently in place is the generic "*your name here*" version. Simply replace it with a new JPEG after you've changed the layered PSD file.

Customizing the Photographer's Name Field

If you have a custom image or graphic that includes your name, as in the example in this chapter, then you can use the photographer's Name field in the Banner Options for other information. You can see this in the final Web gallery of the Autumn Details photos that we made using the customized style. Since Seán's name was already present in the banner image, the name field was used as a subtitle for the main gallery title: "Photographs from the Sierra Nevada."

Creative Use of the Description in File Info

Another thing that we want to point out is that the Description Field in the File Info dialog is not just for descriptions. You can use it for anything at all. In the case of the Autumn Details images, we added information about the available print sizes for the images. This could be very useful if we wanted to encourage print sales through the Web gallery. In the Large Images section of the Web Photo Gallery dialog, we clicked the check boxes for Title and Description. The Autumn Details images already have this information added to them if you want to try it out.

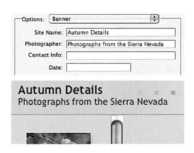

Since the photographer's name appears in the image banner in the customized style, it allows additional information to be used in the photographer's Name field in the Banner options.

The Descriptions field in the File Info dialog: It's not just for descriptions! In this case we used it to describe the print and paper sizes that were being offered with these images.

Portfolio

Berle Stratton

A photographer who moonlights as a pathologist, Berle's photography combines his strong emotional response to landscape with the "cosmic sensuality" of light. These images of Earth, viewed through the heavenly events of weather, capture both a sense of timelessness and the sacred Now. See more of his images at www.berlestratton.com.

34 ◆ Optimizing Images for the Web

Getting your images to look their best on the Web, both in terms of color and detail rendition, is a mixture of art and science. While the methods used to create excellent Web images are firmly based in the scientific realm of software code, it is the eye of the artist that must interpret and guide the process to ensure that the image presented on the Web is as faithful as possible to the finished version of the photograph.

In the previous chapter, we covered the use of the automated Web Photo Gallery feature. But while that feature does a fairly decent job of processing groups of images into a Web gallery, it doesn't give you much control over how the photos are translated into small, Web-sized versions. In this chapter we will focus on the best techniques for optimizing photographic images using the JPEG format. Our ex-plorations will take us into the Save As dialog for basic options, and the Save for Web command for more in-depth controls. Before a file is ready for saving as a JPEG, however, it must first be resized, then sharpened for display viewing, and finally converted from the work-ing space to a profile that is more suitable for images that will be output to the Web. In the first part of this chapter, we'll review these three distinct areas.

Determining Optimal Image Size

The first item of business to settle before you begin creating Web versions of your images is how large they will be in pixel dimensions. The pixel size you use will likely be influenced by the file size of the image (which has an impact on download time), the design require-ments of your Web site, and the presumed display resolution of your intended audience.

The best way to determine what image size to use is to visit other photographers' Web sites. Find a site where you like the size of the images in relation to the rest of the site's design and also how large they appear on your own display. The easiest way to see the pixel dimenions of an image is to right-click (Control-click on a one-button Mac mouse) an image, and from the contextual menu that appears where you clicked, choose View Image in New Window (in the Firefox Web browser this option is called simply View Image). The title bar at the top of the new browser window will list the name of the image and its size in pixels.

Barry's image of Gambier Island near Gibsons, British Columbia, shown here opened in a new browser window. The title area at the top shows the filename and the size in pixels.

Image Size and Monitor Resolution

You should also take into consideration the likely monitor resolution that your intended audience will be using. For example, you might resize your images based on the resolution of your own display (say, 1280x854) and output them at 800x600. While they might look fine on your monitor or on any display using a resolution greater than 1024x768, someone with a display resolution of 800x600 will not be able to see your entire image on screen (remember that the Web browser interface takes up pixels, too).

Current statistics (as of February 2006) indicate that most people are using monitor resolutions of at least 800x600, and many people are using a resolution of 1024x768. To ensure that your site is accessible to the largest number of viewers, however, the conventional wisdom says that the Web site should be easily viewable on an 800x600 moni-tor resolution. If your targeted audience is working in the creative field (for example, art directors, photographers, gallery owners, or art buyers), then it is likely (though not certain) that they are using a resolution of 1024x768 or higher. Keep in mind that many users are not that computer savvy and may never change the default setting (which is often 800x600), or they may use 800x600 because it is easier to read.

Resizing Images for the Web

If you are resizing a master layered file, the first thing you should do is make a copy by choosing Image/Duplicate and clicking the check box for Duplicate Merged Layers Only (this will flatten the layers of the copy file). This is a safe way of making sure that you don't accidentally resize and save your layered masterpiece as a tiny image. Once you've created the duplicate, you can close the master file. If the master was a 16-bit file and the copy file is still at that bit depth, you should go to the Image/Mode menu and choose 8 Bits/Channel.

Bicubic Sharper Interpolation

For resizing images, we generally recommend using the Image Size dialog, which is found under the Image menu. The main reason for this preference is that it is only here that you can specify the interpolation algorithm that will be used when the file is resized. The one that Adobe designed specifically for downsampling images and making them smaller is Bicubic Sharper. Any resizing you apply to a file that is destined for the Web should be done using this interpolation method.

Resolution

For images that are meant for onscreen display, either within an email program or on a Web page, the resolution of the file (for instance, pixels per inch) is one thing you don't have to worry about because it doesn't matter. This may come as a bit of a surprise if you are used to the concept that using specific resolutions is essential for ensuring image quality. The reason resolution doesn't matter for Web images is that Web browsers (and email programs) display the image based on its pixel dimension (say, 600x400). Any specific pixels-per-inch setting you apply in Photoshop is completely disregarded. To see this concept in action, try the following experiment.

> **NOTE**
>
> The only time that resolution is important for Web or email purposes is if you are providing a larger, downloadable image, or emailing a file, that needs to print at a certain quality. For general display images, however, it is not an issue.

The Bicubic Sharper interpolation method (seen here in the Image Size dialog) is the best to use for downsampling images.

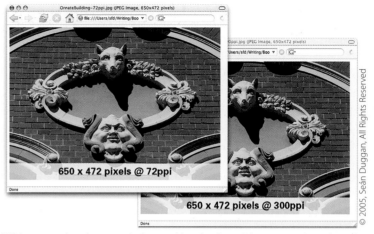

Web browsers and email programs display images based on the pixel dimension, not the resolution. In the example above, two versions of an image with the same pixel dimension but different resolutions display at the same size in the Firefox Web browser.

◆ Launch a Web browser (Firefox, Internet Explorer, Safari, for instance).

◆ From the Chapter 34.Optimizing Web Images folder on the *Photoshop Artistry* DVD, open the folder called Resolution Tests. There are two OrnateBuilding files in this folder. Both have the exact same pixel dimension (650x472) but one was resized at 72 ppi and the other is at 300 ppi.

◆ Drag the 72 ppi version into an open browser window to display it in the browser.

◆ Open a second browser window and drag the 300 ppi version into that window. You'll see that both images display at exactly the same size (some browsers may try to scale the image to fit the window; if that's the case, consult your browser's Help feature to see how you can view the images at 100%).

Another aspect of resolution that you should be aware of (but that you have no control over) is that the monitor resolution of the computer that is displaying the Web site will affect how large the images appear in relationship to the rest of the screen area. If a viewer has a larger resolution set for their display (such as 1280x854), the images on your Web site will appear smaller in relationship to the entire screen than they would on a display that was set to 800x600.

Cropping

We do not recommend cropping to a specific pixel dimension since there is no way to specify the all-important interpolation method using the Crop tool. Any resizing done with this tool will use the setting specified in the Preferences. The default is Bicubic, which is a perfectly good setting to use as a generic default, but is not the best for resizing to Web-sized dimensions.

If you need to crop the image, you should first apply the crop and make sure that no specific size is set on the Options bar (click the Clear button to remove any sizes that may be left over from a previous use of the tool). Then, once the file is cropped to your liking, use the Image Size dialog and resize to the desired pixel dimension using the Bicubic Sharper option in the Resample Image menu at the bottom of the dialog.

Automate/Fit Image

When using actions for processing large groups of images to a specific size, there is a very useful function called Fit Image, which is grouped with the Automate commands in the File menu. This is a very simple dialog that allows you to specify a width and a height in pixels that the image will be constrained within. To make it usable for both horizontal and vertical images in the same action, enter the same pixel value into each field. If you enter 500 pixels for both the width and the height, for example, then vertical images will be 500 pixels high and horizontal images will be 500 pixels wide. The one option this feature is lacking, however, is the ability to specify an interpolation method. Still, for the great benefit you get from automating the resizing of both vertical and horizontal images in the same action, the lack of interpolation choices might not be a big issue. But if you want to have control over the interpolation method, then you will have to use the Image Size dialog.

Sharpening Images for the Web

After downsampling your image to the correct size, whether for email purposes, or for posting on a Web site, you will need to sharpen your images. We will not be showing you how to sharpen images here—that's covered in great detail in Chapter 12, "Essential Photoshop Techniques for Photographers." The purpose of this section is to provide an overview of the three primary methods you might use to sharpen images for the Web and to suggest scenarios when one

method might be more effective, or simply more time-efficient, than the others.

The three methods that make the most sense for sharpening Web images are all found in the Filter/Sharpen menu: Unsharp Mask, Smart Sharpen, and the plain old Sharpen filter. The first two methods give you different controls as well as a preview. The last one gives you no controls or preview at all, but it sometimes does a very good job for Web-sized images—hence its inclusion here.

The Sharpen Filter

Many Photoshop users who relish control probably avoid the humble Sharpen filter simply because it provides no preview and no way to adjust the sharpening effect. Indeed, for what we would call the primary sharpening of an image—that is, the final sharpening you would apply to a file that will be output as a fine art print—we would never use this filter, for just that reason.

But for small images that have been resized to be used in email or for Web sites, the Sharpen filter is worth a look simply because it often does an excellent job on these small files, and with no dialog box or settings to worry about, it's very fast. If you like having the option to tweak the settings, this method may not be for you, but we do recommend that you run some tests on Web-sized images and see what you think.

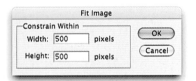

The Fit Image command is perfect for resizing both horizontal and vertical images to a specific width or height using a single action.

Using the Fade Command with the Sharpen Filter

Though the Sharpen filter has no controls, you can use the Edit/Fade command immediately after running the filter to customize the effect somewhat. If one pass of the filter is not enough, but two times is too much, consider running the filter twice and then using Edit/Fade to dial back the opacity of the second application of the filter. With this technique, you can run the filter 1.25 or 1.5 times and often arrive at the perfect amount of sharpening for a Web image.

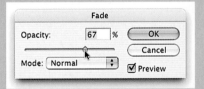

A 200% detail view comparing the effects of an Unsharp Mask Threshold setting of 0 (left) and a Threshold setting of 10 (right). In the second image the blurry background area has not been sharpened.

To apply the filter, simply select it from the Filter/Sharpen menu. To properly view the effects, the display of the image should be set to 100% (View/Actual Pixels).

Smart Sharpen

This filter, which was introduced in Photoshop CS2, is a welcome improvement over the Unsharp Mask filter that had been the main way we sharpened images for years. One of the primary advantages of Smart Sharpen is that it has a more delicate touch in its application of the sharpening effect. The Blur option lets you specify a type of blurring to compensate for, whether lens blur, which is what we normally use, or motion blur (Gaussian Blur makes the filter behave like the Unsharp Mask filter). For images that may have noise problems, Smart Sharpen lets you specify that lesser amounts of sharpening be applied to the shadows, where noise is normally most visible.

The values you use for smaller, Web-sized images will be lower than with larger images you're preparing for printing. Try starting out with the Amount at 75 to 100, and the Radius set to 0.6, and adjust up or down from there.

Unsharp Mask

For some images, the old sharpening standby, Unsharp Mask, may be the better choice because of the presence of the Threshold control. The Threshold setting determines which areas get sharpened based on the difference in value between neighboring pixels. If the difference in tonal or color value between pixels in the same area is less than the Threshold amount, then those pixels will not be sharpened. For images that have areas of intricate detail juxtaposed with relatively smooth areas that you want to remain unsharpened (say, a sky, or the smooth skin of a woman's face), the Threshold slider offers an elegant way to achieve this without the use of selections or masks.

Converting the Color Profile

Web browsers are notoriously fickle about honoring embedded ICC color profiles. Of the three we tested—Firefox, Internet Explorer, and Safari—only Safari honored the embedded profiles of our test images and displayed them identically to the way they looked in Photoshop (our tests were done on a Mac, so results on a PC may vary). The purpose of the tests was not to arrive at ironclad scientific proof, but to illustrate that when creating images for the Web, some things are out of your control.

◆ To see this for yourself, launch a Web browser. If you have more than one browser installed on your computer, you may want to try this with all of them.

A tale of three browsers: Firefox (top), Internet Explorer (middle), and Safari (bottom). The three files display with subtle differences in Firefox and Internet Explorer, but the sRGB file looks the closest to how it should appear. All three files display identically in Safari, and also match how the images look in Photoshop.

- From the Chapter 34 folder on the DVD, open the folder called Color Profile Tests. There are three different versions of the same image in this folder. Each file was saved with a different ICC profile in Photoshop.

- Drag the sRGB file into the browser window. From the browser's File menu, choose New Window twice to open up two new browser windows.

- Drag the ColorMatch RGB and the AdobeRGB files into their own browser windows, and compare how all the files look. You may also want to open all of the files into Photoshop (choose to preserve the embedded profiles when you open them) and see the difference between how Photoshop displays them and how the Web browser displays them.

Since Photoshop understands and honors ICC profiles, all of the images should look identical when viewed in that program. You are likely to see some subtle differences, however, when viewing the three files side by side in a Web browser. In our tests on a Mac, the sRGB profile looked the closest to how it appeared in Photoshop in all three browsers, with Safari providing an identical display for all the images. In Internet Explorer and Firefox, ColorMatch was a bit too dark and AdobeRGB was a bit too light and desaturated. While these differences are subtle, if you care about how your images look on the Web, applying the correct profile is one way to exercise some control in a display medium that offers you very little control.

Because you do not know what Web browsers (or versions of the browsers) people will be using as they view your images, or how well those browsers interpret color profiles (if at all), the easiest way around this is simply to use the profile that most closely represents the vast majority of monitors in the world—and that is sRGB. To convert an image from the color profile of your working space (such as Adobe RGB) into sRGB, use the Convert to Profile command, which is found under the Edit menu (or under Image/Mode in versions prior to CS2) and then select sRGB as the destination space.

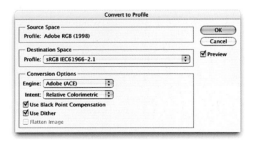

The Convert to Profile dialog.

File Naming Conventions

While the days of the 8.3 naming convention (in which a filename could have no more than 8 characters and a 3-letter file format extension) may be behind us, it still makes sense to use restraint when naming files that will be used on the Web. Modern operating systems can handle longer filenames, but we recommend keeping your filenames limited to 32 characters plus the 3-letter file format extension at the end. Not that we're encouraging you to use the whole 32-character length for all your images. You may be able to get away with a filename of "OllantaytamboTrainStationSunrise.jpg" but it is rather unwieldly, and for Web development purposes, shorter filenames are much easier to deal with.

If you are using other programs to work on your Web pages, make sure that any reference to the file in the HTML code of your Web page uses the same arrangment of upper- and lowercase letters, and never use spaces between words in filenames. If you feel that you must have separations between words to make the name easier to read, use the underscore character or a dash. On Unix systems, it can be even more complicated, because they see a difference between upper- and lowercase letters in filenames. To play it safe, you might want to adopt an all lowercase strategy for naming your Web files.

Saving JPEGs with the Save As Dialog

Photoshop offers two routes to creating compressed images in the JPEG format, and we'll cover both of them in this chapter. The method with the most functionality and options is the Save for Web dialog. The other way to do this is through the regular Save As command. Even though Save for Web has many more features available, if you just need to make a quick JPEG, then the old-fashioned way is still perfectly valid.

- From the Chapter 34 folder on the DVD, open the files called dresden_palace.psd, old_gas_pump.psd, and pink_flower.psd. These files have already been converted to sRGB, so in the color-profile-mismatch messages that appear as you open the files, choose to preserve the embedded profiles.

- From the View menu, choose Actual Pixels for each image to be sure that the view is set to 100%.

- Make the Dresden palace file active and go to File/Save As. In the Save As dialog, choose JPEG from the drop-down Format menu, and click the As a Copy check box. You should also make sure that

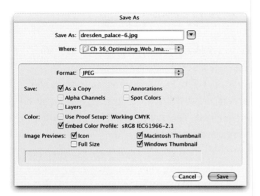

The Save As dialog with the options used for the Dresden palace image.

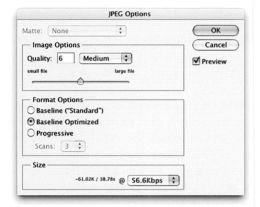

The JPEG Options appear after you select JPEG as the file format and then click the Save button in the Save As dialog.

You need to pay close attention to the details in your images when you save in the JPEG format. The more compression you use, the more likely it is that fine details will suffer. On the Dresden palace image, a JPEG Quality setting of 3 (left) results in obvious artifacts around the edges at the top of the tower. A setting of 6 (right) does a much better job of preserving those details.

the option to embed the sRGB color profile is checked. We're going to save a medium-quality version of the file, so choose a name that reflects what you are doing. Naming the file this way is helpful for identification purposes when you're comparing different-quality versions of the same image. For example, since we knew that we would save this at a medium quality level of 6, we

used "dresden_palace-6.jpg" for the Dresden image to indicate that its quality will be level 6.

◆ If the option for Image Previews appears at the bottom of the dialog, click the boxes for icon and Mac and Windows thumbnails.

◆ Make sure that the Save: As a Copy option is checked and then click the Save button. In the JPEG Options dialog that appears, experiment with different quality settings.

With the preview turned on, you can see how the different levels of compression affect the image quality. Since viewers of a Web site or a multimedia presentation are going to be seeing the images at 100%, be sure that you're zoomed in to 100% so you can accurately judge the compression/quality trade-offs. At the bottom of the dialog box, you can see what the file size of the final JPEG will be when compressed, and also what the download time will be for various connection speeds (this information appears only if the preview is turned on). You can also choose from three different format options: Baseline ("Standard"), Baseline Optimized, and Progressive. For most uses, Baseline Optimized will give you the best result and will do a good job of compressing the image. If you want an image that appears in the browser gradually, looking chunky and pixelated at first and then getting better as more of it loads, choose Progressive.

◆ Choose a Medium setting of 6, Baseline Optimized, and click OK.

Saving a JPEG without Image Previews

For the next part of this exploration, we'll save another version of the Dresden palace image with the same JPEG settings, but this time we won't include any image previwes.

◆ Working from the original PSD file of the Dresden palace image, choose File/Save As once more. In the Save As dialog, choose JPEG as the format, click As a Copy, embed the color profile, but do not check any of the image preview options. Modify the

The file sizes of the Dresden palace images, one with previews (144 KB) and one without (88 KB).

The file sizes of all the JPEG images compared.

The pink flower image yields the smallest file size (64 KB with no preview) due to the fact that most of the photo is out of focus and large areas of the sky are very similar in color and tone.

The Dresden palace photo is a combination of uncomplicated regions, such as the sky, that compress very well, and complex, detail-heavy areas in the ornate tower. The final file size using a Quality setting of 6 and no preview was 88 KB.

The old gas pump file was the largest (100 KB, no preview) simply because the entire image is filled with intricate details and constant changes in color and tone.

filename to indicate that no previews are being saved. We used "dresden_palace-6_nopreview.jpg."

◆ Click Save to bring up the JPEG Options dialog, and use a Quality setting of 6 with Baseline Optimized.

◆ Next, locate the two files in the Finder on a Mac, or in Windows Explorer on a PC, and compare the file sizes.

For the level 6 JPEGs of the Dresden palace photo that we saved, the file sizes are 144 KB for the version with an icon and thumbnails saved, and 88 KB for the version with no previews. Saving the file without the extras of the icon and thumbnails resulted in a savings of 56 KB. The icon and thumbnails are only seen when you are browsing your hard drive, or opening a file into an application that recognizes the thumbnail previews. For Web images, they just take up extra space and make your file larger than it needs to be. While file sizes for images may not be as much of an issue as they used to be, especially as more and more people move to faster Internet connections, keep in mind that not everyone has access to those high-speed on-ramps to the Internet, and there is no point in including extra data that will never be used when the images are served up from a Web site.

◆ Next, save two versions each of the other photos, the old gas pump and the pink flower. Use the same settings as you did with the Dresden palace image: Save: As a Copy, Embed Color Profile, JPEG Quality level 6, and Baseline Optimized. As with the Dresden image, save one version of each image with an icon and Mac and Windows thumbnails and one without.

◆ When you are finished saving the JPEGs, find the files on your computer and compare the sizes.

Comparing File Sizes

Apart from the expected differences in file sizes caused by the presence or absence of image previews, you should notice that each photo in a given category (preview or no preview) has resulted in a different size JPEG file. With JPEG compression, just because you use the identical settings on images that share the same pixel dimensions (as all of these files do), it doesn't mean you'll end up with the same file size. The final file size is influenced by an image's visual complexity. The more complex it is, the less effective the compression; conversely, the more areas of flat color or uncomplicated detail, the better the compression. These files, which are a combination of visually uncomplicated subject matter (the flower) and more complex, detail-rich subjects (the palace and the gas pump), show this principle quite well.

The Save for Web Dialog

For more control over how your JPEG files are compressed, as well as the ability to view side-by-side comparisons of the compressed version with the orginal file, use the Save for Web dialog, which provides a range of options for optimizing images. In the following sections, we'll explore the Save for Web command and take you on a general tour of the dialog and its settings and controls.

◆ In Photoshop, make the old_gas_pump.psd file the active image (or, if you've closed it, reopen the file from the Chapter 34 folder on the DVD). From the File menu, choose Save for Web.

◆ In the Save for Web dialog, click the 4-Up tab in the upper-left corner to view four versions of the file. The upper-left preview is the uncompressed original. The remaining versions, starting in the upper-right corner of the preview area, represent what the image will look like using different formats or compression options (it is possible that your 4-Up arrangement may be four narrow sec-

tions that span the entire height of the preview area, instead of four square sections).

Preview Tabs and Tools

At the top-left side of the dialog are four tabs for switching the preview to display the original image (no compression applied), the optimized or compressed version by itself, and 2-Up or 4-Up layouts that show the original plus one or three optimized versions. You will also see six icons on the left side that represent tools and other functionality.

The Hand tool (H), the Zoom tool (Z), and the Eyedropper (I) will be familiar, since they are the same as in the rest of Photoshop. The Hand allows you to drag the image preview around to see a different area. Moving one preview image will cause the others to move in synchronization. The Zoom tool lets you zoom in or out. The same keyboard shortcuts that work in Photoshop also work in the Save for Web dialog. Pressing the Spacebar will give you the Hand tool, and pressing Command (Ctrl)-Spacebar and clicking a preview image will zoom in. Command-Option-Spacebar (Ctrl-Alt-Spacebar)-clicking lets you zoom out. The Eyedropper allows you to sample specific colors in the image so that those colors can be included in the color table that is used when you're saving in the GIF format. No matter what tool is chosen, however, the cursor location will always display color values on the lower-left side of the dialog.

Below the tool icons is a color swatch that shows you the color sampled by the Eyedropper. This is a feature you would use when creating GIF files and giving priority to specific colors in the image. We will be concentrating only on making JPEGs in this chapter.

Below the color swatch is a button that will toggle the display of slices in the image on or off. Slices are used to divide a larger image into smaller sections so that each can be optimized separately. This

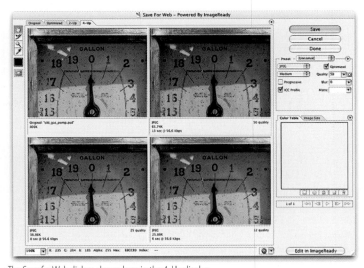

The Save for Web dialog, shown here in the 4-Up display.

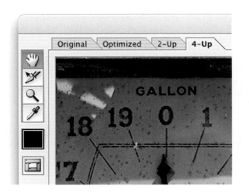

The preview options and tool icons of the Save for Web dialog.

Photoshop feature is for the creation of graphically structured Web pages and is beyond the scope of this chapter.

Optimization Controls and Dialog Menus

On the right side of the dialog are the primary controls for optimizing the image. We'll explore these, and see how we can influence the image's compression and appearance.

◆ In the 4-Up view, click the upper-right preview. If you have thin, vertical previews aligned from left to right intead of the rectangles, click the second preview from the left. This makes that preview active, meaning that any optimization settings will apply only to it. A highlight border will appear around the active preview.

◆ From the Preset menu just under the Done button, choose JPEG High. Next, click the third preview (lower-left corner or third vertical strip from the left), open the Preset menu, and choose JPEG Medium. Finally, click the fourth preview area and set that to JPEG Low.

This is a good, basic setup for evaluating different levels of JPEG quality on photographs. Now we'll set up the Save for Web dialog so that this configuration (JPEG, High, Medium and Low) is the default and will be used every time you enter the dialog in the future.

◆ Hold down the option or alt key to change the Done button to Remember. Click the Remember button. This will tell Photoshop to "remember" the current settings and setup and it will be used the next time you bring up the dialog (if you simply click Done, it will do the same thing, but it will close the dialog).

With the dialog set up to show High, Medium and Low JPEG compression you can start to evaluate how these settings are affecting the image and experiment with changing them. The gas pump image is a good one to use for this because it contains a lot of very fine detail. One thing you will notice as you work with this dialog is that the more complicated an image is in terms of intricate details, the harder it is to get by with a lot of compression as this can seriously impact the quality of how the details are rendered.

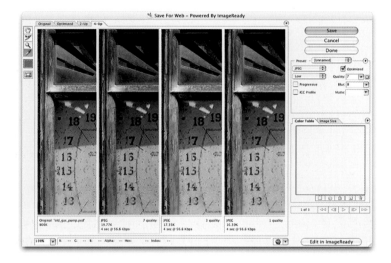

The Save for Web dialog, shown here in the 4-Up display. The light blue highlight border around the second preview from the left shows that it is active.

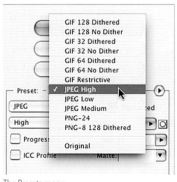

The Presets menu.

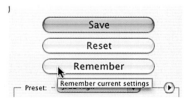

Holding down the Option (Alt) key will change the Done button to Remember. Clicking this button will make Photoshop "remember" the current configurations of settings and apply them the next time you use the Save for Web dialog.

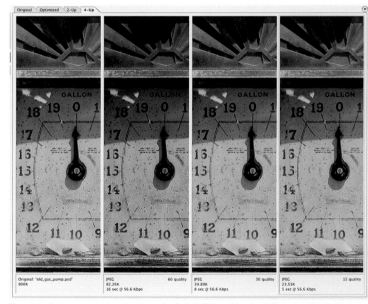

The original, uncompressed version is on the far left, followed by the JPEG High, JPEG Medium, and JPEG Low versions. Under each preview is the file format, quality level, file size, and download time.

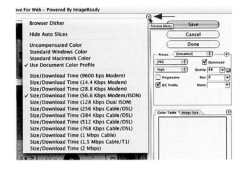

The Preview menu can be found by clicking the small button at the upper-right corner of the main preview window.

The main controls for optimizing JPEGs in the Save for Web dialog.

Crafting a JPEG is always a trade-off between keeping the file size manageable and preserving the subtle details. Although higher speed Internet access is much more common now than it was even a few years ago, you should still keep in mind that some people will be accessing your Web site using a dial-up connection. Keeping the download times for your images reasonable will ensure that people using a slower connection will not have to wait too long for the images to display on the page.

Details, File Size, and Download Time

Underneath each preview image you can see the file format and quality level, the compressed file size, and how long it will take to download the image using a given connection speed. This download time estimate is useful when you are trying to gauge whether a certain file size will be appropriate for someone with a slower connection speed. If you have had the luxury of fast Internet access for a while, it's easy to forget what it was like when you were limited to a dial-up connection!

◆ To see download times using different connection speeds, open the Preview menu, which can be found by clicking the small button at the upper-right corner of the preview window, and select a diferent connection speed.

Optimization Controls

In the upper-right section of the Save for Web dialog are the primary optimization controls. We have already used the Preset menu to select the basic High, Medium, and Low JPEG settings for the gas pump photo.

File Formats

The Format menu lets you choose between GIF, JPEG, PNG-8, PNG-24, and WBMP. For the purposes of our exploration of this dialog, we are limiting ourselves to the JPEG format becuase that is

the one that makes the most sense for photographers who want to prepare good-quality Web versions of their photos.

GIF is limited to a maximum of only 256 colors and is more appropriate for flat-color graphics such as logos, illustrations, or text. PNG-8 is similar to GIF in that it is limited to only 8 bits of information (a maximum of 256 colors). PNG-24 can handle 24-bit color (thousands of colors) and creates good-looking files from photographs, but the files sizes are much larger than with JPEG, and that makes PNG-24 a nonstarter as far as we're concerned. The WBMP format is used for graphics on cell phones and other mobile devices. It supports only 1-bit color, which means that WBMP images contain only black and white pixels. That is obviously not what you want to use for photographs.

Quality Settings and Weighted Optimization

The quality for JPEG files can be set by using the menu just below the format choices, or the slider control just to the right of this. On the far right side of the quality slider is a small icon that is the same as the regular Photoshop mask icon. This feature allows for weighted optimization, where you can specify an alpha channel with which you can apply more compression (less quality) to some parts of the image while optimizing the most important image areas with less compression (better quality). We feel that this is not really necessary anymore unless you are making Web sites where you have strict limits on page size and download time. Since this book is for photographers concerned about crafting good quality images and not a tome for Web developers who are nervously watching every kilobyte, we will not be covering weighted optimization here.

Blur and Matte

The Blur control adds a blur to the compressed image, which can result in smaller file sizes. The JPEG format can more efficiently compress an image without crisp, sharp details. Adding a 0.5 blur to the high-quality JPEG setting reduces the file size of the gas pump image from 85.33 KB to 62.79 KB, but this results in a download time that is only 4 seconds faster on a 56 Kbps connection. And the very significant downside to this, of course, is that you degrade the quality of the image by blurring the details. As photographers who care about the detail in our images, we find this to be an unacceptable sacrifice, and we feel that most of our readers will agree. We recommend that you always leave the Blur setting at 0.

The Matte control defines the color to blend transparent pixels against. Since JPEG does not support transparency, this is a moot point; you should leave it set to None.

Optimized and Progressive

The Optimized check box will create slightly smaller files, but also ones that are less compatible with older versions of some browsers. This is not really a concern with browsers released in the past 4 or 5 years, so we feel it is safe to always have this checked. We should point out, however, that the difference in file size is so small (less than 1K on the high-quality version of the gas pump photo) that it's really a nonissue. We have never run into a problem with this setting.

Using the Progressive option will create a JPEG that will appear very rough and pixelated at first when it begins to download in the Web browser and then will get progressively better as more and more data is downloaded. This setting is a holdover from the days when Internet connections were very slow and it was thought that it was better to have something start to display on the page (even if it was chunky and pixelated) just to let the user know that there was an image on the way. With faster connection speeds, the Progressive option is not much of an issue anymore. We generally do not use it, but there is no harm if you do choose to save JPEGs this way—the impact on file size is neglible.

ICC Profile

Enabling this check box will embed the ICC profile associated with the photo (ideally this should be sRGB for a Web image) in the final compressed file. The impact on the file size is generally quite small. In the high-quality version of the gas pump image, embedding the profile produced a file size of 85.33K, whereas not embedding it yielded a slightly smaller file of 82.26K.

Even though Web browser support for ICC profiles is not what it could be, we strongly recommend that you do use this option. Keep in mind, of course, that if a visitor to your site does not have a properly calibrated and profiled monitor, then even the presence of a profile in your image and a Web browser that understands profiles won't

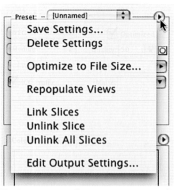

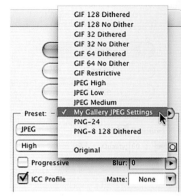

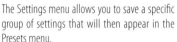

The Settings menu allows you to save a specific group of settings that will then appear in the Presets menu.

Saved settings in the Presets menu.

NOTE

Choosing to embed an ICC profile in the Save for Web dialog does not perform an actual profile conversion to sRGB. To do this, you need to use the Convert to Profile command, which is found in the Edit menu (or under Image/Mode in versions prior to CS2). After resizing and sharpening a flattened copy of your master file, convert to the sRGB profile before using the Save for Web dialog to create the final JPEGs.

guarantee that they are seeing it displayed accurately. But it can't hurt. Since the embedded color tag is of use to those applications that recognize ICC profiles, we feel that any image you send out into the world should have one. As the line in the old commerical goes, "Don't leave home without it!"

The Settings Menu

Just above and to the right of the Optimized check box is the Settings menu. The main utility here for photographers is that it allows you to save a customized group of settings so that you can easily apply them to other images. Once you've saved the settings, they will appear as a menu option in the Presets menu. This is useful if you use the same group of settings on many images.

The Repopulate Views choice is used to refresh all of the previews with new settings if a change is made to one of them. For example, with all of the previews set to JPEG, if you change the high-quality preview to medium quality (30) and choose Repopulate Views, the other two will readjust in proportion, to quality level 15 and 7 (each one is half the quality of the previous version).

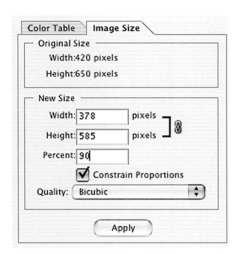

The Image Size controls in the Save for Web dialog. We recommend having your images already sized and sharpened before you enter Save for Web.

The Link and Unlink Slice options and Edit Output Settings all pertain to saving actual HTML Web pages from the Save for Web dialog, which is beyond the scope of what we cover here.

Image Size

Below the main optimize controls are two tabs. The Color Table is only for use with GIF and PNG-8 files, so we don't need to worry about it. The Image Size tab allows you to resize an image as you create the compressed version. We do not recommmed resizing your Web images here for two reasons. The first and most important is that after you resize a file, you need to apply sharpening to it, and resizing the file here does not allow for that. Second, the Save for Web dialog will perform a lot more sluggishly if you are using it with larger files that have not yet been resized. If you do find yourself here and realize that you have forgotten to resize the file, it's best to cancel out of Save for Web. Then resize the file using the Image Size dialog, apply sharpening, and convert to the sRGB profile before returning to Save for Web.

Save for Web: Conclusion

The Save for Web dialog is great for those times when you need to make side-by-side comparisons of how different compression settings affect the image. One advantage of using it is that you can choose to include the ICC profile. Another is that it will not save image previews and icons with the compressed file (these are never seen by people who view an image on a Web site, and including them just makes the file size larger than it needs to be). For many situations, using the JPEG options in the Save As dialog will work just fine, but for those times when you need to exercise the most control in finess-

On the top is the Blackberry Bramble image created by the Web Gallery automation feature...not very sharp. On the bottom is a version of the image that has had custom sharpening applied.

ing the image into a perfect JPEG, then the Save for Web dialog is the place to go.

Customizing Web Photo Gallery JPEGs

In the final section of this chapter, we're going to take a look at the process you would use to replace the automatically generated JPEGs created by the Web Photo Gallery with customized versions that have had sharpening applied to them. The reason we're saving this for last is that we needed to cover the Save for Web dialog first. In addition, this feature really falls under the category of optimizing rather than the automated feature that was covered in the previous chapter. To fully understand this section, you need to read the last part of Chapter 33, "Contact Sheets, Picture Packages, Slide Shows, and Web Photo Galleries," that covers the Web Photo Gallery automation, or already be familiar with that feature and the folder structure it uses for the files it creates.

Web Photo Gallery JPEGs Are Not Sharpened

Although the Web Photo Gallery feature does a great job of quickly and painlessly creating very nice Web galleries, the one thing that it does not do is sharpen the files. Images that are resized smaller for the Web always need careful sharpening to make them look their best. Once the automation has resized the files and created the JPEGs, we can't really go back and sharpen those files, because then we would have to save them (and recompress them) as JPEGs a second time, which is not advisable for good-looking images.

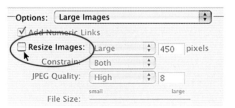

By unchecking the Resize Images option in the Web Photo Gallery dialog, the images will be used as is, with no resizing. This allows you to prepare them in advance, complete with sharpening.

Solution #1: Resize and Sharpen First

There are two solutions to this dilemma. The first, and arguably the easiest, is to resize your images to the exact size that they will be in the Web Photo Gallery and sharpen them before you run the gallery automation. Once in the Web Photo Gallery dialog, in the section that contains the options for Large Images, simply uncheck the box for Resize Images. This will result in the Web Photo Gallery being created with the images as is, with no resizing applied. We would recommend this option simply because it is the most straighforward way to go about sharpening the images, and the one that entails no special effort after the gallery has been created.

Solution #2: Create a Replacement Set of Sharpened Files

If you have already created a gallery, however, and you want sharper images, then you need to replace the existing files with versions that you have sharpened. The following section will detail the steps you need to take to ensure that the new versions are compatible with the HTML code generated by the gallery automation.

Using Actions to Create Sharpened Replacement Images

Manually resizing and sharpening each image would be pretty tedious, especially if you had several large galleries you had to create replacement images for. Using an action to handle the majority of these repetitive tasks is the best way to approach this task. In this section, we'll show you two actions Barry created that will generate new, resized, and sharpened large images, as well as sharpened thumnails. If you have the ArtistKeys loaded into the Photoshop Actions palette, you'll find these actions listed as Horizontal Web and Vertical Web.

◆ In the original images folder that you used for the Web Photo Gallery, create two new folders named "horizontal" and "vertical." Separate your horizontal and vertical images into the appropriate folder.

NOTE

The Horizontal Web and Vertical Web actions are designed to use specific sizes for both the large images and the thumbnails. They will make the large images 475 pixels wide or tall, and the thumbnails 117 pixels wide or tall. To use these to prepare replacement images for a Web gallery, you will need to first create the gallery using those specific sizes for the large images and the thumbnails. You could also edit the actions so that they use different image sizes to match how you like to create your Web galleries.

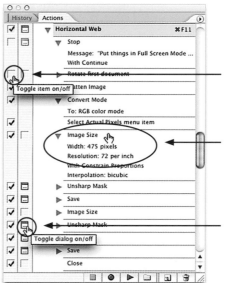

The Horizontal Web action. To turn off a particular step, click the left-most column until the check mark is hidden.

If you want to customize the action so that it uses a different image size, open an image and double-click on that step to change its settings; the action will record your changes and then stop.

To pause the action with a dialog open so you can adjust settings as the action is running, click in the second-to-left column to turn on the dialog icon.

The fastest way to create a new set of images with actions would be to run a batch process on an entire folder. Before you do that, however, you might want to open up a single image first and run the action on it to become familiar with what it's doing.

◆ Start by opening up one of the horizontal images. If the Actions palette is currently in Button mode, open the palette menu and highlight the Button mode choice to change the display of the actions as a named list. Scroll down the list of actions to find the Horizontal Web action, and click the triangle handle next to it to display all the individual steps for that action.

◆ Click the check box next to Rotate First Document to hide the check mark and turn off that step. This action was originally created for images that had already been rotated to vertical in preparation for making inkjet prints. So if your images are already horizontal, they won't need rotating (if you're using the Vertical Web action, there is no step for rotating, and therefore nothing to turn off).

The Horizontal and Vertical Web actions include steps for flattening layers and converting to RGB, so you don't need to do any special preparation to your files.

◆ Click the Play button to run the action on the horizontal image.

It will resize the file to 475 pixels wide (or tall if you're using the Vertical Web action), and pause to allow you to choose a sharpening value (or you can use the ones that Barry has created; they're pretty

These are the files that the Horizontal Web action created for the Blackberry Bramble image. The two top ones are the thumbnail-sized versions. The bottom ones are the larger gallery images. The JPEGs will need to be renamed to the exact same filenames as those produced by the Web Gallery command.

This is the folder structure created by Photoshop's Web Gallery automation.

good for Web images), duplicate it, resize it to a thumbnail 117 pixels wide, then run the Unsharp Mask filter on the thumbnail. Finally, it will save a Photoshop format of the thumbnail (for generating future JPEGs), and then a final JPEG version. Finally, it will switch back to the larger image, save PSD and JPEG versions of it, and close the file when it's done. At each point where a file is saved, it will prompt you for a location to save the file.

When you apply these actions using a batch process, you may want to edit the Save steps so that the images are always saved to the same location, such as a "drop folder" for sharpened Web Photo Gallery replacement images. You should also let the action give the file the default names, and then rename them after it is finished. For more detailed information on working with actions and batch processing, refer to Chapter 10, "Automating Photoshop."

Replacing the Original Gallery Images

Once you've created the sharpened versions of the images and thumbnails, you need to make sure that they have the exact same names as the files that were produced by the Web Photo Gallery automation. Once you've double-checked and changed the names if necessary, replace the original files with the newer, sharpened files.

Find the folder where Photoshop placed your Web Photo Gallery files. Inside it is a folder called images and another called thumbnails. Open up these folders so you can see what the filenames are. Rename the new sharpened files with exactly the same names. When done, you can drag the new files into the appropriate gallery folders and replace the versions that were created by the automation. Just make sure you're putting thumbnails into the thumbnails folder and the larger versions into the images folder. After you've replaced all the images and thumbnails, return to the browser page displaying your gallery and hit the reload or refresh button. You should see a definite improvement in the sharpness of your images.

BIBLIOGRAPHY

Publications

Adams, Ansel. *Examples: The Making of 40 Photographs*. Mill Valley, CA: Ansel Adams, 1998.

Adams, Ansel with Mary Street Alinder. *Ansel Adams: An Autobiography*. Boston, MA: New York Graphic Society Books, 1985.

Adams, Ansel with Robert Baker. *Ansel Adams: The Camera*. Boston, MA: New York Graphic Society Books, 1980.

Adams, Ansel with Robert Baker. *Ansel Adams: The Negative*. Boston, MA: New York Graphic Society Books, 1981.

Adams, Ansel with Robert Baker. *Ansel Adams: The Print*. Boston, MA: New York Graphic Society Books, 1983.

Eismann, Katrin, Sean Duggan, and Tim Grey. *Real World Digital Photography 2ns Edition*. Berkeley, CA: Peachpit Press, 2004.

Evening, Martin. *Adobe Photoshop CS2 for Photographers*. Burlington, MA: Focal Press, 2005.

Fraser, Bruce, Chris Murphy, and Fred Bunting. *Real World Color Management*. Berkeley, CA: Peachpit Press, 2005.

Hunt, R. W. G. *The Reproduction of Colour*. New York, NY: John Wiley & Sons, 2004.

Johnson, Harald. *Mastering Digital Printing*. Boston, MA: Course Technology PTR, 2004.

Krogh, Pete. *The DAM Book: Digital Asset Management for Photographers*. Sebastopol, CA: O'Reilly Media, 2005.

Margulis, Dan. *Photoshop LAB Color: The Canyon Conundrum and Other Adventures in the Most Powerful Colorspace*. Berkeley, CA: Peachpit, 2005.

Margulis, Dan. *Professional Photoshop, The Classic Guide to Color Correction*. New York, NY: John Wiley & Sons, Inc., 2002.

Sammon, Rick. *Complete Guide to Digital Photography*. London: W. W. Norton & Co., 2004.

Threinen-Pendarvis, Cher. *The Painter IX Wow! Book*. Berkeley, CA: Peachpit Press, 2005.

White, Minor. *New Zone System Manual: Previsualization, Exposure, Development, Printing*. Morgan & Morgan, 1998.

Wilhelm, Henry with Carol Brower. *The Permanence and Care of Color Photographs: Traditional and Digital Color Prints, Color Negatives, Slides, and Motion Pictures*. Grinnell, IA: Preservation Publishing Company, 1993.

Willmore, Ben: *Photoshop CS2 Studio Techniques*. Berkeley, CA: Adobe Press, 2006.

Web Sites

Atkinson, Bill. *www.billatkinson.com*. Bill Atkinson Photography.

Cramer, Charles. *www.charlescramer.com*. Charles Cramer Photography.

Haynes, Barry and Wendy Crumpler. *www.maxart.com, www.barryhaynes.com*. Photographers, Imaging consultants and *Photoshop Artistry* authors. See our site for Workshops, Art Gallery, Print Sales and free Latest Tips.

Reichmann, Michael *www.luminous-landscape.com*. Non-commercial site full of beauty and information.

Ross, Denise W. *www.dwrphotos.com*. Great hand-colored black-and-white prints.

Sammon, Rick. *www.ricksammon.com*. Graphic Arts Consultant.

Weinman, Lynda. *www.Lynda.com*. Web books and information.

Wilhelm, Henry. *www.wilhelm-research.com*. Color permanence information.

COLOPHON

This book was produced almost entirely by the authors on three Macs.

Each chapter of this book was set up as a separate document in Adobe InDesign. The text was input directly into InDesign using a template document with Master pages and style sheets. Screen captures were done with Snapz Pro X. Low-res RGB captures were placed in the original documents and sized in InDesign. After design decisions were made as to final size and position, Barry separated the files by hand using scripts he had written. Color correction and separation was done, of course, from Photoshop CS2 using the methods and settings described in this book.

Most photographs in this book are digital, shot with the Canon Digital Rebel.

Most pages were output at 2400 dpi using a 150-line screen. Critical color proofing was done using Spectrum Digital Match Print proofs and less critical color was proofed with Fuji First Look proofs. We used the techniques explained in this book, as well as our GTI Soft-View D5000 Transparency/Print Viewer, to calibrate Photoshop CS2 separations on our LaCie electron 19 blue display and our eMac monitors to color proofs for critical color pages and the cover.

Transfer of files was done primarily using an FTP site. Editing, tech editing and proofing were done from PDFs; copy editing was done using Adobe InCopy. Film was set in signatures of 16 pages starting with the most color-critical signatures first.

Printing was done by CDS Publications in Medford, Oregon, direct to plate with a Creo platesetter, then printed on a Mitsubishi L-750 4 color heat set web press. The book is printed on 70lb Opus Dull and the cover is 12pt C1s with a lay-flat gloss laminate.

Typefaces are Bembo Std and Myriad Pro, both from Adobe.

PHOTO CREDITS

first and/or most prominent occurance of each art piece is listed. Most photos not listed here are by Barry Haynes or Wendy Crumpler.

Jeff Blewett
345

Wendy Crumpler
346

Seán Duggan
113, 118, 122, 128, 132, 132, 267, 279, 285, 287, 289, 291, 298, 299, 302, 323, 437, 486, 507, 512

Maria Ferrari
191

Curt Fischbach
353

Barry Haynes
xx, 111, 150, 172, 177, 237, 238, 248, 253, 324, 334, 335, 344, 354, 360, 370, 375, 388, 406, 435, 437, 448, 451, 451, 452, 465, 467, 478, 483, 506

Carl Marcus
407

Kenda North
43

Mark Reid
75

Kirsten Shaw
171

Berle Stratton
505

James Weiss
277

Index

Quotes About Our Gibsons, B.C. Photography and Photoshop Workshops

What did you like about the workshop?

The intensiveness of the content, knowledge of the instructor, small class size, comfortable setting, great location and scenery, nice people.

Charles H Davies
Seattle, WA

Not much time wasted—plus plenty of time to apply/work on my own images. This class was the best Photoshop learning experience I've had. All in all—this class was extremely inspiring!

James Weiss, African Wildlife Photographer
Chicago, IL

Flexibility to deal with questions—interaction with other students.

Dewey Hess
Beaumont, TX

Focus on photography and printing. Small class size. Barry's background in computer science and ability to solve numerous computer-related issues on the spot.

Hart Kannegiesser
Wheaton, IL

Small group was beneficial, relaxed but intense information and pace.

Jayne Jones, Photography Instructor
Anchorage, AK

Everything. Small group, depth of instruction, atmosphere, hands-on right after instruction chunks. Being able to make prints was very helpful.

Gertraud Gonzales
Sacramento, CA

Examples, working in my own images with help.

John Humphrey
North Liberty, IO

How would you rate your instructor? Why?

Top notch: Knowledgeable, patient, insightful, focused, flexible. When you are pretty comfortable with a Photoshop topic and think you can use it pretty well, Barry adds another layer of knowledge!

Gertraud Gonzales
Sacramento, CA

Excellent—knowledgeable, organized, accessible.

Charlotte Temple, Photographer
St Helena, CA

A+—A storehouse of knowledge and useful information

Jeff Blewett, Landscape Photographer
Garden Valley, ID

A. Knows everything about everything regarding Photoshop for photographers, incredible depth of experience and excellent photographer.

Charles H. Davies
Seattle, Washington

Excellent range and depth of knowledge, patient, genuinely caring whether we were able to take away the skills with us.

Karen Bauer,
Austin, TX

Very knowledgeable, excellent at one-on-one instruction, nice manner.

Sharon Brunzel
Vancouver, B.C.

Excellent. Knows how to make complicated things understandable. Always responsive to inivividual participant's needs

Hart Kannegiesser
Wheaton, IL

Superb—huge breadth of knowledge and lots of patience.

Steve Deering
Vancoucer, B.C.

Photoshop and Photography
Workshops with Barry Haynes and Wendy Crumpler

Technique

Whether you are new to Photoshop or a photographer who needs to improve your knowledge and skill, we have a class that is right for you. Our introductory workshops give you all the information you need to begin making beautiful digital prints of your work. Advanced workshops help you perfect your technique while working with a master printmaker.

Art

Our workshops offer you more than the nuts and bolts of Photoshop. We work closely with you to explore what you want your photography to say. We encourage the individual vision of each student, offering advice and support at a level appropriate to your processs. Lively classroom discussions and lunches together are opportunities to explore photography's place in our lives.

Vision

Come and visit us on B.C.'s Sunshine Coast, we have the beauty and the light. www.barryhaynes.com

Kayak Photography Adventure

Begin this four-day adventure with an optional half-day kayak lesson and/or a half-day photography/digital camera session. Then it's out to the water for some kayaking, hiking, exercise, and photography. We spend time in the studio to work on the shots you took or other images your bring, and you take home two beautiful 16x20 prints.

Digital Printmaking for Photographers

Barry's popular five-day photography, Photoshop, and printmaking workshop. Learn the best Photoshop workflow for photographers using Bridge, Camera Raw, adjustment layers, and masks to get the prints you want from your images. See our Web site for a detailed workshop desciption. Includes test prints and two 16x20 prints.

Digital Paint

For photographers who want to explore new directions in their art, this three-day class examines how Photoshop and Corel Painter work together. Painting is done primarily in Painter; compositing, color correction, and printing are accomplished in Photoshop.

Advanced Digital Printmaking for Photographers

Open to former students of Digital Printmaking for Photographers, this workshop is focused on helping you get what you want from prints of your images. Bring your problem images and all your questions. Learn how to automate your image sorting, Camera Raw, Photoshop, and printmaking workflow with actions, Bridge, and other techniques. In this workshop, we take advantage of tides, ferries, outdoor skills, weather, and student preferences to usually include at least one day of shooting.

Introduction to Photoshop for Photographers

This three-day course is designed for students ready to get serious about digital imaging. You use our examples and your own images to work through and understand the color correction workflow. We also present an overview of Photoshop's many tools and features, then show you which ones are most important to photographers and how to use them in the most efficient ways.

Photoshop or Elements? Which Do I Need?

This one-day class for novice digital photographers looks at the two popular applications and compares the type of work that can be done in each. At the end of the day, you will understand which application is right for you now, and why.